TEXAS

150 Works from the
Museum of Fine Arts, Houston

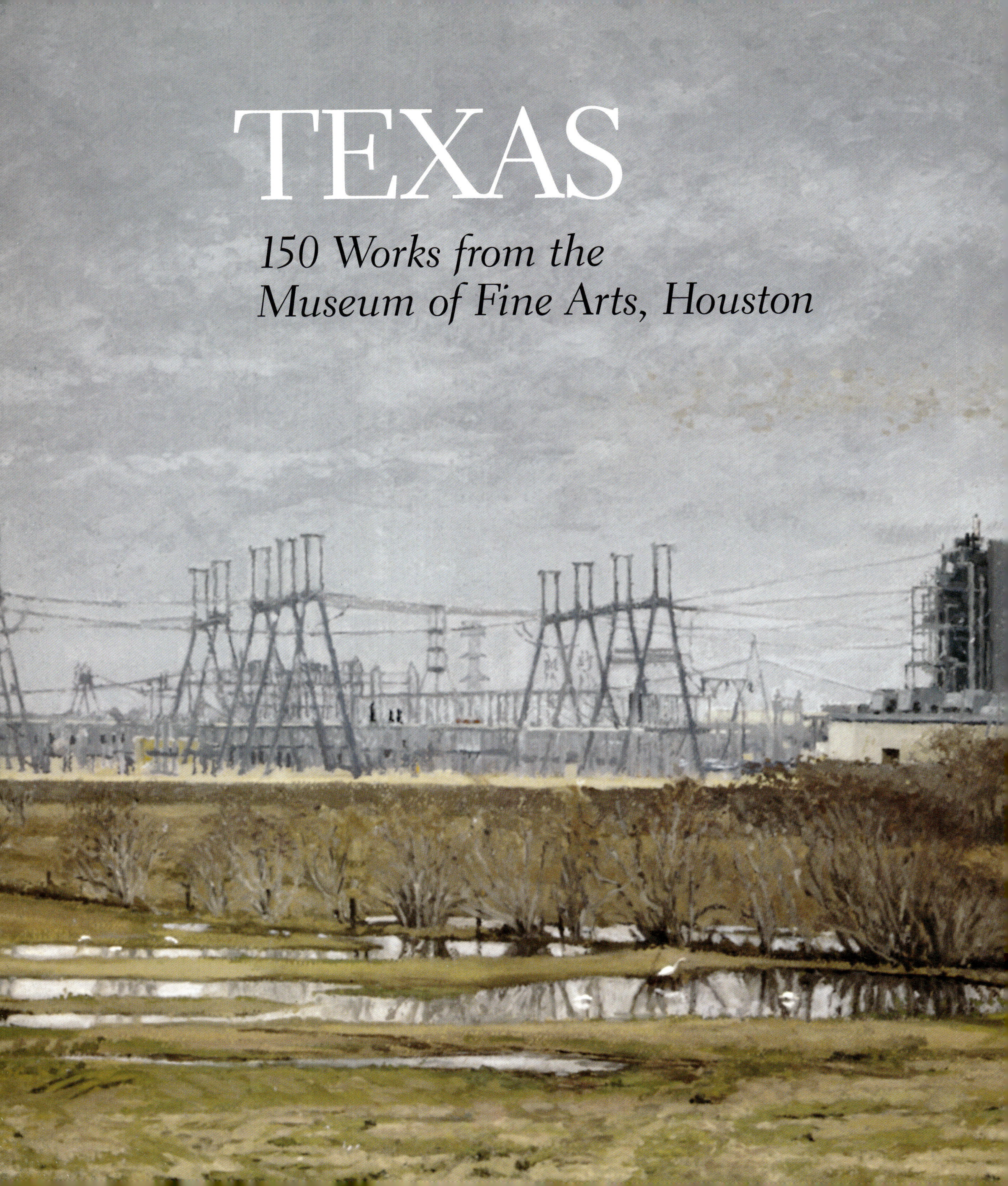

TEXAS
150 Works from the
Museum of Fine Arts, Houston

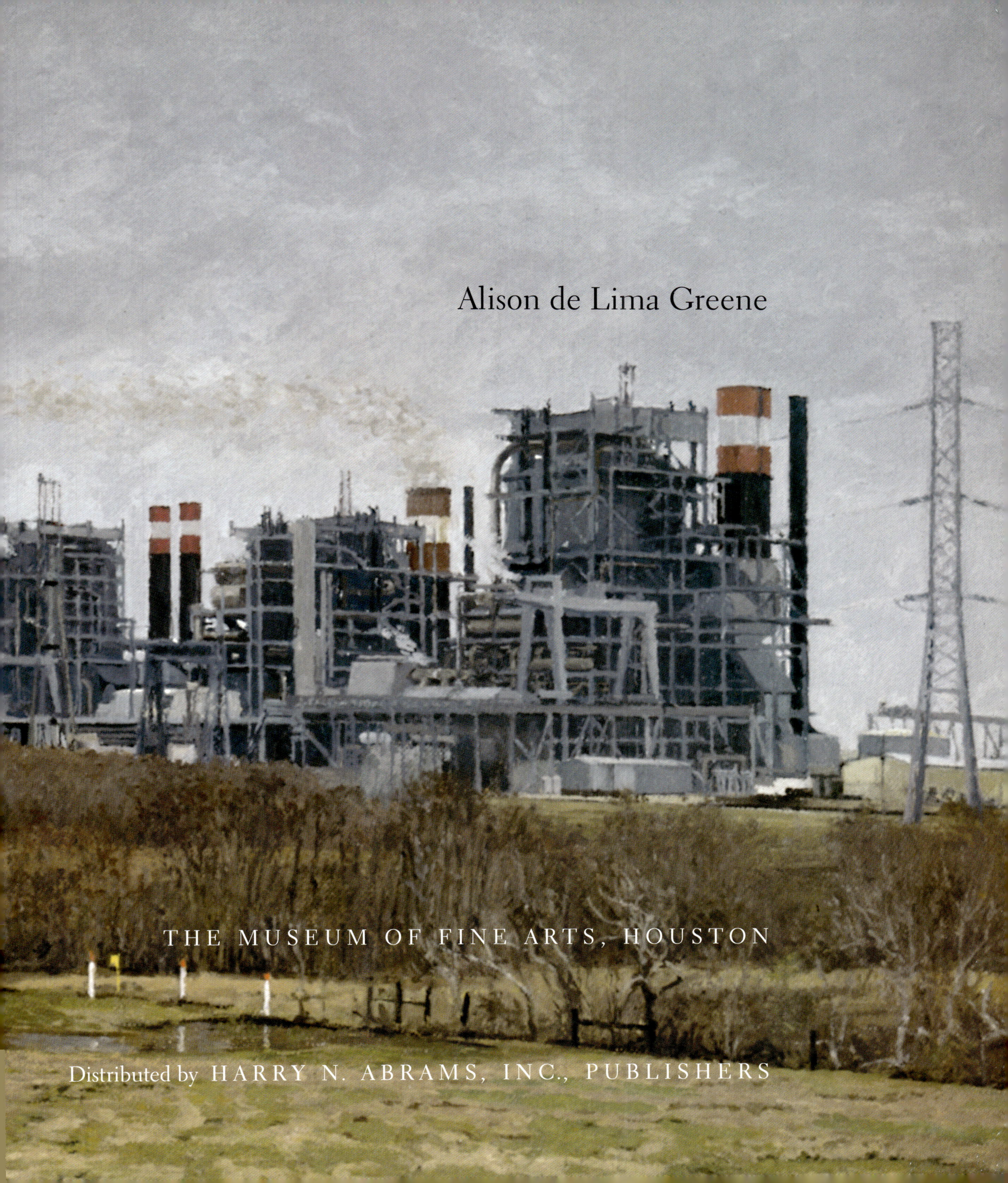

Alison de Lima Greene

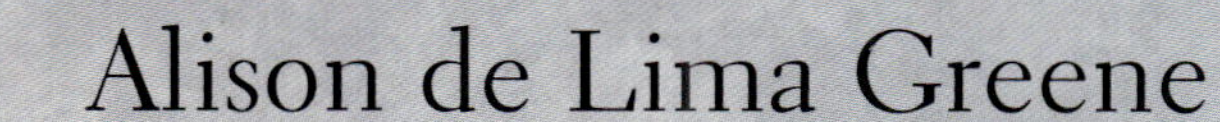

THE MUSEUM OF FINE ARTS, HOUSTON

Distributed by HARRY N. ABRAMS, INC., PUBLISHERS

Library of Congress Cataloging-in-Publication Data

Museum of Fine Arts, Houston.
    Texas: 150 works from the Museum of Fine Arts, Houston /
by Alison de Lima Greene ; foreword, Peter C. Marzio.
       p. cm.
    Introduction by Alison de Lima Greene, Shannon Halwes,
and Kathleen Robinson.
    Biographies by Robert Montgomery, Monica Garza,
Jason A. Goldstein, and Alison de Lima Greene.
    Chronology of exhibitions by Alejandra Jimenez.
    ISBN 0-89090-095-7 (pbk.: alk. paper) –
    ISBN 0-8109-6706-5 (hc.: alk. paper)
    1. Art, American—Texas—Catalogs. 2. Art, Modern—
20th century—Texas—Catalogs. 3. Art—Texas—Houston—
Catalogs. 4. Museum of Fine Arts, Houston—Catalogs.
    I. Greene, Alison de Lima. II. Jimenez, Alejandra. III. Title.

N6530.T4 M87 2000
709'.764'0747641411—dc21

                                 99-88795

Distributed in 2000 by Harry N. Abrams, Incorporated, New York

Printed and bound in Germany

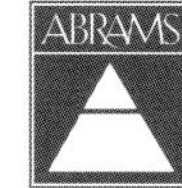

Harry N. Abrams, Inc.
100 Fifth Avenue
New York, N.Y. 10011
www.abramsbooks.com

Cover: Forrest Bess, *Untitled [11A]*, 1958 *(see plate 12)*

Title page: Rackstraw Downes, *P. H. Robinson Generating
Station, Dickinson, Texas: Eight Ibis Feeding with an Egret*
(detail), 1991 *(see plate 37)*

Contents

Peter C. Marzio   10   Foreword

12   Acknowledgments

Alison de Lima Greene, Shannon Halwes,   14   Introduction: Texas Art at the
and Kathleen Robinson   Museum of Fine Arts, Houston

Alison de Lima Greene   TEXAS: 150 Works from the
Museum of Fine Arts, Houston

34   Chapter 1: A Sense of Place

80   Chapter 2: Another Reality

118   Chapter 3: Texas Modern

172   Chapter 4: This State I'm In

206   Notes

Robert Montgomery, Monica Garza,   222   Biographies
Jason A. Goldstein, and Alison de Lima Greene

Alejandra Jiménez   260   Chronology of Exhibitions of Texas Art
at the Museum of Fine Arts, Houston

269   Selected Bibliography

272   Index

279   Credits

Texas: 150 Works from the Museum of Fine Arts, Houston, began as the documentation of two exhibitions of Texas art from the museum's holdings: *Texas Myths and Realities* (October 29–December 31, 1995) and *Texas Modern and Postmodern* (January 21–March 3, 1996). The generous support of the following donors made possible both exhibitions and this catalogue:

Exxon
Goldman, Sachs & Co.
Duke Energy
Mr. and Mrs. Peter R. Coneway
Jeanne and Michael Klein
The Wilder Foundation
Sara Fort Paschall Dodd
The Vaughn Foundation
Texas Commission on the Arts

Texas Myths and Realities and *Texas Modern and Postmodern* were presented as a part of "A Place for All People" at the Museum of Fine Arts, Houston, which was made possible by a grant from the Lila Wallace-Reader's Digest Fund. Additional support for "A Place for All People" was provided by the Charles E. Culpeper Foundation, the Edward and Betty Marcus Foundation, and the National Endowment for the Arts, a federal agency.

Additional support for this catalogue was provided by:

Mr. William James Hill
Victoria and Marshal Lightman
Mr. Frank Ribelin
Mr. and Mrs. Andrew Schneck
Ms. Tara Lewis
Dr. Richard Moiel and Ms. Katherine Poeppel
Mr. and Mrs. Byron Lee
Mr. David R. Stevenson
Ms. Kerry F. Inman
Mr. and Mrs. W. Douglas Ankenman, Jr.
Mr. Jack Jones
Dr. and Mrs. David F. Peterson
Ms. Jan M. Diesel
Carola and John Herrin
Mr. and Mrs. Arthur I. Newman
Mr. Robert T. Greenstein
Ms. Nancy Adams Frye
Ms. H. Joan Ehrlich
Mr. and Mrs. F. Walter Bistline, Jr.
Mr. Derek K. Harmon, Sr.
Ms. Sharon Berryman
Mr. and Mrs. Stephen Weiss
Ms. Nan Lockwood
Dr. K. D. Charalampous
Dr. Gary Freeman and Ms. Candace Collier
Howard and Merle Hunt
Ms. Carol J. Berman

The following donors made gifts to this catalogue in memory of Sigrid de Lima and Stephen Greene:

David Aylsworth and Paul Forsythe, Michael K. Brown, Patricia Clark-Faenger, G. Clifford Edwards, Leslie Field, Margaret Crocker Ford, Monica Garza, Gwendolyn H. Goffe, MariAlice Grimes, Joseph Havel and Lisa Ludwig, Rachel Hecker, Ms. Bernadette A. Henry, Isabell S. and Max H. Herzstein, Katherine S. Howe, William K. and Stephanie R. Joseph, Janet Landay and Edward Hirsch, W. F. Lassiter and Edward B. Mayo, Janie C. Lee and David B. Warren, Christine and Joseph Manca, Celia Martin, Frances and Peter Marzio, Jeannine Maxwell, Ken Mazzu, Barbara Michels, Margaret Mims and Jim Barham, Mary Morton, Jon W. Naylor, Mr. and Mrs. Richard W. Neff III, Nicole O'Bryan, Thomas B. and Linda R. O'Toole, Minnette and Jerome Robinson, Anne-Louise Schaffer, Beth and Michael Schneider, Alice C. Simkins, Margaret C. and Louis Skidmore, Jr., Frances Carter and Nicholas C. Stephens, Cindi Strauss and Chris Ballou, Lorraine A. Stuart, Anne Wilkes Tucker, Barry Walker, and Cyvia and Melvyn Wolff.

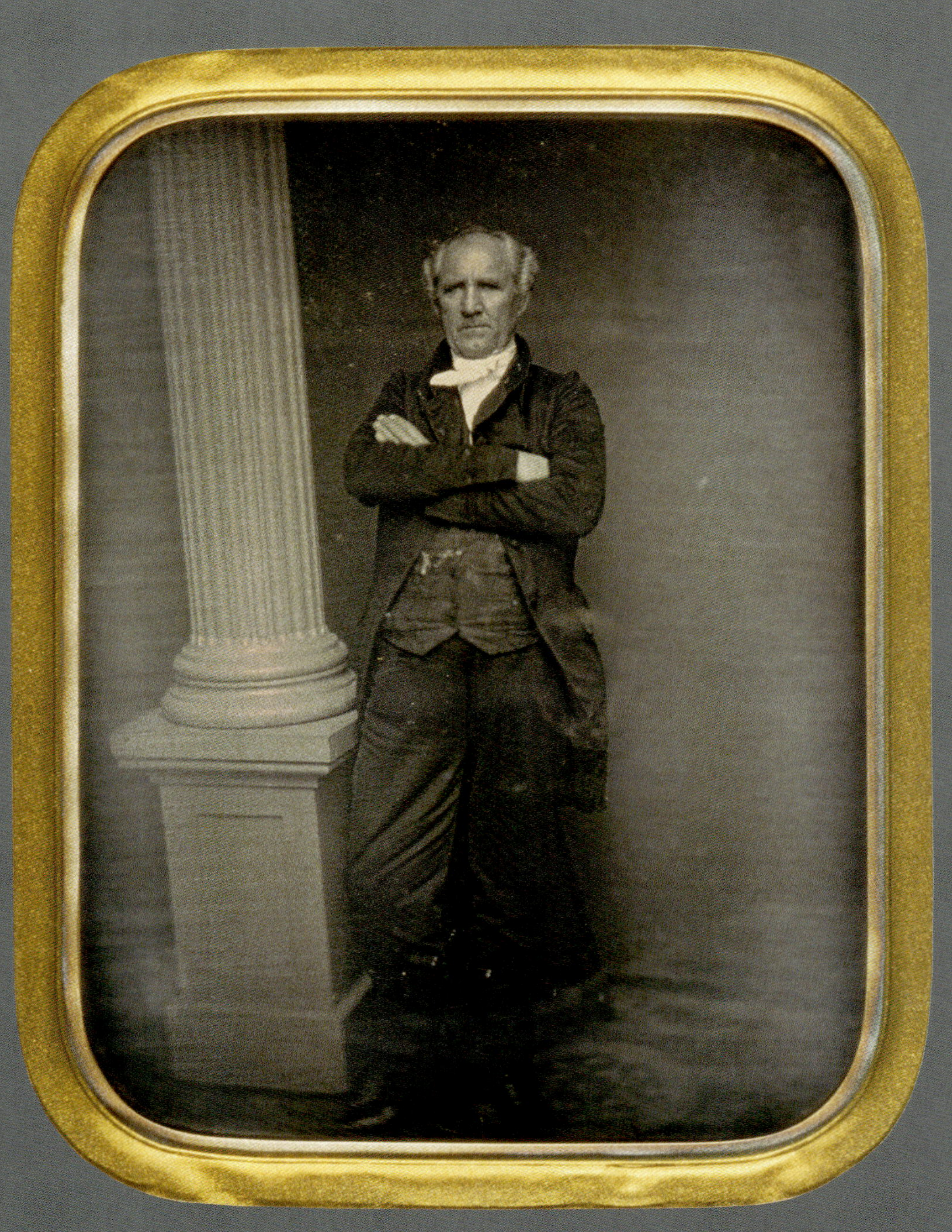

Foreword

The Museum of Fine Arts, Houston, has been committed to the art of Texas since its foundation in 1900: more than 325 exhibitions dedicated to Texas art and artists have been hosted by the MFAH, and today its collection of Texas art consists of over 2000 paintings, sculptures, drawings, prints, and photographs. Published in the museum's centennial year, this catalogue celebrates the range of this enterprise, tracing the history of the institution and highlighting 150 works from the museum's permanent collection. These works will serve to introduce the figures who have shaped our understanding of art in Texas, not only offering a vivid portrait of the state seen through the eyes of its artists, but also challenging us to readdress our assumptions about the nature of regional art.

Alison de Lima Greene, curator of modern and contemporary art and author of this catalogue, has conveyed the rich history of art in Texas. She has swept away the clichés and revealed a diverse palette of talents and skills and media and subjects. The story of Texas art takes many twists and turns, and Ms. Greene has succeeded in offering a comprehensive view of the larger picture. In addition, throughout her fifteen-year tenure at the MFAH, Ms. Greene has consistently pursued outstanding acquisitions that have both extended the historical depth and contemporary breadth of the museum's Texas collection.

The structure of the catalogue grew out of two exhibitions curated by Ms. Greene and drawn from the collection of the Museum of Fine Arts, Houston: *Texas Myths and Realities* and *Texas Modern and Postmodern*, seen at the MFAH in 1995 and 1996. As we reviewed major segments of the collection, we discovered four significant currents ran through the range of Texas art, reflected in the four chapters of this catalogue. The first chapter is devoted to the Texas landscape, to many readers the most familiar aspect of the art of this region; visionary responses to this landscape and the pursuit of the spiritual are discussed in the second chapter; Modernism in Texas is the third topic surveyed; we conclude our overview with a consideration of Postmodernism and the diversity of the present scene. Not surprisingly, these currents frequently echo the evolution of modern and contemporary art both in the Americas and Europe; it is the aim of this publication to integrate the contributions of Texans into this larger history.

This catalogue has been made possible by the generous support of a number of friends. The above-mentioned exhibitions of Texas art in 1995 and 1996 that launched our research received major underwriting from Exxon; Goldman, Sachs & Co.; Duke Energy; Mr. and Mrs. Peter R. Coneway; Jeanne and Michael Klein; The Wilder Foundation; Sara Fort Paschall Dodd; The Vaughn Foundation; and the Texas Commission on the Arts. These exhibitions also fell under the museum's "A Place for All People" initiative; permanent collection exhibitions and public programs for "A Place for All People" at the Museum of Fine Arts, Houston, are made possible by a grant from the Lila Wallace-Reader's Digest Fund. Additional support has been provided by the Charles E. Culpeper Foundation, the Edward and Betty Marcus Foundation, and the National Endowment for the Arts, a federal agency. Deep gratitude is due to these sponsors for the leadership role they took in promoting this project.

Additional thanks are due to the funders of the catalogue: Mr. William James Hill; Victoria and Marshal Lightman; Mr. Frank Ribelin; Mr. and Mrs. Andrew Schneck; Ms. Tara Lewis; Dr. Richard Moiel and Ms. Katherine Poeppel; Mr. and Mrs. Byron Lee; Mr. David R. Stevenson; Ms. Kerry F. Inman; Mr. and Mrs. W. Douglas Ankenman, Jr.; Mr. Jack Jones; Dr. and Mrs. David F. Peterson; Ms. Jan M. Diesel; Carola and John Herrin; Mr. and Mrs. Arthur I. Newman; Mr. Robert T. Greenstein; Ms. Nancy Adams Frye; Ms. H. Joan Ehrlich; Mr. and Mrs. F. Walter Bistline, Jr.; Mr. Derek K. Harmon, Sr.; Ms. Sharon Berryman; Mr. and Mrs. Stephen Weiss; Ms. Nan Lockwood; Dr. K. D. Charalampous; Dr. Gary Freeman and Ms. Candace Collier; Howard and Merle Hunt; and Ms. Carol J. Berman. In addition, many friends and colleagues have made donations in memory of Sigrid de Lima and Stephen Greene, parents of the author, for which I am deeply grateful. Finally, I would also like to salute the many friends who have helped build our collection of Texas art over the years.

Texas artists form a fluid community: some have devoted the major part of their lives to this region, others have worked here for critical—if brief—periods. The museum's holdings emphasize the contributions made by artists who have worked in Houston, but we have also sought to include the defining talents who have worked across—and at times outside—the state as well. New talents emerge and overlooked artists are rediscovered. The men and women who created this rich legacy deserve to be better known; not just in the United States, but throughout the world. We hope that this book will be a significant step in that journey of recognition.

Peter C. Marzio
Director
The Museum of Fine Arts, Houston

1
**Meade Brothers
(Charles Richard and
Henry William Matthew)**
Samuel Houston, 1851
Daguerreotype on silvered
copper plate, full plate size
in presentation glass mat
and frame, 8 x 5¼ in. (20.3
x 13.2 cm). Museum purchase with funds provided by
Vinson & Elkins L. L. P. in
honor of the Firm's seventy-
fifth anniversary, 92.444.

Acknowledgments

This publication has been a five-year undertaking, and many colleagues within the Museum of Fine Arts, Houston, were unflagging in their support. First and foremost, I would like to thank Peter C. Marzio, director, who stood by this project as it evolved from a series of collection installations into a major publication. I am also deeply grateful to Emily Ballew Neff, curator of American art, who shared her research on the more historical collections with friendship and grace. At the museum's Glassell School of Art, Joseph Havel, director, and Valerie Loupe Olsen, associate director, have repeatedly provided information and pointed to new directions in research; the exhibitions and publications programs they have recently initiated have contributed significantly to the literature on contemporary Texas art. Additionally, Michael K. Brown, curator of the Bayou Bend Collection; Charles Carroll, registrar; Gwendolyn H. Goffe, associate director in charge of finance and administration; Marian Luntz, curator of film and video; Edward B. Mayo, registrar emeritus; Barbara Michels, deputy development director; Beth B. Schneider, education director; Margaret C. Skidmore, associate director in charge of development; Anne Wilkes Tucker, the Gus and Lyndall Wortham curator of photography; Barry Walker, curator of prints and drawings; Alvia J. Wardlaw, curator of twentieth-century art; and David B. Warren, director of Bayou Bend, offered insight and encouragement throughout.

Shannon Halwes, former curatorial assistant, deserves great thanks not only for her contributions to this catalogue's introduction, but also for the research she undertook during initial stages of this project. William R. Thompson expertly took up where Ms. Halwes left off, and Robert Montgomery and Monica Garza have gracefully seen this catalogue to its conclusion. Mr. Montgomery and Ms. Garza also wrote the majority of the biographical essays, bringing to this task exceptional care and critical intelligence. Former archivists Kathleen Robinson and Joey Kuhlman pored through the museum's records, confirming details of this institution's history; in particular, Ms. Robinson is to be thanked for her contribution to the introduction. Archivist Lorraine A. Stuart and volunteer Terry Brown have further proved to be valuable colleagues and assisted in finalizing the chronology of the museum's Texas exhibitions. The museum's library staff, headed by Jeannette Dixon and Jacqui Allen, has answered numerous questions with alacrity and good humor. Karen Vetter offered timely administrative support, and G. Clifford Edwards provided secretarial support with his customary expertise and thoroughness; curatorial interns Alejandra Jiménez and Jason A. Goldstein contributed to the chronology of exhibitions and artists' biographies, and Eric Davis, James W. Ellis, and Debbie Fletcher offered much-needed, last-minute research assistance.

Diane Planer Lovejoy, publications director, has overseen this project from its first stages, and Christine Waller Manca has gracefully taken on all editorial duties, ably assisted by Hillery Hugg, Jennifer Lawrence, and Michelle Nichols. Wynne Phelan, conservation director, gave insightful advice on all issues of materials and conservation; Kathleen Crain and the staff of the museum's ever generous preparations department kept works accessible for study and photography. Suzanne Decker, Misty Moye, Marty Stein, George Zombakis, and Celene Reno assembled photographic materials; Thomas R. DuBrock and Jud Haggard are responsible for new photography. Deep thanks are due to Don Quaintance and Elizabeth Frizzell of Public Address Design, Houston; Mr. Quaintance, designer of this catalogue, not only shaped the character of this publication, but also contributed to the editing of the final text with wit, insight, and patience. I also want to thank our partners in printing and distributing this publication: Klaus Prokop at Cantz, and Paul Gottlieb and Elaine Stainton at Harry N. Abrams, Inc.

My colleagues at Rice University Dr. William A. Camfield and Steven Fox proved to be invaluable friends and resources. Galleries were generous in opening their files, including most notably Devin Borden Hiram Butler Gallery, Laura Carpenter Fine Art, Barbara Davis Gallery, David Dike Fine Art, Lynn Goode Gallery, Harris Gallery, Hooks-Epstein Galleries, Eugene Foney, Inman Gallery, James Gallery, Lawing Gallery, Meredith Long & Company, Lyons Matrix Gallery, Adair Margo Gallery, Robert McClain & Company, McMurtrey Gallery, Moody Gallery, New Gallery, Oil & Steel Gallery, Parkerson Gallery, Gerald Peters Gallery, Sally K. Reynolds, Sally Sprout Gallery, Texas Gallery, Valley House Gallery, Barry Whistler Gallery, and Gerhard Wurzer Gallery. I would also like to honor the memories of Richard Bellamy, Charles Hooks, William Graham, and Warren Hadler, art dealers who were instrumental in deepening my understanding of certain artists. Further important conversations with Talley Dunn, Michael Ennis, Dana Friis-Hansen, Nancy Hixon, Michael Grauer, Lynn Herbert, Walter Hopps, Patricia Johnson, Susie Kalil, Patricia John Keightley, Meredith J. Long, George Shackelford, and Clint Willour gave welcome direction as the project evolved.

Many of the artists featured in this catalogue have opened up their studios and their memories to me, and in numerous instances their letters discussing works in the museum's collection proved to be invaluable resources. The artists' interviews and ephemeral materials assembled by the Texas Project of the Archives of American Art, Smithsonian Institution, offered additional insight into the history of the Texas scene. Several friends allowed me to bounce ideas off them, and I received particularly intelligent advice from Terrell James, Ralph McKay, Michael Miller, Betty Moody, and Liz Ward.

The Texas collection at the Museum of Fine Arts, Houston, has been built over many years, guided not only by the museum staff, but also by a wider community of trustees, collectors, and artists, who for close to a century have demonstrated an unwavering devotion to the art of this region. The pioneering work of James Chillman, Jr., first director of the Museum of Fine Arts, Houston, established the museum's commitment to Texas art. I would like to acknowledge his vision and foresight, as well as the great contributions made to this endeavor by successive directors and curators, including most notably Ruth Pershing Uhler and Barbara Rose. Most of the museum's Texas works were acquired through individual sponsors and their names are acknowledged elsewhere. However, I would like to take this opportunity to thank the funders who generously made this catalogue possible and in particular to acknowledge Duke Energy, which has supported many years of Texas acquisitions and exhibitions. Additional thanks are due to the extraordinary collectors Nona and Richard Barrett, who set an example of enlightened patronage: not only have they offered wise counsel and generous support over the years, but recent gifts from The Barrett Collection have transformed the Texas collection at the Museum of Fine Arts, Houston. Marshal and Victoria Lightman were among the first champions of this project, and I am forever grateful to them for their insistence that I finish the manuscript. Alice Simkins's enthusiasm buoyed my spirits time and again, while her scholarly acumen guided my research into new areas. I would also like to acknowledge the deeply generous friendship of Isabell Herzstein, Cecily Horton, Jeanne and Michael Klein, Salle Werner Vaughn, Isabel B. Wilson, Michael Zilkha, and the many others who have served on the museum's twentieth-century subcommittee — their wise care for this project and the museum's twentieth-century collection has been inspiring.

Finally, I thank my mother, Sigrid de Lima, who taught me how to write, and Stephen Greene, my father, who taught me how to look at art.

Alison de Lima Greene
Curator of Modern and Contemporary Art

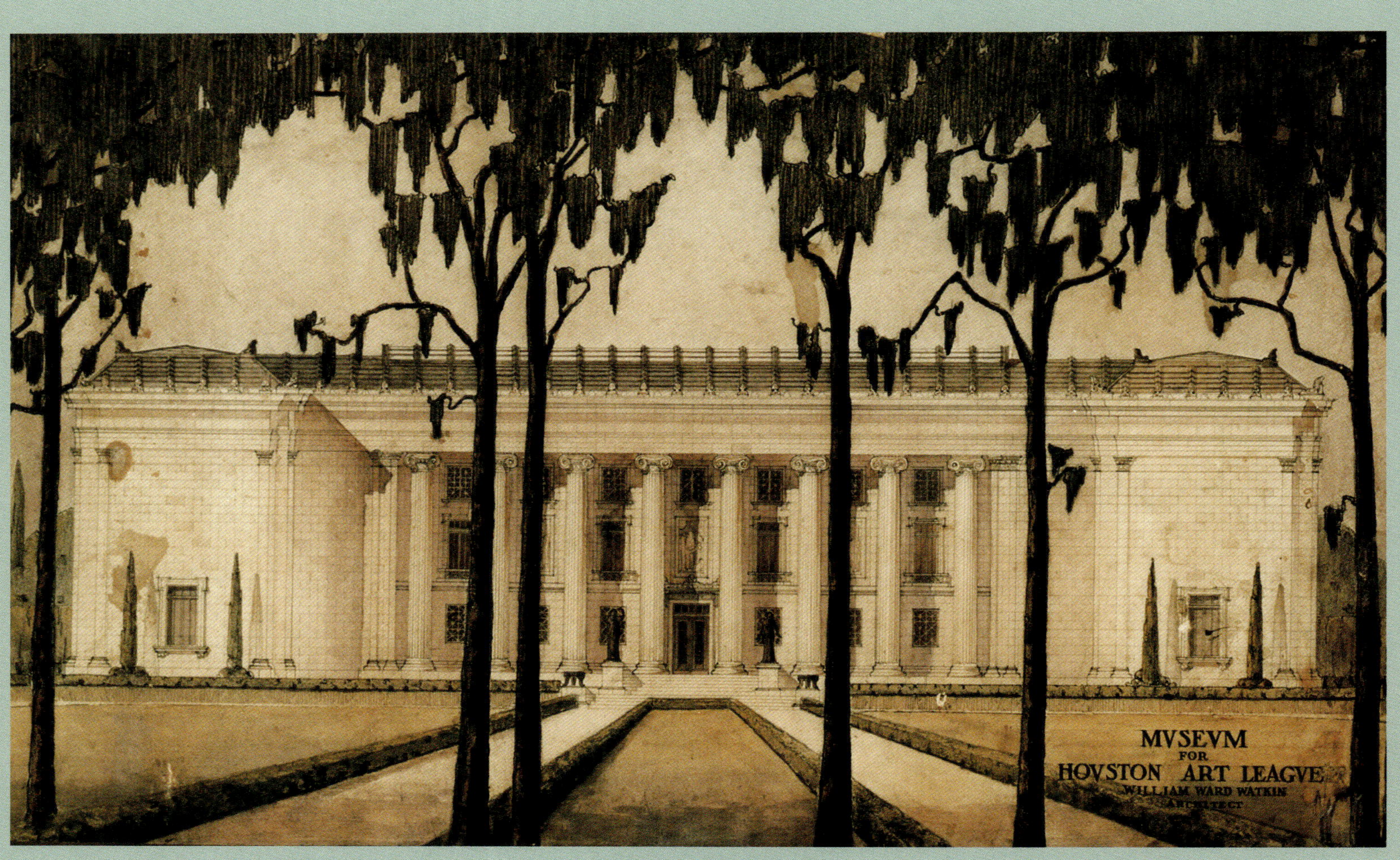

MVSEVM
FOR
HOVSTON ART LEAGVE
WILLIAM WARD WATKIN
ARCHITECT

Introduction: Texas Art at the Museum of Fine Arts, Houston

Nature made Houston rich
Time will make her powerful
Only the Arts can make her great.
    —James Chillman, Jr. [1]

THE FOUNDING YEARS, 1900–1945

When the Museum of Fine Arts, Houston, opened its doors on April 12, 1924, the appetite for art in Houston had reached such a level that an estimated one thousand citizens had to be turned away, and the hundreds of visitors who were able to make their way inside the museum quickly wore the varnish off of the newly polished wooden floors.[2] Displayed in the museum's galleries were approximately one hundred and fifty objects; on opening day visitors would have been able to see a sweeping vista of the Saharan desert, the misty wharves of London, and a pastoral nineteenth-century Dutch landscape.[3] A portion of these works were assembled by the Houston Art League for the museum's permanent collection, but the major part of the installation consisted of loans secured from the founding patrons of the museum, including Robert Lee Blaffer, Joseph S. Cullinan, and Ima Hogg, among others. Works that reflected the museum's location in the Southwest included several Taos School paintings and a group of twelve paintings by Frederic Remington lent by William C. Hogg, Miss Hogg's brother.[4] Six landscapes by the late bluebonnet painter from San Antonio, Julian Onderdonk (1882–1922), offered a glimpse—albeit selective—of Texas. This glimpse proved to be seductive, however, and within two weeks of the opening, Onderdonk's *Bluebonnets* had been voted the most popular painting in the museum.[5]

Although Texas art was not emphasized in the inaugural installation, and no Houston artist was represented at all, the museum had begun to exhibit and collect Texas art well before it erected a building in which to house it. The Houston Art League, at the forefront of the city's fine arts movement since 1900 and the founding body of the art museum, featured Texas exhibitions in its modest annual program as early as 1917.[6] Since an art museum had yet to be built on the newly acquired land at the intersection of South Main Street and Montrose Boulevard, the League leased space in the Scanlan Building, one of downtown Houston's largest office buildings.[7] Two years later, in 1919, the League added its first work by a Texas artist to its fledgling collection through the bequest of Houston industrialist George M. Dickson. The bequest featured nineteenth-century academic paintings by Jean-Léon Gérôme and Anton Mauve, as well as William Merritt Chase's *Emerald Lady*, and it also included a Southwest Texas landscape by Onderdonk (plate 4). In 1925 the Current Literature Club of Houston sponsored the museum's first purchase of a work by a Houstonian, Emma Richardson Cherry's *Portrait of Mrs. Henry B. Fall*. Cherry was generally recognized as one of the city's first professional artists and, together with Fall, was among the most active founders of the Houston Art League.

The commitment to exhibit and acquire Texas art—complementary activities which remained interdependent throughout the museum's history—gained focus following the 1924 opening of the museum. Designed by William Ward Watkin, the neoclassical structure was the initial component of an ambitious building program, and within two years east and west wings had been added to the original south galleries (fig. 1). Having built the first art museum in the state, the board of trustees stated that its mission was in part "to encourage in all ways within its power the efforts of local artists."[8] This would be achieved by bringing examples of great art to the museum, by providing art training and education, and by regularly exhibiting and purchasing work produced by the area's artists. In their role as leaders in the fine arts movement, members of the Houston Art League and other museum patrons saw themselves as bringing culture to a growing but relatively unsophisticated city. They believed that support of local art was critical to the broader goal of cultivating art appreciation and education throughout the city, maintaining that a Houston art community could not be fostered and sustained solely by importing works of art from such well established but distant centers as Paris and New York.

James Chillman, Jr., who served as director from 1924 to 1954, was instrumental in realizing the goals established by the museum's founders. An art historian, artist, and architect who was also on the faculty of the

Fig. 1
William Ward Watkin, preliminary design for the south facade of the Museum of Fine Arts, Houston, c. 1921.

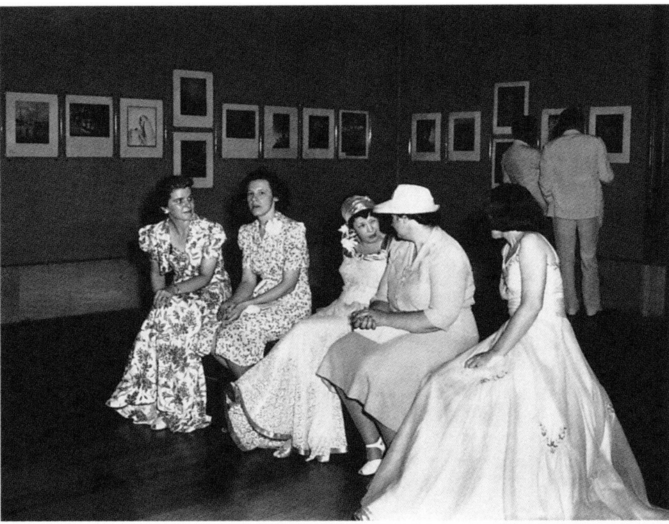

Fig. 2
Opening reception, *4th
Annual Exhibition of the
Houston Camera Club,*
the Museum of Fine Arts,
Houston, June 1941.

Fig. 3
Houston artists Ruth Pershing
Uhler and Grace Spaulding
John on the porch of John's
home and studio, c. 1939.

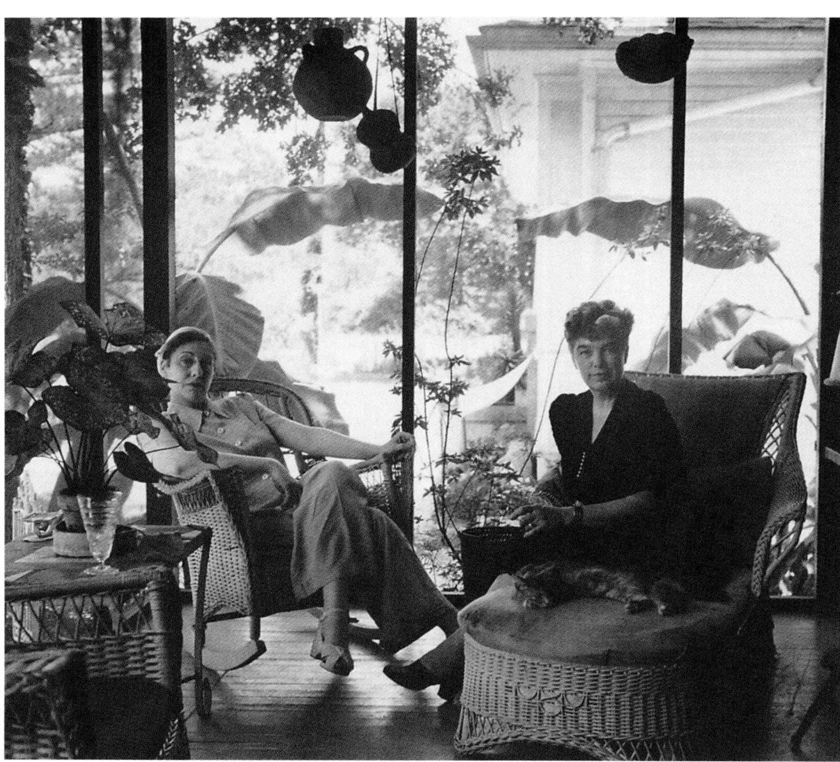

neighboring Rice Institute (now Rice University), Chillman was ideally suited to assume the many roles of a museum director. He embraced the museum's multifaceted educational mission and successfully united the museum's program with the needs of the local community. Soon after the museum opened, Chillman devised a formula for showcasing area artists. He recognized that "without art production, little art appreciation was possible," and he resolved that the museum should support both ventures equally.[9] During its inaugural season of 1924–25, the museum reserved a small gallery for local exhibitions, which was available for two weeks to any artist who requested it. The haphazard result of this policy quickly proved to be problematic, however, and Chillman acknowledged at the end of the first year that much of the work shown in the "independent" gallery was mediocre.[10] In 1925 he adopted the historically established procedure of an annual juried art competition, restricted its participants to Houston artists, and created a popular success that would endure until 1961. The *1st Annual Exhibition of Works by Houston Artists* opened on March 29, 1925, and featured the work of twenty-eight artists. The *Houston Chronicle* hailed the exhibition: "Never has the Museum of Fine Arts held so much of local interest as today. . . . Visitors to the museum will be surprised at the wealth and diversity of local talent."[11]

Photography was a component of the museum's program from its inaugural year as well, and in 1926 Chillman initiated an additional series of annual juried exhibitions for the region's photographers. Throughout Chillman's tenure the museum regularly sponsored local and statewide exhibitions of photographers, both amateur and professional (fig. 2); occasional exhibitions of international photographers were organized as well. However, support for photography did not extend to the permanent collection: the museum did not acquire any photographs until the early 1960s, when an anonymous portrait of Margaret Houston, wife of the illustrious Texan Sam Houston, was added to the Bayou Bend Collection.[12]

As the annual exhibitions were becoming a steady feature of the museum's schedule in the mid-1920s, Chillman developed a complementary series of solo shows of Texas artists. Unlike the first "independent" gallery exhibitions, these presentations were thoughtfully curated and were frequently accompanied by published check-lists or modest catalogues. Among the first Texans profiled were Emma Richardson Cherry, Alexandre Hogue, Julian Onderdonk, and Olin H. Travis, artists who reflected Chillman's ambition to showcase the range of Texas art across the state.[13]

In 1927 the educational mission of the institution was confirmed by the establishment of the Museum School of Art. The school offered art appreciation and studio classes to adults and children, and in 1937 a junior school department was formally designated. Classes were held in the museum's east wing, and the museum's exhibitions and collections became an integral part of the school's program. At the same time, the Museum School offered local artists full- and part-time teaching positions. One of the most influential members of the faculty was the painter Ruth Pershing Uhler (fig. 3), who began as an instructor in 1937. She completed her career thirty years later as the museum's veteran curator of education.

Although the economic crises of the Depression limited many areas of the museum's growth, the institution remained loyal to its artists. In the early 1930s, the museum's exhibition schedule ranged in quality from the popular and decorative, such as the national *Competition of Small Sculptures in White Soap* sponsored by Procter and Gamble and seen at the museum annually from 1929 to 1936, to august and historical presentations, such as *Italian Paintings from the Kress Collection*, seen in 1933. In this context the Houston annual exhibitions became mainstays of the exhibition and acquisition programs, an arrangement that benefited both the museum and area artists. Houston artists could exhibit their best works in an appropriate setting on a regular basis, and many received public recognition and press notices for the first time in their careers (fig. 4). For the museum, an enduring legacy of these exhibitions was the annual purchase prize, established in 1928 with the fourth annual exhibition.[14] The first award was sponsored by an anonymous "friend of art," but purchase prizes thereafter were supported by a board of trustees that shared Chillman's commitment to preserving "a tangible record of the accomplishment and progress of art in Houston."[15]

In addition to purchase prizes, the Texas collection

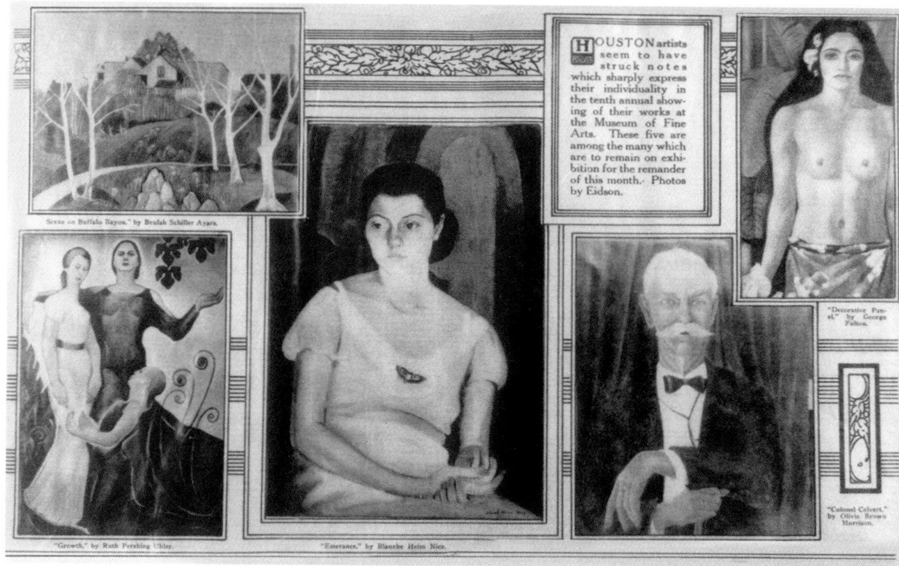

Fig. 4
"The 10th Annual Exhibition of Works by Houston Artists," *Houston Chronicle*, 31 January 1934.

grew through gifts from individual artists and collectors, as well as from organizations such as the Houston Friends of Art, organized in 1926, and the Garden Club of Houston. One of the museum's first formal commissions was awarded to William McVey, Houston's premier Art Deco sculptor. In 1935 the Garden Club commissioned him to create four reliefs to decorate a limestone garden wall for the museum's south lawn; appropriately, the reliefs celebrated the arts of Painting, Sculpture, Music, and Flower Arrangement.

The museum followed the success of its Houston artists' annual with a series of competitions that were broader in scope, including the annual circuit exhibition of work by Texas artists, sponsored by the Texas Fine Arts Association and curated by Chillman from 1929 to 1933, and the annual exhibition of work by Southeast Texas artists, held from 1937 to 1939.[16] These early efforts culminated in 1940 with the first *Texas General Exhibition* (later renamed the *Annual Texas Exhibition of Painting and Sculpture*), which was seen at the MFAH from 1940 to 1961 (fig. 5).[17] The *Texas General Exhibition* was organized jointly by the Dallas Museum of Art, San Antonio's Witte Memorial Museum, and the MFAH with the view that "by collective effort a group of art works could be formed representative of the highest attainments of Texas artists."[18] Similar to the ongoing Houston artists' annual in its juried format and purchase prize award, the

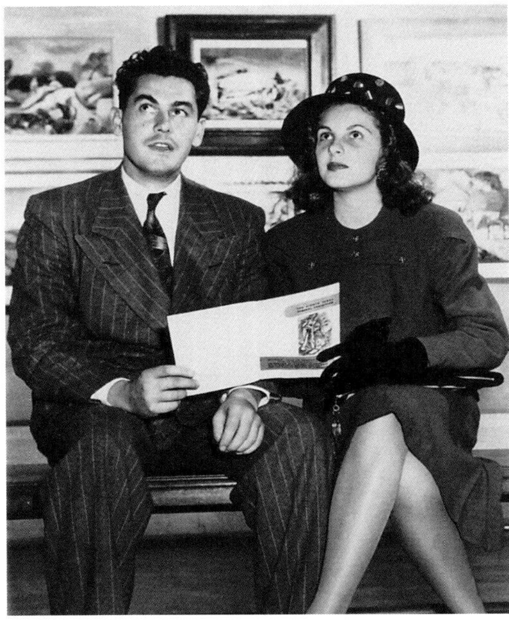

Fig. 5
Dr. Kiechler and Rosemary
Glaviana at the opening
reception, *Eighth Texas
General Exhibition*, the
Museum of Fine Arts,
Houston, 1946.

Texas General Exhibition was the state's most important traveling exhibition. It circulated to Houston, Dallas, and San Antonio annually, as well as to other Texas cities on occasion.

As statewide exhibitions gained momentum, broader support was given to diversifying acquisitions in Houston. In 1939 the museum purchased a number of lithographs by Dallas-area artists, including Alexandre Hogue, Everett Spruce, and Otis Dozier—all of whom were building national reputations along with strong regional ties. By 1940 the museum's Texas collection ranged from works by local favorites such as Evelyn Byers Bessell, to such popular figures as Edward M. "Buck" Schiwetz, to mavericks such as Forrest Bess, Mabel Fairfax Karl, and Robert Preusser.

The commitment to Texas art flourished throughout World War II, when national patriotism fueled regional pride. For example, in 1941 the institution's fund-raising literature reminded the public of the museum's commitment to regional art, and a brochure of that year noted that a typical exhibition schedule was heavily weighted towards the art of Houston and the state.[19] The introductory statement of the 1943 *18th Annual Exhibition of Works by Houston Artists* proclaimed, "No community can realize the full benefits of the Arts unless its local artists are recognized and encouraged."[20] The museum's annual report of 1944 announced that the acquisition of Spruce's painting *Green Hillside* (plate 9) marked the "coming of age of art in Texas," proving that "the Texas artist need no longer go outside the state to obtain his art education or to achieve national recognition."[21]

In a world where communications have cut down time and distance, regional art is fast disappearing. An international style in painting, sculpture, and architecture is practically inevitable.
—James Johnson Sweeney, 1966[22]

THE NEW INTERNATIONALISM: 1945–1982

World War II introduced important economic changes to Houston that would alter the city's identity in the following decades. Known as the "Magnolia City" of the South until the 1930s, post-war Houston shook off its romantic countenance to become America's petroleum capital, the fastest-growing city in the nation, and a leading example of a new sprawling urbanism. Suddenly, Houston's regional identity became a hindrance to its image as a modern urban center of national and international significance.

Responding to changing attitudes within the city, the Museum of Fine Arts, Houston, underwent a critical re-examination and rebirth during the post-war era. Although it continued to champion Texas art during the late 1940s and 1950s, practical factors such as cramped gallery spaces and limited financial resources forced the museum to reassess its priorities. As a result, the museum chose a more cosmopolitan focus for its exhibition and collection programs, making regional art a secondary emphasis. At the same time, however, the annual exhibition catalogues of 1947 and 1948 (fig. 6) document a similar shift in the work of Texas artists: "Gone are the sentimental bluebonnets, gone the pale magnolias, gone the nostalgic bits of Southern landscape," wrote James Chillman in 1947, "and in their places is a modern statement of modern times."[23]

Efforts to draw attention away from regional art carried over into the museum's auxiliary activities. A "Collectors Committee" was formed in the mid-1950s to encourage younger supporters to collect art and to strengthen their ties to the museum. The committee's guidelines included a specific interdiction, however, on purchasing works by Texans.[24] Furthermore, in the 1950s, the museum's acquisitions of Texas art were limited exclusively to the annual purchase prizes and gifts. Some of the prize winners during this decade, such as John Biggers's *The Cradle*, acquired in 1950 (fig. 7), and gifts such as Dorothy Hood's *Warrior's Plumage*, 1957 (plate 49), and Ary Stillman's *Black Magic*, 1953 (plate 50), both acquired in 1957, nevertheless remain cornerstones of the museum's collection.

As the museum gradually withdrew support from Texas art in particular and contemporary art in general, the city's need for an alternative institution became pressing. Venues for local art outside of the museum had existed sporadically since the 1930s with the establishment of small but dedicated groups such as the Houston Artists' Gallery and the Associated Artists of Houston.[25] However, in 1948, fresh impetus was given to the community with the foundation of the Contemporary Arts Association (CAA), now the Contemporary Arts Museum.[26] The first presentation sponsored by the CAA was held at the MFAH; titled *This is Contemporary Art,* it was a fine arts and design exhibition co-organized by one of Houston's leading abstract artists, Robert Preusser, a member of the Museum School faculty. By 1949 the CAA had its first home on Dallas Street in a Modernist building designed by Karl Kamrath; five years later the original structure was moved closer to the museum district when the CAA leased land from the Prudential Insurance Company of America at 6945 Fannin Street, in what is now the Texas Medical Center.[27] The quality of the early exhibitions and the enthusiastic audience for new art were aptly captured by Frank Freed in his *Opening Night: The Contemporary Arts Museum,* 1953 (fig. 8).

While the first CAA exhibitions stressed international developments in contemporary art, highlighting such artists as László Moholy-Nagy, Arthur Dove, Joan Miró, Max Ernst, and—surprisingly—Vincent van Gogh, Texas artists were a significant part of their program as well. In 1952 Chillman, along with Jerry Bywaters, then director of the Dallas Museum of Fine Arts, and Daniel Defenbacher, of the Fort Worth Art Association, organized an exhibition of *Texas Contemporary Art,* which was first seen in New York at Knoedler Gallery before being shown later that year at the CAA. In 1953 the CAA began a juried art competition called the *Art Rental Service,* featuring works that were available on a rental basis with the option to purchase. Acknowledging the importance of

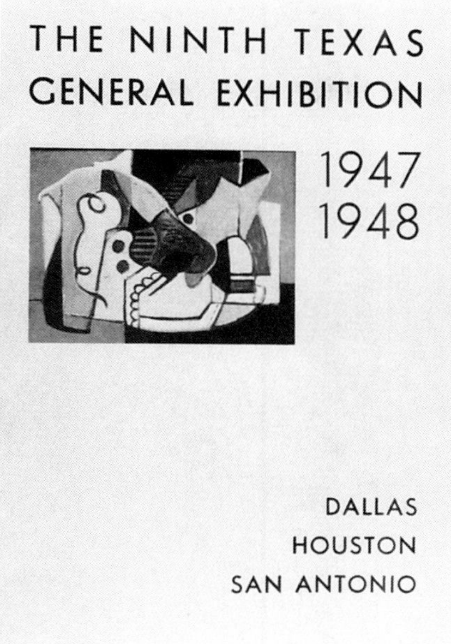

Fig. 6
Catalogue of the *Ninth Texas General Exhibition,* 1947–48. The cover illustration is *Yellow Shoes,* 1947, by DeForrest Judd.

Fig. 7
Catalogue of the *Twenty-fifth Annual Exhibit of Works by Houston Artists,* 1950. The cover illustration is *The Cradle,* 1950, by John Biggers; this drawing entered the MFAH collection as that year's purchase prize.

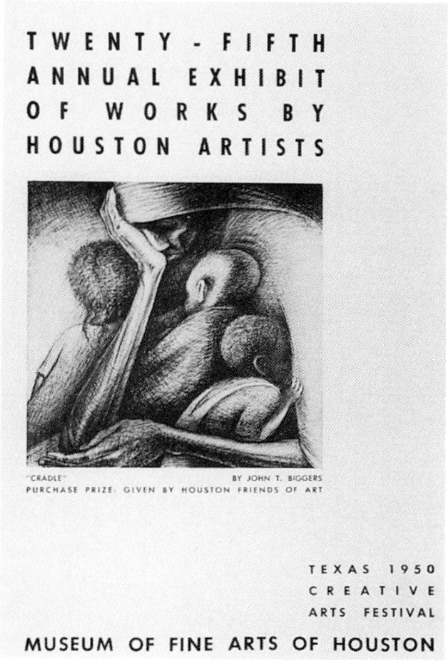

Fig. 8
Frank Freed
Opening Night: The Contemporary Arts Museum, 1953. Oil on canvas, 18 x 25 in. (45.3 x 63 cm). Gift of the Eleanor and Frank Freed Foundation, 93.260.

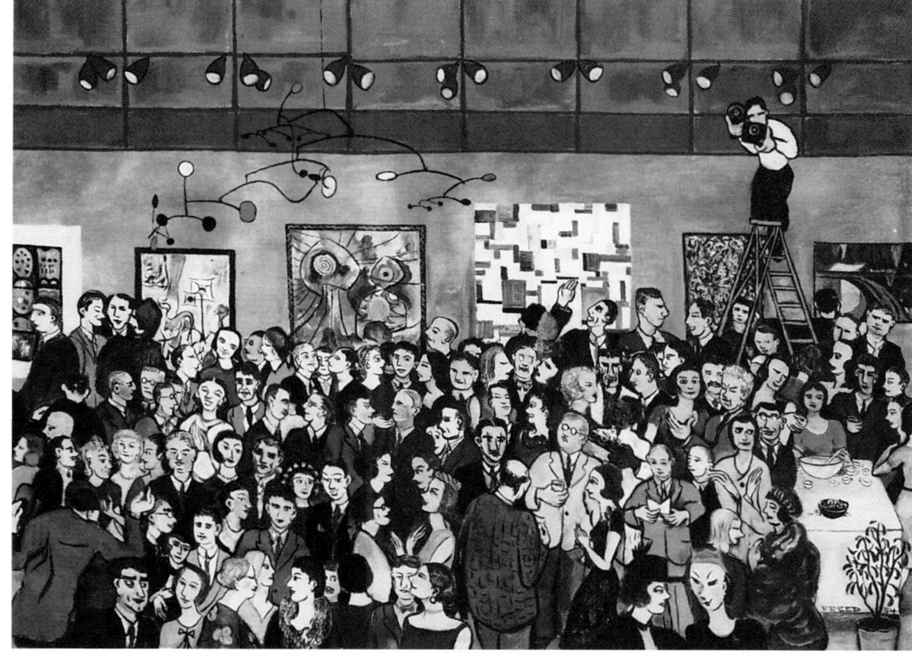

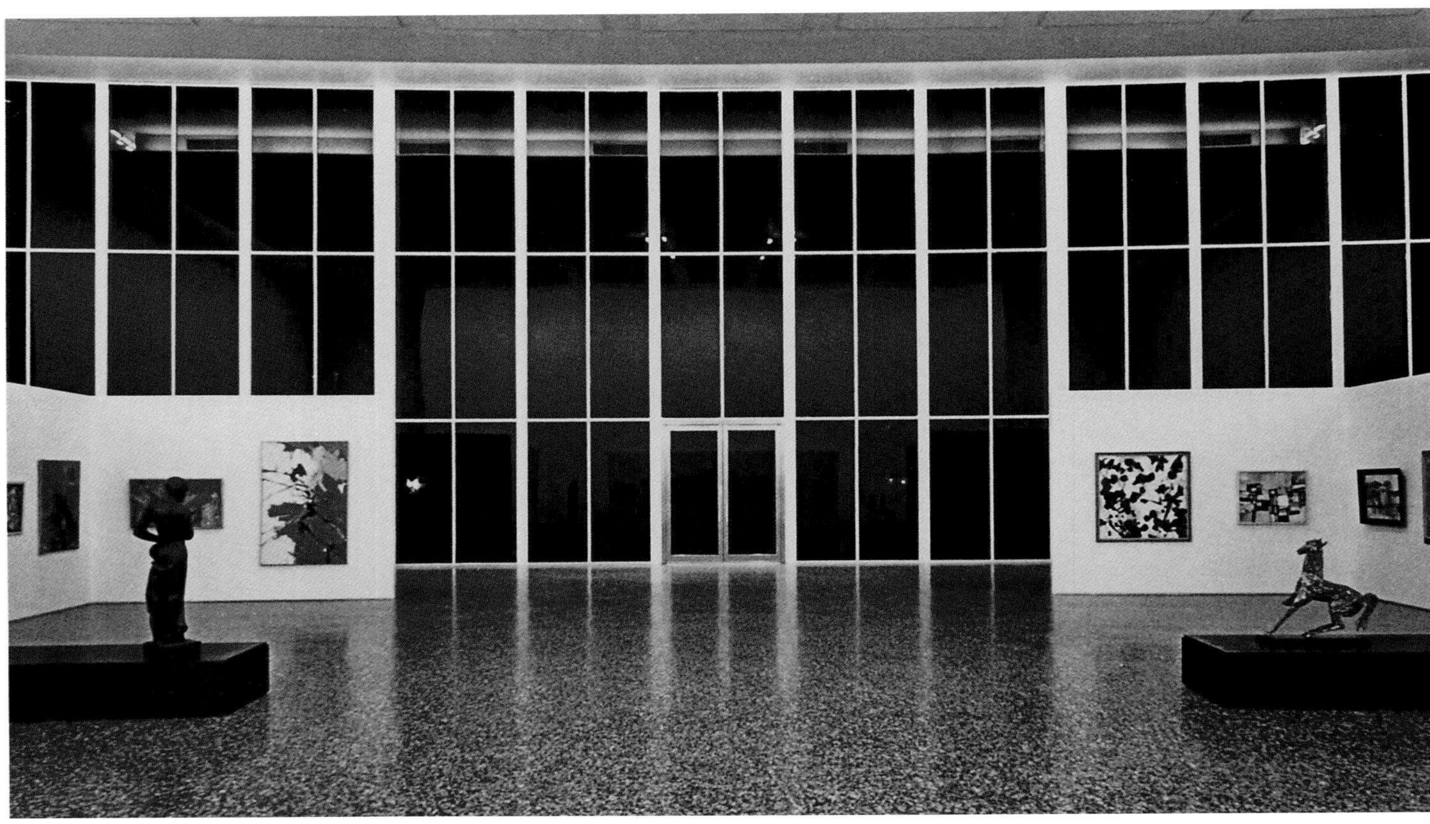

the local community, the CAA designed its art rental program specifically "to encourage a greater appreciation of painting and sculpture by Harris County artists."[28] In addition, through focus shows such as *Painting * Sculpture * Ceramics from the Texas Southern University*, 1953, the CAA offered important opportunities for African-American artists outside the mainstream community. Finally, as a part of its mission to promote contemporary art, the CAA initiated a collecting policy in 1954; not surprisingly works by Texas artists were among its early acquisitions. However, maintaining a permanent collection became a secondary concern as the CAA matured; the collection was only occasionally added to and then was gradually deaccessioned.[29] In 1955 Jermayne MacAgy became the organization's first professional director; her extraordinary talents in mounting exhibitions and her signal support of contemporary artists firmly anchored the Contemporary Arts Association in the Houston community.

As the CAA became more established in the 1950s, the MFAH committed most of its resources to building a historical collection and to erecting additional grand-scale galleries in which to display it. The museum built two major additions in the short span of five years, the first being the Robert Lee Blaffer Memorial Wing, designed by Kenneth Franzheim and completed in 1953. In 1954 the museum undertook a second, more ambitious expansion project. Funds to build the latter addition were donated

by Nina Cullinan, a longtime museum trustee and benefactor, who stipulated that an architect of international stature had to be named to design the new gallery and support spaces. Ludwig Mies van der Rohe was awarded the commission in February of that year; he immediately proposed a glass and steel structure that would transform the nature of the institution (see pages 220–221).[30]

Cullinan Hall, completed in October 1958, was the first phase of Mies van der Rohe's master plan for the museum, and it dramatically changed the museum's relationship to the city. The building's original south entrance, which faced Hermann Park and Rice University, became secondary to the new north entrance, which was oriented toward Houston's downtown. The brightly lit, open Miesian interior, soaring to a height of 30 feet, immediately became the city's preeminent exhibition site and presented a challenge to both the museum and exhibiting artists. Jermayne MacAgy, who was invited to stage exhibitions on behalf of the CAA, was the first curator to realize the potential of the space; her iconoclastic installations in Cullinan Hall were celebrated for their spare drama. Even more traditional exhibition projects took on a new character in Mies's arena, and the annual regional exhibitions were no exception. Installation views of the 1961 *22nd Annual Texas Painting and Sculpture Exhibition* (fig. 9) show a starkly Modernist interior that encouraged artists to work on a larger scale and in a more contemporary idiom.[31]

Lee Malone, who succeeded James Chillman in 1954 to become the MFAH's first full-time director, summarized the changing character of the city and the museum in his 1957 annual report. "Houston has become the great giant of industry and finance . . . we must hope for the finest in the artistic world, to live up to what is expected of us. Very soon we will leave the ranks of 'provincial museums' and join those whose reputation is world renowned."[32] Malone made little effort to increase the representation of Texas artists in the museum's exhibition schedule; however, during his tenure the museum's accessions policy was rewritten to emphasize the collecting of works by leading Texas and Southwestern artists.[33]

It would take James Johnson Sweeney, great champion of avant-garde art and the museum's director from 1961 to 1968, to fulfill the institution's goals of achieving international fame.[34] Sweeney came to Houston just as the city was once again assuming a new identity. The year of his arrival, the petroleum capital was refashioned into "Space City, USA," with the construction of the Johnson Space Center in suburban Clear Lake. The space theme quickly emerged as a new denomination for the city: the baseball team, the Colt .45s, was renamed the Houston Astros in 1964, and the following year the Astrodome, the first domed stadium in the United States, opened with much fanfare. Houston's reputation for being on the frontier of scientific discovery was further bolstered by the Texas Medical Center, which gained worldwide renown for its contributions to medicine, in particular for its breakthroughs in the areas of heart surgery and organ transplants.

Always energetic and often controversial, Sweeney brought a sophisticated vision to the museum's exhibition and collections programs. Exhibitions such as *Three Spaniards: Picasso, Miró, Chillida*, 1962; *The Olmec Tradition*, 1963; *Jean Tinguely: Sculptures*, 1965; *The Heroic Years: Paris 1908–1914*, 1965; and *Not Seen and/or Less Seen of/by Marcel Duchamp/Rose Sélavy (1904–1914)*, 1966, not only featured seminal works, but also showcased Sweeney's brilliantly creative installation techniques. Much as MacAgy revolutionized the city's appreciation of contemporary art in the late 1950s with her installations at the CAA and the MFAH, Sweeney used similarly dramatic techniques on a still greater scale. Exploiting

the theatrical expanse of Cullinan Hall, Sweeney reshaped Houston's perception of both the interior and exterior of the museum. The installation of Picasso's bronze *Bathers* on the north lawn in front of the museum in 1962 stopped passing traffic: the sculptures were posed in and around a shallow swimming pool that Sweeney had built temporarily on the museum grounds. For *The Olmec Tradition*, Sweeney again used the museum's north lawn to introduce the art inside — this time a monumental Olmec head that had been excavated from the jungles of central America specifically for the Houston exhibition.

The extraordinary sponsorship of trustees committed to contemporary art changed the nature of the museum's collection during Sweeney's tenure. Acquisitions such as Alexander Calder's *The Crab*, 1962, a museum purchase, and Eduardo Chillida's *Abesti Gogora*, 1966, funded by the Houston Endowment, were placed on the north and south lawns of the museum respectively, signaling a new ambition for contemporary acquisitions. Prominent patrons and maverick collectors Dominique

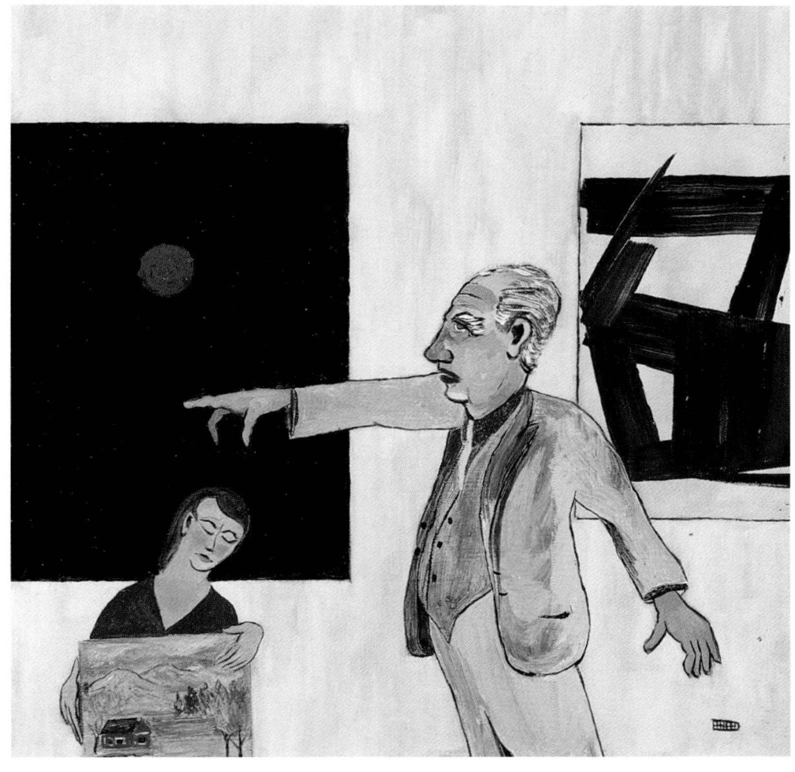

Fig. 10
Frank Freed
Out!, c. 1966
Oil on wood panel, 12 x 12 in. (30.2 x 30.2 cm). Gift of the Eleanor and Frank Freed Foundation, 94.250.

and John de Menil underwrote the purchases of several outstanding modern and contemporary works, including Jackson Pollock's *Number 6*, 1949, a retrospective series of Jean Tinguely's kinetic sculptures, and Claes Oldenburg's *Giant Soft Fan, Ghost Version*, 1967. The de Menils also sponsored a major Texas acquisition, Jim Love's *Paul Bunyan Bouquet No. 1*, 1962 (plate 14).

Sweeney's interests in regional art and the role the museum might play in supporting the local art community were minimal. Evaluating the broader scope of the Texas collection, Sweeney rightly found that many of the acquisitions from the annual exhibitions were of inferior quality, especially for a museum striving to create a world-class collection. He eliminated the Houston annual exhibition from the schedule in 1961 and the annual exhibition of Texas painting and sculpture the following year. In their place, Sweeney organized one major regional survey in 1962, *The Southwest: Painting and Sculpture*, inviting James Brooks and Alexander Calder to act as jurors.[35] For the remainder of his tenure few Texas artists were seen in either solo or group presentations, and exhibitions of local and regional artists dropped from the twenty to twenty-five percentage of previous decades to five percent. The sense of abandonment felt by the local art community was immediate and long-lasting. Frank Freed adroitly captured the mood of the time with *Out!*, c. 1966, in which Sweeney—posed in front of two epic New York School paintings—banishes from the museum a disconsolate woman holding a modest Southwestern landscape (fig. 10).

Sweeney's commitment to the pursuit of quality nevertheless had its positive impact on the Texas collection. Although only a small number of gifts and purchases of Texas art were made during the 1960s, they were of exceptionally high caliber, including works by John Biggers, Jack Boynton, Joseph Glasco, Dorothy Hood, Jim Love, and Dick Wray.[36] In 1962 the museum undertook an ambitious photographic project that became one of the region's landmark publications (fig. 11). Working with Houston architect Howard Barnstone, Henri Cartier-Bresson and Ezra Stoller were commissioned to photograph the historic buildings of Galveston. Their ninety-seven photographs were exhibited and added to the museum's collection in 1965, and the following year they were pub-

lished with accompanying text by Barnstone in *The Galveston That Was*. In his foreword, Sweeney offered one of his few critical assessments of the role that regional art could play in a broader context:

> Regionalism in art is one means toward the protection of individualism against the total encroachment of conformity. Today there is no hope of avoiding an international language in the arts. But one way to keep that international language vital in specific cases is the protection, so far as possible, of the regional spice. Regionalism can no longer be expected to dominate any expression of contemporary art. But where it survives, dominated by the broader international discipline, it can give vitality to our art, as individualism can to our lives.[37]

Perhaps Sweeney's greatest legacy to the museum was a reconsideration of the meaning of regionalism. During the first decades of the museum's history, regional artists were celebrated as a matter of civic pride, but their work was rarely integrated into the larger exhibition and collection programs. As demonstrated by his abolition of the Houston and Texas annual exhibitions, Sweeney abandoned this protectionist attitude, demanding of Houston and Texas artists the same standards that he applied to all museum projects. At the same time, he was expansive in his definition of regional activity, encouraging such internationally established artists as Cartier-Bresson to enter into a dialogue with local history.

Much as the identity of the museum shifted towards a more cultivated internationalism during the 1960s, so too did the contemporary art climate in Houston develop and change. Following her tenure at the CAA, Jermayne MacAgy became chairman of the art department newly founded by Dominique and John de Menil at the University of St. Thomas. In the years between 1959 and her untimely death in 1964, MacAgy carried on the visionary exhibition program which had characterized her work with the CAA. While few of her presentations featured art from the region, her treatment of the gallery space as an intellectual arena proved to be deeply influential on a number of Houston artists.[38]

The early 1960s was a period of flux for the CAA, but the directorship of Sebastian J. Adler (1966–73) saw the renewal and growth of the organization. In 1967 the CAA purchased a lot diagonally across from the museum

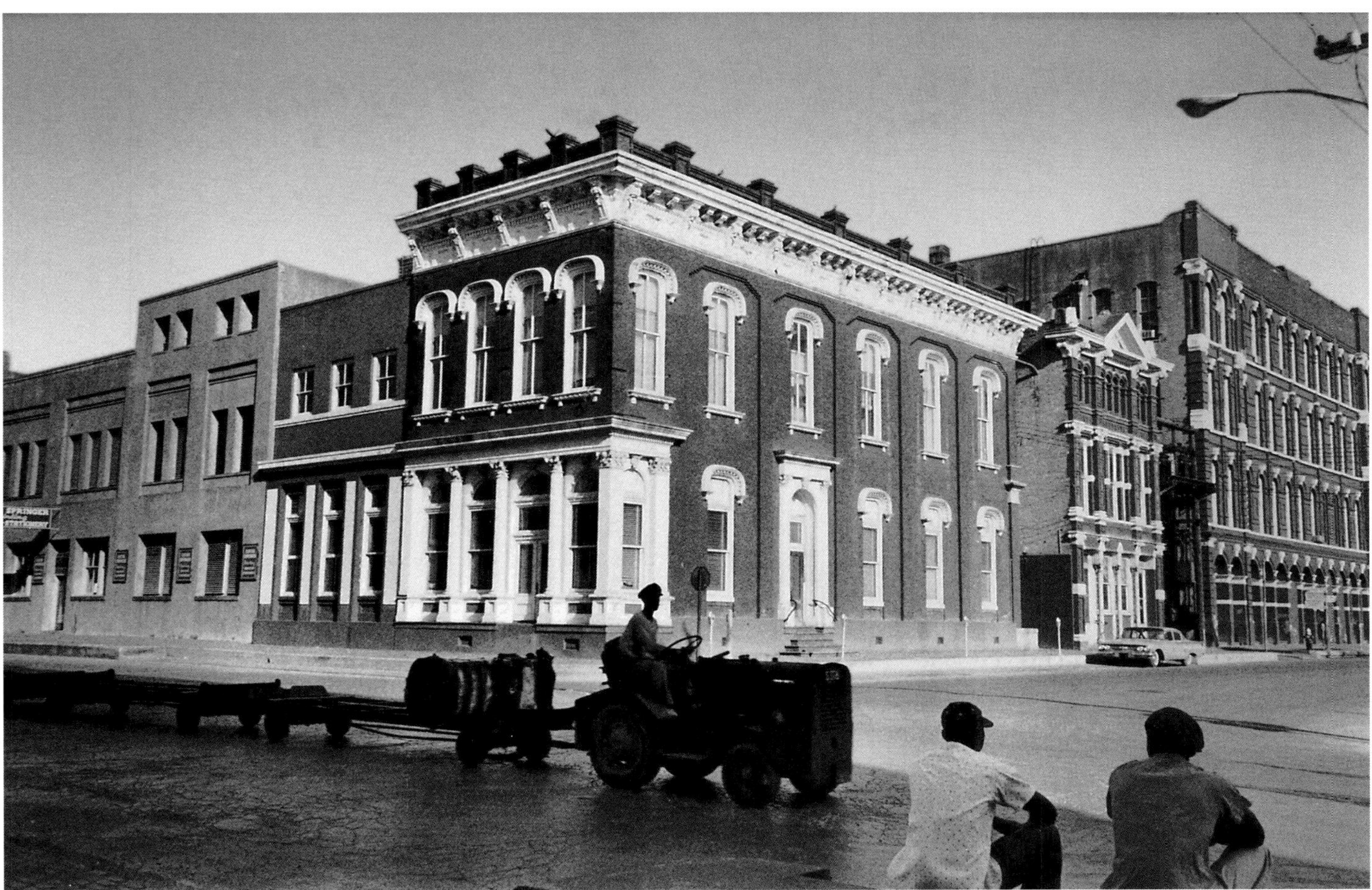

Fig. 11
Henri Cartier-Bresson
The Stewart Title Building and the First National Bank Building, circa 1878, 1962
Gelatin silver photograph, 8 x 12⅛ in. (20.1 x 30.5 cm). Museum purchase, 65.241.

on Montrose Boulevard, and Gunnar Birkerts & Associates was commissioned to create a building that, in the words of Adler, "is not Culture on a corner. I think of the new museum building as a stage environment to house the multimedia in which artists of today are working."[39] The Contemporary Arts Association's new facility opened in March 1972 as the Contemporary Arts Museum; the 10,000-square-foot space of the main gallery, free of dividing support walls, offered Houston an ideal site for the presentation of conceptual and installation art. During the subsequent tenure of James Harithas (1974–78), the Contemporary Arts Museum became a dynamic venue for Texas artists, with introductory exhibitions for such diverse figures as John Alexander, Terry Allen, Luis Jiménez, Julian Schnabel, Myron Stout, and James Surls.

Both Rice University and the University of Houston further demonstrated an increasing commitment to the visual arts during these years. In 1969 Dominique and John de Menil founded the Institute for the Arts at Rice University, which comprised an expanded art department, a media center, and the Rice Museum, which quickly established a reputation as Houston's preeminent arena for the avant-garde.[40] In 1973 the University of Houston completed the Sarah Campbell Blaffer Gallery, and

William Robinson became its first director in 1974. Among other programs, the Blaffer assumed responsibility for hosting the *Houston Area Exhibition*, which became the city's most prominent juried competition. At the same time, under the leadership of George Bunker, the studio department at the University of Houston began to attract such distinguished artists to its faculty as John Alexander, George Krause, the collaborative team MANUAL (Suzanne Bloom and Ed Hill), Gael Stack, and James Surls, among others.

Finally, the opening of the Rothko Chapel in 1971 was a landmark event in the cultural history of Houston. One of the de Menils' most significant acts of patronage, the chapel immediately captured the imagination of the local and international art community. Barnett Newman's *Broken Obelisk*, placed in front of the chapel, and Mark Rothko's somber suite of paintings within, established a vital presence for contemporary art outside of museum precincts, heralding an era of both minimalist and color field aesthetics that were to be major currents in the Houston art scene over the following decade.

The early 1970s also saw an era of growth at the MFAH. In 1974 the second phase of Mies van der Rohe's master plan for the institution was completed with the opening of the Brown Pavilion, and as the museum expanded, it renewed its commitment to collecting Texas art. The acquisition of regional work was reintroduced into the museum's long-range collecting policy in 1973 under the directorship of Philippe de Montebello (1969–74), who was better known for his championship of more historical material. De Montebello also hired the museum's first curator of twentieth-century art, E. A. Carmean, Jr., who served on the staff from 1971 to 1974. De Montebello's and Carmean's tenures coincided with the emergence of new funding sources for contemporary art, giving fresh impetus to the museum's Texas collection. In 1973 the museum received its first purchase awards from the National Endowment for the Arts (NEA) and from the Texas Commission for the Arts and Humanities. In the following year the museum used NEA funds to acquire Dorothy Hood's monumental painting *Sky Locus, 1974*.[41]

William C. Agee's subsequent tenure as director of the MFAH (1974–82) saw the NEA's support of the museum's Texas acquisitions expand dramatically.[42] After the abandonment of the annual purchase prize in 1962, no dedicated funds for Texas art had been allocated in the museum's budget. However, throughout the later 1970s and early 1980s, NEA moneys were repeatedly matched by local sponsors for Texas purchases, which in turn helped revive support for Texas art in the larger Houston community.[43]

Widely recognized as a leading scholar of American art, Agee directed the collecting goals of the museum toward a focused survey of European and American Modernism from 1910 to the present. Agee also initiated the first systematic program for collecting and exhibiting photography. Since *The Galveston That Was* project in 1965, only a dozen photographs had been acquired by the museum.[44] In 1976, with the assistance of a major grant from Target Stores, the museum made a formal commitment to collecting photography. Anne Wilkes Tucker assisted Agee in making the initial selection of photographs for the museum's Target Collection, and she joined the staff as its first curator of photography later that year. By the early 1980s, the photography department led the museum in contemporary Texas accessions.[45]

Although regional acquisitions gained momentum throughout these years, few Texas exhibitions were seen at the museum during the 1970s. The opening of Brown Pavilion had nearly doubled the institution's gallery space, but its galleries were largely reserved for national and international temporary exhibitions. The remaining galleries were committed to showcasing works from the museum's now-encyclopedic collection, as well as the outstanding Impressionist and early Modern paintings from the John A. and Audrey Jones Beck Collection. On average, the museum dedicated four percent of its exhibition schedule to regional art during de Montebello's directorship, and modestly increased that number to nine percent during Agee's tenure. Other than Museum School faculty exhibitions, the only group exhibitions of Texas artists seen at the museum during this era were a 1974 presentation of abstract painting and sculpture in Houston and a 1979 survey of naive artists. Distinguished solo exhibitions were devoted to Ary Stillman, Geoff Winningham, and Dorothy Hood.

The opening in 1979 of the Glassell School of Art, the new home of the Museum School, offered a fresh outlet for the region's artists. The staff immediately took advantage of the school's atrium gallery to develop a regular program of faculty, student, and special exhibitions. By the mid-1980s the combined exhibition schedule of the museum and school harkened back to the first decades of the institution's history, when local and regional artists made up one quarter of the exhibition schedule. Nevertheless, the school's atrium gallery did not have the visibility or prestige of the main museum building. Without exhibitions scheduled in the museum's premier galleries, many members of the Houston community believed that the museum had failed in its support of Texas art.

Painting is Dead, Long Live Painting in Houston.
—Barbara Rose, 1985 [46]

DIRECTION AND DIVERSITY: 1982–2000

Peter C. Marzio, who assumed the directorship of the Museum of Fine Arts, Houston, in 1982, called for all curatorial departments to reassess their collection needs soon after his arrival. The outcome was a major revision to the museum's long-range acquisition goals, including an unprecedented commitment to acquire at least fifteen works annually by Texas artists. At the same time, the museum's long-range exhibition schedule was reevaluated, resulting in a corresponding commitment to showcasing Texas art. *Fresh Paint: The Houston School*, the museum's first major exhibition devoted to surveying Texas art in more than a decade, opened in early 1985 (fig. 12). Curated by Barbara Rose and Susie Kalil, the exhibition featured the work of forty-four Houston area painters, ranging from such senior figures as Joseph Glasco to such emerging talents as Bert Samples. Rose's premise that there was an identifiable "Houston School" incited a storm of local controversy and brought national attention to Houston artists.

Rose, who was on the museum's curatorial staff from 1981 to 1984, astutely took advantage of a change in the national critical climate. The recognition of significant art centers in Chicago and Los Angeles, the wide-ranging exhibitions of such maverick New York curators as Marcia Tucker at The New Museum and Alanna Heiss at P.S. 1, The Institute for Art and Urban Resources, and the continuing growth and diversification of commercial galleries had created new audiences for artists working outside of New York. In her catalogue essay for *Fresh Paint*, Rose noted:

> It is essential to distinguish between Regionalism—the reigning style of thirties realism, based directly on the precedent of the old masters as a conscious opposition to the foreignness of European modernism—and the more complex, introspective individualistic styles of artists working outside New York. . . . Today, the notion of the avant-garde and what it represents is being actively questioned; moreover, the hegemony of New

York is being challenged not only by the emergent art of postwar Germany, Italy, France, Spain, and Great Britain but also by regional schools in America. [47]

Charlotte Moser, writing for *Art in America*, typified the arguments against Rose's insistence on a Houston School: "Influences of pluralism, folk, and ethnic art, and even the climate of Houston are all evident in the work in 'Fresh Paint'—but the paintings don't gel enough to suggest a distinctive school." [48] Thomas McEvilley noted in *Artforum*, "There really is a scene here [Houston]—not a school—which has begun to come out in the open but still waits to reveal itself in its full complexity." [49] In spite of these objections, the exhibition (which traveled to New York's P.S. 1) brought welcome attention to the Houston community, giving the city the contemporary identity that it had long sought. [50]

Before the show opened, Marzio and Rose promoted *Fresh Paint* as a landmark event in the museum's long-range plan, pinpointing new sources of corporate support for ambitious acquisitions. Texas Eastern Corporation (now Duke Energy) was the first major corporate sponsor to take on a long-term commitment to the Texas collection; in 1982 Texas Eastern underwrote the purchase of

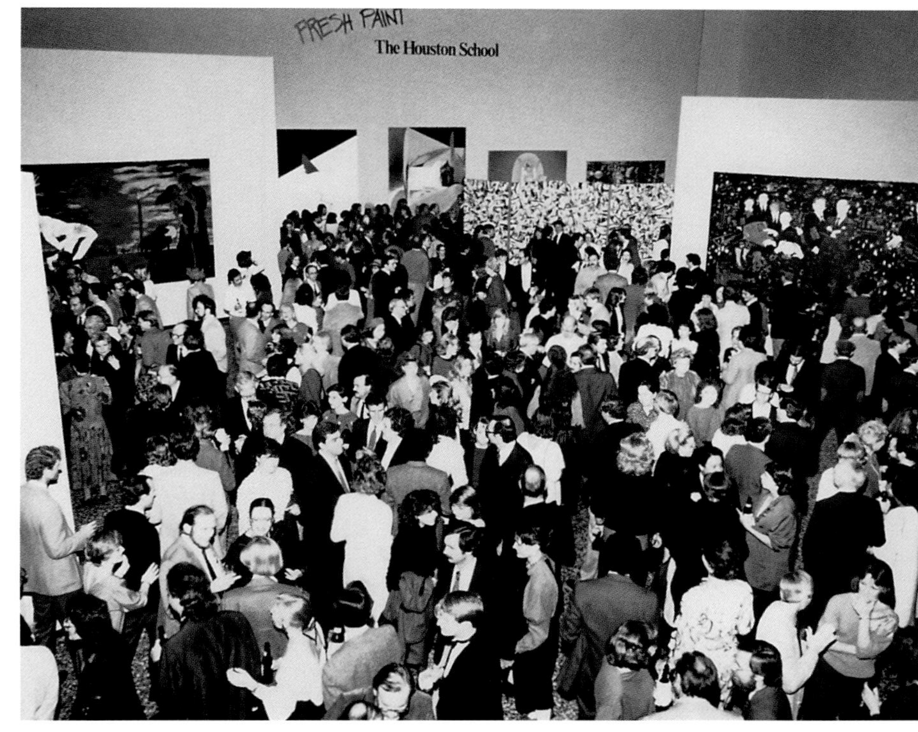

Fig. 12
Opening reception, *Fresh Paint: The Houston School,* the Museum of Fine Arts, Houston, 24 January 1985.

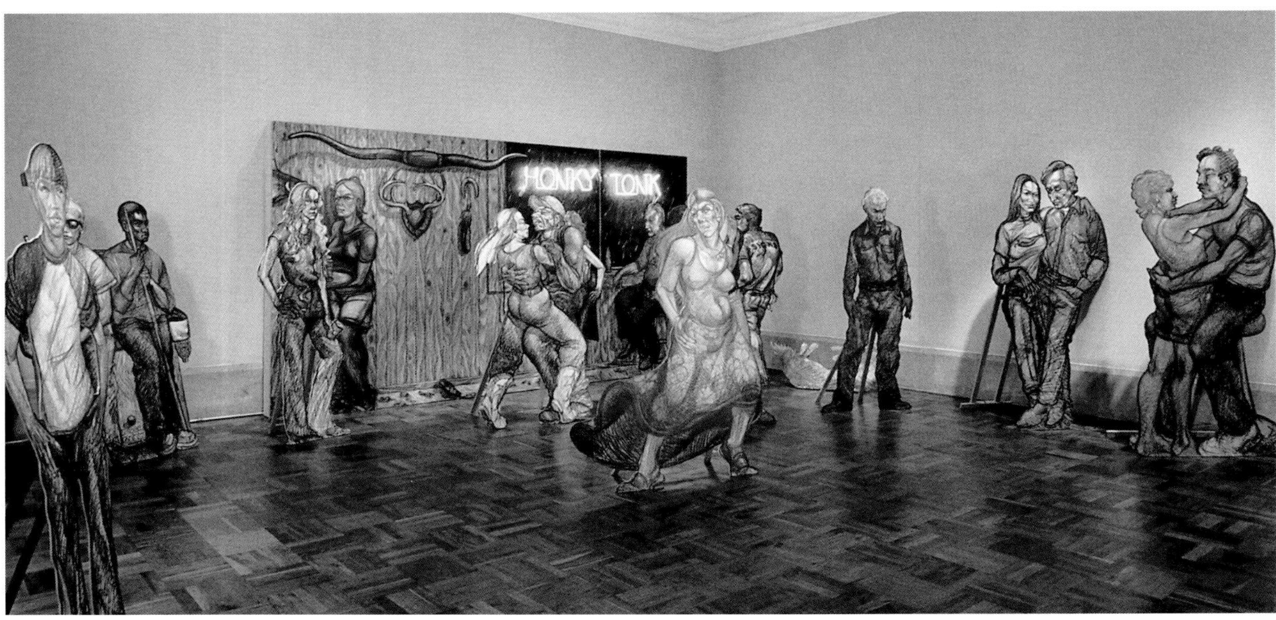

Fig. 13
Luis Jiménez
Honky Tonk, 1981–86
Mixed-media installation,
collection of the artist;
installed in *Hispanic Art in
the United States: Thirty
Contemporary Painters and
Sculptors,* the Museum of
Fine Arts, Houston, 1987.

James Surls's monumental *I Am Building with the Axe, the Knife, and the Needle's Eye* (plate 24), followed in 1983 and 1984 by the purchases of paintings by Melissa Miller and James Drake. In 1985 ten acquisitions were made of works by artists featured in *Fresh Paint* and over the next decade more than twenty major works were acquired through the corporation's generosity.

Although Rose left the museum in 1984, the new emphasis on Texas exhibitions exemplified by *Fresh Paint* was confirmed by two presentations organized by guest curators for the museum: William A. Camfield's *Works on Paper: Eleven Houston Artists,* which was seen at the same time as *Fresh Paint,* and Susie Kalil's *The Texas Landscape: 1900–1986,* which celebrated the 1986 Texas sesquicentennial.[51] *The Texas Landscape* was the museum's first historical survey of Texas art and featured works in all media—from painting, sculpture, and photography to conceptual documentations—including an ephemeral installation by Michael Tracy.

In the years immediately following the *Texas Landscape* presentation, the museum hosted two exhibitions that looked at Texas art in a broader context. In 1987 *Hispanic Art in the United States: Thirty Contemporary Painters and Sculptors,* guest-curated by Jane Livingston and John Beardsley, included the work of five artists associated with Texas: Ibsen Espada, Patricia Gonzalez, Luis Jiménez, César Augusto Martínez, and Jesús Bautista Moroles (fig. 13). In 1988 the museum brought to Houston a mid-career retrospective of Julian Schnabel, by then better known as a New York artist than as a former Houstonian.[52] At the same time, the Glassell School's exhibition program gained in sophistication during the

1980s with presentations organized by the school's curator Janet Landay, including *Collaborators: Artists Working Together in Houston 1969–1986,* 1986, and *One + One: Collaborations by Artists and Writers,* 1988.

The MFAH's renewed commitment to Texas art was matched by other institutions in the city. Despite, or perhaps in reaction to, the oil-market crash that devastated the Texas economy in 1982–83, Houston organizations stepped up their support of area artists in the mid- and late 1980s. Linda L. Cathcart, director of the Contemporary Arts Museum from 1979 to 1988, maintained a balance of sophisticated Texas art exhibitions with presentations of national and international figures. The ongoing *Perspectives* series in the museum's lower gallery showcased many Texas artists; important group exhibitions—such as the 1981 *4 Painters: Jones, Smith, Stack, Utterback* and the 1983 *Southern Fictions*—offered critical assessments of the character of the local art scene. During the 1986 Texas sesquicentennial, the CAM mounted three major retrospectives of artists associated with Texas: Robert Rauschenberg, Joseph Glasco, and Melissa Miller. Following Cathcart's departure in 1988, the CAM undertook a long-range commitment to present significant juried shows of Texas art, beginning with *The First Texas Triennial,* organized by Marilyn A. Zeitlin. Similarly, the exhibition program at the University of Houston's Sarah Campbell Blaffer Gallery gained focus under the supervision of Marti Mayo, who became the director in 1986. A curator at the CAM for much of Cathcart's tenure, Mayo revived the *Houston Area Exhibition* at the Blaffer in 1988 and organized a major retrospective of Gael Stack the following year.

The 1987 opening of The Menil Collection, transferred from its modest quarters at Rice University to a magnificent building designed by Renzo Piano in the Montrose district, brought international attention to Houston.[53] While The Menil Collection's exhibition program reflected the de Menil family's extraordinary collection of ancient, tribal, Surrealist, and contemporary art, the new museum also offered selected but important Texas exhibitions.[54] Walter Hopps, who became the organization's director in 1982, took a special interest in the region's artists and promoted Texas projects both at the Menil and through other venues.

The late 1970s and early 1980s also saw the establishment of a number of alternative spaces, three of which survived to become significant independent entities: the Lawndale Annex of the University of Houston, founded in 1979; the Houston Center for Photography, founded 1982; and DiverseWorks Artspace, founded in 1983.[55] Many of the exhibitions seen at these venues, such as the DiverseWorks retrospective of Mel Chin in 1985, anticipated later museum exhibitions and acquisitions. More importantly, with programs largely determined by advisory boards consisting primarily of artists, alternative spaces provided critical testing grounds for a new era of art in Houston, offering venues for installations and performance that were vital to the evolution of Houston's contemporary scene. In addition, photography in Houston found an expanded forum in FotoFest. A festival of exhibitions and conferences devoted to local, national, and international photography, FotoFest had its first meeting in 1984; under the direction of Houston-based photographers Fred Baldwin and Wendy Watriss, it subsequently became established as one of the city's most celebrated biennial art events.

Nonprofit spaces and independent activities were complemented by a growing number of important commercial galleries dedicated primarily to contemporary art and Texas artists. Between 1970 and 1985 more than twenty significant galleries opened in Houston.[56] While the faltering economy limited gallery expansion after 1982, the commercial scene remained surprisingly enduring, supported by a growing circle of local and national collectors. Newly opened corporate art spaces in the city's newest skyscrapers—most notably the Transco

Gallery, Allen Center, and Cullen Center—offered further sites for exhibitions.

As venues for Texas artists multiplied, the MFAH began to seek additional means of making a distinctive contribution to the community. Not surprisingly, the Glassell School led the museum in reflecting and participating in the increasing diversity of the Houston art scene, providing a vital liaison between more formal museum activities and emerging artists. In 1982, under the leadership of Allan Hacklin (director of the school from 1982 to 1989), the Glassell School initiated the Core Residency Program. Established to encourage young artists to make Houston their home, Core Fellowships were awarded on an annual basis, with the opportunity for a one-year renewal. Artists were provided with working space in the Glassell building and a stipend to cover studio expenses; guest artists and scholars were integrated into the program through studio critiques and public lectures. The Core Program rapidly became a fertile ground for new talent: Core Fellows, many of whom had come to Texas from other regions of the country, as well as from abroad, brought a breadth of experience to Houston. At the same time, Houstonians who entered the Core Program were able to develop their work in a fresh critical climate. The annual Core exhibitions were integrated into the Glassell School's schedule (fig. 14) and over the following decade a number of works by Core Fellows were acquired for the museum's collection.

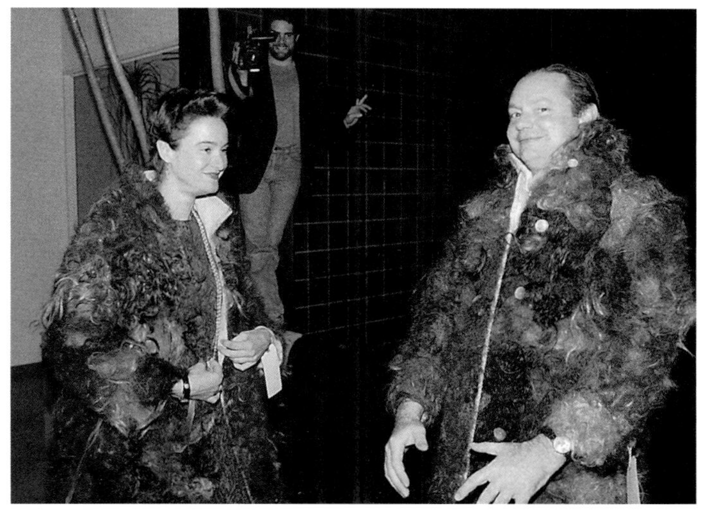

Fig. 14
Opening reception, *Core Fellows Exhibition*, the Glassell School of Art, 15 March 1989. In the foreground are Dean Ruck's *Human Hair Coats*, 1989, modeled by Ramona Fabrigas and Kirk Farris; in the background Ruck films the scene.

Another distinctive aspect of the museum's programs in the 1980s was the rapid expansion of the film department under the supervision of Ralph McKay.[57]   Through McKay's innovative programming, the MFAH began to have an active liaison with such filmmakers as Wim Wenders, and the museum hosted the Texas premiere of Wenders's *Paris, Texas* in 1985. McKay also worked with local filmmakers in the production of Houston-based projects, a tradition that was further upheld by Marian Luntz, who joined the museum's staff in 1990. Among the projects supported by both McKay and Luntz was Robert Ziebell's *This State I'm In*, a visionary chronicle of the Gulf Coast, which premiered at the MFAH in 1990 (fig. 15).

While the exhibition program of the MFAH complemented those of other institutions, one aspect of the museum's support of Texas art was unique: the museum emerged in the 1980s as an unparalleled collecting force of both Houston and Texas artists. The enthusiasm first generated by the *Fresh Paint* and *Texas Landscape*

Fig. 15
Film still from Robert Ziebell's *This State I'm In*, 1990.

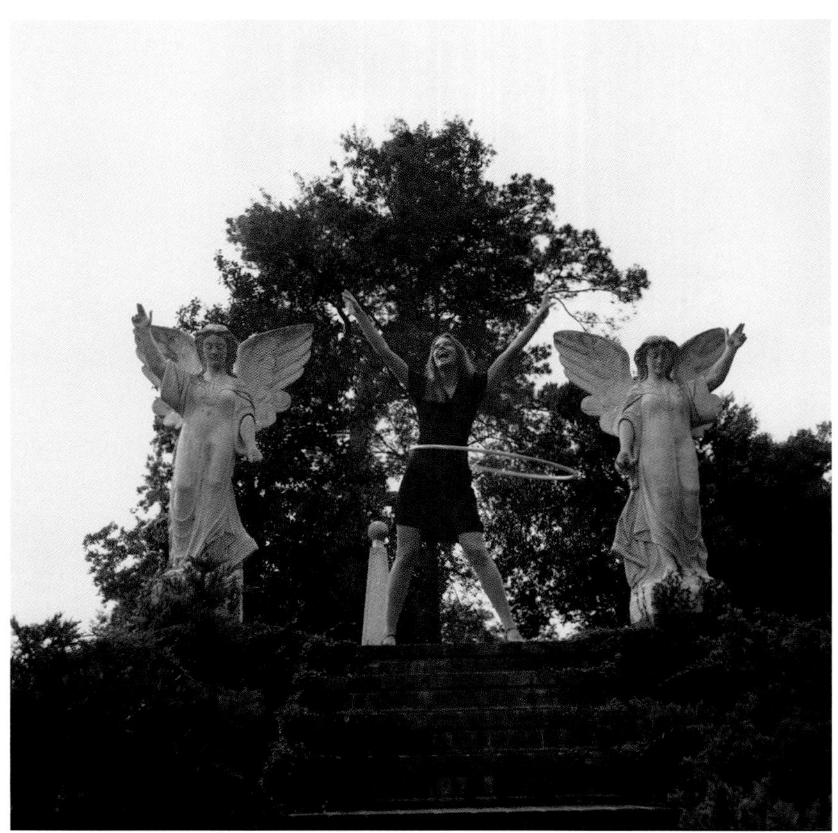

presentations was reflected in acquisitions undertaken by the twentieth-century and photography departments, led by Alison de Lima Greene, who joined the museum's curatorial staff in 1984, and Anne Wilkes Tucker. Building on the strength of annual grants from Texas Eastern Corporation for Texas acquisitions, as well as ongoing grants from the NEA, both curators actively sought additional support from the community. Membership organizations such as the Museum Collectors (founded in 1979) and Photo Forum (founded in 1988) made further significant contributions to the museum's collection of Texas art, and numerous individuals, corporations, and foundations made possible acquisitions on a scale unrivaled by any museum in the region. Houston-area artists were typically accorded first priority, but significant statewide acquisitions were made as well. Furthermore, as the Texas collection became more and more representative of contemporary currents, curators began to take a longer view towards filling in historical gaps. Thus contemporary purchases began to be increasingly balanced by acquisitions of such figures as Forrest Bess, Carlotta M. Corpron, Ben Culwell, Alexandre Hogue, and Toni LaSelle.

The expanding collections put an ever higher premium on the institution's galleries. In 1985 Marzio reorganized the configuration of the permanent collection galleries, devoting the major part of Brown Pavilion to a survey of the European collections. However, the museum's collection of twentieth-century art in general, and works on paper and contemporary art in particular, were without permanent galleries and could only be viewed in intervals as special exhibitions. One of the first and most ambitious of these presentations was a 1988 survey of the collection. Titled *Twentieth-Century Art in the Museum Collection: Direction and Diversity*, the installation was accompanied by a museum bulletin written by Greene, which offered the first historical overview of the museum's twentieth-century collection. Integrated into the survey were selected Texas artists, including Derek Boshier, Vernon Fisher, Melissa Miller, Gael Stack, James Surls, and Michael Tracy.[58]

The opening of the museum's Lillie and Hugh Roy Cullen Sculpture Garden in 1986, created by sculptor Isamu Noguchi to house the museum's collection of outdoor sculpture, provided an alternate forum for the twentieth-century collection. While no Texas artists were placed on permanent display in the sculpture garden until 1991, the *Collaborators* exhibition of 1986 introduced Texas art into the garden, with an installation by Paul Kittelson and Olin Calk, *Anticipating the Drought/An "Untidied" Field*.[59] The first Houston artist commissioned to create a work for the garden was Jim Love; subsequent installations of sculptures by DeWitt Godfrey and Joseph Havel balanced the work of Texas artists with such international figures as Louise Bourgeois, Tony Cragg, and Joel Shapiro.

The museum's policy of aggressive acquisitions and selected exhibitions of Texas art continued into the 1990s, with new support coming from such organizations as the museum's African American Art Advisory Association, established in 1993. The Texas collection numbered more than 1,000 objects in 1990, and close to 1,500 only five years later.[60] The departments of photography and twentieth-century art maintained the momentum of acquisitions established in the 1980s, and Barry Walker, who joined the museum's staff in 1991 as curator of prints and drawings, combined connoisseurship with a sense of adventure to radically transform the museum's collection of works on paper. Unlike the first decades of the museum's history, when the Houston and Texas annual exhibitions generated a limited number of purchase prizes to build the collection, now the exponential growth of the collection created a need for showcase exhibitions. Thus, in 1990 *Tradition and Innovation: A Museum Celebration of Texas Art*, offered a large-scale historical overview of the museum's holdings; recent acquisitions were profiled by the 1990 *Houston Photographers* and the 1993 *Texas Contemporary* presentations; and the seventieth anniversary of the first Houston annual exhibition was commemorated by two collection exhibitions during the 1995–96 season: *Texas Myths and Realities* and *Texas Modern and Post-Modern*. In addition, signal solo exhibitions which reflected collection strengths were devoted to George Krause and Gay Block in 1992, as well as Frank Freed in 1996. In 1995 Alvia J. Wardlaw joined the museum staff and organized a retrospective of John Biggers (fig. 16).

Under the directorship of Dan Gorski, who joined the museum staff in 1990, the Glassell School hosted a

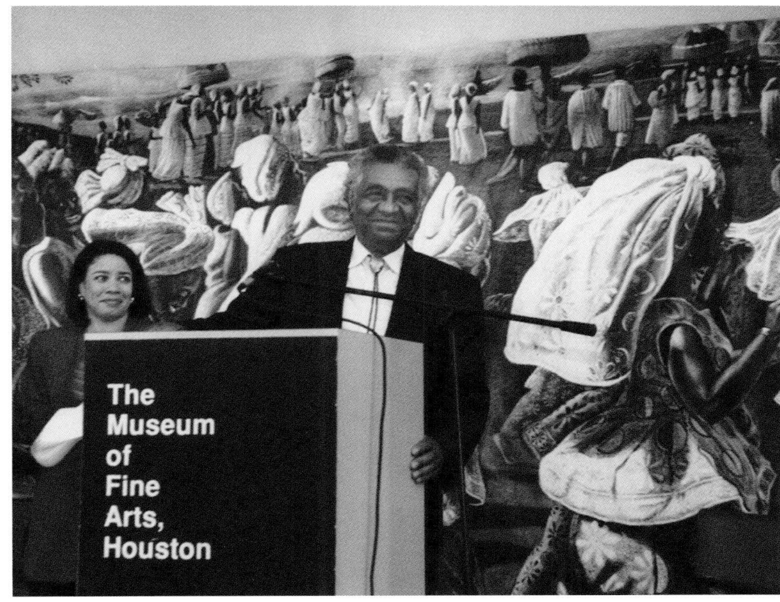

Fig. 16
MFAH curator Alvia J. Wardlaw and John Biggers in front of Biggers's *Jubilee: Ghana Harvest Festival* mural at the Family Day reception for *The Art of John Biggers: View from the Upper Room*, the Museum of Fine Arts, Houston, 2 April 1995.

number of important exhibitions which were revisionist in intent. Chief among these projects were the 1991 *Material as Message*, curated by Liz Ward, the 1992 *Fresh Visions/New Voices: Emerging African-American Artists in Texas*, curated by Joseph Havel and Rick Lowe, and the 1993 *Artists' Progress: Seven Houston Artists 1943–1993*, curated by David E. Brauer.[61] With the transfer of the museum's Junior School to a new building in 1994, the Glassell School's exhibition program was able to expand and undertake more radical installations. Havel, subsequently the director of the Glassell School, and Valerie Loupe Olsen, administrative dean, further added depth to the school's exhibition program by publishing significant brochures and catalogues for such exhibitions as *Genesis in Fire: Works from the Green Mountain Foundry*, 1995–96; *Linda Ridgway: The Poetics of Form*, 1997; and *In Situ: Responses from Charles Mary Kubricht and Ann Stautberg*, 1998.

Other Houston museums and university galleries sustained many of their Texas-based activities into the following decade. The directorship of the Contemporary Arts Museum was held by Suzanne Delehanty from 1989 to 1993; Marti Mayo assumed the position in 1994. Both Delehanty and Mayo continued the balance of exhibitions promoted by Cathcart; the *Texas Triennial* of 1988 was followed up by a second state-wide survey in 1993–94 titled *Texas/Between Two Worlds*, while the *Perspectives* series in the lower-level gallery continued to offer important introductory and mid-career solo exhibitions. In the mid- and late 1990s, the Contemporary Arts Museum initiated such important solo exhibitions as *The Art Guys: Think Twice*, curated by Lynn M. Herbert, and significant surveys that offered a larger context for Texas art, including, most notably, *Abstract Painting Once Removed*, curated by Dana Friis-Hansen. The Sarah Campbell Blaffer Gallery at the University of Houston hosted *Houston Area Exhibitions* in 1992 and 1996, as well as the 1994 *Poison Amor: A Collaborative Installation by Terry Allen and James Drake*. In 1996 Don Bacigalupi joined the staff as director, and the following year he organized a significant survey of University of Houston graduate Michael Ray Charles. The Menil Collection, under the directorship of Paul Winkler, profiled James Reaben and the early work of Robert Rauschenberg in 1990 and 1991. Furthermore, in 1998, The Menil Collection brought to Houston the monumental *Robert Rauschenberg: A Retrospective*: in a unique, citywide collaboration, the work of the first three decades was seen at The Menil Collection; the art and technology and performance work was seen at the CAM; and the recent work, including Rauschenberg's *1/4 Mile or Two Furlong Piece*, was seen at the MFAH.

The larger art community in Houston saw parallel developments. While many corporate gallery spaces had shut their doors by the end of the 1980s, the alternative spaces DiverseWorks and Lawndale both found new homes, in 1989 and 1992 respectively. And while the gallery boom of the late 1970s and early 1980s could not be sustained, the more moderate economy of the early 1990s nonetheless supported a second wave of galleries primarily devoted to regional artists.[62] By the mid-1990s, however, a surge of important new venues opened in Houston, including the restructured Rice University Art Gallery. Kimberly Davenport, who became the director at Rice in 1994, brought a new range of programming to the university's campus. She transformed the institution by hosting a series of site-specific installations by such celebrated figures as Sol LeWitt, Gary Hill, and Nicole Eisenman; she also brought to Houston numerous emerging artists working outside of Texas.

The adaptation of non-art structures for site-specific installations marked Houston's further coming of age as a home to the arts. While temporary outdoor installations and folk-art environments had established an ongoing tradition in Houston in the 1970s, including Jeff McKissack's extraordinary *The Orange Show*, the abundance of unoccupied property within city limits made possible a number of exceptional experimental ventures in the last decade of the century.[63] The most successful of these ventures, Project Row Houses, opened in 1994, and has since become a national model for such enterprises (fig. 17). Following the example of the Spoleto Festival's *Places with a Past* exhibition of 1991 in Charleston, South Carolina, Project Row Houses was conceived by Rick Lowe and a consortium of African-American artists; working with a broad range of support, they reclaimed a block of twenty-two derelict shotgun houses in Houston's Third Ward. The MFAH, the Contemporary Arts Museum, The Menil Collection, as well as the city's alternative spaces, corporations, and private individuals joined in the renovation effort: eight houses were set aside as venues for rotating installations, others were dedicated to start-up community projects.[64] Such activities, which by their nature cannot take place within museum precincts, ultimately attest to the long-term success of the MFAH, which was founded in 1900 "to encourage in all ways within its power the efforts of local artists."[65] Now, a century later, these efforts cannot be confined by any one institution's walls.

Several extraordinary millennial projects extend the Art League's original vision of uniting the Houston community with the larger art world. The opening of the MFAH's Audrey Jones Beck Building, designed by Spanish architect Rafael Moneo, which features two monumental bronze reliefs at its Main Street entrance by Houston sculptor Joseph Havel, and the construction of the Live Oak Friends Meeting House, the result of a collaboration between West Coast artist James Turrell and Houston architect Leslie Elkins, are but two examples of the ongoing and effective dialogue between Texas, national, and international figures. In 1992, art critic Michael Ennis observed:

The myth Texas artists are currently defining is not nearly so simple as a revisionist Texas myth, or even a new Pan-American myth, although it includes elements of both. It is a working model of a Postmodern myth that is at once regional and global. The prototype factory for this myth is Houston, which is arguably the first Postmodern art center; at least it can indisputably claim the first Postmodern skyline. More importantly, Houston is the first art center to emerge in an era marked by two key economic details: a dramatic reduction in the cost of international air travel, and a dramatic inflation in land values and living costs in the world's great cities. . . . Quick, cheap access to the capitals of virtually every epoch and culture is now available to artists living virtually anywhere in the industrial world. This unprecedented mobility has produced the most sophisticated, cosmopolitan generation of artists in history, artists who are studying in a global atelier and then returning to places like Houston—large enough and sufficiently variegated to nourish a community of artists, yet not so densely populated as to crowd them out—to pursue their careers. The age of the cultural capitals is over, at least for the next historical moment. The art of the twenty-first century is likely to be defined in a half-dozen or fifteen or even thirty centers . . . quite similar to Houston.[66]

Ultimately it is the city that shapes the museum and its community. Across the decades, Texas exhibitions and acquisitions have undergone changes which reflect the evolution of Houston. The passionate dedication of the many individuals who make up the Houston art community—patrons and directors, artists and curators, dealers and collectors—has fostered a unique dynamic in which direction is balanced by diversity. The Museum of Fine Arts, Houston, has been integral to this dynamic, in both leading and responding to Houston's commitment to the arts.

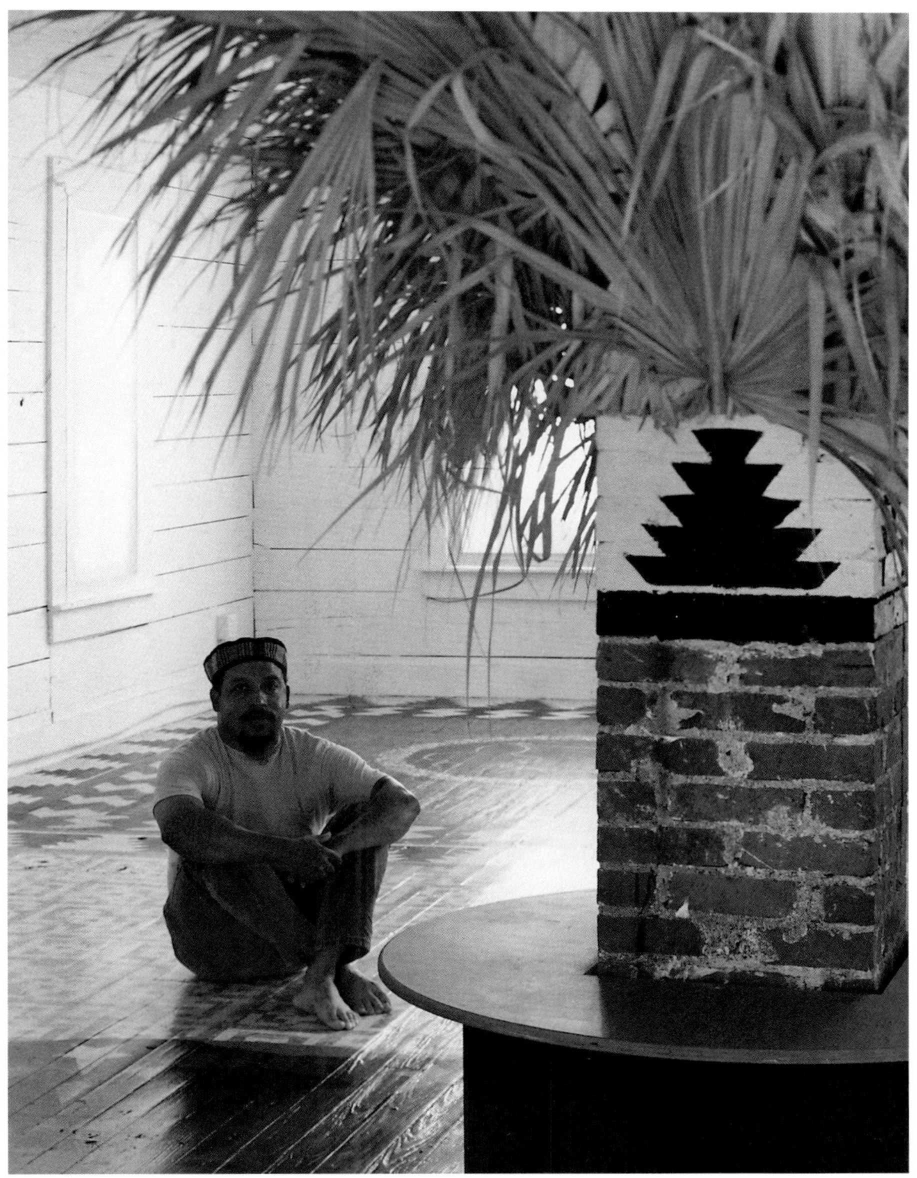

Fig. 17
Bert Samples in his installation *Eyuphuro (Whirlwind)*, 1997, mixed-media installation, Project Row Houses, Houston.

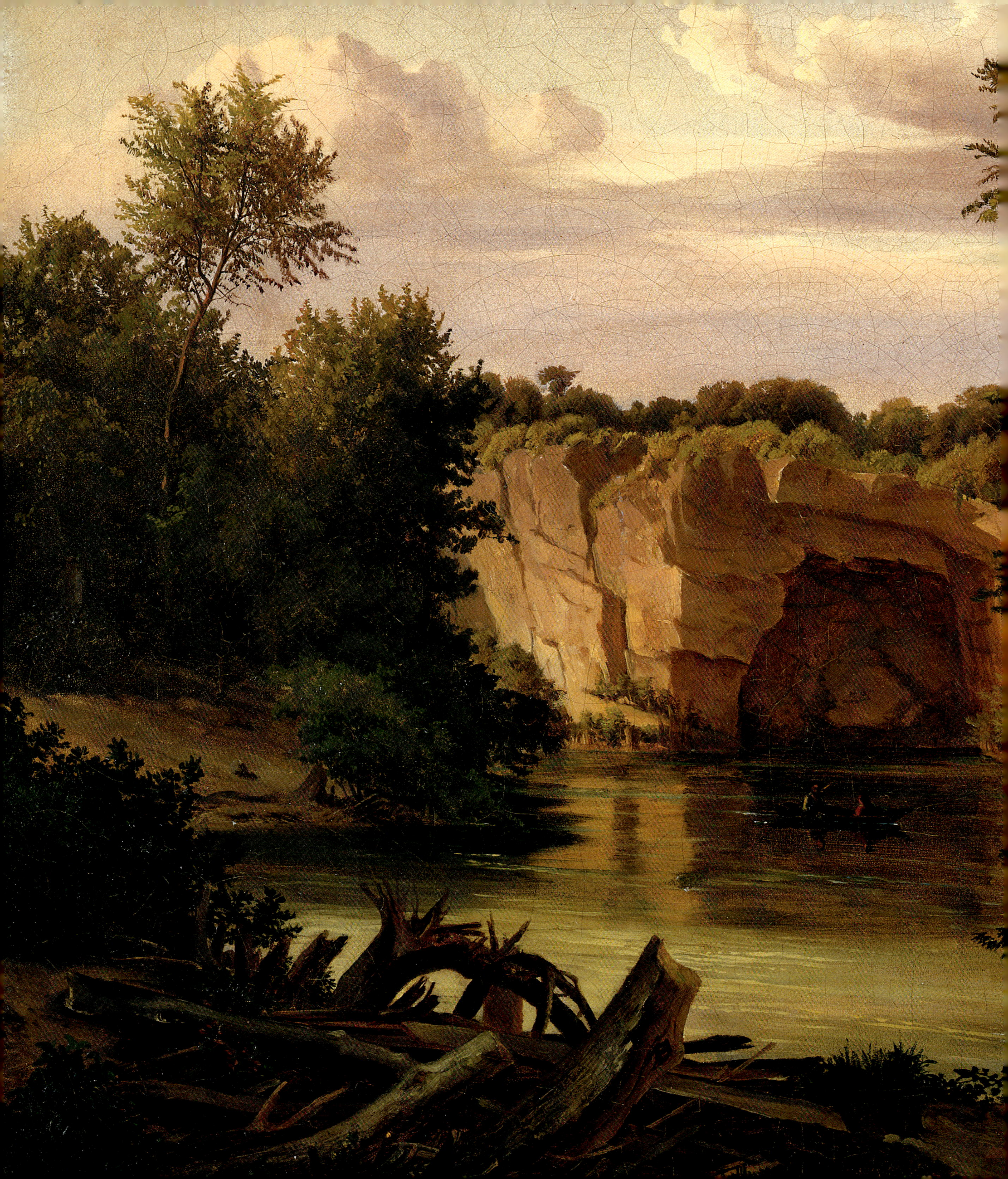

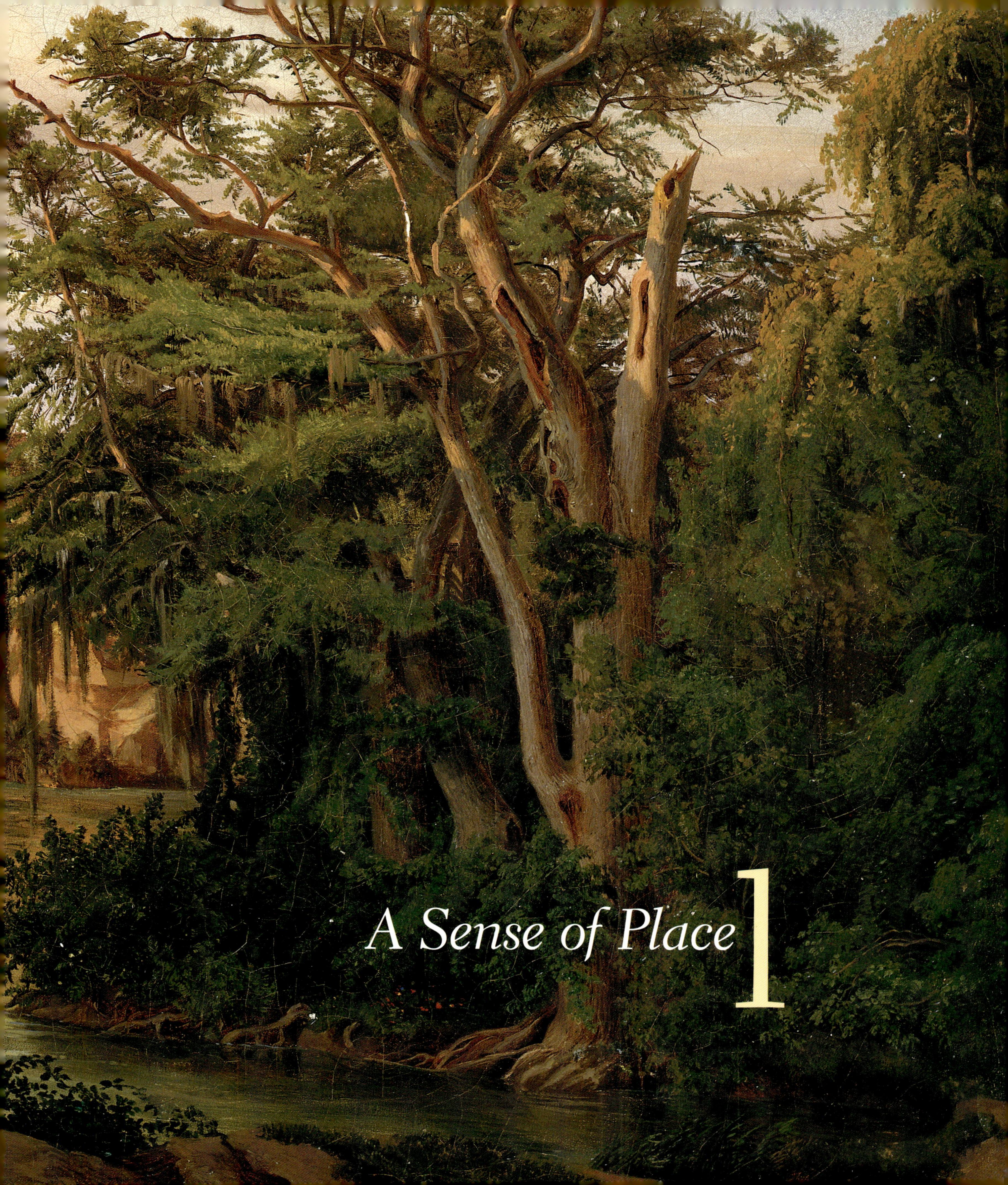
A Sense of Place 1

A Sense of Place

In the past few years the painters of Texas have taken their place calmly in the national art arena without calling attention to their work by symbolically flashing a pair of six-guns or by singing "Git Along Little Dogie" to guitar accompaniment.

—Jerry Bywaters, 1944[1]

The conflict between the mythic fictions and everyday realities of the West animates Texas art across the twentieth century. A state defined in the popular imagination by its landscape, Texas has been cast in heroic terms by artists as disparate as Frederic Remington and Garry Winogrand. Perhaps more than any other medium, film has shaped our view of Texas. Yet the filmic image is frequently a false one: John Ford shot the epic Texas quest of *The Searchers* in Utah's Monument Valley; the Alamo no longer sits alone on a plain; and the battleground of San Jacinto is now surrounded by oil refineries. Ironically, *Dallas*'s Southfork is now an actual tourist attraction, while Houston's Shamrock Hotel, celebrated by George Stevens's *Giant* in 1956, was torn down in 1987.[2]

As Jerry Bywaters's statement reveals, by the mid-twentieth century, Texas artists were conscious of the expectations placed on Texas art, and the clichés of Texas culture have continued to be one of the chief themes faced by ongoing generations of writers and artists. In 1972, critic Dave Hickey wrote on the experience of being a Texan living in New York:

> The words *Texas* and *New York*—as compared to, say, *Oregon* or *Indiana*—do not really represent places. They are semantic categories which include a complex of stances, cultural imperatives and psychological expectations—and these make strange demands upon their inhabitants—extremely complicated ones if you inhabit both categories. It is very strange living in two ideas, participating in two myths. Especially since the myth of New York is self-generated, and many of its inhabitants participate in it, while the myth of Texas is also generated in New York, and while some New Yorkers participate in it, no Texans do without considerable irony.[3]

Art historian Thomas McEvilley picked up on this theme in 1989: "Most states of course don't have the sense of cultural identity that Texas has. It would be less meaningful to speak of Ohio culture or Nebraska culture—not meaningless, but less meaningful.... Texas was once a nation."[4] While more recent writers have tended to reject the regionalist constraints of identifying a "Texas" art, the Texas landscape and the Texas scene continue to offer a means of definition to even the most urban artists committed to working in this region.[5]

The first generations of painters to make Texas their home sought to capture the specific quality of their environment. As Susie Kalil noted in her 1986 essay on the Texas landscape, a modest realism characterized their work in opposition to the example set by such artist-explorers as Albert Bierstadt and Thomas Moran, whose monumental canvases embodied the aspirations of America's western expansion.[6] Indeed, careful examination of early Texas landscapes reveal that few artists identified the region in the western terms that are so familiar today—images of ranchers and cattle drives only begin to appear in Texas art at the turn of the century. This is not surprising in light of the recent work of such historians as Randolph B. Campbell, who have demonstrated that the western identity of Texas is very much a twentieth-century construct.[7] Up through the first decades of this century, Texas maintained close ties to the agrarian economy of the South (an alliance that had brought Texas into the Confederacy in 1861), and it was only in the 1930s that the image of the state was remade into that of a western one.[8] As Debbie Nathan has ably summarized:

> Traditional Texas historians have always found it painful to associate the state with the vanquished, humiliated South. Before the Civil War, Texas was a relatively prosperous state with a thriving cotton-based economy. For years afterward, it was one of the poorest. During the Depression, historians seized on the optimism of the West and tried to put distance between Texas and its Confederate past. This was the era when Texas began to be regarded as Western rather than Southern—a state shaped by ranching instead of farming, cattle instead of cotton, oil instead of timber, the scarcity of water instead of its abundance, the rough egalitarian frontier instead of the genteel planter aristocracy, and of course, heroes instead of losers.[9]

One of the first heroes of Texas is captured in the Meade brothers' daguerreotype portrait of *Samuel Houston*, 1851 (plate 1; see frontispiece). Charles Richard Meade and Henry William Matthew Meade were among the earliest portrait photographers active in the United States; in 1833 they emigrated to New York from their native London, and in 1842, along with their father, they set up their first studio in Albany. Soon thereafter they established additional studios in Buffalo and New York City, and among the subjects who sat for them were Kit Carson, Commodore Perry, and the inventor of the daguerreotype, L. J. M. Daguerre.[10]

Sam Houston, commander-in-chief of the Texas troops at the Battle of San Jacinto, secured Texas's independence from Mexico on the decisive date of April 21, 1836. He was elected the first and third president of the newly formed Republic of Texas, and the city of Houston was formally incorporated in his name in 1837.[11] Houston worked hard to bring the Texas territory into the United States; prevailing in this endeavor in 1845, he represented Texas for fourteen years as a United States senator, and was elected governor of Texas in 1859. However, Houston refused to sign the order to secede from the Union he had so diligently striven to join, and thus forfeited his office in 1860.

Houston probably posed for the Meade brothers during a visit to New York City. The daguerreotype was created during his tenure as senator in Washington, and was commissioned at a time when Houston was seriously considering running for the presidency of the United States.[12] Houston is shown as a figure of stern authority, posed next to a classical column that subtly underlines his strength and republican ideals. This full-length image of Houston, who stood more than six feet tall, is unique; to date only seven other daguerreotypes—all half-length bust portraits of Houston taken by various other studios in smaller sizes—have been located.[13]

Works by Hermann Lungkwitz and Vincent Colyer in the museum's Bayou Bend Collection exemplify the origins of landscape painting in nineteenth-century Texas. Born in Germany, and trained at the Dresden Akademie der Bildenden Kunste, Lungkwitz was among the first professional artists to settle in the newly incorporated state. His engagement in politics had forced him to leave Germany in 1850; after a brief visit to Virginia, he joined the great German migration to the Texas Hill Country and made Fredericksburg his home in 1852. In 1864, when Civil War aggressions were making the rural areas of Texas unsafe, he moved his family to San Antonio, which over the following decades gradually emerged as the first active center for the arts in Texas.

Hill Country Landscape, 1862 (plate 2), is typical of

pages 32–33
Hermann Lungkwitz
Hill Country Landscape
(detail), 1862
(see plate 2)

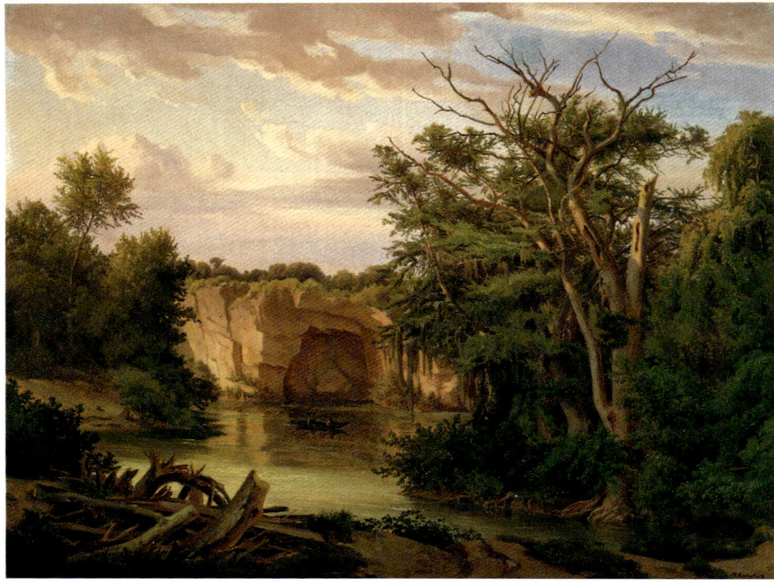

2
Hermann Lungkwitz
Hill Country Landscape,
1862
Oil on canvas, 18⅜ x 23³⁄₁₆
in. (46.7 x 60.5 cm). Bayou
Bend Collection, gift of Miss
Ima Hogg, B.67.39.

3
Vincent Colyer
On the Big Canadian River,
Northern Texas, 1869
Watercolor on paper,
8⁹⁄₁₆ x 13⅜ in. (21.7 x 34 cm).
Museum purchase with
funds provided by the Finger
family in honor of Nanette
Finger at "One Great Night
in November, 1996," B.96.17.

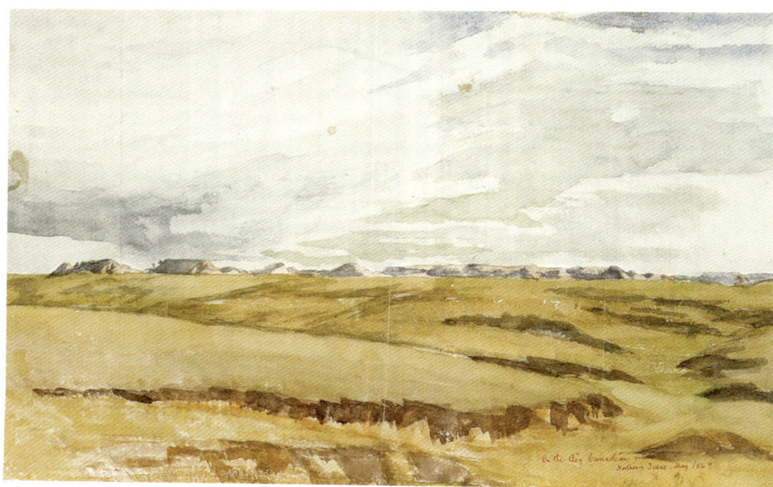

the elegiac cast Lungkwitz gave his depictions of the Texas countryside. Such pictorial devices as the cavern, the blasted tree, and the two spectators gesturing towards the sublimely beautiful scene before them can be traced back to the example of Caspar David Friedrich, the founder of Romantic painting in early nineteenth-century Dresden. The vista is washed in a dappled golden light, and the mood is quietly reflective rather than awe inspiring. The specific location of this landscape has not been identified. However, Lungkwitz brought a sharply observant eye to his compositions; the fact that he sketched on site has been documented, and a study for the barren cypress tree on the right has survived.[14]

Unlike Lungkwitz, whose contribution to Texas painting has been well established, Vincent Colyer's depictions of the Texas landscape are a relatively recent discovery to scholars of Texas art, and only a few sketches from his 1869 visit to the region are known. Born in New York, and a member of the National Academy of Design, Colyer was principally active in the Northeast as a portraitist, landscape painter, and lithographer. After the Civil War, he was hired by the United States government to serve as Secretary of the Board of Indian Commissioners; among his responsibilities was to survey the landscape and customs of the native peoples of the "Indian Territory" that ranged from Oklahoma to New Mexico. *On the Big Canadian River, Northern Texas,* 1869 (plate 3), is from a series of watercolors that he created for the specific purpose of documenting the topography of the high plains. Colyer was a talented recorder of landscape and light, and his Indian Commission watercolors have a vivid immediacy.[15] Largely free of dramatic conventions, Colyer's vista of the Canadian riverbed, north of Amarillo, offers a succinct record of the gently undulating countryside.

The academic polish of Lungkwitz's painting and the informal intimacy of Colyer's sketches are aptly complemented in the museum's collection by the work of two artists who emerged in Texas at the turn of the century, Julian Onderdonk and Frank Reaugh. Onderdonk was among a dynasty of painters that shaped Texas art in the first decades of this century. His father, Robert Onderdonk, moved to San Antonio in 1879, and was quickly established as one of the city's premier portraitists and genre painters. His younger sister, Eleanor Rogers Onderdonk, was active as a miniature portraitist, and was also one of the first curators of San Antonio's Witte Memorial Museum. Julian Onderdonk received his initial training from his father, and enrolled at the Art Students League in New York in 1901; that summer he studied under William Merritt Chase at Shinnecock, Long Island. Following his appointment as art advisor to the State Fair of Texas in 1906, Onderdonk began to divide his time between New York and Texas, and in 1909 he returned permanently to San Antonio.

Sunlight and Shadow, 1910 (plate 4), is characteristic of his landscape compositions. As the title indicates, Onderdonk's first concern was to record the quality of light that animates the landscape, rather than any specific locale.[16] While lacking the bluebonnets that came to be the artist's identifying motif in later years, it is one of Onderdonk's most accomplished early southwest landscapes, and the combination of atmospheric effects and vivid color harmonies link this work to the international style of late nineteenth-century plein-air painting.

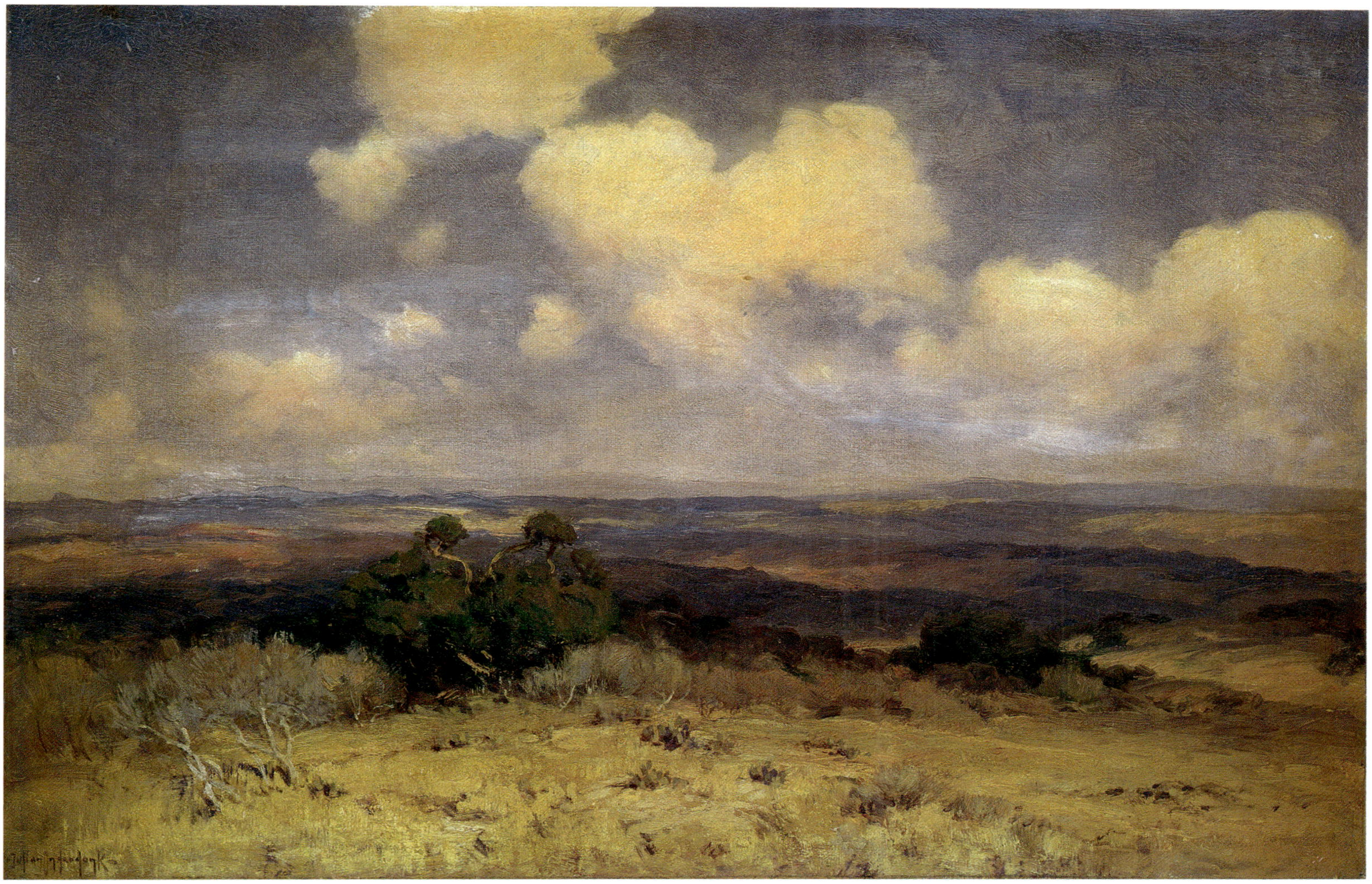

Born in Illinois, Frank Reaugh came to Texas in his early teens in 1876, when his family settled a small ranch in Terrell, southeast of Dallas. He attended the School of Fine Arts in St. Louis, and in 1888 he left for Paris to complete his education at the Académie Julian. Among the artists whose work he came to admire during his year in Europe were the eighteenth-century French pastelist Maurice Quentin de la Tour, and the nineteenth-century Dutch landscapist Anton Mauve. On his return to Texas, he began to devote each summer to travels through West Texas and the Panhandle, rendering the vast landscape in small-scale pastel vignettes. Among his chief subjects was the Texas longhorn, shown during cattle drives or grazing on the unfenced plains of the already vanishing frontiers.

Terrell, Texas, c. 1924 (plate 5), is typical of the artist's more intimate, monochromatic works, depicting the flat landscape and big sky of the countryside around Dallas.

Unlike his travel sketches, which celebrated the unpopulated expanses of West Texas, the scene is essentially domestic. The composition is dominated by the dark clouds of a norther sweeping across the plains; Reaugh also captured with remarkable economy a simple farmhouse shaded by trees and a field dotted with cattle egrets. It was this lucid realism that was to have an effective influence on the succeeding generation of artists who came of age in Dallas in the 1920s and 1930s.

4
Julian Onderdonk
Sunlight and Shadow, 1910
Oil on canvas, 16 x 24 in. (40.6 x 61 cm). Gift of the Houston Art League, the George M. Dickson Bequest, AL.2.

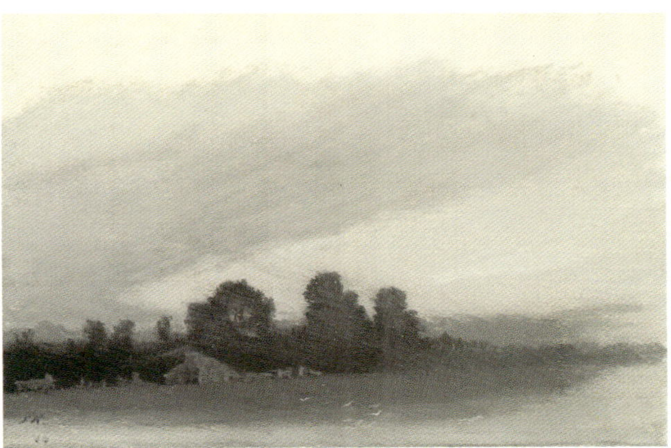

5
Frank Reaugh
Terrell, Texas, c. 1924
Pastel on paper, 6 x 8½ in. (13.5 x 21.7 cm). Museum purchase with funds provided by Blake Tartt III and Mark Elias in honor of Barbara Tartt at "One Great Night in November, 1994," 94.443.

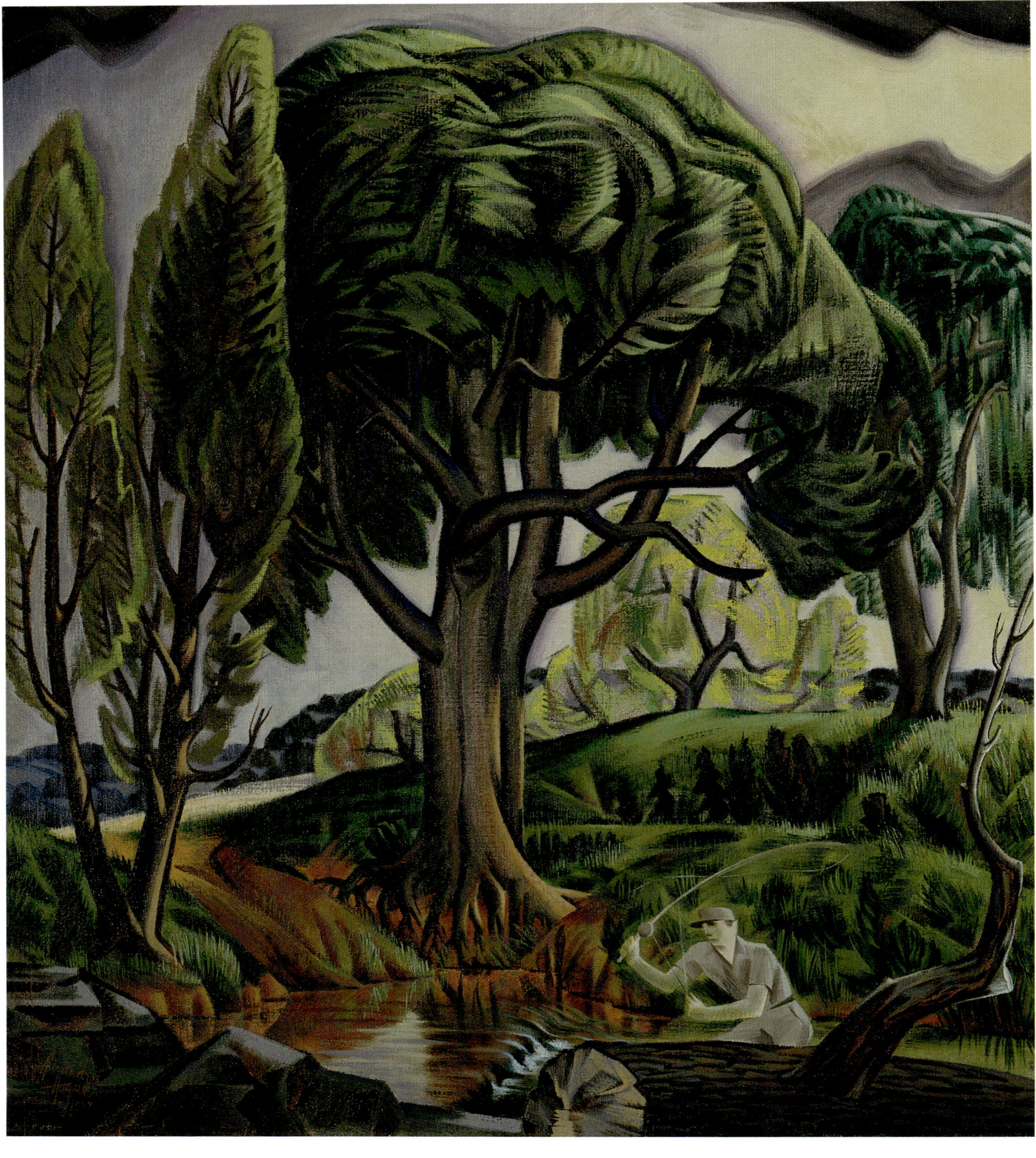

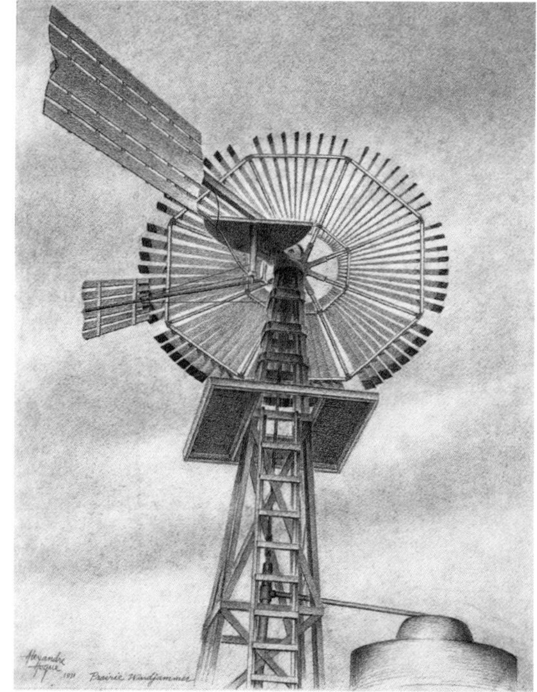

6 *opposite*
Alexandre Hogue
Squaw Creek, 1927
Oil on canvas, 33½ x 29½ in.
(84.8 x 74.6 cm). Museum
purchase with funds provided
by Isabel B. Wilson, 91.1851.

7
Alexandre Hogue
Prairie Windjammer, 1931
Graphite on paper, 18¼ x
13½ in. (46.4 x 34.3 cm).
Museum purchase with funds
provided by Duke Energy,
87.287.

8
Jerry Bywaters
Bone Yard, 1938
Lithograph on paper, 11¾ x
15½ in. (29.8 x 39.4 cm).
Museum purchase with
funds provided by Mr. Alvin
S. Romansky, 87.208.

In the late 1920s, Dallas began to supplant San Antonio as the leading city for the arts in Texas.[17] The publication of the *Southwest Review* at Southern Methodist University beginning in October 1924, the founding of the Dallas Art Institute in 1926, the leadership of such teachers as Frank Reaugh and Olin H. Travis, and the growing careers of such artists as Alexandre Hogue, Jerry Bywaters, and Everett Spruce created an ideal environment for the establishment of a strong and focused alliance. In early 1932, a group of artists committed to a regionalist idiom exhibited at the Dallas Public Art Gallery (later the Dallas Museum of Fine Arts). Dubbed "The Nine" by *Art Digest,* the group included Jerry Bywaters and Everett Spruce.[18] By May of that year, these artists had joined with Hogue to form the Dallas Artists League, fostering what later came to be known as the Lone Star Regionalist movement.

As Rick Stewart has documented, Texas regionalism was bound up with the new Southwestern identity of Dallas in particular, and Texas in general.[19] Writing in the *Southwest Review* in 1929, Henry Nash Smith urged Texas artists to distance themselves from the "Southern Renaissance," as well as the Southwestern schools of Taos and Santa Fe, advocating in their stead a concentration on the local scene: "The secret of culture is an awareness of the immediate environment and a sense of the value of everyday things.... At the bottom must be a tradition built up bit by bit from the heritages of the land where it is to endure."[20] Smith's article reflected a larger current in American aesthetics; in 1920 John Dewey had written on "Americanism and Localism" for the *Dial,* and such artists as Thomas Hart Benton had forcibly rejected the "aesthetic drivelings and morbid self-concerns" of European Modernism in favor of "painting American histories in defiance of all the conventions of our art world."[21]

Alexandre Hogue's *Squaw Creek,* 1927 (plate 6), is an important document of this moment of transition in Texas art. Raised in Denton, Hogue studied at the Minneapolis College of Design, worked as a commercial artist in New York, traveled with Reaugh to West Texas, and in 1920 began to visit Taos, where he became close friends with Ernest Blumenschein. Unlike Benton and other Midwest champions of regionalism, Hogue remained open to Modernist currents, writing admiringly of Rockwell Kent in 1929 for the *Southwest Review.*[22] Blumenschein's and Kent's rhythmic compositional cadences certainly influenced *Squaw Creek;* the landscape and fisherman are rendered with a illustrator's eye for economy of line and silhouette. The setting is a YMCA camp near Glen Rose, southwest of Dallas, where Hogue led summer art classes in the mid-1920s. Hoping to see Glen Rose transformed into a second Taos, Hogue created this bucolic image of Squaw Creek to promote his aspirations for an artists' colony in what he described as the "Queen of the Valley."[23]

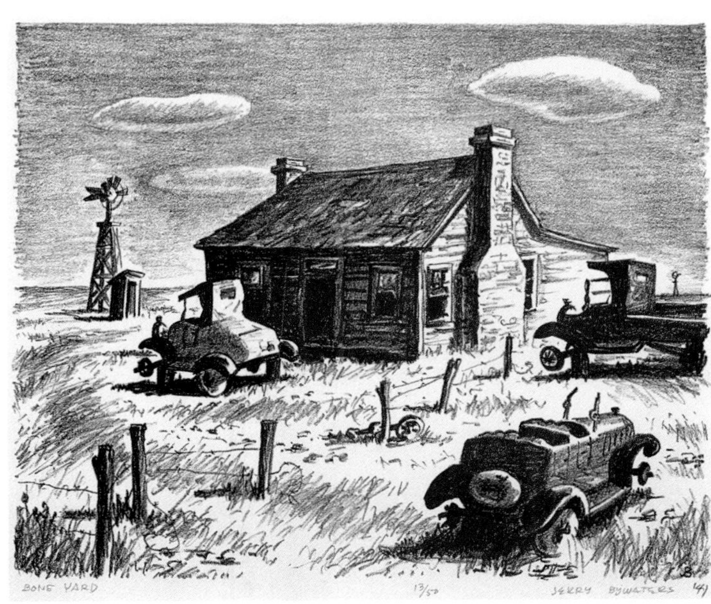

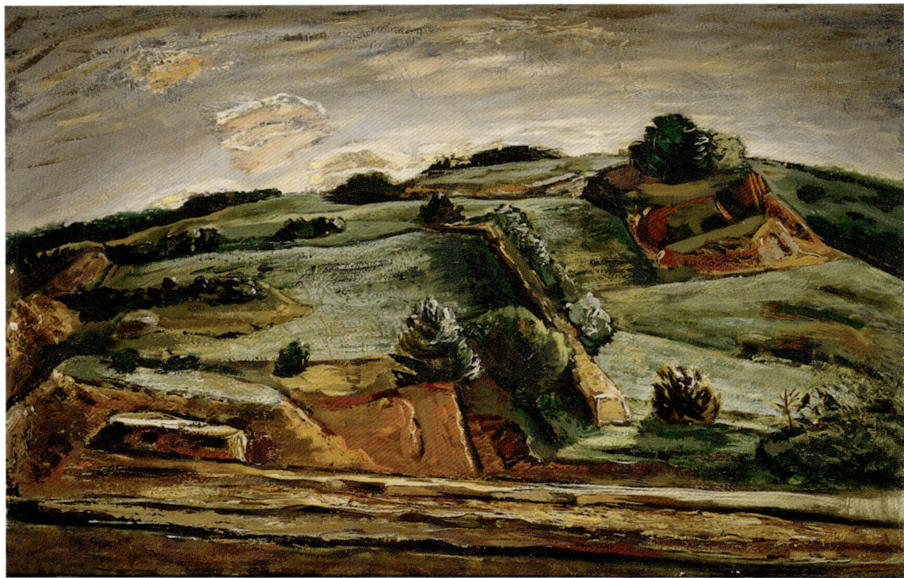

9
Everett Spruce
Green Hillside, 1942
Oil on Masonite, 16 x 24 in.
(40.6 x 61 cm). Museum
purchase with funds pro-
vided by the Houston
Friends of Art, 44.488.

Hogue's drawing *Prairie Windjammer*, 1931 (plate 7), offers a bleaker view of the Texas landscape. Where *Squaw Creek* is a pastoral celebration of the riches of the land, *Prairie Windjammer* is a haunting icon of the dust-bowl era. Most likely a study for the *Drouth Stricken Area*, 1934 (Dallas Museum of Art), where the windmill is shown shattered and broken, *Prairie Windjammer* demonstrates the documentary eye Hogue brought to his work of the 1930s. Much as Benton had insisted on the authenticity of his subjects, Hogue began to identify his work with personal experience. In 1940 he wrote:

> I did not just visit a ranch—I was raised on one and have done all of the work connected with a ranch, including working on windmills from installation to pulling of pump pipe and sucker rod. I was knocked from a mill tower by lightning and landed unconscious. I know when this material has been used with authority and un-derstanding of their function.[24]

And in a 1970 letter to Benton, Hogue recalled:

> In my youth every ranch in the Texas Panhandle had the old-fashioned, 8 section wooden windmills—ours was 18 feet in diameter, direct strike for a 450 foot well. In a high wind its screeching, groaning effort was as ex-citing as an old windjammer straining under the wind. But today the submersible pump has done away with the mills. That pleasant sight on the horizon indicating a distant neighbor is gone and so are all of the wonderful short grasses of the plains.[25]

Jerry Bywaters, eight years Hogue's junior, was one of the catalytic figures of the arts in Texas. In addition to his career as a painter, Bywaters was a contributor to the *Southwest Review*, the *Dallas Morning News*, and *South-western Arts*; a member of the Southern Methodist Uni-versity faculty; and in 1942 he became the director of the Dallas Museum of Fine Arts, a position he held for more than twenty years. His 1938 lithograph *Bone Yard* (plate 8), was among the first editions of the newly formed Lone Star Printmakers. Following the example of the Associ-ated American Artists (AAA) editions of Benton, John Steuart Curry, and Grant Wood, the Dallas-based Lone Star Printmakers hoped to reach a national audience through "the power of the printed line."[26] As Bywaters pragmatically explained in *Southwest Review*, "a first exhibit of thirty unframed black and white prints was of-fered to any regional museum, college, or study group willing to purchase one print and pay the small express charge necessary to secure the exhibit from the previous exhibitor."[27]

Bone Yard displays Bywaters's talent for succinct caricature. The dilapidated jalopies that surround the run-down farmhouse eschew the poignancy of Hogue's dustbowl paintings—rather, Bywaters took Benton's AAA editions as his chief inspiration, delineating the rough-and-tumble aspect of rural life.

Everett Spruce came to Dallas from rural Arkansas in 1925 as a student of Olin H. Travis's. He attended the Dallas Art Institute, and began to work for the newly es-tablished Dallas Museum of Fine Arts in the early 1930s. In 1940 he joined the faculty of the University of Texas at Austin. While allied with the "Dallas Nine," his ongoing commitment to Modernism distinguished his work from that of the other Lone Star Regionalists. His early paintings

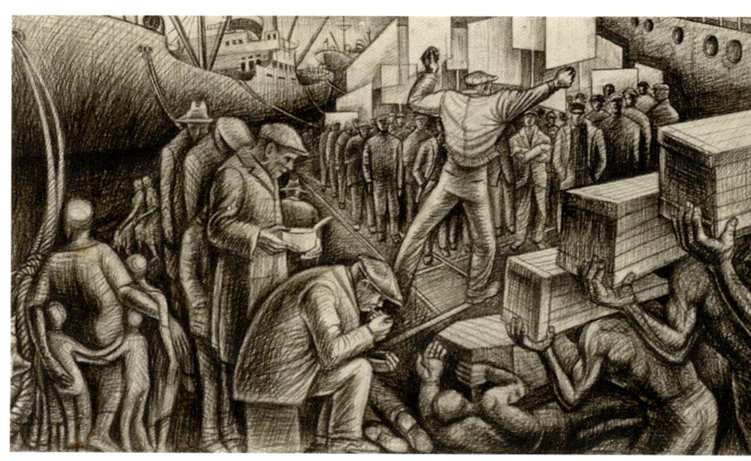

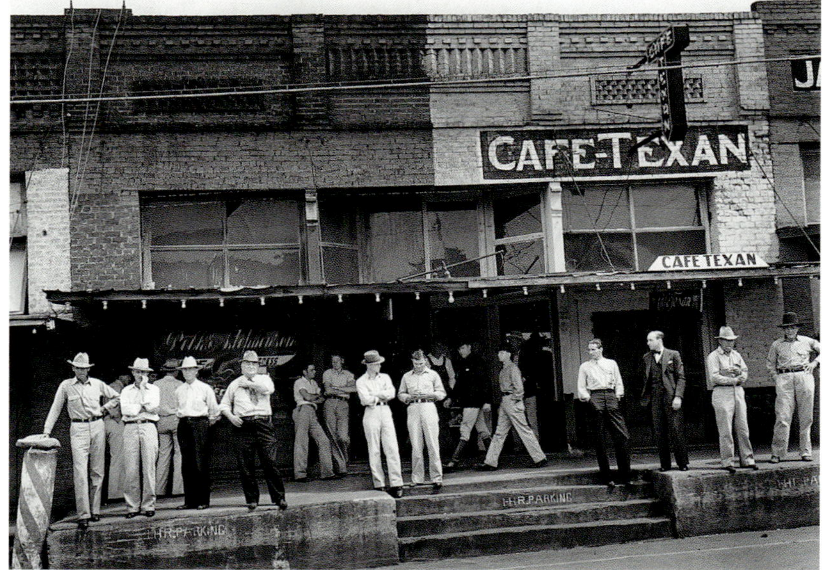

10
Russell Lee
San Augustine, Texas, 1939,
printed 1976 by the Library
of Congress
Gelatin silver photograph,
10 x 13½ in. (25.4 x 34.3
cm). Gift of Mr. and Mrs.
Alvin S. Romansky, 76.405.

demonstrate the influence of the Taos School (see plate 78), and his more mature compositions have a painterly brilliance matched by few of his Texas contemporaries. *Green Hillside,* 1942 (plate 9), is a prime example of Spruce's chiseled landscapes. The paint is laid down in thick layers of impasto, and the composition is built up with an architectonic density, qualities that prompted critics to discuss the formal aspects of his work rather than the subject. Writing in 1944, Gibson Danes described Spruce's compositions: "In many ways Spruce is a true expressionist: each canvas demands a particular solution, a new-born structure, a fresh format of color, pattern, and texture—each is an individual, compact experience."[28]

The concerns of the Lone Star Regionalists were shared by a generation of photographers coming of age in the 1930s. Russell Lee, a contemporary of the "Dallas Nine," came to Texas in the late 1930s on the payroll of the Farm Security Administration (established in 1935 as the Resettlement Administration). One of President Franklin D. Roosevelt's programs to fight the Depression, the FSA hired such photographers as Lee, Dorothea Lange, and Walker Evans to create a portrait of rural life in America. Initially trained as a painter, Lee had joined the FSA in 1936, only a year after he had taken his first photograph. However, Lee immediately evinced an uncommon sympathy with his subjects; unlike the politically charged views taken by other photographers of the FSA, Lee sought to capture the incidental and social aspects of rural life. Simply captioned by Lee as "Street scene," and

dated April 1939, *San Augustine, Texas* (plate 10), distills the rhythm of an East Texas Main Street. Well-dressed men have gathered along the sidewalk in front of the Cafe-Texan, a typical Saturday afternoon ritual in a town that was a trading center for cotton, corn, and timber.

Surprisingly, few artists active in Houston in the 1930s followed the example of the Lone Star Regionalists, despite the fact that their work was frequently exhibited at the MFAH.[29] It was John Biggers, who came to Houston in 1949 to initiate an art department at the Texas State University for Negroes (now Texas Southern University), who came closest to sharing the social and realist vision of the "Dallas Nine."

Biggers arrived in Houston with extensive training in mural design. He had studied with Charles White at Hampton Institute (now Hampton University) in Virginia,

11
John Biggers
Study for the Longshoreman's Mural, 1956–57
Black crayon, graphite, and gouache on artist's board,
16½ x 92 in. (41.6 x 234 cm).
Gift of Mr. and Mrs. Arthur J. Mandell, 94.724.

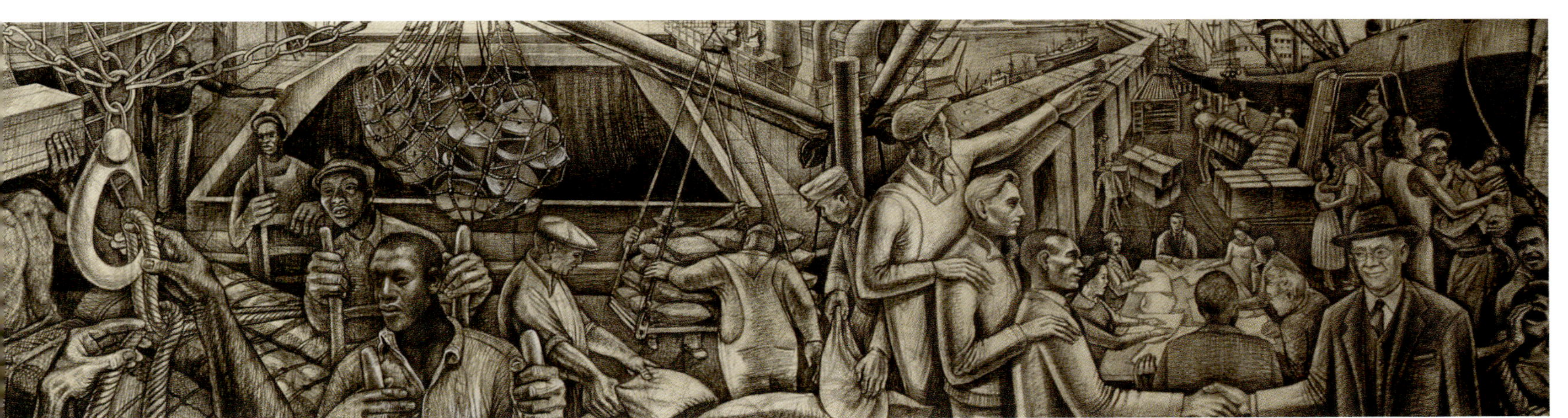

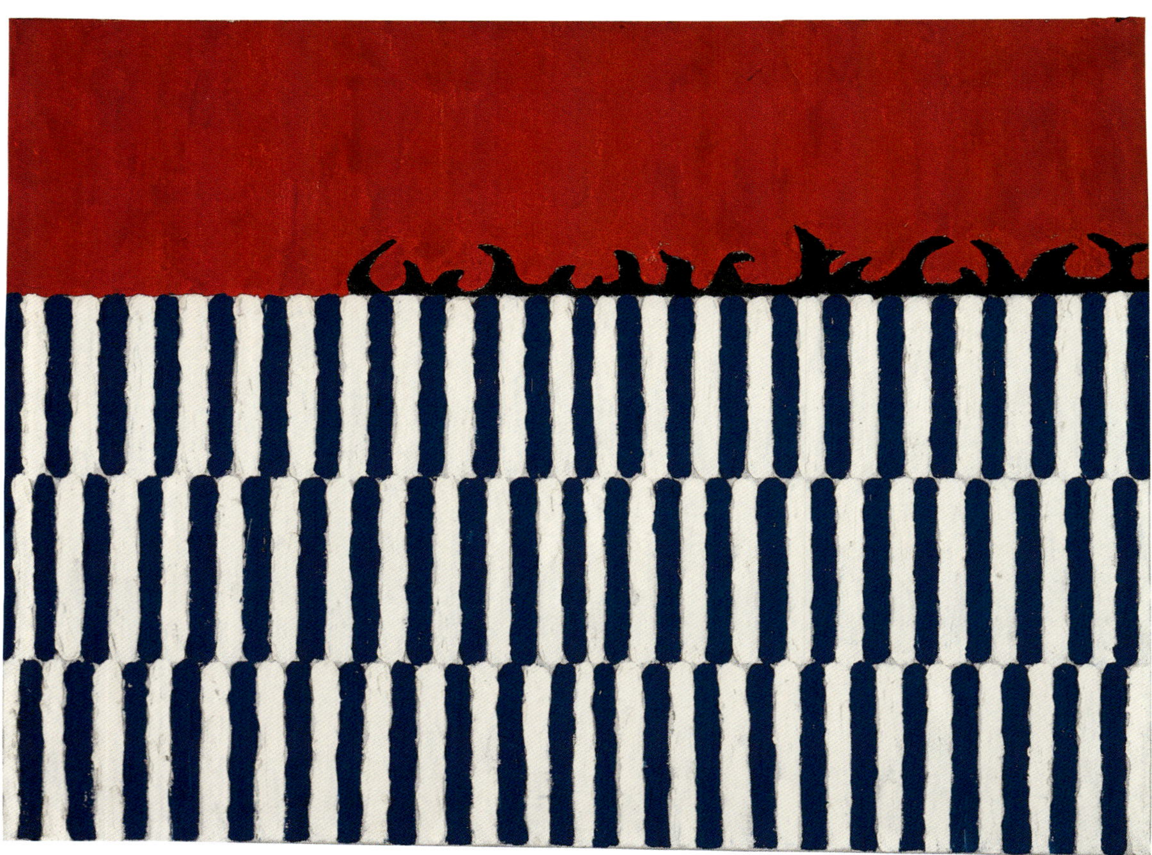

and completed his education at Pennsylvania State University, where Henry Varnum Poor was engaged on a mural project. While at Penn State, Biggers had his first opportunity to create large-scale murals, and had become deeply engaged in the work of the Mexican muralists. Biggers accepted the teaching position in Houston in part because he hoped to establish closer ties with Mexico.

Biggers's first Texas murals depicted themes of African-American history and rural life. His *Longshoreman's Mural,* 1956–57, created for the International Longshoremen's Association Local 872, Houston, and represented in the MFAH's collection by a detailed study (plate 11), is firmly set in the modern realities of Houston's Ship Channel. The most urban of Biggers's murals, the dense dockside activity is captured with a compressed realism comparable to the compact compositions of Diego Rivera. Biggers was undoubtedly familiar with other Houston mural projects, most notably Jerry Bywaters's *Loading Oil,* created in 1939 for the Federal Building, also a scene taken from the Port of Houston. However, where Bywaters chose to focus on the activity of two heroically monumental dock workers, Biggers chose to depict the complex web of activity that unites the Local 872 longshoremen, one of Houston's first African-American unions, and their labor representatives.

The prosperity of the postwar era had many long-range effects on the arts in Texas. Museums began to expand their galleries and diversify their programs, while newly independent galleries and arts associations promoted fresh currents in contemporary art. The formation of the Contemporary Arts Association (now the Contemporary Arts Museum) in Houston in 1948, and of the Dallas Museum for Contemporary Arts in 1956 (which merged with the Dallas Museum of Fine Arts in 1963), offered important challenges to the regional scene. At the same time, such presentations as the Museum of Modern Art's pivotal *Americans* exhibition series and the Whitney Museum of American Art's annuals offered highly prestigious New York venues to artists nationwide.

In addition, an exceptional couple left their marks on both Dallas and Houston: Douglas MacAgy, director of the Dallas Museum for Contemporary Arts from 1958 to 1964, and Jermayne MacAgy, director of Houston's Contemporary Arts Association from 1955 to 1959, and chair of the art department at the University of St. Thomas from 1959 to 1964. Although leading separate lives in Texas, the MacAgys had worked together in San Francisco's budding postwar art scene, and brought with them contacts with such artists as Clyfford Still and Mark Rothko. More importantly, both shared an affinity for Surrealist aesthetics and assemblage, and brought a new sophistication to gallery installations.

Texas artists were not slow to respond to these changes, and international Modernism became an ever more dominant current across the state. While this aspect of Texas art will be discussed in more detail in the third chapter of this catalogue, it is important to take note of at least three artists who offered a new way of looking at the Texas landscape: Forrest Bess, Jack Boynton, and Jim Love.[30] It would be a mistake, however, to assume that these artists formed a school. Rather, as Boynton later recalled:

> Texas has been a place where, other than the Regionalists of the thirties, there has never been much of a group thing. . . . It has been a place where you just do it because you want to do it. There has never been a lot of encouragement, although I guess there has been enough to keep some artists afloat here and there. By the same token there has not been much pressure to do any particular thing.[31]

Forrest Bess, the son of an itinerant laborer, grew up in the oil fields and farming communities of East Texas. After attending Texas A&M University and the University of Texas at Austin, he left school and took a series of jobs in the oil industry. In 1934, Bess set up a studio in Bay City, committing himself to a career as an artist. At the same time, he began to support himself working as a shrimp fisherman. From 1941 to 1945 he served in the Army Corps of Engineers, returning to Bay City in 1947. Living outside the mainstream art community, he developed a body of paintings that were unique in their visionary potency and abstract simplicity. His early work was inspired by the examples of Vincent van Gogh and Maurice de Vlaminck, and he was featured in an exhibition at the MFAH in 1941, prompting Stella Hope Shurtleff to write in the *Houston Post*: "The one-man show of Forrest Bess, in the judgment of this critic, has quite another meaning from that which derives from fine design, interesting color, and a genuine feeling for what is painted. This exhibition affirms clearly, though with utmost modesty, that it is the work of a man of vision. . . . The question logically follows, 'what are some of the characteristics of such an artist?' Among the earmarks, it may safely be said are these: Seeing straight, seeing whole, seeing the world around him."[32]

By the late 1940s, Bess had adopted a highly structured symbolic language in his dense, small-scale canvases. Having experienced visions from the age of four, Bess became increasingly fascinated in integrating his personal experiences with universal symbols, finding guidance and inspiration in the writings of Carl Jung. In 1948, he began to exhibit at Betty Parsons's gallery in New York, a venue which placed him in the context of such artists as Jackson Pollock, Mark Rothko, Barnett Newman, and Richard Pousette-Dart.[33] Over the years he maintained an extensive correspondence with Parsons, as well as with Jung and art historian Meyer Schapiro. In 1962, he scripted an imaginary interview with himself, which he sent to Parsons. Included is a discussion of *Untitled [11A]*, 1958 (plate 12):

> *"What consciously did you feel about the canvas when you painted it; by this I mean before you 'integrated' it?"*
>
> "I felt it had something to do with a lonely beach. The sharp pointed black shapes brought to mind driftwood — the silhouette of driftwood on a beach."
>
> *"Was this what it actually 'integrated' to be?"*
>
> "No. The integration occurred many years ago on a calm, warm summer night. It was the first canvas that I had ever integrated or rather that made itself recall memories visually. Down at camp on the bay. I was in my room and I couldn't take my eyes off this particular canvas for some reason. A sharp wind blew up — I don't know why because it had been calm. My father, mother, and uncle quickly lowered the storm shutters and I still stared at the painting — almost hypnotized. I went to bed — turned off the lights and there in the darkness was a memory so very, very old that the light was very dim. I looked out over a desolate landscape of craters. Almost as if newly cooled white granite had become pockmarked with many many craters with sharp edges — just as if bubbles had bursted [sic] in the granite. . . . The scene was very ancient, so old, so long before man's memory — very lonely — very desolate. Rather like a beginning — after an expulsion."
>
> *"Did this reaction you had from your canvas frighten you?"*
>
> "It did very much. I had no idea of what Jung meant by the integration of the ideogram but here I had experienced one — the happening."
>
> *"Has anyone else ever integrated this particular work?"*

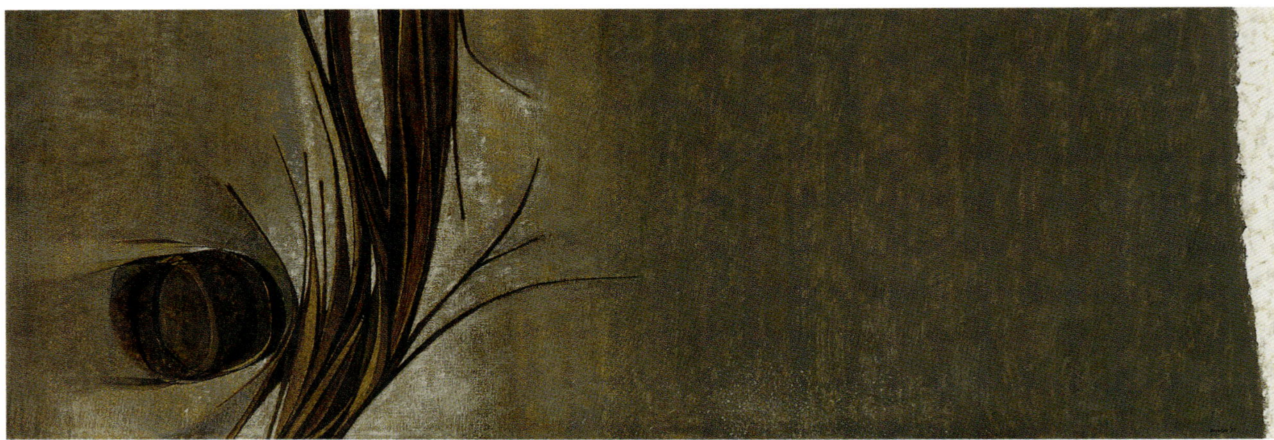

"Only partly. I have seen many cry their hearts out because they felt so very, very alone—after viewing the canvas for possibly half-hour before retiring."[34]

Untitled [11A], with its acid palette and claustrophobic horizon, succeeds in capturing the sense of primal creation Bess sought in his work; his hallucinatory description—the temporal and subjective shifts—mirrors his transcendental aspirations.[35] Only Georgia O'Keeffe, during her early years in Canyon, Texas, had found such liberating inspiration in the Texas landscape. Despite his isolation on the Texas coast, Bess was to have a profound influence on a number of Texas artists, from such contemporaries as Roy Fridge and Jim Love to artists of subsequent generations, including James Reaben and Terrell James.

Born in Fort Worth and a graduate of Texas Christian University, Jack Boynton was one of a handful of Texas artists to establish a national reputation in the 1950s. He first exhibited under the name James Boynton in New York at Knoedler Gallery in 1952; in 1954 he was included in James Johnson Sweeney's *Younger American Painters* at the Guggenheim Museum, and was in the *Young Americans* exhibition at the Whitney Museum of American Art in 1957. He came to Houston in 1955 to teach at the University of Houston, and soon established a friendship with Jermayne MacAgy, with whom he curated *Personal Contacts: A Decade of Contemporary Drawing* at the CAA in 1958.

Like Bess, Boynton drew visionary inspiration from the landscape. An untitled composition from 1957 (plate 13) is unusual in its long, horizontal format; however, the synthesized image is typical of Boynton's work of this period. A heavy, almost toxic orb bursts across the composition, breaking the treelike forms which define the center. On the right, a band of white paint both challenges the illusion of space and adds a disconcerting note of ambiguity. In a catalogue for a 1959 exhibition, Douglas MacAgy wrote: "I know of no other fantast who approaches an imaginary world in quite the way James Boynton appears to confront his. In looking at a number of his paintings, one is led to imagine that the world of his fantasy has a kind of separate existence.... As if he had constructed an occult television receiver, his paintings seem to tune in a remote and fascinating life of the mind with an astonishing sense of fidelity."[36]

Jim Love settled in Houston in 1953 after completing his studies at Baylor College in Waco, where he had been a student of the innovative director Paul Baker, who also was a mentor to Roy Fridge (see plate 60). In 1955, he joined Houston's Alley Theatre as a set designer, and the following year began to work at the Contemporary Arts Association as an installation technician, a position that perfectly complemented Love's growing interest in sculpture. Love actively collaborated on such exhibitions as *The Trojan Horse: The Art of the Machine*, seen at the CAA in 1958; Jermayne MacAgy invited Love to collect and assemble mechanical elements—ball bearings, bolts, cogs, and wheels—which she then juxtaposed with the work of such artists as Gerald Murphy and Max Ernst.

Paul Bunyan Bouquet No. 1, 1962 (plate 14), was created as the centerpiece for MacAgy's *The Age of the Thousand Flowers: An Exhibition of Works by Artists Past and Present*, seen at University of St. Thomas in 1962. MacAgy, with her typical flair for crossing art-historical boundaries, brought together *mille-fleur* tapestries, seventeenth-century still lifes, Henri Matisse, and Florine Stettheimer, along with a dozen of Love's slyly anthropomorphic assemblages. Playing on Gertrude Stein's dictum, MacAgy wrote in the catalogue essay: "In the 'assembled' sculpture of Jim Love we go a step further—a rose is a gear is a brush."[37]

The art of assemblage is very much a twentieth-century phenomenon, finding its origins in the Cubist collages of Pablo Picasso and Georges Braque. However, it is the example of such mid-century sculptors as Richard Stankiewicz, who offer the closest parallels to Love's work. Like Stankiewicz, Love was fascinated by transformation of the object offered by assemblage techniques, and yet, as *Paul Bunyan Bouquet No. 1* demonstrates, the sources of his materials remain evident. Among the most informal of his assemblages of this period, it is also one of the least mediated. Love was among the first artists to successfully discover a visual metaphor for the industrial aspect of Houston; *Paul Bunyan Bouquet* captures both the bravado and the impromptu anarchistic spirit of a city caught in a period of transition and transformation.

While many of the most significant artists working in Texas in the 1950s and early 1960s moved away from the landscape, the late 1960s and 1970s saw a revival of interest in the Texas scene. This revival, however, was not rooted in Texas history. Rather, as Susie Kalil has pointed out: "Texas's reputation for unlimited space and wealth was enhanced to one of rapid, uncontrolled growth.... The plethora of landscape images in subsequent years, then, owes as much to demographics as it does to the sense of romance, independence, and isolation that Texas has acquired. There were simply more artists living in Texas now than in the past.... Their use of landscape is not a revivalist movement, but a means of coming to terms with a shifting existence."[38]

This embrace of the Texas landscape not surprisingly

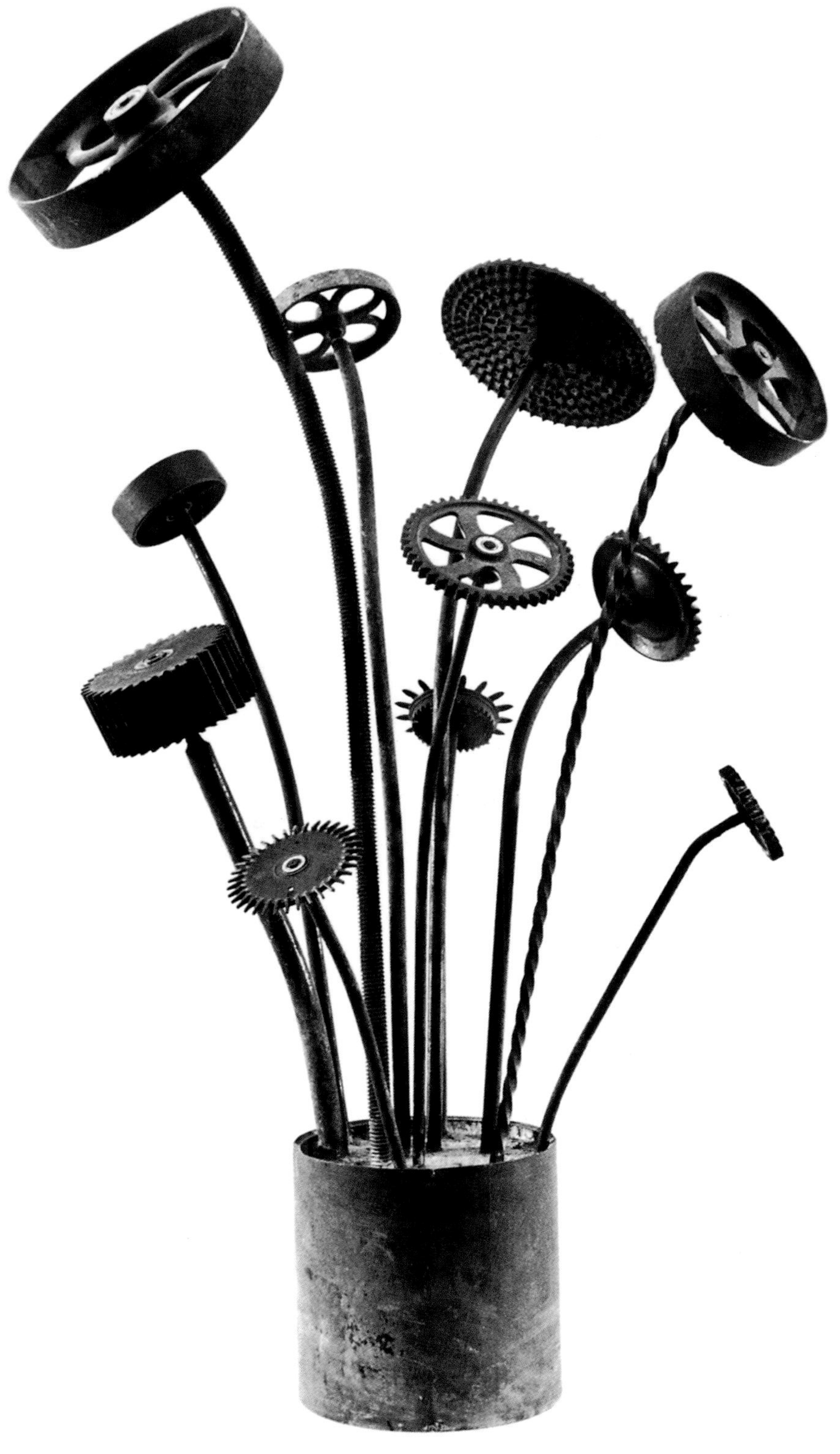

coincided with the increasing urbanization of the region.
A generation of artists had come of age who had very little experience with either ranching or farming, who nevertheless found the fast-expanding cities offered little by
way of history or identity. Dave Hickey, who ran a gallery
called A Clean Well-Lighted Place in Austin from 1967
to 1971, remembered the era in pungent terms: "We created this monster called 'Texas Art' and it nearly de-
voured the whole scene. We had begun by trying to
convince people that there was something special happening in the visual arts here, and reaching for the
metaphor at hand, we invoked the *mythos* of Texas. . . .
Talk about waking the sleeping tiger! Before you could
say 'Look out!' the art was touted as special *because* it was
being done in Texas, because it was *about* Texas. Which
was absolute bullshit. It was special because it was good

art, and all the more admirable because it has been made
in a cultural desert." [39]

Bob Wade was among the first artists to reconfigure
Texas landscape. After attending the University of Texas
at Austin, Wade continued his studies at the University
of California at Berkeley. He returned to Texas in 1966,
and soon became associated with the Dallas artists
known as the "Oak Cliff" group. The Oak Cliff artists,
including Jack Mims, Jim Roche, and George Green,
worked in a wide range of media and styles; however,
they shared a love of humor and low-art aesthetics that
came to be known as "Texas Funk." [40]

Whitney Texas Picturesque, 1971 (plate 15), is a classic early Texas Funk image, typical of what the artist
later called the "Sick Texas Sensibility." As Wade has recounted, he discovered this bizarre "coyote installation"

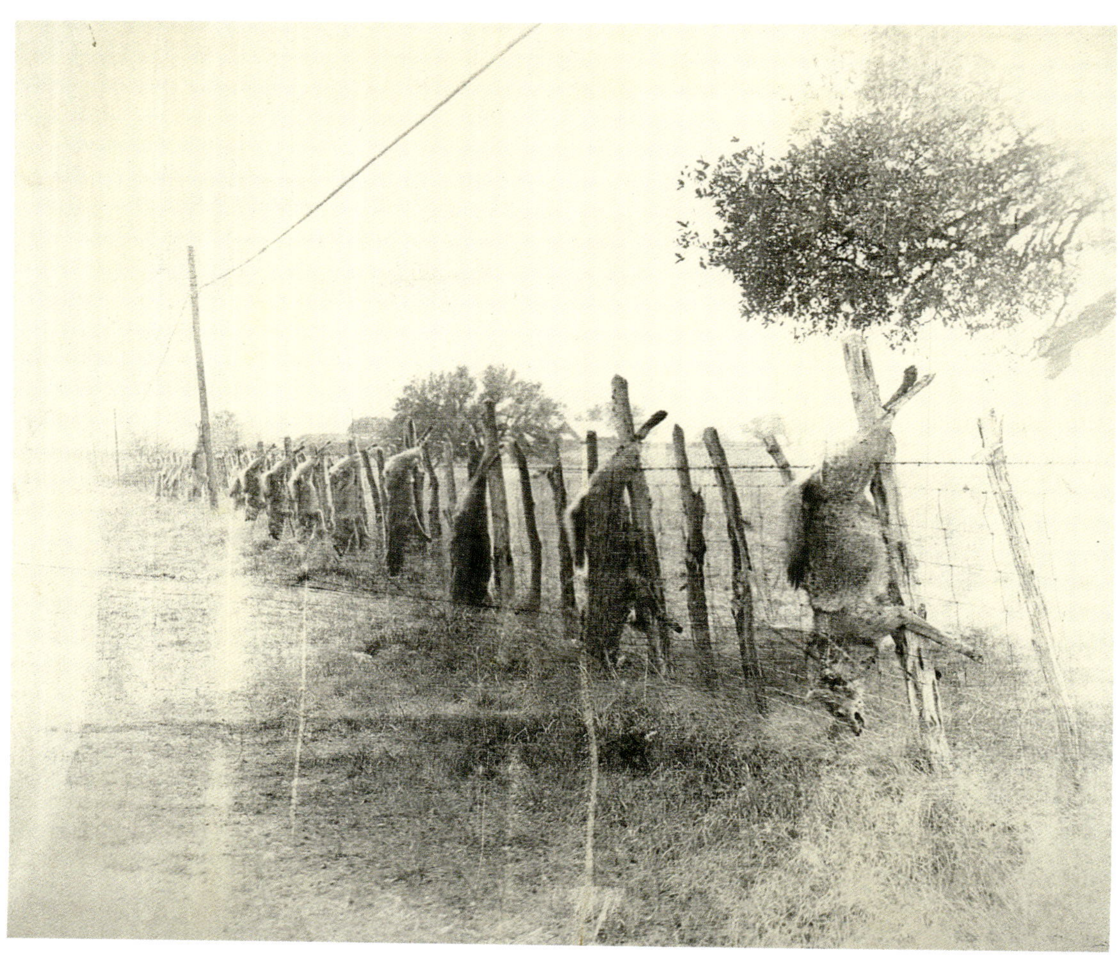

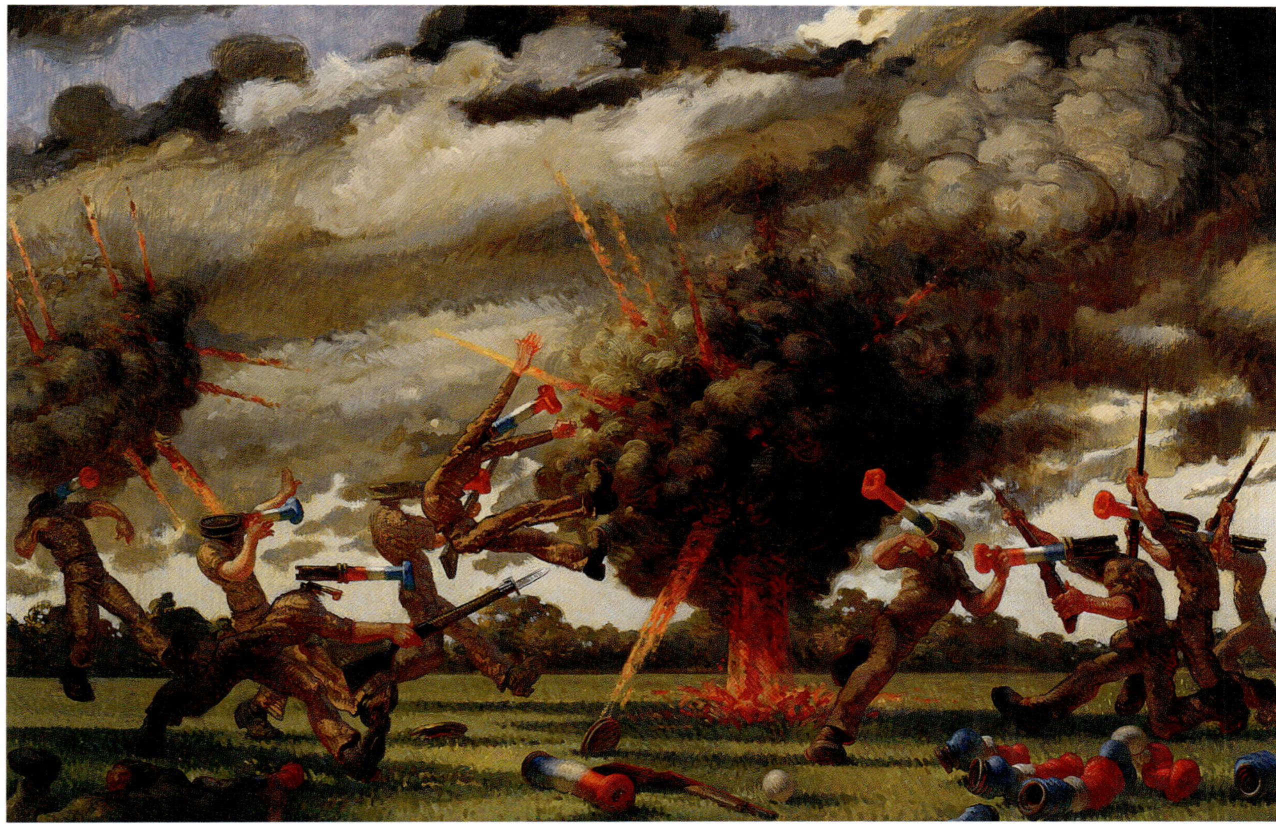

while on a weekend trip near Hillsboro. He photographed the fence from both ends, creating a complementary pair of views, which he then transferred to canvas, adapting the photographic transfer processes pioneered by Robert Rauschenberg.[41] Although rarely found on the main highways of Texas, such coyote fences were not an uncommon sight along Hill Country back roads; the carcasses were used to scare away other coyotes from livestock. At a moment when the atrocities of the Vietnam War had saturated the American psyche, and *Easy Rider* had become the archetypal road movie, *Whitney Texas Picturesque* makes visible the violence that colored the American landscape.[42]

A similar sensibility can be found in the paintings of Robert Levers. Born in Brooklyn, Levers attended both undergraduate and graduate programs at Yale University. He joined the faculty of the University of Texas at Austin in 1961, where he remained for more than thirty years. Levers's compositions combine a surreal naturalism with a brilliantly vivid handling of paint. Pop Art and comic strips offered him an initial point of departure in his works of the 1960s; however, by the mid-1970s his references had broadened to include the larger tradition of Expressionist painting.

The Battle, 1979 (plate 16), is part of an extended series of paintings and drawings dealing with the theme of conflict as the ultimate human folly. The combatants are half-human, half-weapons, with their heads transformed into absurdly phallic instruments of war, ironically painted red, white, and blue; the center of the composition is an exploding fireball. At the same time, the landscape, sky, clouds, and smoke are rendered with a seductively lush painterliness. Unlike some of Levers's compositions, which are specifically situated within famous Texas landmarks, *The Battle* is placed in an anonymous landscape that is only generally suggestive of the countryside around Austin. However, Texas was first a nation founded through war; the battlegrounds of the Alamo and San Jacinto are among the state's most venerated monuments, and an aura of conquest is still popularly celebrated across the region.

Joan Seeman Robinson has commented on *The Battle*: "These goons are out to get each other, their jouncy choreography barely disguising their aggressive group dynamics. They aren't just good ole' boys horsing around, they are players run amok, old grads wrestling for territory, campaigners exhorting constituents, committees wrangling in the air. . . . The stock room of Levers's theater has a musty aura, as if the collegiate experience were endlessly reenacted by generations of graduates who, despite their vaulted educations were merely perpetuating the rituals of many over-inflated enterprises."[43]

16
Robert Levers
***The Battle**, 1979*
Oil on canvas, 48 x 72½ in.
(121.9 x 184 cm). Gift of
Patsy Cravens, 96.1082.

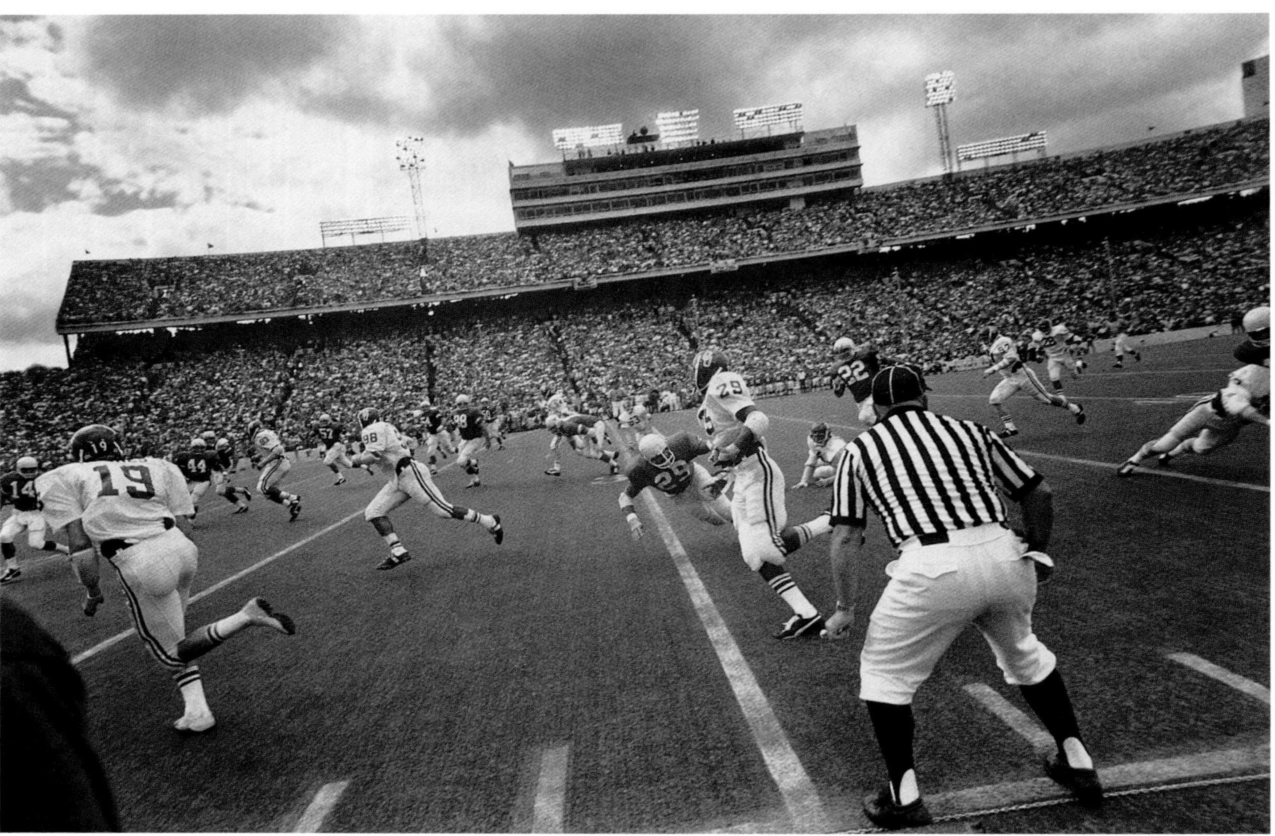

Not surprisingly, photography further answered the need to define the changing aspect of Texas in the 1970s, and over the decade a number of photographers began to create important works in this region. Several factors contributed to this surge in Texas photography: the incorporation of photography by Pop and Conceptual artists encouraged a wider range of artists to explore the medium; active departments of photography at the leading universities drew established photographers to Texas; and such enterprises as the Latent Image and Cronin galleries in Houston and Afterimage and the Texas Center for Photographic Studies in Dallas, as well as the establishment of the MFAH's photography department in 1976, offered more sophisticated venues to photographers, creating a broader climate for the acceptance of the medium among collectors.

Garry Winogrand, Geoff Winningham, Wendy Watriss, and Fred Baldwin were among the leading photographers picturing Texas and Texans in the 1970s. Winogrand, a New Yorker who is most known for his street photography, came to Texas in 1973 to teach at the University of Texas at Austin, where he remained for five years. He disavowed any intent to capture the Texas scene in the photographs he took during this period: "What I am interested in is what is shown and the relationship of what is photographed to how it is photographed."[44] His *Austin,*

Texas, 1974 (plate 17), nevertheless distills not only the drama of college football, but also encompasses the apparently limitless space of the field. This is characteristic of much of Winogrand's work; as Beaumont Newhall has observed: "Winogrand's seemingly haphazard street scenes and flash photographs of public functions demonstrate a use of the camera in which the image seems boundless, not contained within the rectangle of the frame, but stretching beyond it."[45] However, the vertiginous panorama of a game at Texas Memorial Stadium also plays on the clichés of the vastness of the Texas landscape, contained here within the confines of a building.[46]

Geoff Winningham first came to Texas in 1961, and made Houston his home in 1968, when he joined the faculty of the University of St. Thomas. The following year he joined the Rice University faculty, and in 1970 opened Latent Image Gallery, which, while short-lived, was the first serious venue for photography in Houston. Throughout the 1970s, the city of Houston was Winningham's chief subject. *Lamé Pants, Houston Livestock Show and Rodeo,* 1976 (plate 18), was part of an extended series on the Houston Rodeo, and was published with the following commentary by the artist:

For a full two weeks in late February and early March, an epidemic of "Go Texan" fever strikes Houston. Not everyone is affected, to be sure, but none fail to notice there is a lot of it going around. Accountants appear in western outfits, policemen don string ties, service stations sprout rodeo banners and bales of hay, and motel signs say "Howdy" to the visitors who will pump over $15 million into the Houston economy during the two weeks. The show and the people involved in it have style—a friendly, flamboyant style whose symbols are custom-made boots, big western hats kept on through meals and cocktail parties, and a colorful disregard for the niceties of diction and grammar that should not be mistaken for a lack either of intelligence or of formal education.[47]

Many photographers, including Winogrand, have been drawn to the showmanship of Texas's rodeos. However, *Lamé Pants* offers a peerless view of the activities that take place outside of the parade and the arena. Two urban cowgirls are shown shopping in Houston's AstroHall, and one might assume that neither would be flattered by the photographer's point of view. Yet Winningham captures with casual brilliance both the absurd and the appealing aspects of his subject, with much the same affectionate irony as seen in the works of the Texas Funk artists.

In 1971, photojournalists Wendy Watriss and Fred Baldwin settled in Texas and began to work collaboratively. Among their first projects was an ongoing portrait of the Hill Country of Central Texas. Spanning more than a decade, this project grew to include four communities across the state, as Watriss and Baldwin further explored the agrarian towns of East Texas, the border districts of South Texas, and west to the mountains of the Trans-Pecos. As they later recalled, "We came to Texas, symbolic center of the American dream, to scratch away at the surface and see what lay underneath. We wanted to begin to understand the diverse people and forces that had combined to make the American experience."[48]

Stone Duchess and Contestants, Stonewall, Texas, 1980 (plate 19), is part of a photo essay on local beauty pageants. The three young women are shown offstage; on the left is the crowned pageant queen. *Stone Duchess and Contestants* reveals a society caught in transition; not only are the young women awkwardly poised between youth and adulthood, but also between local culture and national stereotypes.

The 1980s saw further contributions to this documentary tradition in the work of Geary Broadnax, Gay Block, and Earlie Hudnall, Jr., all of whom have focused

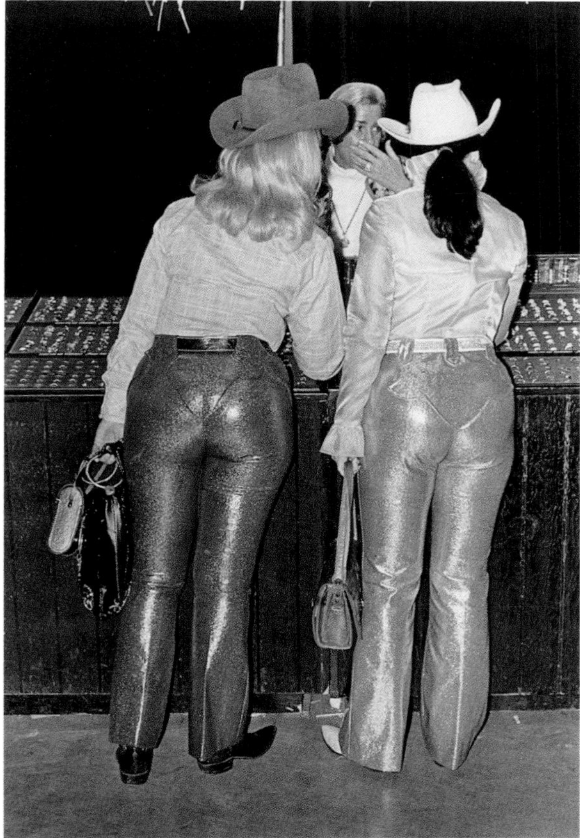

18
Geoff Winningham
Lamé Pants, Houston Livestock Show and Rodeo, from *A Texas Dozen* series, 1976 Gelatin silver photograph, 17½ x 11¾ in. (44.5 x 29.8 cm). Anthony G. Cronin Memorial Collection, gift of the Cronin Gallery, 78.258.13.

19
Wendy Watriss and Fred Baldwin
Stone Duchess and Contestants, Stonewall, Texas, 1980 Gelatin silver photograph, 9 x 13½ in. (22.9 x 34.3 cm). Gift of Clinton T. Willour in memory of Sheila Rosenstein, 93.103.

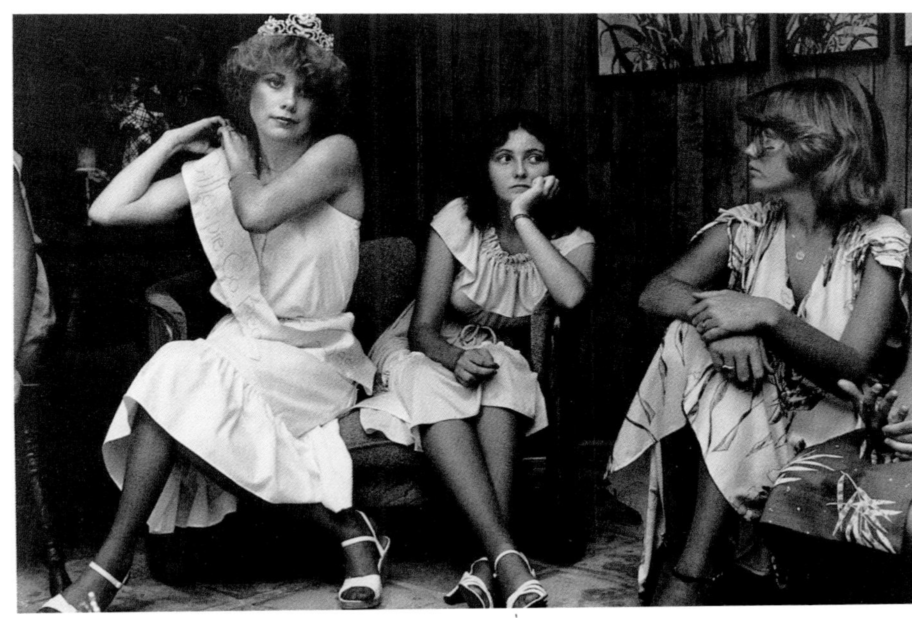

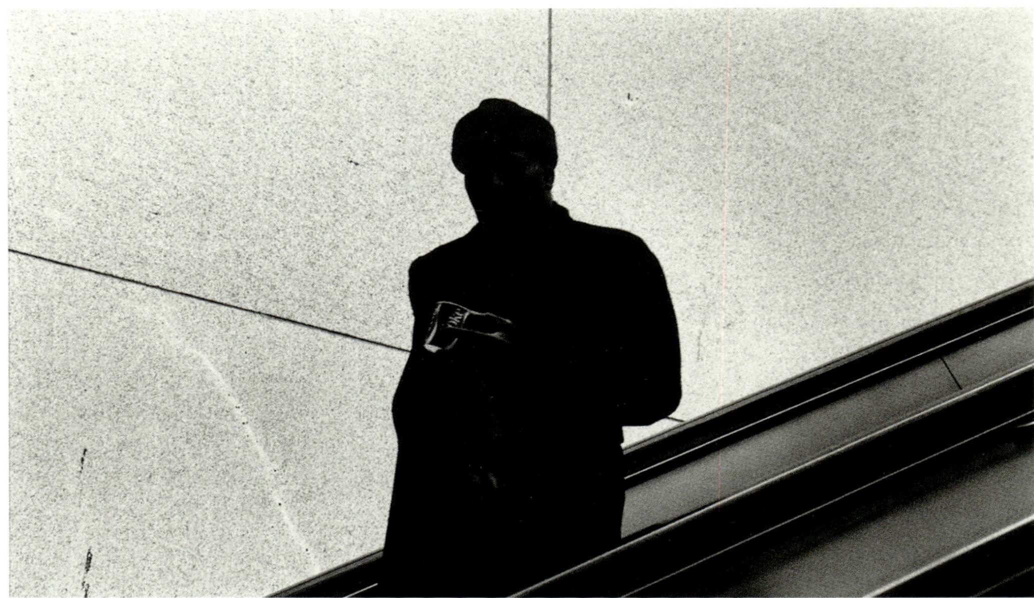

20
Geary Broadnax
The Real Thing, 1980
Gelatin silver photograph,
9⅛ x 13½ in. (23.2 x 34.3 cm).
Museum purchase with
funds provided by Clinton T.
Willour in honor of W. Tem-
ple Webber III, 93.116.

21
Gay Block
*Avilia, H.E.B., McAllen,
Texas,* **and** *Avilia at Home
with Her 10-Year-Old Sons,
Donna, Texas,* **from the**
H.E.B. **series, 1985**
Dye transfer photographs,
12 x 15 in. (30.5 x 38.1 cm)
each. Gift of Gay Block in
honor of Anne Tucker, 86.263.

their lenses on their immediate communities. Geary Broadnax, who worked as a staff photographer at the *Houston Post,* captured the alienating character of Houston's changing urbanism in such photographs as *The Real Thing,* 1980 (plate 20). The image has a formal brilliance and beauty: the central placement of the silhouetted figure is emphasized by the lines between the granite blocks; the diagonals of the escalator rails flow with a streamlined grace. Created at the height of the city's economic boom—when new skyscrapers reshaped the Houston skyline and an expanding tunnel system redirected the downtown pedestrian traffic—the image also offers a subtle criticism of the city's highly artificial environment. The anonymous figure of a black man is descending down the escalator; in his hand is a go-cup of Coca-Cola, which in the 1970s and early 1980s was promoted as "The Real Thing" in a widespread advertising campaign. Broadnax's image is given context by Robert D. Bullard's observations on the economics of the African-American community in Houston of these years: "Although the New South has been portrayed as booming with industrial growth and employment opportunities that were once closed to blacks, and although there has been progress for some southern blacks, very little has changed for the majority of blacks."[49]

Gay Block's career has been devoted to portraiture. After attending the University of Houston's School of Architecture in the early 1970s, Block began to study photography under Winningham and Winogrand. In 1975, she undertook her first oral and visual history project for

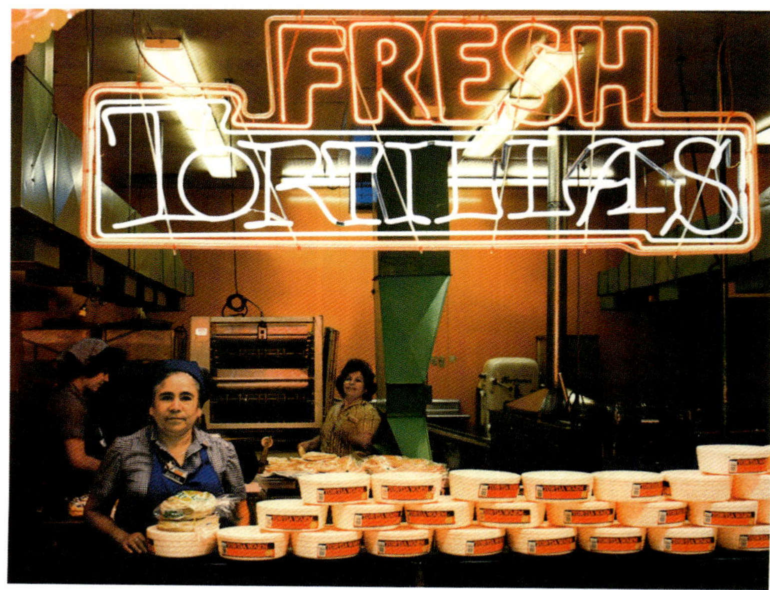

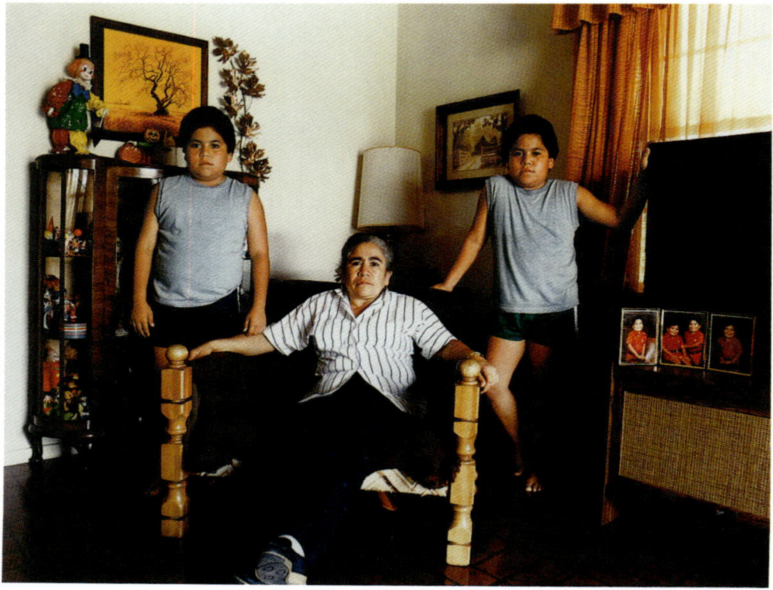

the Congregation Beth Israel, documenting the Jewish community of Houston. In an unpublished statement concerning her work, Block commented, "I am interested in portraying family relationships such as sisters, brothers, mothers and daughters, mothers and sons."[50]

Avilia, H.E.B., McAllen, Texas, and *Avilia at Home with Her 10-Year-Old Sons, Donna, Texas,* 1985 (plate 21), is one of a series of diptych portraits of employees commissioned by H. E. B. Pantry Foods for their corporate headquarters in San Antonio. The diptych format contrasts the two lives of the protagonist: on the left Avilia is shown at work, on the right in her living room flanked by her twin children. Social nuances differentiate these two views: at H. E. B., the protagonist is barred from the viewer by the array of tortillas that fills the frame; in her home, Avilia powerfully dominates the scene. In both instances, the woman is shown as an authoritative figure. Much as John Biggers's *Study for the Longshoreman's Mural* (see plate 11) gave dignity to the laborers of the Houston ship channel, Block's portrait recognizes the individual strength of a single employee.

A similar intimacy is found in Earlie Hudnall, Jr.'s eloquent photographs of the street life of African-American communities. A native of Mississippi, Hudnall attended Houston's Texas Southern University, where Biggers was one of his mentors. Hudnall began to chronicle the city's old Third, Fourth, and Fifth Wards in the 1970s, commenting: "I never pose my subject; I just let my gut level tell me when to take the picture."[51] He further elaborated:

> I chose to use the camera as a tool to document different aspects of life: who we are, what we do, how we live, what our communities look like. These various patterns are all interwoven like a quilt into important patterns of history. A unique commonality exists between young and old because there is always a continuity between the past and the future. It is this commonality which I strive to depict in my work.[52]

Lady in Black Coat, 1988 (plate 22), has a deceptive informality. The anonymous subject appears to have been captured in a casual moment—her gaze calmly meets that of the photographer over her right shoulder, her hand is raised mid-gesture, and her features are set off by her carefully knotted turban and by the contrast-

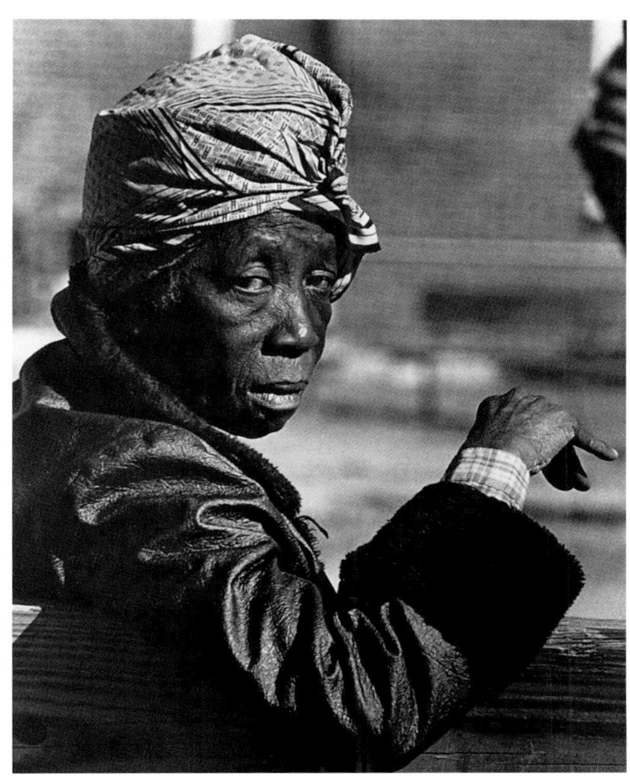

ing textures of her coat. By devoting almost the entire frame of the picture to the figure, letting the background drop out of focus, Hudnall confers a quiet monumentality and authority on his sitter.

The mid-1970s saw the establishment of two artists who were to have a profound influence on Texas art for the ensuing decade: John Alexander and James Surls. Finding their idiom in the flora and fauna of East Texas, Alexander and Surls created works that had their closest parallel outside of Texas in William Wiley's hallucinogenic depictions of the Northern California landscape.[53] Surls and Alexander were first promoted in Houston by James Harithas, director of the Contemporary Arts Museum from 1974 to 1978, who turned the museum over to the two artists in the spring of 1975. Surls exhibited over a dozen roughhewn sculptures in the upper gallery, while Alexander filled the lower gallery with landscapes. To many, their work tapped directly into the local psyche and the land, free of the clichés of boots, cowboys, and rodeo, and offering fresh

22
Earlie Hudnall, Jr.
Lady in Black Coat, 1988
Gelatin silver photograph,
18⅞ x 15 in. (47.9 x 38.1 cm).
The Sonia and Kaye Marvins
Portrait Collection, museum
purchase with funds provided by the Photography
Accessions Subcommittee in
honor of Michael H. and
Michele Sharney Marvins,
90.336.

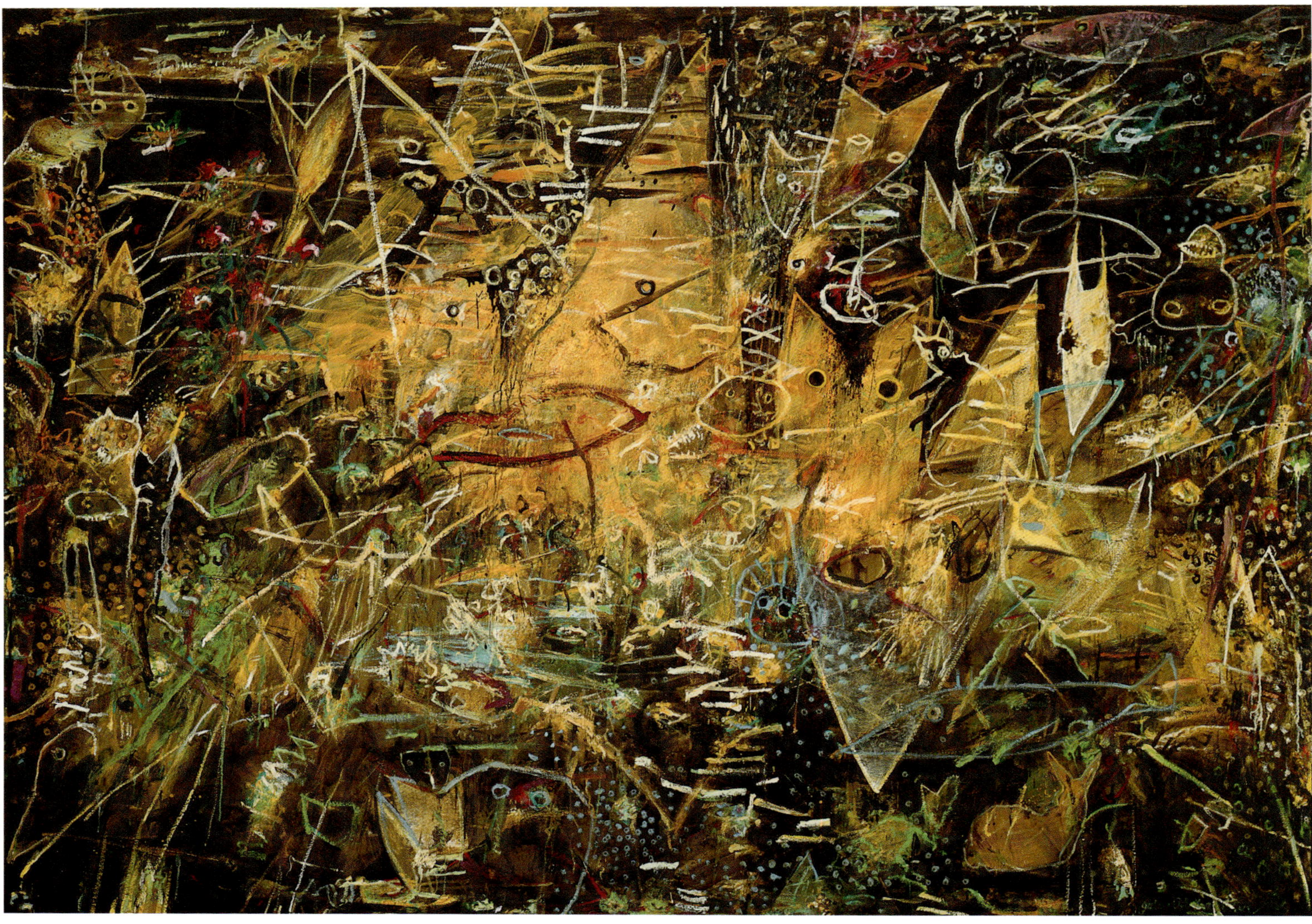

means of exploring the Texas identity. In the CAM's catalogue, Michael Samuels stated: "James's pieces are primal forms of figures which live inside us."[54] And writing later that year, Mimi Crossley predicted of Alexander's work: "Whatever it looks like, it will show the new future of the Texas landscape, out of a past being created now."[55]

John Alexander was born in Beaumont, Texas, one of the "Golden Triangle" cities of the oil boom era. He attended Lamar University and Southern Methodist University, and moved to Houston in 1972 to join the faculty of the University of Houston. His first landscapes emphasized the flat plains and high horizons of the Texas coast; by the mid-1970s, however, Alexander began to adopt a calligraphic, overall treatment of the surface and to animate his compositions with haunting figures and anarchic creatures. As John Beardsley noted in 1983: "Alexander's landscapes are the settings for a series of almost allegorical conflicts: between good and evil, growth and decay, fecundity and death. In the manner of medieval bestiaries, good and evil sometimes take the shape of animals; the former can be a cat named Mr. Friend, the latter a crayfish. . . . Yet death is always present, a gesticulating skeleton, a burning cross or a malevolent creature buried within the layers of painting."[56]

Mr. Friend's Revenge, 1982 (plate 23), has the lush palette of a nocturnal landscape, reminiscent of the dense thickets of East Texas swamps. The artist has revealed, however, that the painting was also inspired by the sight of his cat peering through a fish tank. The specter of the cat is repeated across the canvas, as are images of fish; an inverted death's head on the right indicates the cat's intent. Alexander has commented, "I work with landscape imagery not as an end in itself, but to exorcise the violence and psychosis that have become basic to the human experience."[57]

Like Alexander, Surls has explored the dynamic balance between life and death, creation and destruction. *I Am Building with the Axe, the Knife, and the Needle's Eye,*

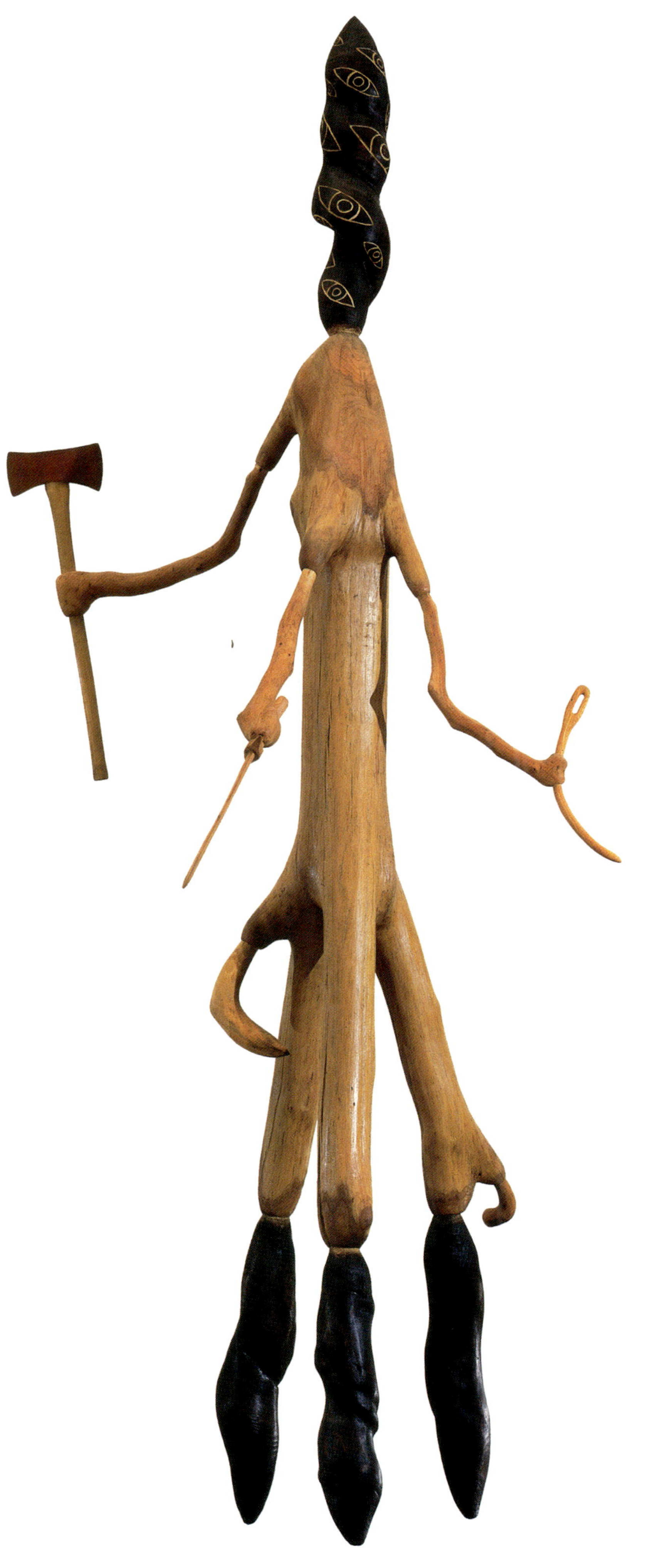

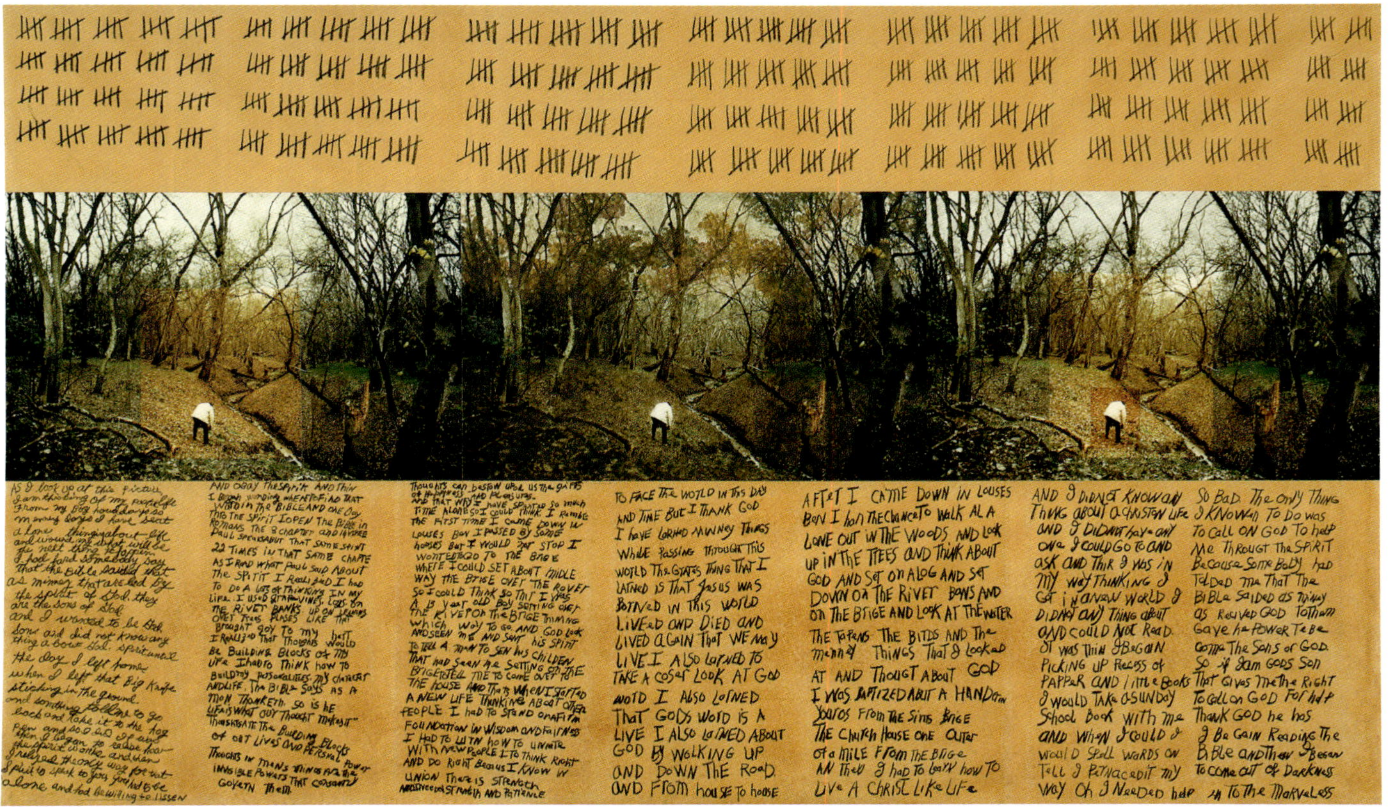

25
Nancy O'Connor
This Is Where I Began to Think of How My Life Would Come to Be, 1979
Color coupler photographs, varnish, photo oil, tempera, and wax pencil, 35½ x 59 in. (90.2 x 149.9 cm). Museum purchase with funds provided by Mr. and Mrs. R. W. Wortham III, 82.49.

1982 (plate 24), can be read as a visionary self-portrait; the wordplay of the title equates the seeing "eye" with the creative "I." Surls was born in Terrell, Texas, near Dallas. He attended Sam Houston State University and Cranbrook Academy of Art; he returned to Texas in 1970 to join the faculty of Southern Methodist University in Dallas. The success of his exhibition at the Contemporary Arts Museum and his growing friendship with John Alexander brought him to Houston in 1976, where he joined the faculty of the University of Houston, and established a studio north of the city in Splendora. The importance of working at the edge of the Piney Woods was critical to Surls, as he later commented:

> Moving to Splendora has affected my life tremendously. For the first time I have an absolute sense of permanence. I have an absolute sense of belonging. I sort of screwed myself to the earth right there. . . . It is East Texas. It has that East Texas sensibility which is what I wanted.[58]

The thirteen-foot tall *I Am Building with the Axe, the Knife, and the Needle's Eye* is constructed out of hickory,

oak, pine, and padouk, materials which Surls was able to gather in the woods around his studio. The combination of "found" elements, such as the inverted trunk that defines the figure's torso and legs, and the more finely worked tools, indirectly emphasizes the distinctions between nature and culture. The twisting forms which define the head and feet evoke at once the physical power of a tornado and the spiritual power of a dervish. What is most remarkable about Surls's sculptures of this period, is their connection to the landscape. Not only are the materials familiar to East Texas, but the figure which Surls has conjured out of them is very much at one with the local myth. In a 1985 interview, Surls considered his place within the Western tradition:

> I really consider myself to be a Western artist. I'm just as much a Western artist as Remington. But, come on, they quit roping doggies 50 years ago. . . . The trail drives are over. I want to be at the forefront of a place, not at the back. I don't want to be in some other artist's vapor trail.[59]

Nancy O'Connor, a native of Victoria, Texas, and daughter of the artist Madeline O'Connor (see plates 61 and 62), was among the first artists to match the vernacular idiom promoted by Alexander and Surls. She attended Trinity University in San Antonio, where she studied film; she then transferred to the University of Texas at Austin, where she studied under Winogrand (see plate 17) and received a degree in journalism. However, as O'Connor's first mature work demonstrates, she brought a narrative immediacy to her documentary essays on the vanishing cowboy communities of Refugio County.

This Is Where I Began to Think of How My Life Would Come to Be, 1979 (plate 25), is part of what ultimately became a six-year collaborative project O'Connor undertook with Milam Thompson.[60] The artwork was titled by Thompson, and as O'Connor has chronicled:

> This piece is part of a documentary on Lewis's Bend—an old black cowboy community in Vidaurri, Texas.... The writing was done by Milam Thompson—75-year-old camp kitchen cook and once part of the Vidaurri community. The photography was taken in Lewis's Bend in the spring of 1979, which was the first time Milam had been back to Lewis's Bend since childhood.[61]

O'Connor shows Thompson walking along the old San Antonio River bottom, his cook's white coat sharply standing out in the wooded landscape. By repeating the image and blocking out color contrasts in the printing process, O'Connor achieves a photographic equivalent to the cinematic tracking shot. Her formal sophistication is matched by the unstudied directness of Thompson's contributions: the top third of the composition is devoted to marks which attest to the passing of time, the bottom third contains his text. Idiomatic eloquence, phonetic spelling, and vivid handwriting bring the narrative to life as Thompson opens with the reflection: "As I look up at this picture I am thinking of my past life. From my boyhood days so menny days I have seat alone thinking about life and the next thing to happen." He continues to recount how he discovered the spiritual dimension of life, concluding with: "I begain reading The Bible and then I began to come out of darkness into the marveless."

As the 1970s progressed into the 1980s, Texas art came to be characterized by an increasingly narrative expressionism, combining the anecdotal qualities of Texas Funk with an autobiographical intimacy. While distinctions can be made within the state—for example, North Texas artists tended to view their surroundings coolly through the filters of appropriation and memory, and South and East Texas artists tended to emphasize the more immediate experience—this trend was recognized in a number of exhibitions and critical articles. The regionalist character of this celebration of Texas themes was debated by historians, critics, and curators, most notably in the catalogue essays of three important exhibitions of the mid-1980s: William A. Fagaly's and Monroe K. Spears's essays for the Contemporary Arts Museum's *Southern Fictions* exhibition; William H. Goetzmann's "Images of Texas," for the Archer M. Huntington Art Gallery's *Texas Images and Visions*; and Barbara Rose's "Painting is Dead, Long Live Painting in Houston," for the MFAH's *Fresh Paint* exhibition.[62]

Fagaly stressed the Texas artists' affinity with a Southern sensibility and literary tradition, an attitude which harkened back to the days when Houston was still known as the Magnolia City. Rose summarized the conflict between the need to identify Texas's unique contribution to contemporary art and to avoid the stigma of regionalism: "Although one can detect a preference for thick paint, strong color, bright light (again, a Southern light), autobiographical content, and a romantic and lyric, rather than urban, expressionism among Houston-based artists, one cannot speak of a regional style. Unlike Regionalism in the thirties, which was a programmatic attack on modernism and its values, current regional schools do not reject modernism and its tenets so much as they are relatively indifferent to it."[63]

However, as Goetzmann noted, the Texas character of Texas art remained an ongoing conundrum: "Shall we declare that Texas itself has vanished into the realm of human fantasy? If so, is that something new...? Can we bear it and still grin? Shall we see it for what it might be—the latest in a long line of Texas tall tales? Is postmodern Texas a rediscovery of our folkloristic roots, or is it nihilism, or self-indulgence; the cry of despair, or the wailing of the hopelessly confused?"[64]

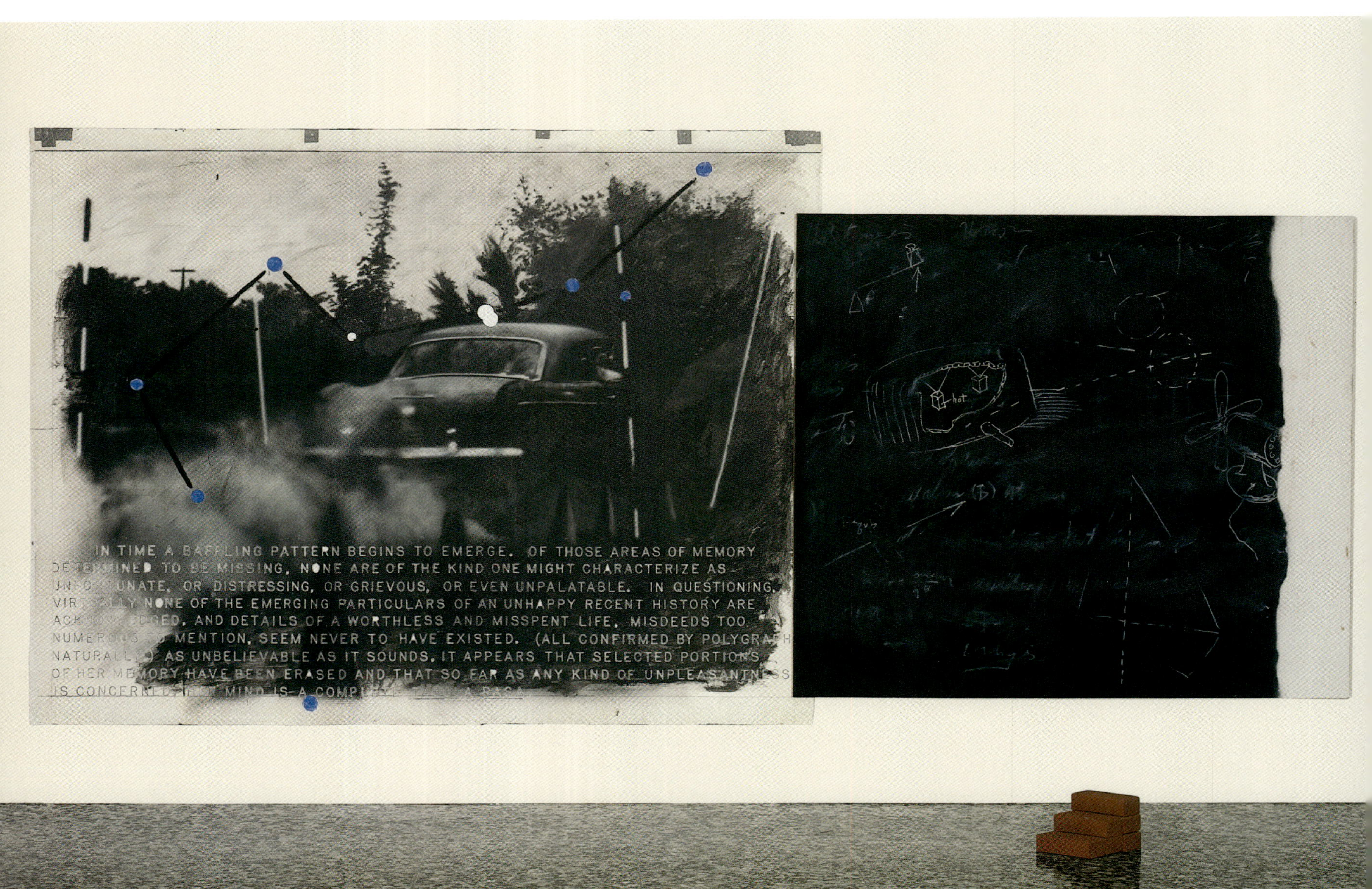
IN TIME A BAFFLING PATTERN BEGINS TO EMERGE. OF THOSE AREAS OF MEMORY
DETERMINED TO BE MISSING, NONE ARE OF THE KIND ONE MIGHT CHARACTERIZE AS
UNFORTUNATE, OR DISTRESSING, OR GRIEVOUS, OR EVEN UNPALATABLE. IN QUESTIONING,
VIRTUALLY NONE OF THE EMERGING PARTICULARS OF AN UNHAPPY RECENT HISTORY ARE
ACKNOWLEDGED. AND DETAILS OF A WORTHLESS AND MISSPENT LIFE, MISDEEDS TOO
NUMEROUS TO MENTION, SEEM NEVER TO HAVE EXISTED. (ALL CONFIRMED BY POLYGRAPH
NATURALLY.) AS UNBELIEVABLE AS IT SOUNDS, IT APPEARS THAT SELECTED PORTIONS
OF HER MEMORY HAVE BEEN ERASED AND THAT SO FAR AS ANY KIND OF UNPLEASANTNESS
IS CONCERNED HER MIND IS A COMPLETE TABULA RASA.

Ironically, this resurgence of Texas themes reflected an international mood, rather than a regional one. Whether as particularized as Roger Brown's Chicago skyline and or as universal as Vija Celmins's night skies, an increasing number of artists in the late 1970s and 1980s turned to the landscape, finding in it a rich source for metaphor and allusion. And much as Anselm Kiefer was discovering a means of recasting the history of Germany through the legends of the Black Forest region where he had grown up, so too were Texas artists mining the histories of their personal landscapes.

Among the most prominent artists to lead this trend was Vernon Fisher, who brought a Postmodernist sensibility to his musings on Western identity. Fisher was born in Fort Worth; after completing his studies at the University of Illinois, Champaign-Urbana, in 1969, he returned to Texas. In the mid-1970s, he began to incorporate written narratives into his work, first in book form, and later as texts accompanying his multimedia installations, paintings, and drawings. Like many of the artists associated with Texas Funk in the 1970s, Fisher employed a cinematic vocabulary and made roadside culture one of his chief themes. However, the increasingly sophisticated narratives, the sense of dislocation, and the layering of allusion in Fisher's work address the existential issues of living in this region. In a 1989 essay, Dave Hickey recounted a conversation with Fisher, "We have been talking about the blessing and curse of growing up in the west, about the first thing you learn, which is that the world you live in, and the words you live by, do not fit, that they never have and never will."[65]

In *Rushing into Darkness*, 1984 (plate 26), the nineteenth-century ideal of Western expansion has evolved into today's stories of the road. On the left half of the composition we see a filmic image of a car plunging down a dark highway.[66] Superimposed over this scene is the Big Dipper pointing towards the North Star, suggesting a search for a guiding principle. Incised into the canvas is a text describing a woman lost in the desert, who has experienced an inexplicable event:

In time a baffling pattern begins to emerge. Of those areas of memory determined to be missing, none are of the kind one might characterize as unfortunate, or distressing, or grievous, or even unpalatable. In questioning, virtually none of the emerging particulars of an unhappy recent history are acknowledged, and details of a worthless and misspent life, misdeeds too numerous to mention, seem never to have existed. (All confirmed by polygraph naturally.) As unbelievable as it sounds, it appears that selected portions of her memory have been erased and that so far as any kind of unpleasantness is concerned, her mind is a complete *tabula rasa*.[67]

The text is complemented by a literal *tabula rasa* (blank slate), recreated on the right panel, with partly erased notations that suggest equations and symbols for various systems of causality. A stack of six bricks is placed in front of the two panels, which can be read as a stairway, or as a reference to the fundamental clay of earth. In a 1989 interview, Fisher discussed the painting:

Rushing into Darkness is the second of two pieces that was excerpted from a longer story I wrote called "Amazing Grace." In this story Grace, who is a stripper named Amazing Grace, has some kind of experience with some phenomenon we're not really sure of—it's some kind of alien, and we're not sure if it's an illegal alien, as in across the border, or from outer space. Nonetheless, she has this experience and apparently loses part of her memory. The part of her memory that she loses is only the bad things that ever happened in her life; she remembers all the good things, so essentially, it's a redemption story.... I made two pieces about this, from which I excerpted part of this text, and one is *Car Impaled on Guardrail* [Collection Anne and Martin Z. Margulies] and the other one is *Rushing into Darkness*.... The two pieces work together, I think, as a sort of heaven and earth.[68]

Even when regarded independently from *Car Impaled on Guardrail*, *Rushing into Darkness* is one of Fisher's most fully realized works of the 1980s. The images and text do not offer a coherent narrative; rather, they prompt an open reading, inviting the viewer to fill in "the areas of memory determined to be missing."

Where Fisher found inspiration in tabloid headlines, film noir, and the highways of West Texas, Lee N. Smith III has tapped his memories of growing up in the suburbs. Born in New Orleans, Smith moved with his family to the city limit of eastern Dallas in 1956. Recalling this childhood, Smith stated, "It was living on the border of expected behavior and the total freedom of the endless flatlands that allowed our adventures to take on greater

26
Vernon Fisher
Rushing into Darkness, 1984
Acrylic on laminated paper on canvas, blackboard slating on wood, and bricks, 87¼ x 112 in. (213.9 x 284.4 cm), 70¾ x 79½ in. (179.7 201.9 cm), and 2¼ x 8⅛ x 4 in. (5.7 x 21 x 10.2 cm) each. Museum purchase with funds provided by Duke Energy, 86.298.

substance and meaning."[69] Smith briefly attended El Centro Junior College in Dallas; stints in advertising and as a rock-and-roll musician led ultimately to a decision to begin painting in 1976.

Smith quickly adopted an illustrative narrative mode in his depictions of suburban children. *In the Eye of the Rebellion*, 1984 (plate 27), distills the adolescent culture of dare and double-dare charted in such 1950s movies as *Rebel without a Cause*. As Emily Todd has noted of this painting, Smith "…brings us from childhood to the frontier of adolescence. Here, the secret clubs of childhood are replaced by the close-knit 'gang' of later years. Having invaded a playground at night, the teenagers explore the forbidden—smoking, drinking and posturing for the opposite sex. The boy who has created the focus of the piece (an eye that invests the concrete culvert with life) has found his niche as an artist, an identity he can cling to in the storm of adolescence."[70]

Unlike the majority of artists discussed in this chapter, Derek Boshier regarded the Texas landscape with the bemused and immediate eye of a foreigner. Born in Portsmouth, England, Boshier was among the first proponents of British Pop. In the 1970s he moved into film, video, and assemblage; however, at the end of the decade he returned to painting with a brilliant post-Pop sensibility. In 1980, he accepted a position on the faculty of the University of Houston, and within a year the Texas scene had became one of the chief themes of his work.

Everyday Opera, 1983 (plate 28), in the words of the artist, "is a combination of things you hear over the media all the time. Formally, two-thirds of it is terror … one third is romance."[71] The montage of images—soap-opera lovers, a phantom jet, the blazing horizon illuminating refineries, offshore rigs, and storage tanks—was inspired by the rapid-fire information of daytime television. The nude figure on the left, a self-portrait, reels away in shock from this panorama. While not a representation of Houston in the strictest sense, *Everyday Opera* captures the spirit of the city on the eve of the oil bust. Boshier later recalled that his work of these years

27
Lee N. Smith III
In the Eye of the Rebellion,
1984
Oil on canvas, 78 x 114 ½ in. (198.1 x 290.8 cm). Gift of Fredericka Hunter and Ian Glennie in memory of Warren Hadler, 86.398.

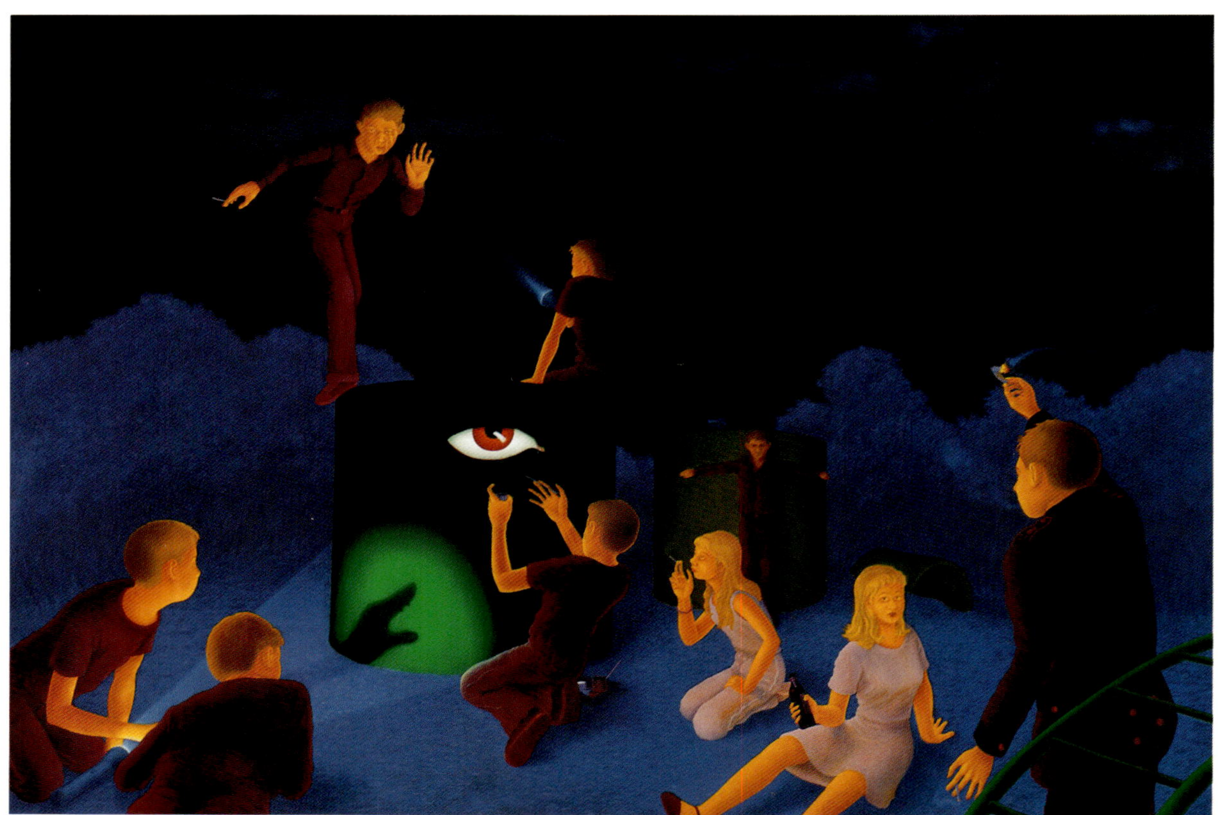

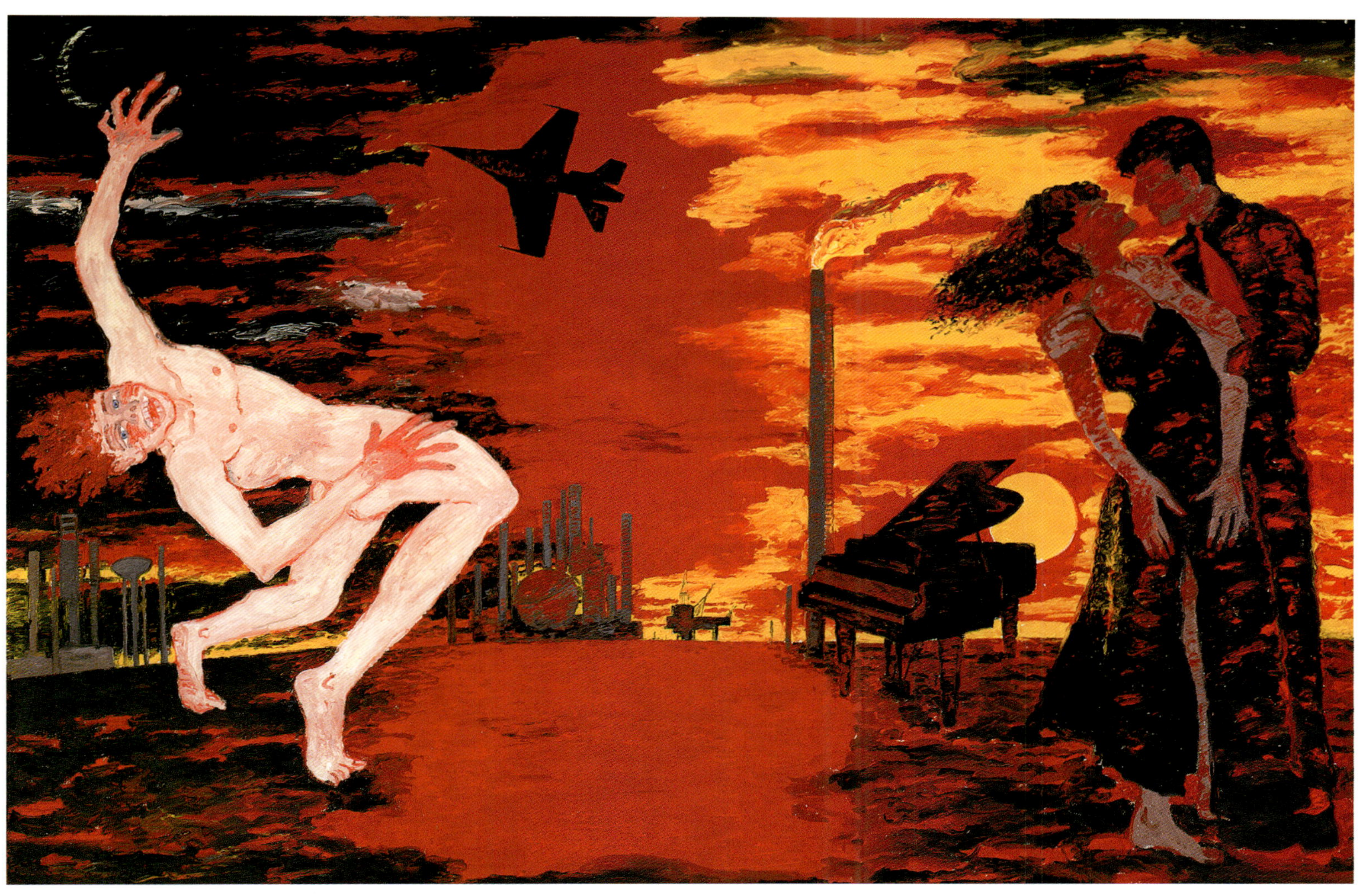

28
Derek Boshier
Everyday Opera, 1983
Oil on canvas, 88¼ x 132½
in. (224.1 x 336.6 cm).
Museum purchase with funds
provided by the Assistance
League of Houston, 84.5.

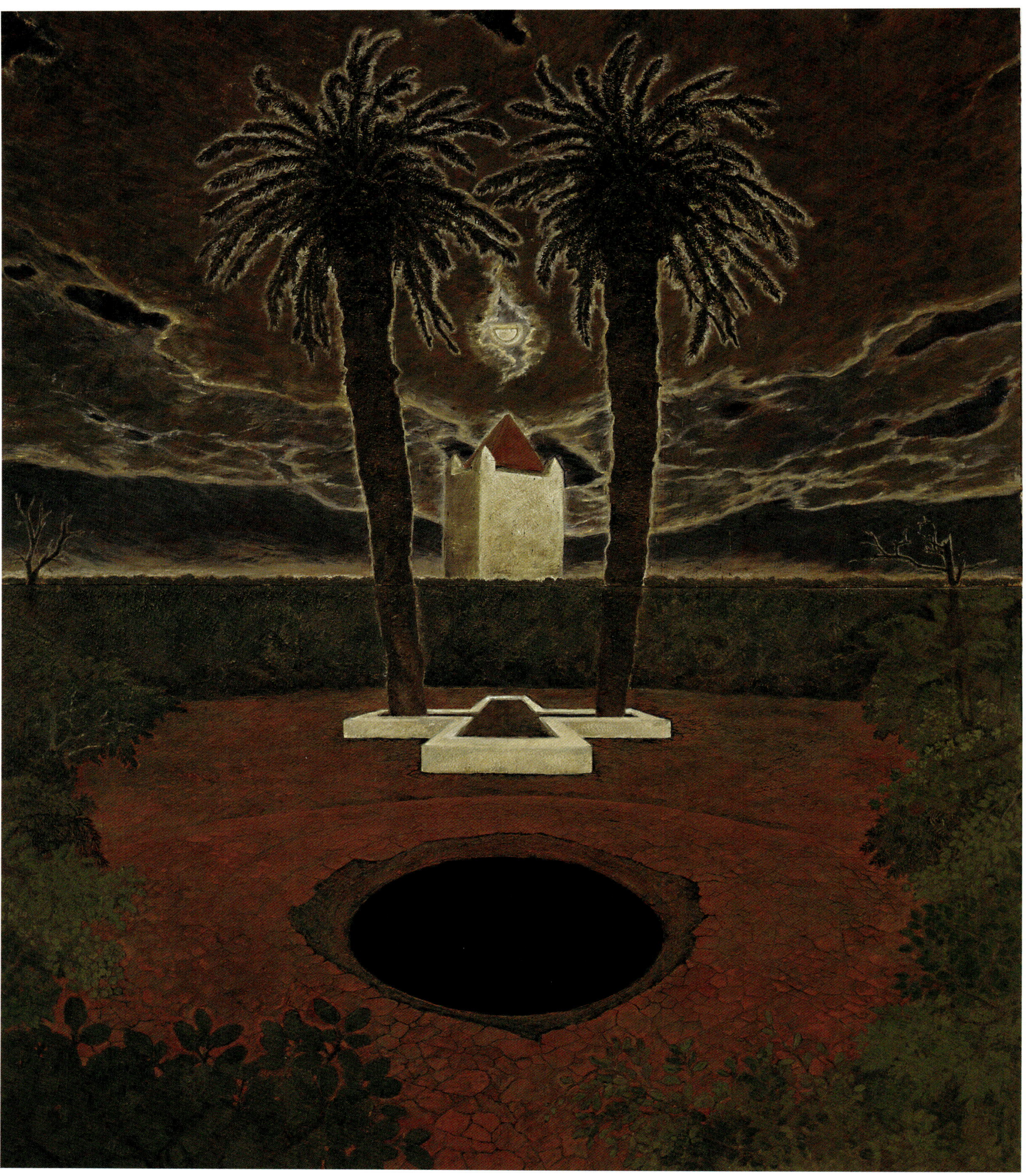

reflected "current events, personal events, social and political situations, and a sense of place and places."[72]

Boshier's media-driven reverie on Houston is appropriately complemented in the MFAH's collection by Mel Chin's *Untitled [Terra Infirma]* diptych (plate 29). A first-generation Chinese-American, Chin grew up in Houston; in 1978 he created one of the city's most exotic public sculptures, *Manila Palm: An Oasis Secret*, which was first sited downtown as part of the Main Street Festival and later placed behind Houston's Contemporary Arts Museum.

Chin's monumental dreamscape revisits some of the formal themes of the *Manila Palm*: both works contrast the image of the palm to an architectural element, both suggest a temporal shift between the here-and-now and the infinite. Chin chose an anonymous Latin poem as the full title for the diptych:

> SUB MAGNA NUBE
> SOMNUS SPIRITUS MEI
> NATURAM TANQUAM
> APARITIONEM INTELLEGERE INCIPIO
> AD LIMEN HUIUS INCUBONIS NOCTURNI
> HORIZON ORITOR SOMNIORUM MACULA
>
> TERRAE INFIRMITATEM SENTIVI
> FIRMAMENTI OBSCURITATEM SCIVI
>
> [Under the great cloud
> The sleep of my spirit.
> I begin to perceive nature
> As an apparition.
> On the edge of this nightmare
> The horizon becomes the blur of dreams.
>
> I have felt the infirmity of the earth.
> I have known the obscurity of heaven.]

Chin depicts a view from the Beth Yeshurun Cemetery of the former Rein Company Building tower along Allen Parkway. The encaustic surface of the painting is heavily built up, dried and splitting apart to mimic terra cotta. *Terra Infirma* was the artist's last painting before he turned to sculpture; he later commented, "The use of a native ingredient (the wax) was important conceptually and economically at the time. Especially in the depiction of the species of the plants that encircle the pool . . . they are all local types and serve as a key identifier for the work."[73]

In early studies for the composition, the silhouette of

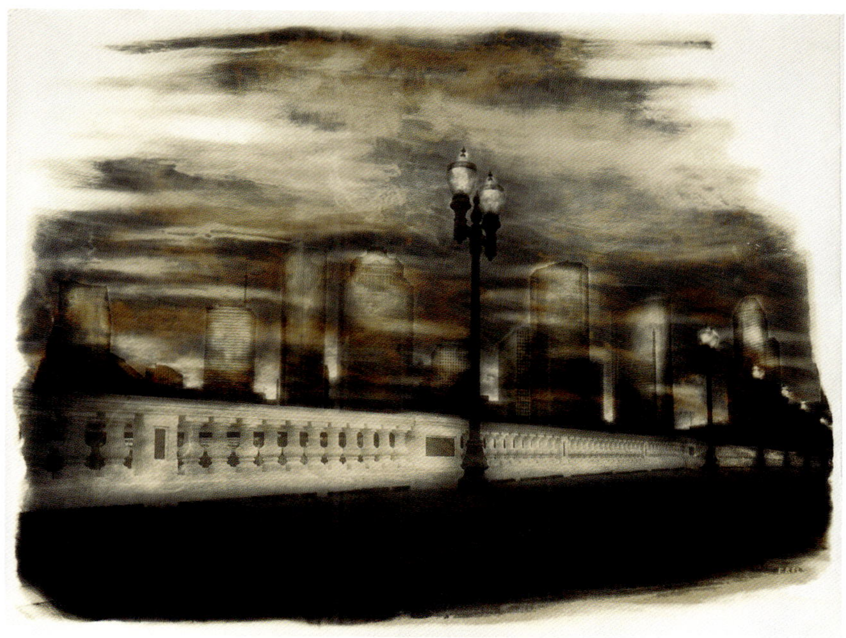

a huddled woman was in the place of the pool. Chin identified the figure as the mythical Myrrha, who in Ovid's *Metamorphoses* had seduced her father by assuming the guise of another woman. Pregnant, she appeals to the gods to save her, and she is turned into myrrh, later splitting apart to give birth to Adonis. Chin has related:

> The parable is more about fusion and transformation, alchemy, rather than incest. I wanted to use this figure in the landscape painting, but I couldn't resolve it. Finally, I did a symbolic metaphor (in the landscape diptych)—the pool, which is a receding image, is feminine, the [tower] and the palm trees are masculine—you know, a polarity.[74]

Regeneration has become one of the chief themes of Chin's career, perhaps most notably in his ongoing *Revival Field* project. Here, the vivid dream image of Houston has a hallucinatory immediacy; through pictorial brilliance and allusion, Chin invests the local landscape with a haunting sense of the timeless and eternal.

A similar elegiac mood characterizes Frank Martin's toned photograph, *Soft Morning City*, 1989 (plate 30). Martin, a native of New Orleans, made Houston his home in 1980. Among his first projects in Houston were portraits of the city's art community—captured at openings, performances, and informal events—which remain among the most vivid documents of that era. He then began a series of photographic monoprints, developing a remarkable ongoing and visionary portrait of the city itself.

Soft Morning City is among a series of views of the downtown skyline, photographed in this instance from the Sabine Street Bridge. Martin has manipulated the print to cloak the vista with a sepia haze and to create an

30
Frank Martin
Soft Morning City, 1989
Toned gelatin silver photograph, 51¼ x 65¾ in. (130.2 x 167 cm). Gift of Alexandra Marshall, 89.121.

29 *opposite*
Mel Chin
Untitled [Terra Infirma], 1981–83
Encaustic on canvas, 154 x 132 in. (391 x 335.2 cm) each. Museum purchase with funds provided by Duke Energy, Mr. and Mrs. Maurice McAshan, Dominique de Menil, Bubba Levy, Sandra Jensen, and friends of the artist, 90.302.

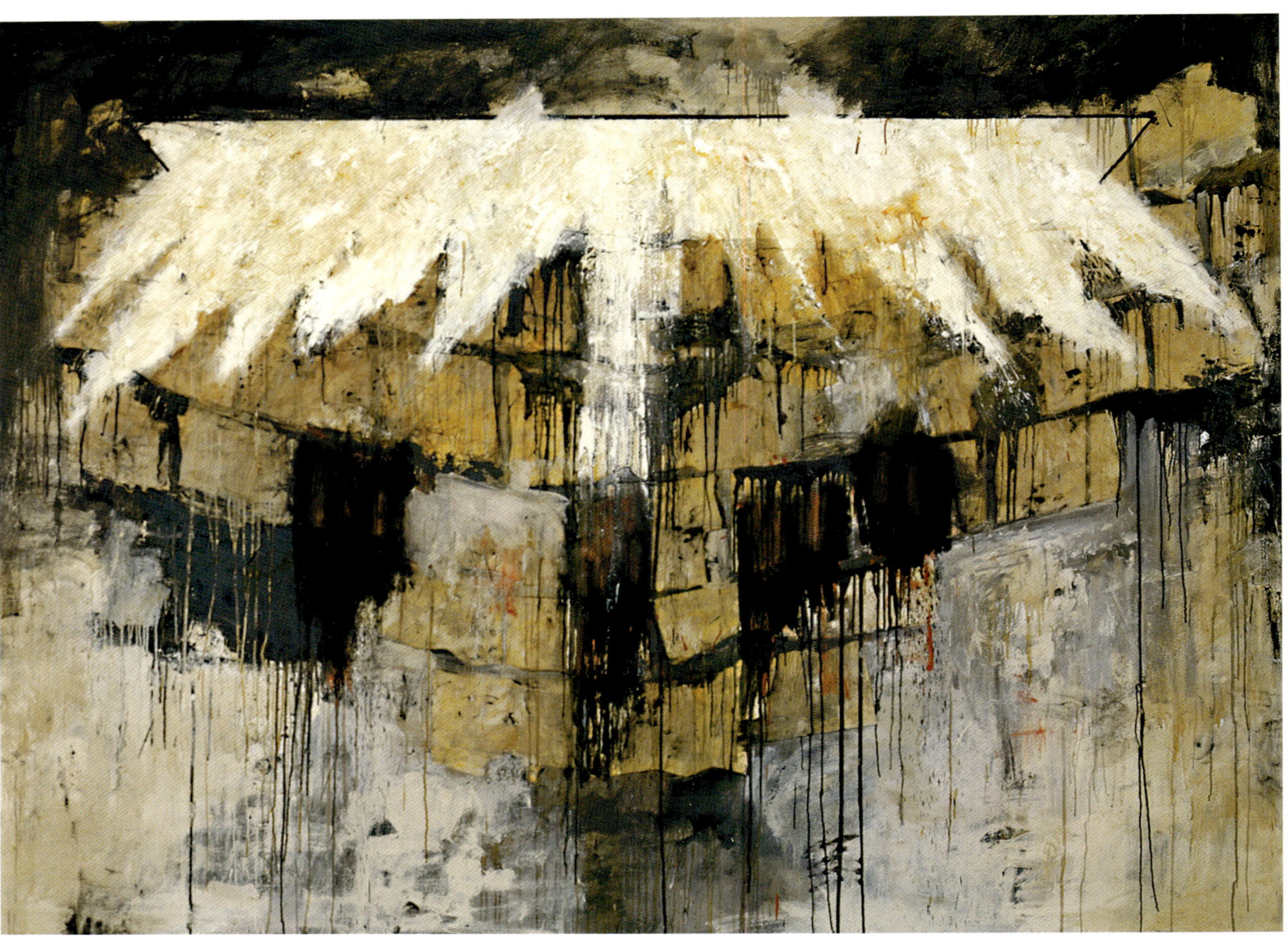

31
Paul Manes
Edge of the Sea, 1987
Oil and collage on canvas,
78 x 105¾ in. (198.1 x 268.6
cm). Museum purchase
with funds provided by Mr.
and Mrs. Maurice McAshan,
87.285.

aura around the buildings, the old-fashioned balustrade and lamps of the bridge offering a sharp contrast to the sleek downtown skyscrapers. Martin captioned a related photograph:

> I did some telephone research a while back and came up with the amazing conclusion that without continued maintenance, modern curtain-wall construction techniques create a building with a life span that is shorter than that of its builders. . . . So this then is a picture of our future's past, muddy, uncertain, though not quite as transitory as the buildings themselves.[75]

The sense of wonder that the Houston skyline inspired in Chin and Martin finds a parallel in the work of two East Texas artists, Paul Manes and Keith Carter, whose early careers followed parallel paths. Both grew up in Beaumont, both attended the business management program of Lamar University in the late 1960s, and both took up photography in the following decade, although Manes turned to painting in 1978. More importantly, both have built their careers through finding revelation in the everyday; in the words of Carter, "I believe in wonder. I look for it in my life every day; I find it in the most ordinary things."[76]

Edge of the Sea, 1987 (plate 31), is among Manes's first mature works. Inspired by the drama of the Gulf Coast horizon, Manes began a series of abstract seascapes in the mid-1980s. While the example of John Alexander's densely knit landscapes of the early 1980s provided a point of departure for Manes, these paintings have a closer affinity to the visionary panoramas of Forrest Bess and Jack Boynton. Throughout the series, light assumes an oracular role, bursting across the composition and evoking the process of creation. The surface is richly worked with layers of oil paint, shellac, and rag paper which has been collaged onto the canvas. Much as photography is a medium defined by light, Manes defines his compositions through dramatic contrast. As Carter Ratcliff has noted, "Manes does not illustrate his experience, nor does he offer exemplary instances of the style called Expressionism. His paintings transpose experience into a pictorial state."[77]

Keith Carter's *Fireflies*, 1992 (plate 32), at a glance appears to cover the same territory as Lee Smith's *In the Eye of the Rebellion* (see plate 27). In both instances, the artist offers a view into the rituals of childhood. However, where Smith distances the image through irony,

Carter closes in for greater immediacy. The two boys, with their treasure trove of captured fireflies, are silhouetted by a wash of light. By focusing on the foreground, Carter confers an anonymity upon the figures, permitting the viewer a degree of identity that would not be possible in a more lucid portrait. Even those of us who have never spent a day of our childhood visiting an East Texas pond cast ourselves in the role of these children.

Fireflies was published in 1992 in *Mojo: Photographs by Keith Carter*, and Rosellen Brown pondered on the meaning of this series: "If photographs are positives, the presence of the negative lies behind them always. As in a good poem, each embodies its antithesis—movement behind stillness, chaos behind clarity, and, inevitably, death behind life.... It isn't surprising that Keith Carter pursues this edgy fascination into a series of photographs in which our memories seem to be filled with things we've never seen."[78]

A complementary current to the narrative landscapes of the 1980s began to emerge by the middle of the decade. As an alternative to the transcendent and autobiographical, artists began to adopt a more neutral view of the Texas landscape. Peter Brown's *H. A. C. Brummett, Lawyer, Dickens, Texas*, 1986, from the *On the Plains* series (plate 33), aptly reflects this shift.[79]

A native of New England, Brown moved to Houston in 1978, when he joined the faculty of Rice University. In 1983, he published a portfolio titled *Seasons of Light*, a series of interior views accompanied by short stories, also written by the artist.[80] Much as Fisher had used narrative in his paintings and installations, Brown employed an autobiographical voice to enlarge the context of his images. *H. A. C. Brummett, Lawyer, Dickens, Texas*, came about through a different working premise. Beginning in 1983, Brown began to photograph the open country, ranches, roads, and small towns of the high plains of Texas, New Mexico, Oklahoma, and Kansas, much as Vincent Colyer had chronicled the topography of the "Indian Territory" more than a century earlier. These images have the documentary directness of the FSA photographs of the 1930s; unlike Russell Lee (see plate 10), however, Brown chooses to elide the figure

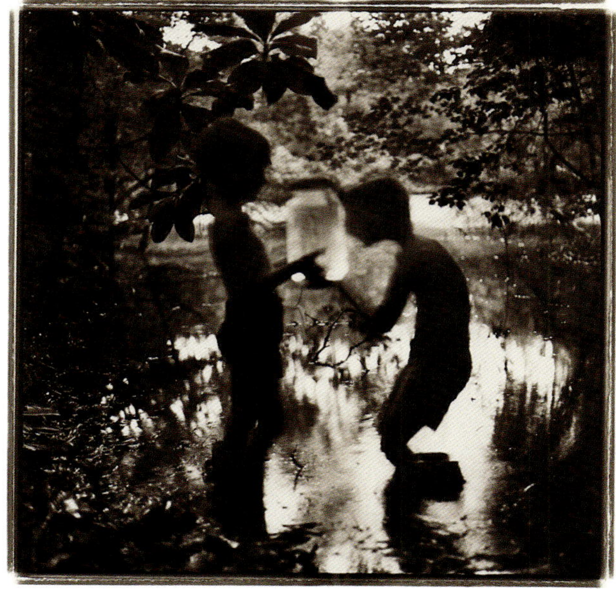

32
Keith Carter
Fireflies, 1992
Gelatin silver photograph,
15¼ x 15¼ in. (38.7 x 38.7 cm).
Gift of Joan Morgenstern in
honor of Sam Lasseter,
93.370.

33
Peter Brown
H. A. C. Brummett, Lawyer, Dickens, Texas, from the
On the Plains series, 1986
Color coupler photograph,
14½ x 18¼ in. (36.8 x 46.4
cm). Museum purchase
with funds provided by Mr.
and Mrs. Joe S. Mundy, 90.16.

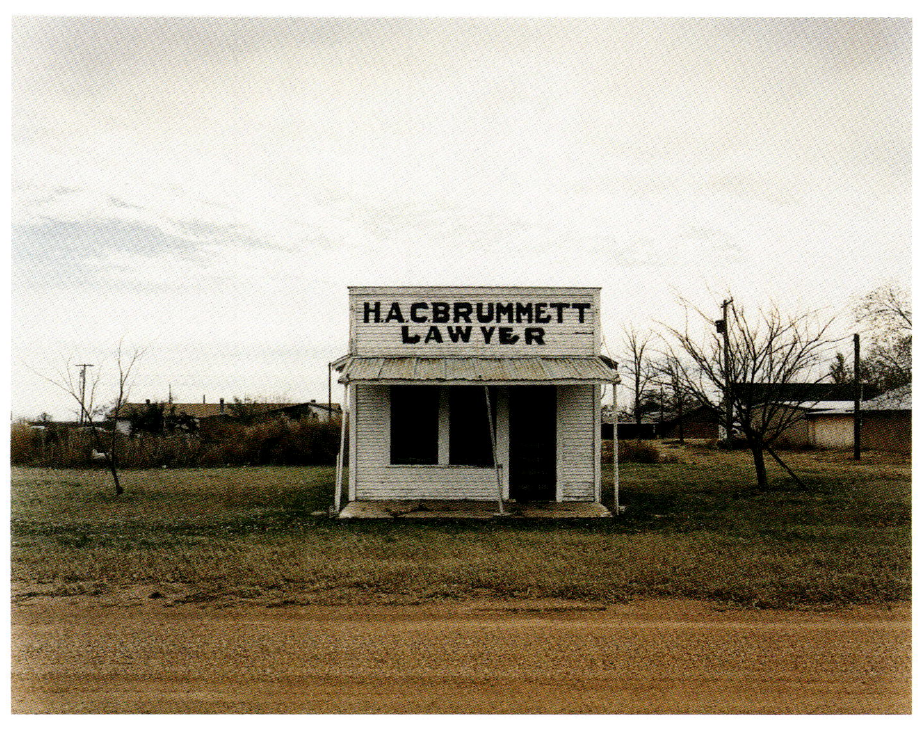

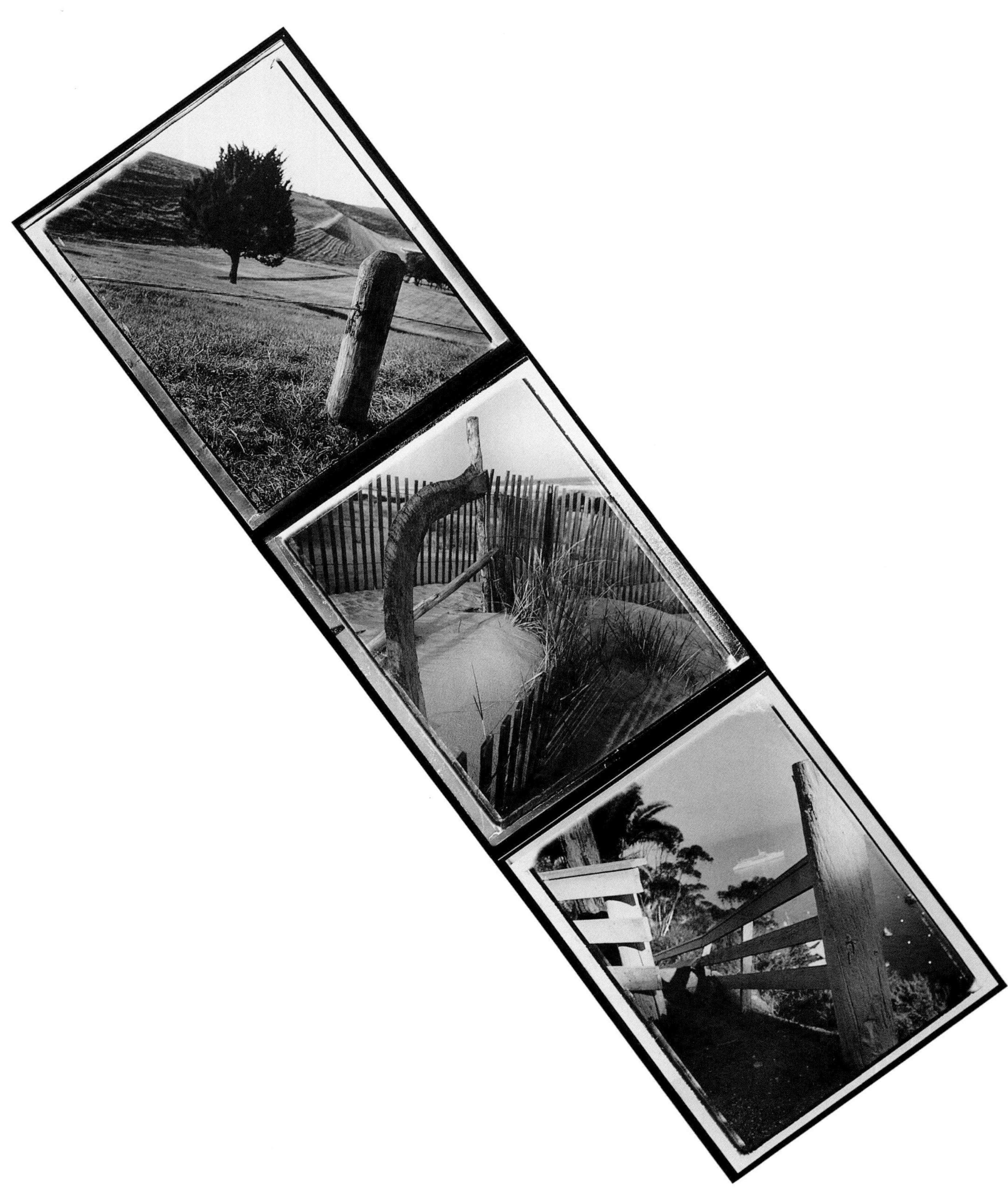

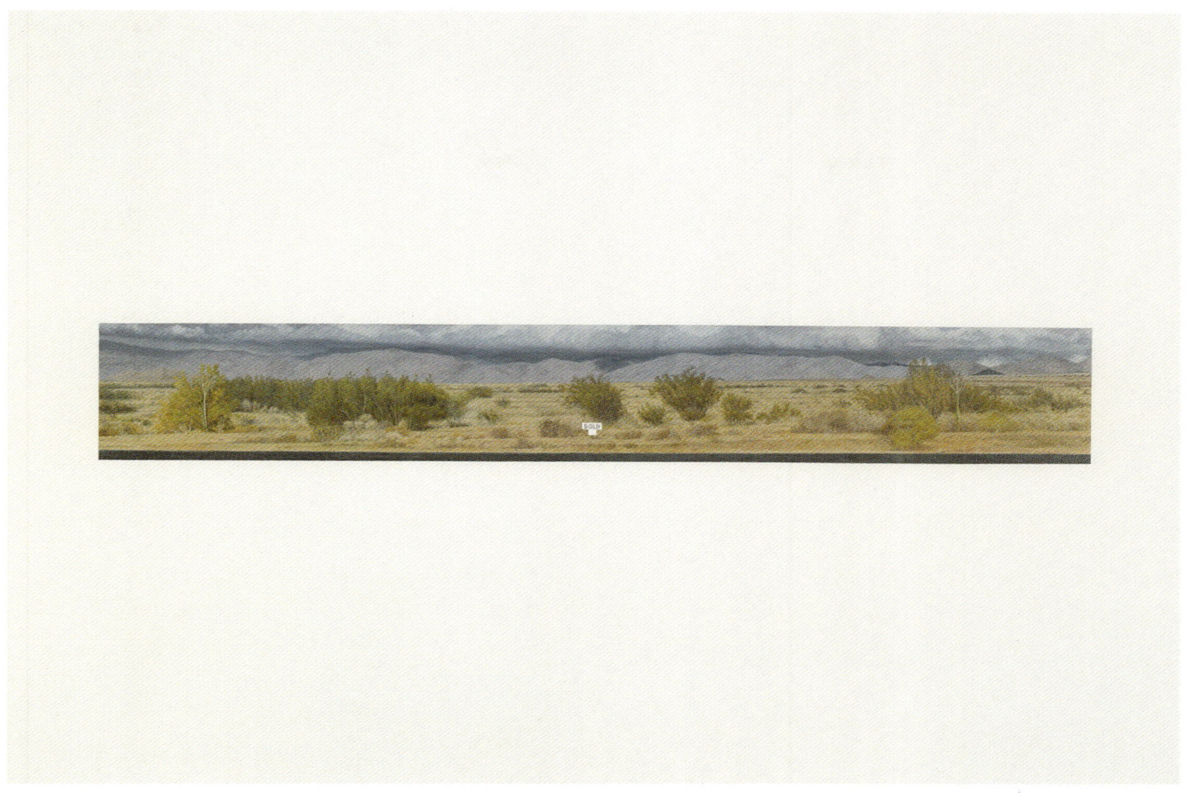

from his photograph. Instead, the ramshackle office and its hand-lettered sign vividly convey the character of this Panhandle community.

Kathleen Norris has commented on how, in Brown's photographs, such structures are "marvels of survival." She continues: "Another building stands improbably by itself, its false front announcing in thick black lettering, H. A. C. Brummett, Lawyer. But the tin roof of the front porch has rusted, and the slender posts holding it up are beginning to buckle and bend. Tufts of grass emerging out of the cement pad at the front door suggest a life's work come and gone in this tiny frame building, an outpost of civil order in an untidy world."[81]

Like Brown, Robert Ziebell has studied the Texas landscape as a part of a larger topography. A graduate of the University of Michigan, Ann Arbor, Ziebell came to Texas in 1983 to attend the Glassell School's Core Residency Program. His early Houston photographs chronicled places of transit—airports and the downtown tunnels—and in 1985 he began working on a film that would record "the ebb and flow of this and that."[82] Released in 1990 as *This State I'm In*, the 80-minute film offers a dazzling montage of a Texas peopled by extraordinary characters (see Introduction, fig. 15). The voices of three narrators recount three different, and at times conflicting, stories, emphasizing the inadequacy of any single version of events.

Ziebell's concurrent *Scenic Details* series suggest a similar multiplicity of views. The series is made up of landscape fragments, framed on a diagonal, and installed serially to suggest film strips. The museum's untitled triptych from this series, 1988–89 (plate 34), juxtaposes the West Texas landscape (top), the Maryland shore (center), and a view from Catalina Island (bottom). When the photographs were first exhibited in 1990, Liz Ward wrote: "Ziebell gave himself a formal challenge to compose in a diagonal rather than a vertical or horizontal format. The idea was inspired by the often unconventional way that space is represented in technical maps in which the north/south axis is not necessarily parallel to the edge of the page and north is not always 'up.' . . . [*Scenic Details*] leave the viewer with a sense of place, and they hint, without being specific, of events, episodes or incidents that might have taken place there."[83]

Julie Bozzi brings a different kind of filmic sensibility to her meticulously drafted panoramas of West Texas. She has acknowledged the essentially cinemagraphic imagination that animates her work:

> Seven years ago I moved to Texas and began collecting panoramic views of the Southwest. It interests me that when foreign directors have come to this country to make films, they have often chosen this kind of landscape as a setting for stories of fugitives.[84]

A native of California, Bozzi graduated from the University of California, Davis, in 1974. The following summer she attended the Skowhegan School of Painting and

35
Julie Bozzi
West Texas II, 1985
Oil on paper, 22 x 30 in. (55.9 x 76.2 cm). Museum purchase with funds provided by Duke Energy, 88.37.

34 *opposite*
Robert Ziebell
Untitled, from the *Scenic Details* series, 1988–89
Gelatin silver photographs, triptych, 24 x 20 in. (61 x 50.8 cm) each. Museum purchase with funds provided by the National Endowment for the Arts and Clinton T. Willour in honor of Alfred C. Glassell, Jr., 89.301.

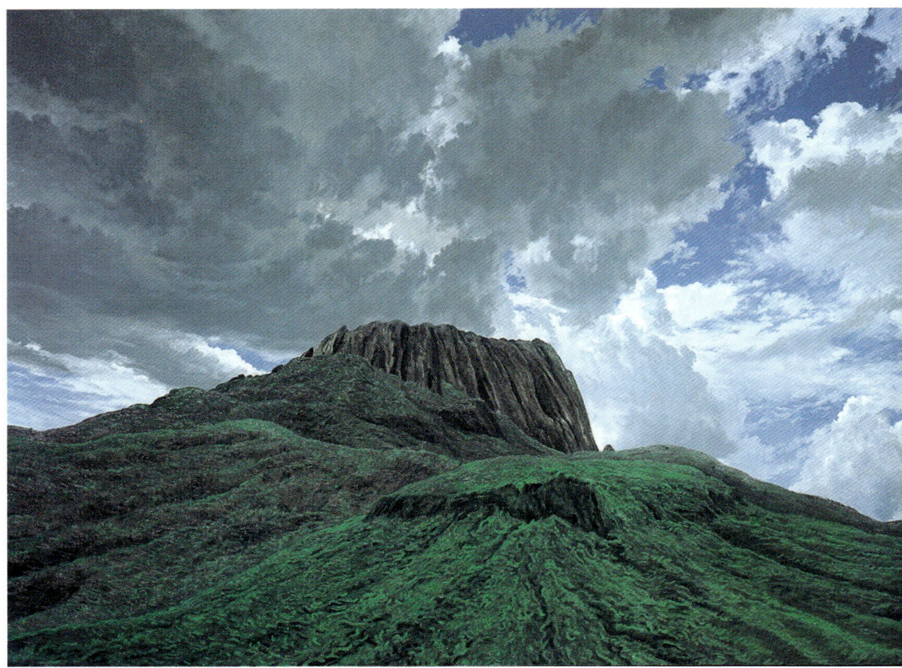

36
Dennis Blagg
Nugent Mountain, 1993
Oil on canvas, 30 x 40½ in.
(76.2 x 102.6 cm). Museum
purchase with funds provided
by William R. Camp in
honor of Frank Hevrdejs and
Louis Tenenbaum at "One
Great Night in November,
1993," 93.384.

Sculpture, in Skowhegan, Maine, where among the resident artists was the landscape painter Rackstraw Downes (see plate 37). She moved to Fort Worth in 1980 and embarked on two major series which continue to define her work: documentations of American foodstuffs and records of landscapes she has visited.

Driving through the Big Bend that inspired Frank Reaugh at the turn of the century, Bozzi discovered a West defined by its highways. In *West Texas II,* 1985 (plate 35), the foreground of the panorama is a narrow strip of asphalt, and it is tempting to identify the scene as a roadside impression. Closer examination, however, reveals the uncommon delicacy of each detail as Bozzi renders the landscape with an astonishing degree of accuracy. At the same time, she indicates the artificiality of her composition by floating it on a much larger sheet

of paper. A sly note of humor enters the scene through the sign which informs the passerby that this vast landscape is "sold."

A different aspect of West Texas is offered by Dennis Blagg's *Nugent Mountain,* 1993 (plate 36). Blagg spent his childhood in the mid-1950s on a cotton farm outside of Seminole, Texas, moving to Dallas, then Fort Worth when he was an adolescent. Largely self-taught as a painter, he made the dramatic topography of the region around Big Bend his chief subject in an extended series of paintings of the 1980s and 1990s.

Nugent Mountain eschews the panoramic vista characteristic of depictions of the West Texas landscape; rather, the artist focuses on the profile of the mountain against the brilliant hard light of the afternoon sky. As Blagg has recalled:

> Nugent Mountain is located in the Big Bend National Park. I have for many years traveled to the park with Vernon Fisher. . . . I have passed this view many times before, so it was on my mind—in my subconscious by now. Suddenly it held me in its grip—the light overcast yet spattered with patches of blue sky, almost a musical flow. The mountain itself is alive with movement that slithers towards the viewer.[85]

Working from photographs, Blagg emphasizes the collapsed spaces created by the camera's lens: the foreground veers out of the picture plane, and the background recedes with equal drama. By selecting a single peak from the Chisos mountain chain, Blagg highlights the contrast

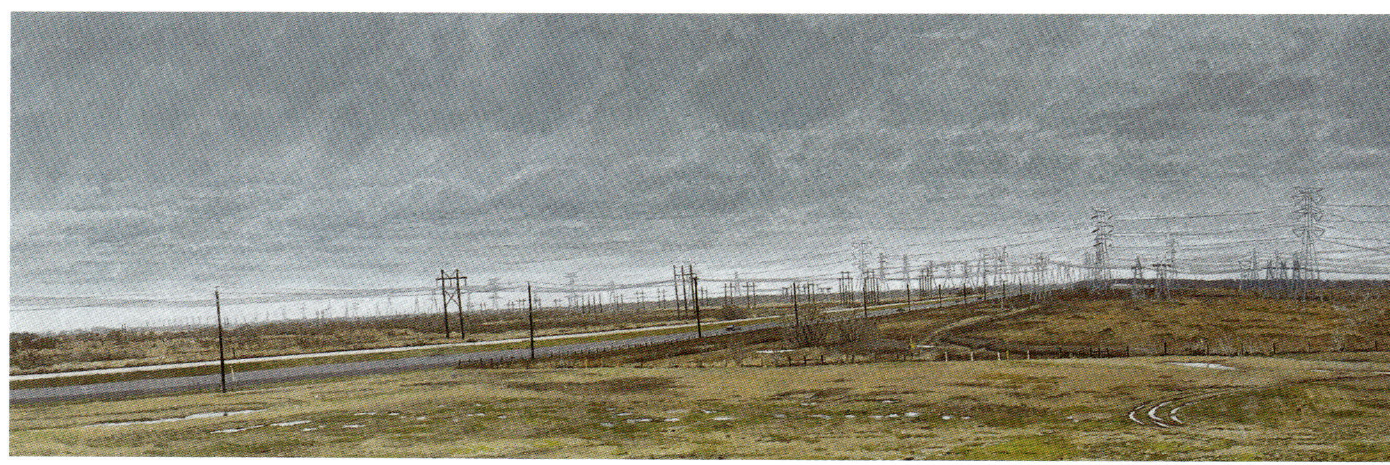

where earth meets sky, capturing the vertiginous scale of West Texas through dramatic cropping and contrasts of light and shadow. As the artist has stated, "I'm not interested in portraying the direct realism of the landscape. Instead, I want to create a *sense* of being there."[86]

Perhaps the most passionately analytical eye to record the Texas landscape is that of New York artist Rackstraw Downes, who began to spend winters in Galveston in the mid-1980s. Born in Kent, England, Downes came to the United States in 1961. He received an M.F.A. from Yale in 1964, and shortly thereafter made the landscape his chief subject. At a moment when photorealism had begun to be a major force in American painting, Downes chose to always work on site, developing his compositions from preliminary studies to finished paintings without the aid of the camera. Typically, Downes seeks out the places where modern industry and urbanism have shaped the land. As Hayden Herrera has recently written, "Coming from the south of England where there is no wilderness, Downes sees America from a particular angle."[87] And Downes has elaborated further, "I don't have what I perceive as a New World sense of antithesis between unspoiled nature and human culture. A landscape to me is a place where people work and live."[88]

P. H. Robinson Generating Station, Dickinson, Texas: Eight Ibis Feeding with an Egret, 1991 (plate 37), is one of Downes's most subtle Texas landscapes. As the title emphasizes, industry and nature coexist in Dickinson side by side. Downes began working on the site thirty miles south of Houston in 1988; he spent three winters on this canvas. Preliminary studies show the Houston Lighting and Power plant from a closer angle, with a greater emphasis on the pylons and high-tension lines that spill across the landscape. Stepping back and further to the south, Downes reframed the panorama to capture the expanse of the generating station, the lines which feed from its power, and the sweep of the surrounding landscape. In a letter from 1992, Downes related what drew him to the site:

Jean Wetta drove me by that plant on route 146 on the way to Houston, and I immediately liked it, mainly because of its isolation on the prairie, the fact that you could see how far away its energy was being distributed. I liked the density of the pylons in the field, and the variety of their shapes, and the plant's symbolic presence which is enhanced by the lack of other industrial structures nearby; just as a hand, or cosmological eye is mesmerizing isolated in the sky of some medieval woodcut.

The time of year is March when the new green grasses start up, but the trees and bushes are still bare.... One thing I like about this area of Texas is the naked, blatant proximity of nature and industry: it is the true metaphor of the state of our planet.... I don't want to sentimentalize either nature or industry, but, in a particular spot, take the measure of either empirically....

In that grass in the foreground, are some tracks that make a big, just discernible oval. They were made by a jeep or pick-up doing "donuts"—driving in a tight circle on the grass. Clearly they got stuck. I liked introducing

37
Rackstraw Downes
P. H. Robinson Generating Station, Dickinson, Texas: Eight Ibis Feeding with an Egret, 1991
Oil on canvas, 16 x 108¼ in. (40.6 x 275 cm). Museum purchase with funds provided by Houston Lighting & Power Company, 92.469.

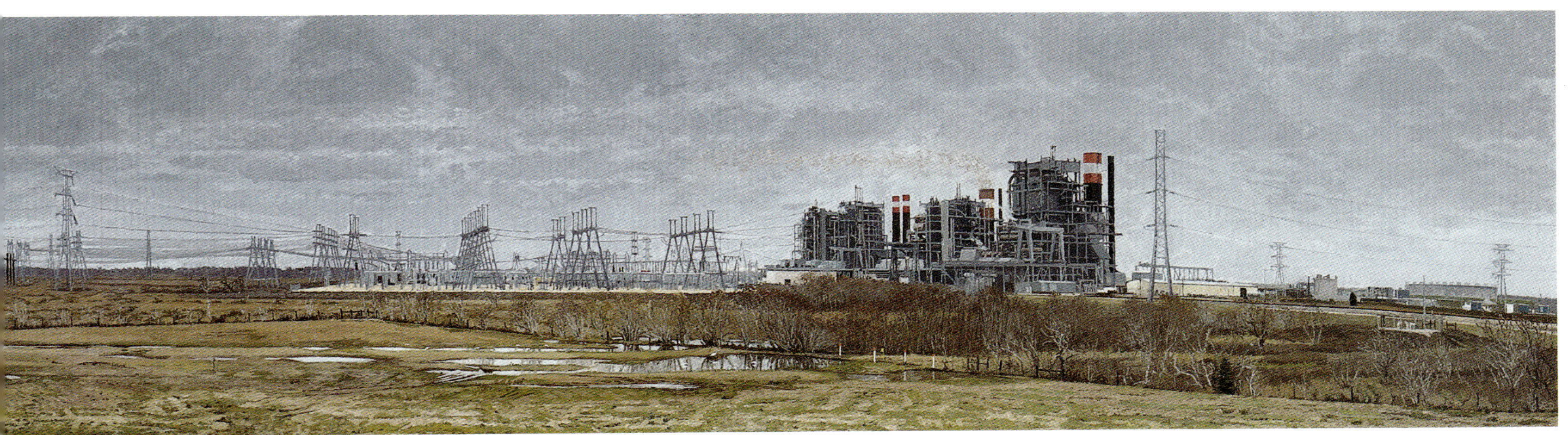

38
Harry Geffert
Zipped Up, 1998
Bronze, 103 x 12 x 116 in.
(261.6 x 30.5 x 294.6 cm).
Museum purchase with funds
provided by Isabel B. Wilson,
Max and Isabell Smith
Herzstein, Bryant M. and
Nancy C. Hanley, Jennifer
and Scott Clearman, Tom
Roupe, and Mr. and Mrs.
Jack S. Blanton, Jr., 99.74.

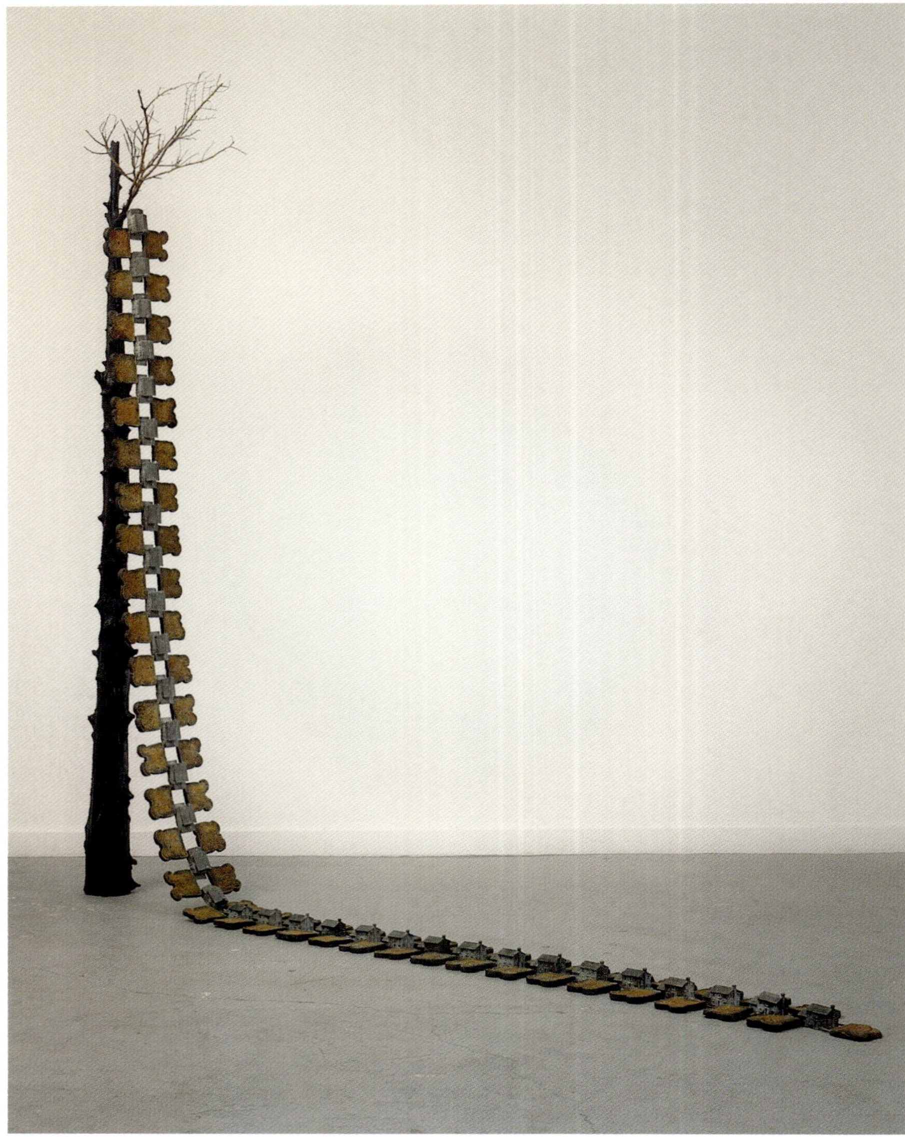

this trace of small-scale boisterousness and high spirits, for me it brought a populist touch to this painting of otherwise impersonal protagonists (and amused visitors . . . who immediately knew what it meant).[89]

Downes balances observation and artistic license. For example, the horizon line is curved, stressing the 180° panorama, as well as suggesting the greater curve of the planet. Details of the landscape are handled with a painterly assurance, and the heavy sky is worked with a subtle impasto, parting for the powerlines that race across it. Ultimately, Downes's dedicated realism, both to his subject and to his medium, results in a genuine freshness and immediacy; rather than transforming the landscape, Downes insists that we regard it for what it is.

If Downes's consideration of the industrial landscape is deliberately neutral, Harry Geffert decries the destruction of the Texas countryside. A native Texan, Geffert attended Southwest Texas State University, San Marcos, and New Mexico Highlands University in Las Vegas, New Mexico. He subsequently made Fort Worth his home, and in 1980 established the Green Mountain Foundry in Crowley, Texas.[90] He adopted bronze as his major medium, and over the following decade became a master of a remarkable range of lost-wax and direct casting techniques. At the same time, Geffert constructed increasingly complex sculptural allegories, conflating the technical and conceptual evolution of his works. "Adjusting the composition—engineering and content—is a balancing act," Geffert has commented. "My goal is to create works that don't look as if they have been engineered, but as if they grew." [91]

Zipped Up, 1998 (plate 38), is a piercing commentary on the dynamics of contemporary real estate. Only one branch is left on the otherwise barren tree as "cookie cutter" houses and lawn plots (wittily represented by slices of Wonder Bread cast in bronze) march across the floor and up the trunk. An effective allegory for the suburban sprawl of Fort Worth that is consuming the open land around Geffert's Green Mountain, *Zipped Up* poses larger environmental questions. The water needed to maintain these artificial lawns is sapping Texas's natural water table, leaving the landscape increasingly sere and desolate.[92]

Other artists have chosen to focus on specific events that have marked our immediate environment. A border incident of 1987 inspired James Drake to create the passionately political *Juárez/El Paso (Boxcar)*, 1987–88 (plate 39). Born in Lubbock, Drake settled in El Paso in the mid-1960s; after attending the Art Center College of Design in Los Angeles, he returned to El Paso, a city in transition between two cultures, dominated ultimately by the much larger Ciudad Juárez on the Mexican side of the Rio Grande.[93]

In the summer of 1987, eighteen illegal aliens suffocated to death when the boxcar they were hiding in was

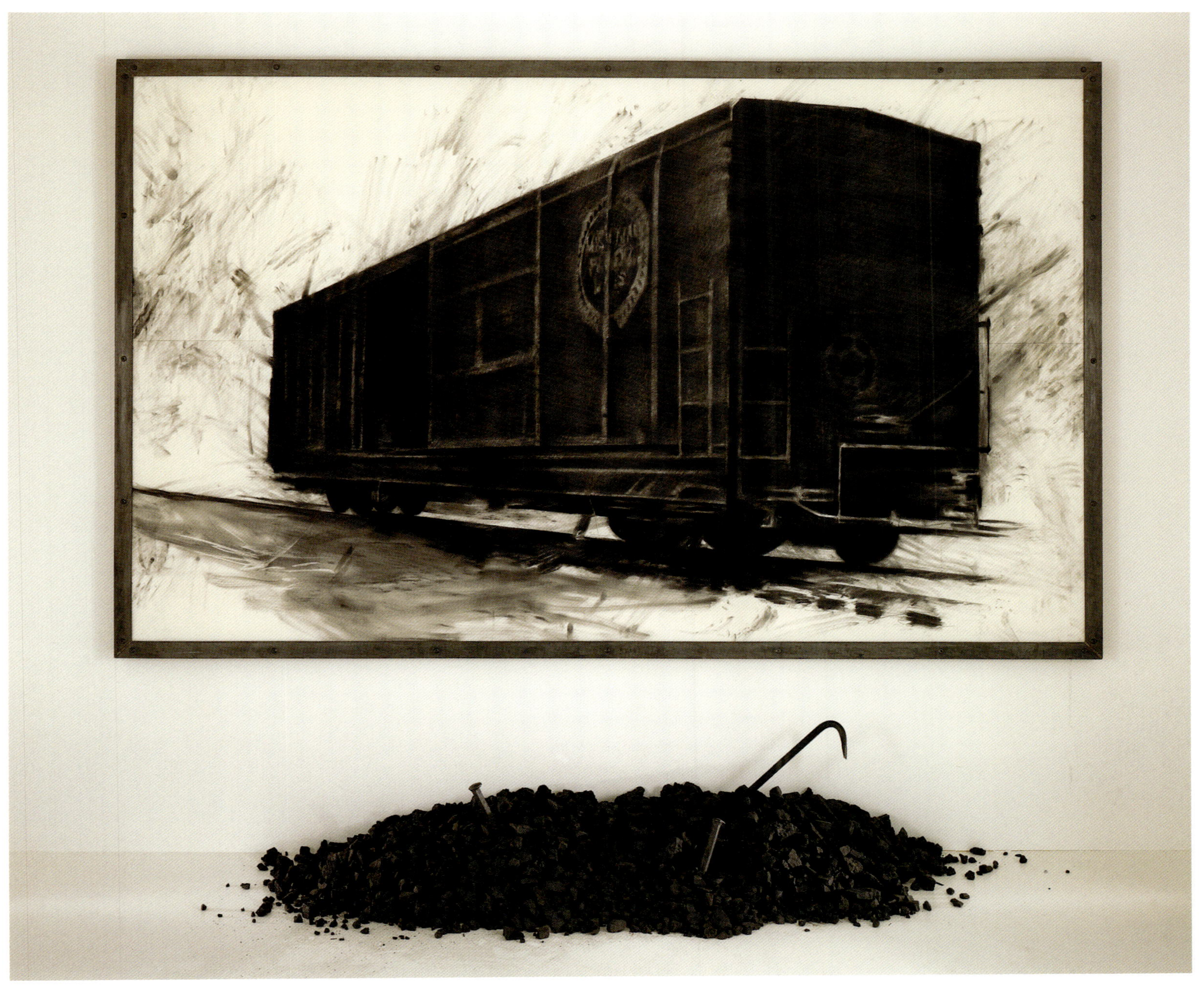

39
James Drake
Juárez/El Paso (Boxcar),
1987–88
Charcoal on paper mounted
in steel frame with coal, railroad spikes, and crowbar,
87 x 110 x 30 in. (220.9 x
279.4 x 76.2 cm). Museum
purchase, 89.3.

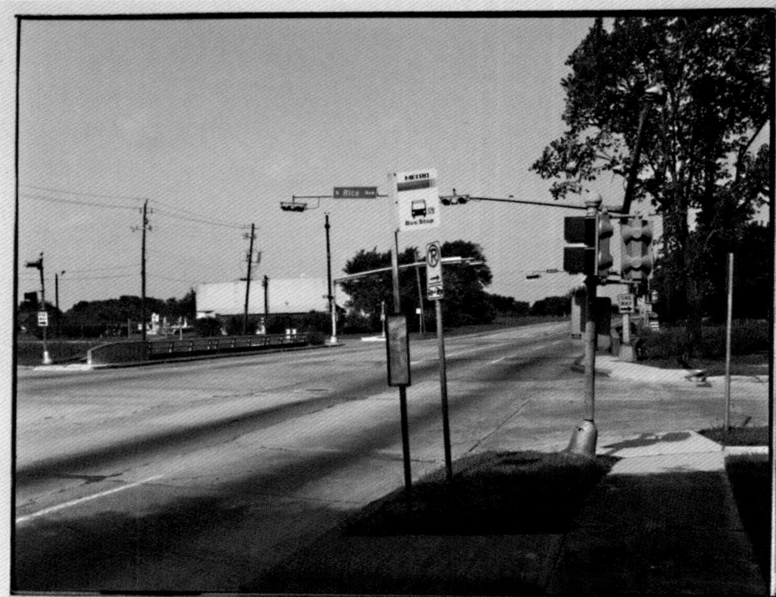

40
Richard Hinson
Untitled (Rice near Braeswood), from the *Violent Places* series, 1992
Gelatin silver photograph with ink, 8¼ x 10½ in. (20.9 x 26.7 cm). Museum purchase with funds provided by Clinton T. Willour, 94.154.

sidelined outside the town of Sierra Blanco, near El Paso. One man survived; he later recounted that the "coyote" who had arranged their passage from Mexico had deliberately locked the Mexicans in the boxcar, throwing them a crowbar before closing the door. One of the victims left behind the following lyrics in a journal he had carried with him:

> Qué lindo es los Estados Unidos,
> Illinois, California y Tenesi.
> Pero allá en mi país
> Un trozo de cielo me pertenece a mí.
> Adiós Laredo, Wéslaco y San Antonio.
> Houston y Dallas están en mi cancíon.
> Adiós El Paso, he vuelto Chamizal.
> Ha regresado tu amigo el ilegal.

> [How beautiful is the United States,
> Illinois, California and Tennessee.
> But over in my country
> A piece of the sky belongs to me.
> Goodbye Laredo, Weslaco, San Antonio,
> Houston and Dallas are in my song.
> Goodbye, El Paso. I am back, Chamizal.
> Your friend the illegal has returned.][94]

Juárez/El Paso memorializes this incident, and was first exhibited in 1988 at the Contemporary Arts Museum as part of a larger installation.[95] Drake offers a vivid image of the isolated boxcar; drawn in charcoal and framed in steel, it has a material affinity with the actual coal, railroad spikes, and a crowbar that are placed in the foreground. With minimal narrative, Drake forces the viewer to empathize with the men who lost their lives trying to enter the United States.

Drake translates a specific event into a monumental tribute; Richard Hinson, addressing much the same subject, finds a fitting analogue for the casual violence of city life through his seemingly informal views of Houston crime scenes. Hinson grew up in Beaumont and attended Lamar University, where he studied music composition. In the mid-1980s, his interest turned to photography, and he received an M.F.A. in the medium from the University of Houston in 1991.

Untitled (Rice near Braeswood), 1992 (plate 40), an image from Hinson's extended *Violent Places* series, is inscribed:

ONE EVENING ON THE WAY HOME A YOUNG ASIAN WOMAN WAS SHOT IN THE HEAD AS SHE WAITED IN HER CAR AT THE TRAFFIC LIGHT. THE TWO MEN, WHO LATER ADMITTED TO KILLING HER, DUMPED HER BODY IN THE STREET AND DROVE AWAY IN HER CAR. WHEN THEY WERE CAUGHT SEVERAL HOURS LATER, THEY TOLD THE POLICE THEY KILLED HER BECAUSE THEY HAD NO MONEY AND THEIR CAR WAS ALMOST OUT OF GAS. I USED TO DRIVE THROUGH THIS INTERSECTION THREE NIGHTS A WEEK ON MY WAY HOME FROM SCHOOL.

The accompanying image is deliberately prosaic; the intersection is vacant, no sign of violence can be traced, and only the darkly shadowed foreground suggests that anything might be amiss. As Hans Staartjes has noted of this work, "The only hint of disorder [is] in the text."[96] The deadpan report and the banal evil of the crime is personalized by the closing line—much as Drake asks us to identify with his subject, Hinson knowingly captures the frisson caused by the knowledge that a familiar place has been the site of a murder.

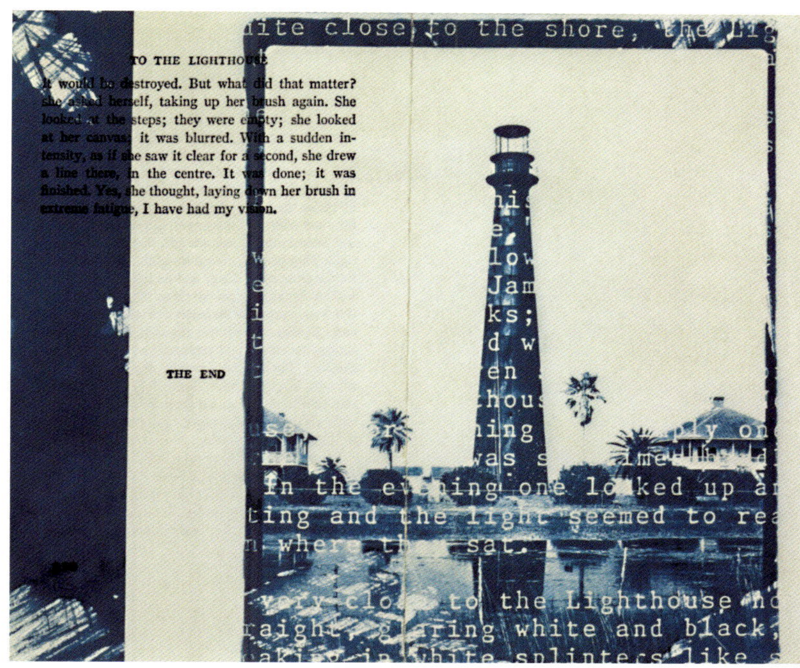

41
Liz Ward
To the Lighthouse
(detail), 1988
153 cyanotypes printed on
pages from Virginia Woolf's
To the Lighthouse, 7¼ x 8¼
in. (18.3 x 20.9 cm) each.
Museum purchase with funds
provided by William and
Virginia Camfield, 91.265.

42
Liz Ward
From the Lighthouse
(detail), 1992
Twelve cyanotypes printed on
Galveston Bay coastal maps,
12 x 15 in. (30.5 x 38 cm)
each. Museum purchase
with funds donated in memory of Moore Murray, 92.498.

The late 1980s and 1990s saw one profound change in the history of the Texas landscape; the subject that, for over a century, had been almost the exclusive province of men suddenly began to be addressed by an increasing number of women. While such historical figures as Ida Weisselberg Hadra, Georgia O'Keeffe, Florence McClung, and Coreen Spellman, among others, can be cited for their early contributions to this genre—the fact remains that most women artists working in Texas chose to depict other subjects.[97] In some instances, women artists who chose to represent the local landscape did so through the filters of abstraction and metaphor, as is demonstrated by the works of Melissa Miller, Madeline O'Connor, and Terrell James (plates 55, 61, 62, and 99). Alternately, many of those who were committed to landscape imagery chose to look beyond the state's borders, as is demonstrated by the works of Ruth Pershing Uhler and Amy Blakemore (see plates 80 and 106).

One reason that more women turned to landscape imagery in recent years has been an increased sense of the fragility of the environment; in claiming the subject, they reclaimed the land.[98] As Liz Ward has recently commented: "The inherently adversarial position of feminism seems inherently sympathetic to an environmentalist point of view," and Ward has been among Texas's leading women artists to make the environment one of her chief concerns.[99]

Born in Lafayette, Louisiana, Ward grew up in Houston. She attended the University of California, Santa Cruz; the University of New Mexico, Albuquerque; and the University of Houston. She also undertook postgraduate studies in printmaking at the Tamarind Institute and Atelier 17, Paris. Her studio methods encompass a range of media—from photography to silverpoint to assemblage—while her thematic concerns remain fixed. Her work celebrates the delicate environment of the coastal wetlands, as well as the native and migratory wildlife that give uncommon character to the region.

In 1988, Ward created an installation titled *To the Lighthouse* (plate 41), a series of 153 cyanotypes printed on pages from Virginia Woolf's 1927 novel of the same title. Four years later, Ward returned to this theme with *From the Lighthouse* (plate 42), a series of 12 cyanotypes

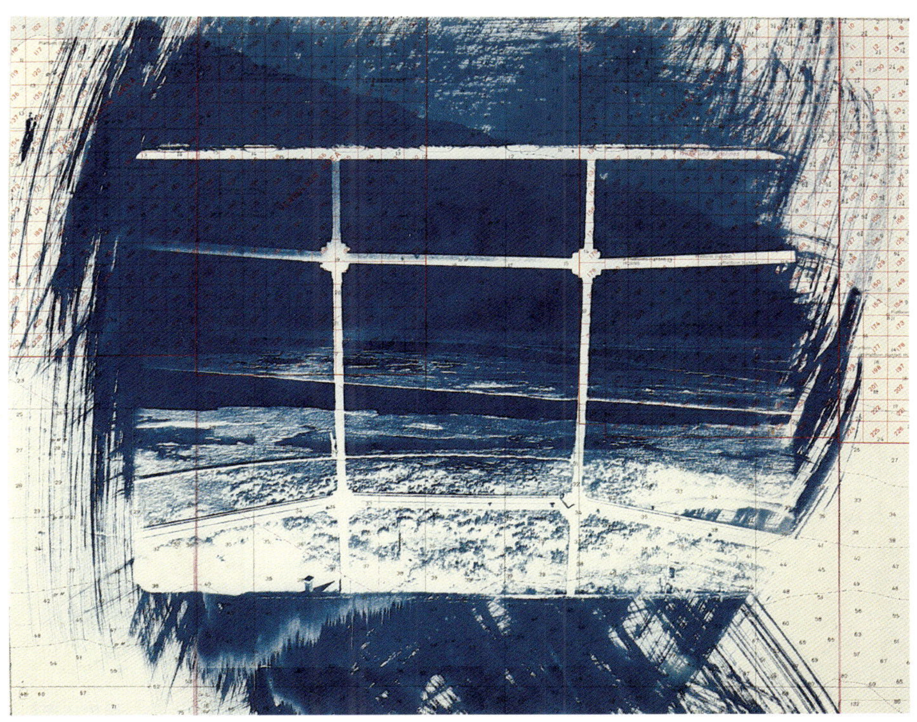

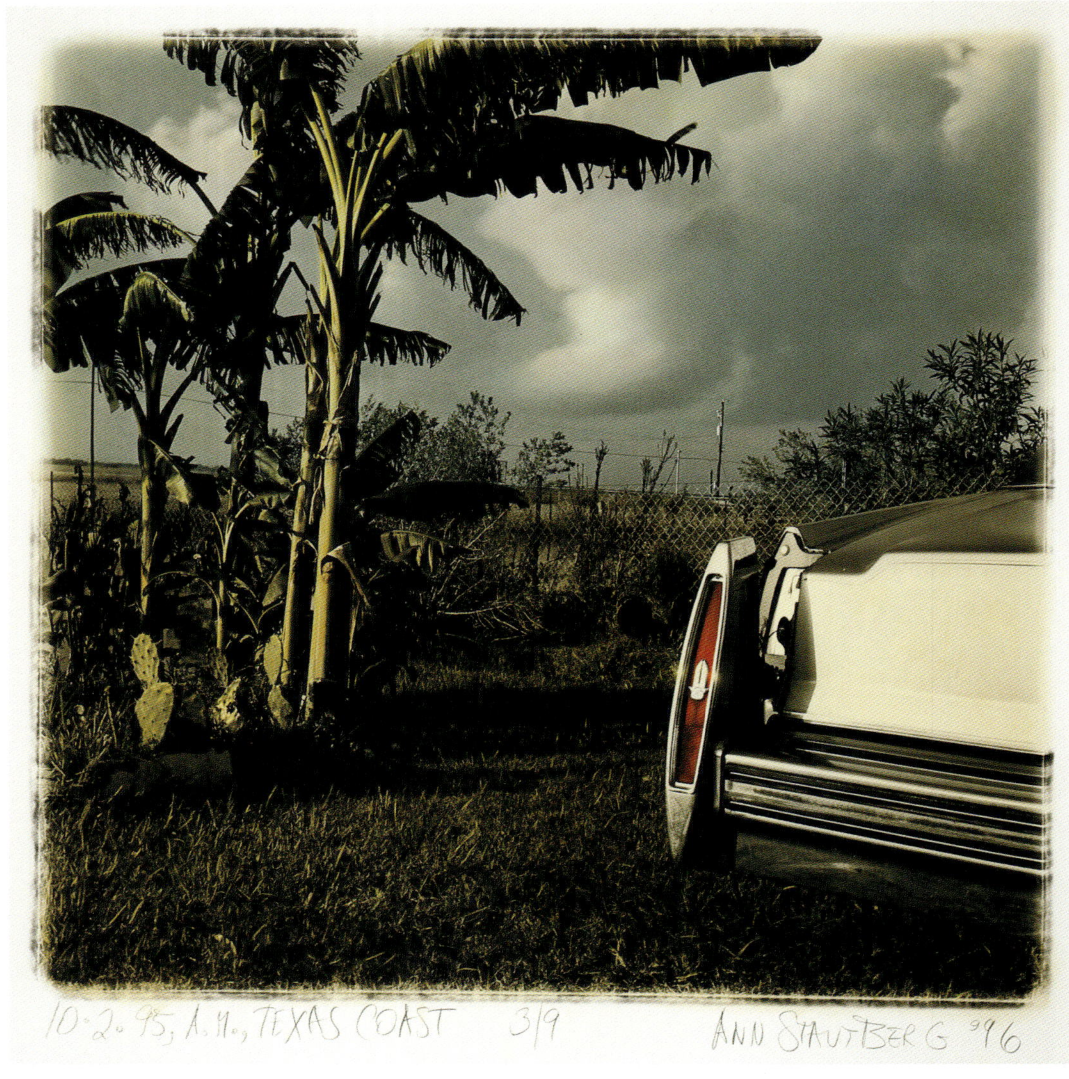

43
Ann Stautberg
10.2.95 A.M., Texas Coast,
1996
Gelatin silver photograph
with applied oil, 41¾ x 42¼
in. (106 x 107.3 cm). Partial
gift of Claude Albritton and
partial museum purchase
with funds provided by Andre
and Sylvia Crispin, Joan
Morgenstern, and Clinton T.
Willour, 97.63.

printed on Texas coastal maps. The earlier work was made up of images of the Bolivar lighthouse and the surrounding coast; the later series records a 360° panorama made from the observation deck of the lighthouse.[100] Ward has stated of the first of these works:

> My piece, inspired by Woolf's novel, is an attempt to possess or to appropriate her text and to remake it into my own. I have overlayed each page of the novel, from beginning to end, with a visual "text" which interferes with the printed words beneath. Importantly, many of the images are . . . sites of my own childhood experiences. Thus, the piece is, in effect, a synthesis of my landscape, location, and language with Virginia Woolf's. . . . Woolf's ironic phrase "Women can't paint, Women can't write" recurs throughout the work, and is simultaneously refuted by it.[101]

Ward also discussed her return to this theme:

> *From the Lighthouse* is a kind of echo of the first piece, made from a new point of view—a new location. In some ways it has to do with having arrived somewhere, having gained perspective on things, as it were.[102]

The cyanotype process, one of the simplest printing methods offered by photography, gives a vivid blue cast to the images, appropriate to the motifs of sky and water pursued by Ward. The two series aptly complement one another, capturing both the Texas landscape and finding in it a fitting metaphor for a coming of age.

In the 1990s, a number of artists working in Houston and Galveston became interested in further exploring the Texas coast, including Ann Stautberg and Jean Carruthers Wetta. Born in Houston, Stautberg attended Texas Christian University and the University of Dallas. Shortly after leaving school, she abandoned painting for photography; in 1977, however, she began to experiment with hand-tinting black-and-white prints, a process that she has continued to refine and expand upon. In 1992, she made Galveston her home, and the lush landscape of the island and the surrounding plains has become her chief subject. Valerie Loupe Olsen has written: "Stautberg's images are rooted in the tradition of photographers who concentrate on the interpretation of place and environment. She has found the means to combine her intimacy of place with the affections for home and channel them into emotionally charged, deeply affecting views of life and landscape in south Texas. Often what she seeks is intangible or elusive; that is, the atmosphere, the feel of place, time passing, silence."[103]

10.2.95 A.M., Texas Coast, 1996 (plate 43), at first suggests a drive-by snapshot of the landscape. The rear fender of a vintage Cadillac slices across the right margin of the composition, much as the car vanishes into Fisher's *Rushing into Darkness* (see plate 26). Closer examination, however, reveals that the car may be the most static element in the composition, as the landscape is swept up in the shifting winds of autumn weather, and the long shadows of the palm and reflective surface of the Cadillac are adroitly played against one another. Stautberg has created what is essentially a memory picture—clearly annotated with the date, time, and place, *10.2.95 A.M., Texas Coast* distills the essence of the gulf landscape with the heightened theatricality of a film still.

Jean Carruthers Wetta, who made Galveston her home in the late 1970s and 1980s, had first established herself as a still-life painter and portraitist. However, in part inspired by a growing friendship with Rackstraw Downes (see plate 37), the Gulf Coast landscape became her chief subject in the late 1980s.

Wetta's painterly nuance belies the conceptual process that governs her work. In many cases, her compositions are grounded in Old Master paintings, found photographs, and preparatory photographic studies. Eleanor Jones Harvey has observed: "Wetta readily acknowledges her debt to earlier artists, finding in them both kindred spirits and guiding hands for her own artistic development. Rather than imitating or updating historical styles, she absorbs an artist's palette or use of light, employing that rich vocabulary to make ordinary objects resonate with spiritually charged energy."[104]

Three Bushes on East End Flats, after Inness, 1990 (plate 44), was derived initially from a detail taken from a nineteenth-century landscape by George Inness. However, Wetta has also infused the scene with the specific qualities of light and atmosphere typical of Galveston. After leaving the island, the artist recalled the "vulnerable, exposed sense of the extreme fury and power of the weather

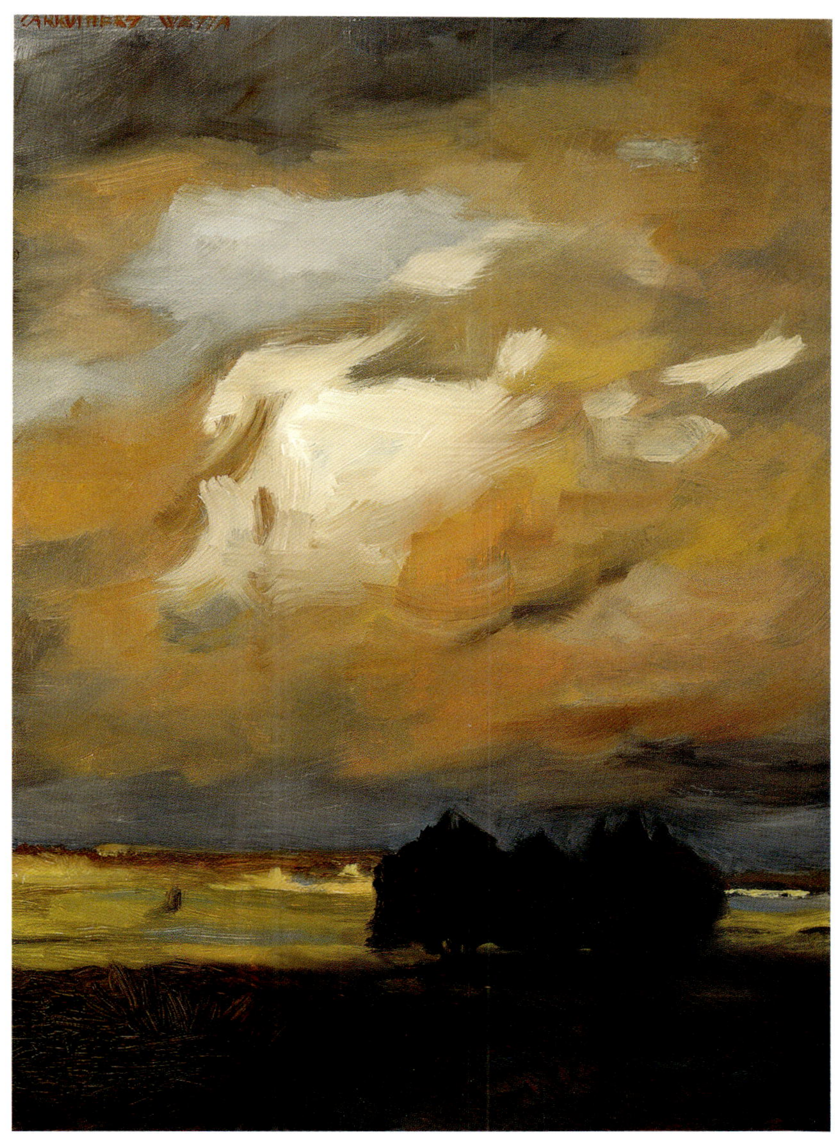

44
Jean Carruthers Wetta
Three Bushes on East End Flats, after Inness, 1990
Oil on wood panel, 16 x 12 in. (35.6 x 25.3 cm).
Museum purchase with funds provided by Eleanor D. McMurtrey and Patti Jones Holloway in memory of Van Jones, 90.511.

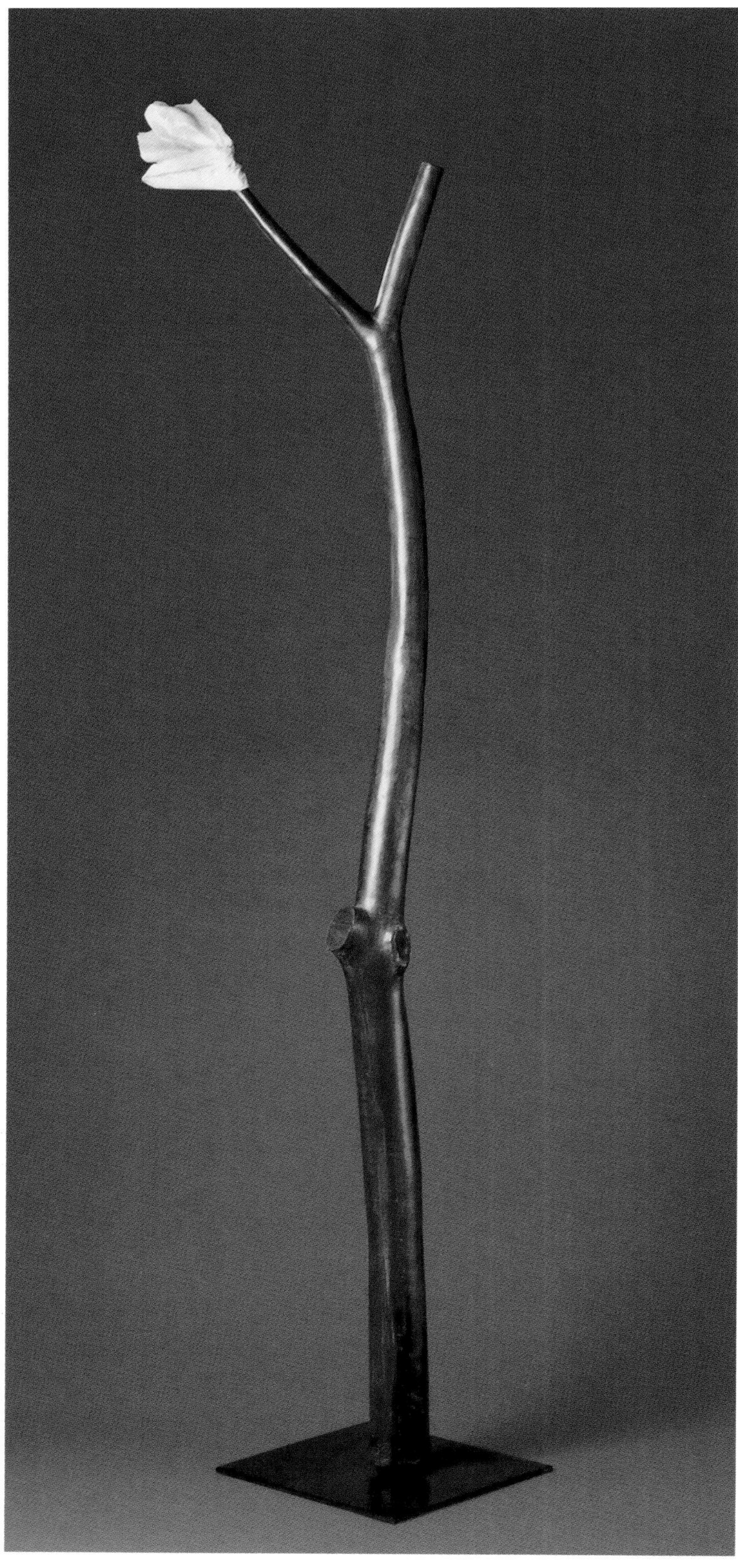

we experienced living in Galveston. . . . I used to dream about the weather."[105] Much as Frank Reaugh made a northern front the focus of his depiction of *Terrell, Texas* (see plate 5), Wetta finds her subject in the fast shifting clouds and dappled light of the Texas coast.

Wind also plays a role in the sculptures of Page Kempner. Born in Houston, Kempner attended Pomona College in Claremont, California; on returning to Texas, she pursued graduate work at the University of Houston. In 1990, Kempner initiated a series of bronzes in which she explored issues of femininity and nature. *The Black Trees Swaying, Slightly # 2*, 1993 (plate 45), was among the first large-scale works of this series, and has been identified by the artist as a response to the Fall of Man. Kempner has stated:

> The trees and twigs are references to the Tree of Knowl-
> edge and, obliquely, to Eve's life in the Garden, with all its
> domestic joys and battles. Due to the scale of the larger
> pieces . . . the tree has become a stand-in for Eve herself.
> These larger pieces are meant to evoke a sense of melan-
> choly tinged, I hope, with a dark kind of humor.[106]

Kempner's prelapsarian metaphor is complemented by the quiet balance her composition strikes between order and chaos. The cropped tree form is reduced to a minimalist silhouette, recalling the careful pruning of a modern-day garden. At the same time, a gust of wind appears to have created the sway of the trunk, and seems to have blown a fragment of cloth into its branches. While not as specifically localized as Geffert's *Zipped Up* (see plate 38), *The Black Trees Swaying, Slightly #2*, nonethe-less captures the character of Houston, where the hand of the gardener and the random forces of nature shape the landscape.

Kristin Musgnug and Robert Ruello came to Houston as a part of the MFAH's Core Residency Program at the Glassell School of Art, in 1988 and 1989 respectively. Un-like the more elegiac mood struck by the artists discussed above, Musgnug and Ruello have emphasized the sense of turmoil characteristic of the quickly eroding Gulf Coast. Both acknowledge how overbuilding and pollution have scarred the landscape. As summarized by Musgnug:

> While my conclusion is that we humans are part of na-
> ture, our behavior towards the land indicates the oppo-
> site. What I found in the contemporary American

middle landscape was far from harmonious. This purgatorial middle ground between the tame and the untame, this devalued netherland on the margins of city and wilderness, is where we perform the act exemplifying the American attitude towards nature—the act of throwing away. In some sense these places are more savage than real wilderness, since the wilderness is of necessity now managed and protected.[107]

Before coming to Houston, Musgnug attended Williams College and pursued graduate studies at the Pennsylvania Academy of the Fine Arts and Indiana University, Bloomington. Musgnug's *Point of No Return*, 1992 (plate 46), pictures the waste that accumulates on Galveston's seawall. The blocks of granite that are supposed to avert the erosion of the coastline have become a catchall for flotsam and jetsam. Musgnug's richly seductive palette ironically highlights her unblinking examination of the antipicturesque. As the title suggests, not only have we reached the limit of land at water's edge, but also the limit of our natural resources.

Ruello, a native of New Orleans, attended Loyola University; he continued his studies at the School of the Art Institute of Chicago, before moving to Houston in 1987. *Atmosphere*, 1993–94 (plate 47), was painted shortly following a drive along the Gulf Coast from Texas to Florida. Ruello used a tondo format to reinforce the cyclical composition of the painting, and orbiting spheres seem to ricochet within the frame. Collage and xerographic images suggest vast shifts in scale, from fingerprints to distant planets, and caught within this dynamic maelstrom are repeated images of a shattered seascape.

Ruello has commented that David Henry Thoreau's "A Winter Walk" was among the immediate sources for this composition: "Thoreau's focus was shifting between actual details of the landscape and his transcendental musings about nature and humankind. The entire story kept expanding and contracting from small details to universal truths." [108] Ruello further explained:

> The work hinges on [the idea of] inhabiting the arctic by building a city covered by a dome . . . As far as I know, that particular project has not been realized, but the absurdity of the idea combined with the bravado spirit . . . makes sense. If we find a place inhospitable, then we will create an atmosphere to make it hospitable—ie: Houston in the summer.[109]

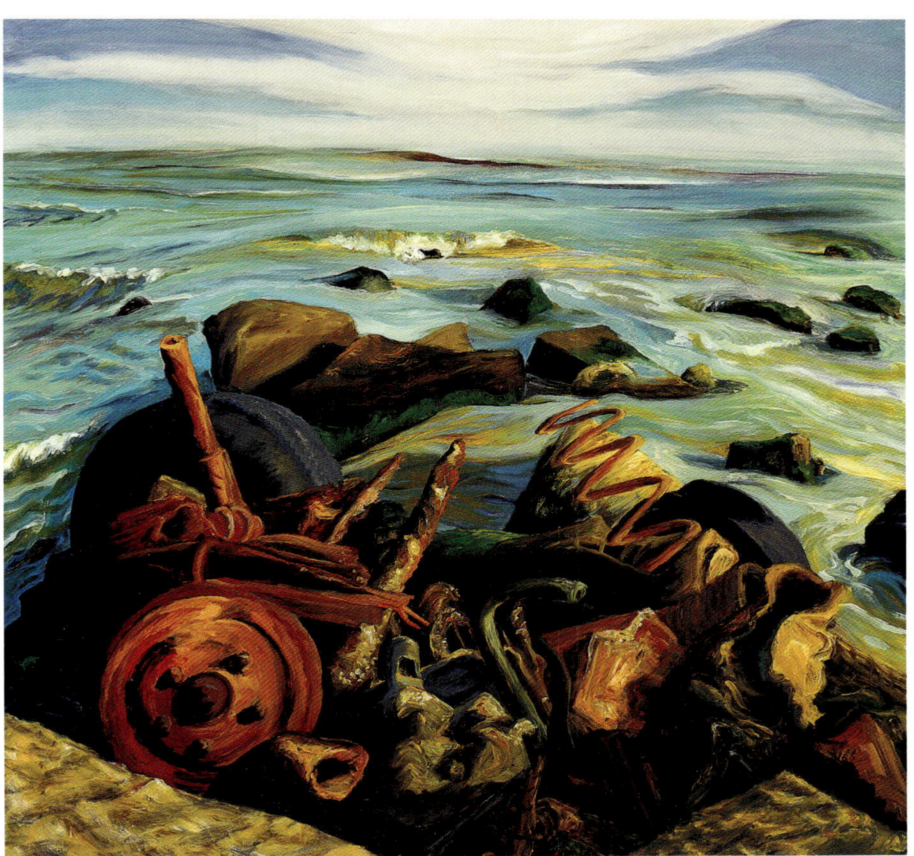

46
Kristin Musgnug
Point of No Return, 1992
Oil on board, 22¾ x 23¾ in.
(57.4 x 60.3 cm). Museum purchase with funds provided by Dr. Kevin Schofield and Kerry F. Inman, 93.423.

45 *opposite*
Page Kempner
The Black Trees Swaying, Slightly # 2, 1993
Bronze, 71 x 29 x 12 in.
(180.3 x 73.7 x 30.5 cm).
Museum purchase with funds provided by a friend of the museum, 94.1.

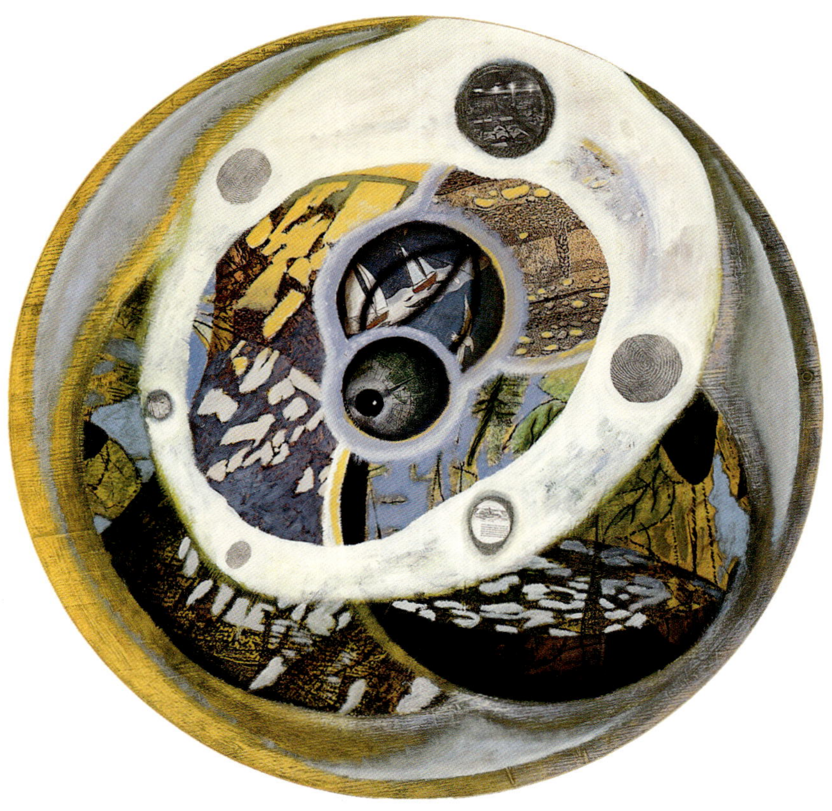

to capture the overall view of the original photograph. *Clouds*, 1998 (plate 48), is Kubricht's most abstract work to date. Paint is thickly laid down in structured blocks mimicking the pixilation of computer-generated reproductions; up close, the image dissolves, but when the viewer steps back, the cloudscape is vividly resolved.

Despite her exploitation of photographic processes, Kubricht's compositions have little to do with current trends in mediated photography; rather, they are best understood as compendia of perceptual shifts. The surface of *Clouds* shimmers with changes in scale and tone, encapsulating memories of changing seasons, fluctuating perspectives, and elapsed time. Susie Kalil has observed of her work, "Kubricht aims to control and take possession of the expanses she paints, to bring them inward and filter them through her own sensibility."[110] Kubricht has clarified further:

> Movement, time, place, and memory have always driven my work. I am attempting a systematic and exhaustive cataloguing of a more precise visual language.... Both the effort of observation as I travel through nature and the detailed cinematic translation as I paint in my studio bring me closer to the landscape I call home.[111]

47
Robert Ruello
Atmosphere, 1993–94
Acrylic, oil, and collage on pine panel, 35¾ in. (90.8 cm) diameter. Museum purchase with funds provided by BP America and Clinton T. Willour in honor of Alison de Lima Greene, by exchange, 94.136.

48 *opposite*
Charles Mary Kubricht
Clouds, 1998
Acrylic on 49 wood panels, 70 x 105 in. (175 x 262.5 cm). Gift of Demian Fore and museum purchase with funds provided by friends of the artist, 99.2.

The atmosphere of Texas is perhaps best captured in its sky, which has been the focus of Charles Mary Kubricht's most recent work. Like Ruello, Kubricht has been deeply interested in photographic processes, and she brings an analytical eye to her landscape compositions. A native Houstonian, Kubricht attended Queens College, North Carolina; she later completed an M.F.A. at the University of Houston in 1983, and was among the first Core Fellows at the museum's Glassell School of Art.

Since the mid-1990s, Kubricht's paintings have evolved out of photographs she has taken during extended walks: each composition is based on a single photographic image which the artist has broken down into a grid. In turn, each photographic segment is then used as a point of departure for a painterly translation of the image onto panel. Kubricht then reassembles the panels

The artists surveyed in this chapter devoted to a sense of place offer a complex portrait of Texas, meditating not only on the character of the land, but our identity within it. As the geographer George F. Thompson, writing in 1997, summarized: "What do we mean by place? For those of us who can see, place is the visual composite of the history of an environment. And that environment is a combination of natural and cultural features and processes.... Place is a valuable way to explain who we are as individuals and who we are as a state and nation. What does an oil rig inside a national wildlife refuge tell us? What does the conversion of a dilapidated downtown into a thriving historic district tell us? We can learn a lot about our collective attitudes, values, and beliefs by viewing the places of everyday existence."[112]

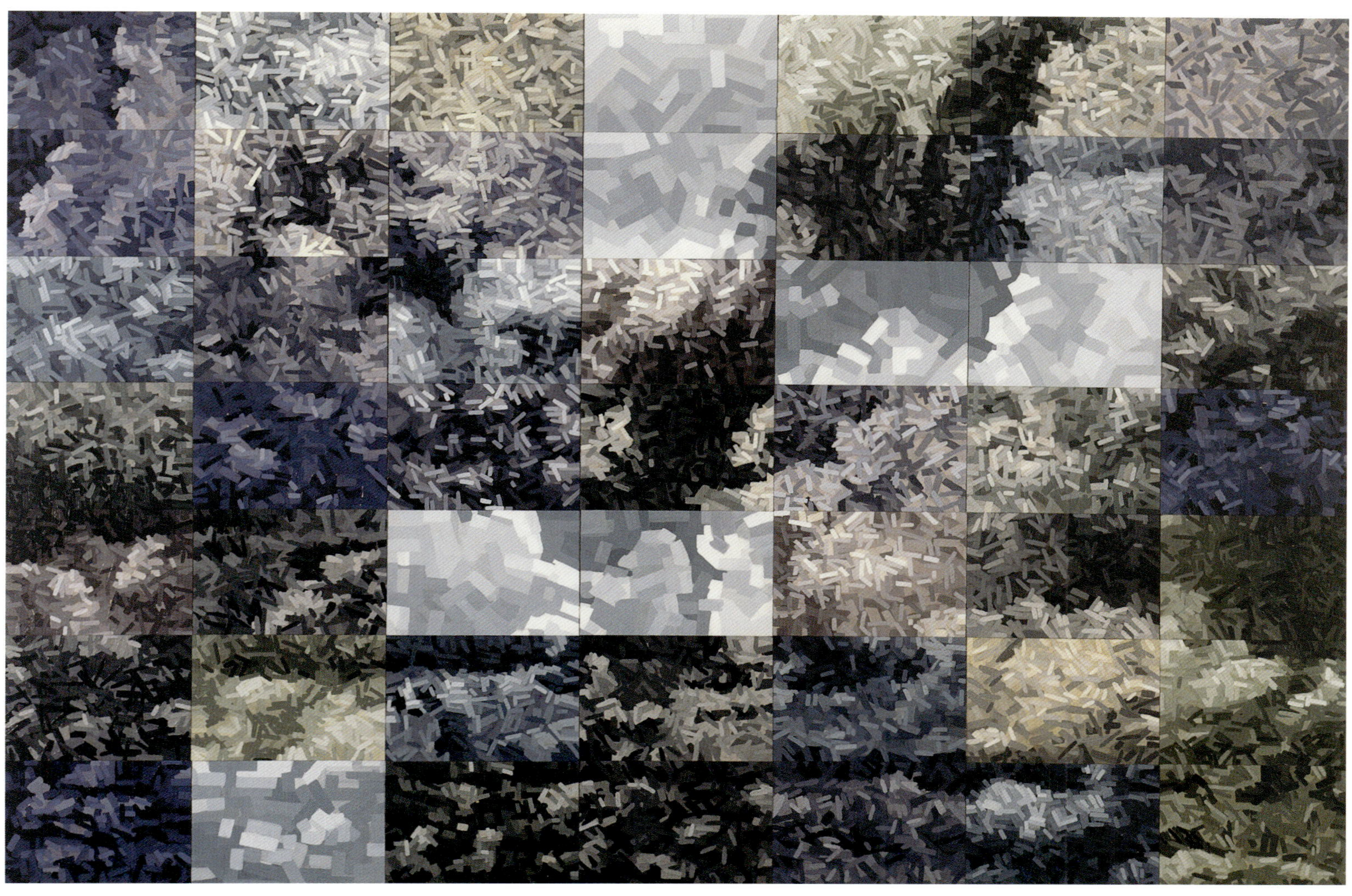

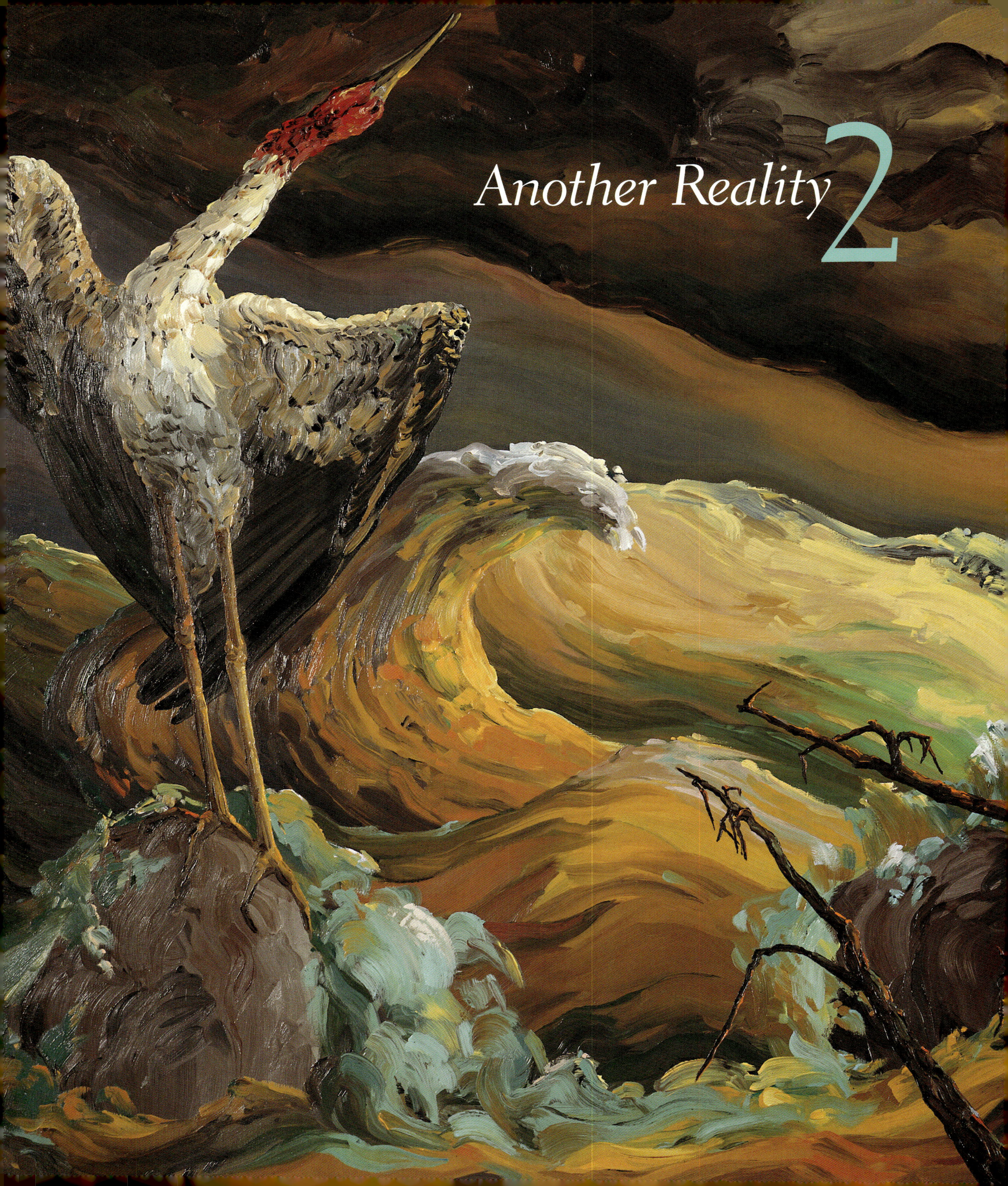
Another Reality
2

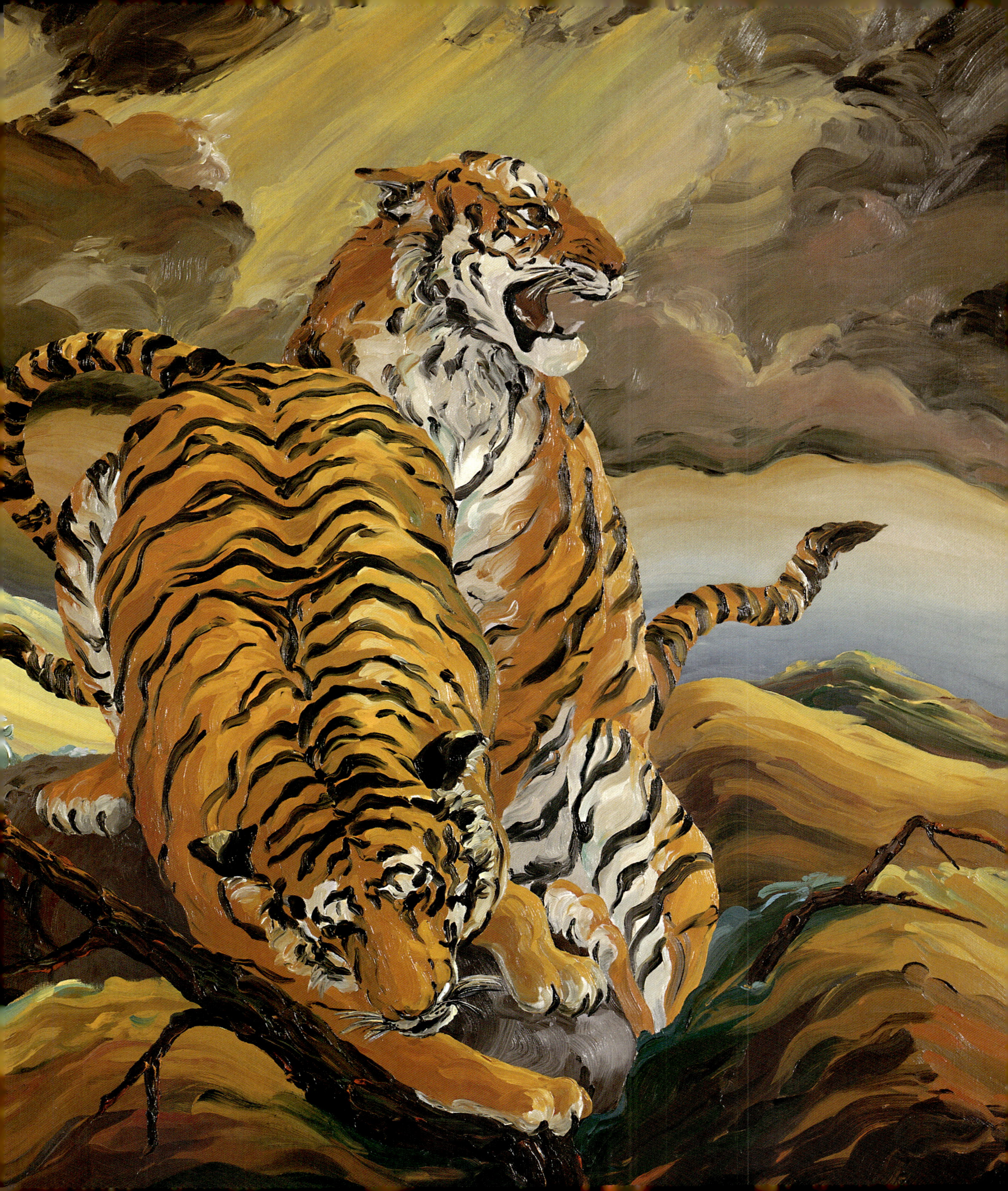

Another Reality

One day, while Ed was napping, I was painting in the camouflage on Feedin' The Hog, and just generally working on the surface. When I finished I went in the house and Ed asked me, "Nancy, did you paint God?" I laughed and said, "Yes, if you mean did I paint the hog?" "Good," he said, and resumed his nap.

—Nancy Reddin Kienholz, 1996[1]

Much as the artists discussed in the first chapter of this catalogue were firmly anchored to Texas by a sense of place, a number of Texans have undertaken a visionary portrait of this region. In so doing, these artists belong to an established tradition within American culture. In 1984, the curator Marcia Tucker, citing the anthropologist Mircea Eliade, observed that mysticism and the western landscape first became deeply entwined in the nineteenth century as Western expansion was seen as "the triumphal march of Wisdom and True Religion from East to West … [identifying] the West with spiritual and moral progress."[2] Recently, Richard Francis has noted that Alexis de Tocqueville's chronicle of his 1831 visit still seems timely: "On my arrival in the United States the religious aspect of the country was the first thing that struck my attention; and the longer I stayed there, the more I perceived the great political consequences resulting from this new state of things."[3]

Most American studies of spiritually motivated art have emphasized the role that spiritual content has played in the evolution of nonobjective abstraction, and certainly such artists as Georgia O'Keeffe, Ad Reinhardt, and James Turrell have made vital contributions to this pursuit across the century.[4] However, exhibitions outside of the United States, including the remarkable *Magiciens de la terre [Magicians of the Earth]*, have demonstrated that this approach neglects the evocative paintings, sculptures, and photographs of the Surrealists, Latin American and African artists, and outsider artists, all of whose work had a critical influence on the development of art in Texas, an area defined both by its proximity to Mexico and by its distance from such art centers as Paris and New York.[5]

By the 1970s, art imbued with a visionary passion was among the strongest currents in Texas painting and sculpture, ranging from the dramatically revelatory altars of Michael Tracy to the meditative and delicately realist compositions of Kermit Oliver. The international resurgence of expressive figuration in the following decade gave additional impetus to this current, and in 1985 Barbara Rose wrote of the Houston art scene, "The nature of representation in Houston is so often dreamlike; an inner world of heightened sensation and emotion, rather than the world of everyday reality, is what these artists care to depict."[6]

The 1987 opening of The Menil Collection in Houston established a unique forum for considering the spiritual in art. Walter Hopps's and Dominique de Menil's thoughtful installations emphasized the connective threads between cultures, and the semipermanent display of the Menil's outstanding collection of Surrealist art continues to fuel the imagination of area artists. Over the following decade, solo exhibitions devoted to Michael Tracy, Mel Chin, and James Reaben celebrated the departures from the ordinary made by Texans, while more historical presentations of such objects as post-Byzantine Greek icons scrutinized the historical traditions of religious art.

In 1989, Houston artists Surpik Angelini and Bert Long curated an exhibition titled *Another Reality*, which surveyed more than sixty Texas artists whose work is dedicated to exploring the transcendental. As Long stated in the introduction to the exhibition's catalogue, "the works of art we were seeking possessed the qualities of magic, mysticism, spiritualism, and alchemical transmutation."[7] Thomas McEvilley commented on the unique function of this work:

> In the curators' opinion many, perhaps most, of these artists regard their work not primarily or exclusively as an aesthetic reality, but as an embodiment of magical or therapeutic energy. They feel . . . as in the milieu of primitive magic, that the work directly—vibrationally as it were—enters the viewer and exerts a unifying or awakening or integrating or softening influence upon the personality. The work is intended to function in the way an icon worked in the view of the Neoplatonist philosopher and occultist Iamblichus—that is, that the deity or force invoked enters the icon and is directly present in it.[8]

He speculated further on what prompted this surge of visionary art in Texas, and the influence that Mexico had in prompting this field of exploration:

> Proximity to an alien culture will always generate the sense that reality is not seamless and conventional but bizarre and interpenetrated. . . . A somewhat isolated living style also contributes to a certain exacerbation of the imagination in which images in the mind may seem to pulse and glow under the focus of loneliness.[9]

In charting an overview of visionary art in Texas, it is difficult to trace a chronological evolution. Rather, as this chapter will demonstrate, certain thematic concerns and friendships unite artists who otherwise pursue different media and formal strategies. And one aspect of the Texas quest for the sublime frequently overlooked by writers concerned with the visionary is the concomitant sense of the absurd explored by many Texas artists. In the spirit of Nancy Reddin Kienholz's statement that opens this chapter, humor, double entendres, and transformation are closely linked. Sources as diverse as the macabre Day of the Dead rituals and the febrile writings of Antonin Artaud have fired the imaginations of these painters, sculptors, and photographers, who through their embrace of the extraordinary have created one of the defining aspects of Texas art.

The first examples of visionary art in Texas can be traced to such turn-of-the-century amateurs as Charles Dellschau, whose fantastic notebooks of flying machines are among the landmarks in the history of outsider art.[10] However, it wasn't until the 1940s that such professional artists as Forrest Bess, who is discussed elsewhere in this catalogue (see plate 12), began to explore the liberating power of visionary experience. In this, Texas mirrored national trends. As the pioneering generation of Surrealists took refuge in the United States and Mexico during World War II, an increasing number of American artists were inspired by André Breton's proclamation, "I believe in the future resolution of the states of dream and reality, in appearance so contradictory, in a sort of absolute reality, or *surréalité*, if I may so call it."[11]

In Houston, Jermayne MacAgy's brilliantly curated exhibitions of the 1950s at the Contemporary Arts Association offered Texas artists an introduction to Surrealist art and thought. For most artists of this generation, casting off local ties was essential to the exploration of Breton's "absolute reality," and for many, Mexico offered an exhilaratingly fresh community, rich in artistic ferment and attuned to the innovations of Surrealism. Dorothy Hood and Ary Stillman were among the artists who made Mexico their home during these years, and both were guided by the search for the psychologically resonant that drove the early Surrealists.

pages 78–79
Melissa Miller
Flood (detail), 1983
(see plate 55)

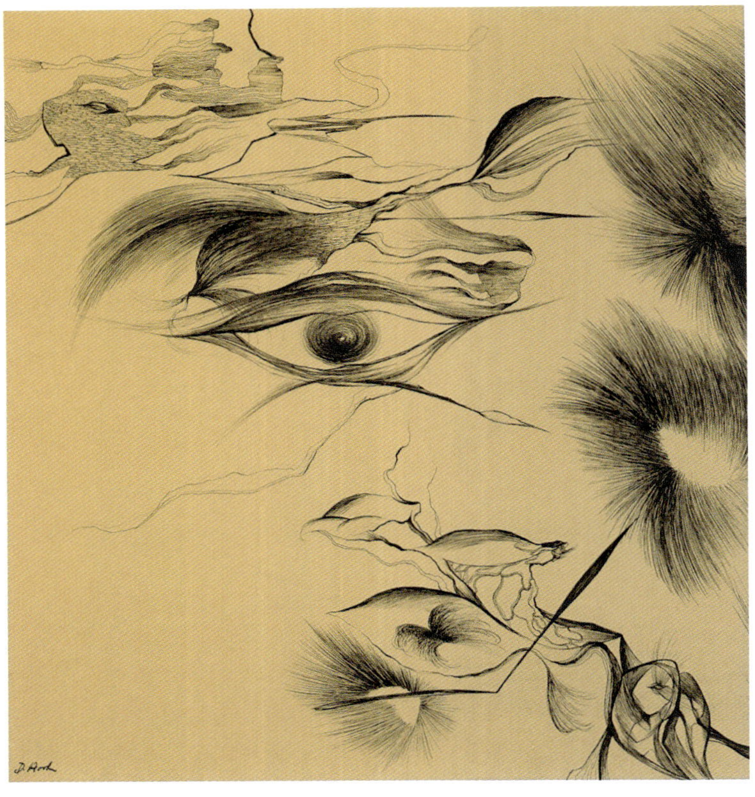

49
Dorothy Hood
Warrior's Plumage, 1957
Pen and ink on wove paper,
20 x 18½ in. (50.8 x 47 cm).
Gift of Mrs. Eugene Wagner,
57.44.

Raised in Houston, and a student at the Museum School, Hood won a scholarship to attend the Rhode Island School of Design in 1937. She completed her formal studies in New York at the Art Students League in 1940; a trip later that year to Mexico City brought her into contact with the leading artists and writers of the Mexican Renaissance. She subsequently made Mexico her home for close to two decades—although she also made extended visits to New York, Houston, and Latin America—and her eloquently mysterious paintings and drawings of these years won her an international audience.

Warrior's Plumage, 1957 (plate 49), demonstrates Hood's early affinity with Mexican Surrealism, most notably such works as Frida Kahlo's *Fantasy,* 1944 (Mexico, D.F., Museo Dolores Olmedo Patiño). Both compositions can be understood as abstract landscapes that spin from the central motif of an all-seeing visionary eye. However, where Kahlo sought to emphasize the physical aspect of even her most fantastic compositions, Hood gave greater primacy to the abstract and the insubstantial. In a later journal entry, Hood recorded:

> How this space of the mind's eye is related to the non-verbal state of painting! . . . At the end, within the Void, is true memory. The psyche, the mute measuring relative to the Void, is also forever active and creating. It is reducing itself, refining itself; it is in itself saying the most, as Kant would, by the least means. It crosses into the Void, into limits, and thus beginnings.[12]

Although Hood does not adopt the psychic automatism of early Surrealism, a certain degree of improvisation animates the composition. Her authoritative draftsmanship pulls across the page, charting seismic shifts in scale and perception. The avian reference—implied both by the title and the images on the lower right—is a recurring theme in Hood's drawings of this period, suggesting at once the Aztec deity Quetzalcoatl (the "feathered serpent") as well as freedom and flight.

Ary Stillman, who only came to Houston after a long and widely itinerate career, similarly spent some of his most fruitful years painting in Mexico. Born near Minsk in Russia, Stillman came to the United States in his teens in 1907. After studies at the Art Institute of Chicago, the National Academy of Design, and the Art Students League, he traveled to Paris, where he remained on and off from 1921 to the early 1930s. He returned to New York in 1933; in 1957, he moved to Cuernavaca, outside of Mexico City; in 1962, he made his home in Houston.

Stillman's work reflects this peripatetic life; his early paintings spring from Post-Impressionism and the School of Paris, while his later nonobjective compositions can be compared to the gestural abstractions of André Masson and Mark Tobey. However, some of his strongest works are a series of gouaches begun in Cuernavaca that chart his growing interest in ritual and myth. *Black Magic,* c. 1957 (plate 50), is among the earliest works of this series. The iconic imagery is rendered with painterly assurance; a silhouetted figure appears caught up in some form of ritual and is framed within a loosely worked cartouche. The image echoes the pictographs of Southwestern cultures: Stillman had visited Santa Fe as early as 1929, and he was also aware of Jackson Pollock's exploration of similar themes. However, it was the experience of working in Mexico that liberated Stillman. In 1965, he recalled:

> Even years before my going to live in Mexico, I had completely broken away from surface realities. But it was in Mexico that the inner reality began more and more to emerge, that I felt more and more its essence. It was for me a period when fantasy became paintable, or when I invaded the world of fantasy. I was completely involved in the mysticism of the subconscious. This mysticism is the inner thing which gives the spark of imagination.[13]

The 1950s also saw a number of significant projects by Mexican artists in Texas. For example, Rufino Tamayo created two important murals in the region: one in 1953 for the Dallas Museum of Fine Arts, followed in 1955 by a commission from Houston's Bank of the Southwest. Notable exhibitions of this era included *Mexican Paintings and Drawings*, hosted by the Contemporary Arts Association in 1953; a Tamayo retrospective, hosted by the Museum of Fine Arts, Houston, in 1956; and the monumental *Mexican Art: Pre-Columbian to Modern Times* exhibition, hosted by the Dallas Museum of Fine Arts in 1959. However, as Houston and Dallas embraced more international trends in the 1960s, fewer works by contemporary Mexican artists were seen in Texas; Houston's single museum exhibition in this area was the Contemporary Arts Association's *Mexico: The New Generation* of 1967. Nevertheless, Americans such as Lucas Johnson continued to make their home in Mexico in the 1960s, and by the 1970s, the richly layered cultures that flourished south of the border seemed once again resonant to such emerging artists as Michael Tracy.

The embrace of Surrealism in Hood's and Stillman's responses to Mexican culture is eloquently complemented by the paintings and drawings of Lucas Johnson. After a childhood spent in Connecticut and southern California, Johnson attended the University of Hawaii, where he studied marine biology. He left school to become an artist, and the defining experience of his career was the decade he spent in Mexico City, from 1964 to 1973. Like the *Nueva Presencia* artists active in Mexico during the 1960s, Johnson united a Surrealist imagination with an exquisite sense of draftsmanship. He adopted the sonorous palette of Rufino Tamayo, and his work developed in concert with that of such contemporaries as José Luis Cuevas and Artemio Sepúlveda.

The student riots of 1968 and the subsequent political climate eventually drove Johnson from Mexico to Houston in 1973.[14] His haunting compositions of barren landscapes and his penetrating figure studies of subsequent years had little direct reference to Mexico; rather, they can be more generally allied with the humanist traditions of Latin American art. However, in 1990 Johnson returned to Mexico for a major exhibition of his drawings in Guadalajara, and the following year he embarked on the *Volcano Series* that revisited his Mexican experiences.

Volcanoes define the topography of the central Mexican plateau and not surprisingly the volcano looms large in Mexican lore, from the legends of Pre-Columbian cultures to the novels of Malcolm Lowry. In the *Volcano Series*, Johnson drew specific inspiration from the startlingly sudden eruption of the volcano Paricutin, which rose up out of the fields of Michoacan in 1947. *Volcano Series, No. 3*, 1991 (plate 51), is typical of the series in that the image of the volcano is tightly framed, and fiery streams of lava bear down on fragile stone walls. The image can be understood as an allegory for the forces of nature that inevitably overwhelm the constraints of civilization. However, the artist has also identified these works as veiled self-portraits, commenting that on his

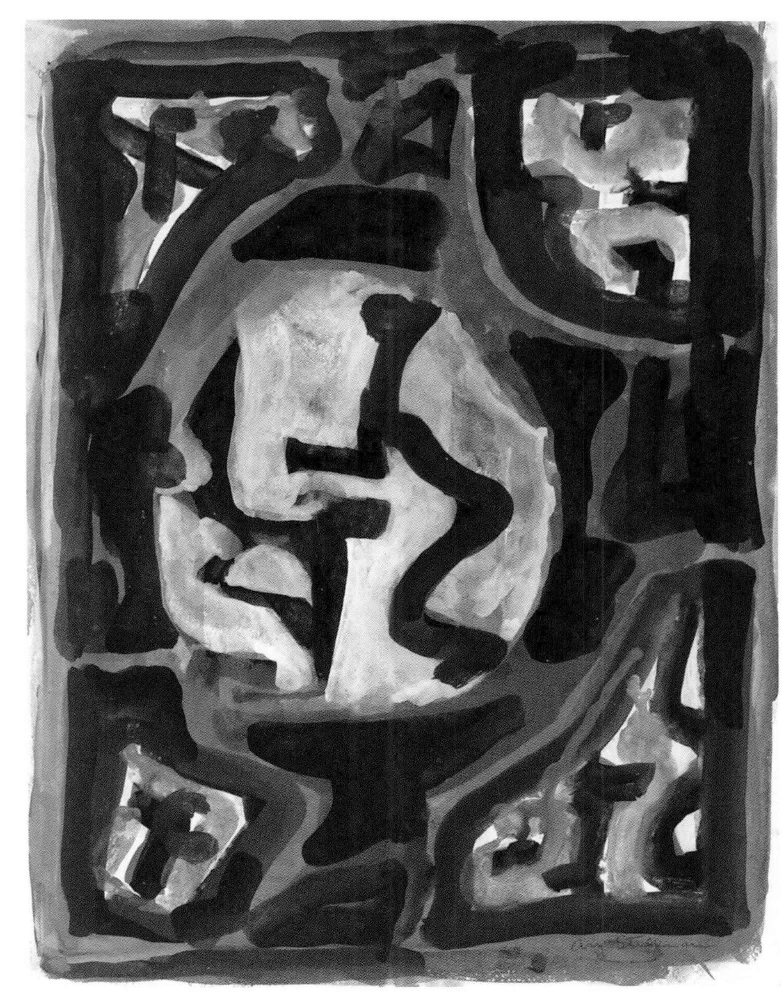

50
Ary Stillman
Black Magic, 1953
Gouache on wove paper, 21¾ x 17½ in. (55.2 x 44.5 cm). Gift of Mr. and Mrs. A. I. Lack, 57.47.

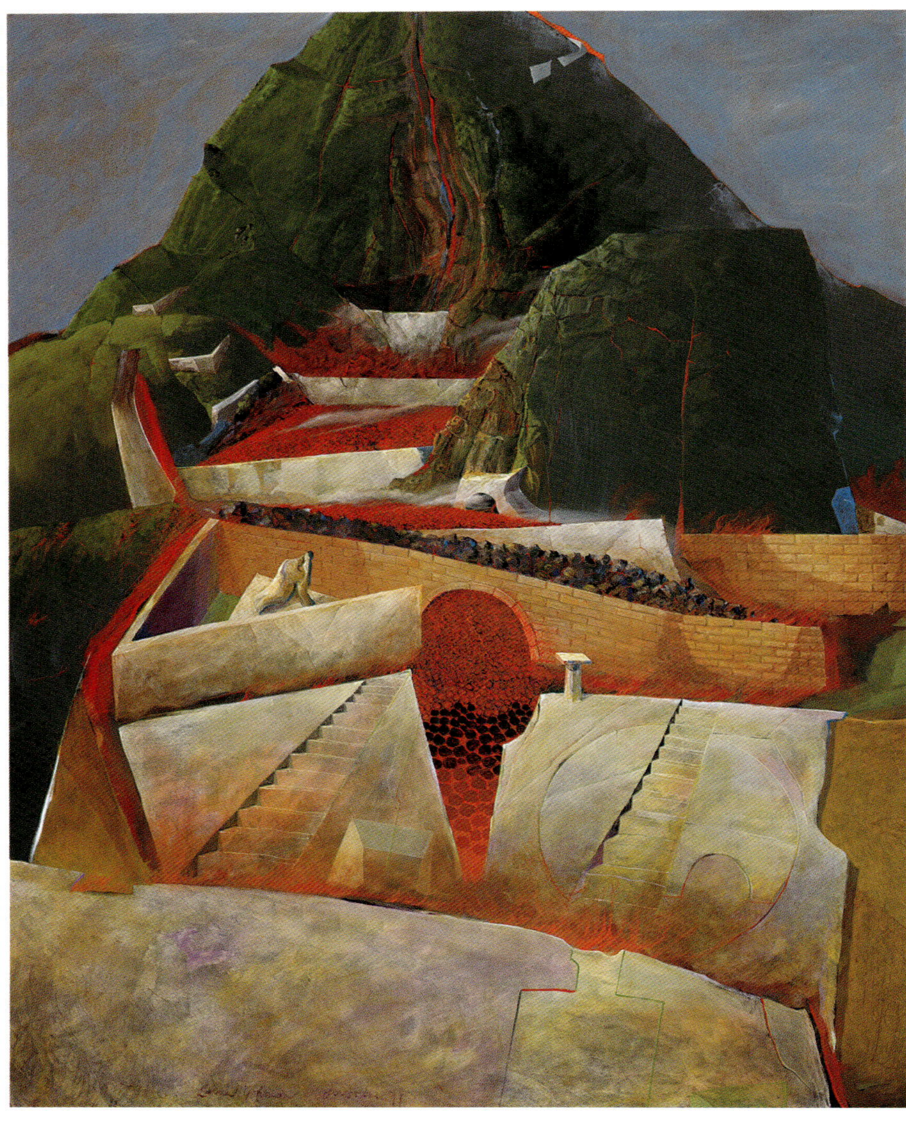

51
Lucas Johnson
Volcano Series, No. 3, 1991
Acrylic on canvas, 59⅞ x
47¾ in. (152.1 x 121.3 cm).
Museum purchase with
funds provided by Crowley,
Marks & Douglas and Pablo
Alvarado in memory of
Diana Faz, 92.120.

Arriving in Mexico almost a decade after Johnson, Michael Tracy looked to the ritual rather than the pictorial traditions of Latin American culture. A native of the Midwest, Tracy came to Texas to study at St. Edward's University in Austin. In 1969 he completed his graduate studies in art at the University of Texas at Austin, and in 1972 he made his first visit to Mexico. While there, Tracy witnessed a *Penitente* procession during Holy Week in Valenciana, Guanajuato, an experience that ultimately led to his first mature series of works, exemplified by *Memento Mori [Agony]*, 1973–79 (plate 52).

Both altar and penitential object, *Memento Mori [Agony]* summons up the dark paintings of the Rothko Chapel. Like Rothko, Tracy was influenced by Gestalt psychology, and his monumental compositions have a dramatic physical presence. However, Tracy looks beyond Rothko to Renaissance art, Catholic culture, and the extreme performances and films of such figures as Antonin Artaud, Rudolph Schwarzkogler, and Pier Paolo Pasolini.[17] *Memento Mori [Agony]* recreates the elevated presentation of a Baroque altar painting; rather than depicting a martyred saint, Tracy treats the support itself (canvas covered with acrylic, oil paint, hair, and Mexican rebozos) as the object of sacrifice, slashing the surface with carefully controlled gestures and plunging spikes into it. In 1979, Tracy stated of his works:

> [They are the] objectified residue of private rituals I have conducted, some in the form of meditations, some in the form of actions—all focused around the idea of Mexico, its history, its displacement into my personal history, and what seems for me a very logical formal development in my work—a binding together of elements which I have been working with these last years.[18]

Memento Mori [Agony] is without precedent in Texas art. Tracy found in Mexico an affirmation of his deepest interests, an affirmation that led him to explore other cultures as well. For example, much as the spikes driven through the canvas reenact the Passion of Christ, they also recall the ritual piercing of the fetish figures of the Congo and Zaire. Thomas McEvilley has astutely commented: "What would become increasingly clear is that it was at least in part Texas's connection with Mexico, with the Third World, that freed [Tracy] to allow the altar boy to anoint himself, to take over the rite, or rather

return from Mexico, "I was a man on fire."[15] Carla Stellweg has written of the fluidity of images in Johnson's work: "As is the case with his Mexican contemporaries, Johnson's oeuvre also shows a pervasive return to or use of the human form.... Nothing is ever just one thing, and there is never only one way to see the people, places, and objects of this world.... Corporeal parts function as architecture: towers, shelters, dwellings, ducts, tunnels, caves, and paths that come and go. Similarly, architecture and landscape become bodyscape."[16]

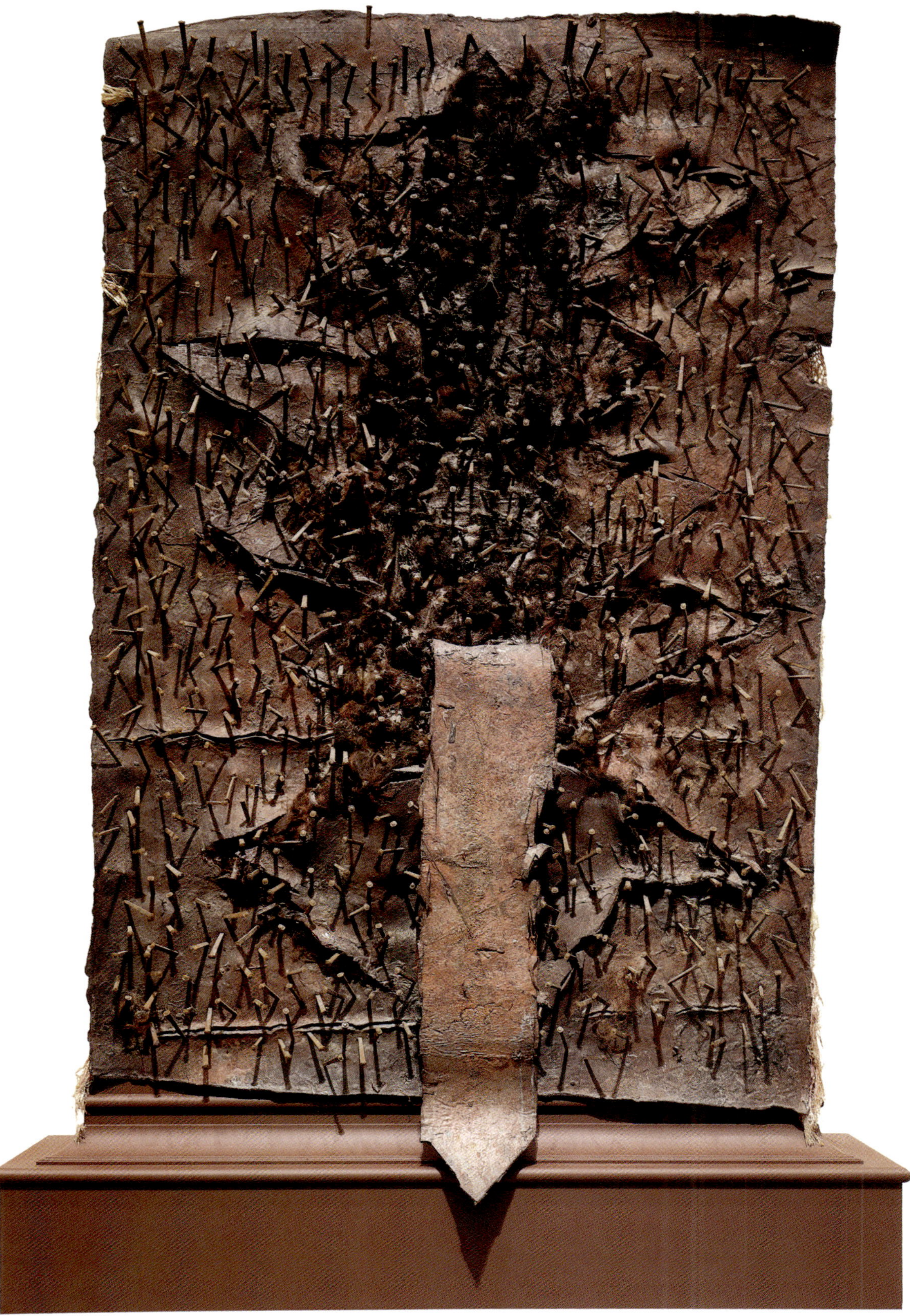

52
Michael Tracy
Memento Mori [Agony],
1973–79
Acrylic on canvas, hair,
metal spikes, rebozos, and
oil mounted on panel, 142 x
85 x 26½ in. (360.6 x 215.9 x
67.3 cm). Anonymous gift,
81.286.

to allow his own rite to emerge from the darkness and find itself in the light. . . . The overwhelming reality of the Third World took over his work and humanized it, while stretching his religiosity into forms where it acquired new meanings."[19]

If Mexico engendered one strand of mystical experience in Texas artists, the landscape of the Southwest gave rise to another. Kermit Oliver, who spent his childhood in Refugio, Texas, developed a form of magic realism deeply imbued with religious belief. A graduate of Texas Southern University, where John Biggers's mural program guided him towards a study of mythology and the history of art, Oliver also attended Elaine de Kooning's classes in Rice University's summer program of 1966.

K. J.'s Calf, 1975 (plate 53), is one of Oliver's first mature paintings and it reflects both the influence of such artists as Andrew Wyeth and a personal rite of passage. Oliver recalls that his father, who had been a cowboy, had always kept a milk cow that calved annually. The year Oliver left home, his father decided to give up the cow, and Oliver has noted that "to me the calf was a metaphor of my father and his life. . . . I've always used the calf or the sheep as representative of a sacrificial animal alluding to those attendant mythological and religious attributes: the restorative and regenerative symbol of the theme of death, birth, and the transformation of the self."[20]

The unusual composition was inspired by a memory of seeing a friend's calf through the high lunette window of the local church. The format, the bird's-eye perspective, and the radiantly rendered sunlight capture this moment with understated eloquence. At the same time, the ornamental frame, the lily, the pail and red cloth, and the directed gaze of the calf confirm the more somber themes of sacrifice and penitence.[21] Art historian Alvia J. Wardlaw has observed: "Oliver requests of the viewer an opening up of the subconscious and a summoning of an awareness of the forces of the universe and its ancient stories. . . . In a time no longer still enough to examine in daylight our dreams, Kermit Oliver sets forth his own dreams and reminds us of the depths of our own complexity."[22]

Oliver's compositions predict the rise of mythological themes that came to dominate Texas art in the late 1970s. However, few artists adopted his mode of magic realism; rather, it was the expressive figuration of such artists as Earl Staley and Melissa Miller that became the

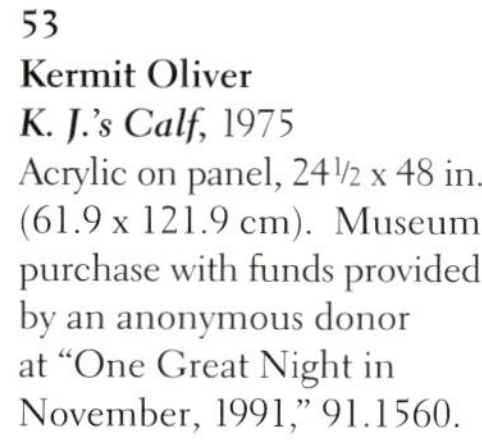

53
Kermit Oliver
K. J.'s Calf, 1975
Acrylic on panel, 24½ x 48 in. (61.9 x 121.9 cm). Museum purchase with funds provided by an anonymous donor at "One Great Night in November, 1991," 91.1560.

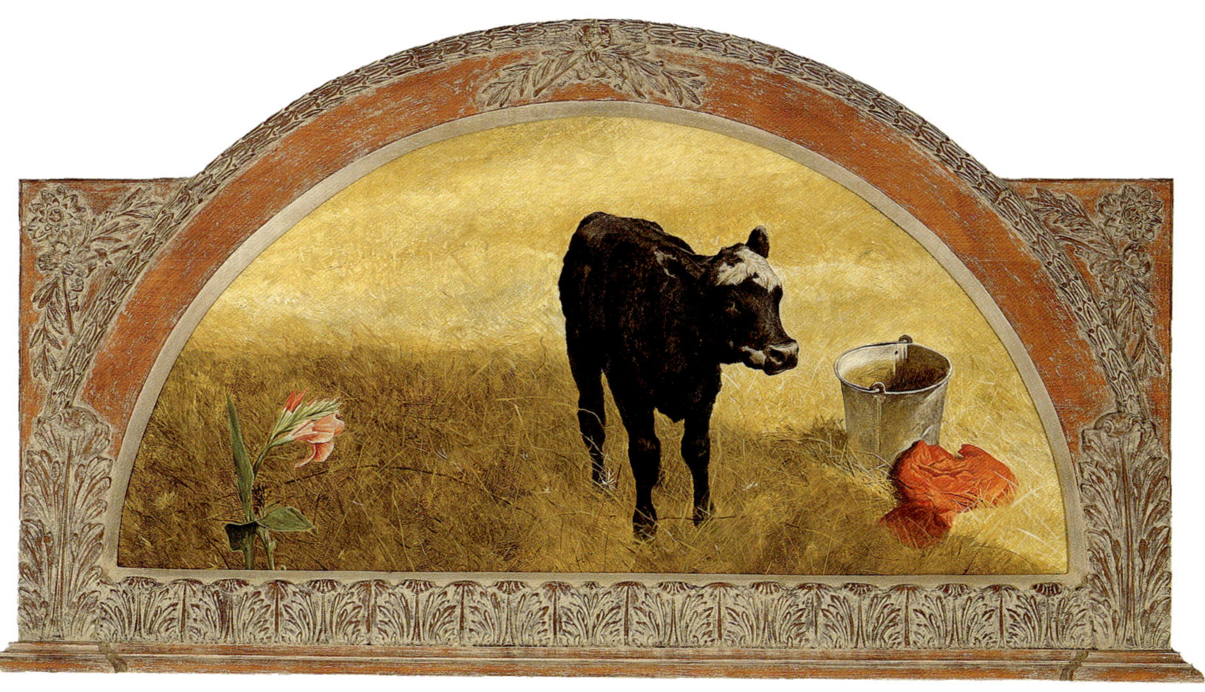

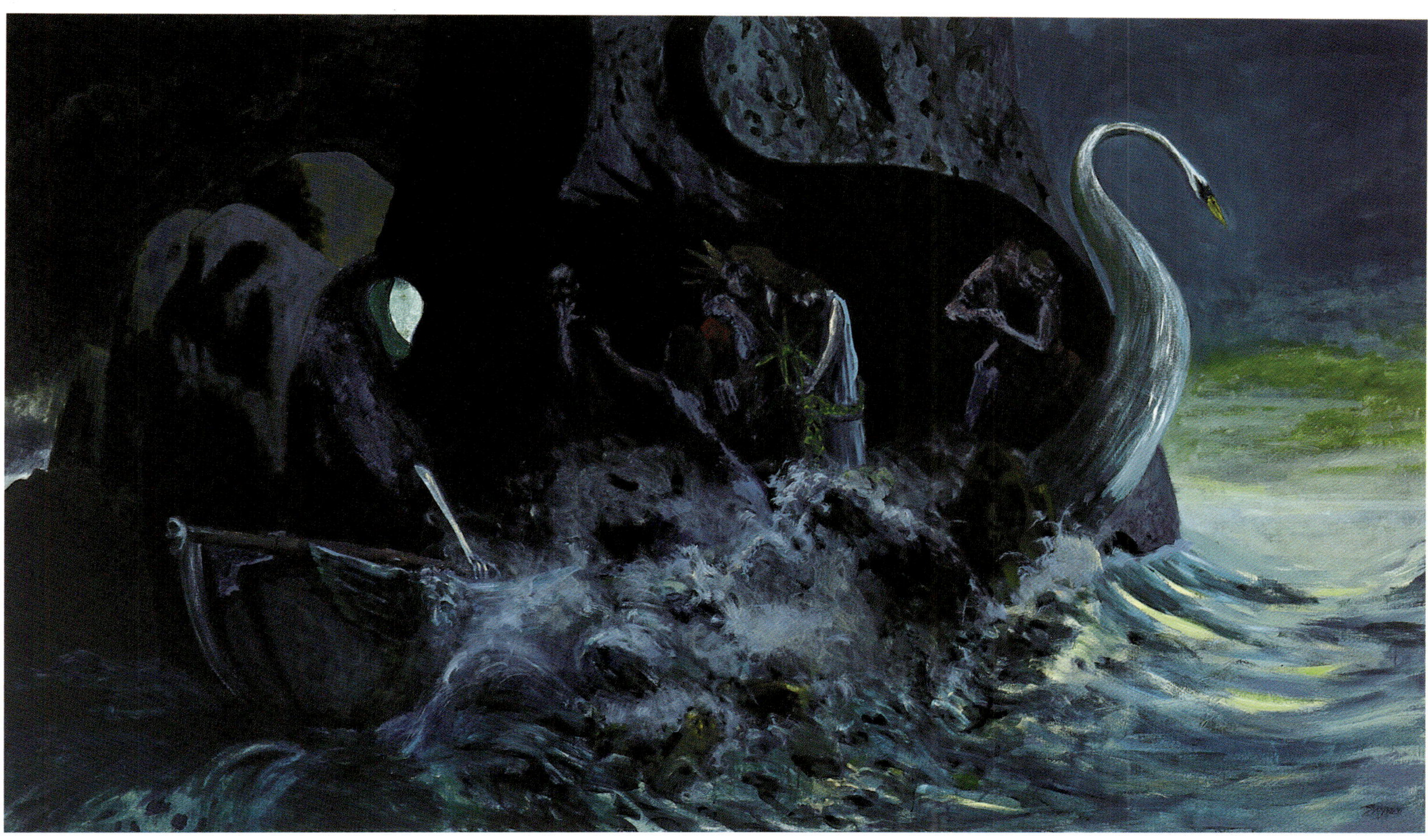

identifying style of this period, recognized locally by exhibitions at Houston's Contemporary Arts Museum, as well as internationally in such presentations as Marcia Tucker's 1984 contribution to the Venice Biennale, *Paradise Lost/ Paradise Regained: American Visions of the New Decade*.

Earl Staley arrived in Houston from his native Midwest in 1966, following studies at Illinois Wesleyan University and the University of Arkansas. He had explored narrative painting early in his career, and by the 1970s the mountains and deserts of West Texas and the folkloric culture of Mexico became major themes in his compositions. His embrace of such non-art materials as glitter and such popular icons as Indian heads, cacti, and skulls led some writers of the period to identify his paintings with the Texas Funk movement. However, mythological subjects had begun to appear in Staley's paintings as early as 1974, and as Tucker has observed: "Staley feels

that the most important event in his career, and the one which had the most profound effect on his work and his attitude toward it, was his decision in 1974 to 'stop making art.' This decision occurred, he says, when he first began to make mythological paintings, and a title like *Dream of Zeus* became more than just an abstraction, but a story to be told."[23]

Staley's deliberate turn towards mythological subject matter had strong art historical precedents, and his decision to "stop making art" was not intended as a divorce from this tradition. Rather, he chose mythological themes to step away from what he perceived as the increasingly formalist and private concerns of contemporary art of the moment.

Ship of Fools, 1978 (plate 54), has no particular mythic precedent, but as a moral conceit it can be traced back to medieval Christian doctrine: the ship of fools represents

54
Earl Staley
Ship of Fools, 1978
Acrylic on canvas, 67³/4 x
113¹/2 in. (172 x 288.2 cm).
Museum purchase with funds
provided by the National
Endowment for the Arts
matched by funds from
Susan Jeffers and Dr. Alice
McPherson by exchange,
84.80.

those whose travel through life is aimless and bereft of enlightenment. Staley has chosen the nocturnal palette and shadowy figures of the nineteenth-century German Romantic painter Arnold Böcklin to frame his rendition of this theme; a figure of Death holds the tiller, and the self-absorbed passengers ignore the waves that threaten to engulf the boat. The prow is shaped like a swan, a reference to Richard Wagner's opera *Lohengrin*, where Elsa's lack of faith destroys her chances of salvation and love.

A similar imagination of disaster characterizes the work of Melissa Miller. A Houston native, Miller attended the University of Texas at Austin, Houston's Museum School, the Yale Summer School of Music and Art, and the University of New Mexico, where she graduated in 1974. She settled in Austin, and the landscape of the Hill Country often offered a background to her painterly investigations; in 1984 Miller remarked: "I live in a hilly part of Texas full of scrubby trees, animals, water, and sky. Each day I observe dramas, contradictions, compromises, tensions, and endearments."[24]

Animals became the chief protagonists of Miller's compositions by the late 1970s; although these early scenes were closely tied to domestic life, her paintings after 1980 became increasingly fantastic. Emulating the fables of Aesop and Charles Perrault, Miller's narratives offered paradigms for the human condition, ranging from images of playful courtship to mortal struggles between species. Typically, Miller would create a unique scenario rather than refer to familiar analogies. However, the biblical theme of the Flood inspired several important works, including the museum's *Flood*, 1983 (plate 55). Miller first approached this theme in 1981 in an extended series of acrylics on paper titled *Studies for the Ark*. As Linda L. Cathcart has chronicled, these works were not intended as preparatory sketches, rather, "the purpose of these drawings was to explore animals in active environments, as well as to express Miller's frustrations about her own world."[25] Miller explained that she wanted to break with traditional renditions: "I never could understand all these ark paintings where everything is going so well —

55
Melissa Miller
Flood, 1983
Oil on linen, 59 x 95 in.
(149.8 x 241.3 cm). Museum purchase with funds provided by Duke Energy, 83.254.

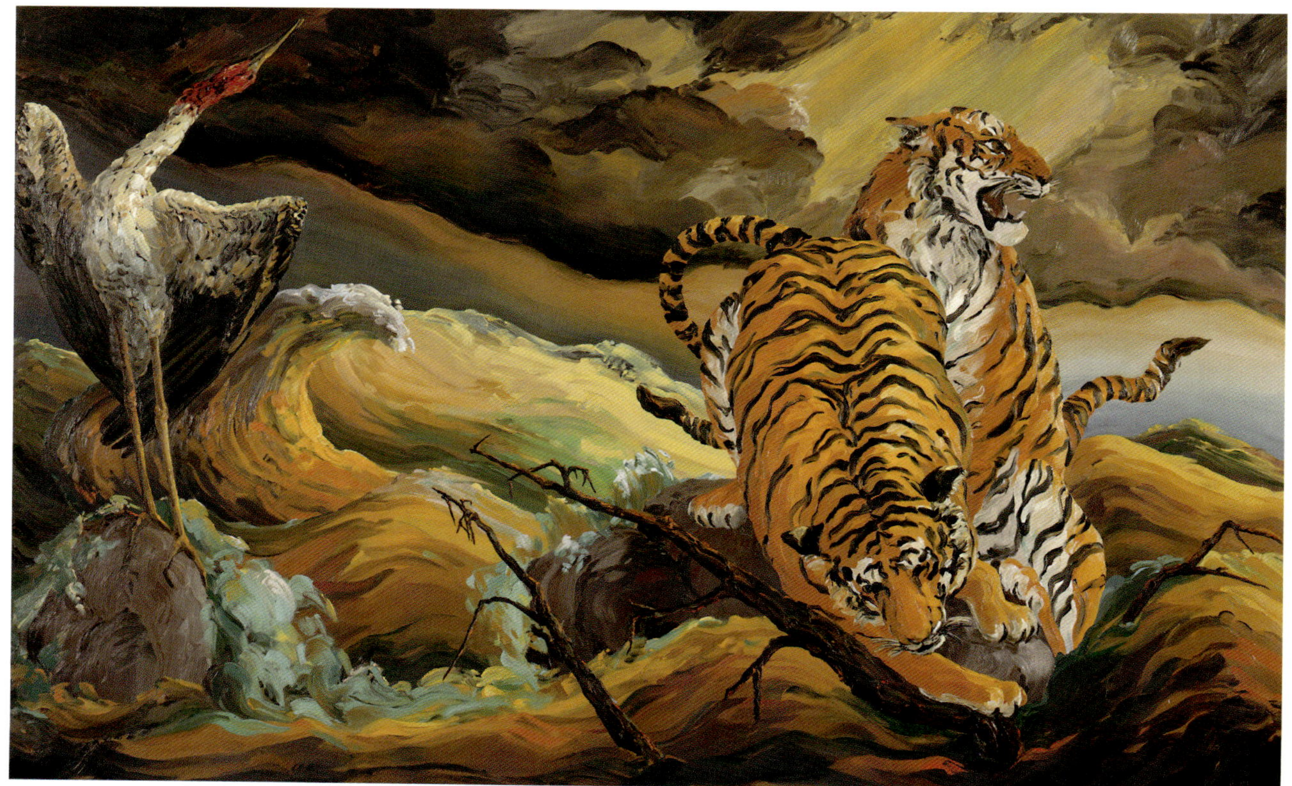

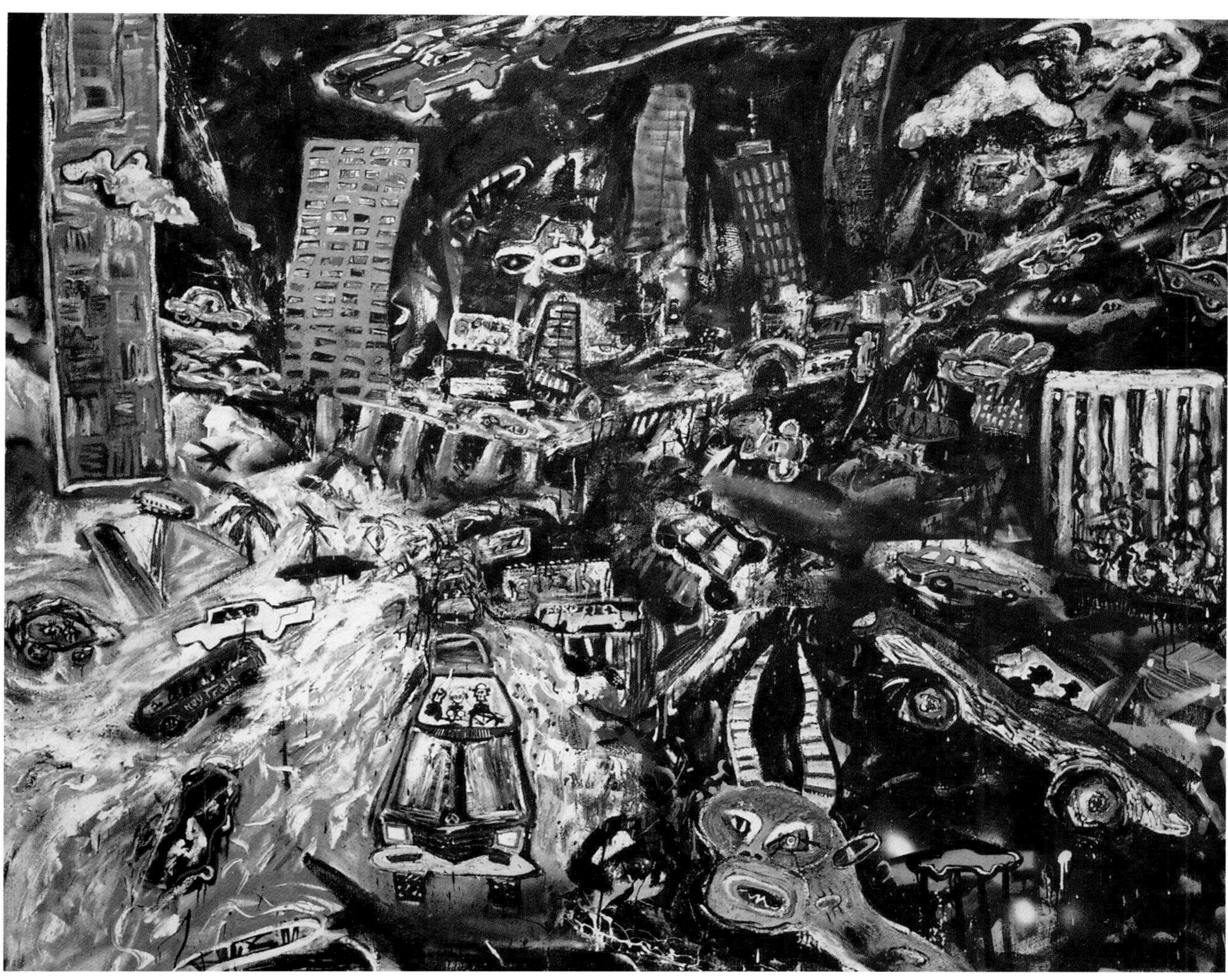

all these animals that would kill each other are together —everyone is behaving beautifully."[26]

Although Miller later returned to this theme in an elaborately detailed and monumental diptych of 1986 titled *The Ark* (Fort Worth: Modern Art Museum of Fort Worth), *Flood* is closer in spirit to the 1981 sketches. Tightly cropped, the painting focuses on the plight of three animals whose reactions to the rising waters chart a range of emotion, from the raging tiger to the crane who seems to arch its neck in despair. The one active figure in the composition is that of the crouching tiger, who tentatively tests a passing branch as a saving foothold. While Miller's paintings are often apocalyptic, Tucker has noted they are also "images of redemption,"[27] and she further links both Staley and Miller to a revived humanism: "It is the intent of these artists to address, once again, the larger issues, ones which are deeply humanitarian, transcultural, and transhistorical.... It is through such haunting images, filled with ambivalence, melancholy, passion, and tenderness, that we are brought together in an expression of solidarity with the human race."[28]

Annette DiMeo Carlozzi has observed that Texas art can been characterized by "an uncensored humor and personal immediacy."[29] Both qualities can be seen in the work of Jeff DeLude and David Bates. Like other painters of expressive figuration, these artists admitted fantastic elements into their compositions. However, their paintings also introduce an anarchic spirit of play, which distinguishes them from those of Staley and Miller. In this, they were closer to such artists as John Alexander and Derek Boshier (see plates 23 and 28), whose celebration of local culture had an added element of parody and caricature.

Jeff DeLude came to Houston in 1979 to attend the graduate program at the University of Houston. He was among the first generation of students to be able to take advantage of the remarkable facility at the university's Lawndale Annex, which under the leadership of James Surls (see plates 24 and 63) was becoming Houston's premier alternative art and performance space.

Under the Sorcerer's Spell, 1980 (plate 56), captures the ebullient and disquieting spirit of Houston's unzoned

56
Jeff DeLude
Under the Sorcerer's Spell,
1980
Oil on canvas, 67⅞ x 84 in.
(172 x 213.3 cm). Gift of
Eleanor Freed, 84.403.

boom era. The artist has cited Jean Dubuffet as an inspiration, and Dubuffet's exploration of children's art and the art of the insane invigorates this composition.[30] DeLude's demonic downtown is a maelstrom of activity spinning out of control; a horned figure on the lower right suggests that it is Devil's Night in Houston. The flying cars, the teetering buildings, and the almost operatic chaos of the city has an unfettered exuberance. DeLude commented on the darker aspects of the shifting urban landscape of Houston:

> What intrigues me most about the city as subject is the often bizarre dislocations of objects in space and the hybrid configurations which result. The use of imagery is recognizable, and therefore easily accessible, but not in a naturalistic manner. . . . The work is about the mania of the city. It refers outside itself, and filters back into the pace, the grind, the noise.[31]

A similar vision animates David Bates's *Mardi Gras*, 1982 (plate 57). A native of Dallas, and a graduate of both Southern Methodist University and the Whitney Museum of American Art's Independent Study Program, Bates is best known for his Arkansas and Texas Gulf Coast landscapes. However, the folkways of East Texas and Louisiana have been consistent themes in his work; Bates's first exhibition of 1976 recreated a Dallas honkytonk lounge, and in 1981 he exhibited over 150 sculptures assembled out of wood and found materials based on folk-art examples. When he made painting his chief medium over the following decade, Bates continued to take his cues from the stacked compositions, flat figures, and brilliant palettes of naive artists.

Between 1982 and 1984, Bates created several paintings using Halloween and Mardi Gras themes, and the museum's *Mardi Gras* is a key transitional work in this series. Bates's move to a monumental canvas deliberately broke from folk-art conventions; instead, like Red Grooms—whom the artist had befriended while in New York—he offers a larger-than-life version of urban experience. Figures fill the frame, masks and floats form a claustrophobic collage, adroitly capturing the hectic and pagan mood of "Fat Tuesday." William A. Fagaly has noted: "There is an undercurrent of the sinister behind this façade of domestic bliss in Bates's large-scale canvasses, particularly in the pictures with the ever-present

gloating smiles on masks. On both festive occasions [Halloween and Mardi Gras] one dresses for the purpose of losing or falsifying one's true identity to create a world of artificiality and to give one license to behave in an abnormal and unrestricted manner."[32]

The questioning of identity, the exploration of myth, and the assumption of alternate personae are themes further explored by such diverse artists as Richard Stout, George Krause, and Roy Fridge. While formally disparate, these artists had all reached mid-career in the early 1980s, and their work shares a similarly reflective mood.

Born and raised in Beaumont, Texas, Stout attended the Art Academy of Cincinnati and the School of the Art Institute of Chicago; a 1957 visit to Houston revealed a burgeoning art scene, and he decided to stay. He received a second degree from the University of Texas at Austin in 1969, and became a member of the faculty of the University of Houston. During these years, he formed important friendships with Dick Wray (see plate 88) and Michael Tracy (see plates 52 and 105).

In 1976, Stout made his first of many visits to Germany, and he found in the contemporary revival of figurative painting in Berlin an affirmation of his own investigation of the figure and the landscape. *Oedipus* (plate 58), which was created over two campaigns in the artist's studio in 1973 and 1984, is characteristic of Stout's work of these years. In a complex scaffolding of spatial relationships, Stout layers and fragments shifting planes, landscape, and figures.[33] In keeping with the title, the imagery is frankly erotic; a segmented fifth-century Greek *kouros* is the central motif of the painting, and the composition thrusts violently towards a central apex. On another level, *Oedipus* suggests the disruptive force of myth and human emotions. The painting was completed during a tragic period in the artist's life; it is both retrospective and regenerative. In 1985, Stout commented: "Often painting is like an earthquake as it can release the tensions and tame the angry forces of our lives. Painting is not communication but more an exorcism."[34]

Unlike Stout, who built his career in Texas, George Krause was an established photographer when he came

57
David Bates
Mardi Gras, 1982
Oil on canvas, 84 x 60 in.
(213.3 x 152.4 cm). Museum
purchase with funds provided
by Duke Energy, 84.8.

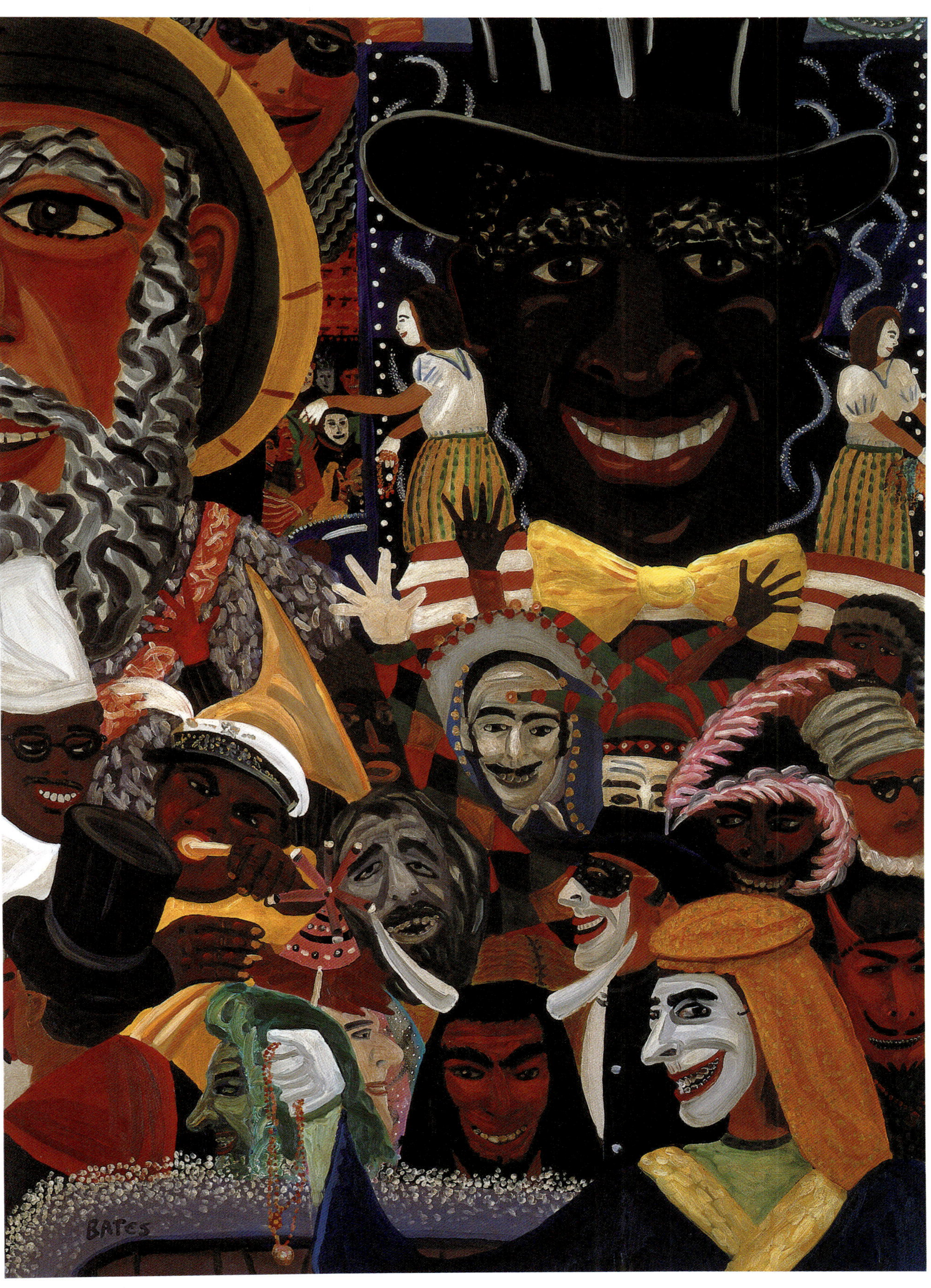

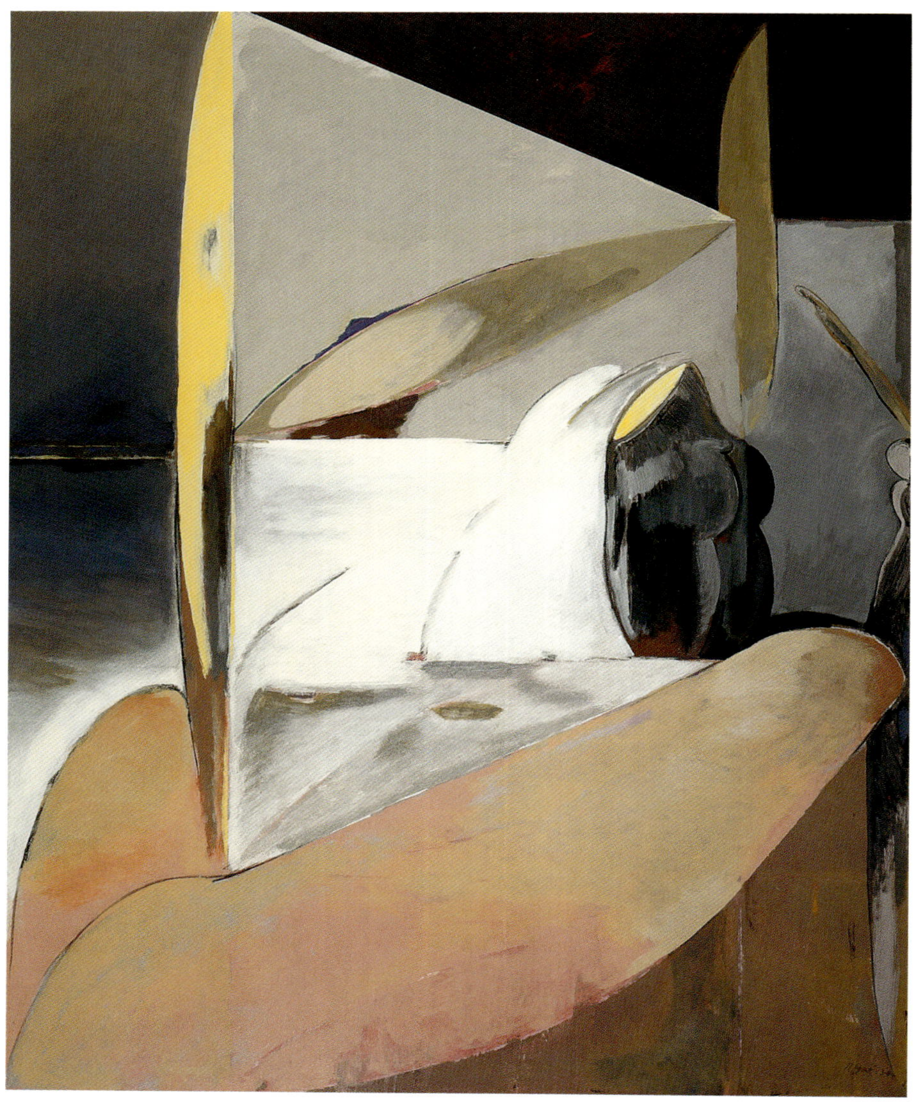

58
Richard Stout
Oedipus, 1973/84
Acrylic on canvas, 100 x 80 in.
(254 x 203.2 cm). Museum
purchase with funds provided
by Duke Energy, 85.10.

to Houston in 1975 at the invitation of the chair of the
art department, George Bunker, to create a department
of photography at the University of Houston. Krause was
born in Philadelphia; after studies at the Philadelphia
College of Art, he began to establish a career in documentary photography, receiving signal encouragement
in this pursuit from Edward Steichen. In the early 1960s,
however, Krause became increasingly interested in expanding the range of his work. During this period, he
continued to respond to documentary traditions, most
notably in the extended series titled *The Street*, but he
also embarked on two ongoing and complementary series
that specifically explored themes of death and salvation:
Qui Riposa and *Saints and Martyrs*. The *Qui Riposa*
photographs began with Krause's 1961 discovery of the
engraved photographic portrait tiles that animate tomb-
stones in Catholic cemeteries; the *Saints and Martyrs*
photographs of religious statuary were initiated by a 1964
visit to Mexico.

Turtle Man, 1981 (plate 59), is part of the artist's extended *I Nudi* series, begun in 1972. Nudes became his
chief subject during two tenures at the American Academy in Rome in 1976 and 1979; the museums and
churches of Rome and daily contact with art historians
in residence at the Academy further confirmed Krause's
interest in Renaissance figure painting. His photographs
of these years take their cues from the dense allegories of
such artists as Piero di Cosimo and Giovanni Bellini, as
well as from Ovid's *Metamorphoses*. Krause emphasized
the studio nature of this series, and Anne Wilkes Tucker
has noted, "Unlike the other three series, the photographs in *I Nudi* are staged and, consequently, depend
on Krause's ability to preconceive a scene."[35]

In *Turtle Man*, which was photographed in Austin,
Krause posed a model holding a 150-pound alligator
snapping turtle; man and beast are conflated into a single fantastic creature. The highly artificial nature of the
image is stressed by the paper backdrop, and by the delicately humorous detail of the fingers at the paper's edges,
revealing the presence of a concealed third figure. The
sexually charged image of the turtle man is oblique in
meaning; Tucker has commented: "Most of Krause's images are too evocative to accept on literal terms alone. It
is implausible that *Turtle Man* occurred because this

man wanted to demonstrate his physical prowess, and a giant snapping turtle was the handiest massive weight to lift. Is it, instead, allegorical? By having a man lift a turtle is Krause inverting the myth of a cosmic turtle supporting the world? Or is he relying on a turtle's primeval associations? Is this a mythic combat between a hero and an animal-monster that must be slain before order can be reestablished?"[36]

Metamorphosis is also central to the work of Roy Fridge, whose early career paralleled that of his friend Jim Love (see plates 14 and 94). Both attended Baylor University in Waco, where the theater director Paul Baker was a deeply influential mentor, and by the mid-1950s, both had found that careers in stage design were leading to sculpture. Unlike Love, who settled in Houston, Fridge made Dallas his home during this era; he further worked in commercial advertising and film, experiences which made him particularly receptive to the nascent Pop Art movement of the following decade.[37]

In 1961, Fridge began to retreat from the urban art community, and started working on the beaches of Port Aransas, Texas, close to Beeville, where he had grown up. In 1963, he built a studio on the beach, and off and on over the following decade he made the Gulf Coast his home, settling permanently in Port Aransas in 1973. During these years he befriended Forrest Bess (see plate 12), whose visionary paintings further prompted Fridge to explore a more independent path. In the mid-1970s, boats became one of the chief metaphors of his work, evolving into increasingly personal symbols as the development of beachfront property prompted Fridge to explore the Coleto Creek woodlands of Victoria County. As Fridge moved into greater isolation, he became fascinated with the possibility of linking performance and sculpture; he created private shrines, which became settings for a series of solitary dramas.[38] Michael Ennis has observed: "Fridge found his forest venue and started turning it into a retreat from his retreat.... Like his description of himself as an amateur hermit, Fridge's forest role as the pseudo-shaman reveals a good deal about his approach to life and art. His escapes are acts, and yet, like good drama, their meanings are believable when one accepts the staging."[39]

Shamanic Ritual Voyage, 1983 (plate 60), created in the Port Aransas studio, evolved out of Fridge's performances in the Coleto Woods. Boat and figure are inextricably united; made of bones and wood gathered from the local forest, the figure is presented with arms outstretched, a crucified or exultant form. In a related photodocumentation, Fridge chronicled:

> Shamanic Ritual Voyage—Journal Notes, 1983: A ritual re-enactment of the remembered voyage...an odyssey in search of wholeness...uniting the duality of black/white, male/female, consciousness/unconsciousness. The androgynous boat/shaman relic recalls the ritual voyage... recalls the putting on of the power of helping spirits "power animal"...an evocation of the remembered ritual and the necessity of continued voyaging into the unconsciousness seeking the elusive self.[40]

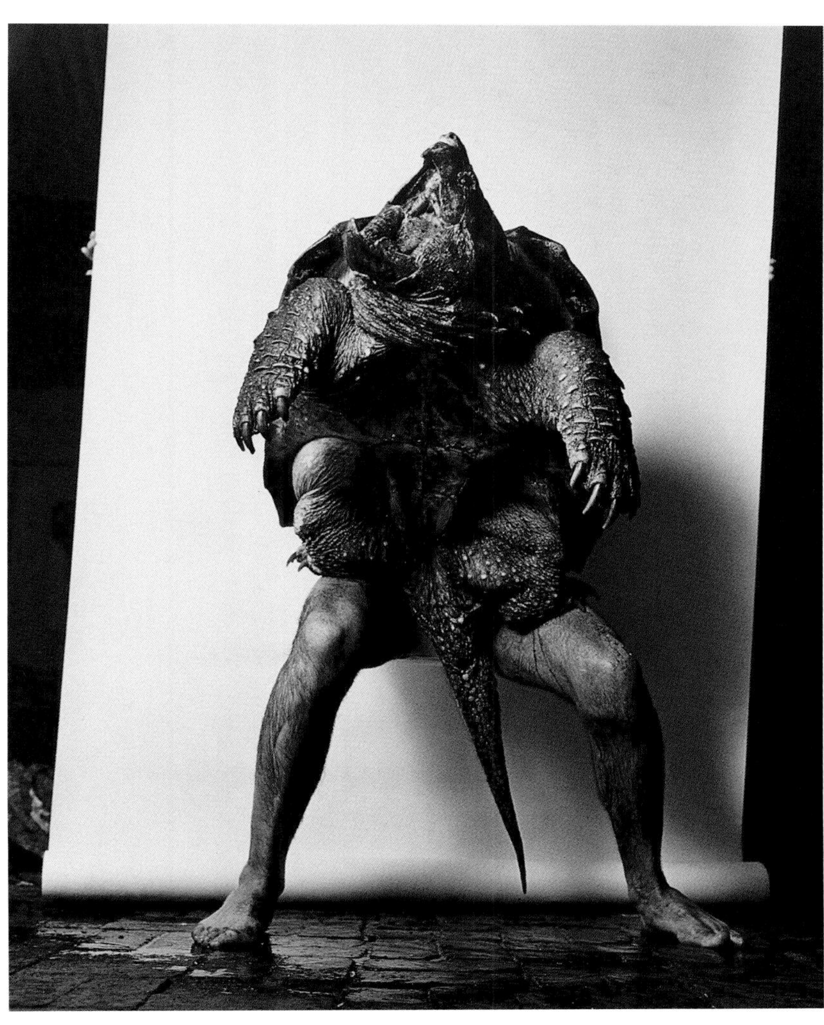

59
George Krause
Turtle Man, 1981
Toned gelatin silver photograph, 13¾ x 17¼ in. (34.9 x 43.8 cm). Museum purchase with funds provided by Patsy Arcidiacono, Barbara Chilton, Bernie Dutton, Sally Horrigan, Jewel McCullough, Muffy McLanahan, Marty Rau, and Beth Schlanger, 82.578.

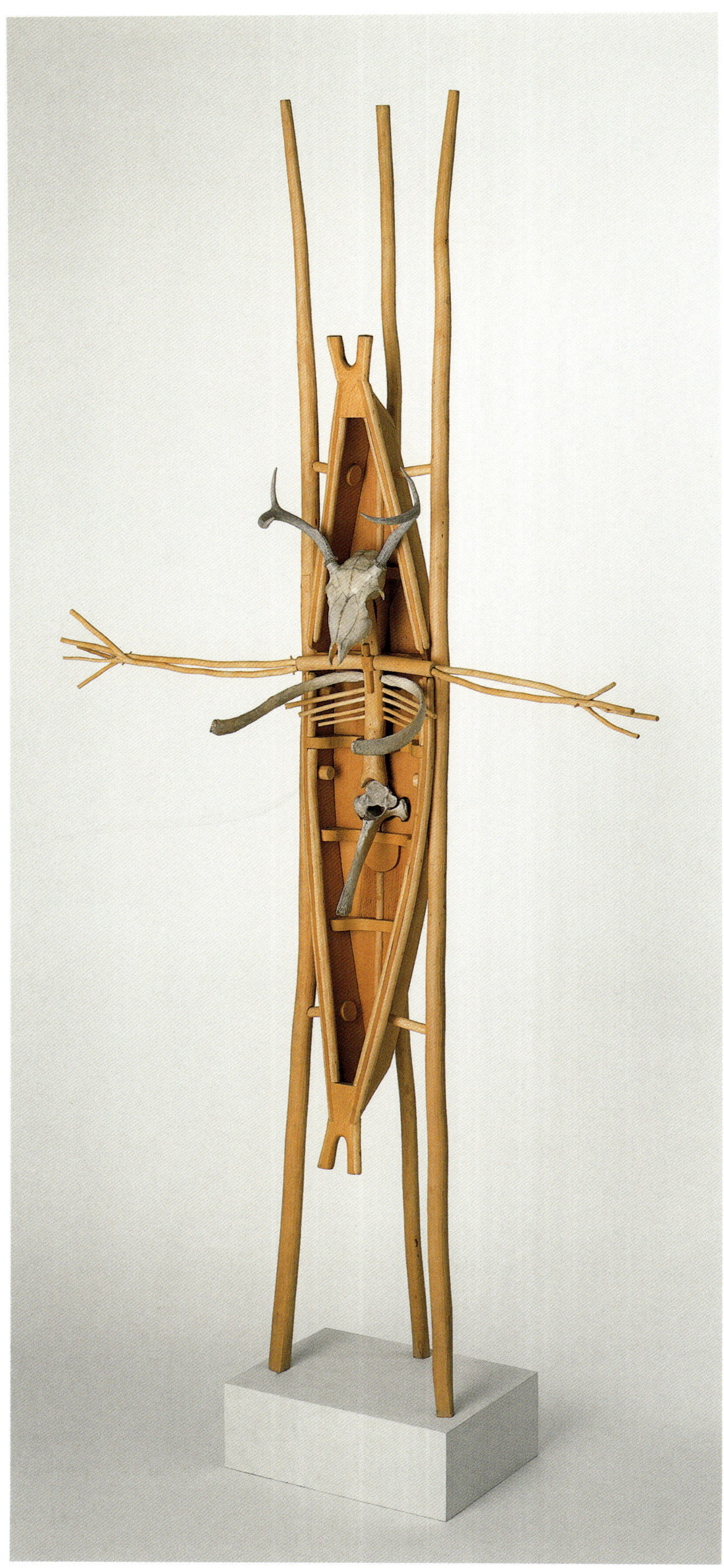

Fridge's mystical embrace of the landscape in part propelled the career of his close friend Madeline O'Connor, who has also chosen to draw her subjects from the woods of Victoria County. However, where Fridge finds in nature an arena to explore the self, O'Connor brings a naturalist's eye to her studio compositions.

Born in San Antonio, O'Connor was largely self-taught as an artist. A convent education and deeply held religious beliefs guided her initial approach to art and her engagement with nature. However, other interests brought her work to maturity, most notably an admiration for the paintings of Mark Rothko and a friendship with Donald Judd (see plate 91), which led O'Connor to explore serial and monochromatic compositional structures.

O'Connor's recent work evolves out of her investigation of the local and migratory birds of South Texas. Using the methodology of a practiced ornithologist, she abstracts from nature essential forms and brilliant color harmonies. At a glance, her finished paintings appear to belong to the reductivist aesthetics of Minimalism; however, as her *Studio Wall* drawings reveal, her compositions grow from diaristic notations, research, and field study. O'Connor has reflected on her working processes:

> My life has been spent walking the woods and marshes of South Texas, sketching the forms, making notations, and observing the cycles of our environment. Through this observation and study I feel I am able to go to the heart—the core—the essence withdrawn from nature.... I use my studio wall to pin a collage of color references, drawings, ornithologist's observations, and mythology notes before arriving at the final geometric form, the long series of the overlapping canvases approximating the shimmering color of an indigenous bird.[41]

O'Connor did not begin to exhibit the *Studio Wall* accumulations until the mid-1980s; in the early 1990s, she brought a new formality to these compositions, exemplified in the museum's collection by *Cross/Shrike*, 1993 (plate 61), from the *Studio Wall* series. Using a cruciform frame that suggests both the Passion of Christ as well as the four points of the compass, O'Connor displays the materials that fed her investigation of the predatory bird that kills by impaling its prey on thorns and barbed wire. As Frances Colpitt has noted, *Cross/Shrike* can best be understood as a reliquary that "houses a collage of skeletons of the bird's victims."[42]

The related *Shrike*, 1993 (plate 62), demonstrates O'Connor's process of paring away from the specific references of the *Studio Wall* studies. Nine triangular canvases are mounted seamlessly to the wall. The metallic palette is drawn from the particular coloration of the shrike, the single, dark bronze canvas at the center of the composition reflecting the bird's darker mask. The complementary pairing of forms subtly evokes a multipaneled altarpiece; the triangular shapes slice into the viewer's space, suggesting the violence and grace of the subject.

The solitary nature of visionary art rarely yields to artistic collaborations; however, collaborations are not unusual in Texas art, and in 1988, curator Janet Landay and author Donald Barthelme invited thirteen pairs of artists and writers to create works jointly for an exhibition at the Glassell School of Art.[44] Among the astonishingly fruitful results of this project was James Surls's and Cynthia Macdonald's *At the Round Earth's Imagin'd Corners*, 1988 (plate 63 and text on pages 96–98).

Cynthia Macdonald, a poet who published her first anthology in 1972, came to Texas in 1977 as a consultant to the Department of English at the University of Houston. In 1979 she was instrumental in founding the university's extraordinary Creative Writing Program. Her writing combines formal brilliance with narrative immediacy; her poem "At the Round Earth's Imagin'd Corners"—later subtitled "A Stack of Marriage Boxes"—is one of Macdonald's *tours de force*.

James Surls first established his career through his monumental and fantastic sculptures made of wood (see plate 24). Drawings were of equal importance to the artist, and he matched the physical power of his wooden figures with extraordinary feats of draftsmanship. Typically, his graphic compositions depend upon contour line, which by the 1980s had become Surls's most fluid means of expression. Wordplay had always had a role in his titles—which were incorporated into the finished drawings—however, when invited to collaborate with Macdonald, Surls was formally challenged by the length of her text.

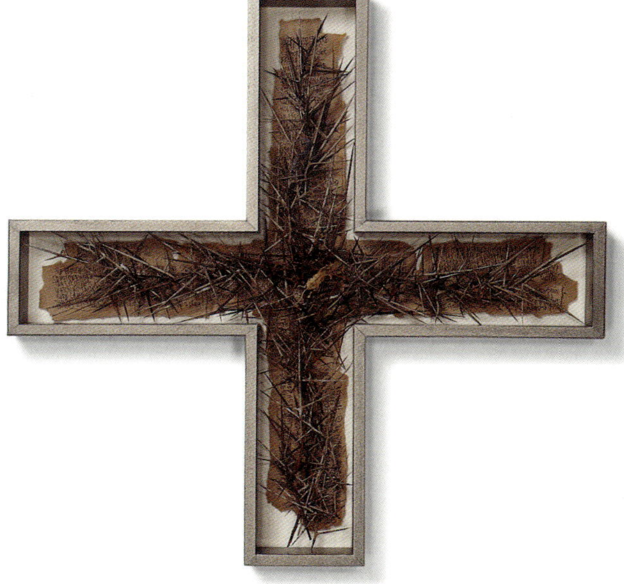

60 *opposite*
Roy Fridge
Shamanic Ritual Voyage, 1983
Wood and mixed media, 83¼ x 40½ x 22 in. (211.4 x 102.9 x 55.9 cm). Gift of Moody Gallery, 85.138.

61
Madeline O'Connor
Cross/Shrike, from the *Studio Wall* series, 1993
Thorns, ink on paper, animal skeletons, galvanized tin, and Plexiglas, 40 x 40 x 4½ in. (101.6 x 101.6 x 11.6 cm). Museum purchase with funds provided by a friend of the museum, 94.243.

62
Madeline O'Connor
Shrike, 1993
Metal powder and acrylic on canvas, nine panels, 44¼ x 14 x 2 in. (112.4 x 35.6 x 5.1 cm) each. Museum purchase with funds provided by a friend of the museum, 94.244.

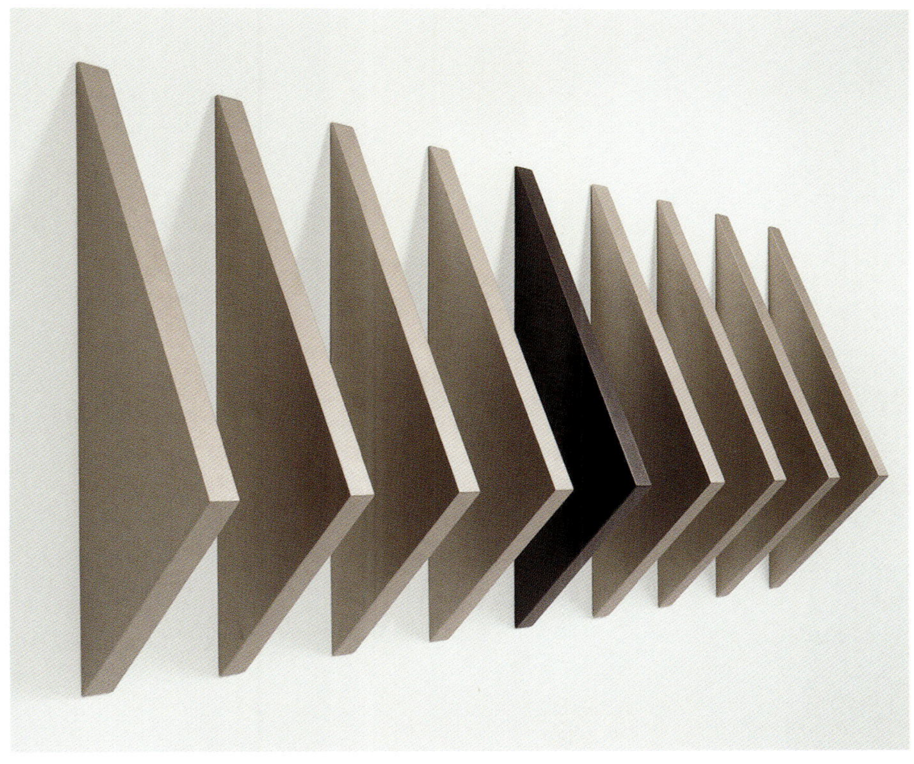

At the Round Earth's Imagin'd Corners is both a compositional triumph and a deeply sonorous reflection on the transcendent nature of union. Macdonald's text offers lucidly rendered vignettes of a shifting relationship, concluding with an absolute reconciliation of her two protagonists. The text is appropriately matched by Surls's layered imagery and shifts in scale and focus. These shifts occur not only between the three sheets of the triptych, but also in the flowing metamorphoses engendered by the artist's use of line. On the left sheet Surls pictures a builder/creator, in the center is an unfurled flower, on the right is a seated figure who appears to be enlarged by and dissolved into a cerebral and physical coupling with another. Macdonald's text is threaded throughout the composition, mediating between image and ground.

Sight is the unifying metaphor that ties the three pages of the triptych together. On the outside sheets images of paired eyes are the nexuses of the compositions, on the center sheet Surls has added "See Cynthia." Surls has commented, "The eye is like an all-seeing kind of phenomenon. It also gives life to something."[45] Unlike Dorothy Hood's visionary eye (see plate 49), which opens out into the void, Surls finds in vision an analogue of communication and communion.

Ocular imagery haunts the work of James Reaben, a self-taught Houston artist whose intense and brief career was dedicated to visionary experience. Reaben emerged from a difficult childhood with a deeply nihilistic view; as his close friend William Steen has recalled, his first works exhibited at Houston's Studio One in the early 1980s were literally wired to explode.[46] However, in 1987 Reaben exhibited a series of drawings, collages, and small sculptures that revealed a far more complex integration of his fascination with destruction, regeneration, and transcendence. A study of Voodoo, Eastern mysticism, ancient religions, and the writings of Artaud had given direction to Reaben's pursuit, and over the following two years, he produced a remarkable body of work that willfully transgressed the boundaries of art into the unknown.

Allotropic Cabinet, 1988 (plate 64) exemplifies Reaben's earlier work of this period. He has taken common materials, and like an alchemist, has transformed them into something extraordinary: allotropy is a chemical term for

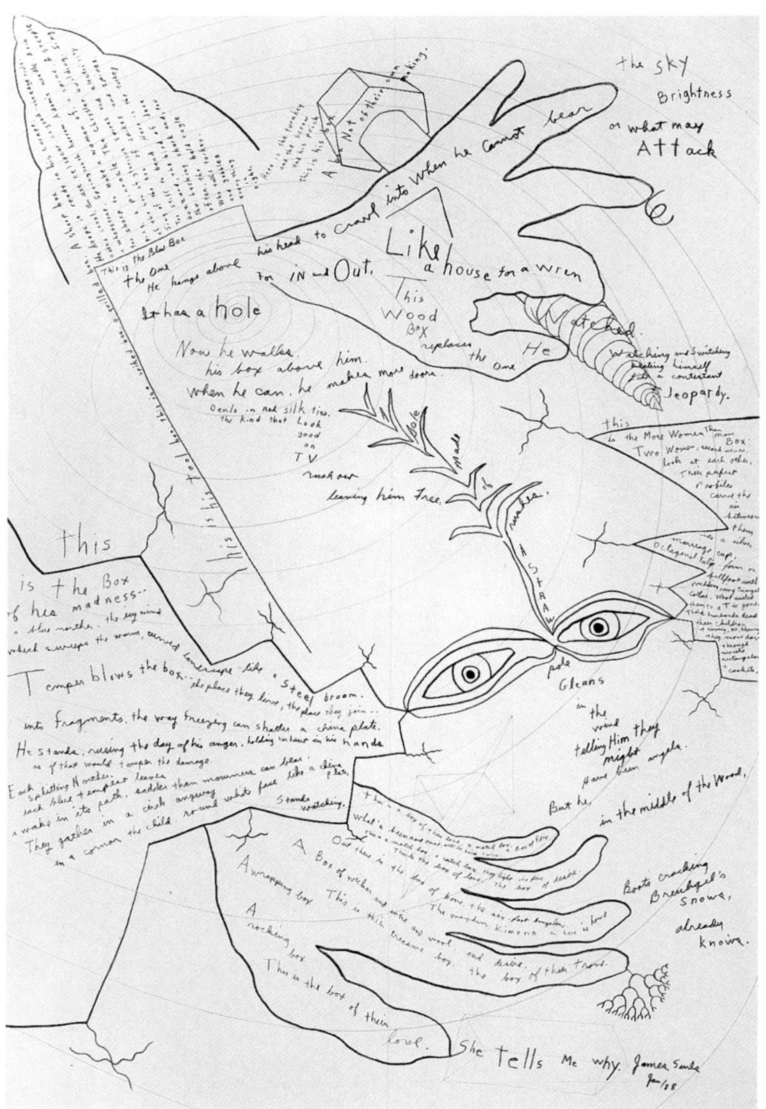

At the Round Earth's Imagin'd Corners

1.

This is the mother, *a Round box, a Wrapping box, a Swaddled box,*
This is the cradle, *a Swaddled box, a Rocking box,* a box squared,
Then lengthened into what the rest of your life will be. The span
Of your life, your mother's pointed fingers bridging the cradle,
A Wrapping box, a Rocking box. When the wind blows the cradle,
She may be there, leaning down, reaching for you, catching you
Like a trapeze artist, like a cold, like a lover, or like a mother.

2.

This is his tool box; this is a spiked box, a quilled box,
A sharp box. He keeps it ready in his corner: naked steel,
An axe, eelspear, oxgoad—the edge tools—a whetstone,
Springtooth harrow, Adam's needle, a rib too sharp to
Make a woman of, a spine, a steeple, pins, a pinnacle,
The Chrysler building. Sing of the box of glorious spires
And electricity. Sing of the box of spikes and spines

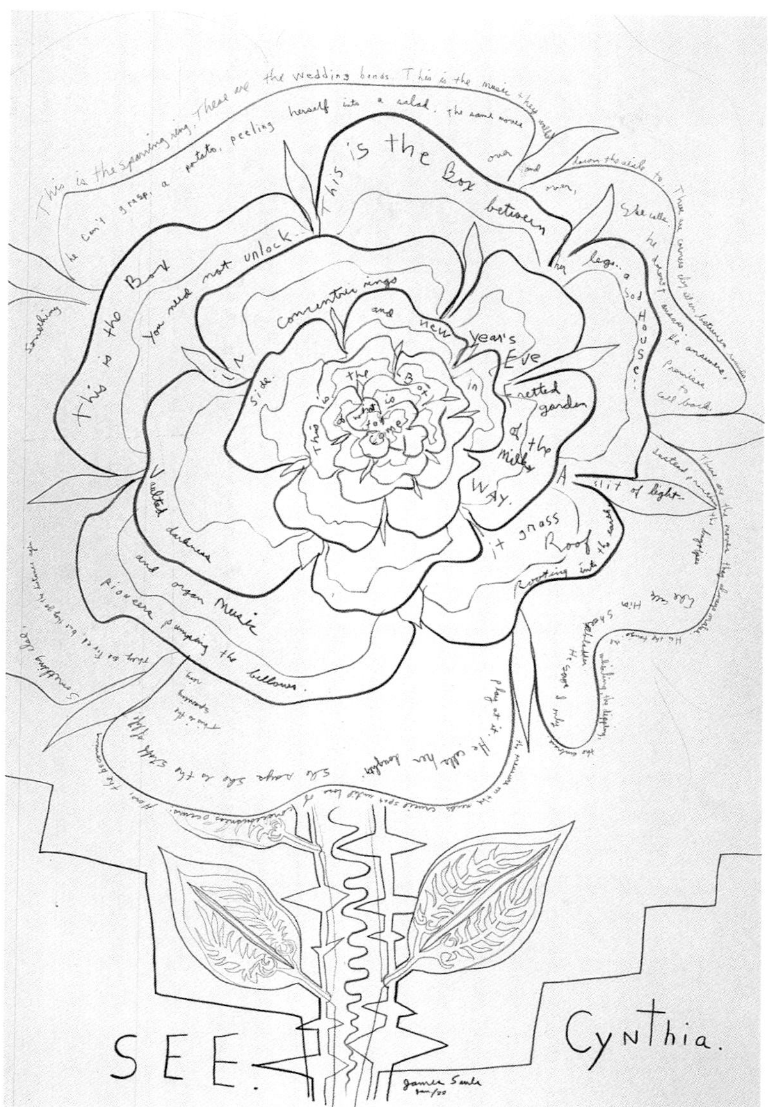

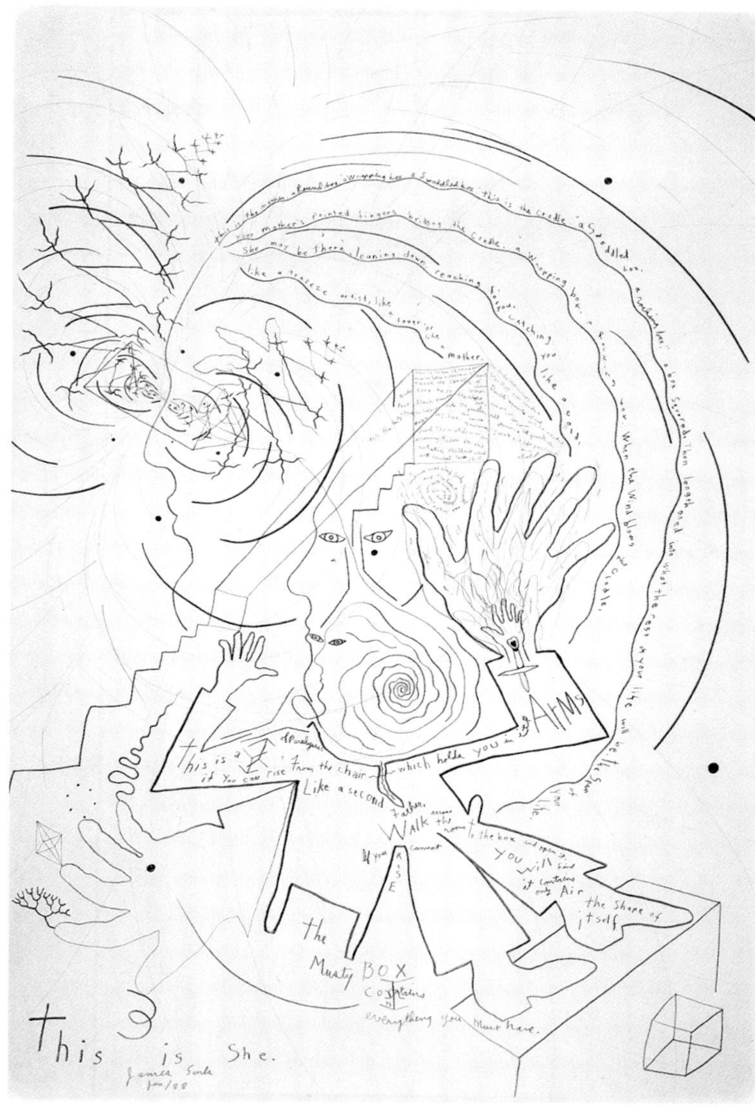

Too stiff to bend. Here is the turkey buzzard, the bird of
Jove, the basking shark and, too often, the bald eagle
Who talks turkey and gobbles everything in sight.
Here is the turnkey and the screw and his prick;
This is his box, a box not of their own making.

3.

This is a George III Fitted Necessaire: A high quadrangular
Box, the hinged cover with four turtle finials and steep
Encrusted gable roof surmounted by pine cones,
Chased all over with rococo cartouches, embellished
On the cover with floral festoons around beckoning hands;
The sides with landscape vignettes, and peacock and peahen
Amid flowering quinces and dead lilacs, drooping; the front
With Pan playing his rush pipes while mounting a maiden
Whose long hair sweeps around to the back where it forms
The pubic cover of Pander arranging a liaison between
Catherine the Great and Li Po who is offering her the moon
As a mirror. *This is a box where sweets compacted lie.*

4.

This is the box
between her legs—
a sod house,
a slit of light—
its grass roof
rooting into earth,
vaulted darkness
and organ music,
pioneers pumping
the bellows.
This is the box
you need not unlock—inside,
concentric rings
and New Year's Eve
in the fretted garden
of the Milky Way.
This is the box
of what is to come.

63
**James Surls and
Cynthia Macdonald**
***At the Round Earth's
Imagin'd Corners,*** 1988
Graphite on paper, triptych:
60 x 40 in. (152.4 x 101.6 cm)
each. Museum purchase
with funds provided by
Duke Energy, 88.36.

5.

This is the box of his madness—a blue norther, the icy wind
Which sweeps the warm, curved landscape like a steel broom.
Temper blows the box—the place they live, the place they join—
Into fragments, the way freezing can shatter a china plate.
He stands, ruing the day of his anger, holding her heart in
His hands as if that would temper the damage. Each splitting
Norther, each blue tempest leaves a wake in its path, sadder
Than mourners can bear. They gather in a circle anyway.
In a corner the child, round white face like a china plate,
Stands watching.

6.

This is a blue box, the one he hangs above
His head to crawl into when he cannot bear
The sky's brightness, or what may attack.
It was a hole for *in* and *out*, like a house for
A wren. This is a wood box, replacing the one he
Watched, watching and switching, beating himself
Like a contestant on *Jeopardy*. Now he walks,
His box above him. When he can, he makes more
Doors. Devils in red silk ties, rush out, leaving him
Free. A pole made of rushes, a straw pole
Gleans in the wind telling him the devils might
Have been angels. But he, in the middle of the wood,
Boots cracking Breughel's snows, already knows.

7.

This is the box of her madness. She checks instructions:
How to Tattoo a Heart on His Chest: Sterilize your needles.
Check the spectrum of colored powders. Double amounts of
Red will be needed. Make sure he is the right one, the one
You can never rid yourself of. Pour black powder into
The mortar, add glycerine. Ask him how big a heart,
The colors he likes, the name of his love. Swab
His left pectoral with alcohol. Begin. Prick
The motifs in the skin, allowing room for
The artistic accident which will reveal
Your skill. Continue until blood leaks
Through the right ventricle, and
The heart convulses. Then you
Will know you are
finished.

8.

There is the More Women Than Men Box:
Two women, second wives, look at each other,
Their perfect profiles carve the air between
Them into a silver marriage cup, octagonal
Tulip-form on bellfoot with wedding ring
Triangular collar. What suited them to a
T is gone. Their husbands dead, their children
Thriving, no, flourishing, they move dazed
Through months rectangular as caskets.

9.

This is the sparring ring.
These are the wedding bands.
This is the music they walked down the aisle to.
These are the corners they sit in between rounds.
These are the moves they always make:
His the tango, the whirling, the dipping,
The embrace, the pressure on the neck's
Crucial spot until loss of consciousness occurs;
Hers, the becoming something else, something he
Can't grasp, a potato, peeling herself
Into the salad. The same moves over and over.
She calls, he doesn't answer. He answers,
Promises to call back, instead practices
The bagpipes. She calls him *sheepsbladder*.
He says I only play at it. He calls her *doughy*.
She says she is the staff of life.
This is the sparring ring. They are
Tired, but they go the distance again.

10.

This is a box of paralysis: if you can rise
From the chair, an indifferent father who
Holds you in his arms, walk across the room
To the box and open it, you will find it contains
Only air the shape of itself. If you cannot rise,
The musty box contains everything you must have.

11.

This is the box of their love.
A match box, a box of rice.
What's been said once
Will be said twice.
This is a match box,
A catch box. They light
The fire. This is the box of love,
The box of desire.
Out there is the box of bone,
The six-foot bungalow,
The wooden kimono.
In here is home,
A box of wicker and wire
And wool, and desire.
This is their treasure box,
The box of their trove,
A *wrapping box*,
A *rocking box*.
This is the box of their love.

—*Cynthia Macdonald* [43]

a substance that can exist in two or more different forms. The cabinet—an old handmade nail box that had belonged to the artist's father—was imbued with personal meaning for Reaben. His father had been an amateur inventor; by converting an ordinary container from his workroom into a ceremonial object, Reaben both paid tribute to his father's hobby of invention and in Oedipal fashion outstripped his artistry. The original drawer pulls are replaced by gilded bones and the side and interior of each drawer is decorated with a symbol. (Additional symbols, including the psi sign of the Greek alphabet and the astrological sign for Cancer, are painted on the back of the cabinet, upon which also is inscribed: "Dream strange and clear here on earth.") Painted on the top of the cabinet is a floating ladder. Eyes, which animate the front face of the cabinet, are cut into the wooden surface and painted with phosphorescent paint.

Exploring the drawers and reading the inscription and various signs on *Allotropic Cabinet* implicates the viewer in a disquieting and hermetic ritual, recreating the artist's own dream life. In an undated journal entry, Reaben recorded:

> I woke up one night dreaming a strange dream, I opened my eyes and their [*sic*] were these two eyes. Floating in front of my face, gold eyes staring at mine. And they could be a hallucination, so I had to watch it just to see what it did, and it wasn't a hallucination it didn't just dissolve. It pulled itself back just a bit and I could see its features, like the face was sorta like purple light. The eyes were definitely a metallic luminous gold—I looked into the eyes and they were made up of scales—that became individual flames—the eye became huge and I could see people walking with candles.[47]

When Reaben created *Allotropic Cabinet* he was already aware that he carried the HIV virus; in the summer of 1989 Reaben died of complications due to AIDS. Among the last works he left behind was a remarkable notebook of thirty-one drawings that chronicled his confrontation with death; the notebook came to be titled *Death Threats* and entered the museum's collection a year later. William Steen acted as partial collaborator in this series; he had discovered the original notebooks (apparently 1930s lecture notes and diagrams from science classes) in a garage sale, and knowing Reaben's interest

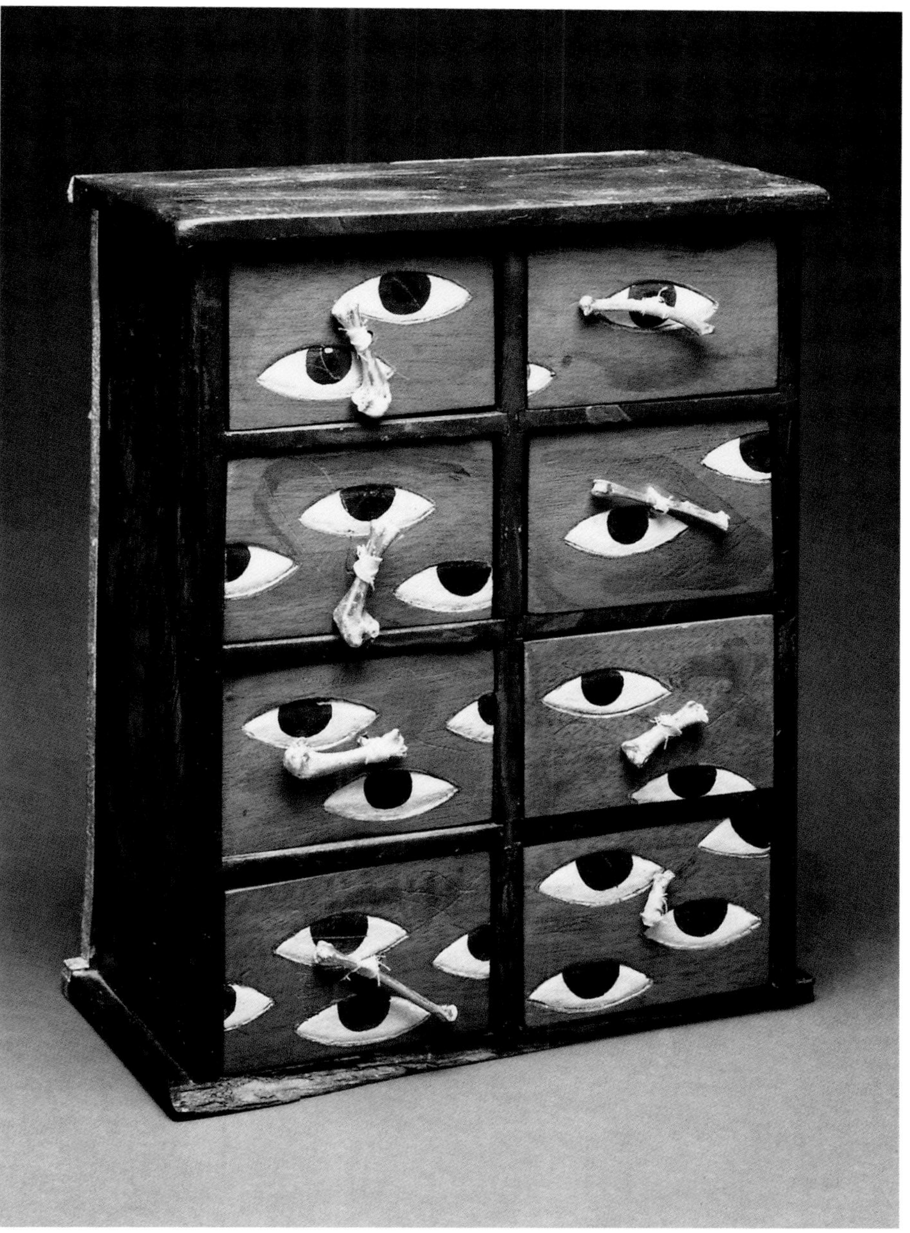

64
James Reaben
Allotropic Cabinet, 1988
Gouache, gold leaf, phosphorous, and collage on mahogany and pine box, 12½ x 10 x 5 in. (31.4 x 25.2 x 12.9 cm). Gift of Katie Kaim Kitchen, 92.237.

in used materials, offered them to him.[48] Reaben then began to rework the pages; the first sheet is washed in dark ink, an ankh-like icon fills the page and inscribed across the top are the words "Mother [fate] Father." Shortly after beginning this series, Reaben's right arm became paralyzed, and the subsequent drawings offer an increasingly vivid record of the artist's physical degeneration and spiritual resolution. Aided by Steen, he introduced gold-leaf on page four, in part a tribute to Arthur Rimbaud's "Illuminations," and gold became both image and ground as the series progressed. A stabbed figure, an all-seeing eye, and a crucifix are among the images that appear on the following pages. The final two pages are just sheets of gold. *Death Threat* (plate 65), page 26, is the most starkly revelatory of the series. Louis Dobay has noted that Reaben's act of confrontation was also his salvation:

We hear the cry of Reaben, who is "Whispering the forgotten name" of God. He describes a "silence burning [the] whole sky." He hears this silence, and at last, whispers, "I Have Opened the Gates." If we can read this as his final overcoming, then we can understand the image as conveying the breakdown of separation between Reaben's material existence and his visionary experience of the greater beyond. In fulfillment of his Artaudian self-symbol, the threat of death is an irony because Reaben remains in mortality long enough to leave a sign of his overcoming.[49]

While few could follow Reaben into the absolute abandonment of his last works, his interest in investigating alchemy and ritual imagery was shared by a number of contemporaries, including Danny Williams, Virgil Grotfeldt, Sharon Kopriva, and Dee Wolff. While formally disparate, these artists are united by their quest for spiritual resonance. Archetypes drawn from non-Western or ancient civilizations have provided powerful metaphors for these artists; as Williams has recently written, "During the twentieth century, the concept of archetypes has refocused attention upon, and perhaps also dulled the mystery of [antiquity's] vital rites and symbols. In a modern world awash with images, in the face of an incalculably vast and frequently insoluble body of scientific, technological and sociological information, have fundamental human yearnings really changed? Is it not our ancient and continuing responsibility to discover those touchstones which speak again to our deepest and most lasting concerns?"[50]

Danny Williams brings a scholarly understanding of world cultures to his studio. He studied anthropology at Southern Methodist University before receiving a graduate degree in painting from the University of Iowa. In 1977, a Fulbright grant took Williams to India, where he was fascinated by the juxtapositions of "stupendous antiquity and modern industrialization, time-tested cultural mores and a thickening veneer of urban Westernization."[51] His paintings of the following years explored the formalist grids of modernism, while related collages and drawings embraced more idiomatic imagery. By the mid-1980s, Williams began to incorporate decorative elements from Islamic art and schematic imagery from literary sources into his paintings; by the end of the

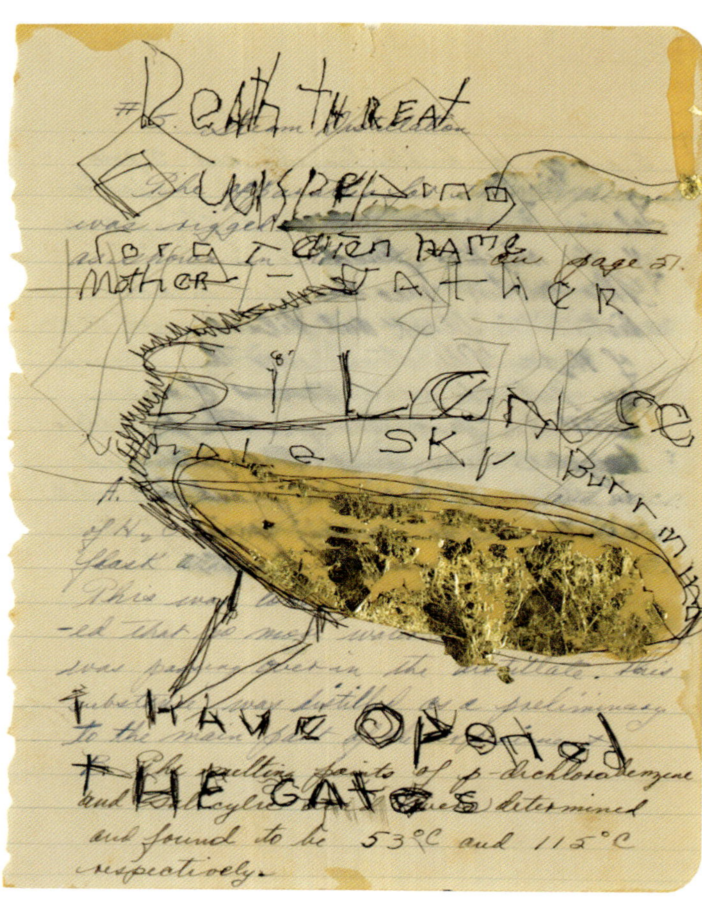

decade he began to investigate sculpture as well.

Wand, 1995 (plate 66), displays Williams's exacting craftsmanship and allegorical command. Created in collaboration with Harry Geffert (see plate 38) and Ken King at Green Mountain Foundry, *Wand* combines direct and lost-wax casting techniques to create an image of seamless delicacy. The brilliant verdigris patina gives *Wand* the appearance of the bronze artifacts of Hellenistic civilizations, while the image is drawn from Sir James George Frazer's 1890 anthology of myth, *The Golden Bough*. Also one of the chief sources of T.S. Eliot's "The Wasteland," *The Golden Bough* is a detailed exploration of magic and religion, centered on the ideas of kingship and power. As Frazer chronicles, "The Golden Bough" has persisted through civilizations as an emblem of the unity between authority and natural order, an image of renewal and rebirth from one generation to the next. Williams has further commented:

> The image of a truncated, leafing branch is a hoary symbol suggestive of regenerative potency, mystic rebirth, and transubstantiation. From classical representations of divining rods held by Didyma's priesthood and Aeneas' magical branch in Virgil, through Medieval Golden Legends and variations on Adam's Tree of Mercy, to more recent appearances in Wagner's *Parsifal* and Frazer's extensive treatment in *The Golden Bough*, the power of this image persists.[52]

Virgil Grotfeldt has pursued related themes of regeneration in his drawings, paintings, and sculptures. A native of Illinois, Grotfeldt moved to Houston in 1977, following extensive studies at Eastern Illinois University and Tyler School of Art. As the artist later recalled, he spent a number of years purging his work of the artistic conventions he had learned in school, and in the early 1980s he discovered that the element of chance could liberate his imagination.[53] Using sheets of wet paper, Grotfeldt would coat them with unstable materials—including salt, bronze powder, and coal dust. As the paper dried, images would emerge from the ground that could then be silhouetted and elaborated upon. In an interview in 1990, Grotfeldt stated: "Almost every time there's some human face or forms already there. At that point I come in and define them, identify them, and start painting out things I don't want any longer."[54]

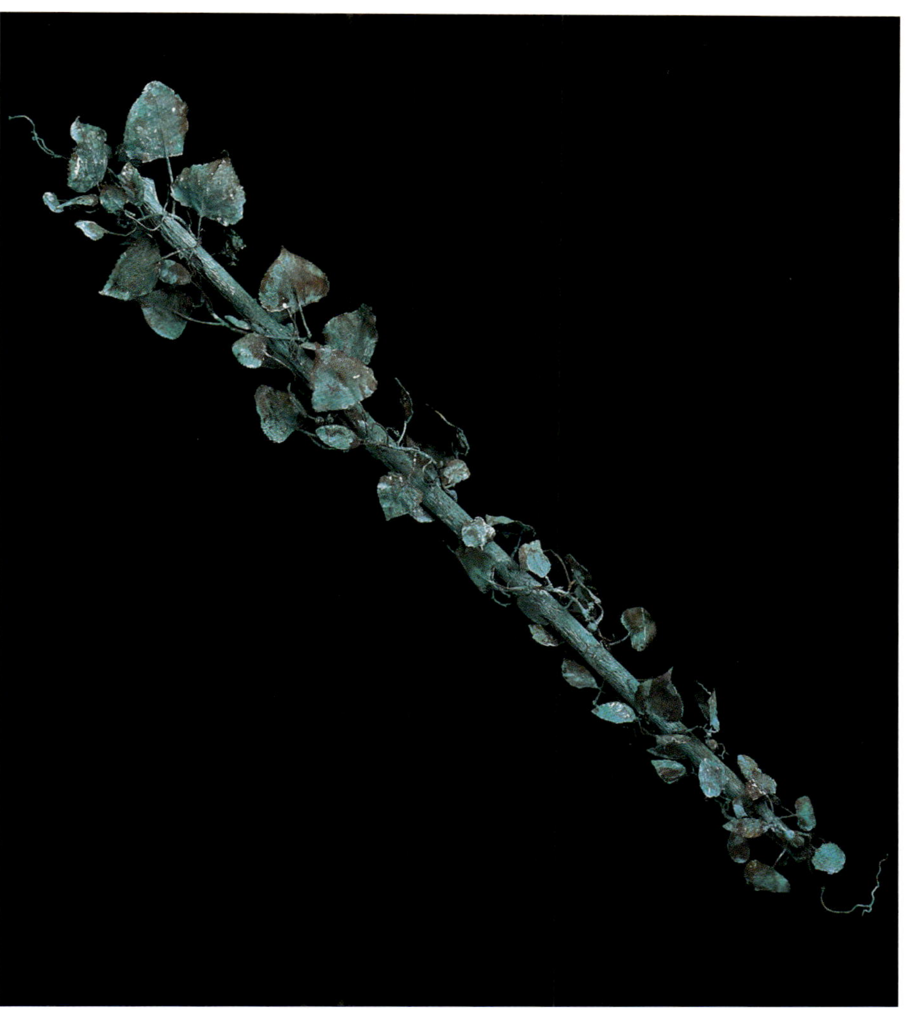

66
Danny Williams
Wand, 1995
Bronze, 62 x 9 1/2 x 6 1/4 in.
(157.5 x 24.1 x 15.9 cm).
Museum purchase with
funds provided by Nona and
Richard Barrett, 98.437.

This method of discovering and editing images is central to understanding Grotfeldt's work, and he has stated that "the psychology of the process" was as interesting to him as the resulting compositions.[55] The first works of this series were intimate in scale and evoked a deliberate primitivism; as the series progressed, the imagery became more unified and Grotfeldt began to use increasingly large sheets of paper.

Burning Crosses, 1988 (plate 67), is among Grotfeldt's first monumental drawings, and it is both specific and provocatively ambiguous in its imagery. Grotfeldt has identified the Symbolist Odilon Redon as among the artists to have the most profound influence on this work of this period, and like Redon, Grotfeldt explores the

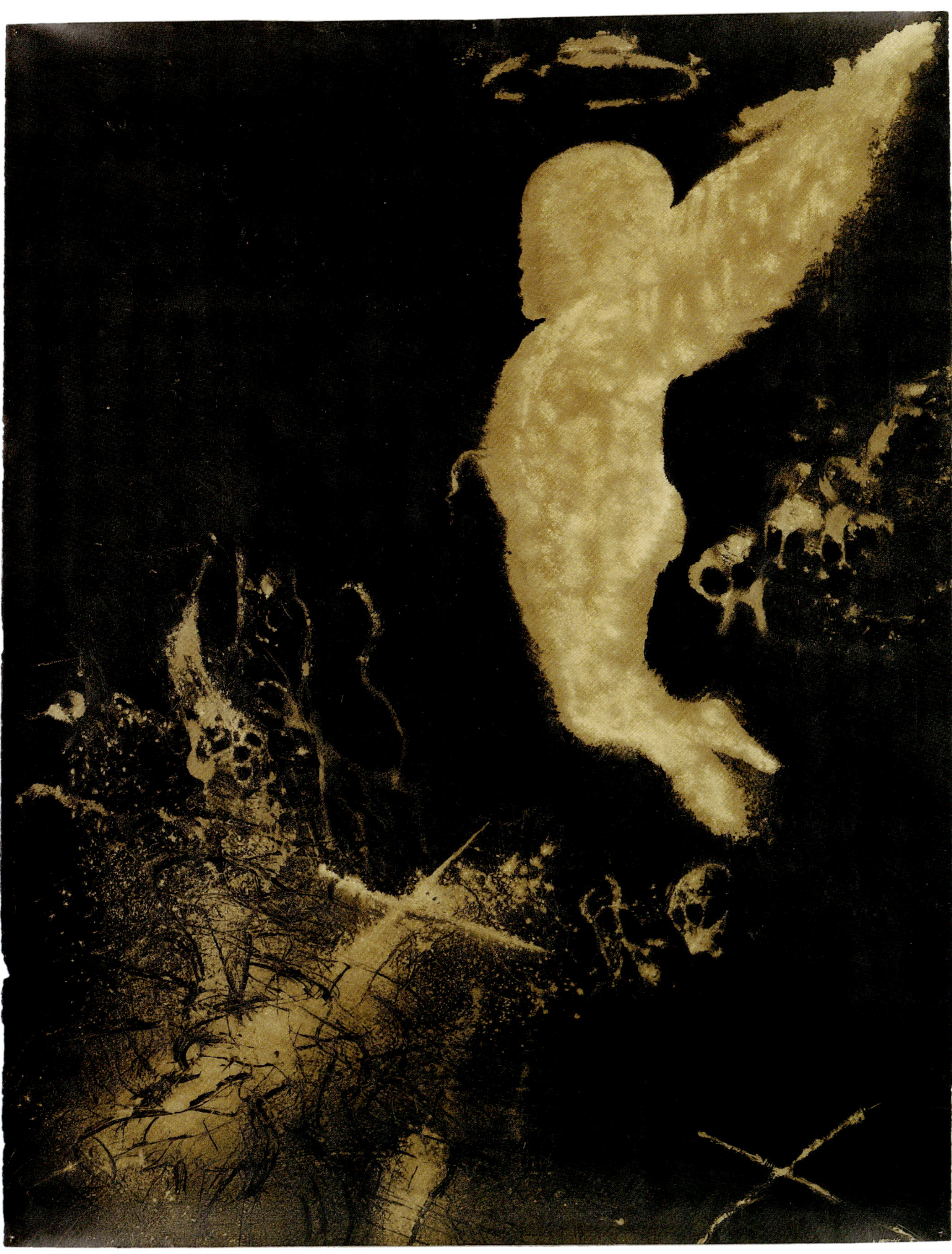

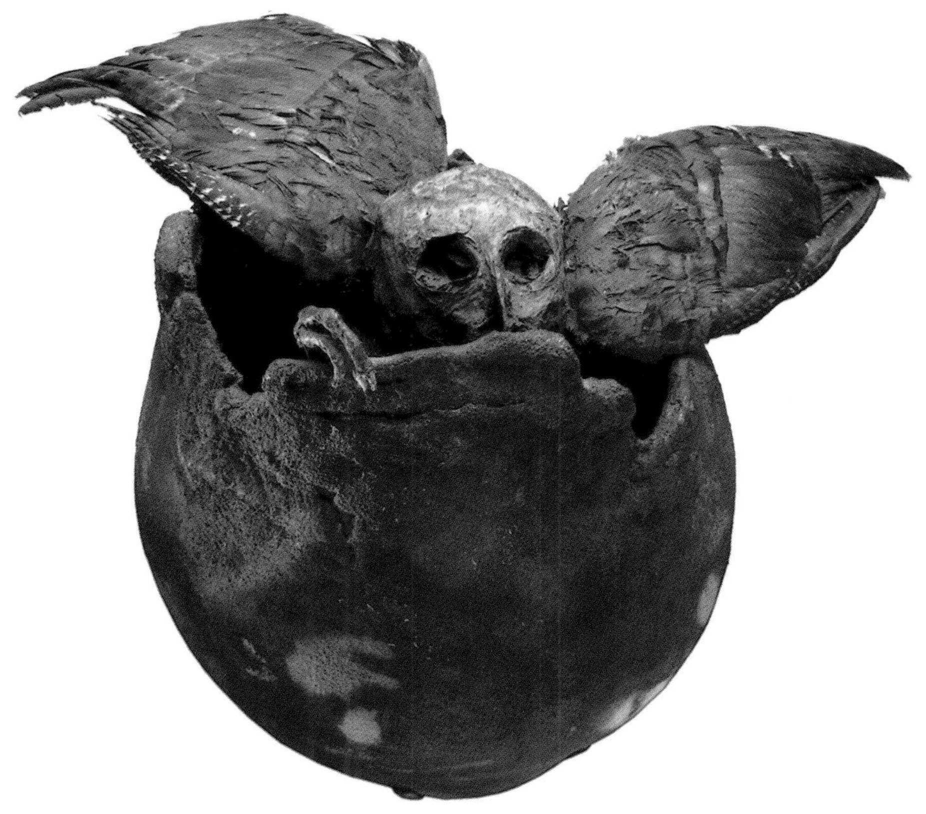

realm of dreams and the unconscious. A cherubic figure dominates the composition, hovering over what can be read as a pile of burning crosses, and a large X is also inscribed on the lower right. Skulls seem to emerge out of the darkened ground, appearing as a macabre chorus behind the main figure. Grotfeldt gives images of destruction and redemption equally free rein; by leaving the narrative implications of these images unresolved, he charges the composition with a starkly emotive power.

Sharon Kopriva similarly examines the mystery of death. Kopriva attended the University of Houston, where John Alexander (see plate 23) and James Surls (see plates 24 and 63) were among her mentors, and the university's Lawndale Annex provided a testing ground for her early work. A 1982 visit to the ancient Nazca burial sites in Peru confirmed an interest in ritual imagery; burial figures became the central motifs of her compositions, and Kopriva mined both Nazca and Catholic cultures for metaphors of transformation. In the mid-1980s, encouraged by a growing friendship with Edward and Nancy Reddin Kienholz (see plate 77), she translated her work into three dimensions, using such humble media as cloth, papier-mâché, wood, and clay to create theatrical tableaux of remarkable immediacy.

Dusk, from Kopriva's *Urn* series, 1989 (plate 68), is among Kopriva's most eloquent and haunting images. The artist has commented: "Most [of the works in this series] are burial pots with figures resting peacefully inside. *Dusk* instead is emerging from his enclosure. He is bird/human, giving him the ability to free himself from his vessel. He is non-violent, but definitely a creature of the night."[56]

At a glance, Kopriva has created a convincing simulacrum of an ancient artifact; however, *Dusk* cannot be mistaken for a Pre-Columbian relic. The winged and hollow-eyed figure emerging from the urn is clearly fantastic and summons up the creatures of Francisco de Goya's *Caprichos*. Furthermore, the artist has invested the work with a certain ambiguity: as much as the figure appears to have come from the grave, the egglike shape of the urn suggests that the figure is being hatched into the world. Thus death and regeneration are subtly balanced, and Kopriva has acknowledged that these works offer a resolution to her Italian Catholic upbringing: "It's

kind of a dark religion in a way. . . I've retained a lot of things that are negative. But I think the end is positive. I think my work is positive. I think of it more as a personal resurrection or rebirth."[57]

A reappraisal of Christian belief also lies at the heart of Dee Wolff's work. A graduate of the University of Houston, she also studied at the Museum School, Houston's C. G. Jung Educational Center, and the Oomoto School of Traditional Art in Kameoka City, Japan. Beginning in 1974, *The Stations of the Cross* became her focal theme in an extended series of works on paper and paintings. For Wolff, an investigation of the passion of Christ was not only a means of coming to terms with Christian ideology, but also a personal journey and spiritual resolution.

Selah. Station IV. Meeting the Mother, 1990 (plate 69), takes as its point of departure the Fourth Station, the moment when Christ meets his mother on the road to Golgotha. Wolff renders this emotionally charged encounter in triptych format, working from a dark ground to capture the effect of an illuminated manuscript. The artist has described her imagery as improvisational rather than strictly iconographic.[58] Three black silhouettes can

68
Sharon Kopriva
Dusk, from the *Urn* series, 1989
Mixed media with terra cotta urn, 25¾ x 31 x 26 in. (65.4 x 78.7 x 66 cm). Museum purchase with funds donated by James Surls and Charmaine Locke, 91.1600.

67 *opposite*
Virgil Grotfeldt
Burning Crosses, 1988
Enamel and bronze powder on paper, 80½ x 60 in. (204.4 x 152.4 cm). Museum purchase with funds provided by Dr. Eric Scheffey, 90.409.

be discerned in the background of each sheet: on the left masked figures cascade across the page like fallen angels; the center page is filled with images of crosses paired with glowing symbols of Buddhist enlightenment; on the right four figures descend upon a womblike haven, which also draws the crosses to it—crowning the entrance to this haven is a radiant dove. The word "Selah" is taken from Psalms; it is a Hebrew word used to designate a pause or moment of silence between the musical lines of the prayers. Wolff has reflected on her *Stations of the Cross* series:

> I use the theme not as an homage to the tradition of Catholic thought, but to explore the common denominators in world religion and in-depth psychology. I find the correlation between the passion of the life of Jesus and the movement towards consciousness to be the truth of the Stations of the Cross. I believe that the idea of "nowness" or "the timeless moment" is the uniting factor of mystical thought not only in Eastern religion but also in Western religion, and that is the impetus of my work. Each painting represents a moment of self-realization, insight, an epiphany, which is one person's own small truth and also a universal truth. It is, I believe, a very basic human desire to unite with the "other," to honor the transcendent function of our consciousness.[59]

The 1980s saw a blossoming of Hispanic culture in Texas and North America, a development recognized by such exhibitions as the Museum of Fine Arts, Houston's 1987 *Hispanic Art in the United States: Thirty Contemporary Painters and Sculptors*. Among the chief themes of this presentation were the ways in which Hispanic identity has been shaped by both native cultures and the Catholic church. Octavio Paz wrote of the spirituality that has threaded through Pre-Columbian, European, and Hispanic traditions:

> For the ancients, the *phantasma* was the bridge between the soul, prisoner of the body, and the exterior world (worlds). For the surrealist poet and painter, the oneiric image is the messenger of the inner man. Poetry and art allow that prisoner, transfigured, to escape. . . . The apparition of these images in the works of Hispanic artists is disturbing. They are hieroglyphs of vengeance, but also of illumination, poundings on a closed door. Their paintings are neither metaphysics nor the knowledge of inner man nor poetic subversion, but rather something more ancient and more instinctual: icons, talismans, altars, amulets, effigies, travesties, fetishes—objects of adoration and abomination.[60]

In the 1988 *Ceremony of Memory* exhibition that traveled to Texas in 1990, curator Amalia Mesa-Bains focused

69
Dee Wolff
Selah. Station IV. Meeting the Mother, 1990
Gouache on handmade paper, triptych, 28¼ x 62¾ in. (71.8 x 159.4 cm) each. Museum purchase with funds provided by Crowley, Marks & Douglas in memory of Alice Dziadul Banker, 91.1421.

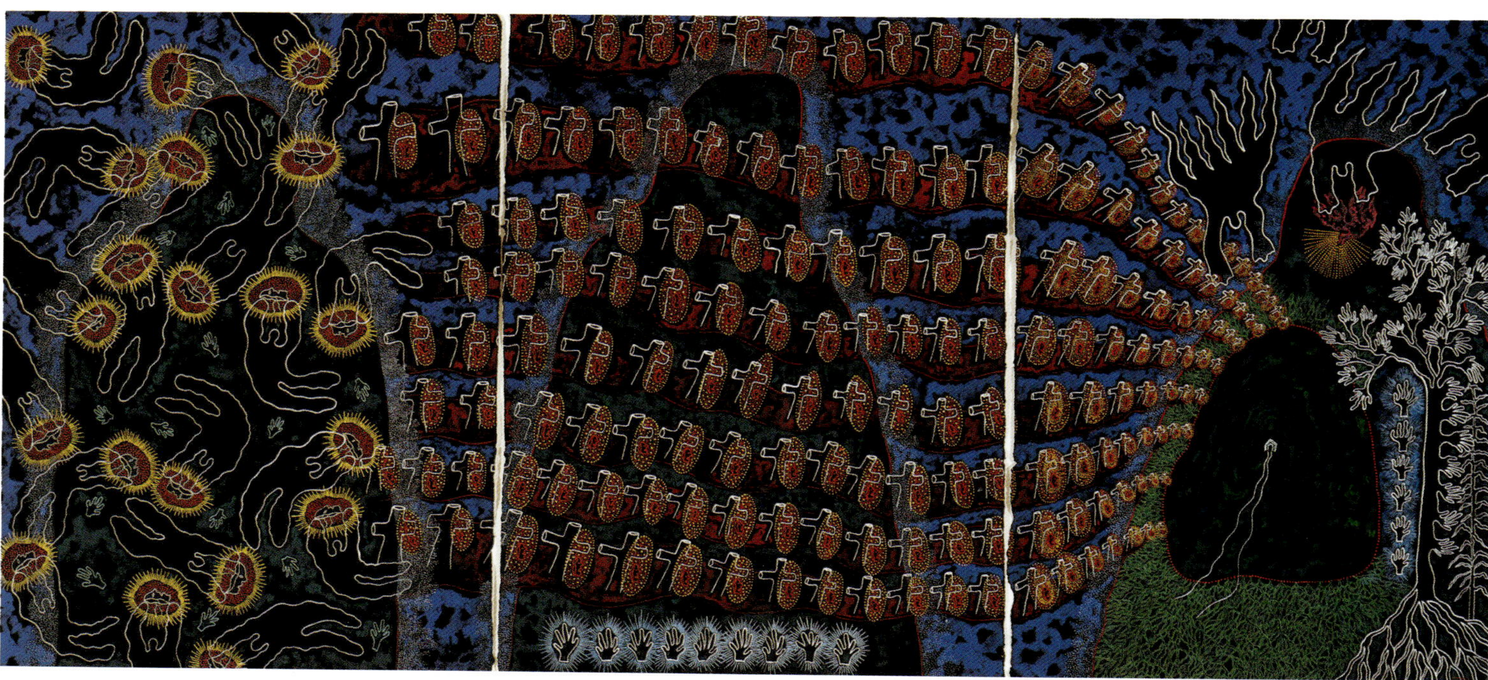

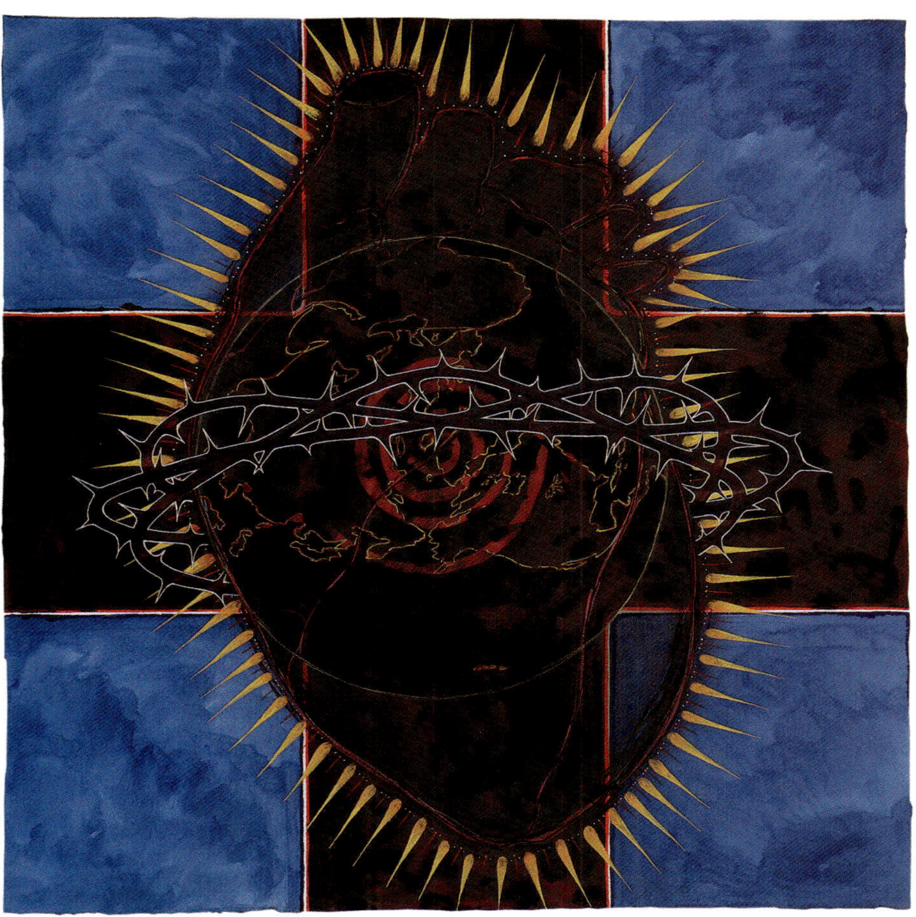

70
Benito Huerta
Corazón de la Tierra, 1989
Gouache, graphite, spray
paint, and ink on paper,
36 x 36 in. (91.4 x 91.4 cm).
Museum purchase with
funds provided by Roman
and Paula Martinez, 90.303.

her presentation on the "vital phenomenon of the ceremonial and spiritual art of contemporary Hispanic artists." She further commented: "Within this genre of work is the aesthetic of fragmentation, recollection, and ceremony. It is an aesthetic which springs from the experience of the émigré, the *curandero* and the lost devotional. In the experience of separation and expatriation lingers the sense of loss. Fragments of childhood secrets, cherished family rituals are recollected and joined with images, icons, and phenomena."[61]

Benito Huerta, Kathy Vargas, and Celia Alvarez Muñoz have all drawn upon cultural memory, and the familiar iconography of domestic *ofrendas* and *retablos* has fueled their work. Unlike the earlier generation of Texas artists who went to Mexico to investigate the historic traditions of Indian and Catholic cultures, these artists drew upon intimate experience. And as their work demonstrates, their appropriation of religious iconography yielded to a range of meaning, reflecting not only the artists' shared heritage, but also their individual pursuits.

Benito Huerta was born in Corpus Christi.[62] A graduate of the University of Houston, he continued his studies at New Mexico State University, Las Cruces. He returned to Houston in 1981, and over the following decade he became established both as artist and curator. Among other projects, he organized the important *Chulas Fronteras* exhibition for Houston's Midtown Art Center in 1986, and in 1994 was among the founding editors of *ArtLies* magazine.

Huerta's early paintings reflected the raucous junk-aesthetics of Texas funk and the parallel *rasquachismo* of Hispanic border artists; as his work progressed, drawing took on a more primary role and his direction became more cross-cultural. In the late 1980s he began to use specifically Catholic iconography while responding to the dialectics of postmodernism; as Michael Ennis observed, Jasper Johns and pious calendar art became equally important points of reference: "The two cultures that Huerta actually mediates are the secular and the sacred. He creates what is basically a religious art in the profoundest sense, transforming the symbols of his Catholic upbringing into a global passion play in which the entire planet is scourged and sacrificed."[63]

Corazón de la Tierra, 1989 (plate 70), conflates the "Sacred Heart" icon with an urgent political message. Huerta depicts a crucified earth—literally "The Heart of the World"—as an object of sacrifice, ringed by a crown of thorns. The polar ice cap seems to dissolve in a red maelstrom, warning of the loss of the protective ozone layer. Huerta has recorded:

> The drawing's idea is about our earth being our heart and vice versa. It is a planet that we are currently and slowly nailing to the cross. What we do, as individuals and as citizens of the earth, we do unto ourselves. The somewhat religious metaphor is used simply because the planet, our earth, is sacred, for it gives us life. And yet we do not see that, therefore, our predicament.[64]

The iconography of Christian shrines is also central to the photographs of Kathy Vargas. Born in San Antonio, she received both undergraduate and graduate degrees from the University of Texas at San Antonio. In 1985 she became the director of the Guadalupe Cultural Arts Center, one of the largest community-based centers for Chicano studies in the United States. After a period devoted to painting, Vargas launched her career as a photographer in 1980–81, documenting the vernacular architecture and elaborate yard shrines of the Mexican neighborhoods of East San Antonio. Following this series,

71
Kathy Vargas
St. Frog Sandwich, from the
Seafood Saints series, 1989
Hand-colored gelatin silver
photograph, 23 x 17½ in.
(58.5 x 44.5 cm). Museum
purchase with funds provided
by Clinton T. Willour in
honor of Marlee Miller,
93.18.

she began to create her own shrines in her studio, not as objects in themselves, but as subjects for photographic study. Vargas combined the themes of *vanitas* found in classic still-life arrangements with an acute awareness of the commemorative function of shrines, and a number of works were specifically dedicated to departed friends. Vargas further used in-camera montage techniques and tinted the resulting prints to give added resonance to her compositions.[65] These formal devices permitted a ghostly layering of images and atmospheric tones that can be allied with the literary devices of Magic Realism. Diana Emery Hulick has observed: "Vargas's montages reflect

the reality of the human spirit and the imagination. Like [Gabriel García] Márquez, Vargas is concerned with creating ritual out of daily life. Common objects and experiences are reexamined in new contexts and from different viewpoints."[66]

St. Frog Sandwich, 1989 (plate 71), from the *Seafood Saints* series, injects a lighter note into Vargas's oeuvre. As Vargas has recalled, her previous series had included a number of images of small dead creatures. On showing these works to New York dealer Ivan Karp, she asked if such themes would be too morbid for a New York audience. Karp's assured her to the contrary: "We have frog's legs for lunch here." This offhand comment inspired Vargas to create *Seafood Saints*, dedicated to her favorite seafood items, "the martyrs of my appetite."[67] In *St. Frog Sandwich* two frogs caught in a *danse macabre* are displayed on an old-fashioned sandwich tray that the artist had found in a flea market in San Antonio—flowers are arranged around the edges in the place of garnishes. A *trompe l'oeil* overlay of broken glass (created through montage) enhances the illusion that the artist has photographed an actual shrine. As subjects for consumption—whether for lunch or as still-life objects—the frogs are posed between life and art, the profane and the sacred.

Celia Alvarez Muñoz's photographs and installations explore her identity as a Mexican-American woman. Muñoz grew up in El Paso and earned a B.A. from the University of Texas at El Paso in 1964. Over the following decade she lived on both the East and West coasts; she moved back to Texas in 1975, making her home in Arlington. Shortly thereafter, she returned to school at the University of North Texas, Denton, where Vernon Fisher (see plates 26 and 125) was among her mentors. Fisher encouraged Muñoz to explore various narrative strategies, and her artist's books and captioned photographs of the early 1980s recount family history, fairy tales, and popular legends. Much like Kathy Vargas, she arranged her photographic subjects in a studio setting, staging tableaux and still-life arrangements that both reflect and diverge from the conventions of Hispanic visual culture.

"Ella" y 'El,' 1987–89 (plate 72), is on one level an essay on the rights of passage which women and men face as they come of age and marry. The front panels of the cabinet frame photographs of the kinds of arrangements

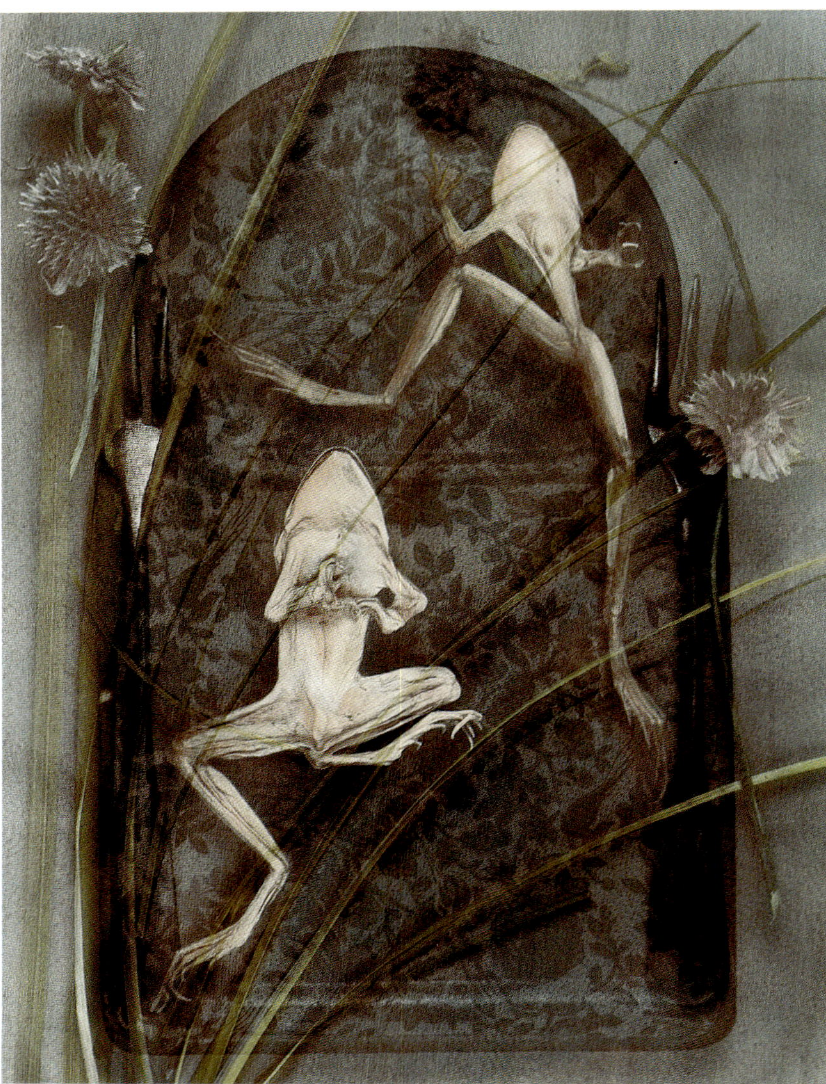

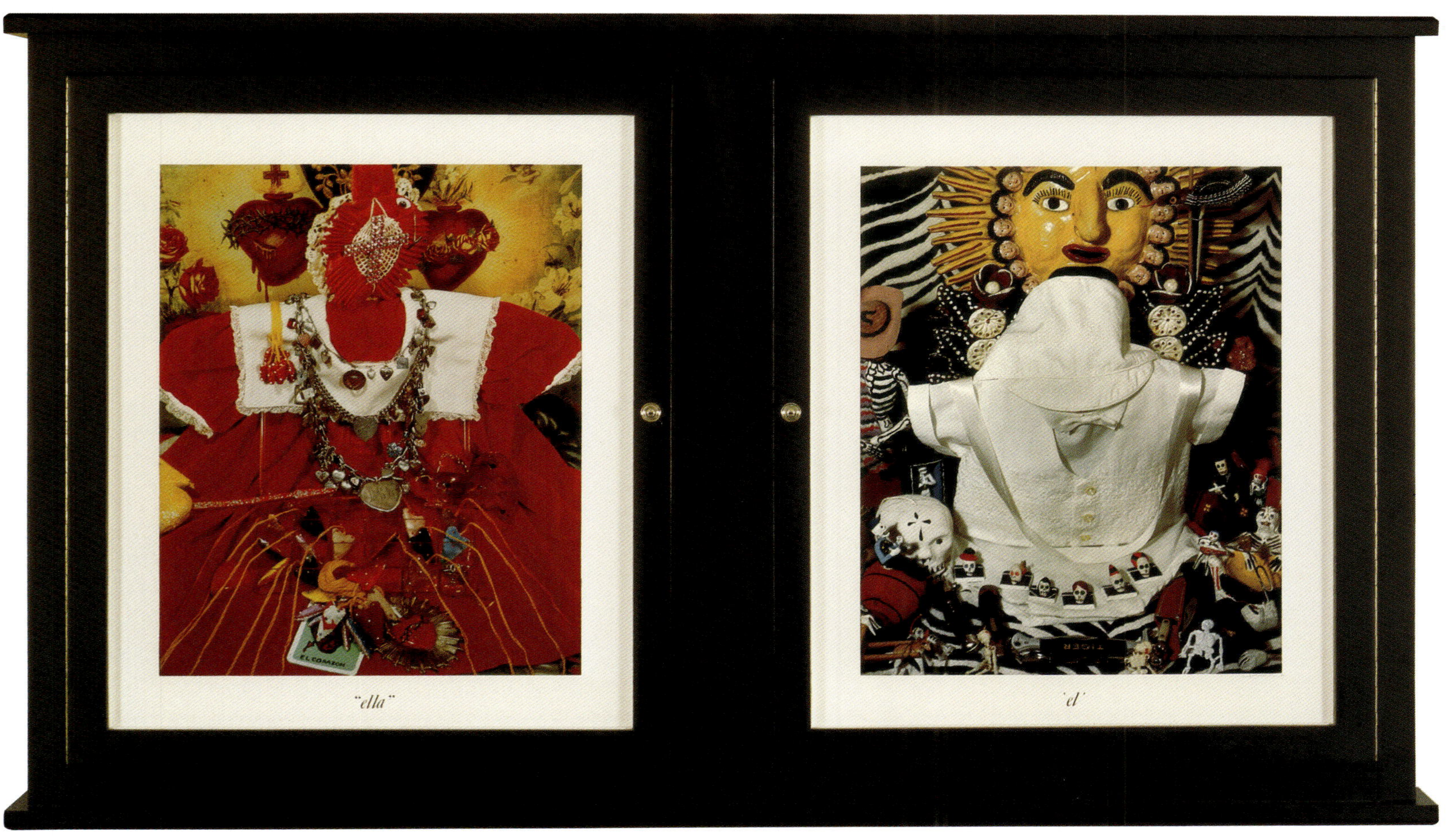

72
Celia Alvarez Muñoz
"Ella" y 'El,' 1987–89
Maple cabinet, Cibachrome
photographs, letterpress type,
fabric, ribbon, buttons,
amulets, and found objects,
31$\frac{1}{2}$ x 54 x 4 in. (80 x 137.2
x 10.2 cm). Gift of The
Barrett Collection, Dallas,
Texas, 98.720.

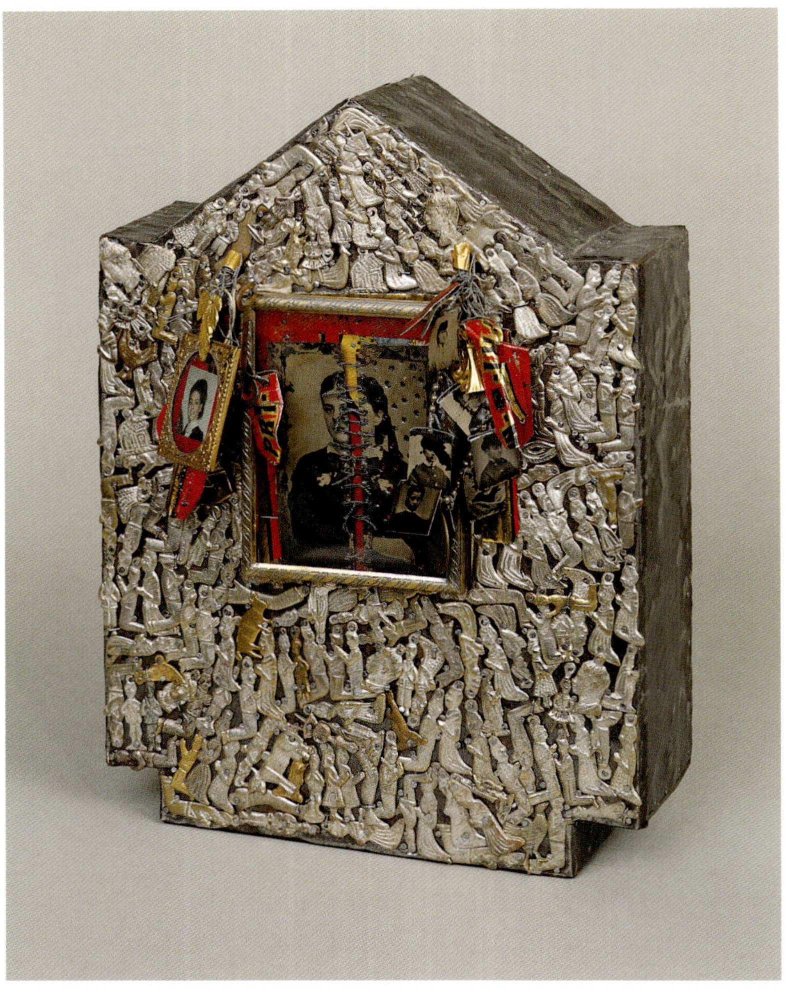

calaveras (skulls). She (Caterina) fancies fine old funeraries. To start a new life together, they roamed old countrysides, looking for old cemeteries.'"[69]

At the same time, Muñoz invites the viewer to deconstruct her stereotypical images of sacrifice, sexuality, and violence. Michael Ennis has commented: "In *"Ella"* *y 'El*,' Muñoz appropriates a number of conventions from Mexican art.... But the richly layered Mexican elements in *"Ella"* *y 'El*,' aren't intended as declarations of Muñoz's bicultural identity. Instead, the photographs of ornately costumed his-and-hers *santos*, framed on the outside of this secular folding altarpiece, and the elaborate symbolic attributes displayed inside, ironically emphasize a pan-cultural theme, the complex expectations and conflicting roles imposed on modern relationships."[70]

Appropriating Mexican religious icons as a means of delving into autobiography is not limited to Hispanic artists; Karin Broker, who is best known for her monumental drawings and graphic work, has also created a number of boxes that owe a debt to the *cajas* that act as informal reliquaries in Hispanic households.

Born in rural Pennsylvania, Broker attended the University of Iowa, Atelier 17 in Paris, and the University of Wisconsin, before coming to Houston in 1980 to join the faculty of Rice University. Houston introduced Broker to Mexican culture, and her Catholic background made her particularly receptive to the religious art of Mexico. In 1986 she began creating boxes out of found materials. Diane Kett has described the evolution of these works: "The physically aggressive arrangement of scrap metals, hammered nails, and twisted wire almost camouflage the spiritual intensity of these pieces. Gleaming metal *milagros*—the tiny embossed images historically offered in prayer to the saints—were initially used by Broker simply as decoration. But [more recently] the spiritual significance of the milagros became an integral part of the work's content. The production of each box is no longer mere creation, but now sincere supplication—a private religious ritual that invokes salvation from human misery."[71]

Self-Portrait on Valentine's Day, No. 1, 1991 (plate 73), reflects a particularly difficult moment in the artist's life. Shortly before Valentine's Day, she was attacked by a

of religious objects and personal mementos found in domestic *ofrendas*. However, as suggested by the titles printed on each image, these constructions address sexual archetypes: *"Ella"* shows a little girl's dress, shockingly crimson, surrounded by romantic charms and images of the Sacred Heart; *'El'* shows a boy's white christening gown surmounted by a sun god and surrounded by knives and Day of the Dead skeletons.[68] The cabinet doors open to reveal additional texts and a collection of talismans that complement and reinforce the images seen on the front panels. Created to honor the marriage of friends, Dallas artists Kay and James Chefchis, *"Ella"* *y 'El'* celebrates the union of male and female. As Moira Roth has documented, "When the tabernacle doors open, we read in the narrative that 'Jaime collects dog who bit her face, prompting her to reexamine her childhood expectations about beauty, romance, and courtship.[72] The central image is an anonymous tintype portrait—split down the middle—that Broker had noticed resembled an older version of her high-school prom portrait. A copy of the prom portrait and other vintage tintypes are also attached. Blood-red ribbons frame the portraits, and the box is covered with traditional *milagros*, hammered in by the artist both in invocation and entreaty. Much as Michael Tracy reconstructed the grand-scale ecstasy of religious experience in such monumental works as *Memento Mori [Agony]* (see plate 52), Broker adopts the intimate folk customs of Hispanic culture, finding in the traditional acts of expiation a means of personal renewal.

Austin artist Steve Brudniak addresses the existential with a tongue-in-cheek sense of humor. Born in Topeka, Kansas, Brudniak grew up in Houston and worked both as a musician and songwriter before making assemblage his chief means of expression in the mid-1980s. In a biographical statement of 1988, Brudniak wittily encapsulated his career in sculpture: "Work in three-dimensional construction began as early as age 6, until more serious work in clay became recognizable as art. Experimental work in clay on cubist and realist themes eventually led to works in mixed media. Application of surrealist and other subconscious means of creation, combined with scientific elements mostly involving electricity, quickly became the obvious niche for creative exposition."[73]

Divining Implements for Prophets, Messiahs, and Physicians, 1989 (plate 74), appears at a glance to be an unaltered found object—an old-fashioned cabinet of medical instruments, perhaps. However, upon closer examination, each instrument is revealed to be a highly crafted construction, combining the handles of bakelite utensils with various tools, including the workings of a pressure gauge, a microphone, and an electric meter, and a modified projector bulb reflector lens. The ordinariness

74
Steve Brudniak
Divining Implements for Prophets, Messiahs, and Physicians, 1989
Altered tools in wooden case, 3½ x 17¼ x 11 in. (8.9 x 43.8 x 27.6 cm). Museum purchase with funds provided by Crowley, Marks, & Douglas in memory of David Lee Nitcholas, 92.234.

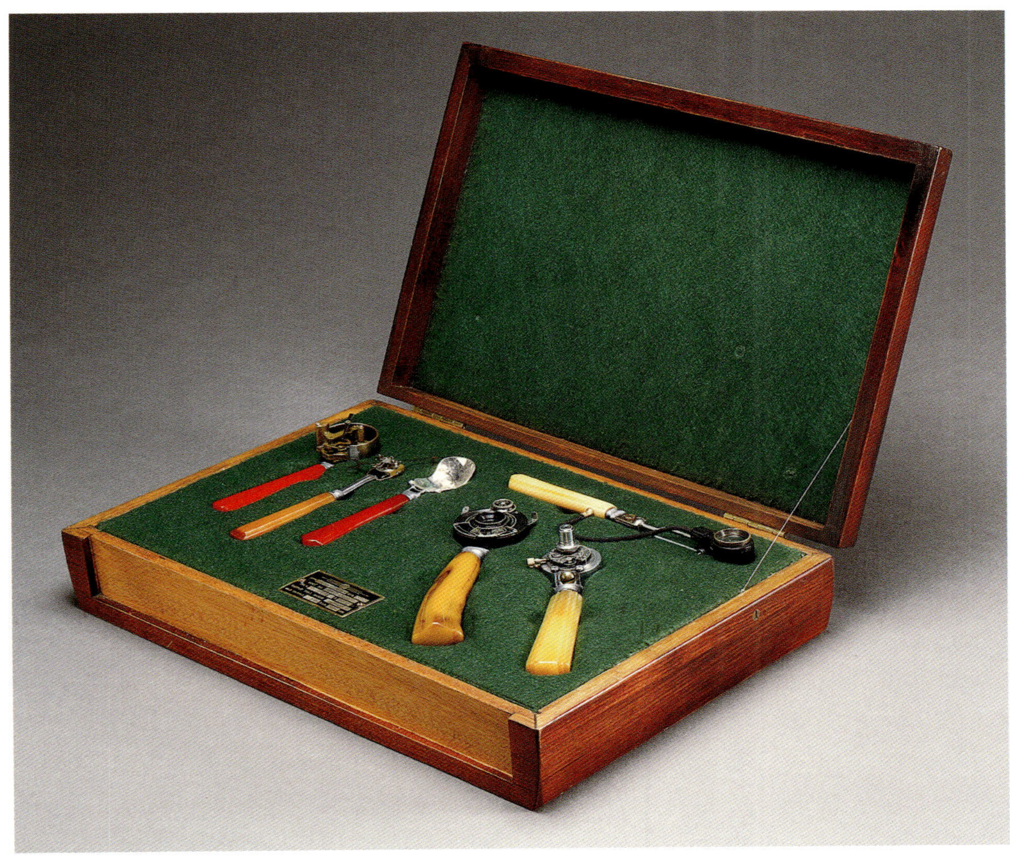

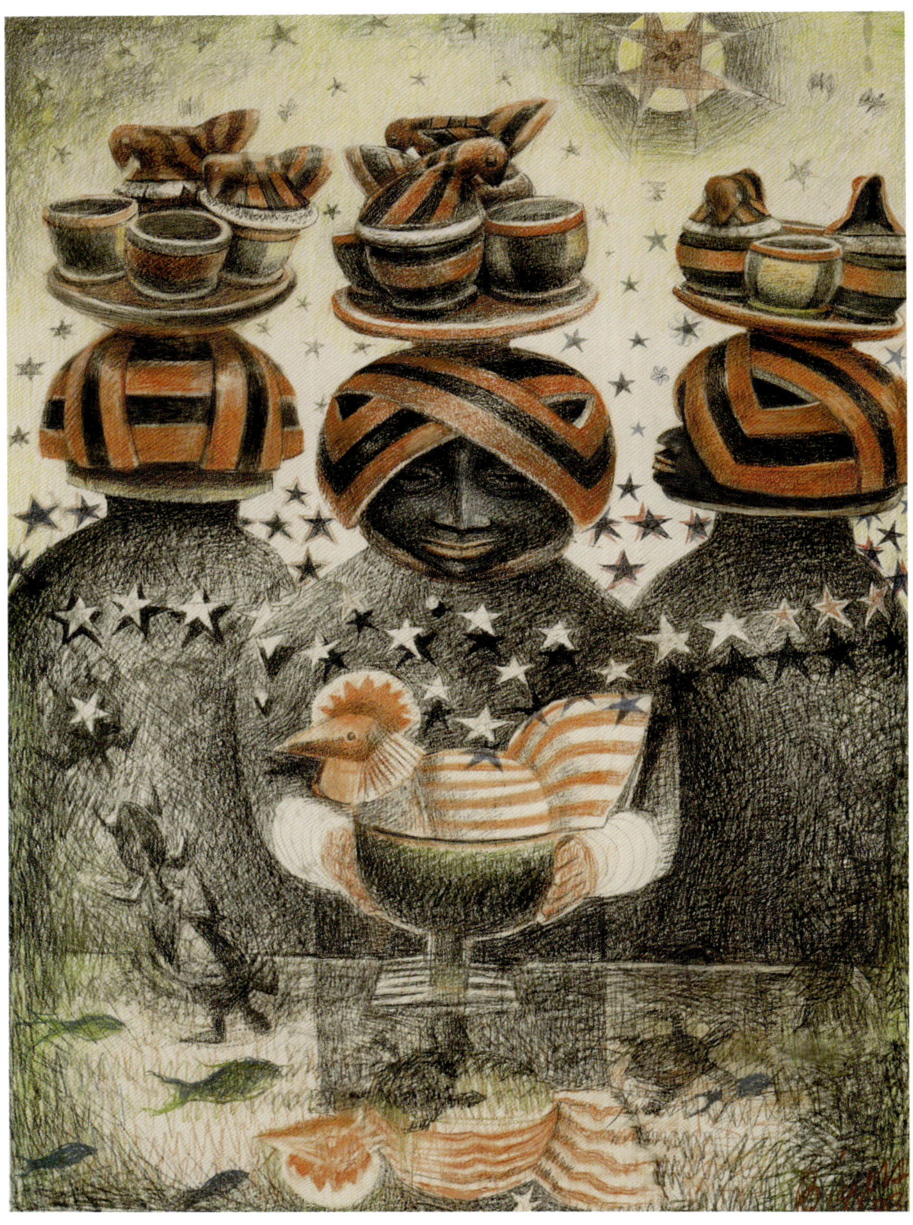

75
John Biggers
***Study for View from the
Upper Room***, 1994
Conté crayon and pastel on
paper, 41³/₄ x 30³/₈ in. (106.1
x 77.1 cm). Museum pur-
chase with funds provided by
African American Art Advisory Association and partial
gift of the artist, 94.187.

of the felt-lined cabinet that cradles the objects confers
authority upon them—by exploiting the viewer's recognition of the familiar, Brudniak convinces us of the util-
ity of his extraordinary assemblages. The implications of
the title are gently subversive; the artist has commented:

> *Divining Implements for Prophets, Messiahs, and Physi-
> cians* represents quackery at the personal level. The parts
> are condition indicators, magnifiers and reflectors. They
> are the self deceptions, knivings, and manipulations gone
> through to insure specific desired outcomes in the future:
> Lies, people pleasing, spying, impersonating, brownnosing,
> codependency, enabling, premeditated conversation, flat-
> tery, ladder climbing, idolatry, incantations, and worthless
> repentances, to name a few. All normal human re-
> sponses to fear and need. I look for a cure. I look for love
> and truth, I look for the future. I am a physician, a mes-
> siah, and a prophet, and therefore I need a set of tools.[74]

Much as Hispanic artists looked to Pre-Columbian
cultures as a means of understanding their
heritage, so too did African-American artists
study the cultures of Africa to trace their ancestral traditions. The sources of African pride can be traced back to
such authors and artists of the Harlem Renaissance as
W. E. B. Du Bois and Alain Locke, and Aaron Douglas and
Lois Mailou Jones. In the 1990s, a renewed interest in
the spiritual heritage of African-Americans was promoted
by such exhibitions as *Black Art—Ancestral Legacy: The
African Impulse in African-American Art*, organized by
the Dallas Museum of Art in 1990, and *Face of the Gods:
Art and Altars of Africa and the African Americas*, organized by the Museum of African Art, New York, in 1993.[75]

Both these exhibitions carefully examined the ways
in which African religious customs survived in American
culture. Robert Farris Thompson observed:

> In pain and terror West and Central Africans came
> across the waters to the Americas. The Middle Passage,
> endured from the sixteenth to the nineteenth centuries,
> was horrific. . . . But Africans arriving on the shores of
> North and South America did not forget their ancestors
> or their gods. Covertly at first, they honored them at
> points of reverence and honor. In North America,
> under pervasive oppression, they managed to establish
> altars to their dead even while blending with the Christi-
> an world.[76]

Edmund Barry Gaither, writing on the evolution of the African-American identity, noted that as Africans were bereft of their heritage through the diaspora to the Americas, "the African creative impulse of American black artists was directed into folk and utilitarian art, especially in objects for personal use, such as canes and other small decorative items. The artistic impulse to express personal, often religious visions later became objectified in paintings, sculpture, and the constructed environment."[77]

John Biggers, who first came to Houston in 1949 hoping to establish a link to the Mexican mural renaissance that formed his early work (see plate 11), ultimately found his greatest inspiration in Africa. A UNESCO fellowship allowed Biggers to travel to West Africa in 1957, a journey that the artist described as "the most significant of my life's experiences."[78] This visit, enriched by the artist's first-hand encounter with the emergence of Ghana as an independent nation, was chronicled in such murals as the 1958 *Web of Life* (Texas Southern University, Houston) and the 1959–63 *Jubilee: Ghana Harvest Festival*, now in the collection of the Museum of Fine Arts, Houston (see Introduction, fig. 16).[79] However, the naturalism of these paintings gave way to an increasingly complex vision over the following decades, as Biggers began to explore the art and rituals of the Dogon and other African cultures as both formal and conceptual sources. At the same time, the customs of African-American folkways became increasingly central to Biggers's work, and by the mid-1980s he achieved a remarkable synthesis between African references and American culture.

Study for View from the Upper Room, 1994 (plate 75), takes its title from the traditional spiritual, "The Upper Room." The Yoruba headdresses, the astral imagery, and the tripartite presence of the figure (viewed frontally, in profile, and from the back) are mystical evocations of the cycles of nature, indicating both physical and spiritual renewal. The artist has commented that both time and space are key concepts for this composition: the headdresses echo the ideograph of the Great Serpent, who bites its tale to form an eternal circle, and the stars and waters encompass both heaven and earth.[80] Alvia J. Wardlaw has written of Biggers's work from this era: "Rebirth, another act of transformation, is most clearly represented in the ritual of baptism in water, which occurs in Christian and in ancient African traditions. In African cultures, as in other civilizations, water is associated with power and life.... The green water is the source of life, the home of the crocodile and the turtle, a place where humans can no longer dwell but to which they must return for nourishment. Just as the waters of the womb serve as the first home in each human life, this reconnection with water signifies a return to one's pure beginnings."[81]

Biggers's pioneering investigation of African cultures broke the ground for the following generation of artists; however, as the work of Vicki Meek demonstrates, many African-American artists who addressed similar themes in the 1980s and 1990s adopted a radically different pictorial language. A native of Philadelphia, Meek attended the Tyler School of Art, the University of Wisconsin, Madison, and Queens College, New York. She moved to Dallas in 1980, and quickly became involved with the community, acting as an administrator and independent curator for such organizations as the Dallas Visual Art Center, the African American Museum, and the South Dallas Cultural Center. Beginning in the mid-1980s, Meek took her sculptures into the broader context of installation art. Combining ideographs drawn from Yoruba cultures with topical news items, Meek discovered a means to probe the history and present-day realities of African Americans.

The Crying Room: A Memorial to the Ancestors, 1992 (plate 76), was originally created for the *Fresh Visions/New Voices* exhibition at the Glassell School of Art. Among the most complex of Meek's installation works, it offers a sophisticated layering of sources, ranging from the bleak records of the European slave ships to the survival of Yoruba culture in the new world. Meek uses each element of the installation to subtle yet dramatic effect: the floor is covered with sand and a path of charcoal leads to the rear wall. As viewers follow this path, they are confronted by an elaborate ideograph on the rear wall and a line of memorial candles. As Bruce D. Kurtz has chronicled, this ideograph signifies "The Lifting of the Plate," or the final ascension that takes one from death into the realm of the ancestors.[82] An overturned flowerpot is an added symbol of death and resurrection. On the right-hand wall three panels of sardine tins represent slave

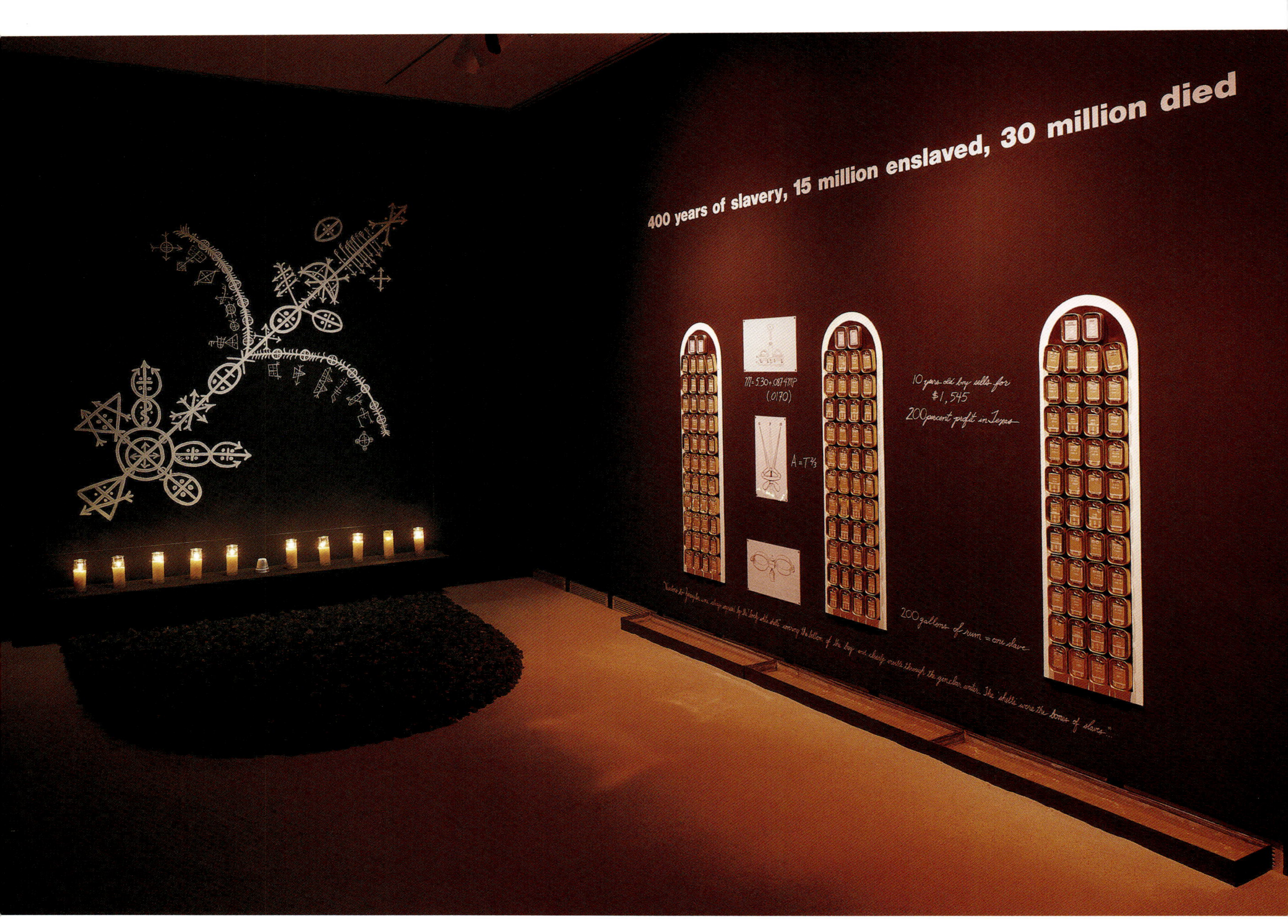

ships, and Meek has added inscriptions of the horrifying mathematical calculations of slavers who estimated acceptable losses. Below is a line of cowry shells. On the left-hand wall, Meek inscribed the words of a Yoruba chant, and a recording of this chant can be heard as well. Upon leaving the gallery, the visitor is invited to add a comment to the memorial wall.

The Crying Room: A Memorial to the Ancestors is a powerful commemorative statement, celebrating the survival of the spirit in the face of adversity. The artist has written:

> Public memorials are important because they allow a society or a community to reconcile its grief. The collective grief over the loss of the millions of ancestors lost during the Middle Passage and through the mass lynchings of the 20th century has never had an outlet. Consequently, this pent up grief manifests itself in many inexplicable ways.... *The Crying Room: A Memorial to the Ancestors* is meant to allow us to remember and grieve for all those many ancestors whose lives were sacrificed. The Yoruba ideographs all relate to the passing of loved ones to the ancestral realm. The lava rock walkway to the *Lifting of the Plate* ideograph provides a purifying path to the eternal ascent. The shells represent our return to the Motherland, by sea, as we arrived here. The overturned flower pot symbolizes the way death turns life upside-down.[83]

It seems fitting to conclude this chapter with Edward Kienholz, one of the great innovators of American art, who time and again examined the forces that turn life upside-down. Born in Idaho and educated in the Pacific Northwest, he moved to Los Angeles in 1952. Coming of age at a moment when Abstract Expressionism dominated the international avant-garde, Kienholz both appropriated the painterly strategies of the New York School and undermined them through a brilliant use of found materials. His first assemblages were created in 1955; he soon shifted from the abstract mode of these early constructions to reliefs and freestanding sculptures made of the detritus of junk culture, eerily animated by mannequins, doll parts, and dress forms. In 1961–62 he created his first major tableau, *Roxys* (Collection Reinhard Onnasch). Over the following decade his wry humanism found expression in such works as *The*

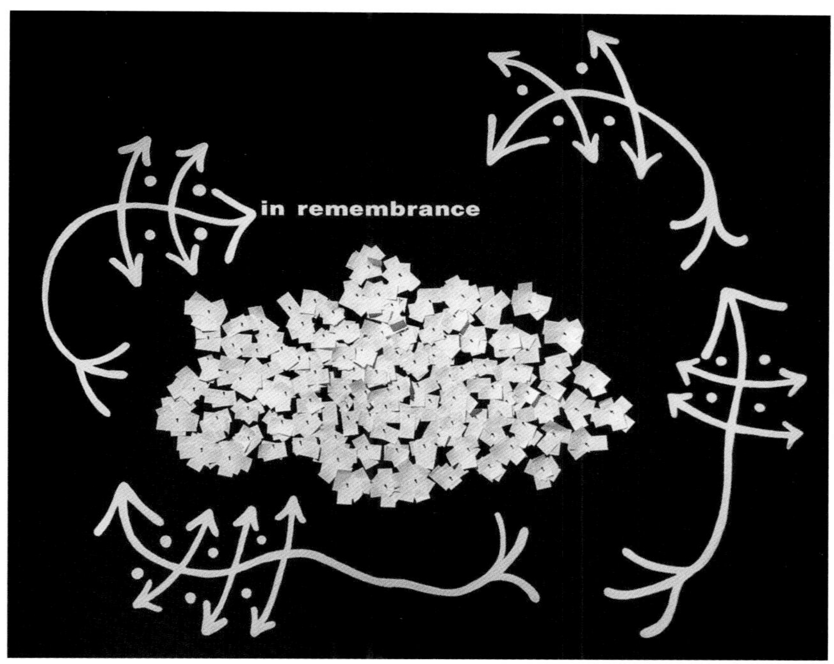

Illegal Operation, 1962 (Betty and Monte Factor Family Collection), *The State Hospital*, 1966 (Moderna Museet, Stockholm), and *The Portable War Memorial*, 1968 (Museum Ludwig, Cologne). In 1972 the artist Nancy Reddin became both Kienholz's partner and full-time studio collaborator.

Friendships with Walter Hopps, then director of The Menil Collection, and collector Marilyn Oshman drew the Kienholzes to Houston a number of times in the 1980s. In 1988, the Kienholzes made an extended visit to jury the Blaffer Gallery's *Houston Area Show*, an experience that brought them into contact with an increasing number of Houston artists, and three years later they made Houston their winter home. Their engagement with the Houston community had an immediate impact: in 1993 the Museum of Fine Arts, Houston, exhibited the Kienholzes' *Merry-Go-World or Begat by Chance and the Wonder Horse Trigger*, a literal merry-go-round that reflected their world travels and moral concerns, and in 1995 Walter Hopps organized *Edward Kienholz: 1954–1962* for The Menil Collection. Perhaps more important to local artists was their encouragement of emerging talent and their friendships with such established figures as Sharon Kopriva and Lucas Johnson, who created major

76 *opposite and detail above*
Vicki Meek
The Crying Room: A Memorial to the Ancestors, 1992
Mixed-media installation, dimensions variable. Museum purchase with funds provided by AT&T New Art/New Visions and the Wilder Foundation, 93.255.

works during visits to the Kienholzes' summer home in Hope, Idaho.

Feedin' the Hog, 1994 (plate 77), is among the Kienholzes' final great collaborations. Created in Houston at a time when Edward Kienholz was coming to terms with his own mortality, the assemblage can be regarded as a veiled self-portrait. The repeated use of mirrors evokes the convention of the artist's self-portrait rendered as a mirror image, and the distorted mannequin of Howdy Doody in the center can be understood as an Everyman figure.[84] The lowering curtain in the background not only serves as a theatrical device, but also as an image of closure. Concrete objects are given illusionistic context by the painted backdrop of an empty room, and with dramatic bravura, the Kienholzes pit the image against the actual. For example, the chair back seems to cast a shadow on the support panel (contradicting the pictorial illusion of the curtain and the receding space behind it); at the same time, however, the lamp below the chair casts a real shadow over the painted shadow. Finally, inscribed in low relief in the curtain is the hauntingly ambiguous phrase, "The Fish is Always Time"; on the right panel of the composition the dummy is feeding a fish to a ferocious hog.[85]

If the fish of *Feedin' the Hog* is to be understood as time, the tableau takes on another reality, as time becomes a finite quantity about to be consumed by a force both rude and rapacious. The Kienholzes could be unsparing in their criticism of sanctimony, and a concurrent work titled *76 J. C.'s Led the Big Charade*, 1992–94 (collection of Nancy Reddin Kienholz), reflects Edward Kienholz's cynicism about "the hypocrite who prays in church on Sunday and then preys on his neighbors and associates the rest of the week."[86] However, Edward and Nancy Reddin Kienholz's art never mocked the spiritual, and frequently addressed the existential and moral issues of our times. As Marcus Raskin has noted, "For Kienholz, the material about us is not denied. It becomes the creative spirit's practical tool for a common good which includes the wretched, the excluded, and the forlorn. Mastery of the artistic scream and the material is the beginning of social regeneration. Kienholz was the master."[87]

In 1991, Miguel Cervantes organized *Mito y magia en América: Los Ochenta [Myth and Magic in America: The Eighties]*, the inaugural exhibition at the Museo de Arte Contemporáneo in Monterrey, Mexico, which surveyed artists from across the North and South American continents. One of the chief aims of this presentation was to posit a different history of Modernism, one that focused on content rather than formal concerns; as Cervantes stated in the introduction, a point of departure for understanding the twentieth century could be Paul Gauguin's query "Who Are We? Where Do We Come From? Where Are We Going?"[88] Charles Merewether elaborated: "Modernism can be rewritten as a series of excursions into hitherto uncharted domains of experience, consciousness, and knowledge. Primitivism, the savage, wildness and the mythic were informing concepts of this excursion."[89]

The history of twentieth-century art has been constantly invigorated by digressions from the mainstream and explorations of other realities. The Texas artists who have taken such excursions challenge us to reconsider who we are, where we come from, and where we are going.

77
**Edward Kienholz and
Nancy Reddin Kienholz**
Feedin' the Hog, 1994
Mixed-media assemblage with electric lights, two panels, 65 x 73 x 21 3/4 in. (165.1 x 185.4 x 55.2 cm). Museum purchase with funds provided by the Caroline Wiess Law Accessions Endowment Fund, 95.326.

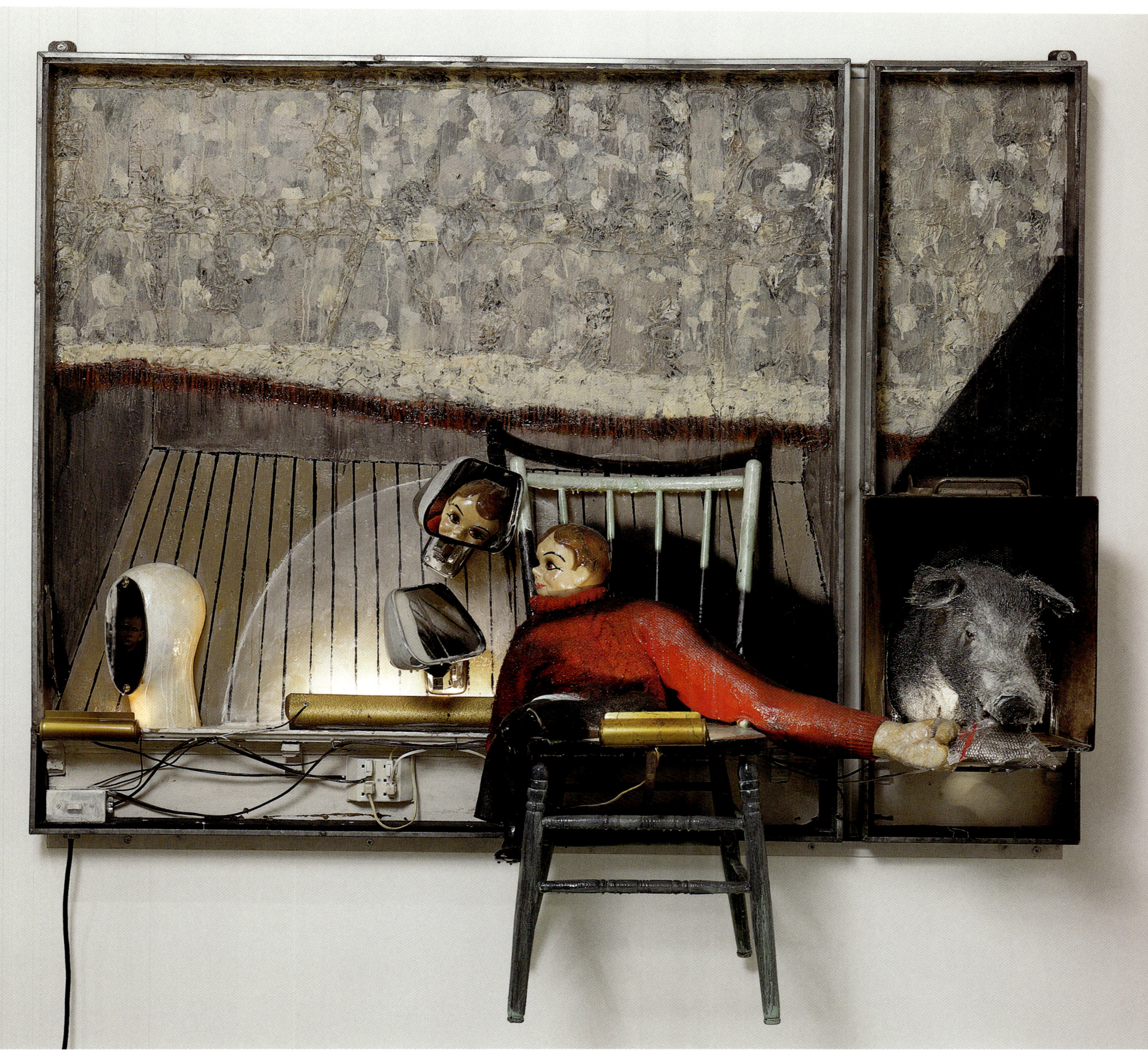

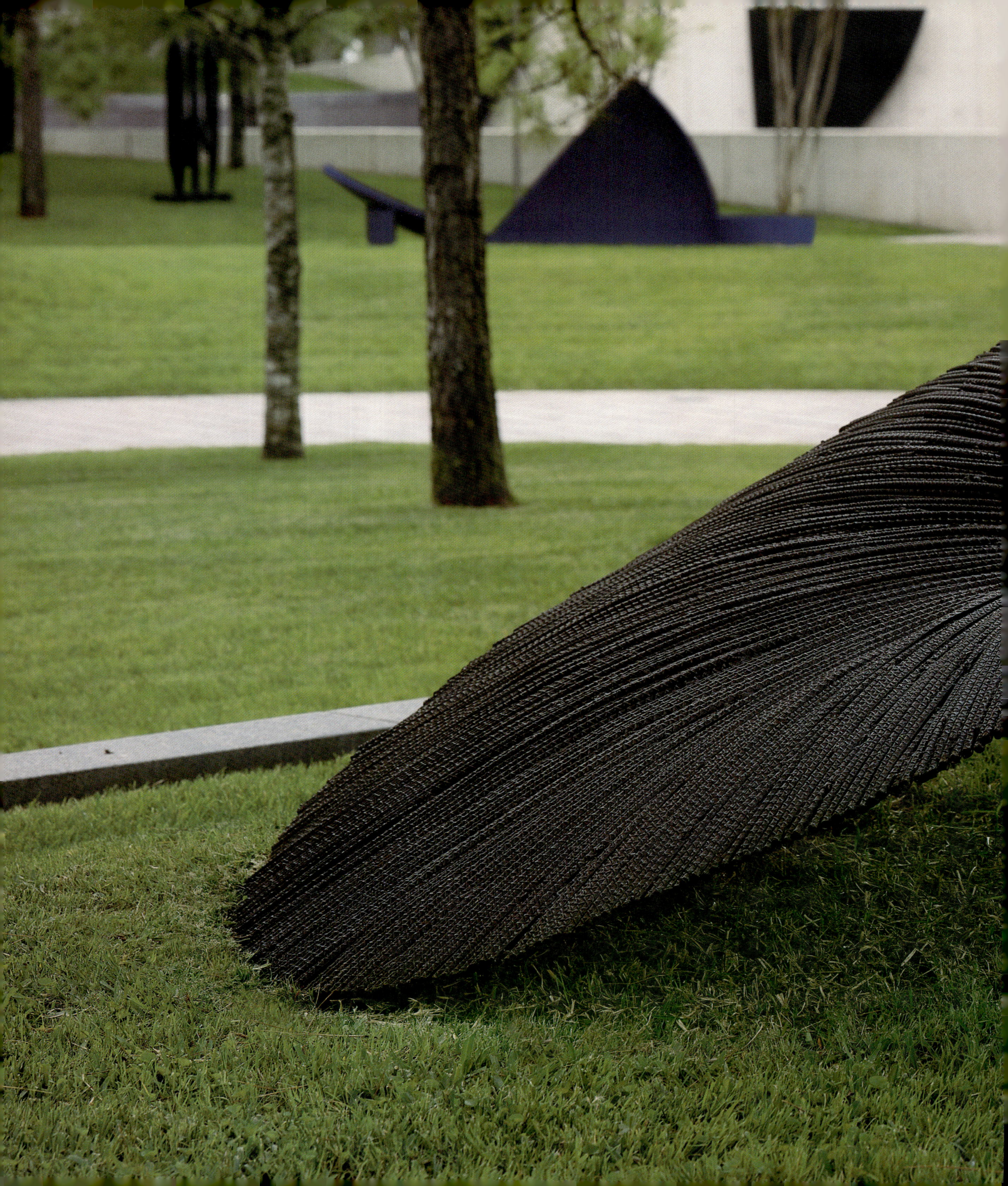

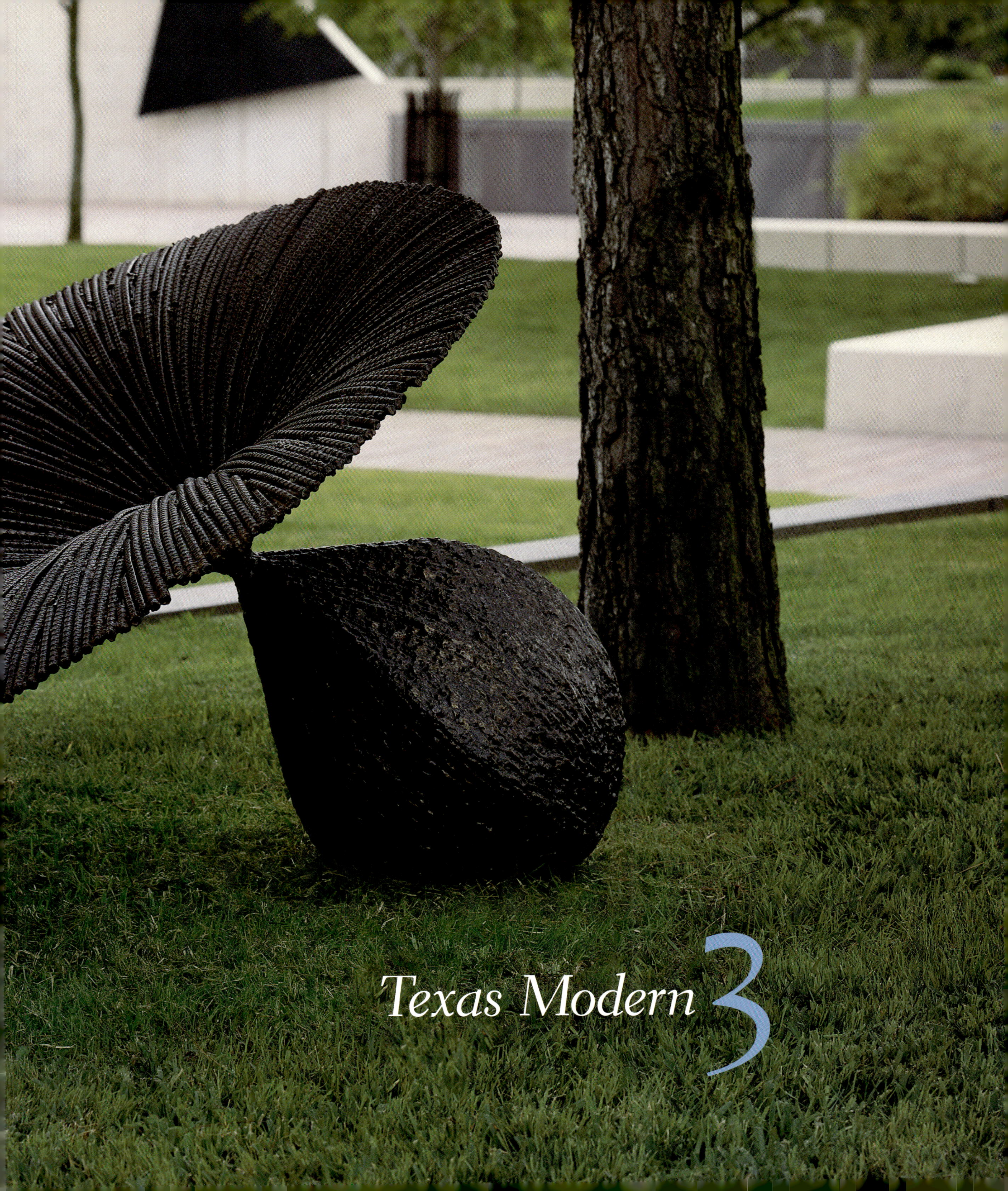
Texas Modern 3

Texas Modern

In the Southwest—in Texas, there is so little in one's surroundings to repeat and give substance to what the culture we inhabit—and study so assiduously—tells us are the real things, the valuable things in the surroundings where that culture grew. In Texas you have to make those things up. Texas is not only provincial— it's a province with little or nothing you can tie into that everything you learn (which always comes from somewhere else) tells you you should be tying into.

—Myron Stout, 1957[1]

Mark Rosenthal noted in his survey of abstraction in twentieth-century art that one of the tenets of Modernism was best summarized by Eva Hesse's description of her work as "total risk, freedom, discipline."[2] From Kasimir Malevich and Piet Mondrian to Agnes Martin and Gerhard Richter, the evolution of Modernism has been tied to that of abstraction, as successive generations of twentieth-century artists have sought meaning in the artwork itself. Or, as Clement Greenberg famously described the goal of Modernism in 1939, "Content is to be dissolved so completely into form that the work of art or literature cannot be reduced in whole or in part to anything not itself."[3]

Risk, freedom, and discipline are also qualities that have shaped Modernist art in Texas. While the first two chapters of this catalogue have addressed the aspects of Texas art typically defined by a sense of place—whether realist or visionary—there were also artists emerging from and working in Texas who sought to cast off geographical ties. Unlike such artists as Forrest Bess, Michael Tracy, and Vernon Fisher, who accepted and successfully overcame the challenge of reconciling a local identity with international currents, the artists discussed in this chapter annexed their work to the increasingly abstract and conceptual progress of Modernism.

Modernism was slow to gain an audience in Texas, and the first artists to move into abstraction received little encouragement, despite the pioneering efforts of such institutions as the Contemporary Arts Association in Houston and the Dallas Museum for Contemporary Arts. In 1947, for example, visiting artist George Biddle stated of the Texas General Exhibition in Dallas, "We felt that all too many of the dozen or so abstract or nonobjective paintings…fail to appeal to the senses or to the intellect."[4] As late as 1968, the *Houston Chronicle* reported: "The [Museum of Fine Arts, Houston] played to a big house last year—more than 230,000 visitors. They tuned in on the masters, pop and op, with varying degrees of enthusiasm. Many of them grooved on such recent accessions as paintings by Motherwell, Miró, Pollock, Kline and Mondrian, and sculpture by Brancusi, Calder, Chillida, Tinguely and Picasso. But others sneered at the 'crazy modern paintings and sculpture.'"[5]

This climate of opinion prompted many artists to

spend significant portions of their careers outside of Texas, assimilating into the national scene with little trace of their Texas heritage. Myron Stout, Robert Wilson, and Melvin Edwards are among the most famous artists who fall into this category. As Stout's comment from his journal attests, for these artists, Texas was a vacuum, and they had to move beyond the state's borders to find a context within which to develop their work. However, the story of Texas Modernism is not exclusively a story of expatriates. Many artists—including Joseph Glasco, Ben Culwell, and Dorothy Hood—returned to Texas after sojourns elsewhere. Experienced artists also came to Texas, introducing fresh perspectives into the local scene, including Toni LaSelle, Carlotta M. Corpron, and Donald Judd, just to mention a few. Finally, as this chapter will demonstrate, a generation of artists for whom the dialectics of regionalism and representation had little meaning came of age in Texas in the 1980s and 1990s.

Nonobjective art did not make an appearance in Texas until the late 1930s. However, a number of Texas painters and sculptors working in the late 1920s and early 1930s began to experiment with a new means of representation that echoed the concerns of the modernist vanguard. As the work of Everett Spruce, Grace Spaulding John, Ruth Pershing Uhler, and Mabel Fairfax Karl demonstrates, decoration, artifice, and formal unity were the defining qualities of early Texas Modernism. It was to Taos, rather than New York or Paris, that these artists looked, and their work reflects both the example of first generation of such Taos painters as Ernest Blumenschein and E. Martin Hennings as well as that of the second generation, represented by Andrew Dasburg, Marsden Hartley, and Georgia O'Keeffe.

Everett Spruce, who devoted the major part of his career to celebrating the Texas landscape, was perhaps the most sophisticated painter of the Dallas Lone Star Regionalist movement of the 1930s (see plate 9). Spruce began his career precociously with the remarkable folding screen *Catalpa Tree Landscape*, 1929 (plate 78), created when the artist was only twenty-one years old. The main face of the screen shows a stylized autumn landscape in which a catalpa tree is framed by a rocky promontory.

The verso is decorated with a cubistic pattern of interlocking abstract forms. The bold silhouette of the landscape and the Art Deco cadences of the composition echo Blumenschein's stylized New Mexican vistas, which Spruce would have known through reproductions and exhibitions in Dallas, while the function of the folding screen places the work at the forefront of contemporary American design.

Catalpa Tree Landscape is a unique object in the history of Texas art. Few artists in Texas successfully bridged both decorative and fine art traditions of this era, and it was probably Thomas Stell, a former assistant to the muralist Augustus Vincent Tack and Spruce's teacher at the Dallas Art Institute, who guided his work in this direction. The fresh route Spruce took was quickly recognized; as Rick Stewart recounts, "By 1930, Spruce's work was being described as strongly modernistic and was in fact very expressionistic.... Like the others [of the Lone Star Regionalists], Spruce was forging his own style, concerned more with experimentation and ideas rather than with representation."[6]

As is discussed in the first chapter of this catalogue, the Dallas artists who investigated modernist currents in the 1920s adopted the Regionalist style championed by Thomas Hart Benton during the bleak Depression era of the 1930s. In Houston, however, Regionalism never took a firm hold. Instead, led by a number of extraordinary women, Houston's contemporary art community promoted a hybrid form of Modernism initially inspired by the Taos School, but also informed by such artists as George Bellows and Rockwell Kent, who were seen in solo exhibitions in the 1920s at the fledgling Museum of Fine Arts, Houston.

One of the first professional artists active in Houston, Grace Spaulding John was among the city's most vibrant personalities. She made Houston her home in 1920, after extensive studies in art academies around the country, and the following year she married Alfred John, great-grandson of General Sam Houston. The *Houston Post* welcomed her arrival with gusto, noting that her studio was "a bit of Greenwich Village transplanted into the conventional suburb of Houston."[7] She made the first of many tours of Europe in 1927; the following year she visited Mexico; and in 1931, she made her first trip to Taos.

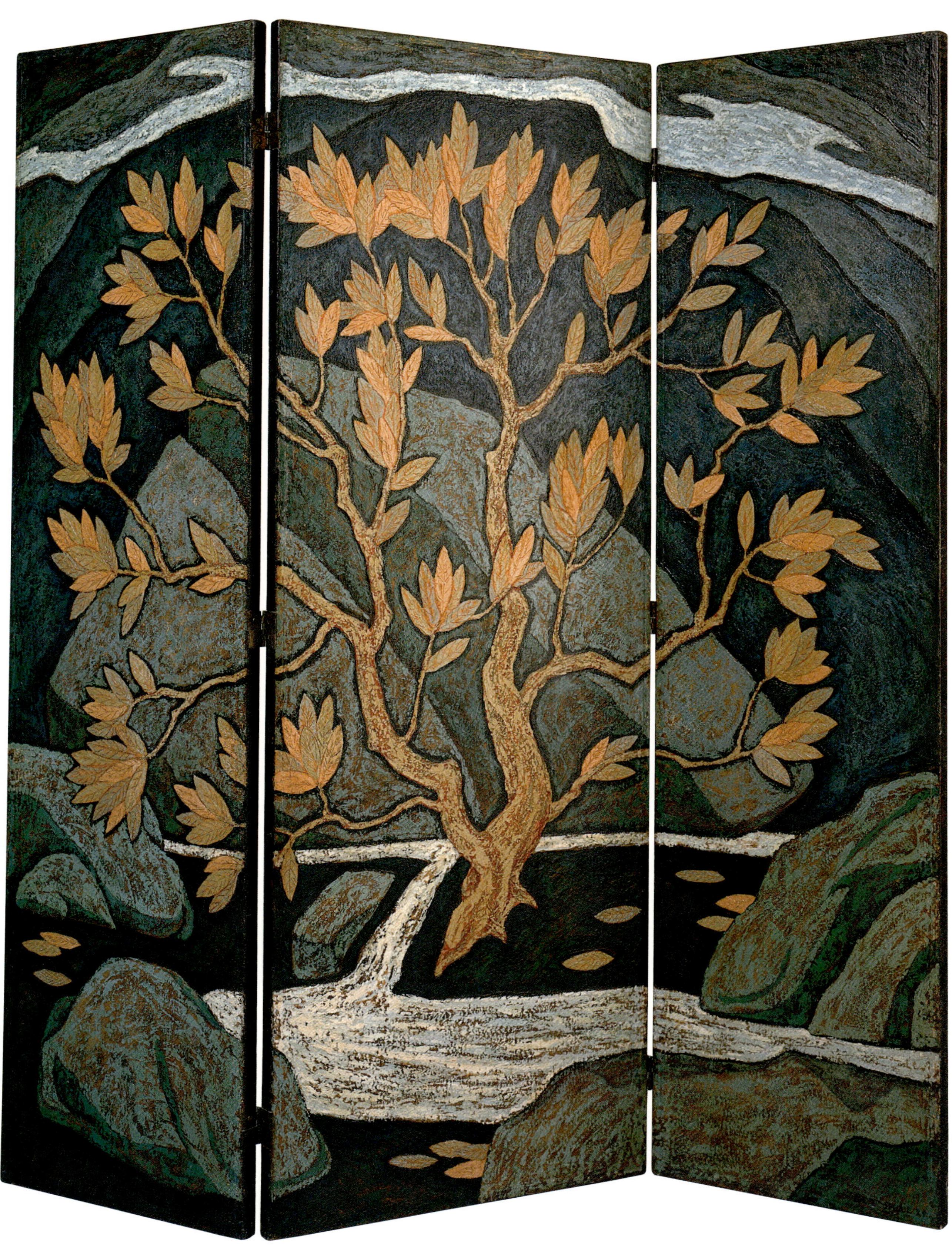

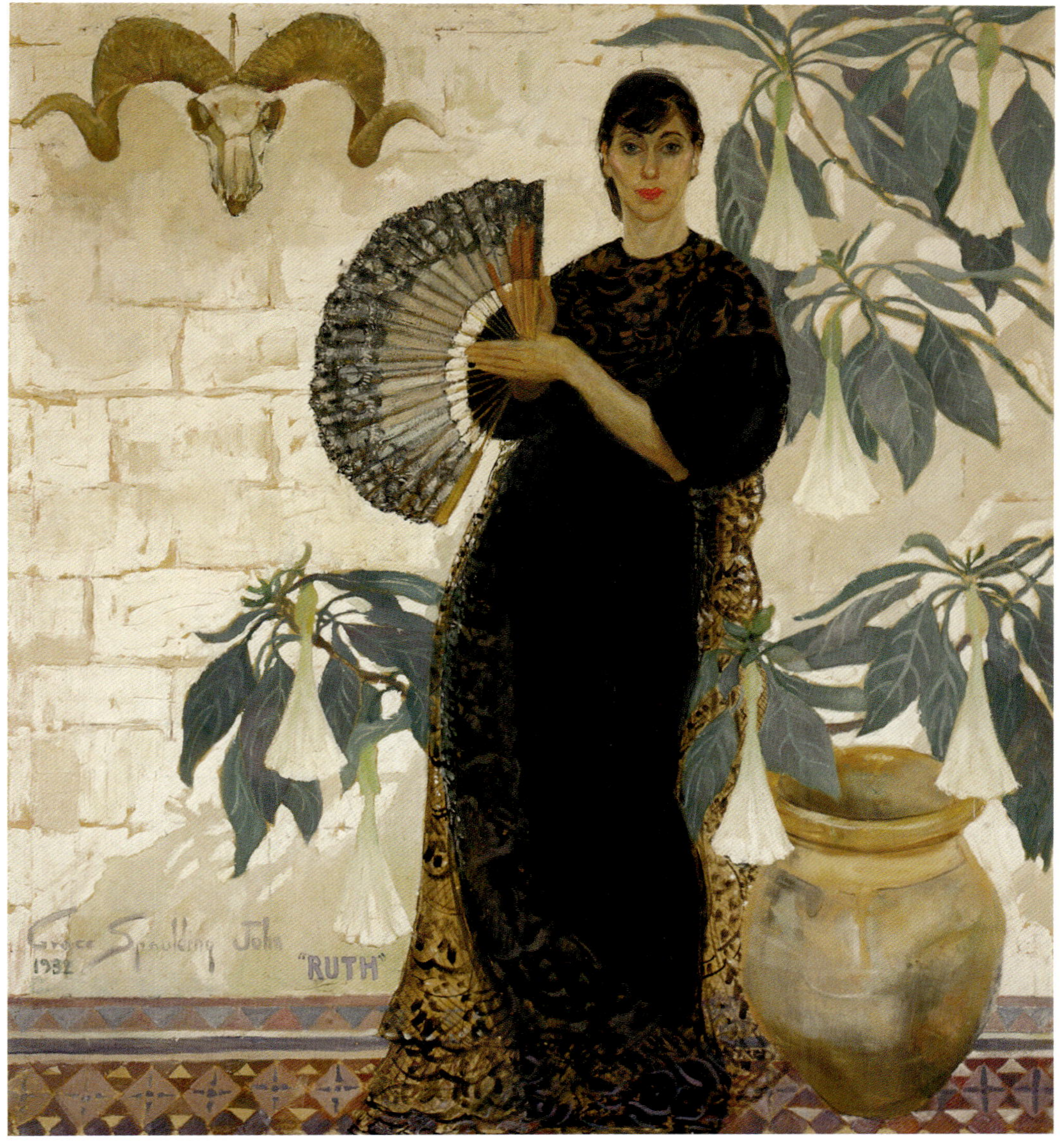

79
Grace Spaulding John
*Patterns: Portrait of Ruth
Pershing Uhler,* 1932
Oil on canvas, 60 x 54 in.
(152.4 x 137.2 cm). Gift of
Patricia John Keightley,
98.315.

John devoted a major part of her multifaceted career to portraiture, and *Patterns: Portrait of Ruth Pershing Uhler,* 1932 (plate 79), is her most vivid and resolved composition. The subject of the portrait, Ruth Pershing Uhler, was a close friend and fellow artist (see plate 80 and Introduction, fig. 3). Much as Charles Demuth animated his "poster portraits" with calculated symbolic allusions, so too did John in this deeply felt tribute. The layered images referencing Spain, Paris, and New Mexico mirrored both artists' experiences and aspirations. As Patricia John Keightley, John's daughter, has recorded:

The artist, Grace Spaulding John, posed her good friend Ruth Pershing Uhler in the patio of her studio/ home at 1306 Barbee. Ruth holds in her hands a fan of black Chantilly lace, mounted on gold lacquer sticks, which the artist brought back from the famous *Marché aux Puces* in Paris, in 1927. The black lace mantilla draped over Ruth's shoulders, as well as the large Spanish oil jar in the lower right corner were brought back from Spain by the artist the same year.

On the wall, in the upper left corner, hangs a ram's skull, found by the artist's son, John, while Grace was painting the Indian pueblo at Taos, New Mexico, in 1931. . . . The white flowers in the background are

78 *opposite*
Everett Spruce
Catalpa Tree Landscape,
1929
Oil on canvas, three-panel
screen, 66 x 20 in. (167.6 x
50.8 cm) each. Museum
purchase with funds provided
by the Museum Collectors,
95.173.

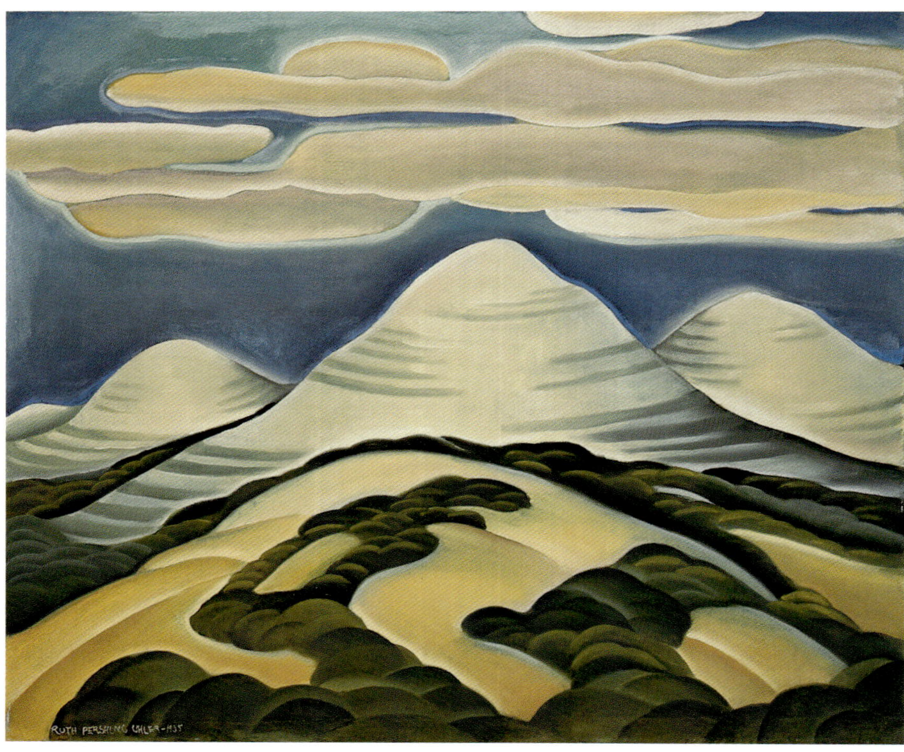

80
Ruth Pershing Uhler
Earth Rhythms No. 3, 1935
Oil on canvas, 25¼ x 30½
in. (64.1 x 77.5 cm). 12th
Annual Houston Artists
Exhibition, Museum
Purchase Prize, 1936, 36.2.

Brugmansia, or "Angel's Trumpet," a member of the family of flowering plants sometimes called nightshade. A source of belladonna, their graceful shapes remind one of the model herself. Ruth's myopic eyes, unusually large, with dark pupils, give her face an expression of serenity. She, like the flowers, appeared at her best in the evening.[8]

Uhler was born in Philadelphia, and she moved to Houston with her family in 1909. She graduated from the Philadelphia School of Design for Women in 1921, after which she returned to Houston. Like John, Uhler was featured in the MFAH's first *Annual Exhibition of Works by Houston Artists* in 1925, and was awarded the purchase prize at the twelfth *Annual Exhibition* in 1936 for *Earth Rhythms No. 3*, 1935 (plate 80).

Earth Rhythms No. 3 was created following an extended visit to Santa Fe, where Uhler had gone to recover from tuberculosis. One of a series of nine paintings, it was inspired by the landscape surrounding an Indian turquoise mine between Santa Fe and Albuquerque. Where her earlier paintings were infused by a dreamy and decorative delicacy, *Earth Rhythms No. 3* has a compositional tautness and arid palette that make it one of her strongest works. Uhler had most likely become familiar with the paintings of O'Keeffe; the composition has the artificial synthesis characteristic of O'Keeffe's early Southwestern landscapes. The suggestion of musicality in the series title reflects not only the example of O'Keeffe, but also that of such artists as Marsden Hartley and Arthur Dove.[9]

In 1937, Uhler joined the staff of the Museum School, becoming the first curator of education at the MFAH in 1941, a position she filled brilliantly for over two decades. However, the demands of the institution led Uhler to abandon her career as an artist. Patricia John Keightley has recalled: "In 1940, Grace Spaulding John went to California, and Ruth, who was staying at Grace's home, performed the double duty of guarding the house and chaperoning me.... One afternoon I came home and found Ruth in the backyard standing in front of a bonfire. Onto its flames, she was busily tossing paintings—her own. Asked what she was doing she said, 'Well, I want only my best work to survive.'"[10]

Other established painters to emerge in Houston during this era included Emma Richardson Cherry and Kathleen Blackshear. Of this generation, Mabel Fairfax Karl was one of the first professional sculptors. A native of San Diego, Karl came to Houston after her marriage in 1927, and over the following decade she divided her time between the two cities. Her *Orpheus* and *Eurydice* figures, c. 1933 (plate 81), were awarded the purchase prize at the MFAH's tenth *Annual Exhibition of Works by Houston Artists*. The two complementary figures are delicately modeled with subtle sophistication. Karl exploited the grain of the wood to emphasize the bowed postures of the sorrowful couple, evoking a somber emotional tenor with remarkable economy. As Patricia D. Hendricks has noted, the specifically classical theme is unusual in Texas art of the period; it wasn't until the grand-scale centennial commissions were unveiled in Dallas in 1936 that Art Deco classicism found an arena in Texas.[11]

Two important events in Houston at the end of the 1930s signaled a shift in aesthetics and a new commitment to the European avant-garde. In 1938, MFAH director James Chillman, Jr., brought to the museum its first exhibition of abstract art. Curated by the London painter Eileen Holding, the *International Exhibition of Abstract Painting and Sculpture* focused on works by artists who were featured in Ben Nicholson's and Naum Gabo's 1937 *Circle* manifesto, including Alexander Calder, Naum Gabo, Jean Helion, László Moholy-Nagy, and Piet Mondrian, among others. The following year, Miss Ima Hogg made an outstanding gift to the MFAH of a remarkable series of twentieth-century prints and watercolors—including works by Lyonel Feininger, Paul Klee, and Wassily Kandinsky, among others.

Over the subsequent decade, Texas Modernism reflected the shifts that characterized the larger American scene, and both nonobjective and Expressionist tendencies found proponents in Texas. Robert Preusser, Carlotta M. Corpron, Toni LaSelle, and Myron Stout were pioneers of nonobjective abstraction. Ben Culwell and Joseph Glasco exemplified the move into expressive figuration. The experience of World War II bred a new internationalism in this generation of artists; not only were Culwell, Glasco, Preusser, and Stout posted overseas, but the proximity and influence of such émigré artists as Moholy-Nagy, Gyorgy Kepes, and Hans Hofmann had a powerful effect on the evolving careers of Preusser, Corpron, LaSelle, and Stout.

Robert Preusser was a remarkably precocious artist, first exhibiting in student shows in the mid-1930s at the MFAH when he was still in his early teens. He studied under McNeill Davidson, Houston's earliest champion of abstract art, and in 1938 wrote a letter congratulating Chillman on the occasion of the *Abstract Painting and Sculpture* exhibition: "The present show of abstract painting and sculpture has arisen in me such a tremendous stimulation that I am prompted to voice my thanks to you for bringing this most vital exhibition to Houston. The stimulation of which I speak is one of painting and delving deeper into the meaning of today's art. . . . I by no means stand alone in this opinion, for I have sat up late hours discussing the show with other active artists of Houston, and we agree upon its value to us as young painters."[12]

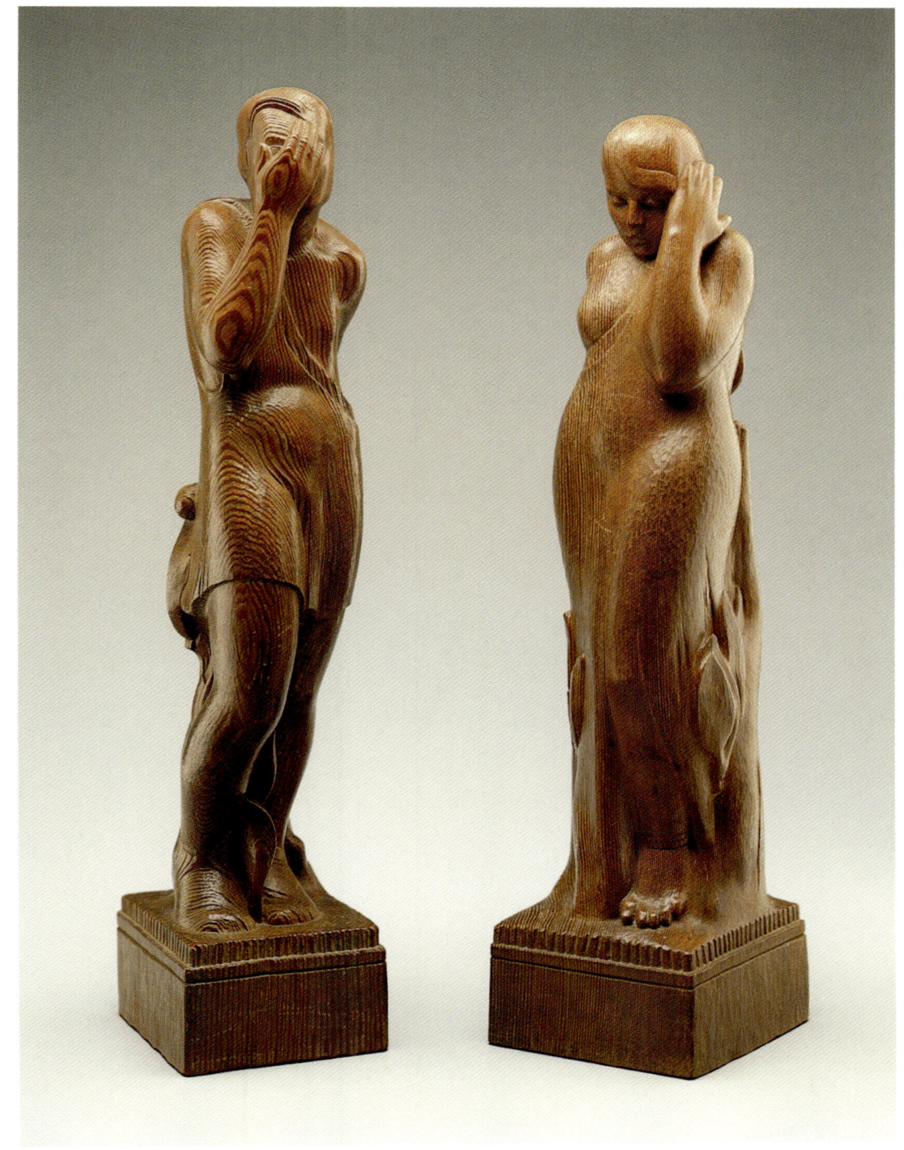

81
Mabel Fairfax Karl
Orpheus and *Eurydice*,
c. 1933
Wood, 20⅛ x 4¼ x 5⅛ in. and 19½ x 4¾ x 5¼ in. (51.1 x 10.8 x 13 and 49.5 x 12.1 x 13.3 cm). 10th Annual Houston Artists Exhibition, Museum Purchase Prize, 1934, 34.1, 34.2.

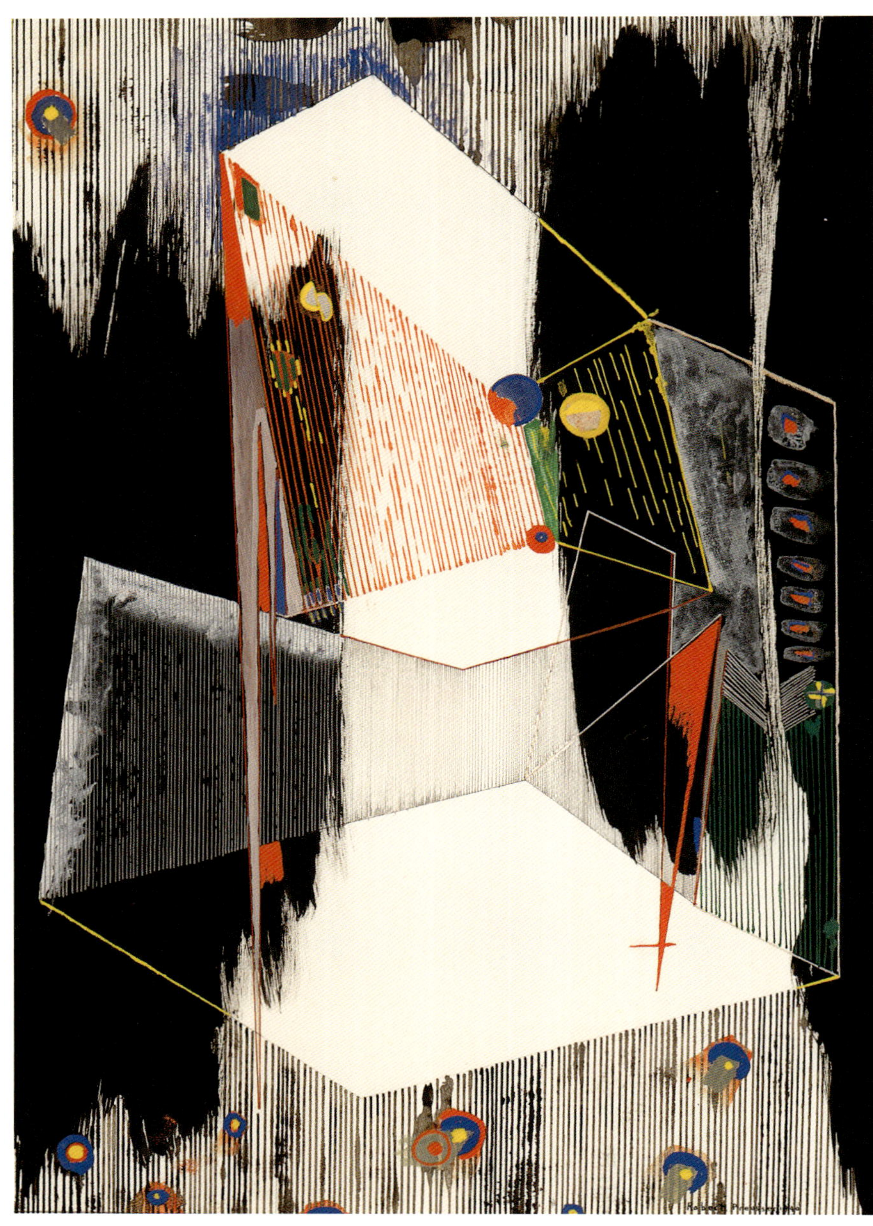

82
Robert Preusser
Composition No. 1, c. 1940
Casein and tempera on wove
paper, 21³⁄₈ x 14¹⁄₂ in. (54.3
x 36.8 cm). 16th Annual
Houston Artists Exhibition,
Museum Purchase Prize,
1940, 40.212.

Composition No. 1, c. 1940 (plate 82), is one of a series of nonobjective studies that Preusser executed while
attending the newly established Institute of Design,
Chicago, under the direction of Moholy-Nagy and Kepes.
Along with two other studies from the same series, it received the purchase prize at the sixteenth *Annual Exhibition of Works by Houston Artists* in 1940, thus becoming
the first nonobjective work purchased by the MFAH. An
essay in transparency and structure, *Composition No. 1*
owes a clear debt to such works as Moholy-Nagy's *Space
Modulator*, 1923–30, and the related film *Light Display:
Black and White and Gray*, 1930.[13]

Preusser later became one of the strongest advocates
of Houston's Contemporary Arts Association (CAA).
Formed in 1948, the CAA's first exhibition, *This is Contemporary Art*, was curated by Preusser and described the
Bauhaus model for the arts in which architecture, design, photography, and fine arts would be fully integrated. The second show mounted by the CAA was a
memorial exhibition dedicated to Moholy-Nagy.[14]

In contrast to Houston's gradually increasing embrace of contemporary European art, Dallas remained
largely committed to a local aesthetic—a tendency confirmed by the appointment of the "Lone Star Regionalist" painter Jerry Bywaters in 1943 as director of the
Dallas Museum of Fine Arts. Nevertheless, an extraordinary circle of independent artists emerged in Denton, including Corpron and LaSelle, and less directly Stout.[15]

Like Preusser, Carlotta M. Corpron was one of the
first artists in Texas to adopt the program of "The New
Bauhaus." Born in Minnesota, and raised in India, Corpron moved to Texas in 1935 to take up a teaching position at Texas State College for Women (now Texas
Woman's University), and as part of her design studies,
she began to work in photography. Her photographs of
the early 1940s reflect a Precisionist aesthetic, but she
also began a more radical extended series of light abstractions that are among the unparalleled achievements
of American Modernism. Corpron's move into abstract
photography was encouraged first by Moholy-Nagy, who
in 1942 and 1943 conducted summer workshops at Texas
State College for Women, and later and more importantly by Kepes, who came to Denton in 1944 to teach at
North Texas State University. Kepes later recalled:

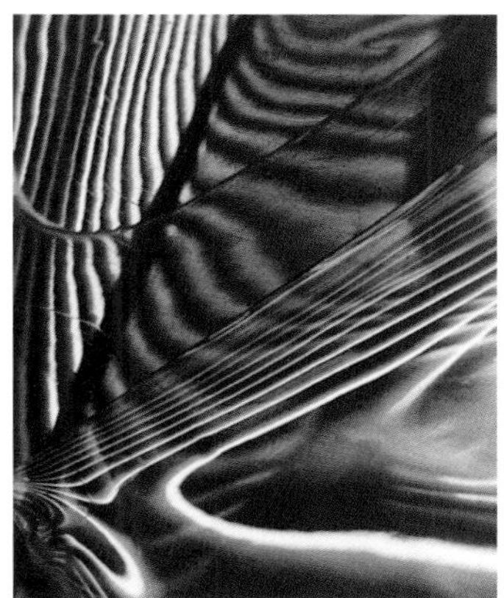

We shared the belief that photography could offer important aspects of a poetry of light which could add a new quality of sensibilities to the achievements of some great artists of the past who had worked with light. . . . For photography can do more than render the inexhaustible richness of material appearance. There are endless ranges of expressive light-poetry that are not limited to optical facsimiles of external phenomena.[16]

Corpron's untitled photograph of around 1947 from her *Fluid Light Design* series (plate 83), addresses the phenomenological basis of the medium, focusing on the play of light itself. Unlike her earlier series of abstract works, which evolved slowly through experiment and accidental effects, the *Fluid Light Designs* were directly inspired by the sight of light falling on plastic as it filtered through the slats of the venetian blinds of the artist's studio. The series became increasingly complex as Corpron exploited the transparency and reflective qualities of the plastic and the striated pattern of the light. Corpron also chose to make contact prints directly from her negatives; while as a result her prints were very small in scale, they have an exceptional density and resolution. She emphasized the discerning nature of her processes, "It's a matter of selection. So much of modern painting has been that. The painters who splash paint on a canvas will find a part that's very good and frame it off. When I did the Fluid Light pictures my control was not complete and so I had to select certain details of my negatives."[17]

Perhaps an even more remarkable member of the Texas State College for Women faculty was Dorothy Antoinette (Toni) LaSelle, who came to Denton in 1928 after completing her studies at the University of Chicago; in the 1930s she was the only artist working in Texas committed to nonobjective abstraction. In 1942–43 she returned to Chicago to work with Moholy-Nagy at the Institute of Design, and she was responsible for bringing him to Denton.[18] In 1944, however, LaSelle moved in a fresh direction; that summer she visited Hans Hofmann's workshop in his Provincetown studio, an experience which proved to be a turning point in her mature career. She fell in love with Provincetown, and made a second home there; she revisited Hofmann's classes in 1946 and again from 1950 through 1953. As LaSelle has recalled, she began to "feel the modern opening up," and over the

following decade she brought a unique painterly sophistication to her elemental abstractions.[19]

Puritan, c. 1947–50 (plate 84), was created during the extended summer visits LaSelle made to Provincetown. As the title suggests, the composition has a stringent and pared down purity. In a later poem inspired by the Provincetown landscape, "Coincident to Hour and Place," LaSelle wrote:

The sky and shore
Repeat each other's contours
By frequent counterfeits
Of shape and detail
Coincident to hour and place.[20]

In much the same way, *Puritan* evokes the cool balance of the rhythms of nature. The paint is laid down with a forceful assuredness, while the angular and rounded forms are gracefully pitted against one another. LaSelle returned later to this palette of green, black, and white in an extended series of gouaches.

A third artist to emerge from Denton in the 1940s was Myron Stout. A native of north Texas, Stout attended art school in Mexico City, where he studied under Carlos Merida; he continued his studies later in New York. In 1943, he was drafted; after the war, he followed the advice of LaSelle and began to attend Hofmann's classes, both in New York and Provincetown, making Provincetown his home in 1952.[21]

Stout worked with painstaking slowness, frequently spending as much as a decade on a single drawing, yet at

83
Carlotta M. Corpron
Untitled, from the *Fluid Light Design* series, c. 1947
Gelatin silver photograph, 2⅛ x 1¾ in. (5.4 x 4.4 cm). The Allan Chasanoff Photographic Collection, 91.508. *Illustrated at actual size*

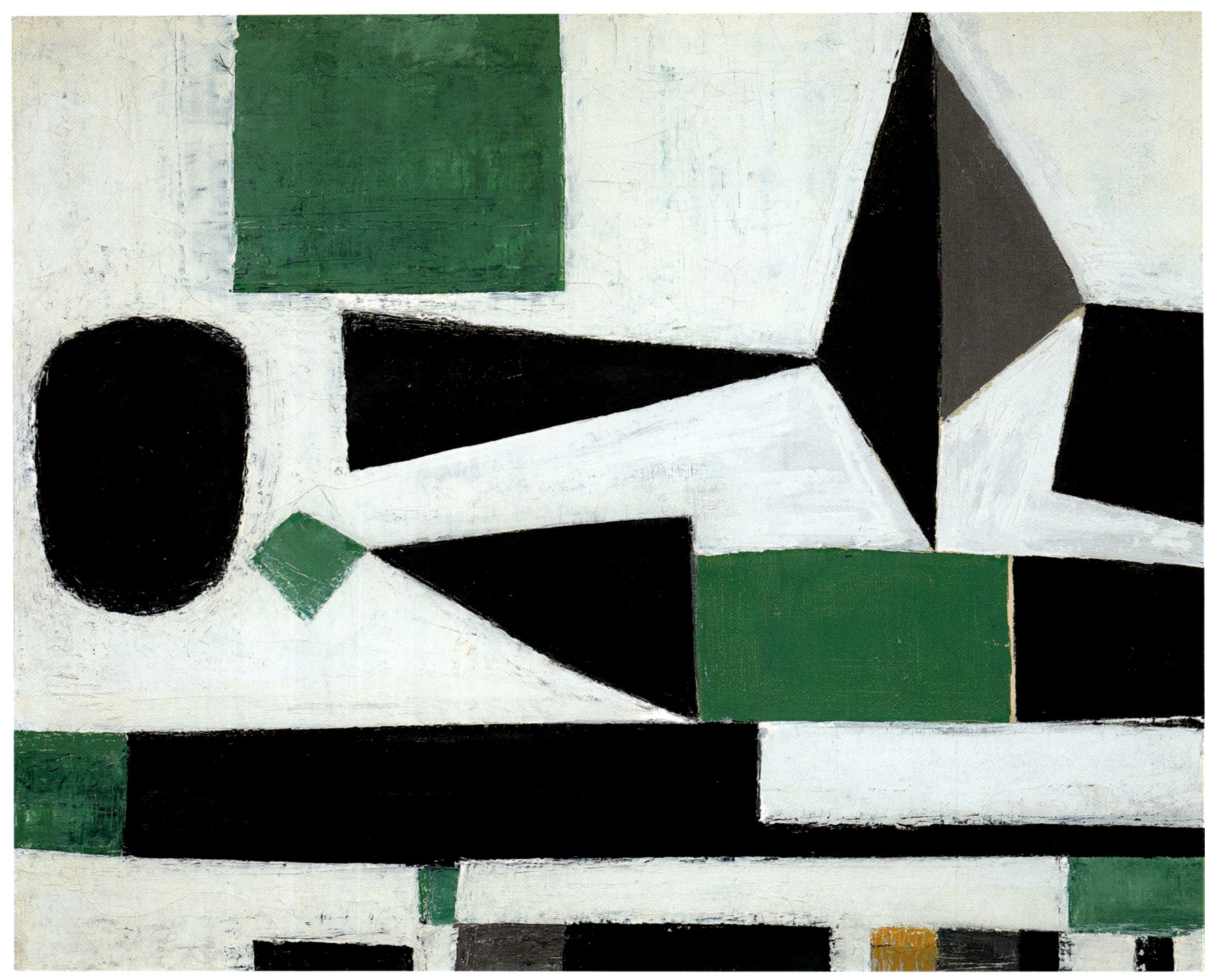

84
**Dorothy Antoinette
(Toni) LaSelle**
Puritan, c. 1947–50
Oil on canvas, 25 x 30 in.
(63.5 x 76.2 cm).
Museum purchase with
funds provided by the Frank
Freed Memorial Painting
Fund, 95.45.

the same time keeping the page remarkably pure. As Sanford Schwartz has observed, "The eye takes in a Stout very fast.... Each of his pictures is about a single incident, and the power of his art is in making that incident appear essentialized, focused, concentrated."[22] An untitled drawing, from around 1957–62 (plate 85), exemplifies both his relationship to and independence from Hofmann and LaSelle. The two black forms are densely rendered with concentric circular strokes, establishing an Hofmannesque vibrancy between the two tones of white and black. And like LaSelle, Stout preferred to work in small formats, acknowledging that landscape fueled his spatial sensibility:

> The flatness of my native environment had affected my imagination so powerfully. The flatness—or rather the successively endless, low-rolling character of north Texas and of all the areas of Texas that I went to in my young years—had the effect of giving promise in every direction.[23]

However, Stout introduced a meditative quality into his hard-edge abstractions that was as much about the process of creating the image as the image itself. In this, his work radically diverges from that of his mentors, predicting the departures that Minimalism was to promote in the 1960s.

Expressionist currents also began to emerge in Texas art in the 1940s, notably in the work of Ben Culwell and Joseph Glasco. Culwell was raised in San Antonio, Houston, and Dallas; he attended the Dallas Art Institute in 1934 and completed his artistic education in New York. In 1941, he enlisted in the Navy, and from 1942 to 1944 he was on active duty in the South Pacific on the *USS Pensacola*. While at sea, he maintained a passionate diary of drawings capturing all aspects of his experience, from the carnal reveries of the lonely sailor to the adrenaline-filled terrors of bombardment. This series was featured in Dorothy Miller's *Fourteen Americans* exhibition of 1946 at the Museum of Modern Art, New York. Among the other artists included in this exhibition were Arshile Gorky, Robert Motherwell, Isamu Noguchi, and Mark Tobey.

In the catalogue of the exhibition, Culwell wrote of serving in the Pacific arena: "As the stimuli recurred from

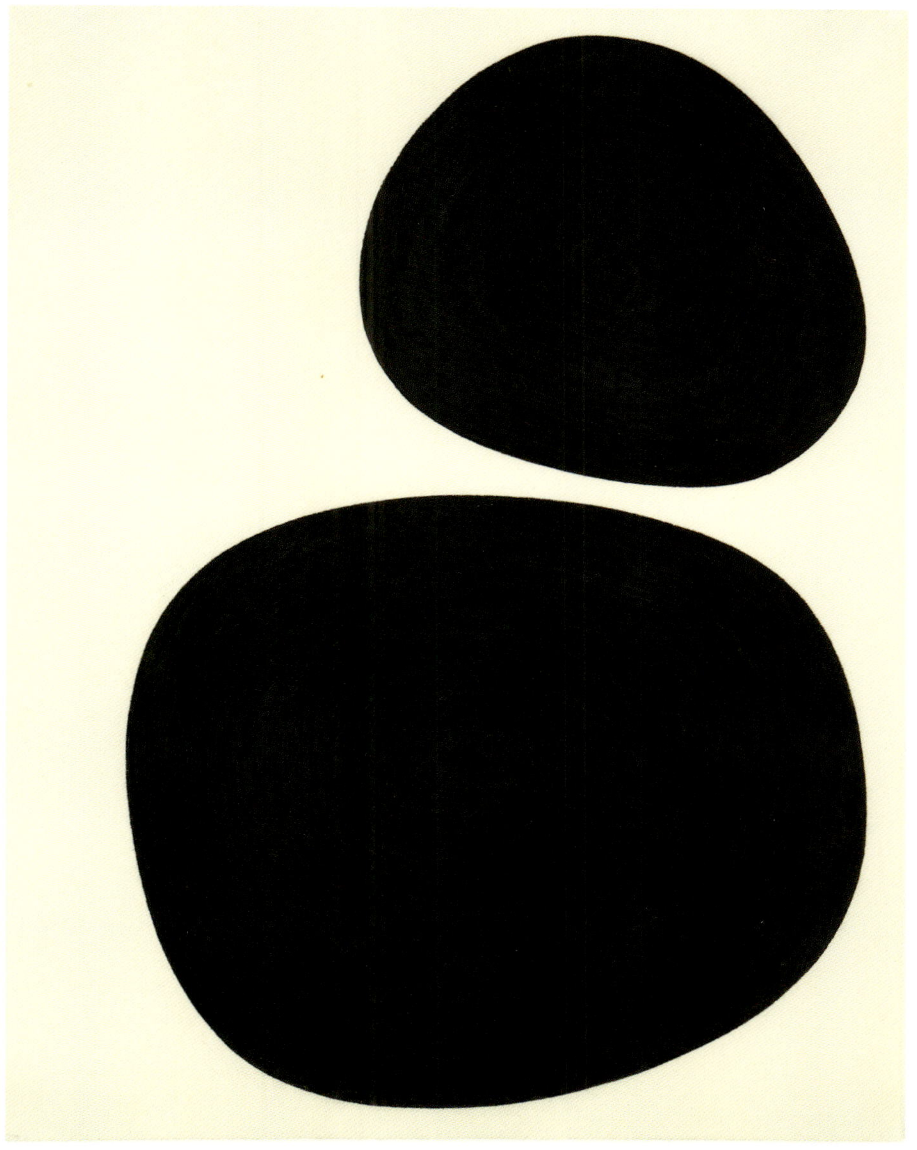

85
Myron Stout
Untitled, c. 1957–62
Charcoal on paper, 25 x 19 in. (63.5 x 48.3 cm). Museum purchase with funds provided by the Caroline Wiess Law Accessions Endowment Fund, 92.450.

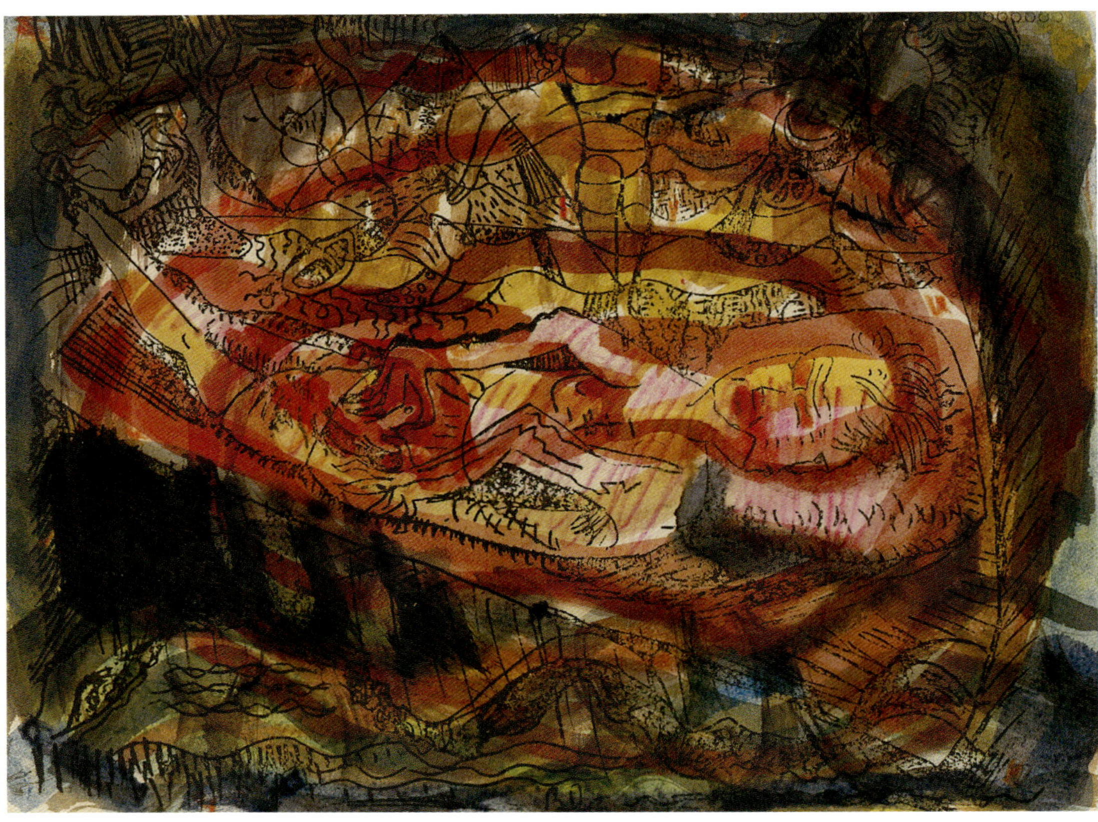

86
Ben Culwell
Sleep Sailor: Seventy-six
Days at Sea, 1942
Mixed media on paper,
6 x 8⅛ in. (15.2 x 20.6 cm).
Museum purchase with
funds provided by William
and Virginia Camfield, 91.66.

87 *opposite*
Joseph Glasco
Salome, 1968
Colored ink on paper, 96½ x
48½ in. (245.1 x 123.1 cm).
Gift of Mr. and Mrs. Anderson
Todd, 69.1.

day to day in the well-known cycle of battle, routine, battle, I set down relationships of the life which I was in, in
the full perspective afforded by the simultaneous viewpoints of assimilated familiarity and fresh impression."[24]
Sleep Sailor: Seventy-six Days at Sea, 1942 (plate 86), is
representative of the series in its display of acid color,
nervous line, and visionary imagery—a sailor is shown
dreaming of women in his bunk. The frank eroticism of
the scene is reinforced by the red, yellow, and roseate
washes of color that cradle the figure. Culwell reworked
this theme a number of times; a related drawing was titled *Oh God, if I could only be there now—tonight, to
awake this morning from her bed.*[25] The influence of
such artists as André Masson, George Grosz, and Paul
Klee can be traced in these drawings. However, as much
as Culwell drew on Surrealism and German Expressionism to record his encounter with war, these works also
stand alone with a passionate intimacy unknown in the
work of any other Texas artist up to that time.

If Culwell was impelled to record his wartime experi-

ence with the immediacy of a polygraph, Joseph Glasco
chose a more oblique approach in his tightly structured
paintings of the 1950s. Born in Oklahoma, Glasco moved
with his family to Tyler, Texas, in 1931. He was drafted
into the US Army in 1943; after the war, Glasco briefly
attended the Portsmouth Art School in Bristol, England,
before returning to the United States. Between 1946 and
1949, he continued his education in Los Angeles, Mexico,
and New York. His densely patterned figure studies captured the attention of Dorothy Miller, who purchased
one of his drawings and included him in the Museum of
Modern Art's *Fifteen Americans* exhibition of 1952. This
landmark presentation also featured the work of Jackson
Pollock, Mark Rothko, and Clyfford Still.

However, Glasco's work had little in common with
the gestural expansiveness of the New York School.
Poised between decoration and figuration, Glasco's compositions of the 1950s offered a synthesis of painterly nuance and psychological penetration. In 1955, he
dedicated almost a year to a painting of Salome dancing

before King Herod.[26] The last major work Glasco created before leaving New York, *Salome* is a deeply disquieting composition, in which monumental forms are pitted against tautly drawn details. Glasco returned to the theme thirteen years later in the MFAH's *Salome*, 1968 (plate 87).[27] While the later version exemplifies the exoticism of Glasco's work of the 1950s, it is further imbued with a febrile eroticism by the veils of color that wash over figure and ground. The monumental adolescent dancer fills the compositional frame; on the lower right rests the head of John the Baptist. In an interview of the mid-1950s, Glasco commented, "Painting *can* deal with violent subject matter, of course, but the organic building of the picture, its relationships and its order, must be achieved first."[28]

The 1950s was a boom era for Houston, a prosperity which was also reflected in the city's support of contemporary art. Lee Malone replaced James Chillman, Jr., as director of the MFAH in 1954, and with the visionary support of Nina Cullinan, the museum was able to commission Ludwig Mies van der Rohe to create an ambitious master plan for the museum later that year.[29] In 1955, the CAA hired its first professional director, Jermayne MacAgy. John and Dominique de Menil also emerged as significant patrons during this era; not only did they support MacAgy's ambitious exhibition program at the CAA, but along with Nina Cullinan and Stanley Marcus, they also were instrumental in bringing The American Federation of Arts (AFA) Convention to Houston in 1957.[30]

The AFA Convention, held at the Shamrock Hotel from April 3 to 6, marked a turning point in Houston's involvement with contemporary art. As the program records, the theme of the convention was "Perpetual Discovery," reflecting upon "many aspects of the development of style: its philosophical basis, its psychological origins, its dissemination and establishment, and—in the case of the visual arts—the means by which it is presented to the public by the contemporary museum."[31] The guest list of speakers brought together some of the leading artists, writers, and psychologists of the era, ranging from Marcel Duchamp, Jimmy Ernst, and Stuart

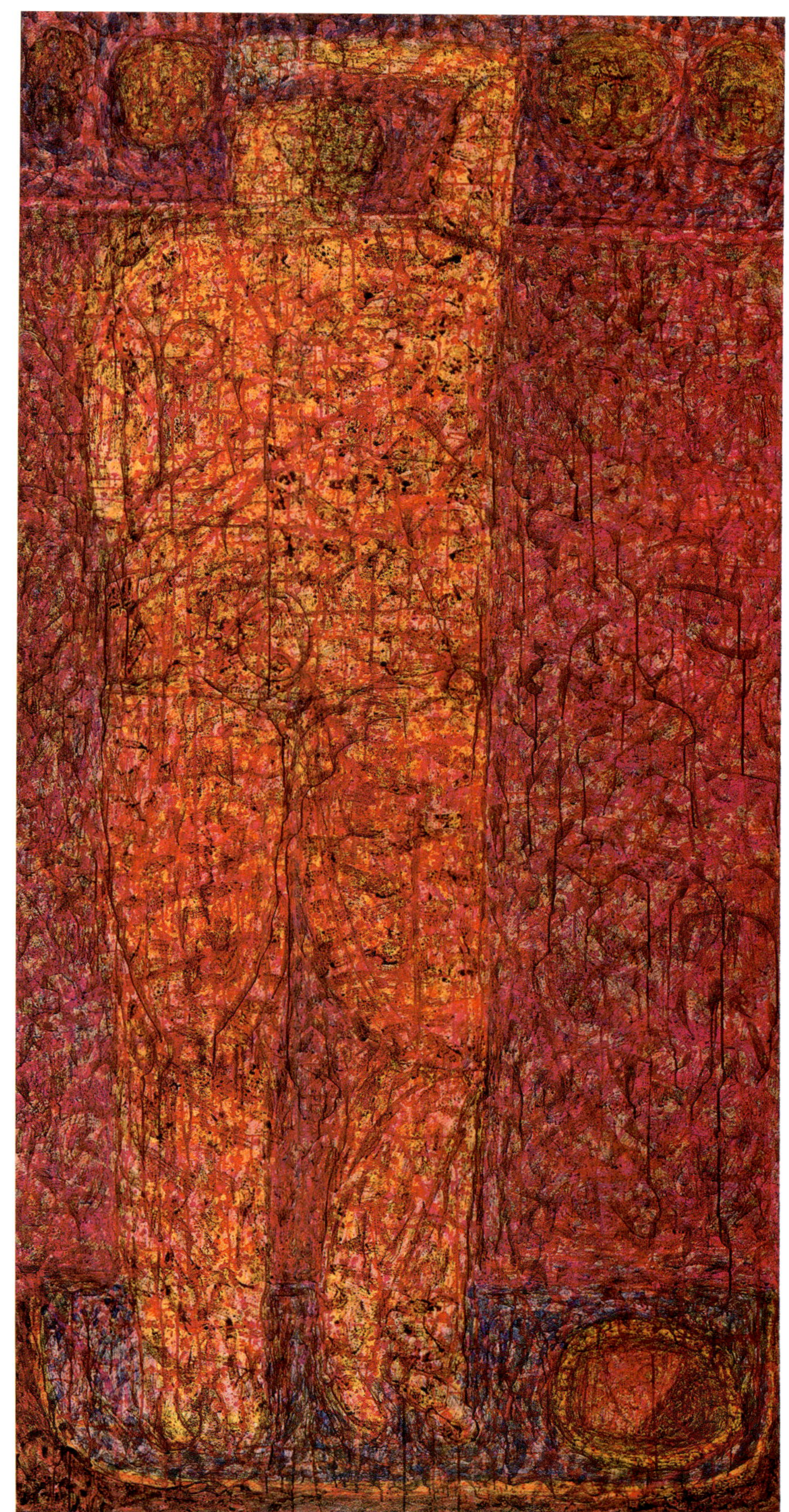

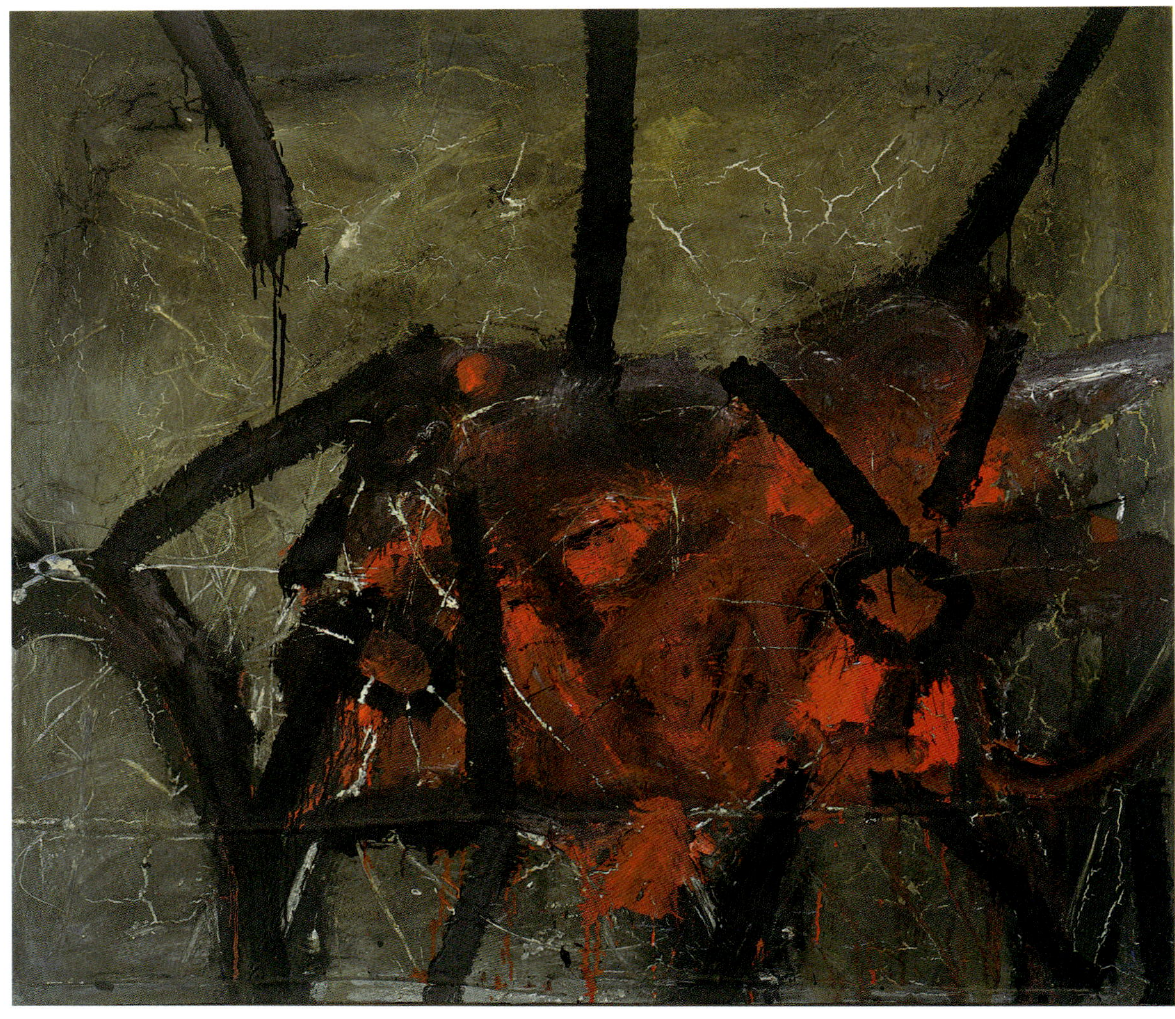

Davis to Randall Jarrell and Gregory Bateson. Among the art historians and curators in attendance were Meyer Schapiro, William Seitz, and James Johnson Sweeney, who was then director of the Solomon R. Guggenheim Museum. Vincent Price, celebrated as a connoisseur as well as an actor, was invited to speak at the closing banquet. The museums took advantage of the international audience to open two major exhibitions: the MFAH hosted *Three Brothers: The Work of Marcel Duchamp, Jacques Villon and Raymond Duchamp-Villon*, which had been organized by the Guggenheim Museum, and the CAA presented *Pacemakers*, a survey of new talent organized by MacAgy, which included Forrest Bess, Jack Boynton, Walter Kulman, and Hassel Smith, among others. The convention concluded with a chartered jet tour of Texas, with stops at San Antonio, Fort Worth, and Dallas. The events attracted an audience of 1,400, the largest in the history of the organization. *Life* and *Artnews* ran extended features on the meeting, and *Harper's Bazaar* published a photo-essay by Henri Cartier-Bresson on the attendees.[32]

In the wake of these activities, the arts in Houston enjoyed a surge of energy. Two important commercial galleries were established at this time—Meredith Long & Co. and New Arts Gallery—and the Art League of Houston opened its first permanent exhibition space. Artist Richard Stout (see plate 58) has recalled:

> I came in November of 1957. After I got out of school, I sort of checked around: "Where am I going?" I had no intention of ever coming back to Texas, but after checking around Texas—and on my way home—I stopped in Houston for the first time in years. Saw the Mies van der Rohe building going up and visited the Contemporary Arts Museum, and I was so impressed by the show I saw, *Irons in the Fire . . .* that I decided that I would come here.[33]

The role that Texas artists were to play in this expanded climate for contemporary art was still evolving, however. Sweeney, who became the MFAH's director in 1961, cancelled both the Texas and Houston annual exhibitions. In their place, he undertook a single ambitious survey of Southwestern art, inviting James Brooks and Alexander Calder to join him in selecting the works. Out of 889 submissions, they chose 83 examples, with an emphasis on nonrepresentational work that at its best reflected a genuine independence.[34] As Sweeney wrote in the catalogue introduction: "Facilitated travel and communication had unquestionably made its inroads into geographical limitations. What was also notable here was the fact that this wide acquaintance did not result in a mere reflection of fashionable trends as is so frequently recognizable in certain regional exhibits and in the most interesting examples took on a personal character and individuality."[35]

Houston-born Dick Wray was among the artists featured in Sweeney's *The Southwest: Painting and Sculpture* exhibition. After enrolling in the architecture program at the University of Houston in the late 1950s, Wray completed his studies at the Kunstakademie Düsseldorf in 1958. Over the following year, he traveled through Europe, encountering in Paris the pivotal *New American Painting Exhibition*, organized by the Museum of Modern Art, which was the defining survey of Abstract Expressionism. As David E. Brauer has chronicled, "This was Wray's first exposure to the breadth of contemporary American Modernism," an encounter that was enriched by his knowledge of such European artists as Pierre Alechinsky, Jean Dubuffet, and Antoni Tàpies.[36] Wray returned to Houston in 1959, where he worked in an architectural office, but he was increasingly committed to becoming a painter, a shift encouraged in 1961 by Donald Barthelme, then acting director of the CAA. Wray later recalled, "In those days nobody even thought about being an artist. There weren't any artists."[37]

Klee Gone Mad, Almost Berserk, 1963 (plate 88), is characteristic of Wray's early paintings. The cracked and densely worked surface relates to the example set by Tàpies, while the scale, gestural authority, and structure of the composition relate to the paintings of the second generation Abstract Expressionists.[38] The reference to Paul Klee in the title, whose work was presented in Houston in an exhibition organized by MacAgy in 1960, suggests both an homage and a break with the past.

Wray's painterly dexterity was matched by such contemporaries as Jack Boynton and Dorothy Hood, both of whose work of the 1950s is discussed in earlier chapters (see plates 13 and 49). In the 1960s, Hood moved to the forefront of the Houston community. She had settled in the city in 1962, following extended sojourns in Mexico and Latin America. Over the following decade, Hood reconciled the Surrealist roots of her work with the stain techniques pioneered by the Color Field painters. Unlike such artists as Helen Frankenthaler and Morris Louis, however, who celebrated the transparency of the medium, Hood sought a more theatrical layering of space, pitting opacity against transparency.

By the mid-1960s, additional possibilities began to open up for the arts in Houston. Newly established galleries (most notably Louisiana Gallery, David Gallery, and Kiko Gallery) promoted a range of contemporary art. In 1964, Dominique and John de Menil began to discuss with Mark Rothko the possibility of creating a chapel. And in 1966, the CAA brought in Sebastian J. Adler as director, and made a commitment to embark on an ambitious building program.

In 1969, buoyed by Adler's offer of a solo exhibition to be sponsored by the CAA, Hood moved into a dramatic scale in her work.[39] *Haiti*, 1969 (plate 89), is one of the artist's first truly monumental paintings; psychological space and physical space are united through sonorous colors and sweeping compositional gesture. Created at a time when the island republic of Haiti was experiencing severe social repression, *Haiti* was an unusually political statement for the artist. The uneasy balance of color and the sharp compositional breaks result in an eloquently foreboding work of art. In an interview of 1970, Hood stated:

> I feel that I have met my scale. I have now been able to do what I have never done before. We're too distracted in our daily lives to let this largeness come out.... It's been a thrilling experience. I guess that for me this has been the difference between small orchestra and full symphony.... It takes all your guts and courage to make them come off.[40]

Psychological space was also central to the concerns of another artist who came of age in Houston in the 1960s, Charles Schorre. Schorre graduated from the University of Texas at Austin in 1948, and moved to Houston later that year. Working both as a commercial illustrator and as an educator, Schorre embraced a range of

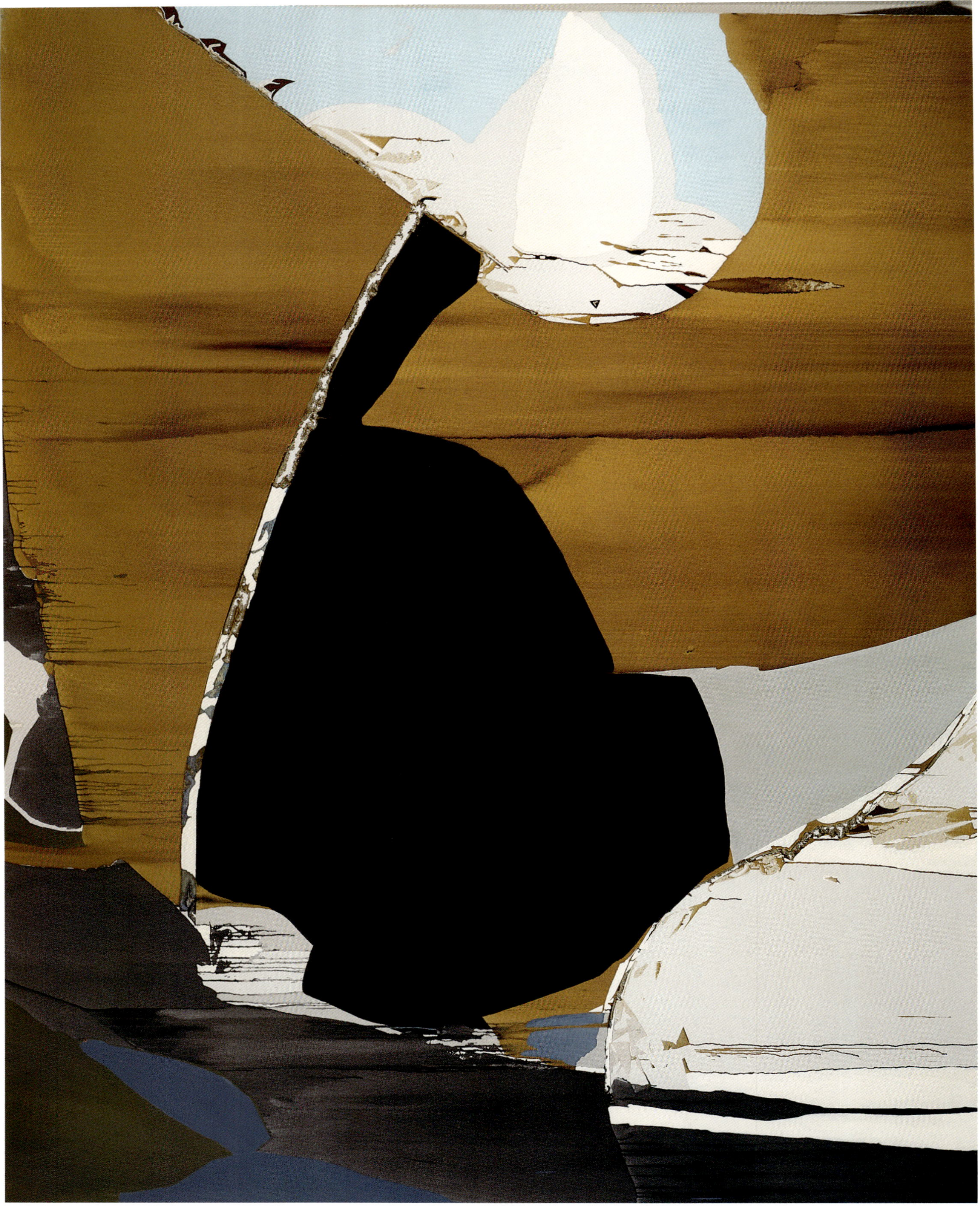

materials and techniques, from photography and collage to painting and drawing. In a 1985 statement, he commented:

> Houston has influenced the direction of the work only in that it has been a visual wasteland. I like this because it causes one to be more innovative—the work has to come from within.... The work seldom refers to the immediate environment. It comes from visions, dreams, discoveries, and from the omnipresence of nature.[41]

Moonavel, 1984 (plate 90), while a later work, complements his paintings of the 1960s.[42] Like many artists active in Houston during the "Space City" era, Schorre found in astral imagery a metaphor for creation. *Moonavel* is a reverie in part inspired by the lunar landscape, and in part based on his studio practice, as Schorre maintained a commitment to life drawing throughout his career. In *Moonavel*, the suggestion of a woman's torso in the central orb serves to unite the particular and the universal forces of nature. The brilliant, high-contrast palette and the assured use of line confer a celebratory spirit onto this image of gestation and renewal.

The late 1960s and 1970s saw many Texas artists embracing regional narrative and visionary currents, and such figures as Lucas Johnson, John Alexander, and James Surls were among the defining influences during these years. However, this era also saw the emergence of two artists whose work was ultimately to challenge expectations about art in Texas: Donald Judd and Robert Wilson.

Born in Missouri, Judd had established a reputation in New York as a writer and artist by the mid-1960s. He had begun his career as a painter, deeply influenced by the example of such artists as Barnett Newman. Seeking, however, to purge his work of painterly illusion, Judd adopted industrial materials and methods of fabrication. The resulting works, which Judd did not classify as sculpture, pointed to a new direction in American art. In 1965, Judd wrote for the *Arts Yearbook 8*:

> The use of three dimensions makes it possible to use all sorts of materials and colors. Most of the work involves new materials, either recent inventions or things not

89 *opposite*
Dorothy Hood
Haiti, 1969
Oil on canvas, 120 x 96 in. (304.8 x 243.8 cm). Gift of Mr. and Mrs. Meredith J. Long, 70.68.

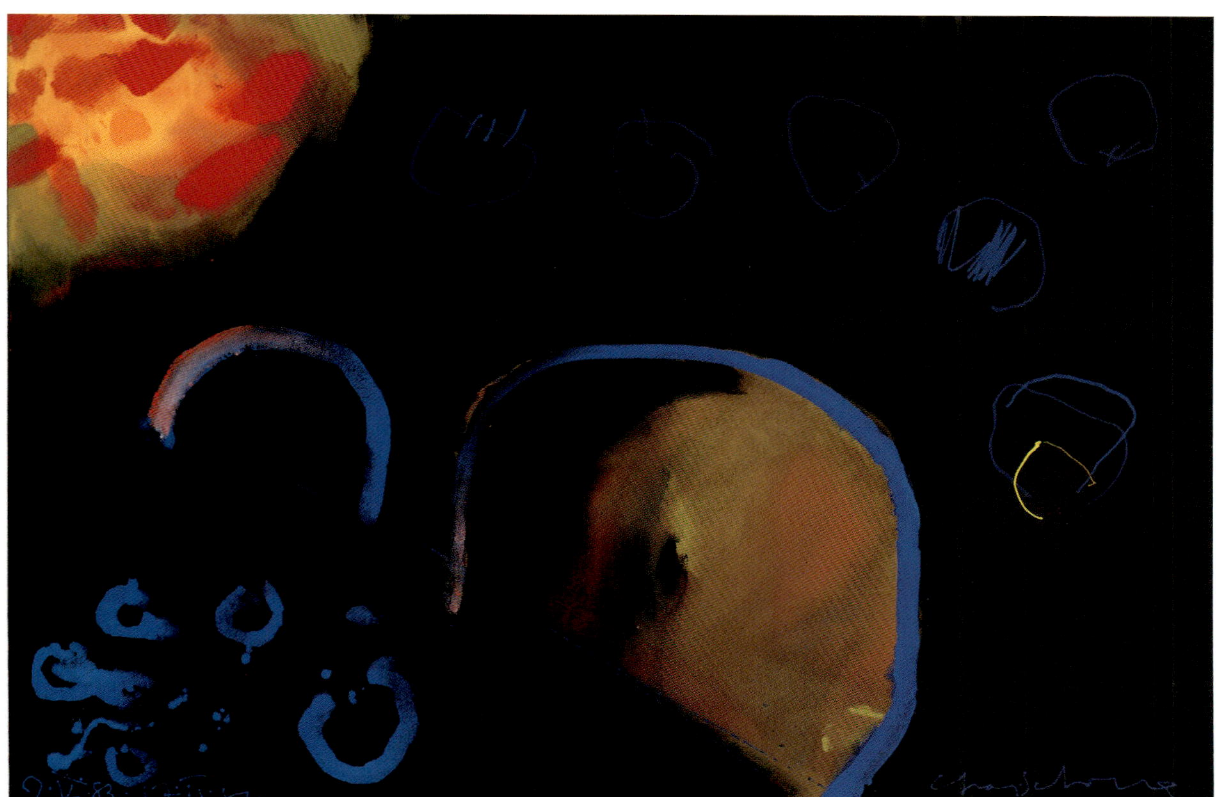

90
Charles Schorre
Moonavel, 1984
Acrylic on canvas, 48 x 72¼ in. (121.9 x 183.5 cm). Museum purchase with funds provided by Duke Energy, 85.8.

used before in art. Little was done until lately with the wide range of industrial products. Almost nothing has been done with industrial techniques and, because of the cost, probably won't be for some time. Art could be mass-produced, and possibilities otherwise unavailable, such as stamping could be used.... Materials vary greatly and are simply materials—formica, aluminum, cold-rolled steel, plexiglas, red and common brass, and so forth. They are specific. If they are used directly, they are more specific. Also, they are usually aggressive. There is an objectivity to the obdurate identity of the material.[43]

The authoritative and reductive geometry of Judd's pieces, as well as their method of fabrication, prompted some writers to classify his work as Minimalist or Conceptual, both terms that the artist rejected. Rather, as Barbara Haskell has pointed out, "Judd correctly protested that the creative act was not an exclusive attribute of execution, but could be as potently expressed through the artist's decisions about composition, color, and materials."[44]

In 1971, Judd began to seek a Southwestern site where he could create a studio retreat from New York. He had passed through West Texas while a soldier en route from Alabama to California in 1946, and in 1972 he decided to settle in Marfa, Texas, a town established in 1881 as a tank stop for the Southern Pacific Railroad. Marfa had been developed in the first decades of the century as a border post; in 1929, Camp Marfa was renamed Fort D. A. Russell, and during World War II was the site of a P.O.W. camp. The post was closed in the years following the war, and by the early 1970s, it was possible for Judd to purchase several buildings both in the town and at Fort Russell. Over the following two decades, Judd dedicated his major efforts to developing his work—and that of selected colleagues—at Marfa. With the support of the Dia Foundation in the late 1970s, he was able to take over the Fort Russell site, and later through the establishment of the Chinati Foundation, was able to accomplish one of the most powerful artistic statements created in Texas.[45]

In 1975, the MFAH commissioned Judd to create a work for the collection; the result was an untitled piece made from polished brass and painted aluminum (plate 91). The open top of the piece invites the viewer to look down and into the work, and Judd noted that in revealing the box structure:

It would open the top surface up. I was always interested in edges and flanges.... It defines what the boxes are made of by showing the thickness of the sheet metal, and thus becomes less arbitrary, more rigorous, with a more precise knowledge of the thickness of the material.[46]

The bottom aluminum panel is enameled cadmium red, a color that Judd adopted as early as 1961 for its visual clarity.[47] By exploiting the reflective property of the brass and the radiant quality of cadmium red, Judd fuses light and surface. At the same time, the lucid structure effectively complements the illusionism inherent in the materials.

While largely critical of Judd's work, Michael Fried's seminal essay "Art and Objecthood," published in *Artforum* in 1967, brought up an interesting issue in regard to Minimalist art. Fried objected to the theatrical or situational aspect of what he identified as "literalism," asserting: "Someone has merely to enter the room in which a literalist work has been placed to become that beholder, that audience of one—almost as though the work in question has been waiting for him."[48] It was this quality of theatricality that was to fire the imagination of Robert Wilson.

Born in Waco, Wilson attended the University of Texas at Austin, before moving to New York in 1962. In 1965, he designed sets and costumes for an off-Broadway production, embarking on a career in the theater which has continued to expand over the subsequent three decades. Wilson's iconoclastic approach to stage direction runs counter to the rapid acceleration of modern life, and his monumental stage productions have taken some of the concerns defining Minimalism as a point of departure. Much as Judd had exposed the specific qualities of his materials, Wilson explored the factor of time as it relates to performance. Similarly, as Judd had laid open the structure of his works, Wilson clarified the dramatic structure of his productions. However, Wilson's move into sculpture ultimately broke with Minimalist precedents. He began to create permanent pieces out of his stage designs in the mid-1970s, creating works that heralded the New Image movement. Among his most famous sculptures are the *Stalin Chairs* (plate 92), which stemmed from the 1973 production of *The Life and Times of Joseph Stalin*, a twelve-hour compilation of Wilson's theater work since 1969. Two draped chairs were the

91
Donald Judd
Untitled, 1975
Polished brass and painted aluminum, 36⅛ x 60 x 60 in. (91.8 x 152.4 x 152.4 cm). Museum purchase with funds provided by the National Endowment for the Arts and the Brown Foundation, 75.370.a–.e.

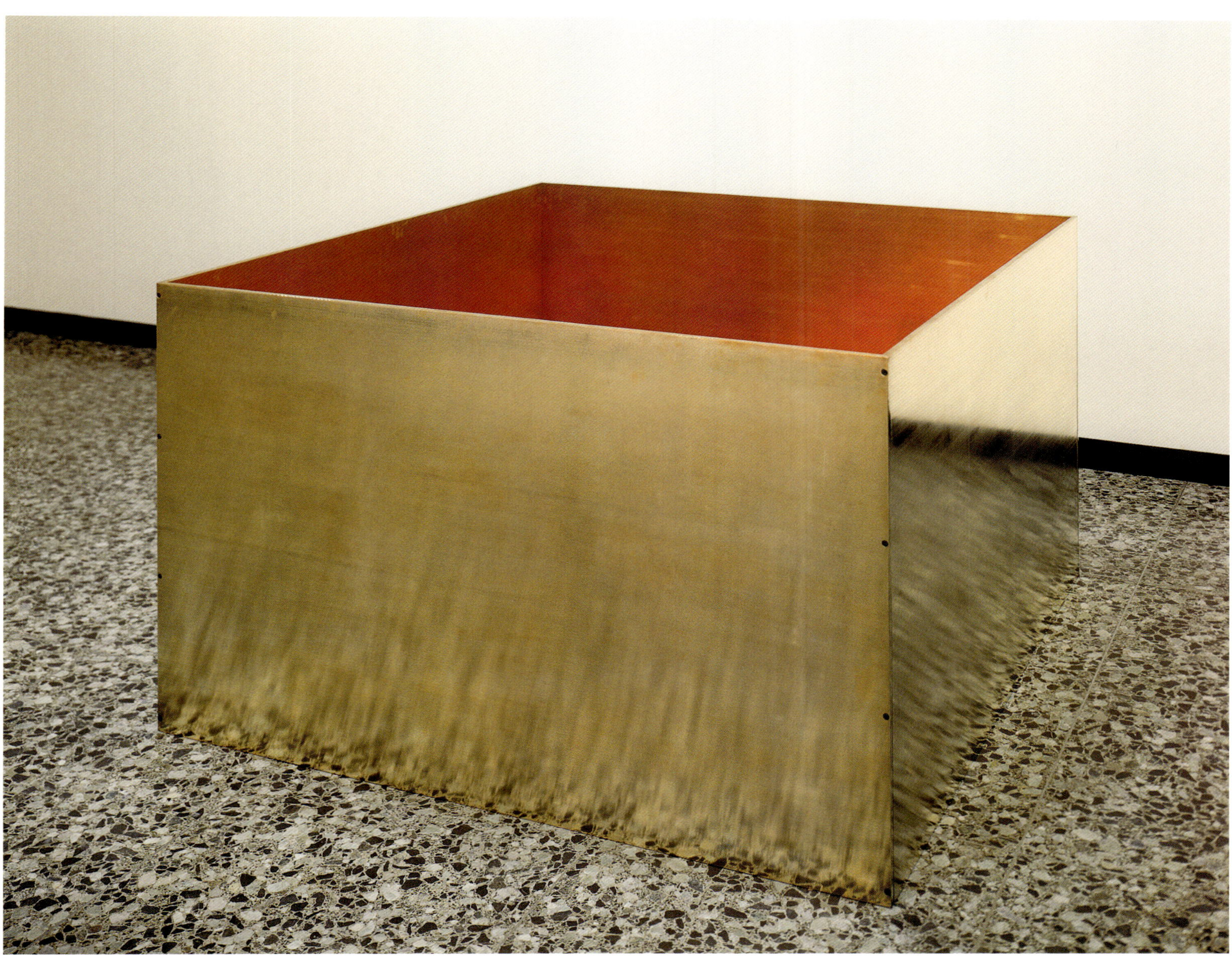

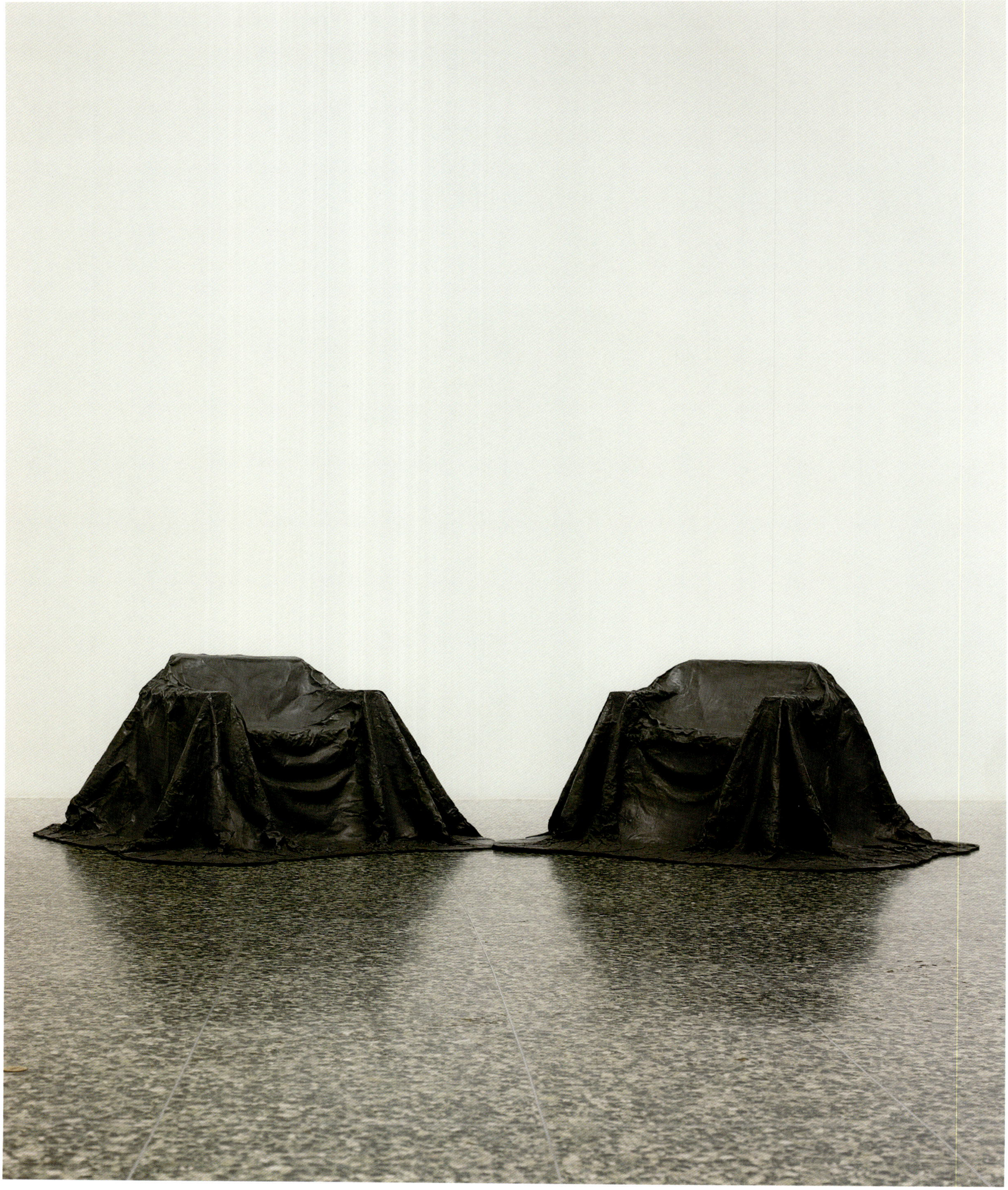

focal point of the stage production; as Trevor Fairbrother has recounted: "Wilson created a degree of structural symmetry by building parallels into the settings or actions of acts 1 and 7, 2 and 6, and 3 and 5. Act 4 was thus the center, and at its midpoint he staged the death by poisoning of Stalin's first wife. Because Stalin had kept two identical apartments, each with an armchair draped in white fabric, his wife's death was witnessed on stage by two identically costumed Stalin figures … seated in identical draped armchairs."[49]

These stage-props were in turn the prototypes of the lead sculptures which the artist created in a limited edition in 1977. The spare geometry of the forms relate to Minimalist aesthetics, while the draped lead lends a quality of disquieting verisimilitude. These pieces function independently from the stage production. Robert Stearns has observed: "The *Stalin Chairs*, posed at an informal angle to each other, suggest covered furniture at the summer house. Draped in lead they appear funereal. The lead reminds us that Wilson does not deal in theatrical *trompe l'oeil*. We are not being fooled by crafty imitation in sculpt-metal. This is cold, dense, and poisonous lead."[50]

Although Judd and Wilson were not an established part of the art community in Texas in the 1970s, by the late 1980s their activities began to be integrated into the local art scene. With the opening of the Chinati Foundation in 1987, Judd's efforts in Marfa became known to a more general public, and in 1989 the Dallas Museum of Art hosted the Whitney Museum's retrospective of the artist. Wilson had his first performance in the Houston area in 1977, when the University of Houston at Clear Lake hosted Wilson's coproduction with Lucinda Childs of *I was sitting on my patio this guy appeared I thought I was hallucinating*. In 1986, Wilson's first retrospective exhibition traveled to the Laguna Gloria Art Museum in Austin, and in 1991, the Contemporary Arts Museum in Houston hosted the monumental exhibition *Robert Wilson's Vision*. Beginning in 1992, Houston Grand Opera and the Alley Theatre began to sponsor outstanding performances of Wilson's productions, including world premieres of *Danton's Death*, 1992, *HAMLET: a monologue*, 1995, and *Four Saints in Three Acts*, 1996.

Despite the fact that Minimalism and Conceptual art came to dominate the American scene in the 1970s, several key events in the first years of the decade promoted an ongoing engagement with abstract painting in Houston, most notably the opening of the Rothko Chapel in 1971, and the *Post-Painterly Abstraction* exhibition that inaugurated the Brown Pavilion at the MFAH in 1974.[51] William C. Agee's subsequent tenure as director of the MFAH, from 1974 to 1981, saw further exhibitions of American abstraction, ranging from Patrick Henry Bruce to Helen Frankenthaler. Consequently, even into the 1980s, a number of senior artists and emerging talents continued to explore issues in abstraction without breaking from the Modernist canon.[52]

Joseph Glasco, whose *Salome* is discussed earlier in this chapter (see plate 87), made Galveston his home in 1972. Over the following five years he underwent a period of stringent self-evaluation, and his compositions assumed a different sense of weight and monumentality as he abandoned the figure. In 1974, he began a series of overall abstractions, which in 1977–78 led to his first collaged canvases. Glasco exploited the collage technique primarily as a means of breaking up the illusion of depth, affirming the primacy of the picture plane. The applied layers of collage drew attention to the surface of the canvas in much the same fashion as Hans Hofmann's color blocks anchored his compositions.[53] Furthermore, the cut-and-paste technique was a clear break from the flowing gestural style advocated by the Abstract Expressionists of Glasco's generation. In 1983, he recalled:

> I really never thought I'd paint the rest of my life with glue. It was just something that I wanted to do at the time. Also, there is a need in me to do sculpture and it somehow comes out when I paint and use material on top of material … which is what sculpture is about. The collage paintings were constructed as such and I wanted to block out any action painting and any references to that in my own work.[54]

Screen, 1983 (plate 93), is the culmination of Glasco's exploration of these themes. Consisting of ten double-sided panels stretching over forty feet, the freestanding format allowed the artist to address the canvas as a physical entity. One face is devoted largely to primary colors and white. The opposite face is monochromatic. When

92
Robert Wilson
Stalin Chairs, 1973/77
Lead folded over wood and fiberglass armature, 32 x 71½ x 69½ in. and 32 x 77¾ x 66½ in. (81.3 x 181.6 x 176.5 and 81.3 x 197.4 x 168.9 cm). Museum purchase with funds provided by Max and Isabell Smith Herzstein, 93.331.

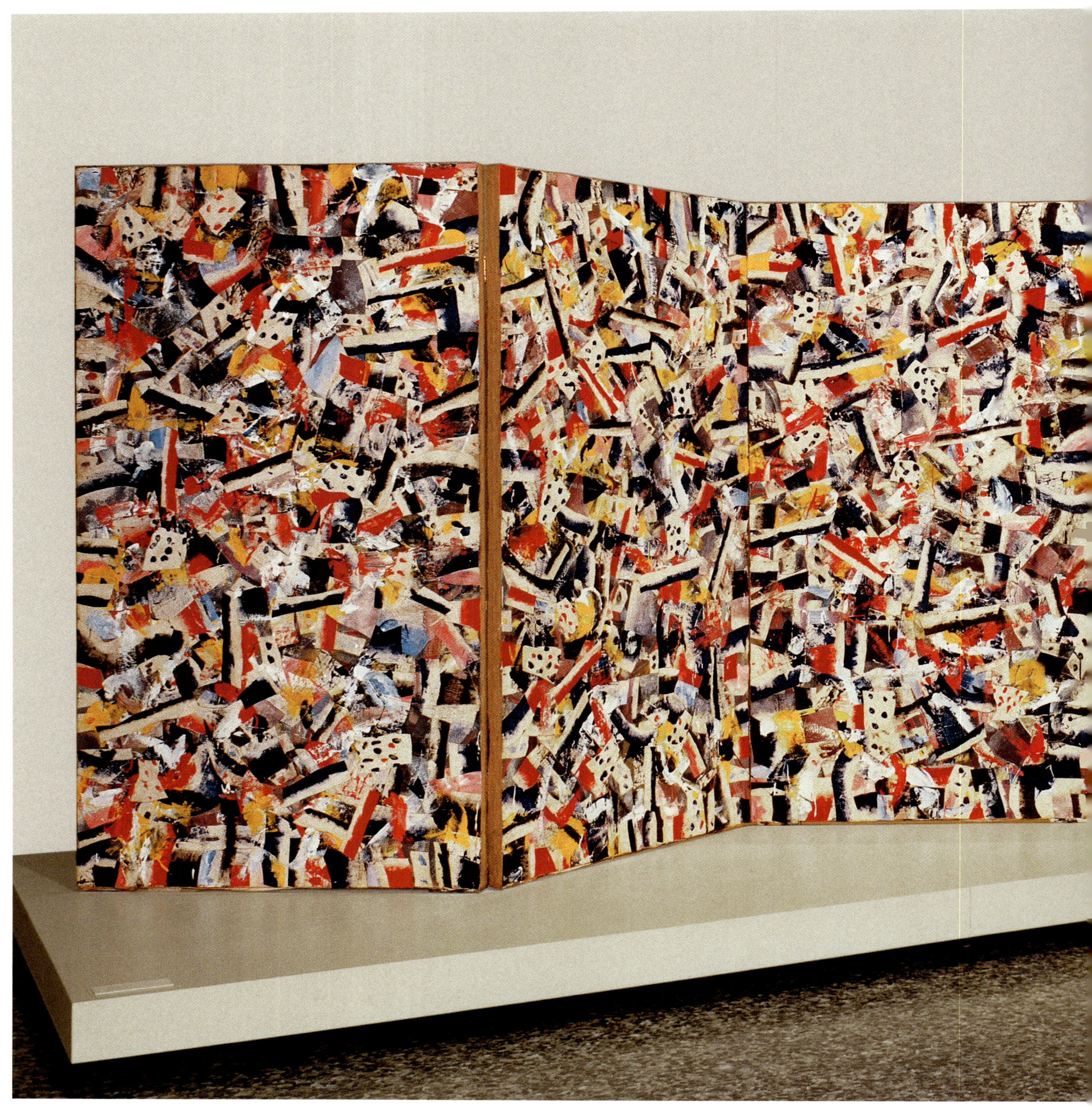

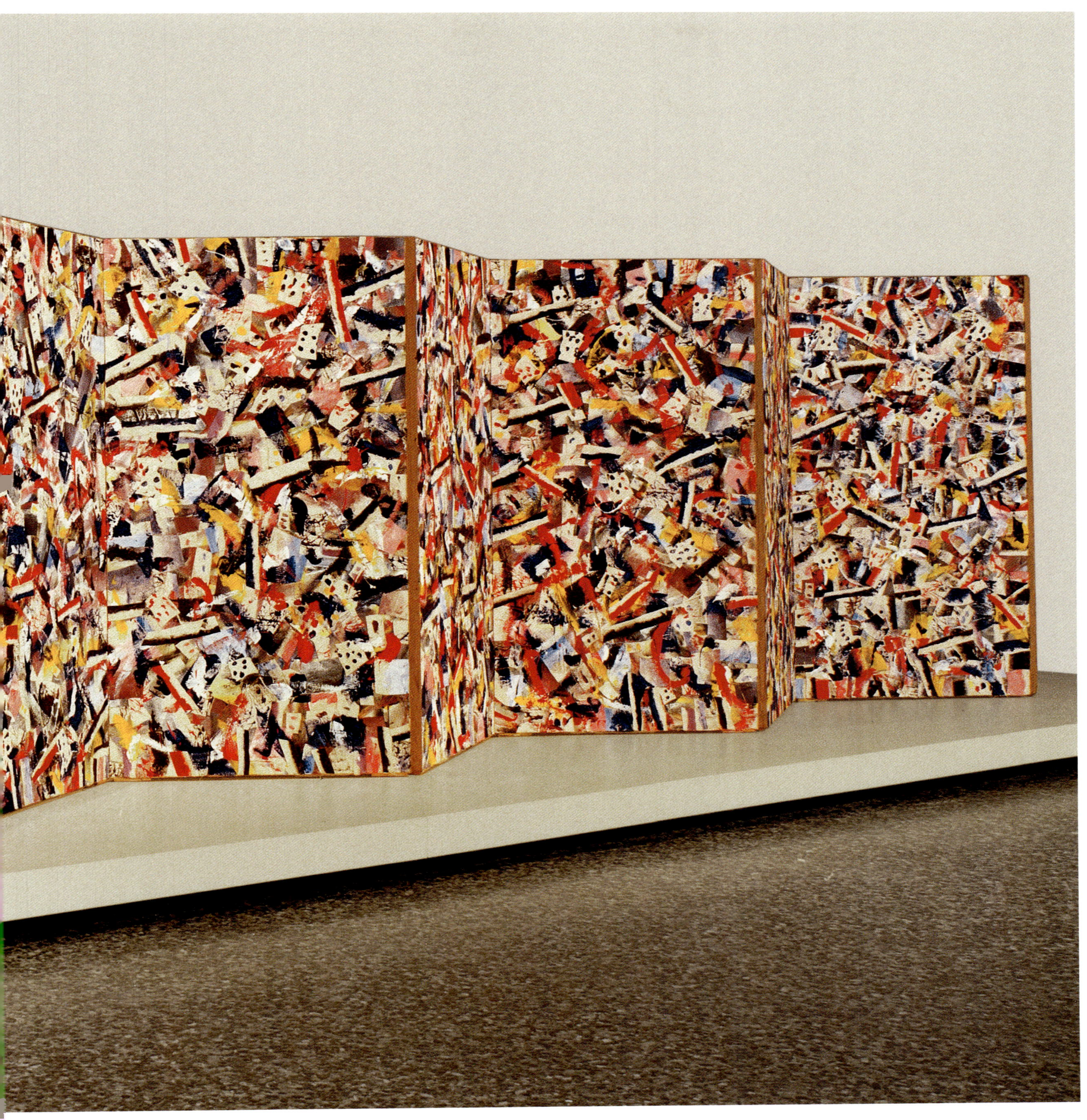

93 *pages 138–139*
Joseph Glasco
Screen, 1983
Acrylic and collage on canvas,
ten-panel screen, 88 x 48 in.
(223.5 x 121.9 cm) each.
Museum purchase with funds
provided by Duke Energy,
85.4.

94
Jim Love
*Can Johnny Come Out
and Play?*, 1990–91
Bronze, 107 in. (281.1 cm)
diameter. Gift of Caroline
Wiess Law in memory of
Theodore N. Law, 90.419.

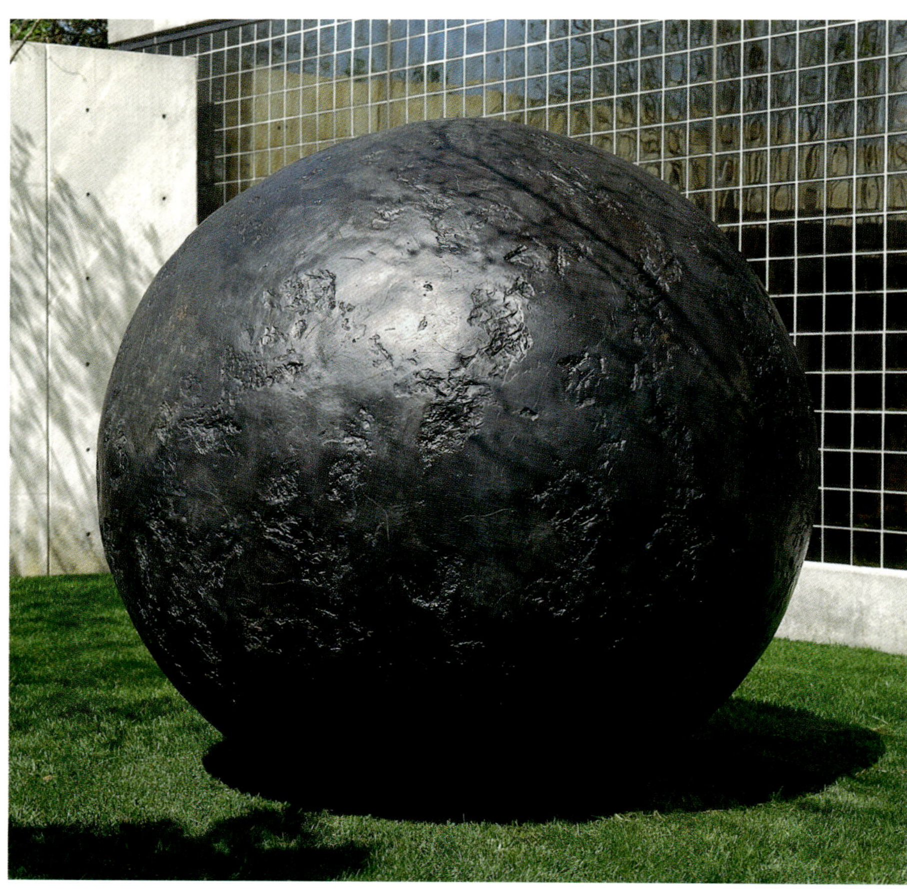

installed, the painting sweeps across a gallery space with authority and bravura, recalling the best work of the Action Painters of the 1950s. The syncopation of the layered tones and surfaces capture the celebratory spirit of Fernand Léger's first ventures into abstraction. At the same time, Glasco's *Screen* is liberated from these precedents; as he deliberately encapsulated the history of Modernism, he also pushed his painting into new directions by freeing it from the wall.

Glasco's embrace of monumentality and the roots of Modernism finds interesting parallels in the work of Jim Love, whose earlier contributions to Texas art are discussed in the first chapter of this book (see plate 14). In 1990, he undertook a major commission for the MFAH. Asked to create a work for the museum's Cullen Sculpture Garden—which houses bronzes by such artists as Louise Bourgeois, Lucio Fontana, and Ellsworth Kelly—Love chose to abandon the assemblage aesthetics which up to that time largely defined his work. *Can Johnny Come Out and Play?*, 1990–91 (plate 94), wittily responds both to the nonobjective sculptures of other artists seen in the garden and to larger issues. As William R. Thompson has observed, "Although its simple geometry departs from the more elaborate nature of the artist's past assemblages, the enormous sphere, like much of Love's work, evokes the experience and perspective of youth. The title suggests the innocence of children at play, while visitors to the garden confront its enormous scale in a manner similar to that of a child discovering the intimidating world of adults. In contrast to its allusions to childhood, the sphere's dark, mottled surface appears aged and distressed. Is it the abandoned plaything of an imaginary giant, a small model of the planet earth, or perhaps a counterpart to the enormous toy jacks Love made two decades ago?"[55]

Robin Utterback, a graduate of Rice University's B.F.A. program, made a commitment to nonobjective painting in Houston in the 1970s, and his work has continued to develop in new directions in abstraction. Utterback's early works were explorations of unified fields, characterized by a monochromatic expanses animated by a play of surface and light. In the 1980s, he opened up the structure of his compositions, literally stripping the canvas off the frame, and layering pigment over an armature of wood, cloth, and plaster. In 1989, Utterback embarked on a new series of paintings in which drawing assumed a primary role. Exhibited at the Contemporary Arts Museum in 1992, these works displayed a remarkable freshness of touch and a graphic immediacy. Suzanne Delehanty wrote for the gallery notes of the exhibition: "Each of Utterback's pictures is an invented world where light and dark, order and chaos, calm and intensity follow laws of his creation. For Utterback, the blank sheet of paper or empty canvas is like a game board where an infinite number of permutations exist within the changing combination of forms, colors, and touch."[56]

Untitled [No. 404], 1990 (plate 95), is the most nuanced painting of the series. In it, Utterback accepted a set compositional restraint: the entire palette was dependent on the tones that could be derived from one tube of red acrylic paint and one tube of black. Working on raw canvas, Utterback achieved a range of tones from the fully saturated red to the palest washes of gray. The interlocking and overlapping arabesques confer a subtle exoticism to the composition, while the complex spatial relationships attest to his ongoing concern with structure.

The graphic authority of Glasco's and Utterback's work is complemented by that of Ibsen Espada, who emerged on the Houston scene in the 1980s. Like Utterback, Espada came to painting with an acute sense of the achievements of previous generations of abstraction. Born in New York, Espada was raised in San Juan, Puerto Rico, where he studied under the Cuban painter Rolando Lopez Dirube. In 1975, Espada moved to Beaumont, Texas, and shortly thereafter made Houston his home, continuing his studies at the Museum School, where Dorothy Hood became his mentor.

Three Studies for a Cockfight, 1987 (plate 96), is one of the artist's most somber compositions. Like much of his work of the 1980s, the title refers to the Latin culture in which he was raised. However, compositionally *Three Studies for a Cockfight* evinces a greater kinship with the work of such artists as Jackson Pollock and Pierre Alechinsky. Espada adopted Pollock's method of controlled gesture, painting on sheets of rice paper placed on the floor. Then following Alechinsky's example, Espada laid down on canvas the completed drawings. The result is a balance between chance and structure. In an interview of 1990, the artist commented:

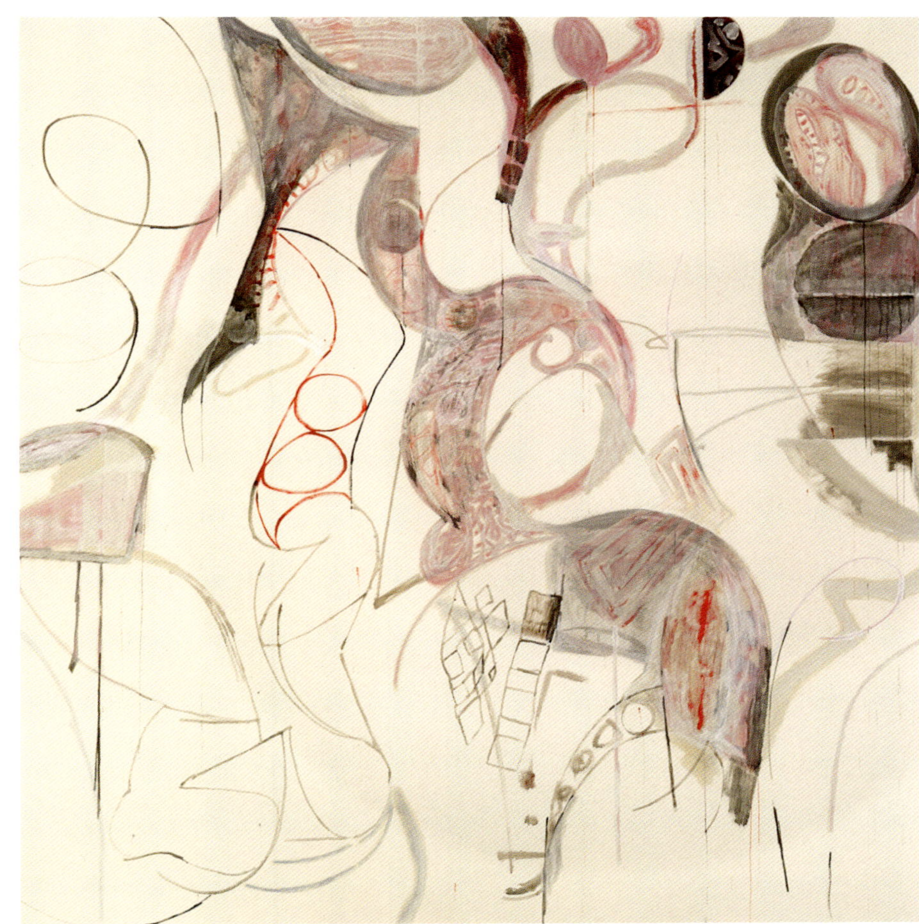

95
Robin Utterback
Untitled [No. 404], 1990
Acrylic on raw canvas, 79¼ x 76⅝ in. (201.2 x 196.6 cm). Museum purchase with funds provided by the George Bunker Living Trust, 92.189.

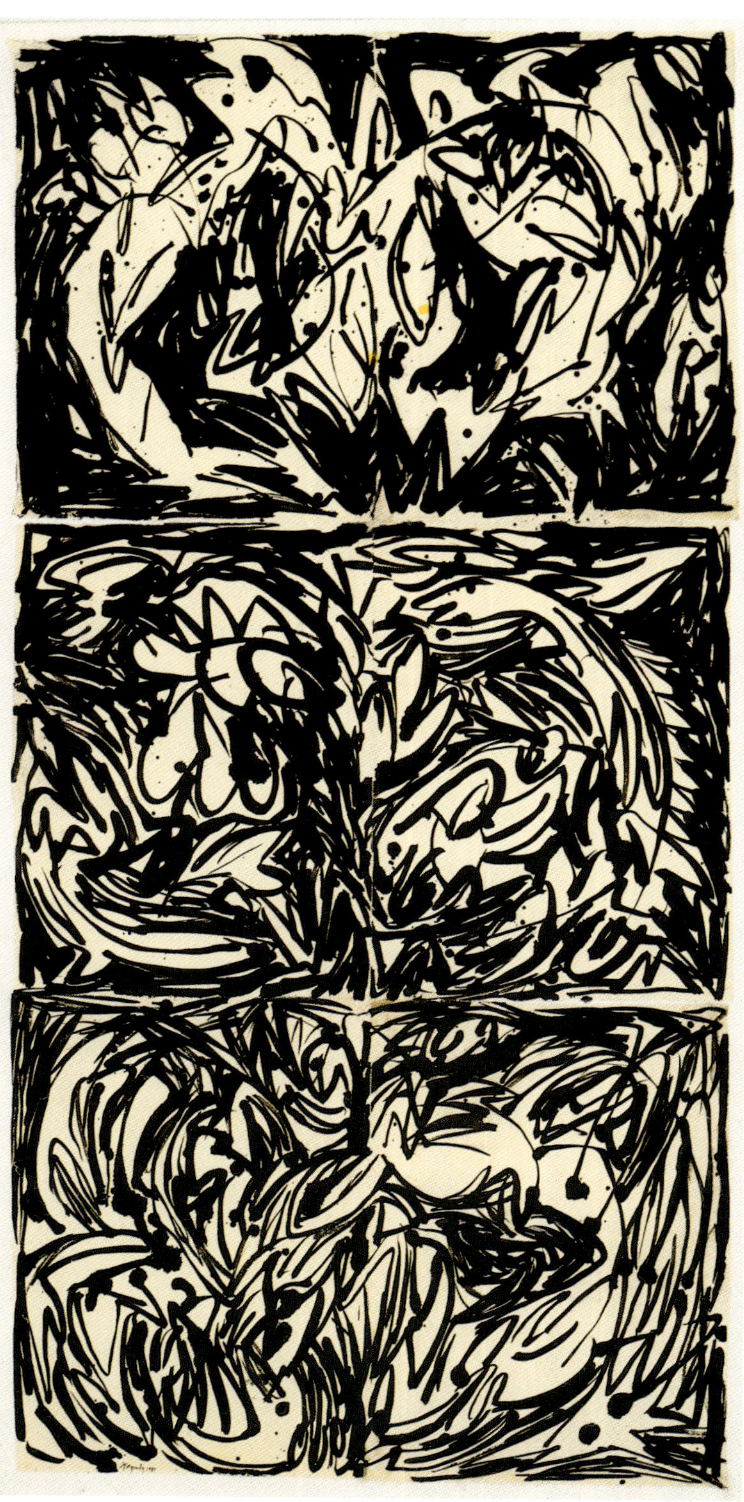

In the beginning I was involved with printmaking and sculpture. When I began to paint, I felt that I could put my ideas down quickly and not be forced to stop and analyze the process or direction. Maintaining a flat surface in the most important consideration in the work. It seems the shapes in my paintings come automatically and I give emphasis and direction to certain shapes as the painting grows.[57]

In the late 1980s and 1990s, a shift occurred in abstract art in Texas, one that reflected a larger national phenomenon. As Lisa Phillips commented in 1988: "Today, the once optimistic ideal of linear progress has been abandoned as we seek to counter the destructive side effects of technological advancement. In art, as well, the notion of forward progress has been replaced by a new model of invention, one borne of antithetical forces that create friction, irresolution, ambiguity, and fluctuation. It is within this dynamic tension that artists must work, seeking some consolation in the metaphors of growth, eroticism, and personal identity that the natural realm provides."[58]

Phillips made this statement in the catalogue of an exhibition at the Whitney Museum of American Art titled *Vital Signs*, a survey that examined the primacy of organic abstraction in the history of American Modernism. This presentation not only featured the works of such early Modernists as Arthur Dove and Joseph Stella, but also those of such contemporaries as Terry Winters, Bill Jensen, and Elizabeth Murray, who probed nature to find paradigms for the generative force of abstraction.

A number of Texas artists similarly found organic abstraction to be a means of reinvigorating painting and sculpture. Unlike the artists discussed in the first chapter of this catalogue, few of these artists chose the local landscape as a point of departure; instead they found in the exotic an impetus to explore fresh directions in their work.

Salle Werner Vaughn brings an essentially Surrealist sensibility to her studies of nature. She attended Texas Woman's University, where she was a student of Carlotta M. Corpron and Toni LaSelle (see plates 83 and 84). In the early 1970s, Vaughn made Houston her home, and over the following decade she produced a range of work exploring the mythic and the sensual. Following the footsteps of such artists as Jean Cocteau and Yves Tanguy,

Vaughn created both paintings and installations that transport the visitor into hermetic realms resonant with allusion. William Kelly Simpson has described Vaughn's paintings: "Shapes exist in their own formal essence, related only to each other and subtly graded. The sure hand of the draftsman rules this world, a private, intense, and intimate theatre sustained not only by these metaphysical voyages, but also by flowering forms."[59]

Flower of Namaqualund, 1989 (plate 97), was inspired by a trip to South Africa, and the strange botanical images that punctuate the composition are based on studies of the flora of the region. Vaughn conjures up a mystical response to the exotic, and the composition reflects a visionary rather than a scientific sensibility. The nuanced veils of color both reveal and conceal images that are poignant in their ambiguity; brightly hued geometric planes, spheres, and the suggestion of plunging perspective create a sense of unanchored space and vertigo.

DeWitt Godfrey's sculptures also balance organic abstraction with a measured geometry, however to a startlingly different effect. After graduating from Yale University, he came to Houston in 1982 as a fellow in the newly established Core Residency Program. In 1985, he created a major outdoor installation, a series of three monumental abstract "drawings" made out of sheet steel and installed along Buffalo Bayou, as a part of the annual Houston International Festival.

Godfrey's work explores the positive and negative spatial relationships between such basic forms as the circle, the cone, and the helix. At the same time, his sculptures ratify Minimalism's insistence on the nature of the material itself. A 1989 untitled sculpture (plate 98), is made up of welded steel rebar, a labor-intensive industrial process pioneered by the artist. In a 1988 statement, Godfrey commented:

> Steel provides a grudging physical resistance that results in work that embodies a natural growth and rhythm; decisions cannot be made spontaneously but must survive the process of fabrication. As my aesthetic has matured, I have developed an approach that recognizes the integrity of materials and process, guided by a continuing refinement and evolution of ideas about form. The initial pure conceptualization of a sculpture is inevitably transformed by the practical demands and logical considerations inherent in building an object.[60]

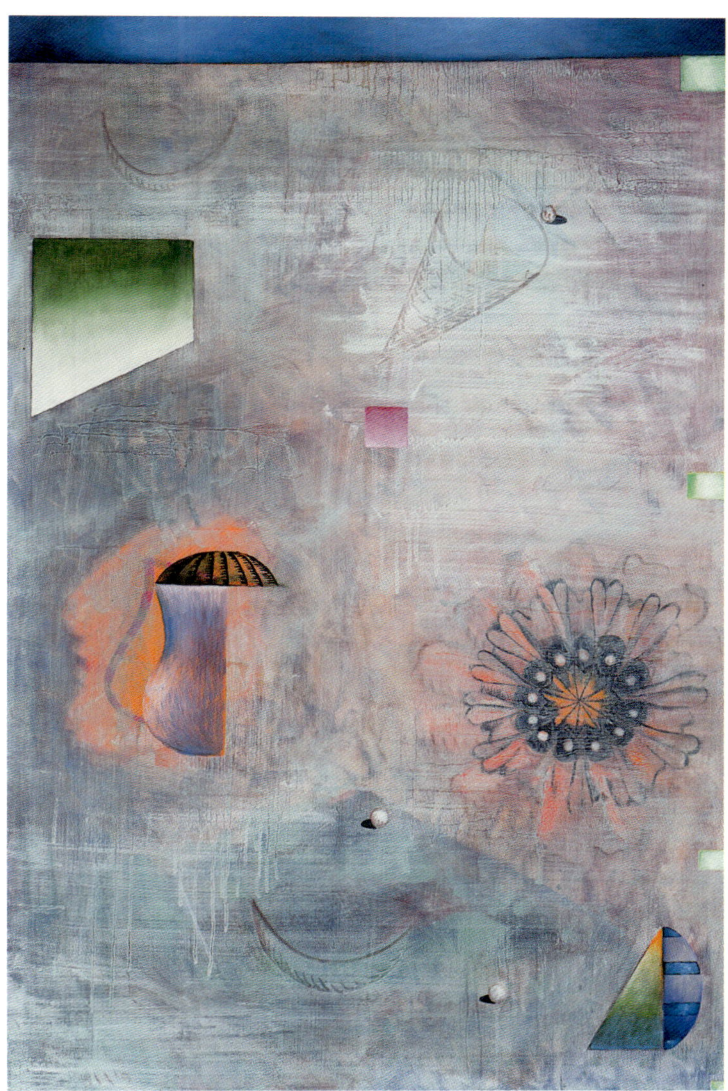

96 *opposite*
Ibsen Espada
Three Studies for a Cockfight,
1987
Mixed media on canvas,
80⅛ x 40 in. (203.5 x 101.6 cm). Museum purchase with funds provided by Dr. and Mrs. Anthony Henfrey and Simmons and Company International, 87.240.

97
Salle Werner Vaughn
Flower of Namaqualund,
1989
Oil on canvas, 50¾ x 36½ in. (128.9 x 92.7 cm). Museum purchase with funds provided by the Charles Engelhard Foundation in memory of E. Rudge Allen, Jr., 90.330.

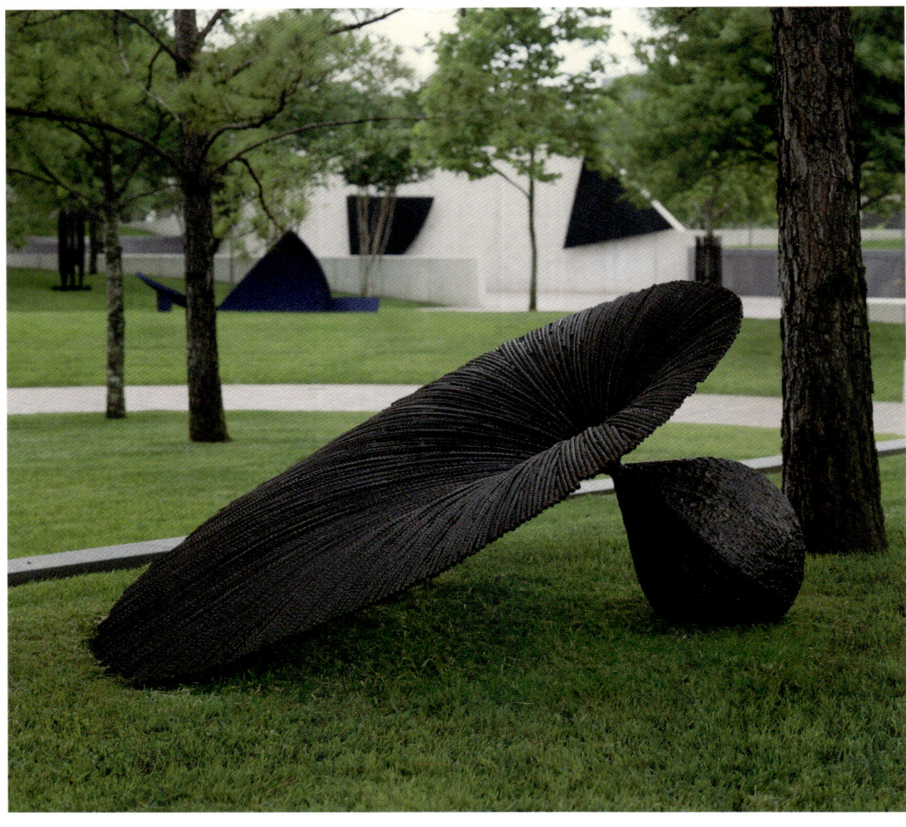

98
DeWitt Godfrey
Untitled, 1989
Welded steel, 33 x 69 x 65 in.
(83.8 x 175.3 x 165.1 cm).
Museum purchase with
funds provided by Duke
Energy, 91.1341.

99 *opposite*
Terrell James
A License to Thought, 1992
Oil and graphite with collage
on gessoed paper, 50 x 38 in.
(127 x 96.5 cm). Gift in
memory of Elizabeth
Bellows, 94.254.

Appropriately placed in the museum's Cullen Sculpture Garden, the work reads as a blossoming biomorphic form—such as a ripening seed pod—when seen in profile. Seen from straight on, Godfrey's sculpture reveals the pure geometry that provides the structural and conceptual basis of the composition, with the radiating rebars forming a perfect cone.[61] Michael Kimmelman wrote of these works: "His shapes are spare but their surfaces are varied in ways that endow these sculptures with a curious lightness and flexibility. There's something sexual about the curvaceous, budding forms and also something threatening about their tough unbendable rusting steel."[62]

In formal terms, Terrell James, Sally Gall, and Michael Kennaugh are primarily concerned with the spatial layering revealed by a study of landscape. James, a native of Houston, attended the University of the South, Sewanee, Tennessee, where the painter Edward Carlos was among her mentors. A stint as assistant director for the Smithsonian Institution's Archives of American Art Texas Project

in the early 1980s led her to compile a comprehensive archive on Forrest Bess (see plate 12), whose work has profoundly affected James's largely independent evolution.

In 1990, James embarked on a series of large oil drawings on paper that drew their inspiration from landscape imagery. The later drawings of the series, including *A License to Thought*, 1992 (plate 99), were based upon sketches the artist made while visiting the Monte Verde cloud forest reserve in Costa Rica. James synthesized careful observations taken from nature with an essentially abstract imagination. The L-shaped form which dominates the center of the composition was taken from a study of a waterfall, while other notations reflect plant forms.[63]

The compositional restraint of *A License to Thought* invites close examination. James uses washes of pigment and passages of collage to chart a remarkable depth of surface with minimal means. This process of examination becomes associative, as James scrutinizes the way in which memory is triggered by even the most tenuous evidence: "I am interested in the viewer's participation in my work. There is the painting, then there is something that happens between the viewer and the painting: a sort of second painting."[64] Daniel Stern commented further: "To gaze at a painting of Terrell James's is to enter into an experience in the making: painting in which the act of painting continues on as the eye wanders the finished surface. Each painting is completed by each individual encounter."[65]

Sally Gall grew up in Houston, and completed her studies at the Rhode Island School of Design. She first received recognition for her photographs of Houston's urban landscapes and the formal gardens of France, sites where nature and culture meet. Gall's work has prompted comparisons with the pictorialist photographers of the turn of the century. However, as Marilyn A. Zeitlin has noted: "While Gall's photographs may resemble those of the pictorialists on a formal level—blurred focus, diffused light—it is a superficial correspondence. Gall's images speak of contemporary life. She does not erase reference to the material world in search of a poetic equivalent of thought or the otherness of nature; she looks at the physical presence of humans in the landscape and sees a psychological dimension."[66]

Andrea, 1989 (plate 100), marks a departure from

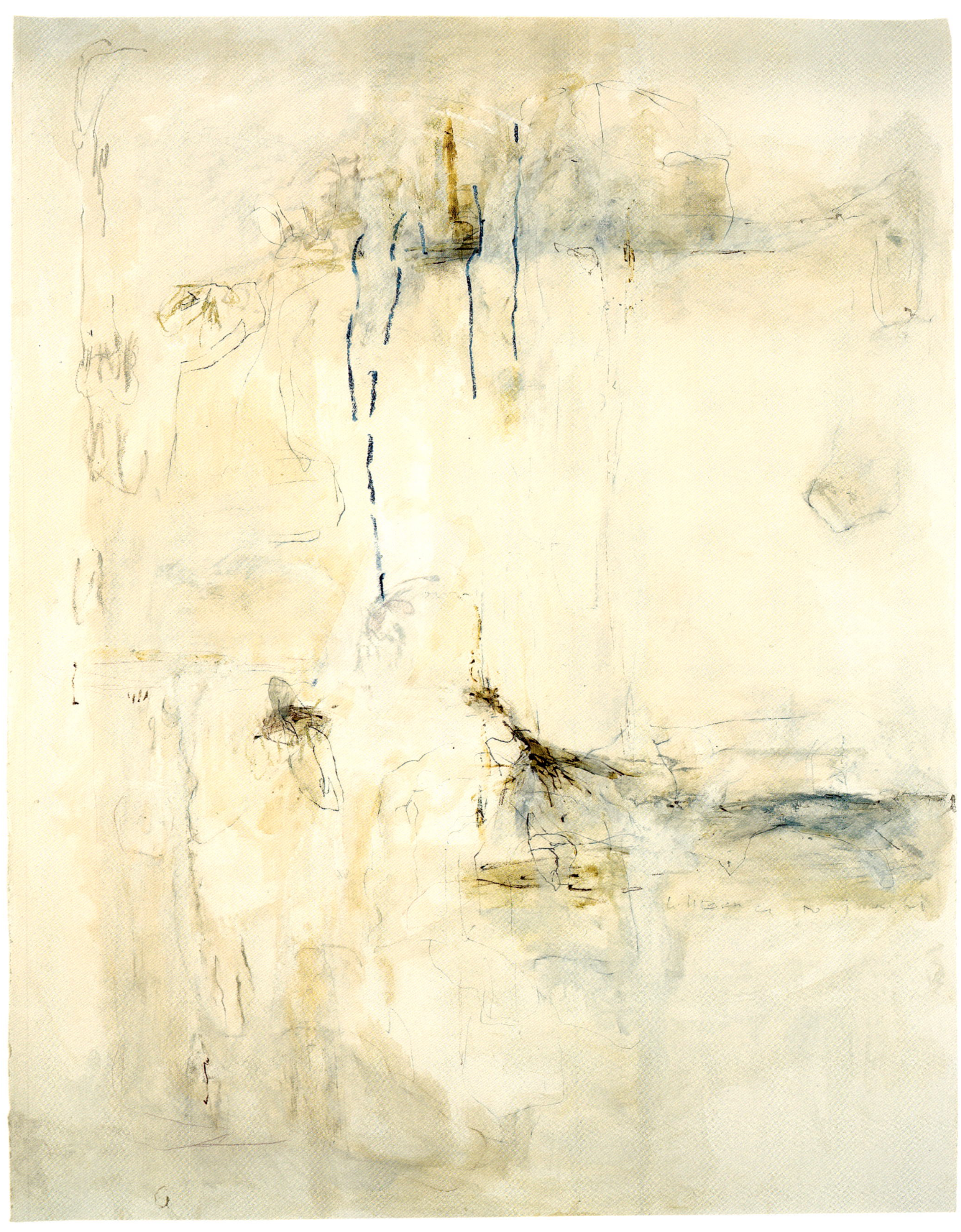

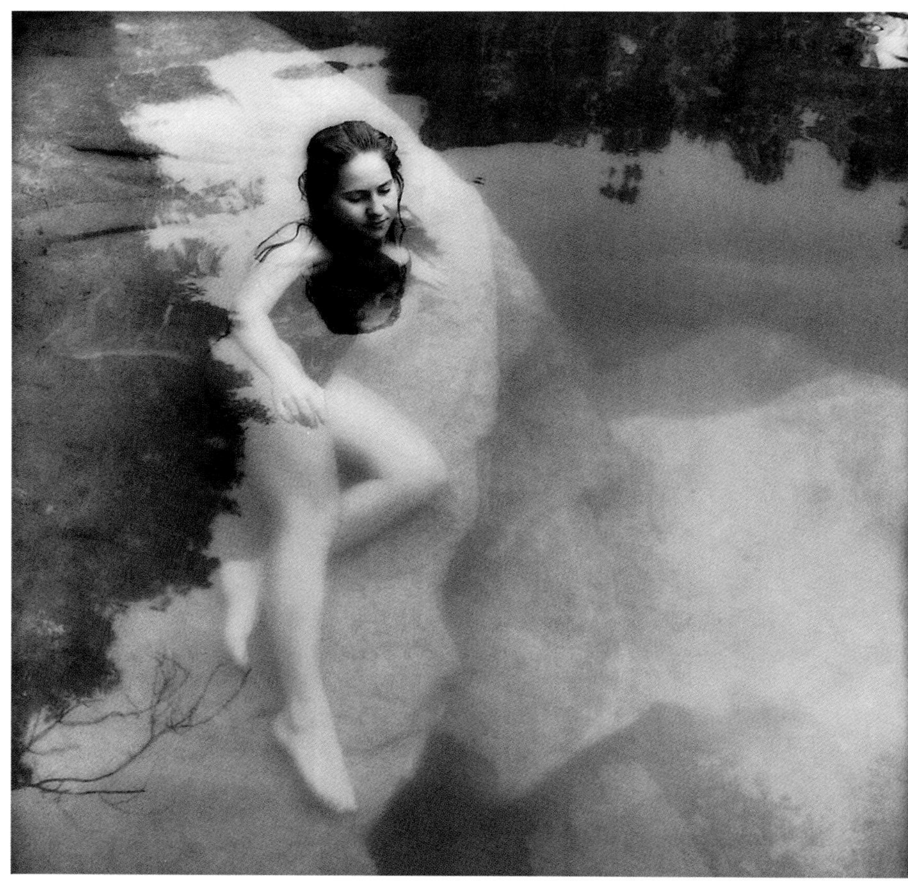

100
Sally Gall
Andrea, 1989
Gelatin silver photograph,
19 x 19 in. (48.3 x 48.3 cm).
The Allan Chasanoff Photo-
graphic Collection, 91.639.

much of Gall's work of the 1980s in that the landscape is closely cropped and lacks the specificity of place (whether Texan or exotic) that characterized much of her earlier work. The image invites several readings. On a literary level, it is tempting to identify the figure as a Nereid or water nymph. At the same time, Gall challenges such an interpretation through her emphasis on the structure of the composition. The mirroring of the figure's head is at once psychologically disturbing and formally succinct, drawing the viewer's eye to the sophisticated layering of transparency and reflection that collapse pictorial space. James Salter has written of these works, "They seem to describe solitude, the fields, the old things, nature herself, the nature which Tolstoy said was 'a friend you will never lose until death — and even then you die and disappear into nature.'"[67]

Michael Kennaugh also seeks the abstract in nature. Like many artists who grew up in East Texas, Kennaugh attended Lamar University; Paul Manes (see plate 31) was among his early mentors, and Kennaugh briefly worked in New York as Manes's studio assistant. *Amstel Dam*, 1995 (plate 101), is among the artist's most seductive paintings. Like much of Kennaugh's work of this period, it reveals his thoughtful assimilation of artists who have made drawing central to the structure of their compositions, including Paul Klee and Mark Tobey. A memory picture, *Amstel Dam* records both a visit to Holland and quotidian experiences. (The Amstel is one of the canals of Amsterdam.) The dappled play of light on water is evoked by the tonal washes of the composition; a journey is suggested by the traveling lines and arrows of graphite that transverse the canvas. Kennaugh has commented on his work of this period:

> The paintings evolve as a visual diary, recording those images and colors that emerge as recurring motifs. The forms are a record of the visual profundities of daily observations. Painted out of the conscious experience, they often reveal the subconscious, alluding to the larger concept. Most of the paintings take from three to five months to complete. The element of time is extremely important to the works as current experiences often develop into a formal language. Painted over time they begin to represent a development of an idea rather than a specific moment.[68]

   The formal power of *Amstel Dam* is carefully structured through the taut balance of contrasting compositional strategies: sharply nuanced graphic marks are pitted against looser gestural washes, while layers of transparent tones are punctuated by opaque dabs of paint. Indeed, Kennaugh's work can perhaps be best understood as a amalgam of the organic and the synthetic, the autographic and the referential.

   The 1980s and 1990s saw the emergence of a number of artists who brought to the Modernist canon a distinctly Postmodern sense of cultural and personal singularity. Among the artists to pioneer this reappraisal of form and content was Melvin Edwards, who in a 1994 interview stated: "Nobody gets away from identity, but it's not always declared."[69] Jesús Bautista Moroles and George Smith have similarly explored cultural archetypes through their otherwise severely minimal work.

   Melvin Edwards was born in Houston, where he spent the majority of his childhood. He was one of two students from Phyllis Wheatley High School selected to study at the Museum School in 1953, the first year that African-American students were admitted into the museum's classes. Following his graduation from Wheatley, he moved to Los Angeles, where he came of age as a sculptor. In 1963, Edwards initiated the *Lynch Fragment* series, an ongoing project that now comprises close to two hundred sculptures. The title of the series refers directly to America's appalling history of lynchings—and the series was prompted in part by the violence of the Civil Rights era—but each relief has its own frame of reference.

   Good Word from Cayenne, 1990 (plate 102), is dedicated to the poet Léon Gontran Damas, a friend and philosophical mentor of Edwards's who was born in Cayenne, French Guyana.[70] The dense composition and the evident weight of the iron and steel reflect precedents in twentieth-century assemblage such as Julio González and Richard Stankiewicz; the masklike shapes of the *Lynch Fragments* series allude to African sculpture. More importantly, Edwards has declared that the emphasis on metaphor in African art has been at the core of this own outlook, "the only realism in creation is procreation, all

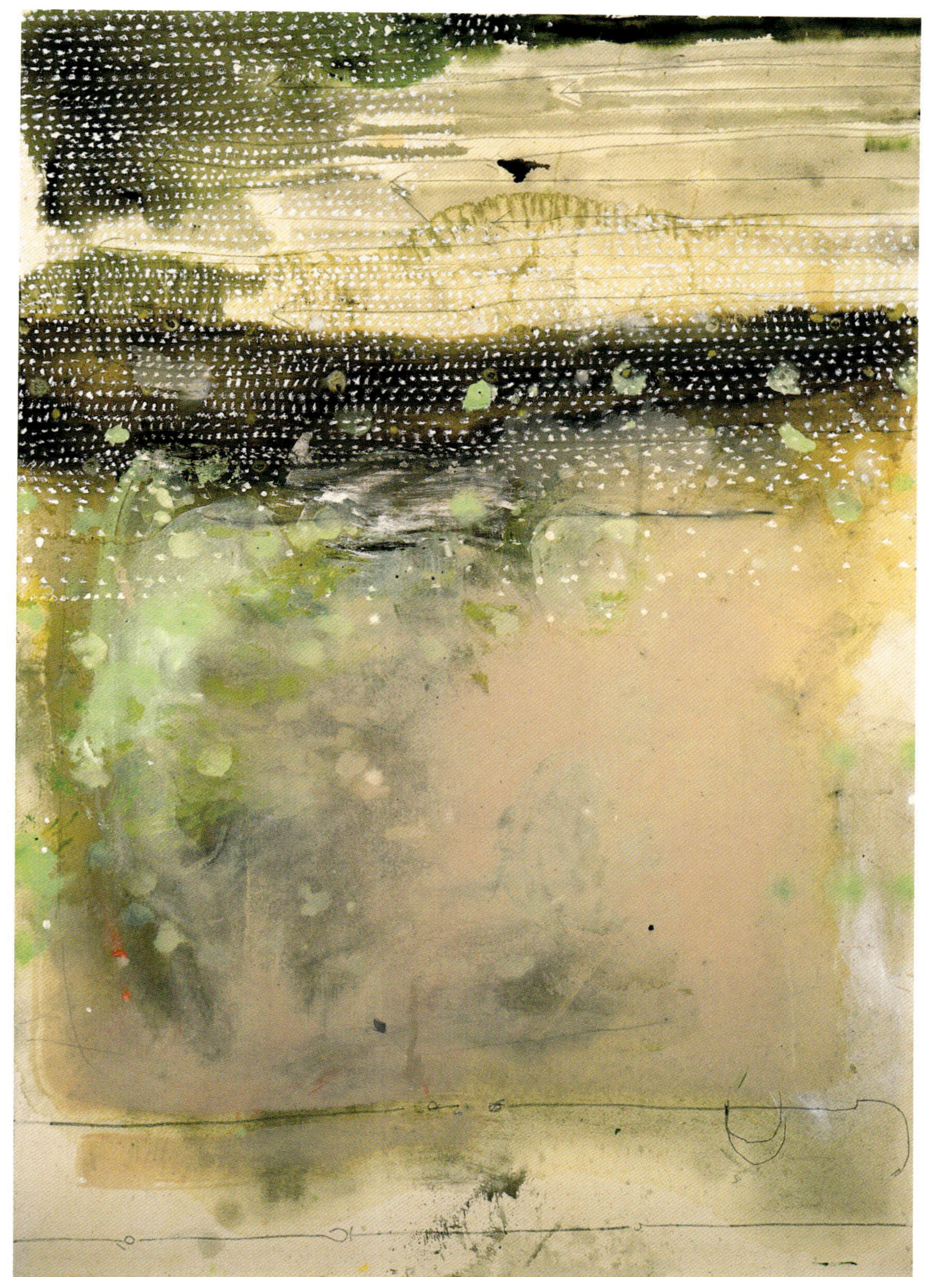

101
Michael Kennaugh
Amstel Dam, 1995
Oil and graphite on canvas,
66 x 46½ in. (167.6 x 118.1
cm). Museum purchase
with funds provided by
Steven J. Snook, 96.615.

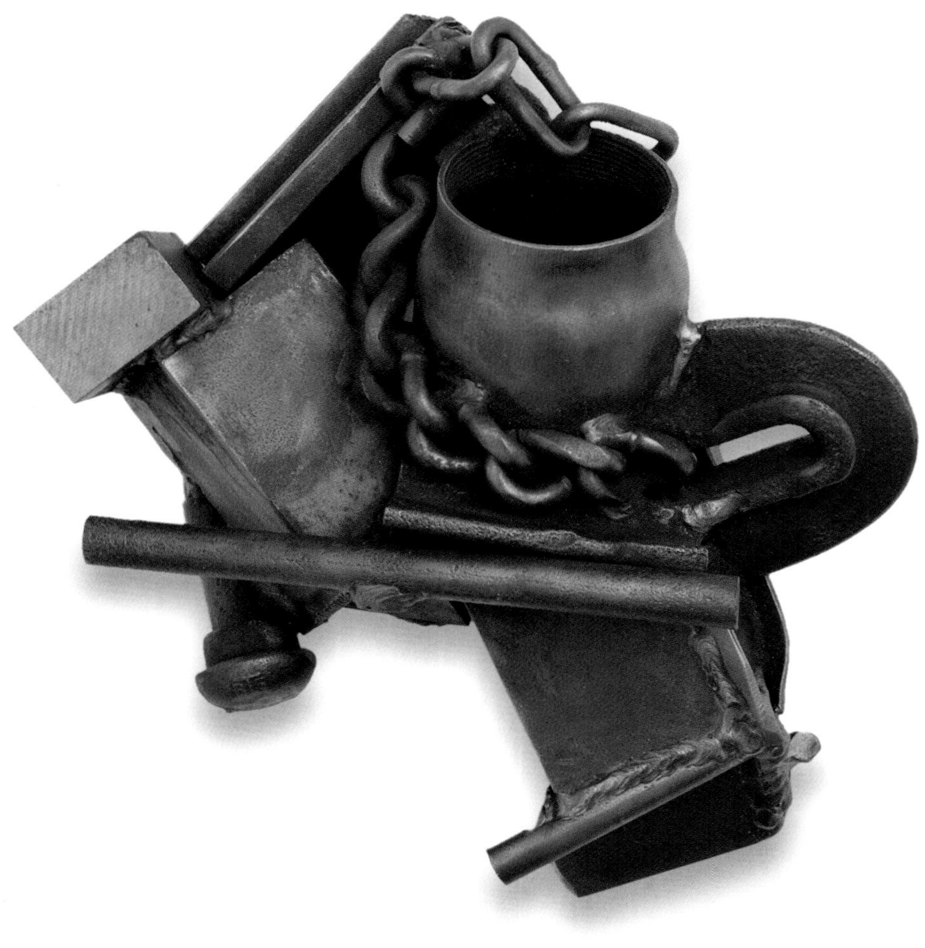

102
Melvin Edwards
Good Word from Cayenne,
from the *Lynch Fragments*
series, 1990
Welded steel, 13½ x 11¼ x
7 in. (34.3 x 28.6 x 17.8 cm).
Museum purchase with funds
provided by the Eleanor
Freed Stern Estate, 94.134.

103 *opposite*
Jesús Bautista Moroles
Texas Shield, 1988
Texas granite, 44⅛ x 24¼ x
23¾ in. (112.1 x 61.6 x 60.3
cm). Gift of Frank Ribelin,
88.292.

else is metaphor," and his use of found objects carries a range of allusions.[71] As Michael Brenson has pointed out: "The *Fragments* are emphatic, yet wide open. Chains can evoke the corrosiveness of slavery and also the supportiveness of bonding; scissors can suggest severing and disconnection and also piecing together; spikes and nails can communicate impaling, even crucifixion, and also be a call to constructive action. Because of their compositional dynamism, almost everything destructive and oppressive in the *Fragments* suggests the possibility of liberation and creation."[72]

In *Good Word from Cayenne* a chain snakes through the assemblage, vividly standing out as both a sign of pro-

tection and imprisonment; a cup can be understood as a vessel and a mouthpiece. The relief is otherwise made up of nonspecific elements that cascade together in a syncopated rhythm, forming a vibrant silhouette against the mural support.

Metaphor is also key to understanding the work of Jesús Bautista Moroles. Born in Corpus Christi, Moroles graduated from North Texas State University, Denton. He continued his exploration of sculpture first in the El Paso studio of Luis Jiménez (see plate 130), and later at the great marble quarries in Carrara, Italy, where he studied traditional stone carving. He returned to Texas in 1980, and opened a studio in Rockport in an old monument workshop. Over the following decade he developed a signature style of simplified forms and architectural motifs, using local granite and industrial techniques of hardstone cutting.

Texas Shield, 1988 (plate 103), is a variation of a motif that first appeared in the artist's work in 1986.[73] The interlocking forms suggest at once an architectural fragment and a protective buttress. While not specifically referencing Pre-Columbian architecture or sculpture, the hierarchic austerity of the work summons up the monoliths of ancient civilizations. As Jane Livingston has noted: "[Moroles's] obsession with monumentality and with the physical properties of quarried stone, together with a sure grasp of geometry, place him in a familiar modernist context. But alongside (really underneath) this aspect of Moroles's artistic heritage and concern is something else, some characteristic that definitely separates him from the art-historical mainstream.... Moroles somehow makes contemporary, makes new, and quite clearly makes *culturally specific*, his version of polished stone sculpture."[74]

George Smith similarly investigates correlations among the different facets of his artistic heritage. A native of upstate New York, Smith attended Hunter College, where he studied under Tony Smith, later becoming his studio assistant. He emerged as an artist of note in New York in the early 1970s, and in 1981 his work was the focus of a ten-year retrospective exhibition at the Studio Museum of Harlem; later that year he came to Houston to join the Rice University faculty.

As Thomas McEvilley has pointed out, the artist's

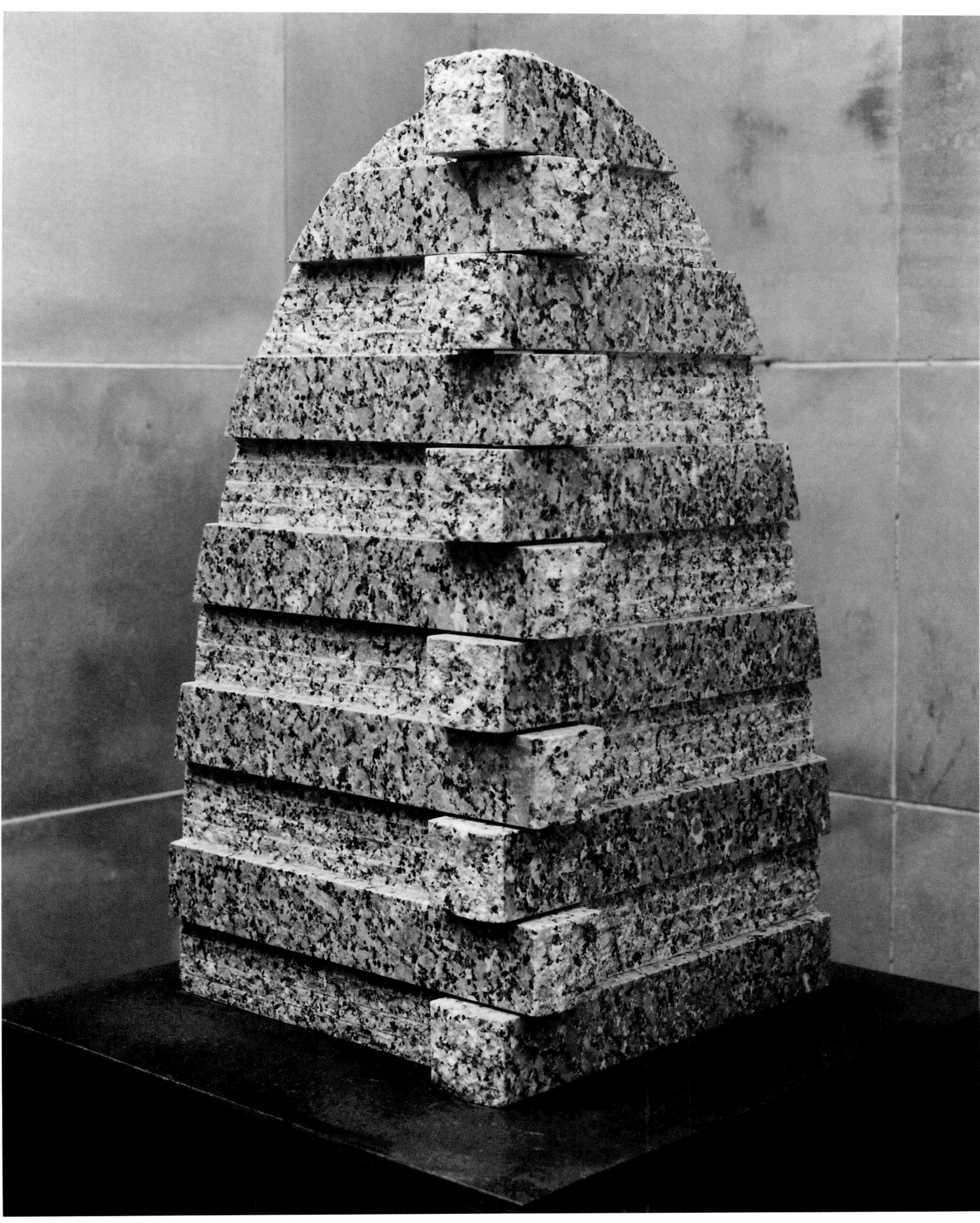

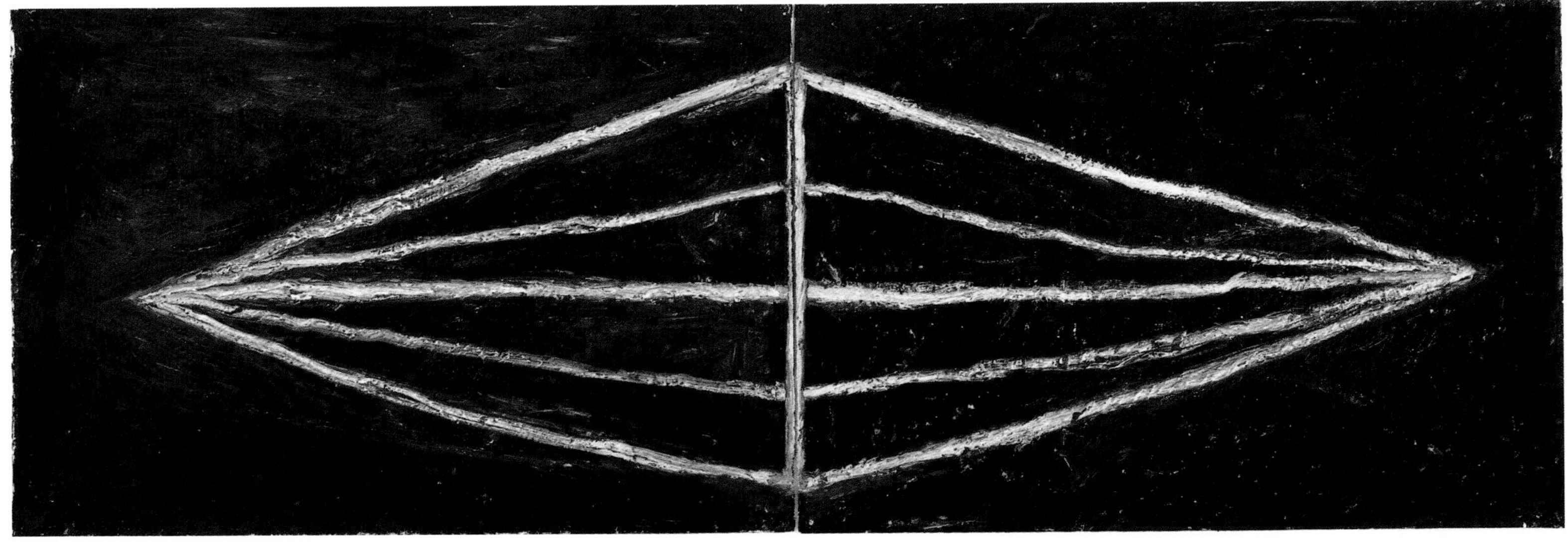

104
George Smith
Untitled Diptych, 1994
Oilstick on paper, 30 x 96 in.
(76.2 x 143.8 cm).
Museum purchase with funds
provided by the Eleanor
Freed Stern Estate, 94.649.

aesthetic evolved from an essentially Modernist to Postmodernist sensibility: "Smith's work has made this difficult and challenging transition from a non-referential to a referential mode of existence, from a sense of abstract purity to an acknowledgment of the personal nature of the work as simply 'mine.'"[75] One of the chief sources that Smith turned to in order to give context to his exploration of reductivist forms was Dogon architecture and sculpture. Smith has stated, "I was attracted to the art of the Dogon because of the geometry of it. The shapes of the carved figures, the posts, and the door locks. . . . I do not copy these forms, but instead use them as inspiration to express something that I have experienced."[76]

An untitled drawing of 1994 (plate 104), reflects Smith's dual allegiance to Modernism and African art. The taut pull of the lines and the thick buildup of pigment give this drawing a sculptural weight akin to the work of such artists as Richard Serra; the diptych format emphasizes the support material. At the same time the monochromatic composition summons up the batik drawings of West Africa, while the conical forms are derived from the architecture of the Dogon granaries. The mirroring of images between the two sheets further reflects Smith's investigation of Dogon cosmology, where one of the central myths is that of the twinning of terrestrial and celestial existence.[77]

The 1987 opening of The Menil Collection offered a benchmark in the history of the arts in Houston. Permanent installations of works by such artists as Barnett Newman directed attention to colorfield aesthetics. At the same time, the Menil's deep holdings in Surrealism, as well as special exhibitions dedicated to such figures as Joseph Beuys, promoted a heightened awareness of artists who chose to challenge the Modernist canon through an exploration of the spiritual. This emphasis also reflected larger national trends. In 1978, Rosalind Krauss had stated, "we find it incredibly embarrassing to mention 'art' and 'spirit' in the same sentence."[78] However, the AIDS crisis, which struck the world community over the following decade, redirected a new generation of artists towards the spiritual. While many chose diaristic and narrative approaches, as is discussed elsewhere in this catalogue, Amy Blakemore and John Wilcox were among those who chose Modernist compositional strategies to address existential issues. At the same time, such senior artists as Michael Tracy, who had dedicated his career to exploring the spiritual, addressed like subjects with continuing passion.

Tracy, whose work is introduced in the second chapter (see plate 52), created some of his most eloquent installations as a tribute to victims of oppression, including the *Requiem para los Olvidados [Requiem for the Lost Ones]*, seen at the Contemporary Arts Museum in Houston in 1983. *Flores de Guatemala I–IX*, 1986–92 (plate 105), can be understood as an extension of such works, memorializing the victims of years of civil war in Guatemala.[79] Each sheet contains an explosive burst of color: Tracy took his inspiration for his palette from the *flores de sangre* [flowers of blood], which grow in the mountains of central Mexico. These wildflowers are traditionally associated with Day of the Dead rituals, their crimson petals taking on symbolic connotations of sacrifice and renewal. The tripartite arrangement of the drawings and the rich gold frames evoke the panels of traditional Mexican altarpieces. However, as is typical of Tracy's drawings, imagery is discarded for more directly expressive gestures. Individually the drawings have a compact grace; taken as a whole they embody a fiery drama.

Amy Blakemore moved to Texas to attend the graduate program at the University of Texas at Austin; in 1985 she came to Houston as a fellow in the Core Residency Program. Her photographs of children, stripped of sentimental convention, first brought her broad recognition. These works took an oblique angle to depict the private rituals of childhood, and Blakemore commented in 1991, "These pictures offer information in a conciliatory manner—they read the way memory reads, with a measure of fact and a degree of abjuration. In this way, it is the viewer's task to complete the picture through her or his own experience."[80]

One of the chief themes of Blakemore's work is her ongoing examination of what motivates the leap of faith

105
Michael Tracy
Flores de Guatemala I–IX,
1986–92
Watercolor, gouache, and oilstick on paper, nine sheets, 22¼ x 30¼ in. (56.5 x 76.8 cm) each. Museum purchase with funds provided by the George Bunker Living Trust and Mrs. Susan McAshan, 93.259.

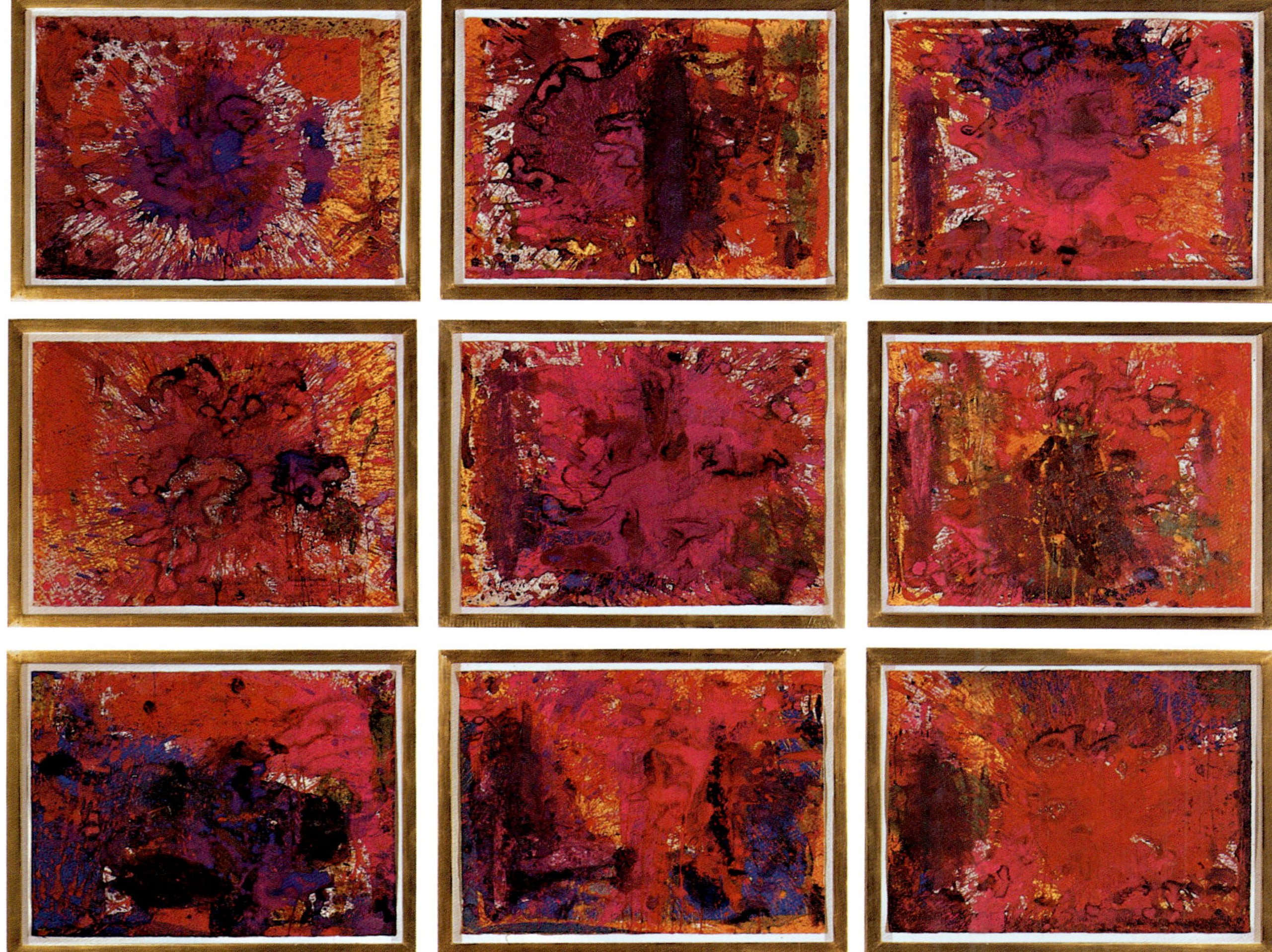

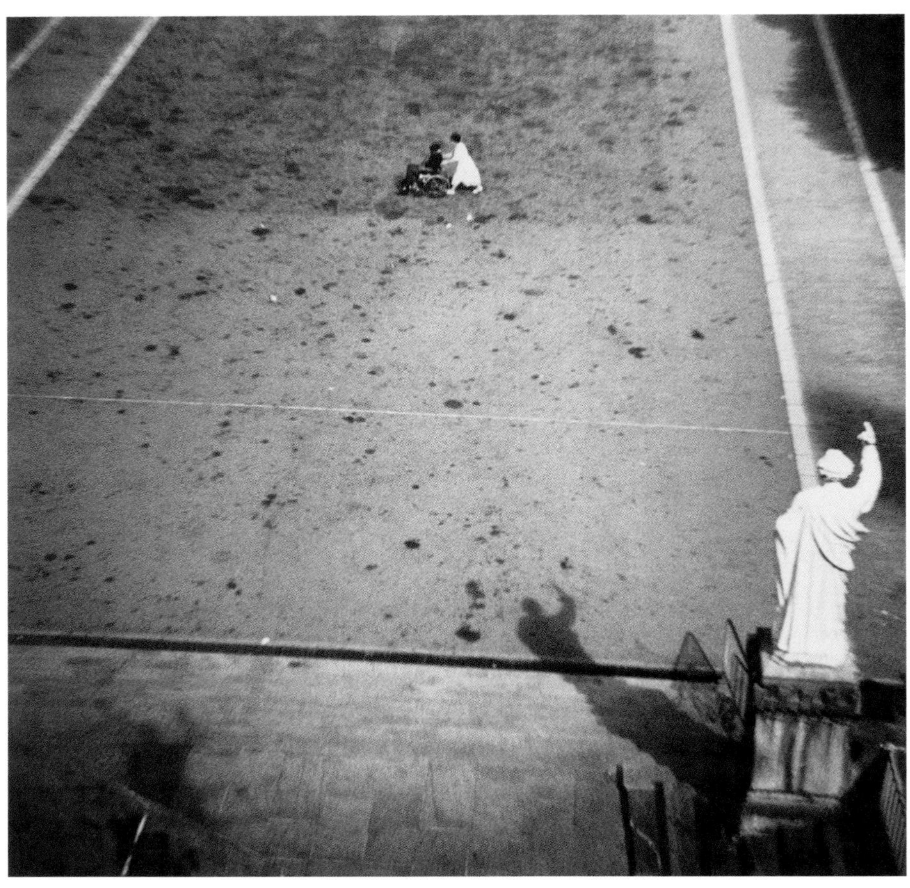

106
Amy Blakemore
Plaza, 1992
Selenium-toned gelatin silver photograph, 15⅛ x 15 in.
(38.4 x 38.1 cm). Museum
purchase with funds provided
by Clinton T. Willour in
honor of Mark Petr, 93.272.

in our time. She has credited an image of snake handlers as her first mature work, and in 1992, Blakemore took a series of photographs of Lourdes, initiating a series dedicated to pilgrimage sites. In many of the Lourdes images, the composition is without a central focus and figures are spun to the edge of the picture frame. Blakemore does not disguise the fact that the majority of pilgrims come to Lourdes to seek not only redemption, but also physical healing.

As *Plaza*, 1992 (plate 106), reveals, Lourdes can be a disturbingly vacuous place. The tilted bird's-eye view of the camera—a hallmark of early Modernist photography—flattens the visual space of the composition: the empty ground; the diminished figure in a wheelchair; and the distorted shadow of the gesturing saint suggest the intangibility, or even impossibility, of solace in this world. Susie Kalil has written of these works: "These are twilight places, where what we see is about to be transformed or transported into something or somewhere else. We search for something that might be holy, or at the very least a place were we can feel the presence of an expressive force that moves us to think about our memories and blind spots, our feelings and follies. Blakemore's images reveal that the destination is quite likely to not be nearly as meaningful as the journey itself."[81]

John Wilcox combines a Minimalist sense of process with a deeply sensual command of color. A native of North Texas, Wilcox attended Colorado College in Colorado Springs and the University of Texas at Austin, ultimately making his home in Dallas. *Untitled (The Tomb Is Empty)*, 1995 (plate 107), is among a series of works of the mid-1990s in which Wilcox sought to bring new content to monochromatic composition. While these works appear to be a single field of color, they have a radiance that is achieved by multiple applications of layers of paint. Frances Colpitt has explained:

> [Wilcox's] newest, luminous monochromes resonate with layer upon layer of color, which, along with the paintings' intimate scale, is conducive to slow, quiet contemplation. Although Wilcox admits to being influenced by the gestalt theory embraced by Minimal artists (which demanded that a work of art be first and foremost a single, whole shape), he is inspired by more personal and transcendental concerns. *Untitled (The Tomb Is Empty)* was painted during the hospitalization of a friend who was HIV positive. Each day the artist applied a layer of brilliant yellow paint. . . . The following day the paint was sanded and another layer laid down. The process and the radiant painting it engendered are Wilcox's means for coming to terms with death and achieving a balance of the tragic and the transcendent.[82]

The yellow field is given further visual impact by the fact that it does not continue to the edge of the canvas. Rather, Wilcox floats the field slightly within the frame of the composition, allowing a white margin to be revealed. The artist has identified the yellow palette as the color of his friend's truck—as well as that of New York taxicabs—but it is also the revelatory color used by Mathias Grünewald in the *Transfiguration* panel of the *Isenheim Altarpiece*. Grünewald frames the resurrected Christ in a brilliant, yellow halo, and Wilcox's reference to this masterpiece is made clear by his choice of subtitle.

The 1990s saw further developments in organic abstraction, moving away from the landscape imagery that propelled such artists as Terrell James and Michael Kennaugh (see plates 99 and 101), and towards more biological and corporeal metaphors. Brian Portman, Joe Mancuso, Tracy Harris, and Jackie Tileston have explored the ways in which abstraction can reflect the physical parameters of the body. While many artists made the frailty of the body a focus in the post-AIDS era, these artists emphasize the essential power of the human anatomy.

Brian Portman's paintings are unabashedly provocative: warm tones, earthy forms, organic images evoke the realm of the senses. Portman came to Houston in 1983 as a fellow of the Core Residency program, and by the mid-1980s, he had established a reputation as an extraordinary draftsman. Over the following years he devoted himself almost exclusively to working in charcoal; beginning in 1992, however, Portman returned to painting, creating works which seem inspired by a *horror vacui*. The densely layered spaces of his compositions recall the baroque labyrinths of Piranesi's *Prisons*, and at a glance his work appears to be so rich in painterly allusions as to be almost indecipherable. On closer examination, however, it is possible to discern the luminous dialogue Portman establishes between line and structure, reference and content.

With *Vertical Dances*, 1994 (plate 108), Portman strikes a delicate balance between lucidity and complexity. He exploits the elastic qualities of painterly media, contrasting the dark shadowy ground with the tense calligraphy of the surface. While avoiding any direct reference to the human anatomy, Portman delves into the sensual. Michael Ennis has commented on this painting:

> Portman shows what a talented young artist can do with the entire history of twentieth-century art at his disposal. Layered almost like an archeological site, the image reveals its cubist ancestry in the faceted, gridlike structure visible beneath the translucent dark glazes; at the surface is a dancing pattern of calligraphic strokes recalling Cubism's American descendent, Abstract Expressionism. But Portman's contemplative work isn't animated by nostalgia for Modernism's glory days. Instead, it asserts the continuing capacity of paint, form, and gesture to evoke the deepest emotions.[83]

107
John Wilcox
Untitled (The Tomb Is Empty), 1995
Oil on canvas, 39¼ x 30¼ in. (99.7 x 76.8 cm). Museum purchase in memory of Joe Fawbush with funds provided by friends of the artist, 96.798.

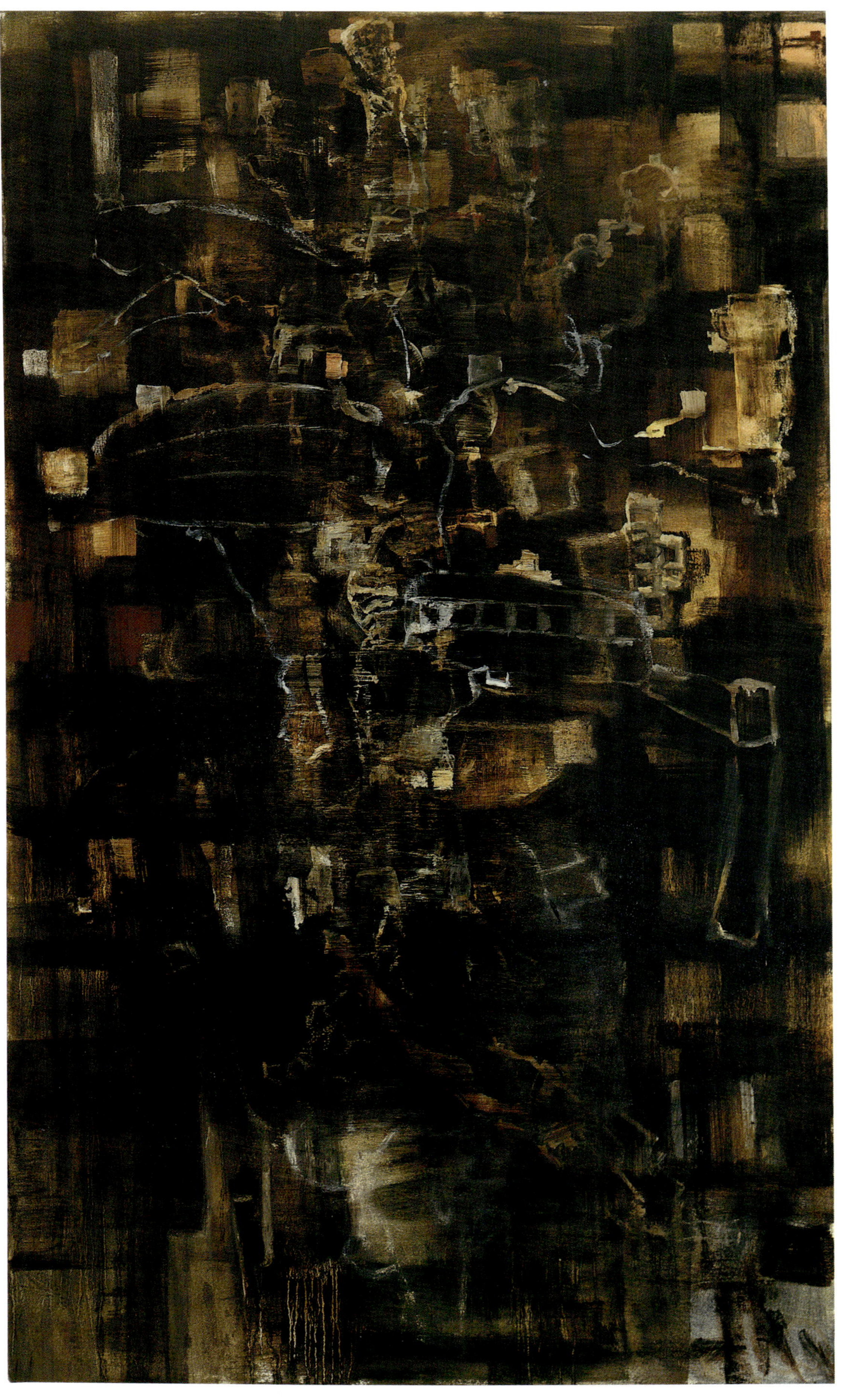

Like John Wilcox (see plate 107), Joe Mancuso has adopted Minimalist strategies in both his paintings and sculptures. A native of the Midwest, Mancuso came to Houston in 1982; his work evolved through an increasingly nuanced play between two- and three-dimensional forms. An ongoing series of paintings from the early 1990s were structured around concentric circles, defined by the width of the artist's brush and animated by shifts in touch and density of medium.

Mancuso's sculptures of this period are similarly conceived; *Vessel*, 1993 (plate 109), is made up of wooden lathes that the artist has shaped into a column. Using found materials from local building sites, Mancuso introduces a random element into his otherwise tightly controlled construction: while equal in width, the lathes are of different lengths, and are variously weathered. The dimensions of the column echo the artist's height and girth, with the central portion of the column offering a slight anthropomorphic curve.

While the vessel image has become a familiar identifier for a number of women artists, Mancuso finds in the process of constructing his sculpture a mirror for his concerns. Aaron Parazette has written of Mancuso's work, "The circle is the most demanding form in nature. Proposing motion while arresting the passing glance, a circle creates a field of focus and a measure of perfection. It is a standard against which Joe Mancuso measures himself."[84] Valerie Loupe Olsen has further elaborated, "Mancuso wants the viewer to appreciate a sense of beauty, which is based on simplicity and harmony.... Mancuso's odyssey as a perpetual seeker of the worthless or the common is rewarded by his redemption of the seemingly irredeemable, and by making the common beautiful. As he pursues this pilgrimage, Mancuso also seeks the spirit of life within the materialism of human existence."[85]

Tracy Harris, a native of Oklahoma, was raised in Dallas. Both her father and her grandfather were architects, and her compositions are characterized by a sense of the plasticity of space. Michael Ennis describes Harris's compositions of 1990: "[Harris's painting and drawings] might be best approached as still lifes pushed to the metaphysical limit, familiar shapes peeled, dissected, and permuted into models of uncertainty. The reticent, virtually monochrome fields are scratched and scrawled

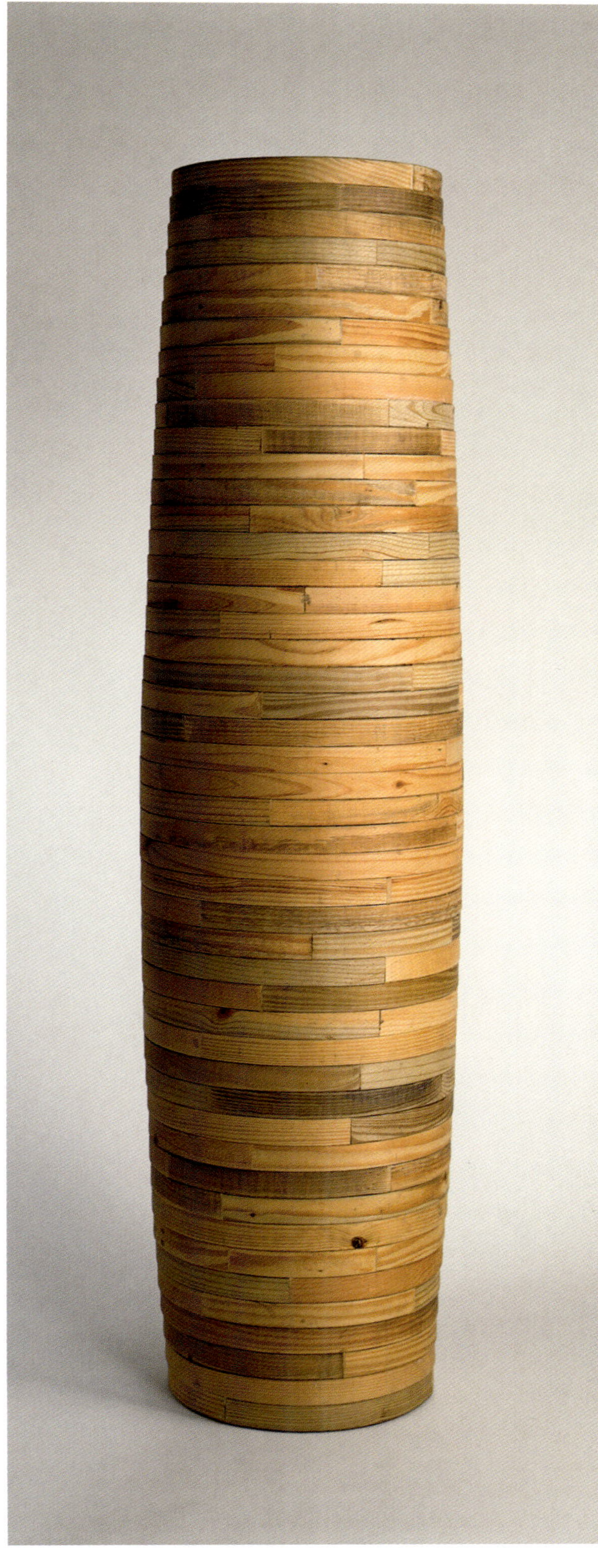

108 *opposite*
Brian Portman
Vertical Dances, 1994
Oil on acrylic on canvas, 72 x 47¾ in. (182.9 x 121.3 cm). Museum purchase with funds provided by Christopher J. Gongolas in memory of Helen R. Gongolas, 94.650.

109
Joe Mancuso
Vessel, 1993
Wood, 72 x 18 x 18 in. (182.9 x 45.7 x 45.7 cm). Museum purchase with funds provided by Diane S. Baker, Mr. and Mrs. Louis B. Cushman, Dr. and Mrs. Clive Fields, Dr. Alton and Emily Steiner and The May Department Stores Company Foundation, 95.198.

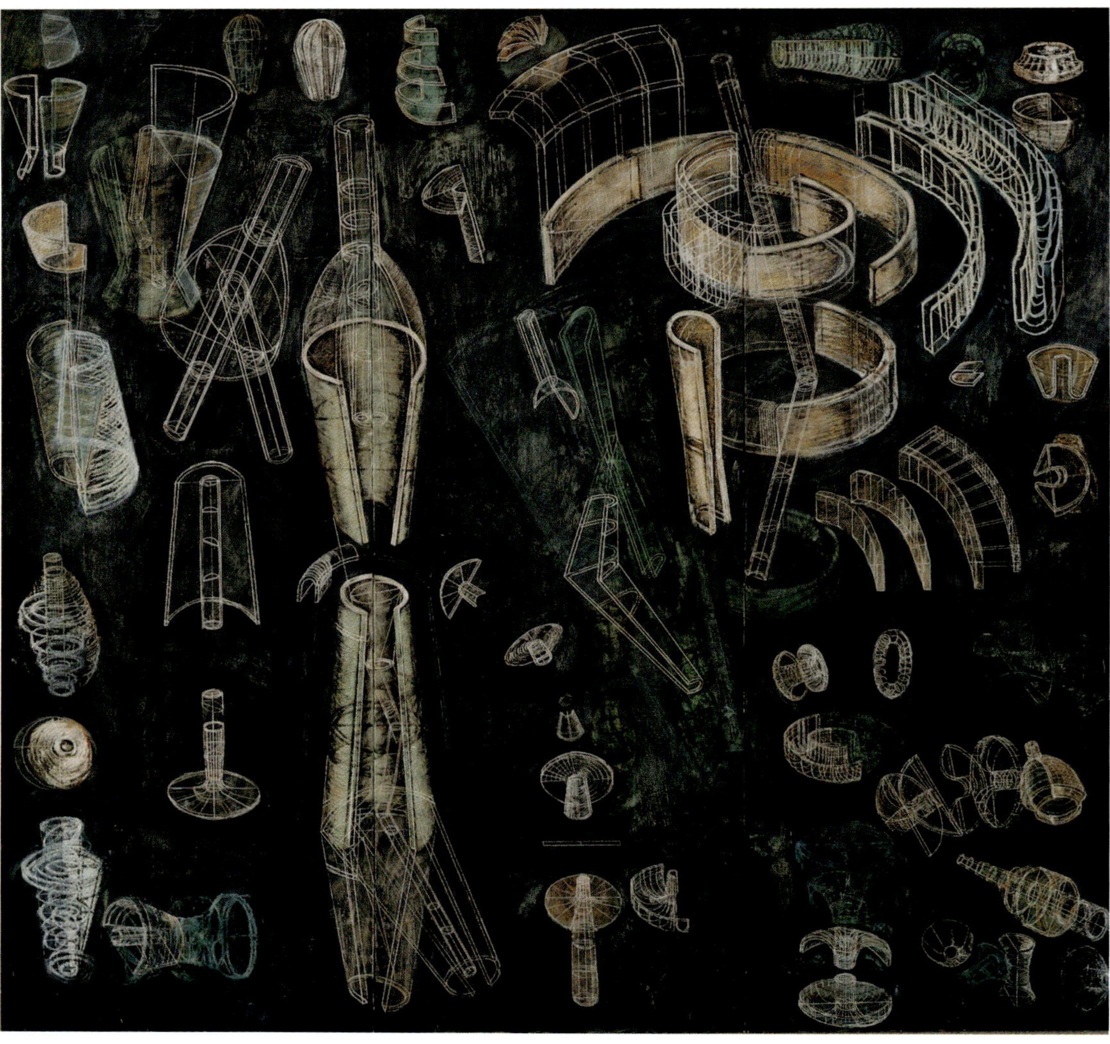

110
Tracy Harris
Cup for Inversion of Choice,
1989–90
Oil and encaustic on wood,
80 x 84 in. (203.2 x 213.3 cm).
Museum purchase with
funds provided by
Duke Energy, 90.408.

with what looks like a cross between Leonardo da Vinci's anatomical studies and computer-drawn engineering schematics. Objects that initially seem mechanical evolve into organic sensuality; solid forms explode into skeletal components."[86]

The impact of Harris's passionately analytical compositions is derived from the masterful quality of her draftsmanship. Transparent planes reveal interior structures, and the artist has recalled, "I was always interested in the paper buildings my father was working with. For a long time I didn't understand the difference between a plan and an elevation, so I tried to combine them in my own drawings."[87]

Cup for Inversion of Choice, 1989–90 (plate 110), resonates with figurative and architectonic connotations. For example, the repeated cylindrical forms suggest exoskeletons, girdles, and buttresses. In adopting such metaphors, Harris knowingly deconstructs a humanist tradition in architecture that stretches from Vetruvius, to Michelangelo, to Le Corbusier. In an essay on Renaissance architectural proportions, Oswald Mathia Ungers has noted: "Those who theorized on architecture turned to

nature's own forms—and particularly the human body—to deduce the elements of proportion as much for the architectural orders as for buildings as a whole. The essential geometrical figures remained the circle and the square, as representations and synonyms for the cosmos."[88]

Harris finds a wholeness in her examination of forms. *Cup for Inversion of Choice* is constructed with no reference to scale, and the order implied by Harris's structures ranges from the microcosmic to the universal.

Similar perceptual shifts characterize the work of Jackie Tileston. Born in the Philippines, Tileston traveled widely before coming to Houston in 1988 to take part in the Core Residency Program. Her compositions frequently use emblematic forms as a point of departure, and the artist has stated that she is interested in "invented and organic forms and their variations that for me are evocative of vessels, the body, artifacts, the Trix Rabbit, etc. . . . All of these paintings play with dualities between what is and what isn't, background/foreground, physical/immaterial, solid/atmospheric, sexual/spiritual."[89]

These dualities are aptly reflected in *Love's Function,*

1991 (plate 111).[90] Tileston imbues her composition with a mystic sensuality: a cosmological vista is framed within sexually charged forms. Frances Colpitt has stated of slightly later works: "[Tileston] operates outside the skeptical mainstream of contemporary painting. Admitting to an optimistic attitude and indulgence in beauty (only recently admissible in discussions of contemporary art, a revival that spirituality has yet to attain), she seduces her viewers with spectacular optical displays."[91]

As the 1990s progressed, a number of Texas artists began to create works that exposed an increasing self-consciousness in regard to the history of abstraction, a shift that was reflected in such exhibitions as *Buttered Side Up*; *Analogs of Modernism*; *Texas Abstract: New Painting of the Nineties*; and *Abstract Painting, Once Removed*.[92] The work of these artists reflected a change in emotional tenor, and as Tom Moody has noted: "None of these artists find it possible to believe in abstract art the way their predecessors did. Our culture has become too ironic, our expressions too self-critical to permit the religious feelings that Malevich, say, had for his art."[93]

Interestingly, this line of investigation attracted few women artists in Texas. Dave Hickey has speculated that the shallow picture plane is a masculine conceit,[94] and David Pagel has noted that "until very recently, if an artist was a woman who also made abstract work, it was assumed that . . . her art offered a critical commentary on the obvious macho problems posed by Minimalism, Abstract Expressionism, and other unfriendly styles from which women had been excluded."[95]

Pagel goes on to observe that in the mid-1990s, a number of women emerged on the West Coast who made important contributions to Postmodern abstraction, including Ingrid Calame, Monique Prieto, and Pae White. In Texas, however, only a handful of women artists emerging in the 1990s have addressed abstraction on an ambitious scale, and while there are notable exceptions, Postmodernist abstraction in Texas became a largely masculine pursuit.[96]

David Aylsworth, Giles Lyon, and Michael Miller are among those whose paintings exemplifies this shift. All fellows of the Core Residency Program in the 1980s,

their work followed certain parallel developments. However, as the work of Casey Williams, Joseph Havel, and Tad Griffin demonstrates, these concerns were not the exclusive property of artists who emerged out of the Glassell School.

David Aylsworth came to Texas in 1989 from Ohio, where he had studied at Kent State. Taking inspiration from such early Modernists as Marsden Hartley, his paintings of the early 1990s were typically intimate in scale. These works displayed an extraordinary visual wit, balancing an ebullient palette of pastels and secondary colors with taut compositional structures. In 1994, Aylsworth, Giles Lyon, and Bill Davenport organized an exhibition of their work for Houston's Lawndale Art and Performance Center. Titled *Buttered Side Up*, the exhibition featured

111
Jackie Tileston
Love's Function, 1991
Oil and lead white on canvas, 82¼ x 69½ in. (208.9 x 176.5 cm). Museum purchase with funds provided by Tim Crowley and Lynn Goode in honor of Bill Graham, 92.246.

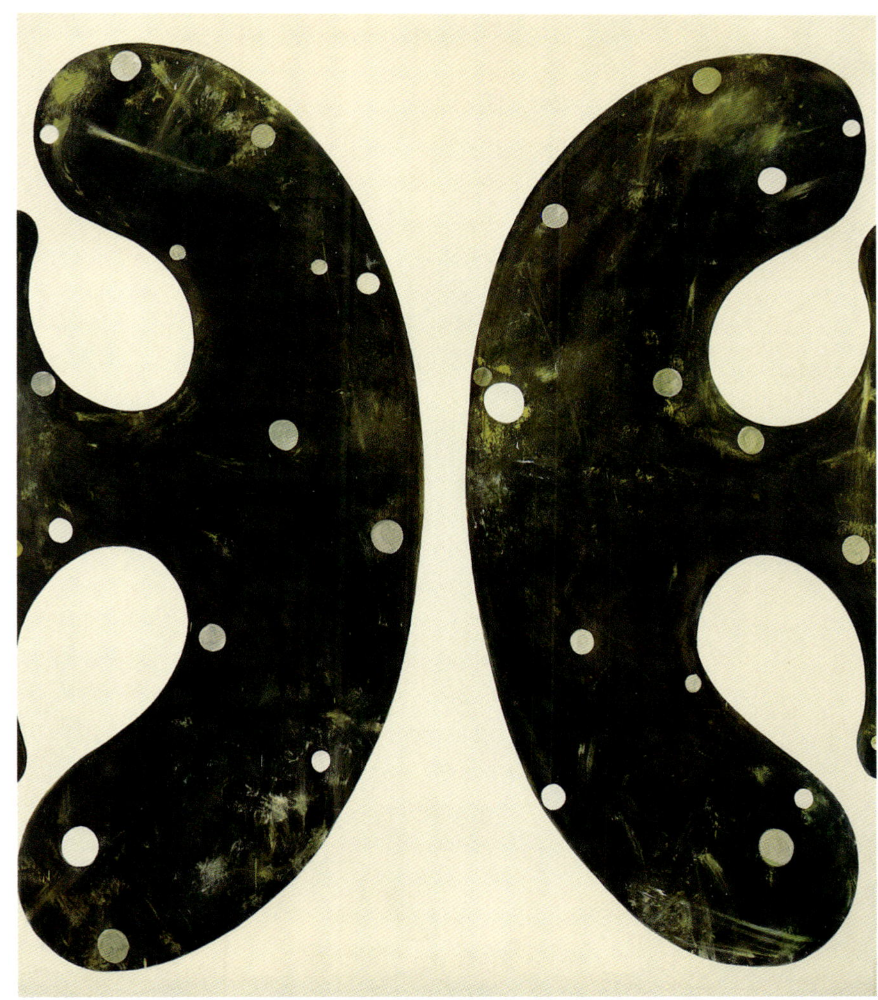

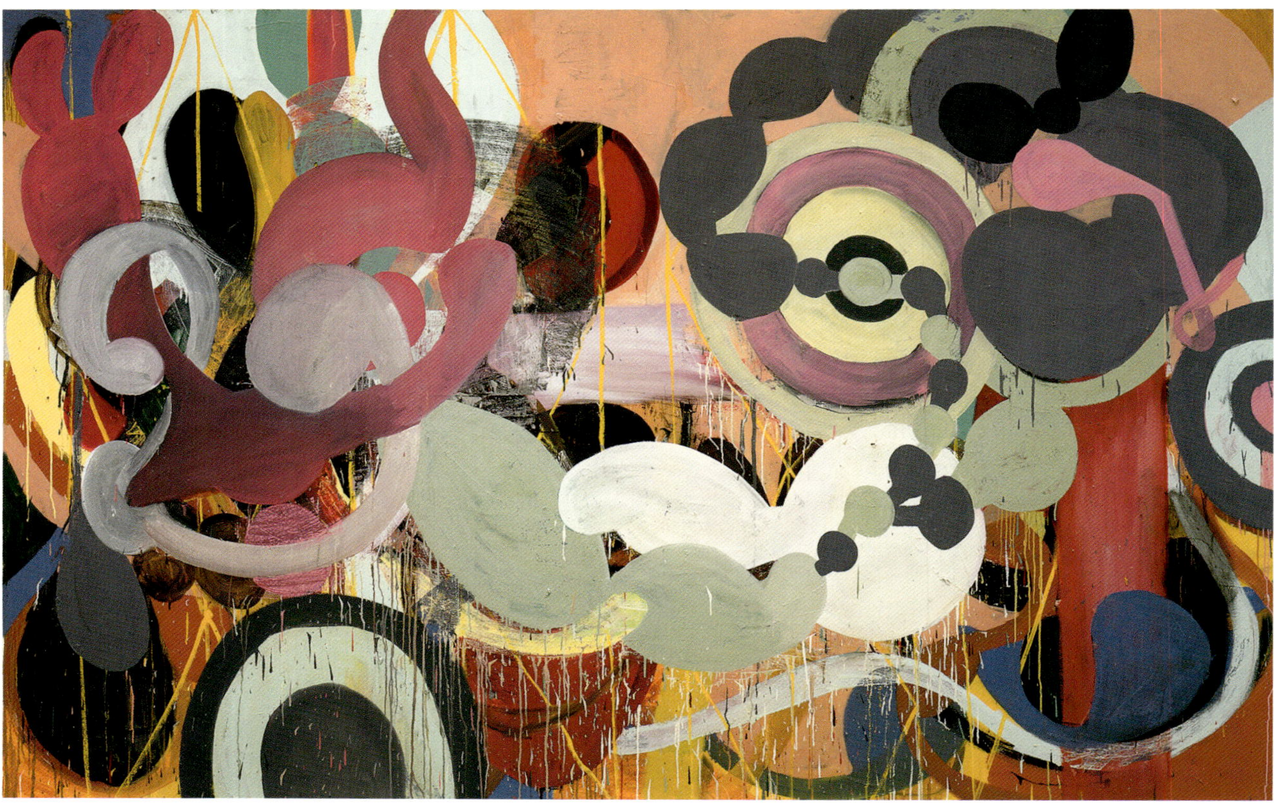

112
David Aylsworth
Bereft of F., 1994
Oil on canvas, 74 x 116 in.
(188 x 294.6 cm). Museum
purchase with funds provided
by Alton and Emily Steiner,
Kerry F. Inman, and Kevin
Schofield with matching
funds provided by The May
Department Stores Company
Foundation and BP America,
94.655.

the artists' most ambitious projects to date. Bernard Brunon observed in the catalogue that these artists were linked by "a similar attitude in front of the medium, refusing to control it totally but rather allowing the painting to be part of the creative process. Actually, all their works evidence an obvious pleasure in the act of painting.... Pleasure seems in fact to have been part of the act of painting from the very beginning, and this might be one of the main reasons why 'the death of painting' seems to be a pure intellectual speculation."[97]

Bereft of F., 1994 (plate 112), was among Aylsworth's contributions to the show, and marked a departure in scale and resolution.[98] The elongated format of the canvas offers a panoramic compositional field, and, working wet on wet, Aylsworth achieves a vivid, painterly immediacy. Surfaces are scraped and layered; pentimenti and semi-opaque overpainting create an active ground; forms spin into one another, generating new shapes and cadences. While the artist keeps figurative elements at bay, the suggestive silhouetting of his forms gives further animation to the composition. In an unpublished statement, Aylsworth placed his work in relation to the history of Modernism:

It's intoxicating to work at the end of the century and look back at the beginning of the century. Gertrude Stein talked about how she personally brought writing out of the nineteenth century and into the twentieth. I'm not sure at all how to do the similar thing into the twenty-first century, but I do believe that she and other writers and artists did . . . and we can find some help from their examples.[99]

Giles Lyon, a native New Yorker, attended the Rhode Island School of Design before coming to Houston in 1989. By the mid-1990s, Giles Lyon had embraced a deliriously hybrid signature style, aptly described by Marek Bartelik: "[Lyon's] paintings combine high seriousness of purpose with a playfully cryptic use of material. They absorb a profusion of sources—from Pollock's allover drips, Warhol's 'found' abstractions modeled on Rorschach inkblots, and Taaffe's decorative motifs to Japanese animation and Dr. Seuss illustrations—into an intensely nervous stylistic mélange reminiscent of Texas Funk."[100]

In his most successful works, Lyon embraces chance and celebrates draftsmanship; he randomly stains the canvas, and then builds a densely locked composition from images he discovers within the stains. *Memory Quilt*, 1996–97 (plate 113), demonstrates Lyon's intuitive balance of the freewheeling and the purposeful. Passages of pure abstraction and suggestive reference rambunctiously crowd the canvas: cartoonlike figures emerge from the loosely worked ground, while brilliant colors and delicate shades create a visual pulse across the composition. John Goodman has written of this painting: "Here the many odd elements, which can look like body parts, color patches or classically gestural abstract forms, coexist uneasily, yet somehow remain connected. Despite the painting's funkiness, the simple areas of color at its borders . . . imply a sensibility as lyrical as it is rough."[101]

Much as Aylsworth and Lyon were seeking to reinvigorate abstraction through an exuberant frame of reference, Casey Williams used montage techniques to similar ends. Williams was born in Houston, and he established a career considerably earlier than the artists discussed above. He graduated from the University of Texas at Austin in 1970, where among his most important teachers was Russell Lee (see plate 10).

Williams's first photographs were landscape essays in mood and memory; in the early 1980s, Williams began to hand-tint his compositions, giving them at once a nostalgic quality while also heightening their immediate impact. At the same time, he enlarged the format of these works, exploring the true and illusionary scale of foreground and background relationships. In the early 1990s, Williams began to experiment with in-camera montage, physically blocking part of the lens, and then running the film through a second series of exposures. The process introduced an element of randomness into the resulting works; however, as the series progressed, the layering of images became more highly structured. Peter Doroshenko has observed of these photographs: "Williams pits the concept of chance against his own artistic control and choices, not only to exploit the particular characteristics of photography but to reexamine the history of the medium. Apart from the questions these disarming images pose, Williams's layering of images is a meditation on modernist photography."[102]

CWP4 (Hoover Dam/Houston), 1993 (plate 114), is among the most conceptually and technically resolved compositions of this series. A trip to Las Vegas drew Williams

113
Giles Lyon
Memory Quilt, 1996–97
Acrylic and mixed media
on canvas, 57 x 117 in.
(142.5 x 292.5 cm).
Museum purchase with funds
provided by Minnette and
Jerome Robinson, Mr. and
Mrs. Andrew Schneck, and
Mr. and Mrs. John W.
Johnson, 99.73.

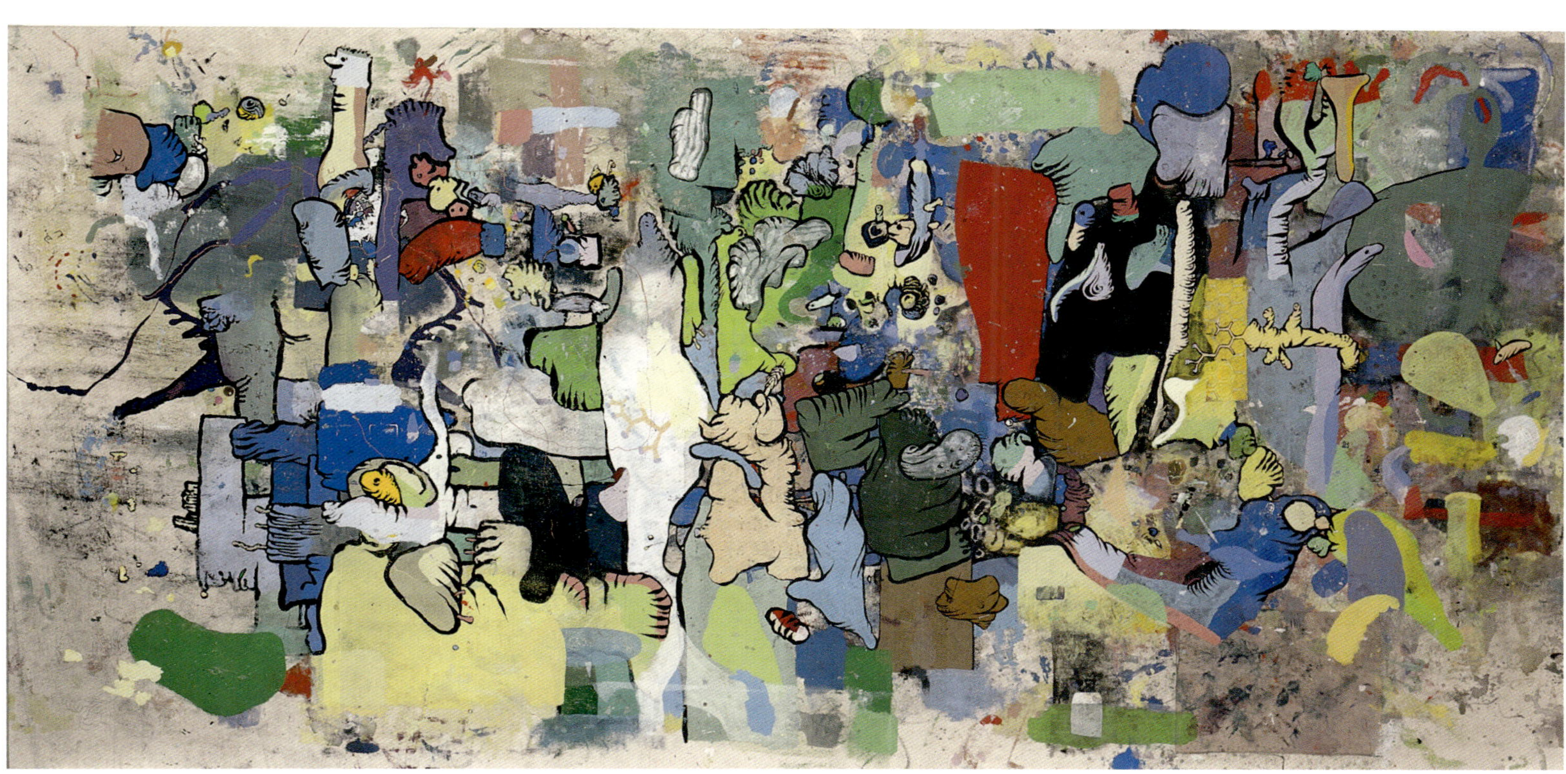

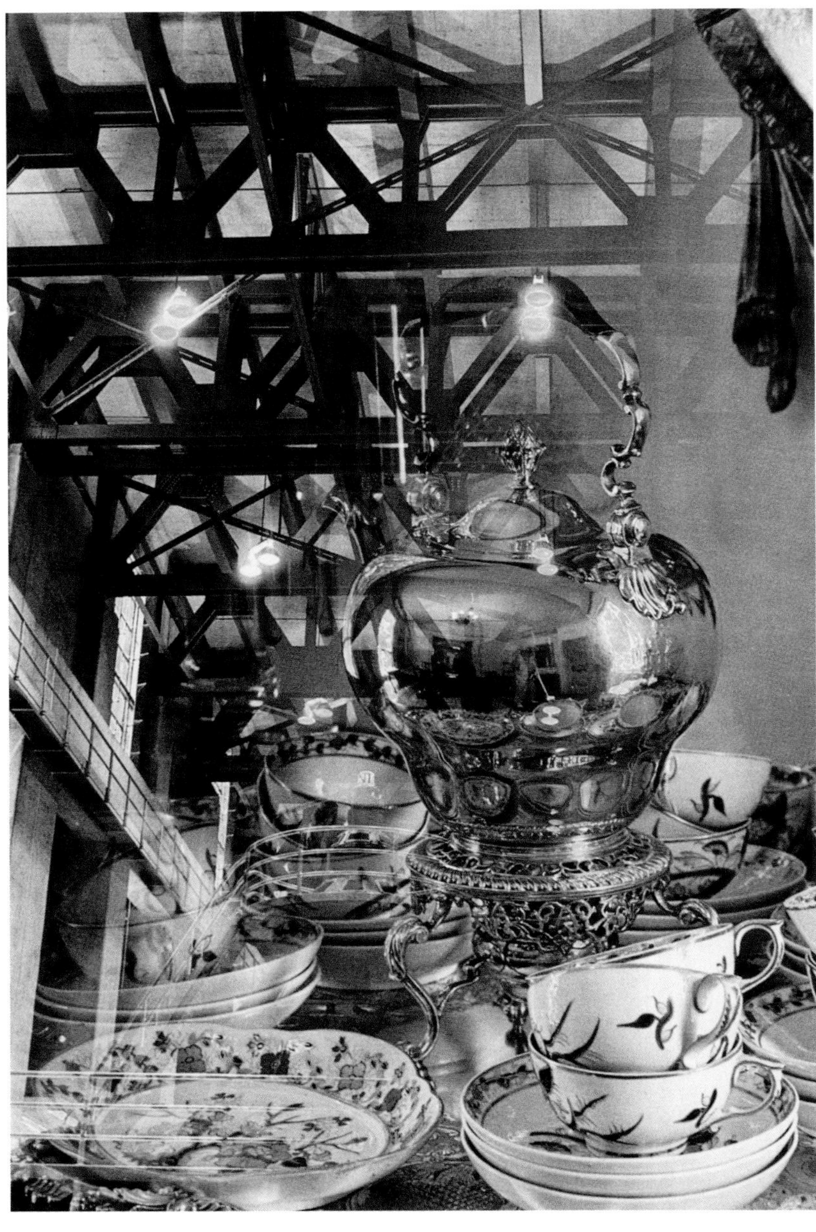

114
Casey Williams
CWP4 (Hoover Dam/ Houston), 1993
Gelatin silver photograph on canvas with acrylic, 30½ x 20 in. (76.2 x 50.8 cm). Museum purchase with funds provided by Marion and Joe S. Mundy, 94.149.

reflect on the disparate sources of his visual memory, "While poles apart, I admired both aesthetics so much it made sense to draw them together into one image."[103]

Layering of image and decoration is also of interest to Michael Miller. A native of North Texas, Miller completed his studies at the University of California, Davis. By the end of the 1980s, he had adopted a method of building up and rubbing away the surfaces of his compositions, allowing a remarkable degree of interplay between image and ground. In 1991, the Corcoran Gallery of Art featured Miller in the *42nd Biennial Exhibition of American Painting*, and Terrie Sultan noted in the catalogue: "Michael Miller's programmatic gestures and diagrammatic arabesques blend the distinctive territories of style and process."[104] In 1996, Michael Odom commented on Miller's compositional strategies: "It is tempting to read Miller's patterns as effaced art-historical reference . . . and to read his sanding back and painting out as a Postmodern concern for the palimpsest, the partially erased surface so popular in the '80s. But even if they are clearly acknowledged, Postmodern endgames do not appear to be of overriding importance in Miller's aesthetic. . . . Rather, the complex intersections of form and color and the abrupt transition from figure to ground operate on the picture plane like mutually harmonic, melodic lines to produce a set polyrhythmic visual music that is satisfying in itself."[105]

An untitled painting of 1993 (plate 115) is among Miller's most lucid compositions. Adopting a process in the artist's words "to make and make fun of," Miller lays open the structure of his composition with humor and delicacy.[106] Using a Kool-Aid blue as a ground tone, he constructed a weblike network of circles as the middle ground, and introduced a fantastic wreathlike decoration as the final defining element. By articulating chains and clusters into spheres—with highlights—that thrust upwards, Miller creates an effect that is at once spatially dynamic and absurdly dramatic.

A similar sensibility characterizes the work of Joseph Havel, with whom Miller studied briefly. A native of the Midwest, Havel moved to Sherman, Texas, in 1979 to teach at Austin College. Over the following decade his work developed as a poetic response to the vernacular landscape of the North Texas region. In 1986, Havel

to the Hoover Dam and, conscious of the work of such American Modernists as Charles Sheeler and Ralston Crawford, Williams took a number of shots of the vast internal structure. The still life of a tea service was later photographed in the home of P. F. and Audrey Graves, friends of the artist in Houston, who collected Rococo silver and china. Combining an icon of modern industry with the decorative arts of another century allowed Williams to

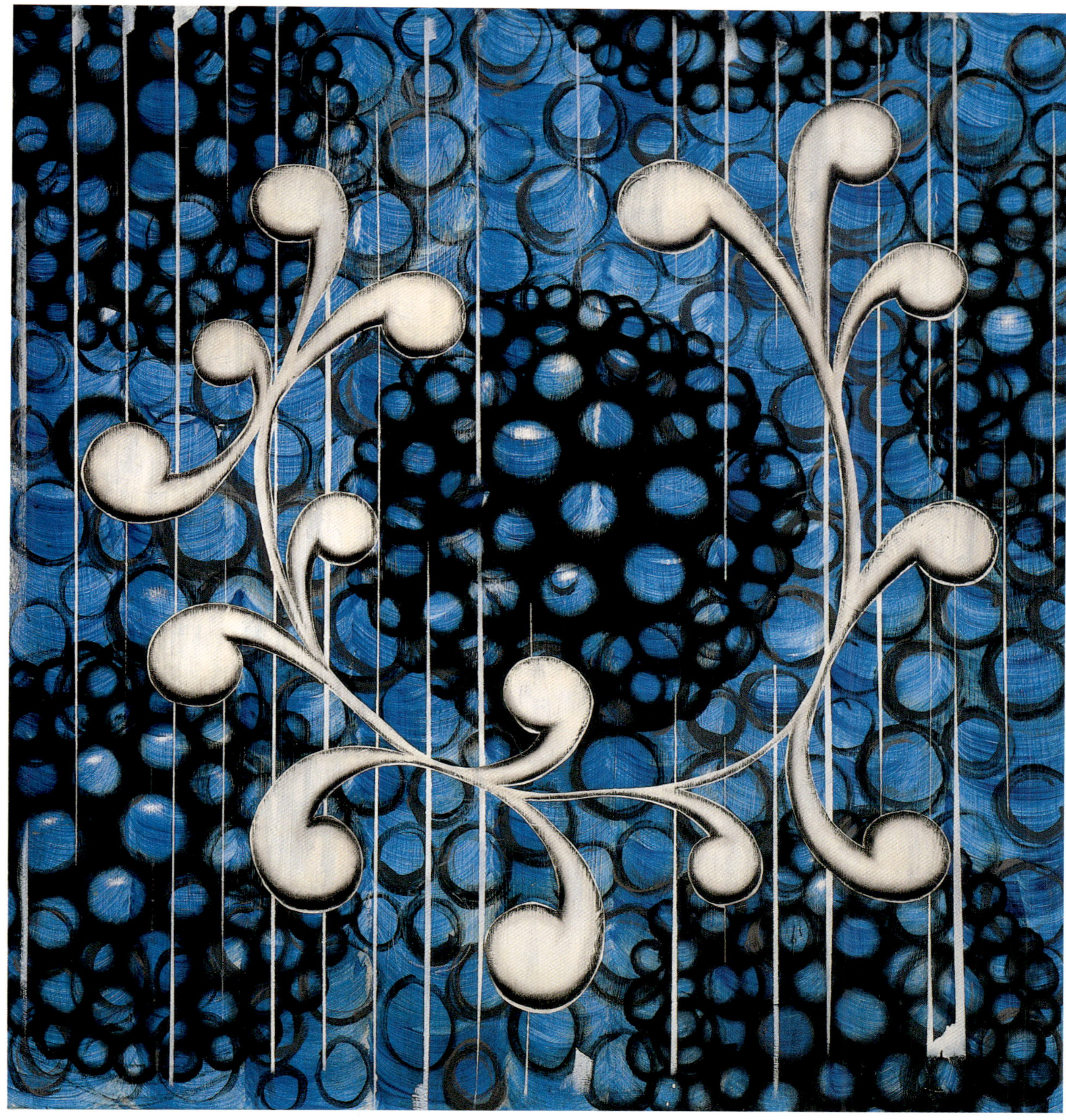

began to cast his work at Harry Geffert's Green Mountain Foundry (see plate 38), using direct and lost-wax casting techniques to render his sculptures in bronze. Direct casting can recreate found materials with vivid realism, capturing every nuance of surface and form. The tensile strength of bronze allowed Havel to liberate his compositions, while the fluidity of the medium made it possible to amalgamate otherwise incompatible objects into seamless assemblages. Havel moved to Houston in 1991, a shift reflected in his work by an increasing use of industrial and urban subjects.

Exhaling Pearls, 1993 (plate 116), is both monumental and capricious. Asymmetrically balanced and delicately taut, it reflects the artist's concern with the transformation of inanimate objects into animated forms. The central support was direct cast from a ship channel rope; Japanese paper lanterns were used to create the two "pearls" which anchor and crown the composition. Placed on a berm in the center of the Cullen Sculpture Garden, the hybrid form of the sculpture appears to be eerily alive as the braided rope rises in a gesture of aspiration. Havel has commented on this work:

> Conceptually, the piece is the culmination of the heroic end of a group of pieces that used the Japanese lanterns.... It seemed important to have something that was ironically grand and heroic around for a while. It was made

115
Michael Miller
Untitled, 1993
Acrylic and oil on canvas, 48 x 45 in. (121.9 x 114.3 cm). Museum purchase with funds provided by Crowley, Marks & Douglas in memory of Opal Mae Hanks, 93.333.

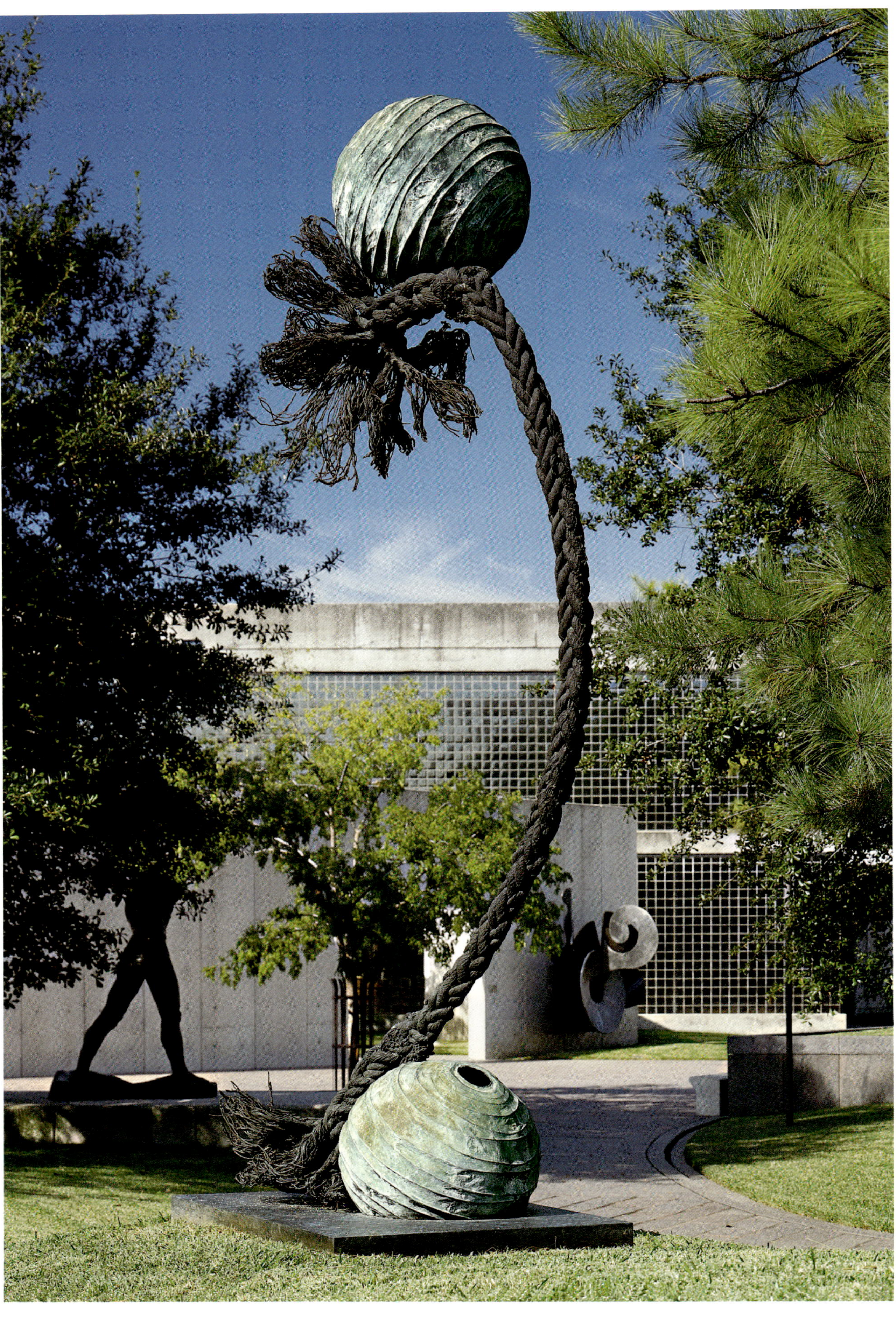

to be a grand gesture that was both casual and formal.... I was interested that the title reflect both western and eastern cultural readings, that it suggested a figure through implying human activity, and that it had a broad range of other associations that all shared a similar tone. It also combines the "pearls of wisdom" saying with sexual slang.[107]

Tad Griffin takes organic imagery into the context of our technological present. Griffin completed his studies at East Texas State University, Commerce. In 1991, he returned to his native Houston and embarked on a series of paintings characterized by strong optical rhythms of black and white. These works appear to be the result of a mechanized process: their horizontal patterns contain nuances of form which seem to relate to digital or genetic information. Dana Friis-Hansen has written of these paintings: "Griffin finds inspiration in the conceptual distance and visual texture of technological data, a mediated language that describes an object or phenomena impossible for human sense to perceive.... Musing about the digital data that helps us cross phenomenal, perceptual, and conceptual distances, Griffin has observed that by 'extending our senses beyond wonder, into the realm of understanding, our awe at the works of nature is renewed.'"[108]

In 1995, Griffin embarked on a series of drawings in which the grid is more subdued and serves as the background for the gleeful bursts of color the artist has wiped across the surface. The smooth autographic gesture of these drawings suggests organic form—the bloom of some flower across the landscape of the grid—and they become optimistic and even celebratory in tone. An untitled drawing from this series, 1995 (plate 117), demonstrates the nuance that Griffin brings to these works. The ground is largely erased and a gestural wipe of orange pigment dominates the composition. Close examination reveals further information as the artist uses almost transparent medium to punctuate the surface with barely perceptible motifs of circles and wavy lines. Griffin has compared himself to "a sensitive listener, a delicate seismograph in tune to the subtle rumblings of our culture," and this drawing provides a fascinating metaphor for the ways in which we process information, through perception, emotion, and memory.[109]

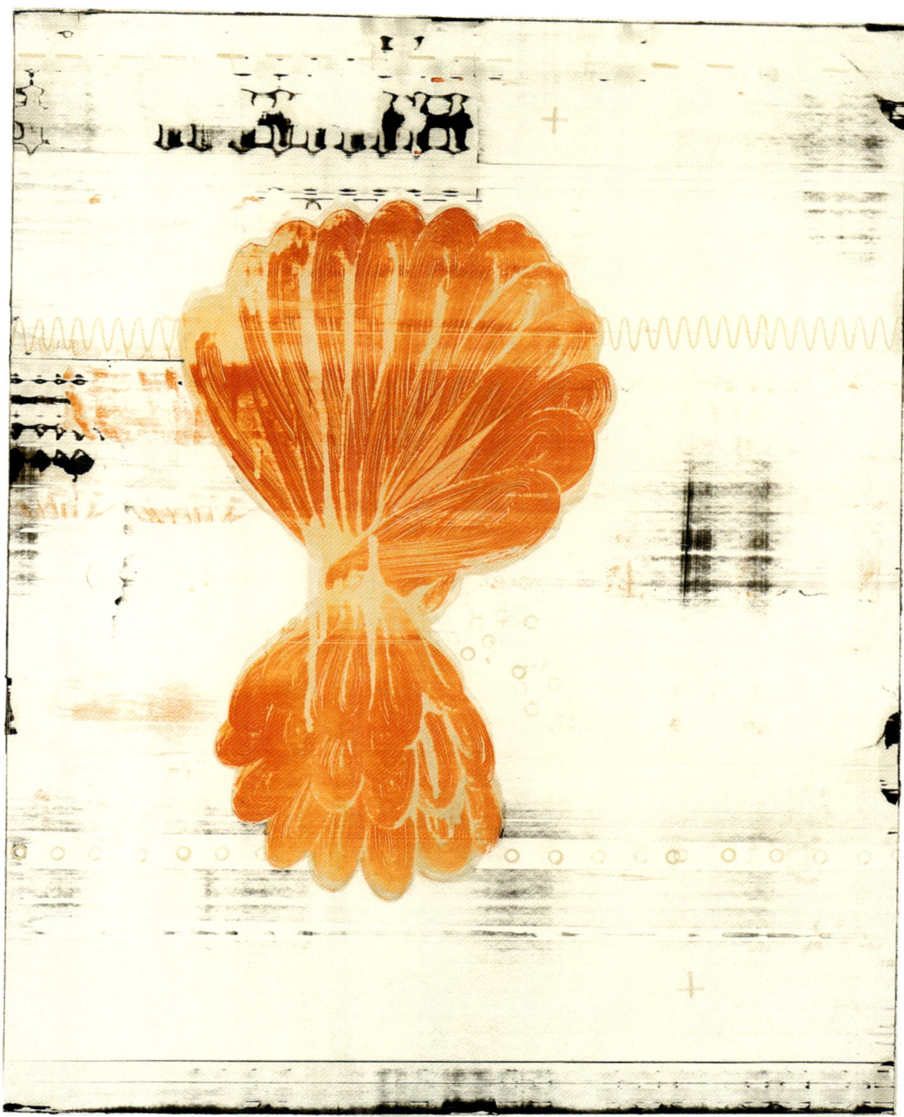

The issue of appropriation as it relates to abstraction is a complex one. As Mark Rosenthal has observed: "The tendency of so-called postmodernist artists to select abstract passages to imitate when quoting or parodying modernism indicates that abstraction is fundamental to the outlook of modern art. And, despite these postmodern manifestations, there is no neo-abstract movement, because abstraction has never ceased to exist. It continues to be an enticing and viable alternative for artists."[110]

David Pagel has further commented: "It's important to distinguish what's going on in abstract painting today ... from the once prevalent Postmodern notion of art-in-quotation-marks. The primary purpose of the latter's predominantly abstract works was to make grand (tongue in cheek) propositions, and then by means of a sly wink, knowing nudge, or ironic twist, let insiders know that

117
Tad Griffin
Untitled Drawing, 1995
Oil on paper, 36 x 28 in. (91.4 x 71.1 cm). Museum purchase with funds provided by Randal E. Bell and Patrick H. Reynolds, 97.119.

116 *opposite*
Joseph Havel
Exhaling Pearls, 1993
Patinated bronze, 130 x 55 x 33 in. (330.2 x 139.7 x 83.8 cm). Museum purchase with funds provided by the Caroline Wiess Law Accessions Endowment Fund, Isabell and Max H. Herzstein, Isabel B. Wilson, Nona and Richard Barrett, and friends of the artist, 94.115.

such goals were ridiculously overblown, even dangerously authoritarian."[111]

The artists discussed in the conclusion of this chapter do not hide their sources, and at a glance their work may be seen as an ironic commentary on the history of Modernism. And yet—as the work of Aaron Parazette, Bill Davenport, Robert Montgomery, Paul Kittelson, and Jeff Elrod demonstrates—these artists do not divorce themselves from the Modernist practice. Rather, in looking back on the intellectual history of a century, they feel free to combine the appropriative strategies of Marcel Duchamp with the compositional purism of Piet Mondrian and Donald Judd.

Aaron Parazette is fascinated by the conscious act of composition and constructs his paintings through an astute manipulation of "found" motifs, from the neutrality of stripes to the banality of decorative wallpaper design. A native of California, he attended the Claremont Graduate Program, before coming to Houston in 1990 to join the Core Residency Program. Beginning in 1995, he adopted clip-art graphics of paint splashes as the defining motif of his work. In a recent interview, Parazette commented on this choice of motif: "I couldn't ignore the issue of image entirely, so making a painting which references 'Painting' seemed right. Robert Ryman once said, 'I paint the paint.' I am doing that in a contemporary way."[112]

Parazette's appropriative strategy is further underscored by his choice of titles in this series, all of which are taken from the Abstract Expressionist paintings featured in the Museum of Modern Art's *The New American Painting* exhibition, which toured Europe in 1958–59. *Soft Night*, 1996 (plate 118), was originally the title of an Arshile Gorky painting, now in the collection of the Hirshhorn Museum and Sculpture Garden, Washington, D.C. Parazette's *Soft Night* has little in common with Gorky's original: where Gorky used transparent layers of oil medium and an exquisitely nuanced calligraphy, Parazette uses enamel house paint that disguises any mark of the artist's hand. Where Gorky embraced rich organic tones, Parazette adopts the deliberately dull palette of artificial colors. However, Parazette is not interested in making a bland replica of Gorky's work. Rather, much as the artists of Gorky's generation created a signature style, so too has Parazette striven to make a distinc-

tive statement that overrides the triteness of his clip-art sources. Parazette has stated:

> The decision to appropriate titles from *The New American Painting* catalogue is intended to highlight the implicit comparison between two periods and approaches to abstract painting. Abstract Expressionism is arguably the high point of the European painting investigation/tradition, while it would seem that we are currently in a period of confusion and searching. My curiosity is in how these two very different painting epochs relate to one another. That there is a relationship is clear. The specifics, however, remain elusive, and therefore seem worthy of consideration and contemplation.[113]

Bill Davenport questions both the form and content of Pop Art and Minimalism with a sharp, critical wit. A native New Englander, he completed his studies at the University of Massachusetts; like Parazette, he entered the Core Residency Program in 1990.

Davenport has embraced a range of media—from needlepoint to painted wooden constructions—to explore contemporary visual culture. In 1995, he commented, "My source is the commonplace: the grubby paint on Houston's slapdash architecture, signs, graffiti, and the little enigmatic illustrations in the Yellow Pages."[114] Roy Lichtenstein could lay claim to similar sources; however, where the Pop artists fetishized the deliberate finish of commercial production, Davenport cherishes the worn and the handmade.

Davenport challenges the cool authority of art of the 1960s with *Yellow Box*, 1992 (plate 119). Unlike Donald Judd's sleek untitled box (see plate 91), *Yellow Box* looks thrown together, industrial materials are replaced by the ordinary stuff of hardware stores, glowingly polished brass is replaced by yellow paint. Indeed, in its ordinariness, *Yellow Box* also invites comparison with Andy Warhol's 1964 *Brillo Boxes*. Davenport is keenly aware of these sources, and in a recent statement offered a guide to art historians:

> My work may be compared profitably with several periods in art history: **Pop Art** with its use of the commonplace as a fit subject for art, and its playing with the distinction between high and low culture. **Minimalism** with its effort at paring down to essentials in search of some existential truth. **Folk Art** for its easy, unpolemic ignorance of artistic conventions; its simplicity and directness of manufacture.[115]

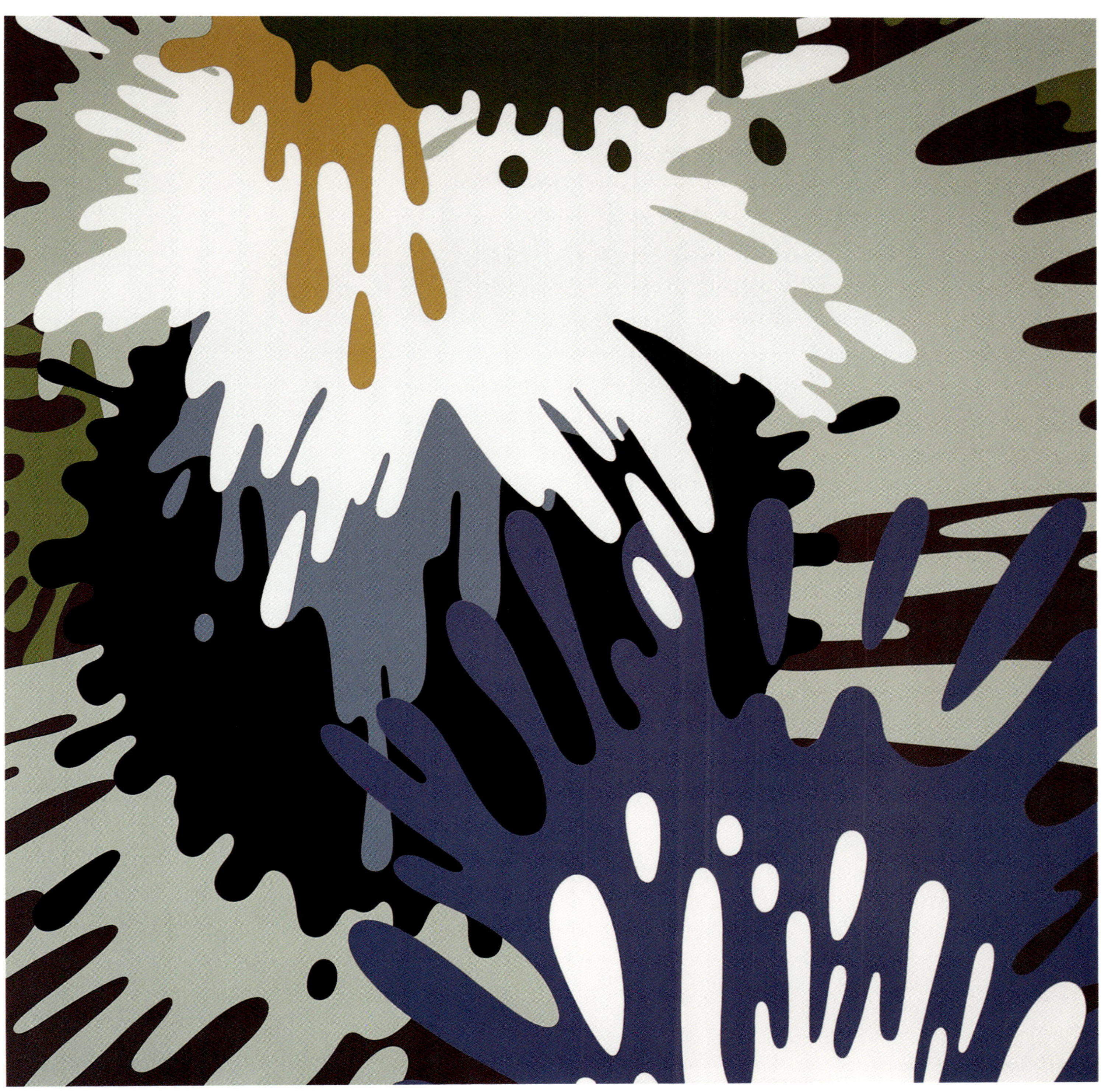

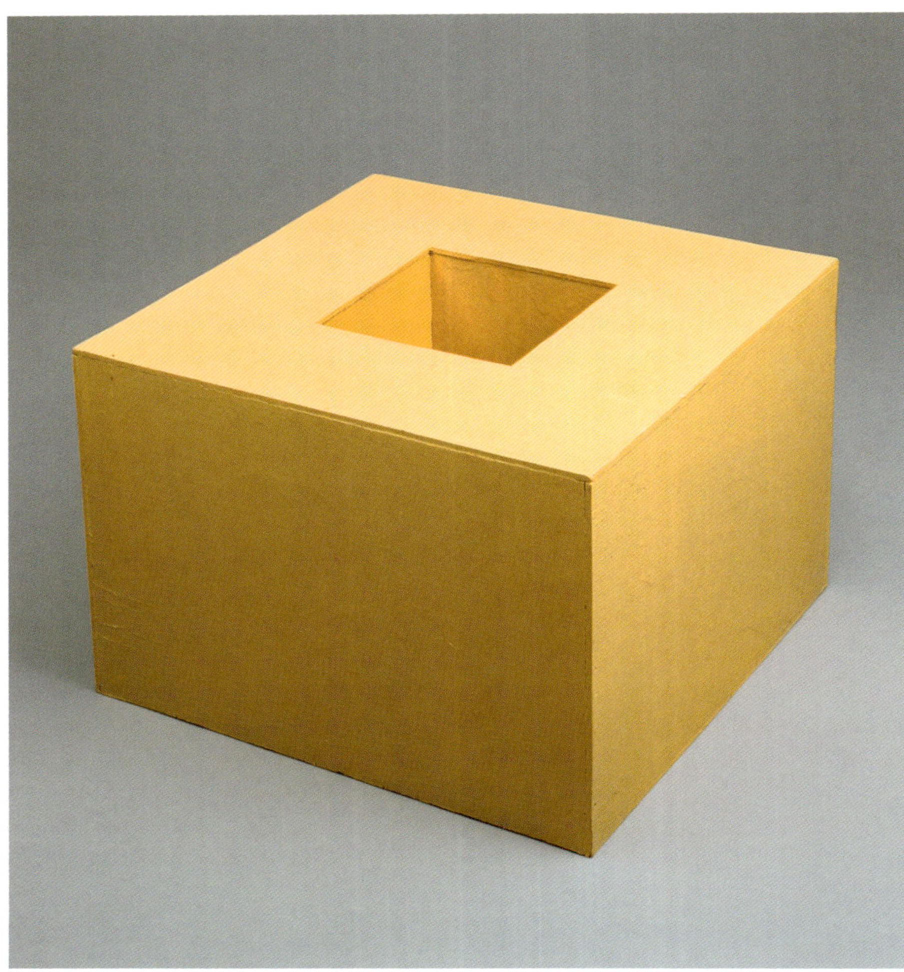

119
Bill Davenport
Yellow Box, 1992
Plywood with enamel, 12¼ x
17½ x 17½ in. (31.1 x 44.5 x
44.5 cm). Museum purchase
with funds provided by
Steven J. Snook, 98.183.

Davenport, who is anything but ignorant of artistic conventions, takes what he wants and departs from Pop, Minimalism, and folk art in subtle and perverse ways. *Yellow Box,* measuring just over a foot high, is an awkward scale for gallery installation: too small to "hold" a place on the floor, too large to place in a vitrine, and too humble to place on a pedestal. Lacking a bottom panel, *Yellow Box* also fails as a container in the practical sense of the word; yet metaphorically it accommodates meaning with delicate humor.

Robert Montgomery, who came to the United States in 1995 from his native Scotland, regards Modernism with a knowing but romantic eye. He entered the Core Residency Program that year in part because Houston appealed to Montgomery as a city with little history. Traveling across the urban landscape, he has used installation art, video, appropriation, and drawing as a means to explore, in the words of Randy Watson, "The ordinary out of which the extraordinary arises."[116]

Towerblock, 1997 (plate 120), frames Minimalist drawing in a socially engaged context. A failed experiment in urban renewal, towerblock (or high-rise) housing in Britain became a symbol of the social disenfranchisement of the British underclass in the 1980s. As the artist has recorded:

> The towerblock is a tragic symbol for me. . . . The drawing comes from a series of objects and drawings exploring the potential for objects within a minimalist stylistic paradigm to carry literal meanings. The style of the drawing is, obviously, very close to that of Agnes Martin, which is culturally disparate, for me, to the motif of the towerblock. The tension between the immediately perceived abstract reality of the drawing, and its hidden potential as the representation of a towerblock was my primary interest. It should feel almost as though the representation was smuggled into the drawing as contraband information.[117]

Towerblock is also a deeply beautiful object. The blue field suggests infinite space, and the grid records with delicacy the variegated touch of the artist's hand. While rejecting the progressive notion of Modernism, which found its most signal failure in urban planning, Montgomery pays tribute to the idealism that motivated the original Modernist quest.

Paul Kittelson is among the generation of artists who came of age in the mid-1980s for whom a serious sense of play is an essential aspect of their work. A native of the Midwest, he came to Houston to complete his studies at the University of Houston's graduate program. He first captured the attention of the city with his improbable public sculptures: *Stegosaurus*, a "life-sized" dinosaur made from discarded foam (situated in 1986 clandestinely beneath the 59 Freeway overpass on Montrose Boulevard) and *Mindless Competition*, a row of giant, headless, black-rubber bodybuilders that were lined in front of the Contemporary Arts Museum for the *First Texas Triennial* exhibition of 1988.

Kittelson's more intimately scaled work conveys a similar Pop sensibility: since the mid-1990s, he has focused on recreating common snack foods: donuts, potato chips, cakes, and candy. These tributes to junk culture are indebted to Claes Oldenburg's heroic lipsticks and cigarette butts; however, Kittelson explores the disjunction between the preciousness of his objects and their common sources. Highlighted in a recent exhibition titled *Too Good to Be True*, Kittelson has remarked of this work, "You see them for one thing, and experience them in a different way."[118]

M&M, 1998 (plate 121), is an artwork of rare elegance and humor. At a glance, it appears to be a refined abstract sculpture in the Modernist tradition of Constantin Brancusi and Barbara Hepworth. The title, however, throws the work into a different context. As Catherine Anspon has observed: "One appreciates *M&M* foremost as a reductive object which mesmerizes for its lush golden [and] highly polished surface which acts as a mirror serving up perfect reflections of its surroundings. Only secondarily do we discover its candy associations."[119]

Jeff Elrod takes his inspiration from MTV, computer games, and video arcades, as well as from the history of art. A native of North Texas, he entered the Core Residency Program in 1991, and a 1993 tenure at Amsterdam's Rijksakademie brought him into contact with the masterworks of early and mid-century Modernism. Such artists as Frank Stella and Kenneth Noland further motivated his work as he became fascinated by the influence they had on commercial design, and Elrod's paintings of this period mimicked the supergraphics of the 1970s.

120
Robert Montgomery
Towerblock, 1997
Watercolor and ink on Bristol board, 38 3/4 x 29 in. (98.4 x 73.7 cm). Museum purchase with funds provided by Steven J. Snook, 98.519.

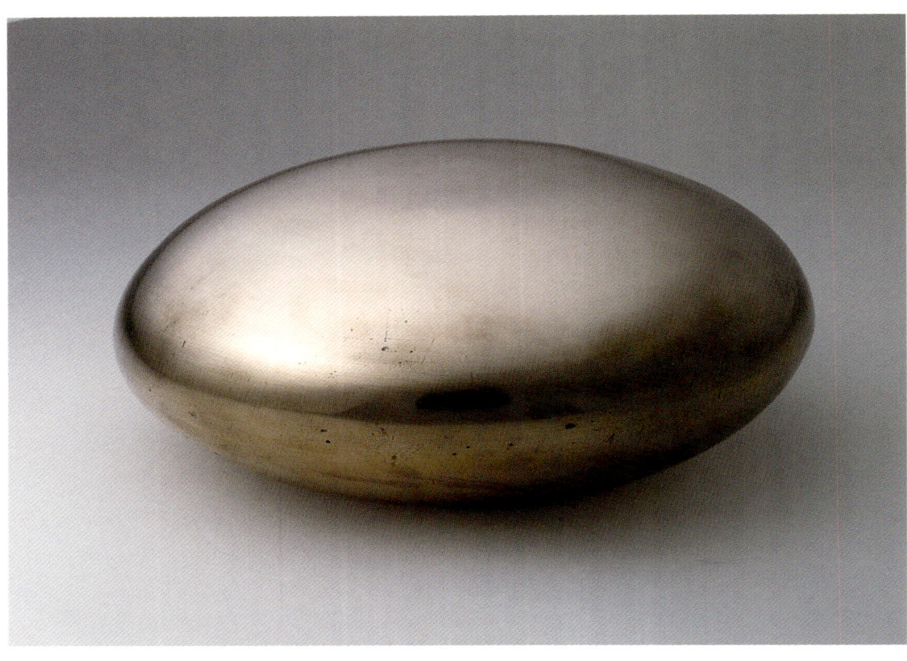

121
Paul Kittelson
M&M, 1998
Polished bronze, 5 x 10 x 10
in. (12.7 x 25.4 x 25.4 cm).
Museum purchase with
funds provided by Minnette
Robinson in honor of her
husband, Jerome, 98.185.

As *Turning Japanese* demonstrates, the computer can duplicate motifs, and has a tendency to clean up the artist's gesture (i.e., make straight lines, 90° angles, and perfect arcs). Conversely, the program also allows an enormous degree of improvisational freedom, and *Turning Japanese* adroitly reconciles the worlds of the subconscious and technology. Perhaps coincidentally, the composition resembles an Etch-a-Sketch version of the lower half of Marcel Duchamp's *The Bride Stripped Bare by Her Bachelors, Even* (1915–23, Philadelphia Museum of Art). The looming mechanical form in *Turning Japanese* echoes that of Duchamp's bachelors, and the computer allows the element of chance provided by the cracked glass. Elrod has commented, "The machine freed my repressed nature. It liberates my drawing in a way I have never been able to achieve with pen on paper. It's smooth, it's clean, there's no friction."[121]

Beginning in 1996, Elrod turned to the computer as a means of creative release. Unlike many artists, who use computer imaging processes to create layered and dense compositions, Elrod exploited the blunt and effective simplicity the computer could provide. Using a drawing program that allows him to sketch using a mouse, Elrod created the composition that became the basis of *Turning Japanese*, 1997 (plate 122), by improvising around the word "Japanese."[120] Working from a computer printout, Elrod then projected the composition onto primed canvas, taped the lines, and rolled paint across the surface.

Elrod's deft combination of Duchampian themes, contemporary technology, and Modernist aesthetics adroitly captures the dialectics of abstraction today. In 1989, Arthur C. Danto posited in his seminal essay, "Narratives of the End of Art," that the development of Modernism, as well as the larger history of Western art, had been irreparably broken by the pluralism of the Postmodernist era.[122] However, Danto saw this rupture in the most liberating terms, echoing the spirit of the early twentieth-century manifestos of the Futurists and Dada artists: "Once art makers are freed from the task of finding the essence of art, which had been thrust upon art at the inception of Modernism, they too have been liberated from history, and have entered the era of freedom."[123]

122 *opposite*
Jeff Elrod
Turning Japanese, 1997
Acrylic on canvas, 92 x 83 in.
(233.6 x 210.8 cm). Museum
purchase with funds provided
by Mr. and Mrs. Andrew
Schneck, 98.68.

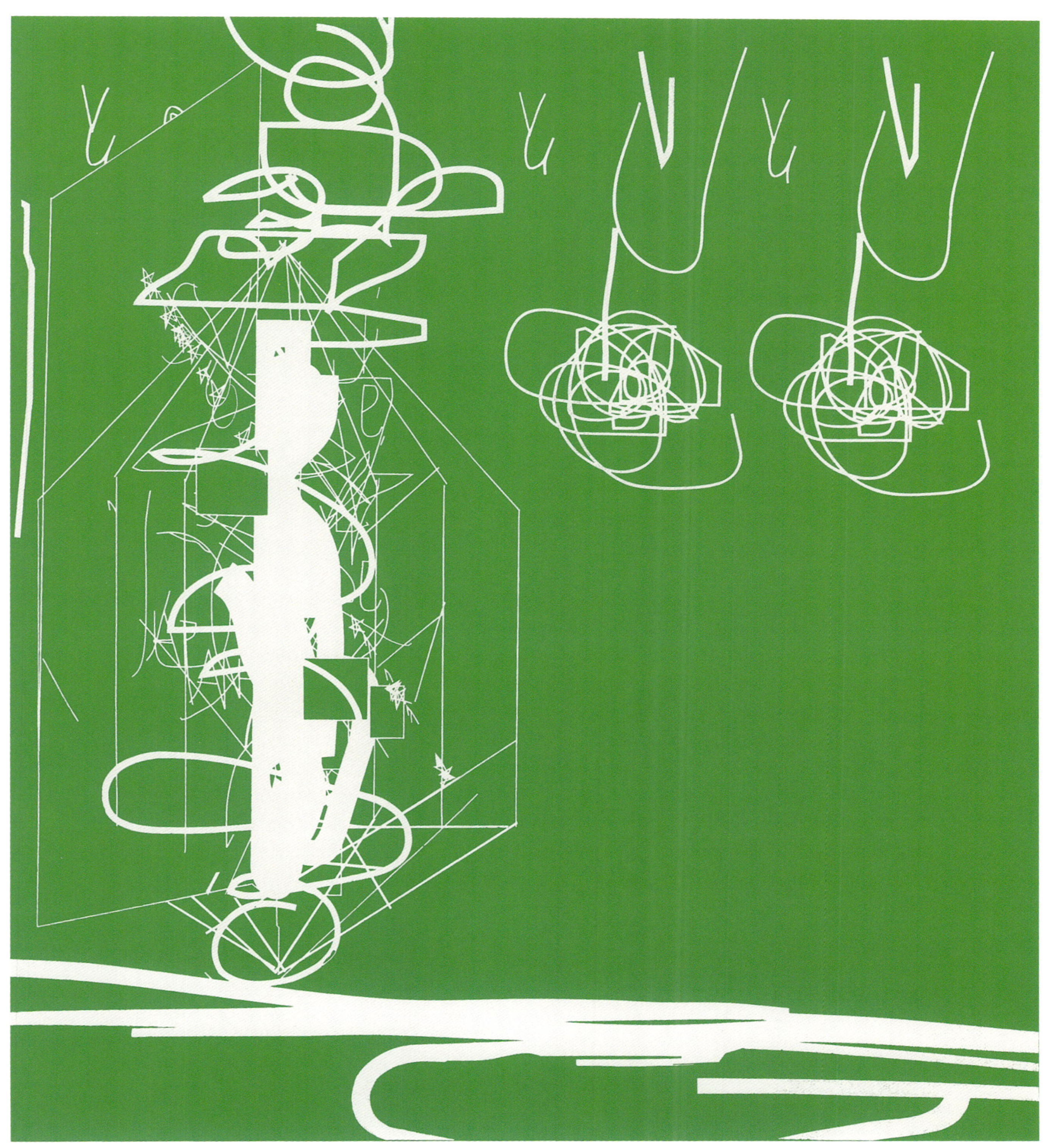

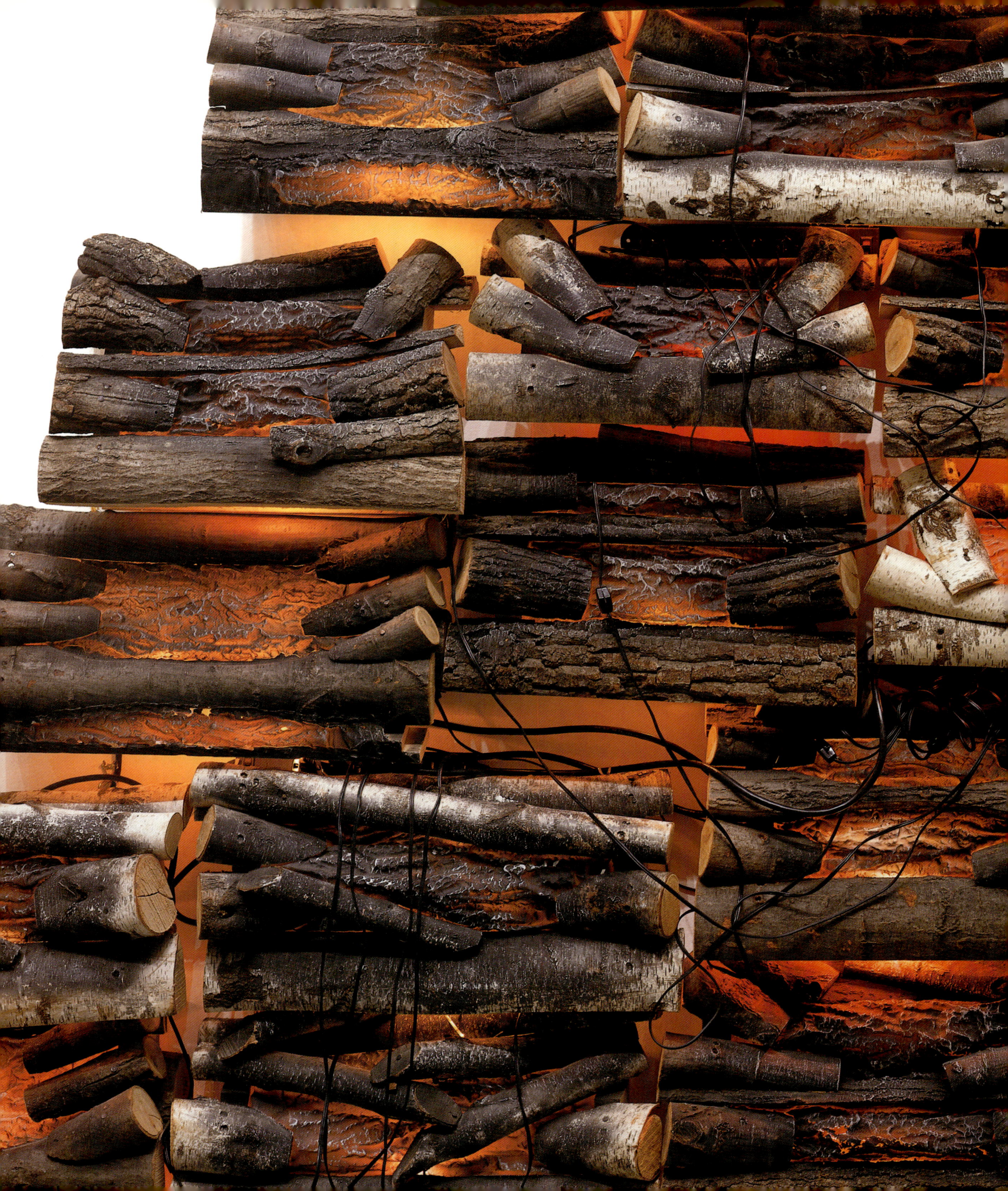

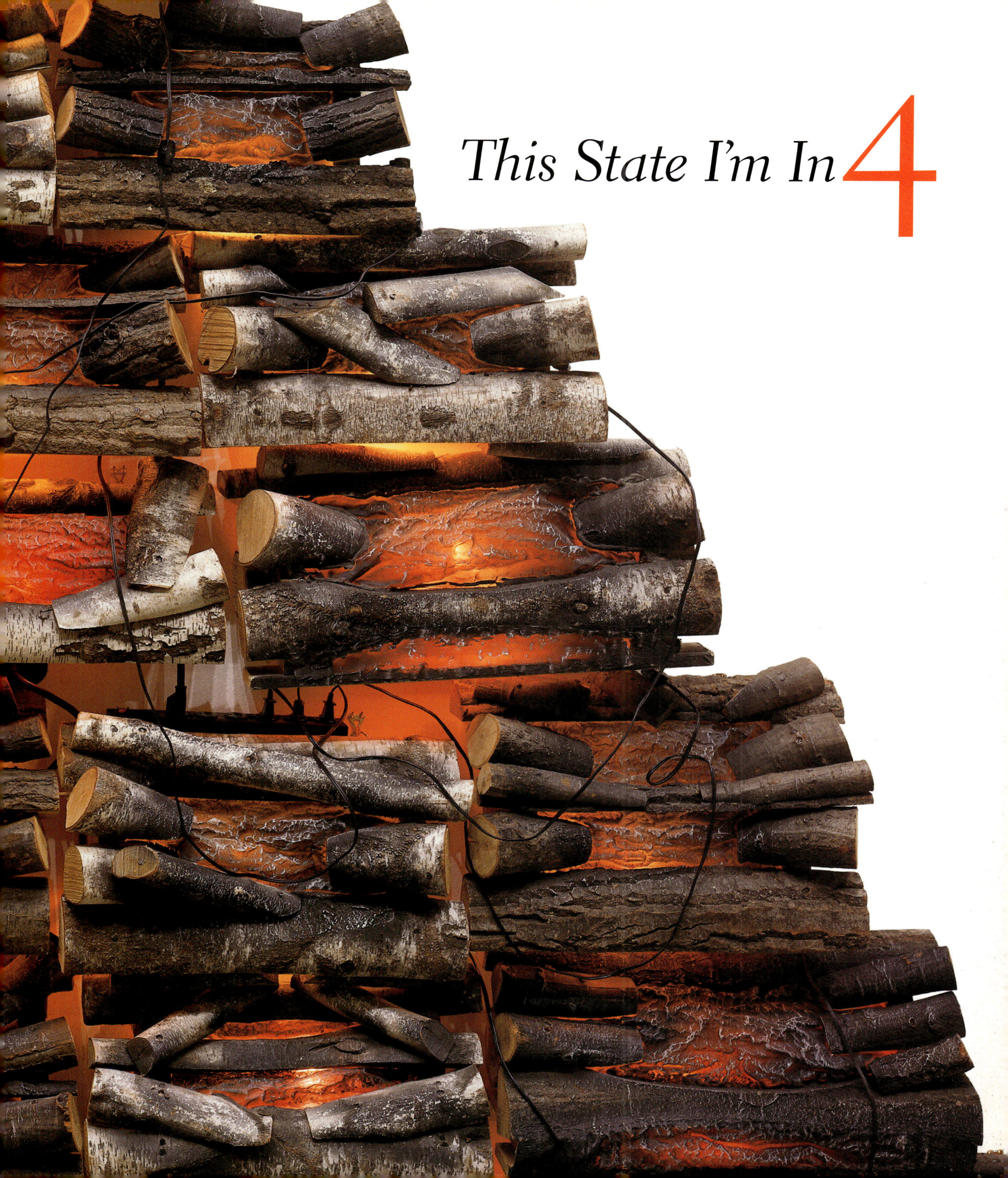

This State I'm In 4

This State I'm In

When I was a kid I was never any good at

finding Easter eggs. At the class Easter egg

hunt, everyone would run yelling and screaming

after the eggs, finding them right and left

until their baskets practically ran over, while

I stumbled around never finding any unless it

was one that had been stepped on. It never

occurred to me that in a big grassy field the

eggs weren't just scattered at random. Later I

discovered that because we were SUPPOSED to

find them, they were always placed next to other

objects: the bases of trees, fence posts, water

faucets, etc. I know that now, but back then,

I was unable to break the code.

—Vernon Fisher, 1981[1]

In 1972 Leo Steinberg was among the first critics to apply the term "post-Modernist" to the visual arts.[2] Writing about Robert Rauschenberg's and Andy Warhol's appropriation of found imagery, Steinberg commented: "The picture conceived as an image of an image. It is a conception which guarantees that the presentation will not be directly of a worldspace, and that it will nevertheless admit any experience as the matter of representation. And it readmits the artist in the fullness of his human interests, as well as the artist-technician." Steinberg continued with the crucial observation: "The all-purpose picture plane underlying this post-Modernist painting has made the course of art once again nonlinear and unpredictable."[3]

Steinberg's recognition of this state of flux proved to be prophetic, and over the following two decades issues of appropriation, autobiography, and critical meaning became central to contemporary art.[4] However, defining the larger phenomenon of Postmodernism has challenged numerous writers, philosophers, critics, historians, and artists. Hal Foster has asked: "Postmodernism: does it exist at all and, if so, what does it mean? Is it a concept or a practice, a matter of local style or a whole new period or economic phase? What are its forms, effects, place? How are we to mark its advent? Are we truly beyond the modern, truly in (say) a postindustrial age?"[5]

Foster responded to these questions by gathering an anthology of contemporary writings on Postmodern culture. Among the featured essays were Jürgen Habermas's "Modernity—An Incomplete Project," Douglas Crimp's "On the Museum's Ruins," Craig Owens's "The Discourse of Others: Feminists and Postmodernism," Fredric Jameson's "Postmodernism and Consumer Society," and Jean Baudrillard's "The Ecstasy of Communication." These essays were among the defining writings on Postmodernism and the visual arts in the early 1980s, and while wide ranging in their lines of inquiry, Foster noted that these writers shared "a will to grasp the present nexus of culture and politics and to affirm a practice resistant both to academic modernism and political reaction."[6]

Although Postmodern currents can be discerned in the work of Texas artists as early as the mid-1970s, Postmodernism in Texas art was not recognized by any significant exhibitions until the early 1990s.[7] Such presentations as *The Perfect World*, curated by Jim Edwards for the San

Antonio Museum of Art in 1991, and *Texas/Between Two Worlds* curated by Louise Dompierre, Peter Doroshenko, and James Fisher for Houston's Contemporary Arts Museum in 1993, established new thematic criteria for understanding the art of the region. These exhibitions featured the artists MANUAL, Vernon Fisher, Jesse Amado, and Helen Altman (see plates 124, 125, 140, and 150), among others, who have made the disjunctions that color day-to-day existence the central theme of their work. Jim Edwards remarked that these artists celebrate "the illusionary nature of image and meaning.... Their art represents an individualized human response to the seemingly undifferentiated flood of objects, images, and language of our postmodern world."[8] In the foreword of the Contemporary Arts Museum's catalogue, the curators observed, *"Texas/Between Two Worlds* is about looking at that which is real yet difficult to actually *see*. It is about looking at aspects of human life that are quantifiably authentic but for which there are no clear answers or explanations."[9]

Vernon Fisher's text from his 1981 installation *Easter Egg Hunt* (plate 125), quoted at the opening of this chapter, exemplifies this shift in mood. Fisher describes his awareness of being an outsider, "unable to break the code," a predicament that reflects not only the artist's childhood memory, but also Postmodernism's rupture with the progressive notion of history and social evolution. Indeed, an argument can be made that Texas art by its very nature is largely Postmodern, as an admission of regionalism breaks with the Modernist canon, and certainly many artists discussed in prior chapters can be termed Postmodernists. This circumstance was deftly acknowledged by Texas photographer and filmmaker Robert Ziebell in the title of his film *This State I'm In*, released in 1990 (see Introduction, fig. 15). Ziebell's wordplay, with its self-consciousness clearly asserted, captures the double entendre of "state," which can imply both a condition of being and a physical boundary.[10] As this concluding chapter will demonstrate, a growing number of Texas artists in the 1980s and 1990s deliberately addressed Postmodernist concerns beyond the issues of locality, spirituality, and abstraction discussed earlier in this book. They adopted a broad range of compositional strategies to question the nature of art, to reflect upon personal identity, and to analyze our larger culture.

Robert Rauschenberg embraces the maelstrom of contemporary existence. His engagement in every aspect of artmaking—painting, drawing, sculpture, and printmaking, as well as performance and political action—has made our times, in the words of Charles Stuckey, "Rauschenberg's Everything, Everywhere Era."[11] In an interview in 1968, when he was asked, "What is your greatest fear?" Rauschenberg replied, "That I might run out of world."[12]

Rauschenberg was born in Port Arthur, and he grew up among the oil refineries of the Texas Gulf Coast. In 1943 he entered the University of Texas at Austin, but left shortly thereafter, and was drafted into the US Navy the following year. A visit to the Huntington Library and Art Collections while he was stationed in San Diego confirmed Rauschenberg's interest in art, and following his discharge in 1945 he pursued an itinerate education that took him to the Kansas City Art Institute, to the Académie Julian in Paris, to the Art Students League in New York, and most famously, to Black Mountain College in Asheville, North Carolina, where he could count among his mentors Josef Albers, John Cage, and Merce Cunningham. A visit to Italy and North Africa with fellow student Cy Twombly in the fall and winter of 1952–53 marked the end of Rauschenberg's apprentice years; however, he continued throughout his career to seek new techniques and technologies to advance his art.

Rauschenberg met the publisher Tatyana Grosman in New York in 1961; Grosman, through her Universal Limited Art Editions (ULAE), had just begun to foment an American print renaissance through collaborations with such artists as Larry Rivers, Robert Motherwell, and Rauschenberg's close friend and associate of these years, Jasper Johns. Their meeting came at a critical juncture in Rauschenberg's career; by the end of the late 1950s Rauschenberg had brought a new sophistication to collage aesthetics through such landmark works as *Monogram* (1955–59; Moderna Museet, Stockholm), a three-dimensional assemblage that took painting off the wall and into the physical—and psychological—space of the viewer.[13] However, just as the real stuff of Rauschenberg's environment (including his own bed) became the materials of his art, he shifted his attention to transfer drawings, which, as Julia Blaut has noted, allowed him to bring

pages 170–171
Helen Altman
Signal (detail), 1992
(see plate 150)

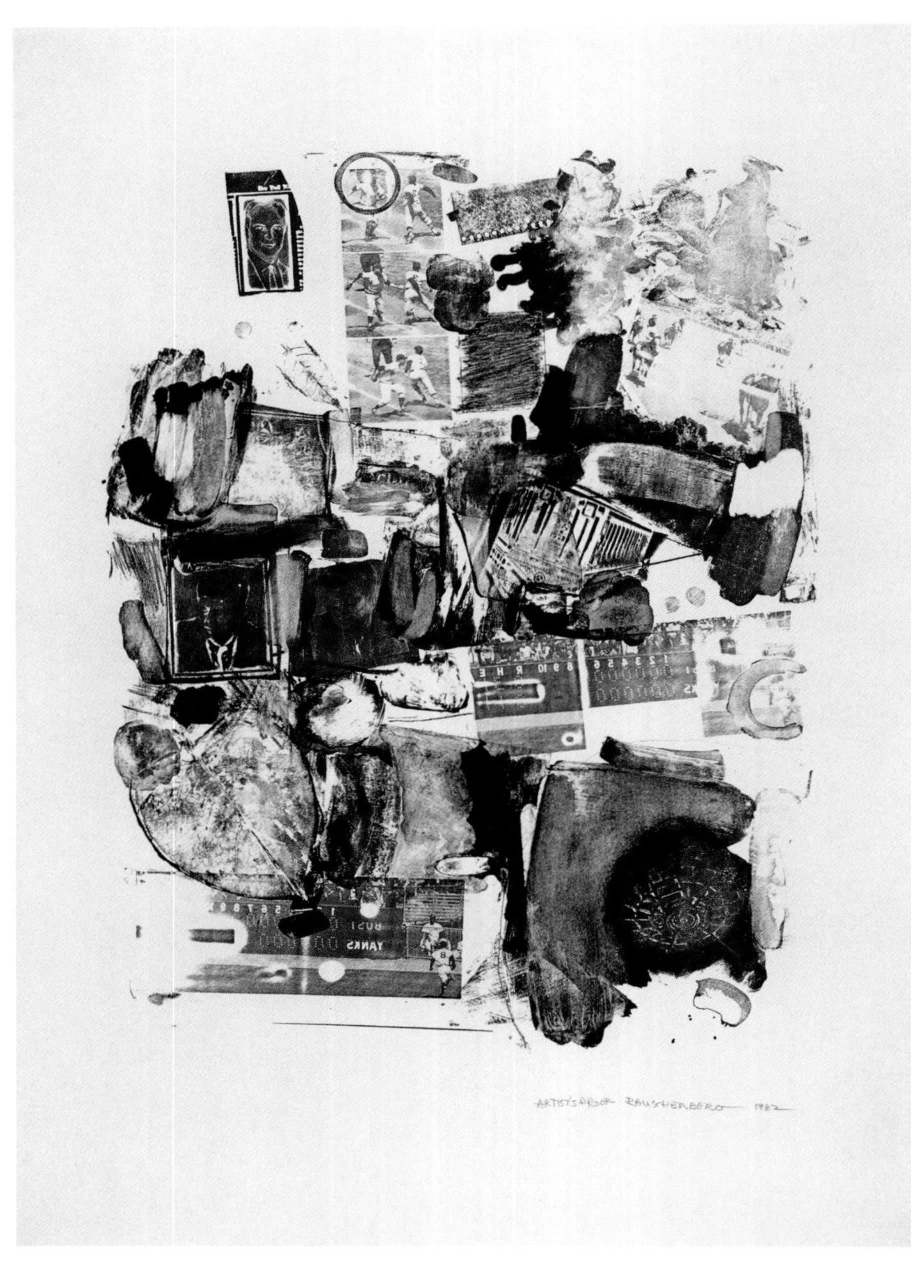

123
Robert Rauschenberg
Urban, 1962
Lithograph, published by
Universal Limited Art Editions; edition 38, 41¼ x 29¾
in. (104.7 x 75.5 cm). Gift
of Barbara Rose, 79.136.

"the element of collage onto a two-dimensional plane; photographs, comic strips, and reproductions of artworks now became continuous with the picture surface."[14]

Grosman, recognizing the affinity between Rauschenberg's transfer drawings and printmaking, immediately invited him to undertake a series of lithographs at her West Islip studio on Long Island, New York; *Urban*, 1962 (plate 123), was among the first results of their collaboration. Esther Sparks has noted:

> With *Urban* . . . it became evident that Rauschenberg could and would change the very definitions of lithography and that, in turn, lithography would influence his work in other media. . . . For Rauschenberg, the graphic equivalent of the infinite world of objects in which we live are the millions of photographs that roll off the press every day. He gave his first prints a *cinéma verité* look by helping himself to a supply of used printers' mats from the *New York Times*. . . . The photographic transfers and films he used . . . are equally anonymous. For example, the baseball players in *Urban* are rarely identifiable nor is the outcome of their actions clear. But the work itself is interesting.[15]

Urban offers a montage of baseball players, horse races, spectators, scoreboards, captions, architectural fragments, direct prints from leaves, and on the center left, paired photographs of President Kennedy. Rauschenberg's autographic working of the lithographic crayon and inks knit the composition together, and the reversed texts and images attest to the nature of the printmaking process. However, Rauschenberg (who is dyslexic) has added an inscription that is not inverted—"Kennedy"—in block letters above the center image of the president, which acts as a foil to the other transferred images. These elements not only add up to create an analogue for the urban environment, but also emphasize the varying reproductive sources appropriated by the artist.

As mentioned above, Rauschenberg's improvisatory manipulation of found images opened up a realm of possibility to future artists. The collaborative team MANUAL (Suzanne Bloom and Ed Hill), Vernon Fisher, Terry Allen, Gael Stack, and Al Souza were among the Texas artists who came of age in the 1970s who recognized the potential of a narrative layering and montage. The fact that the majority of these artists also held long-term teaching positions in Texas—Fisher at the University of North

Texas in Denton; MANUAL, Stack, and Souza at the University of Houston—further promoted an interest in appropriation and narrative among Texas artists emerging in the 1980s and 1990s.

MANUAL took Rauschenberg's montage strategies in a fresh direction, using critical theory to direct their examination of the uses of photography and reproduction. Bloom and Hill met in 1970 while both were teaching at Smith College in Northampton, Massachusetts; in 1974 they adopted the name MANUAL to signal their collaborative works and embarked on the ongoing series *Art in Context: Homage to Walter Benjamin*.[16] Two years later they joined the newly dynamic faculty of the University of Houston's art department.

French TV, 1976 (plate 124), from the *Art in Context* series, is a witty commentary on how art is regarded when the reproduction is more familiar than the original. An image of Jean-Auguste-Dominique Ingres's 1814 *Odalisque* (the original of which is preserved in the Musée du Louvre in Paris) appears on the screen of a small portable television; the logo of television's maker—Sony—is as evident as the odalisque, and the background field is filled with the floorboards upon which the television set rests. Also clearly visible are the antennas, and the electric and video cords connected to the set. As the artists have revealed, the choice of the Ingres was in part dictated by the fact that it was reproduced in the standard textbook of the era, H. W. Janson's *History of Art*; the image has further relevance in that Ingres himself made several replicas of this composition, so that even in its own time the painting was not unique.

As its subtitle acknowledges, this series has been guided by Walter Benjamin's writings, most notably his 1936 essay "The Work of Art in the Age of Mechanical Reproduction," which gained currency among a number of American artists and critics in the 1970s. Benjamin contended that the authority or "aura" of the original is radically altered through reproduction, that the speed of perception is fundamentally changed by the camera, and that film, with its ability to shift perspective and create a montage of imagery, was a disruptive force.[17] Of particular importance to MANUAL's *Art in Context* series was Benjamin's observation: "Even the most perfect reproduction of a work of art is lacking in one element: its presence in time and space, its unique existence at the place where it happened to be."[18] Ed Hill has stated:

> The phrase "art in context" could almost become a motto for MANUAL. It relates to everything we do. We've used it rather specifically in a particular series relative to well-known works of art. But the overriding concern in all our work is context.... Modernism was really born out of art for art's sake, and it makes a basic division between form and content. Modernism levels content, equalizes it all, and never raises the question of context; it can't—being art for art's sake, its context is always Art.[19]

Vernon Fisher, whose work is also discussed in the first chapter of this book (plate 26), is similarly fascinated by the possibilities of montage and shifting meaning. As Madeleine Grynsztejn has pointed out, Rauschenberg's procedure of altering "our experience of art from one of seeing to one of reading" had a strong influence on Fisher, who has paid tribute to Rauschenberg by appropriating both imagery and compositional strategies from his work.[20] Fisher was also interested in Rauschenberg's selected use of his personal history, and by the mid-1970s Fisher's autobiographical narratives had become the distinguishing characteristic of his drawings, paintings, and installations.

124
MANUAL (Suzanne Bloom and Ed Hill)
French TV, from the *Art in Context: Homage to Walter Benjamin* series, 1976
Toned gelatin silver photograph, 14½ x 18¾ in. (37 x 46.9 cm). Gift of Clinton T. Willour in honor of Kathy Reiser, 90.524.

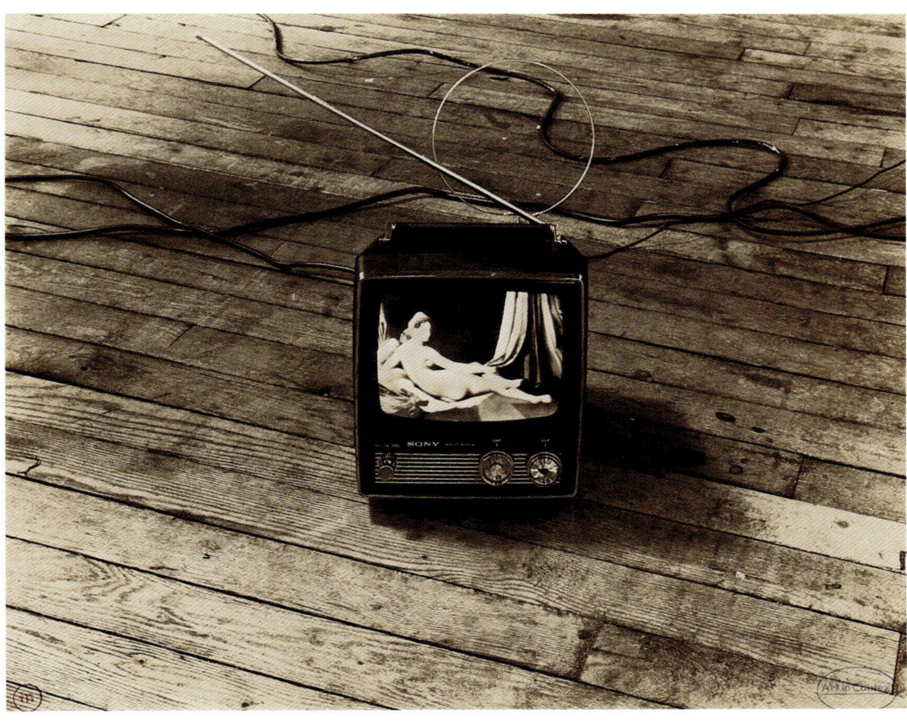

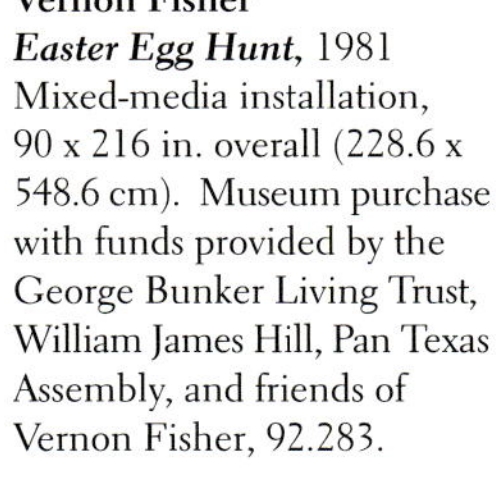

In 1981 Fisher wrote a series of three texts that he titled *Breaking the Code*.[21] Cast in an anecdotal idiom, these narratives describe situations in which a protagonist is frustrated by his or her inability to understand a pattern that is patently clear to others. *Easter Egg Hunt*, 1981 (plate 125), features the most autobiographical of these texts (see page 172). An anomaly among Fisher's compositions, *Easter Egg Hunt* was originally created for an exhibition at Franklin Furnace in New York; Fisher incorporated conspicuously non-art materials into a wall-mounted installation complementing the narrative, forgoing the pictorial illusionism typical of his work of the period.[22] On the left one egg is camouflaged on a square of "grass"; on the right the ordinary detritus of an urban environment—including a well-worn sneaker, an empty cigarette pack, and a crumpled Metropolitan Museum of Art shopping bag—serve as signposts for a series of easily distinguished purple eggs.

Fisher's use of ordinary objects comes in the wake of Marcel Duchamp's 1915 *In Advance of the Broken Arm*, as well as Andy Warhol's 1964 replicas of ordinary Brillo boxes; Marge Goldwater has noted that for Fisher, the use of objects "introduce a foil, what Fisher describes as the 'reality factor.'"[23] However, Fisher's overriding intent is to call attention to the mutability of memory and perception. In a 1989 interview he read the text of *Easter Egg Hunt* and then stated:

> There's no such thing as an objective viewer. That is part of the basic point of all these pieces. Everything we see is completely colored, and we bring this coloration to the work, and then as we participate in the work, the way we see it changes: an existent object changes as we look at it. It is all about things not adding up. Better put, it is about setting up situations where apparently things are going to add up, but they never do.[24]

Like Fisher, Terry Allen is a storyteller who builds his compositions around vividly sketched narratives. A native of Kansas, Allen grew up in Lubbock, Texas. He enrolled

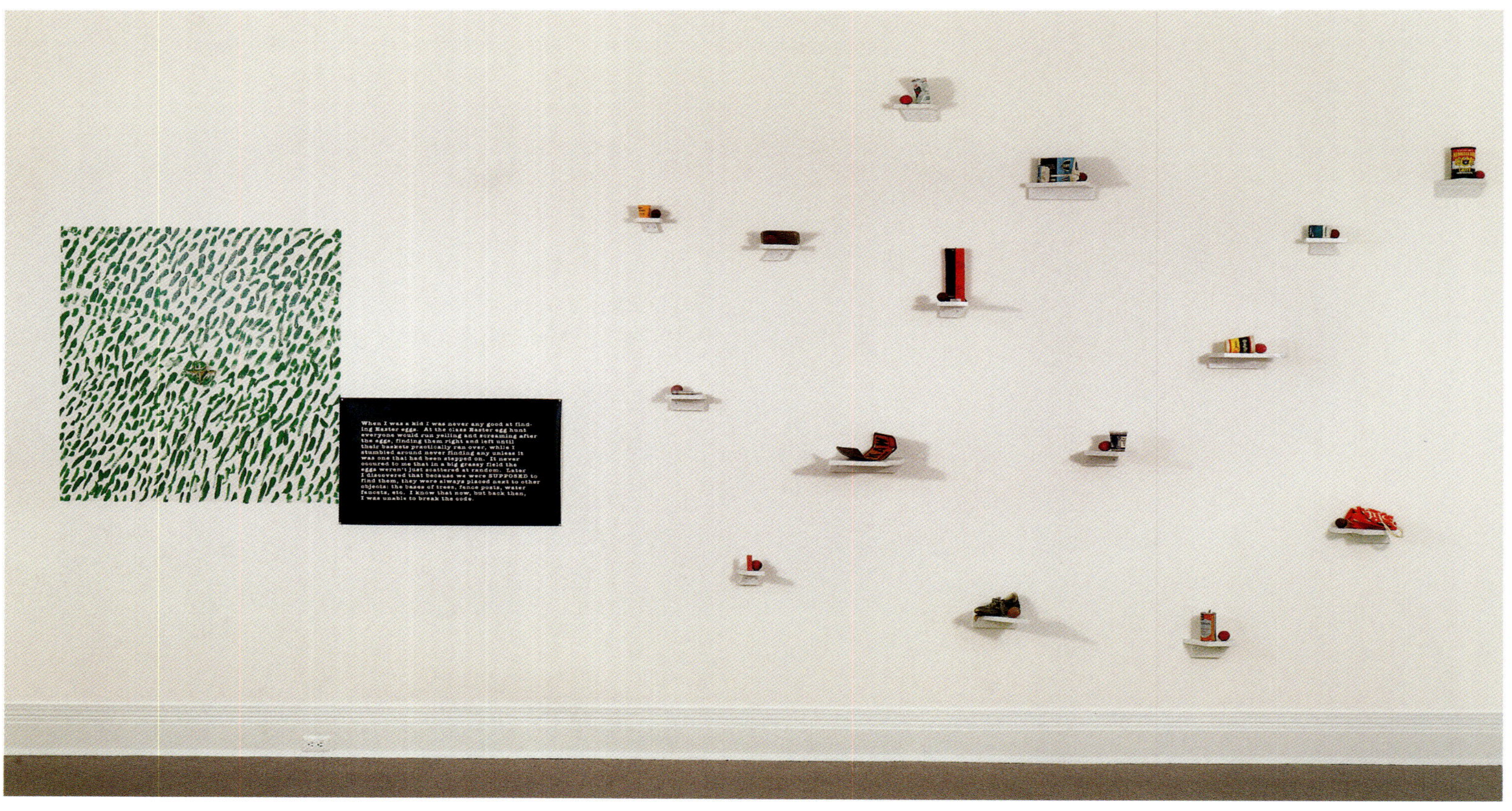

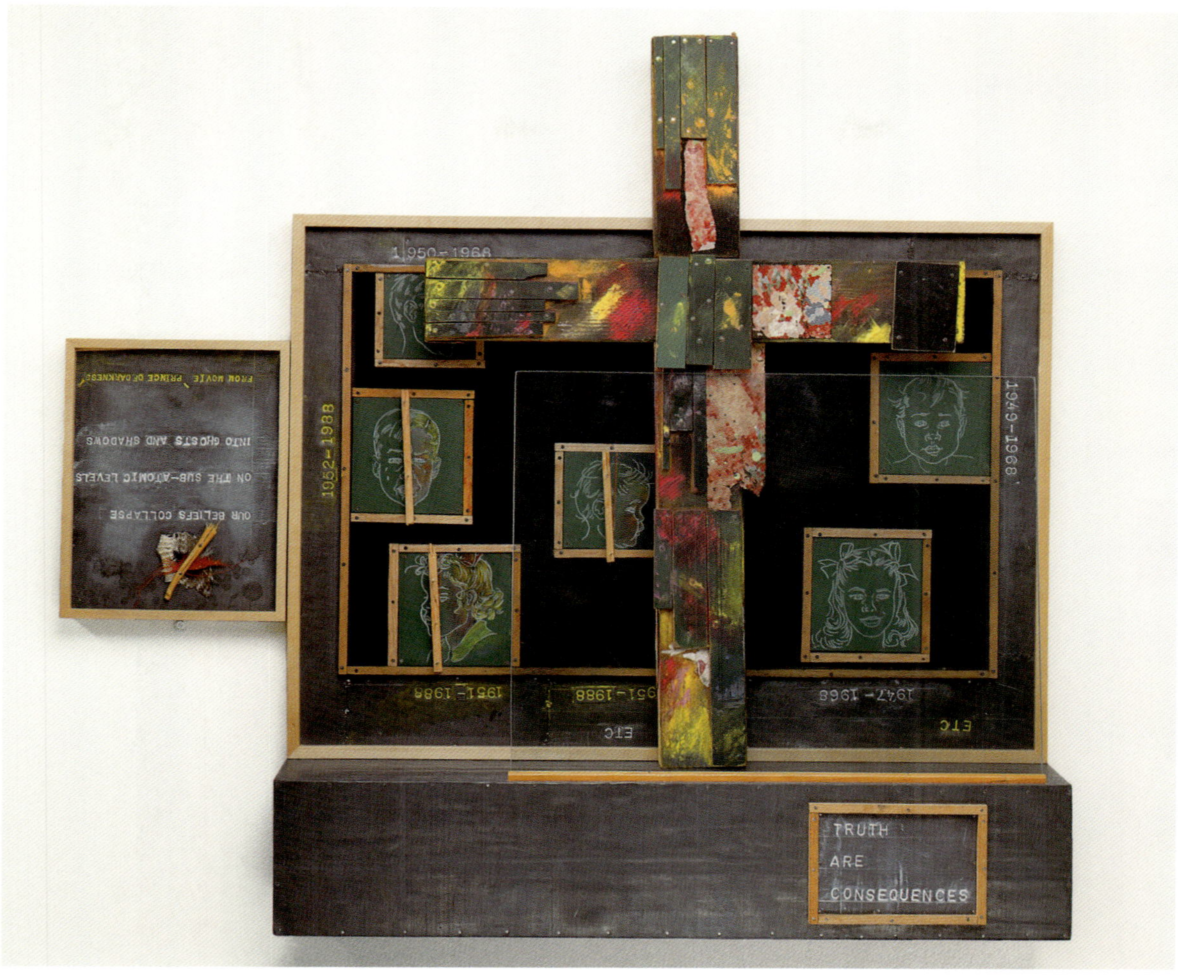

briefly at Texas Tech, and graduated from the Chouinard Art Institute in Los Angeles in 1966. Over the following two decades he made his home on the West Coast, developing a wide-ranging body of work in music, video, painting, performance, sculpture, and installation art. He maintained ties with Texas, however, exhibiting with the Oak Cliff artists of the Texas Funk movement in the early 1970s. And as his 1975 debut album *Juarez*, and the accompanying exhibition seen at the Contemporary Arts Museum demonstrated, Texas—its stories and its inhabitants—remained central to his interests.[25]

In 1982, the German filmmaker Wolf-Eckart Bühler commissioned Allen to create a soundtrack for a documentary on American veterans of the Vietnam War and their Amerasian children living in Thailand. As the project developed, Allen began an extended series of mixed-media works titled *Youth in Asia* devoted to the generation of Americans whose lives were forever changed by the Vietnam War. *Truth Are Consequences*, 1988 (plate 126), is part of this series.[26] Allen assembles the elements of the composition in the manner of an informal shrine: the roughly made crucifix, the upside-down panel on the left, and the partially obscured features of the textbook illustration children indicate the disrupted lives of one small group of classmates.

The function of the *Youth in Asia* series, however, goes beyond that of a memorial to the soldiers who fought in Vietnam, and Allen totals up the toll that years of conflict and subterfuge has had on the American people. The inverted text on the left panel is taken from the 1987 movie *Prince of Darkness* and reads, "Our beliefs collapse on the sub-atomic levels into ghosts and shadows." The toxic lead material of the support and the inversion of imagery suggest a pervading degradation of integrity. As Craig Adcock has noted, "Betrayal of innocence is a primary leitmotif in . . . *Truth Are Consequences*. School children, with the blackboards and chalk, illustrate consequences that were reached in Asia Minor—consequences resulting from distortions of truth in such social institutions as elementary school and high school. Little kids are easily fooled."[27] In an interview of 1988, Allen commented more fully on the corrosive aftermath of the Vietnamese war: "The war generated a climate of betrayal that's with us still. The credibility of everything we

126
Terry Allen
Truth Are Consequences, from the *Youth in Asia* series, 1988
Mixed media, 36¼ x 40 x 6¾ in. (92 x 101.6 x 17.1 cm). Gift of William James Hill in honor of Peter C. Marzio, Director, 91.1846.

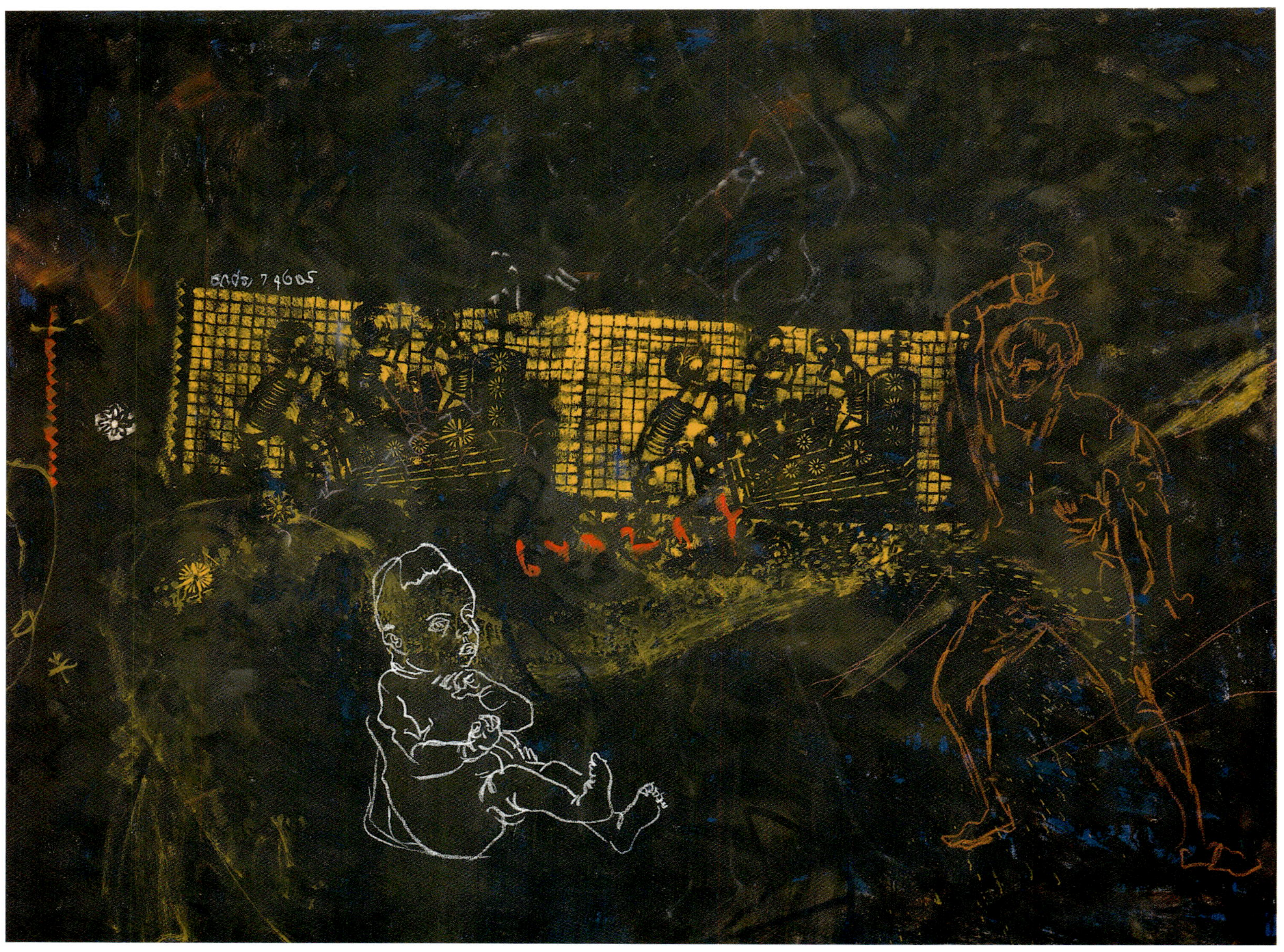

127
Gael Stack
The Christmas Picture,
1987–88
Oil on canvas, 64 x 84 in.
(162.5 x 213.36 cm). Gift of
Betty Moody and Bill Steffy
in memory of George
Bunker, 91.1847.

were raised to believe during the '50s suddenly fell apart and there was a collective psychological reshuffling that people are still trying to sort out."[28]

Gael Stack also explores the twists and turns of memory. A native of Chicago, Stack attended the University of Illinois and Southern Illinois University; she moved to Houston in 1973 and joined the faculty of the University of Houston the following year. While eschewing the direct appropriations of many of her contemporaries, Stack balances gestural abstraction and deliberate reference in her densely structured compositions. As Marti Mayo has pointed out, Stack's dialectical layering corresponds to Charles Jencks's definition of Postmodernism: "Its best works are characteristically double coded and ironic, making a feature of the wide choice, conflict and discontinuity of traditions, because this heterogeneity most clearly captures our pluralism."[29]

Stack stated in 1985: "Art about itself is ultimately boring.... The paintings are based on particular ideas, experiences, or feelings, and the starting point is almost always verbal. I wish to communicate with people some of our common stuff."[30] *The Christmas Picture*, 1987–88 (plate 127), exemplifies this approach. Stack began the composition during Christmas 1987; the figure of the child appears in other paintings of that period, and, as Mayo has chronicled, the image in part reflects a visit with a young nephew.[31] It is set in contrast to the stenciled skeletons taken from Mexican Day of the Dead decorations that dominate the center of the composition, and it is tempting to draw the conclusion that the artist is suggesting a temporal and cyclical continuity between death and new life. However, Stack complicates this equation by adding a third, more shadowy figure on the right, who appears with one arm raised in the classic stance of a Samurai warrior. Whether the figure is to be understood as a threat to or defender of the child is left open. The dark ground, in which blue and brown tones form an uneasy alliance, gives the composition a further sense of tension and irresolution.

Stack, who raised two sons as a single mother, has frequently explored the mixed emotions attached to motherhood, and in her hands the image of the child becomes a potent one. She has commented on the authority of this icon in Western art:

I've ... always liked the Renaissance babies.... I call them "creepy babies" because here they are, supposed to represent God, but they're so powerful (in body) and also always detached from the mothers. And babies are about time. They are the past and they are the future.[32]

Al Souza tests the visual codes that surround us. A native of New England, Souza began to study art in the mid-1960s after completing undergraduate studies in engineering. He attended the Art Students League and the School of the Visual Arts in New York, and received a graduate degree in painting from the University of Massachusetts in 1972. Various teaching positions brought Souza to Texas in the early and mid-1980s; in 1992 he joined the faculty at the University of Houston.

As Sue Graze has observed, Souza's first mature work was devoted to analyzing "the deceitful nature of photography."[33] His compositions of the mid-1970s, for example, followed in the footsteps of such Conceptual artists as Joseph Kosuth, contrasting photographs of an object with the actual object. Other works revealed the ways in which photographs can manipulate the viewer's perception of scale, space, and color, casting the documentary function of the medium into question. In the early 1980s, he turned to painting, bringing to his canvases a similarly deconstructive sensibility.

Marco's Gift, 1989 (plate 128), was the first in a series of diptychs in which Souza introduced a reduced formal clarity to his work. Unlike his earlier paintings of the decade, where transparent images and texts were layered one over the other, Souza split his compositions into two canvases, creating a dramatic dichotomy between image and text. Michael M. Floss has related these paintings to filmic montage, citing Sergei Eisenstein's statement, "From the collision of two given factors arises a concept."[34] In *Marco's Gift*, Souza contrasts the tattooed features of a Maori aborigine with the enigmatic words "The Encyclopedia of Contest Pictures" (the actual title of a 1940s image source book given to the artist by a friend named Marco). The surface of the upper half of the diptych is heavily impastoed; the lower half is executed with thin washes of paint. Souza has pointed out that a nineteenth-century text on ornament by the English architect and theoretician Owen Jones, cited by Ernst Gombrich in his *The Sense of Order: A Study in the*

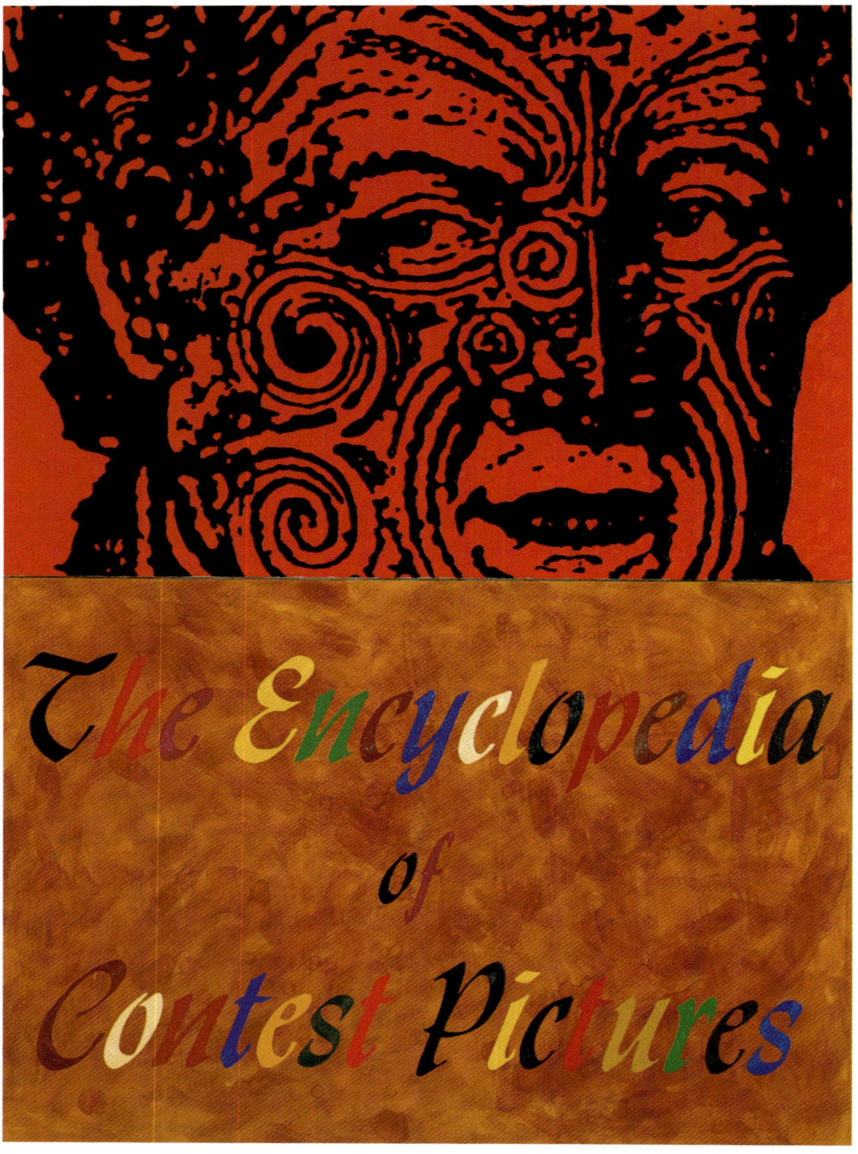

128
Al Souza
Marco's Gift, 1989
Oil on canvas, diptych: 84 x
60 in. (217.2 x 152.4 cm).
Museum purchase with funds
provided by Duke Energy,
89.108.

Psychology of Decorative Art, was the textual source for this composition.[35] Jones observed:

> The ornament of a savage tribe, being the result of a natural instinct, is necessarily always true to its purpose; whilst in much of the ornament of civilized nations, the first impulse which generated received forms being enfeebled by constant repetition, the ornament is oftentimes misapplied, and instead of first seeking the most convenient form and adding beauty, all beauty is destroyed, because all fitness, by superadding ornament to ill contrived form. If we would return to a more healthy condition, we must even be as little children or as savages; we must get rid of the acquired and artificial, and return to and develop natural instincts.[36]

However, unlike Jones, who sought to redeem modern decoration, Souza is fascinated by the acquired and the artificial, recognizing in them the natural expression of contemporary life.

A second aspect of the Postmodern era is the promotion of cultural differences in the arts. The critic Craig Owens observed in the early 1980s, "Decentered, allegorical, schizophrenic… —however we choose to diagnose its symptoms, Postmodernism is usually treated, by its protagonists and antagonists alike, as a crisis of cultural authority, specifically of the authority vested in Western European culture and its institutions."[37] Dana Friis-Hansen, who explored this theme in a 1999 exhibition titled *Other Narratives* at the Contemporary Arts Museum in Houston, reviewed the range of this shift: "The 1980s and 1990s marked the publication of important bodies of theoretical writing under the diverse headings of Feminism, Black Studies, Latino Culture, Asian Studies, Cultural History, Postcolonial Criticism, Lesbian and Gay Studies, and the like, all of which broadened the discussion of new ideas about the roles gender, race, culture, sexual orientation, and class play in shaping identity and society. These challenges to the status quo from artists and theorists alike shaped the defining parameters of Postmodernism."[38]

The 1980s saw a number of exhibitions across the United States that examined Hispanic and African-American themes. As discussed in the second chapter of this catalogue, many these presentations focused on the ways in which artists defined identity through the religious and ritual traditions of their cultures. Of equal importance, however, were the artists who chose to confront pop-culture clichés and, more controversially, negative racial stereotypes.

César Augusto Martínez and Luis Jiménez have seized upon the working-class imagery of Chicano culture. The curator John Beardsley linked the two figures in his 1987 essay for the exhibition catalogue *Hispanic Art in the United States: Thirty Contemporary Artists*. After describing the evolution of Hispanic identity in the United States, from the heavily politicized movements of the 1960s to the more individualized developments of the 1970s, Beardsley observed:

> César Martínez manifests a slightly more detached perspective: because the *pachucos*—Mexican-American rebels—he depicts are rigidly frontal and isolated, as with *Bato con Sunglasses*, they are nearly iconic. One senses that these are historical rather than intimately observed personages, a feeling confirmed both by the fact that *pachuco* culture reached its apogee in the years immediately after World War II, and by the fact that the characters are composites created from, among other sources, back issues of *Lowrider* magazine and old high school yearbooks. Luis Jiménez has likewise depicted the *pachuco*, but also reached back to one of the original Mexican-American character types, the *vaquero*—cowboy—and forward to one of the most recent—the illegal alien.[39]

The son of Mexican émigrés, Martínez grew up in the border city of Laredo; after attending Laredo Junior College, he received a B.A. in 1968 from the Texas Arts and Industries University in Kingsville. Martínez reflected tellingly on his childhood: "When I was a kid, I thought every town had a Mexican counterpart across the river, an *otro lado*. It wasn't until I was in my teens that the meaning of being Mexican American began to sink in."[40] Following a term of military service, Martínez returned to Texas and worked as both a commercial and a fine arts photographer in San Antonio. In the mid-1970s he abandoned photography for painting; however, photographic sources remained an inspiration for his subsequent memory portraits.

Bato con Sunglasses, 1984/91 (plate 129), is one of over

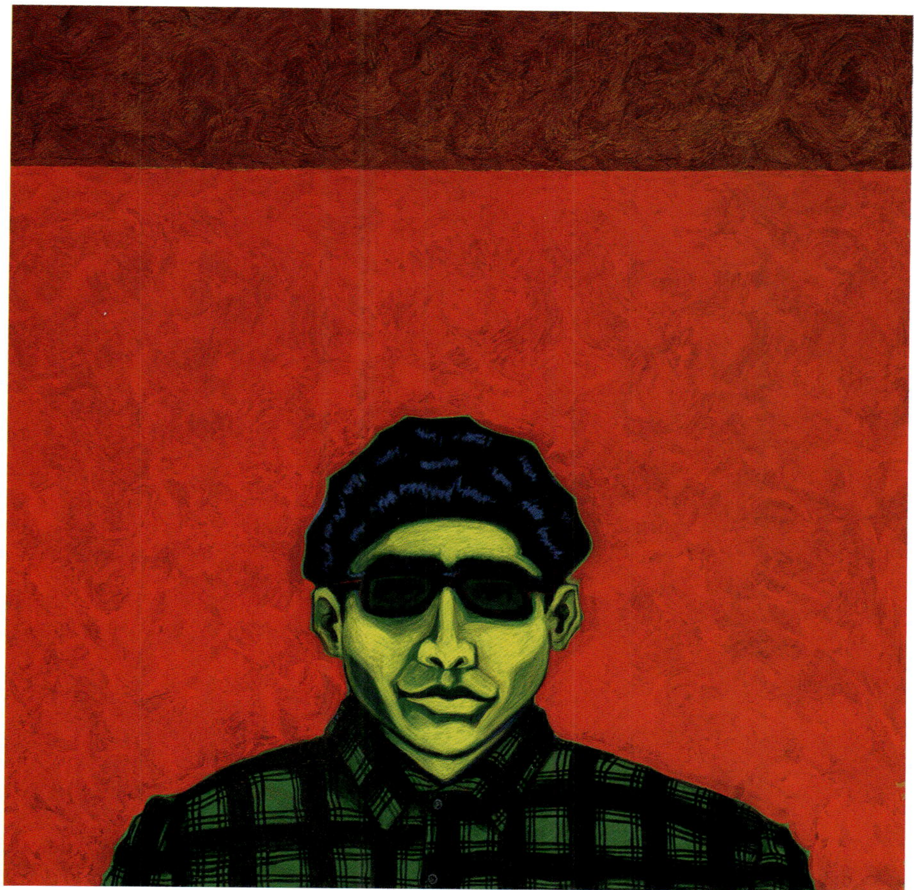

129
César Augusto Martínez
Bato con Sunglasses,
1984/91
Acrylic on canvas, 50 x 50 in.
(127 x 127 cm). Museum
purchase with funds provided
by Crowley, Marks & Douglas
and Pablo Alvarado in
memory of Froilan and Juan
Joaquin Aguirre, 91.1852.

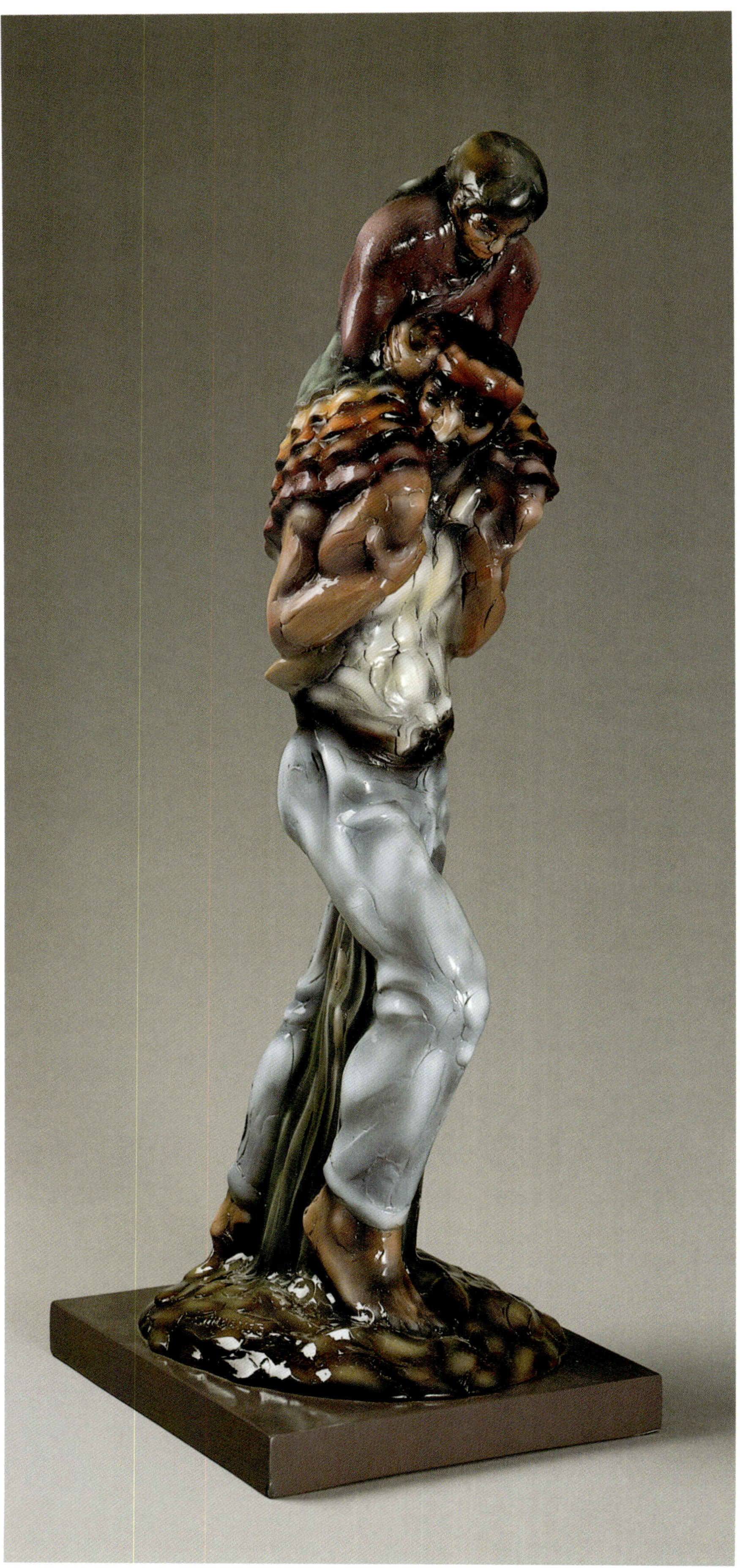

sixty portraits Martínez created as part of his extended *Bato* series dedicated to the figures he remembered from his childhood in Laredo. (*Bato* can be loosely translated into English as "guy.") The first *Bato* portraits date from 1978, although the artist has recalled that "it had been on my mind for a good few years."[41]

The composition of *Bato con Sunglasses* underwent a period of adjustment; originally titled *Bato Weathering a Storm of Controversy*, the painting was reworked in 1991, and Martínez has documented: "Although the figure remained pretty much the way it is now, the colors changed several times and the background went through several repaintings. Finally, [in] 1991 I got it right."[42] The vivid contrast between the warm tones of the background and the acid green of the figure push the *bato* into the foreground—veiled by sunglasses, he nonetheless engages the viewer with a direct gaze. Jacinto Quirarte has observed of this series: "These are single half-length portraits of easily recognized barrio types.... They are presented against a dark background with a band of color across the top of the visual surface. The key element of the image is the eye contact between the sitter and the viewer who is asked to acknowledge the presence of someone from the barrio."[43]

Border issues have defined much of Luis Jiménez's work. Jiménez grew up in El Paso, where his father worked as a sign painter and creator of the neon "spectaculars" that animate the nighttime highways of the Southwest. Jiménez received his first artistic apprenticeship in his father's shop; he later attended the University of Texas at El Paso and the University of Texas at Austin, where he graduated in 1964. Between 1966 and 1971, he worked in New York City; in response to Pop Art and the political climate of the time, Jiménez created his first fiberglass sculptures of such figures as an intoxicated Statue of Liberty and a man on fire (which had evolved from a figure of a protester bearing a Molotov cocktail).

On returning to Southwest, Jiménez turned his attention to public sculpture, enshrining, as the curator and artist Benito Huerta has noted, "working-class heroes." Not only did Jiménez use such populist materials as fiberglass, familiar to the Lowrider culture of the Southwest, but as Huerta has described, his themes are imbued with an essential humanism: "Jiménez's work . . .

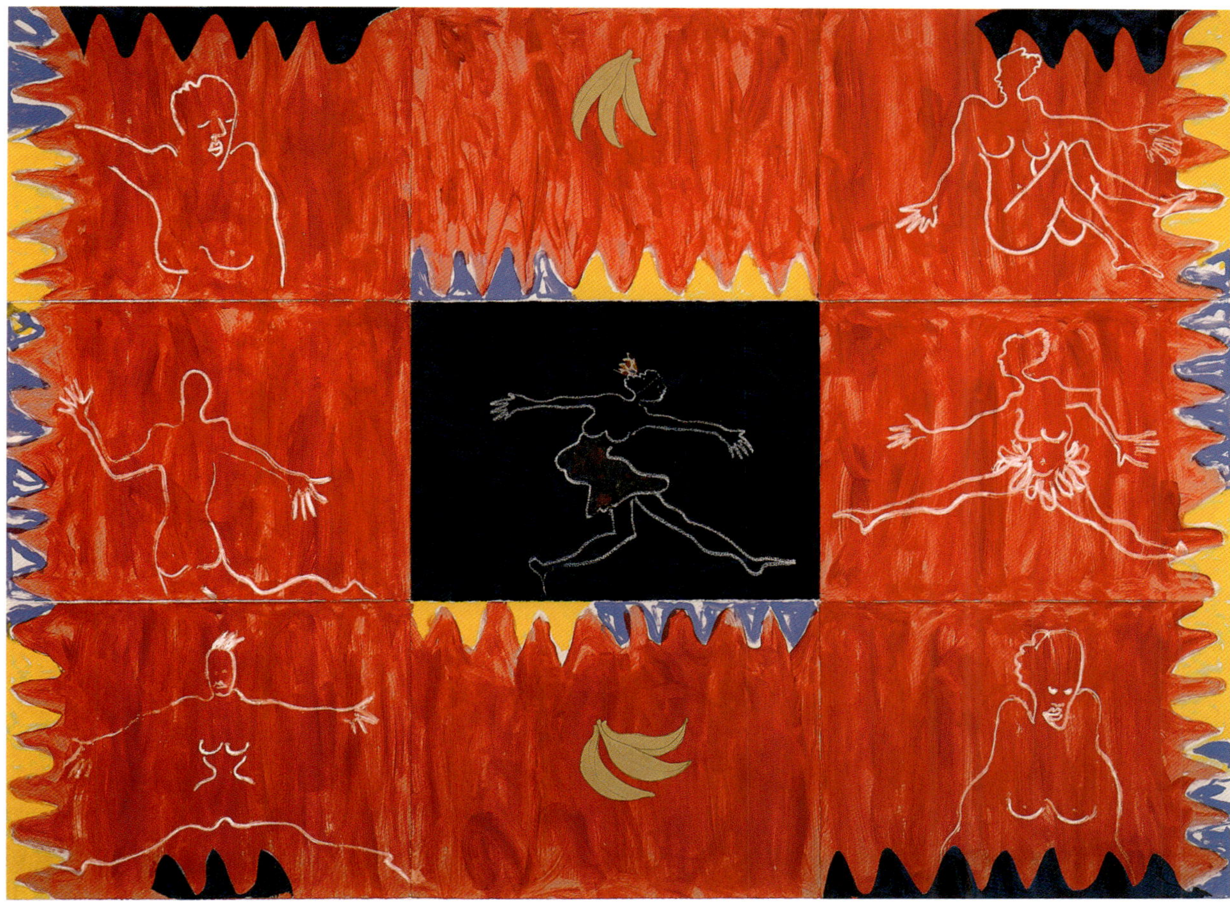

reflects an examination and celebration of the culture and myths from both sides of the Mexican/United States border. From the settlement of the western United States to the political upheavals that continue into the present, Jiménez's work explores the ways in which these elements impact the everyday individual."[44] As Dave Hickey has further observed, Jiménez's sculptures have a revisionist function: "Luis Jiménez's West is fully embodied and full of life. The theatrically 'empty' Western landscape of American mythology—populated by roaming murderers and visionaries, by Billy the Kid and Brigham Young, Bugsy Siegel and John Ford—is replaced in Jiménez's art by a landscape of living creatures, animals and humans, who live and work and dance together."[45]

Border Crossing [Cruzando el Rio Bravo], 1986 (plate 130), is a small-scale study for one of the artist's most eloquent sculptures. Reflecting on his own Mexican heritage, Jiménez pays heartfelt homage to the laborers who face exploitation, exportation, and even death by crossing the Rio Grande (or seen from the Mexican side, the Rio Bravo) into the United States.[46] A man bears his wife and child on his shoulders, an ensemble that recasts the flight into Egypt into secular and present-day terms.[47] The artist has recalled:

I had wanted to make a piece that was dealing with the issue of the illegal alien. People talked about aliens as if they landed from outer space, as if they weren't really people. I wanted to put a face on them; I wanted to humanize them. I also wanted to deal with the whole idea of family. . . . I went back to my experience in El Paso where this is a common sight.[48]

Floyd Elbert Newsum, Jr., Annette Lawrence, and Michael Ray Charles similarly probe memory and cultural signifiers as they explore the evolution of contemporary African-American identities. At the same time, they accept the challenge of framing their work within the conventions of contemporary art and theory. Greg Tate, writing about African-American modernism, has commented tellingly: "In the visual arts, acceptance of Blacks as Moderns depends upon artists producing work that both resonates with Black acculturation and conforms to the definitions of style and abstraction considered current and marketable in the contemporary art world. The invention of metaphoric, iconic and expressive means to accomplish these tasks has been the triumph of a relative few."[49]

Newsum, the most senior artist of this group, has grounded his work in the celebratory spirit of the Harlem

131
Floyd Elbert Newsum, Jr.
Josephine Sho' Can Dance,
1991
Acrylic, oil stick, and collage on paper, 67 3/4 x 89 3/4 in. (172 x 227.9 cm). Museum purchase with funds provided by Crowley, Marks & Douglas in honor of A. Y. Woodard, 92.40.

130 *opposite*
Luis Jiménez
Border Crossing [Cruzando el Rio Bravo], maquette, 1986
Fiberglass with pigment and glitter, 31 3/4 x 10 1/4 x 11 3/4 in. (80.64 x 26 x 29.8 cm). Gift of Frank Ribelin 90.410.

Renaissance, although the later collages of such artists as Henri Matisse and Romare Bearden have also been key influences. A native of Memphis, Tennessee, he attended the Memphis Academy of Arts and the Tyler School of Art in Philadelphia, where he received a graduate degree in 1975. A position on the faculty of the University of Houston brought him to Texas the following year.

Josephine Sho' Can Dance, 1991 (plate 131), dedicated to the great dancer and chanteuse Josephine Baker, is the first of a series of large-scale compositions that marked a breakthrough shift in Newsum's work.[50] His earlier paintings and drawings were more intimately scaled and densely structured, with a greater reliance on collage aesthetics. In *Josephine Sho' Can Dance* collage is kept to a minimum: nine sheets are mounted in a grid—framing seven images of Baker—while two brown-paper cutouts of bananas (which allude to the dancer's most notorious costume) wittily puncture spatial illusion.

Despite its compositional lucidity, *Josephine Sho' Can Dance* is richly textured in reference and meaning. The overall format and palette of the composition relates to West African textiles; Baker appears as an exuberant dancer and a forceful image of sensuality. Newsum is certainly aware of the complicated readings prompted by Baker's role as an unrestrained personification of the primitive, and as Andrea D. Barnwell has recently noted, "Although many people celebrate Baker's career, many could argue that her initial success was achieved at the expense of her integrity and the principles of African-Americans.... The interplay between her self-produced images and those created by others complicates, and often detracts from, her self-agency as a performer." Barnwell concludes, however, "As the epitome of a woman who utilized self-agency in order to attain personal satisfaction, Baker was re-creation and reconceptualization personified. This ability to metamorphose secures and implants her standing as the ultimate self-propelled icon of renaissance, within and beyond the boundaries of Harlem's rebirth."[51]

Annette Lawrence, a native of New York, attended the University of Hartford in Connecticut and received a graduate degree from the Maryland Institute in Baltimore in 1990. A Texas Commission on the Arts grant brought her to Houston later that year, where she became an

artist-in-residence at the Community Artists' Collective. Her first exhibition in 1991 at Houston's Barnes-Blackman Galleries, where she traced her personal growth through a chronicle of her menstrual cycles, captured the attention of numerous critics, and the following year she was featured in *Fresh Visions/New Voices: Emerging African-American Artists in Texas* at the Glassell School of Art.

Rock Writing, August 1992 (plate 132), was first seen in an exhibition at MexiArte in Austin in 1992; the specificity of the date of the work reveals that it was created during the summer of riots in Los Angeles that followed the Rodney King verdict, a time when race relations across the United States were deeply strained. Lawrence spells out the phrase: "They Must Don't Know Who We Are" in lava and limestone rocks arranged on the floor of the gallery space.[52] The formal qualities of *Rock Writing* can be linked to the work of such installation artists as Richard Long; however, it is the text that resonates for Lawrence:

> The phrase "They Must Don't Know Who We Are" expresses the indignity of those who have been inappropriately received on account of the vanity and presumptuousness of Western Culture. The syntax indicates a point of view that cannot be expressed using "correct" English. Must is used to emphasize the attitude of the speaker. The attitude comes from the feeling that "They" should know better than to not acknowledge "We" with due respect. "They" and "We" are applicable as the reader chooses.
>
> The words in *Rock Writing* are literally written in stone. The permanence implied by writing in stone, and the value placed on permanence in Western Culture are debased by the form as an installation that changes each time it is assembled and disassembled. The value of *Rock Writing* is found in the meaning not in the materials used.[53]

Michael Ray Charles grew up in rural Louisiana; after attending McNeese State University in Lake Charles, he came to Texas to complete his graduate studies at the University of Houston, where he received an M.F.A. in 1993. Like Lawrence, he was among the artists featured in the Glassell School's 1992 *Fresh Visions/New Voices: Emerging African-American Artists in Texas*. It was in this exhibition that Charles introduced the Little Black Sambo figure that has evolved into one of his chief motifs

132
Annette Lawrence
Rock Writing, August 1992
Lava and limestone rocks, 72 x 136 in. (182.8 x 345.4 cm). Museum purchase with funds provided by AT&T New Art/New Visions and the Wilder Foundation, 93.254.

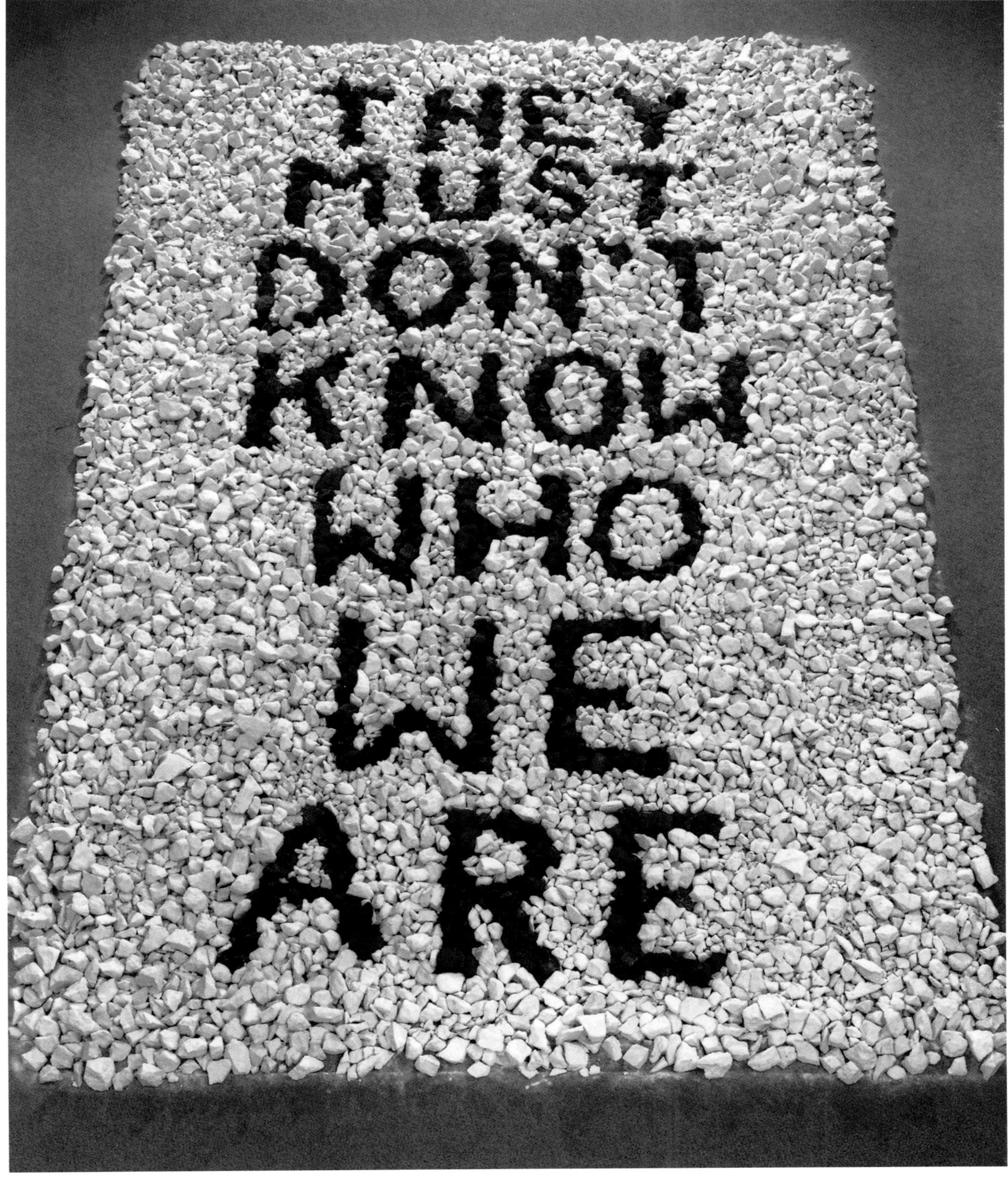
THEY
MUST
DON'T
KNOW
WHO
WE
ARE

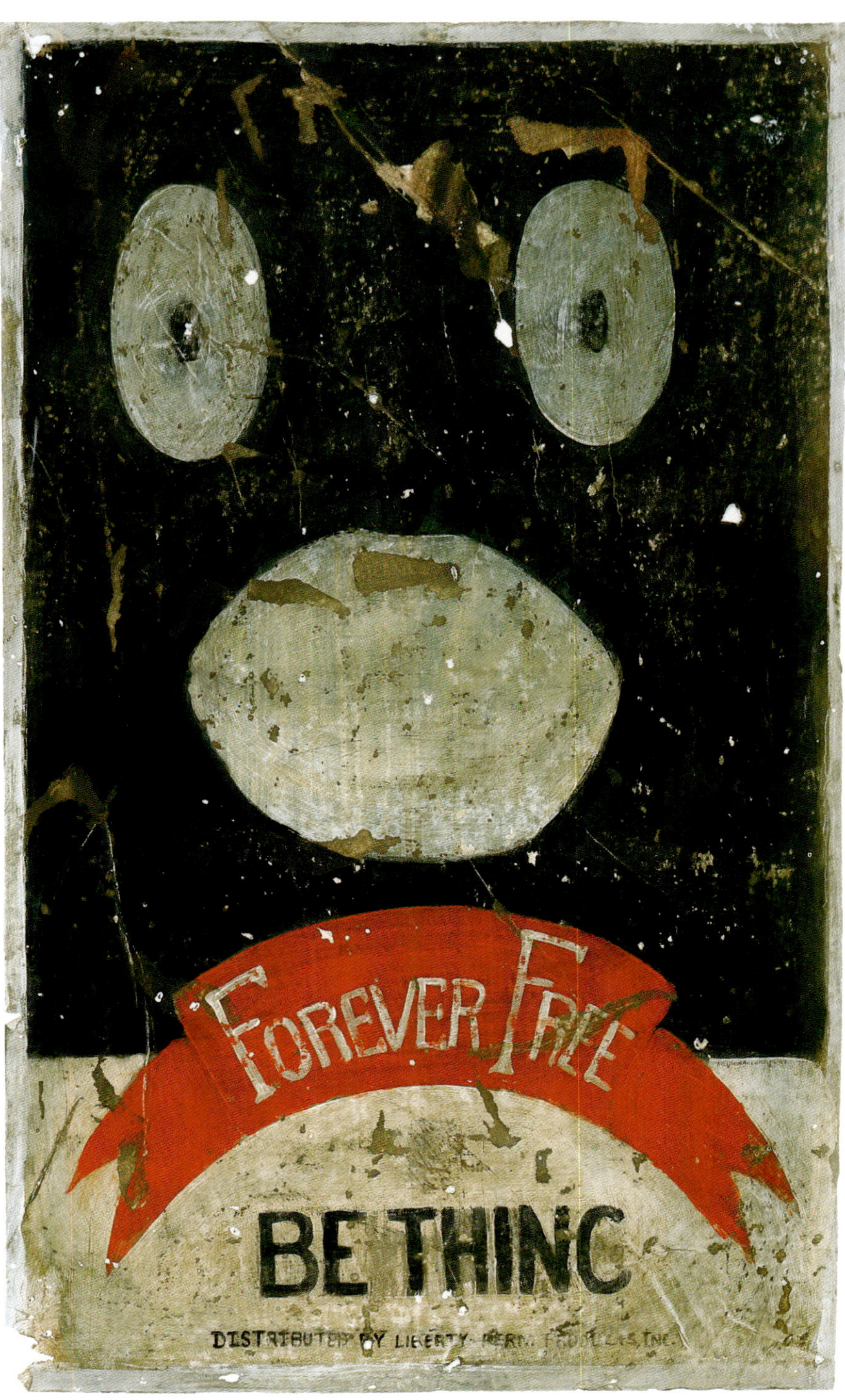

in a series of increasingly confrontational paintings that address racial stereotypes.

Be Thinc, 1993 (plate 133), from the artist's extended *Forever Free* series, is among Charles's most abstract works.[54] Working from a black ground, Charles fills the field with the round-eyed and opened-mouth features of a Sambo caricature. The distressed surface and the pictorial style of the image hearken back to the graphics of vintage editions of *The Saturday Evening Post*, a publication which the artist has acknowledged presented a world utterly alien to his own experience.[55] As in every work of this series, Charles has affixed a penny into the background of the composition; Charles has noted that not only does the penny feature Abraham Lincoln, the great emancipator, but also that it is the "black" coin and the cheapest of American currency.[56] He has stated of this series:

> The "Forever Free" series started out of my attempts to deal with the Sambo image, the multiple meanings involved in its existence both past, present, and possibly in the future. That was the first step towards what has become a thorough search for an understanding of what constituted what an African-American appeared to be in past societies.... I question how and why these derogatory images were used and consumed.... I believe these paintings will help us all to understand elements that exist around us that contribute to determining factors which describe who we are, and what we are to become.[57]

Charles's images are not easily understood by all audiences, and like such contemporaries as Kara Walker, he has been accused of perpetuating racism through his investigation of racial stereotypes. However, Charles's revisionist intent is confirmed by the phrase "Be Thinc," which not only extols the viewer to "bethink oneself" but also suggests a pun on "Be Ethnic." Calvin Reid has noted: "In a Michael Ray Charles painting, racial symbols clash and butt against one another to create an impression combined of past and future, reality and perception.... The works track the ebb and flow of racial symbolism through mass culture and its expression in the smallest daily activities. His appropriated signifiers collide in a reduced version of a kind of race war, without guns but fought with images and ossified stereotypes still rumbling around in the American subconscious."[58]

In 1990, the Musée d'Orsay in Paris mounted an exhibition of nineteenth-century sculpture that examined the body in fragmentary form. Titled *Le Corps en morceaux* [*The Body in Pieces*], the exhibition surveyed the range of anatomical studies—from devotional talismans, to medical mannequins, to the magisterial work of Auguste Rodin—that saw the body as segmented, vulnerable, and at the same time a potent site of meaning. This presentation reflected the concerns of many artists of the 1980s and 1990s, and over the following decade a number of exhibitions focused on contemporary paintings, sculptures, and photographs that deconstructed the image of the human body. Among the most notable of these presentations were the 1992 *Corporeal Politics* and *Post Human* surveys and the Venice Biennale's 1995 centennial exhibition *Identity and Alterity: Figures of the Body 1895–1995*.[59] Writing of this phenomenon, art historian Linda Nochlin commented: "In postmodernist production, the fragment assumes new, and differently transgressive, forms.... The postmodern body, from the vantage-point of [Cindy Sherman and Robert Mapplethorpe] and many others, is conceived uniquely as the 'body-in-pieces': the very notion of a unified, unambiguously gendered subject is rendered suspect by their work."[60]

A number of artists working in Texas, including Rachel Hecker, Jeffrey Cowie, Sharon Engelstein, and Lynn Cazabon, have responded to this essentially Postmodern understanding of the body. For these artists, the body is a political arena, affected not only by sexual mores, but also by the larger issues of what makes us human.

Rachel Hecker manipulates icons from popular culture to investigate our preconceptions about consumerism and sexual identity. A graduate of Moore College of Art in Philadelphia and the Rhode Island School of Design in Providence, Rhode Island, Hecker came to Houston in 1982 at the invitation of Allan Hacklin to act as assistant director of the Glassell School of Art. In 1992 she joined the faculty of the University of Houston. Using the airbrush and montage techniques of such artists as James Rosenquist, Hecker looked to both *film noir* and Saturday morning cartoons in her paintings of the late 1980s and early 1990s. The appropriative strategies of David Salle further influenced on her work, and as Hecker has commented, the intent of her paintings of this period was disruptive:

My paintings are derived from and rally against the things I have been spoon-fed, the things I embrace, and the things that have insinuated themselves in my head. This includes a Max Factor-esque ideal of beauty— "Friends I can believe in" thanks to Walt Disney—eight years of a president who perpetrated the dangerous fiction of bad "B" movies on the will of the people, followed by a man who has been asking me to read his lips, but in four years has yet to speak the truth.[61]

In the mid-1990s Hecker's paintings became more self-reflective, and figuration became increasingly important as demonstrated by *.5 .4 .9*, 1994 (plate 134), the most complex of the *Pleasure and Commerce* series created between 1994 and 1995. Hecker used art-instruction manuals of the 1950s as source materials throughout the series, and despite the charged subject matter of the female nude, these paintings exude the cool gloss of commercial art.[62] The tautly organized composition of *.5 .4 .9* suggests a voluptuous coupling between the two dazzlingly idealized Amazon figures, a unity subtly underscored by the title (five plus four equals nine). The blue-movie palette—as well as the logos of a popular candy and the cash-register numbers that occupy the foreground—can be understood as codes for the pleasures and commodification of sex, while the shocked features of the caricature on the lower right suggests the breaking of a taboo. Nevertheless, the segmentation of forms and the discrete angles chosen by the artist, which also invite the viewer to identify with the subjects, act to diffuse the shock of two women about to be engaged in a sexual act, and as Ann Cvetkovich has observed, Hecker's figures seem serenely oblivious to the jarring images that surround them.[63]

Jeffrey Cowie was in the undergraduate program at the Rhode Island School of Design the same years that Hecker was in the graduate program, and in 1982 he came to Houston as a member of the newly established Core Residency Program at the Glassell School of Art. His paintings of these years moved from figuration into lushly layered abstraction; however, in 1990 Cowie shifted his attention to collage. He later reflected: "My paintings gradually lost their resonance. I saw that I had become too comfortable with the beauty of paint. So I decided to try to make work that was harder edged."[64]

133
Michael Ray Charles
Be Thinc, from the *Forever Free* series, 1993
Acrylic and penny on paper, 36⅝ x 22 in. (92.9 x 55.8 cm). Museum purchase with funds provided by the Wilder Foundation, 93.251.

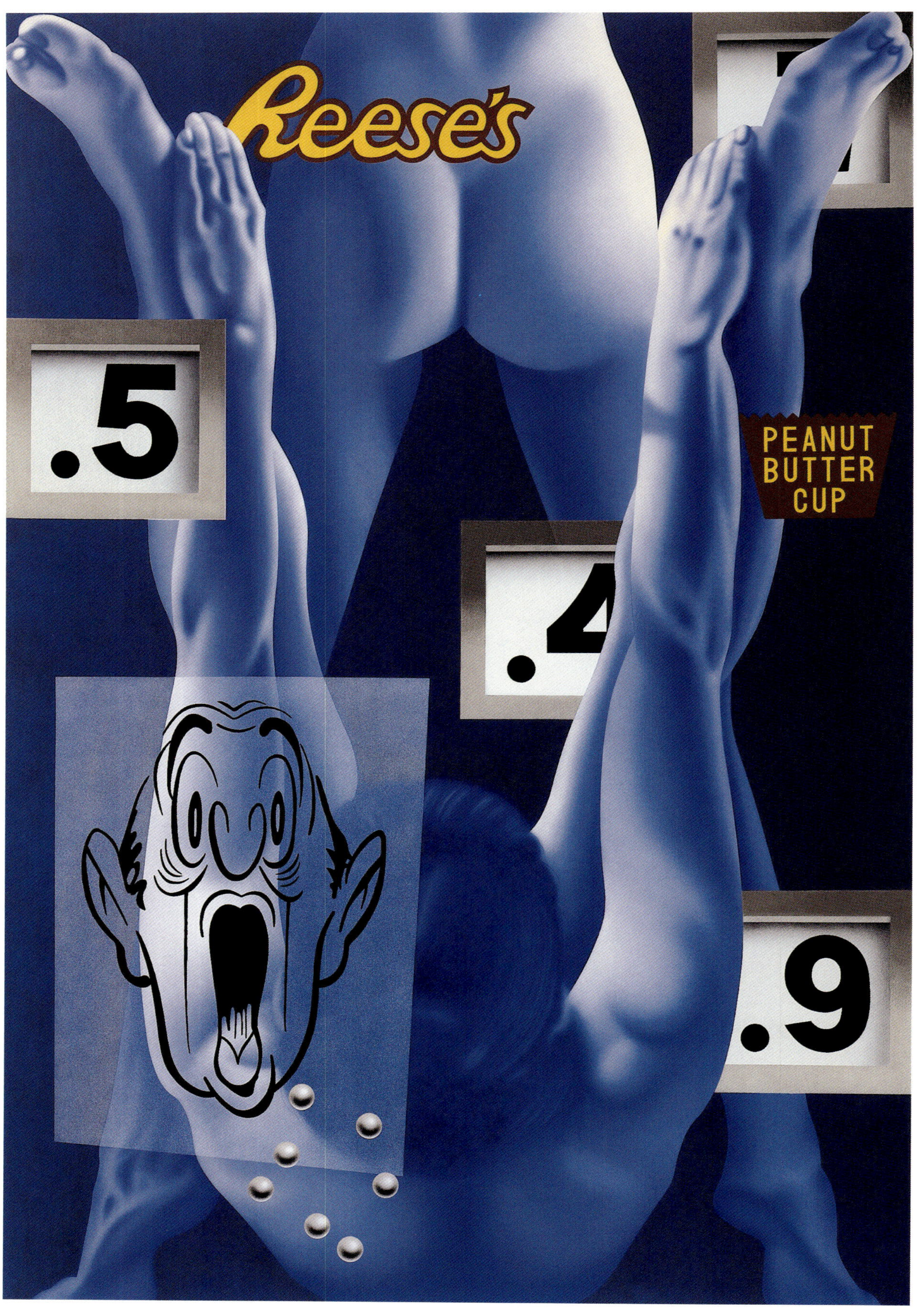
Reese's
PEANUT
BUTTER
CUP
.5
.4
.9

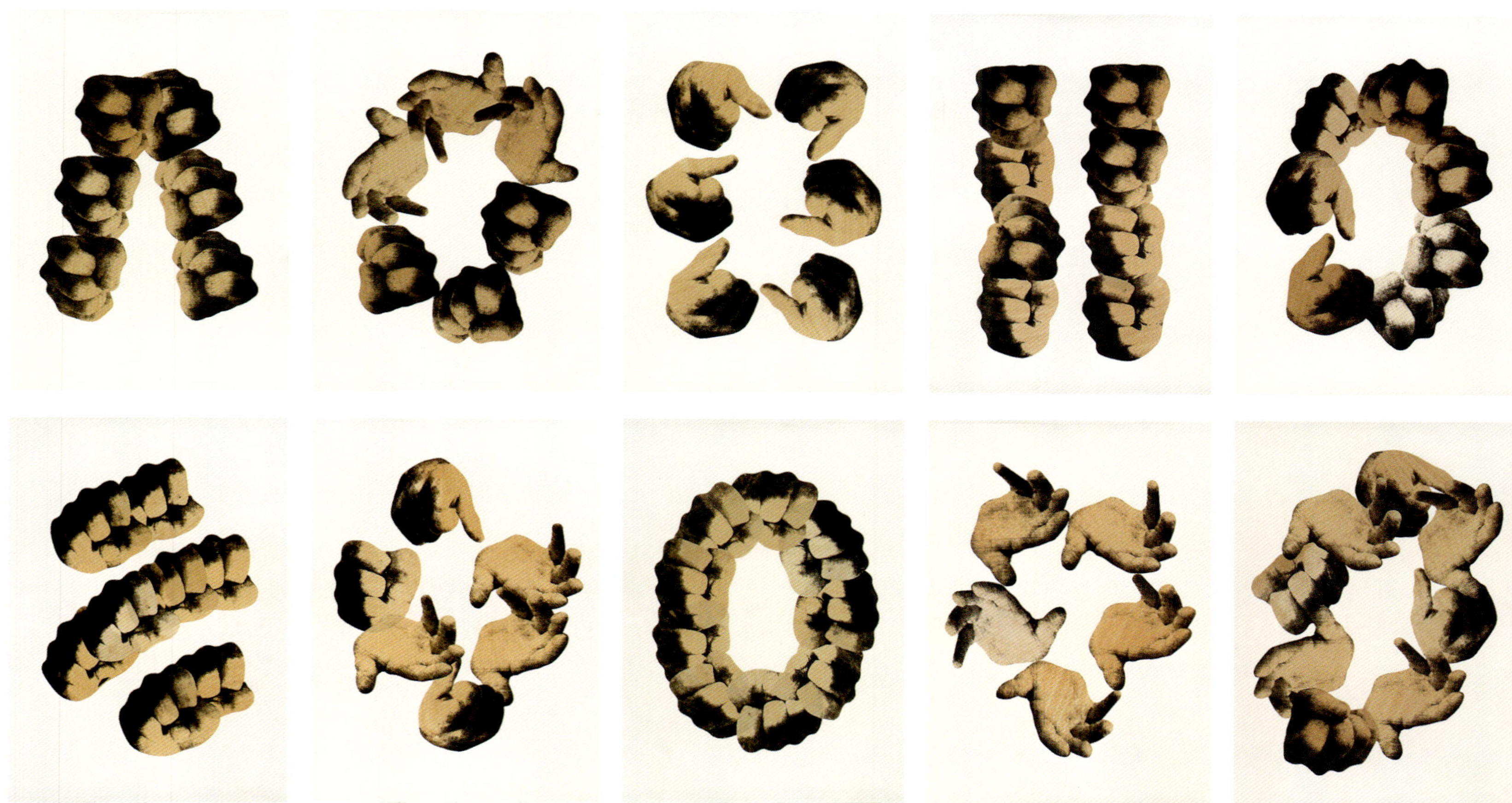

His first works exploring collage featured silkscreened elements integrated into shaped canvases; as the series progressed, Cowie pared down his compositions, giving them greater graphic force.

Keep Talking (For Sheila Rosenstein), 1992 (plate 135), is one of the artist's most powerful works.[65] Using large-scale sheets of paper for support, Cowie collaged onto them a series of images of hands (created and enlarged through photographic and silkscreen processes), ranging in gesture from open-handed greeting to aggressively tight fists. The eloquence of these fragmented gestures recalls the manual alphabetic codes of the American Sign Language; the ten sheets ranged together on the wall have a pugnacious force. Cowie has commented on these works:

> It's about secret societies quietly plotting, power kept in check, secret languages. Hands are a sign for "human," and I chose them as a way of communicating "this is about you" to the viewer. What I like is how much these hands move, how different they look placed this or that way, upside-down or side-ways, and the associations brought to each change in position or combination. Fists refer to violence (always). An open hand is begging or accepting, or a slap. But the hands aren't doing anything. They float, discrete. They make no reference to the things that go in hands, or the places hands go; they simply flap and wave. For me these collages are about talking.... I was trying to get the most from a limited vocabulary of images, to give the sense that there are many different hands when in fact it's the same four over and over.[66]

Sharon Engelstein brings an essentially Surrealist sensibility to her exploration of anatomical fragmentation. A native of Canada, Engelstein studied at the University of South Florida in Tampa before attending Claremont Graduate Program in Southern California. The Core Residency Program brought her to Houston in 1990, where her serial sculptures of biomorphic forms immediately brought her widespread attention.

Untitled III, 1992 (plate 136), is a disturbingly anomalous object. Unlike Engelstein's earlier sculptures that suggested internal organs, *Untitled III* is a perfect sphere, eerily brought to life by the insertion of a prosthetic glass eyeball. The white shell-like surface suggests that the sculpture is an egg—the eye peers out from within, conferring sentience on the otherwise inanimate form. Engelstein commented:

135
Jeffrey Cowie
Keep Talking (For Sheila Rosenstein), 1992
Silkscreen and collage on paper, ten sheets, 46 x 38½ in. each (116.8 x 97.7 cm). Museum purchase with funds provided by the George Bunker Living Trust, Jeri Nordbrock and Mark Peterson, and with funds donated in memory of Moore Murray, 93.66.

134 *opposite*
Rachel Hecker
.5 .4 .9, from the *Pleasure and Commerce* series, 1994
Acrylic on canvas, 108 x 72 in. (274.3 x 182.8 cm). Gift of Michael A. Caddell and Cynthia Chapman, 99.260.

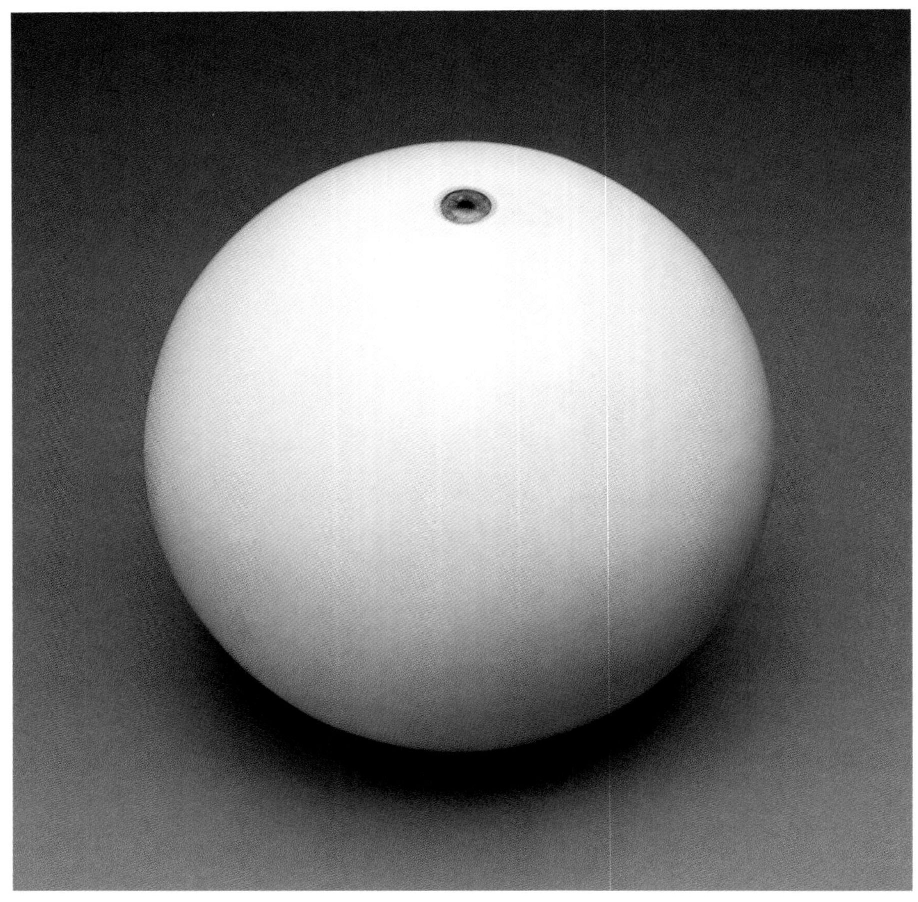

136
Sharon Engelstein
Untitled III, 1992
Plaster, wood, and glass eye,
6¹/₂ in. diameter (16.5 cm).
Museum purchase with funds
provided by Crowley, Marks,
& Douglas in memory of
Valente Viscalno Hernandez,
Jr., 92.233.

consciousness, "Standing near . . . you feel ungainly and tentative; there's an Alice in Wonderland quality to the ensemble, a sense of dislocation and changeability."[68]

Theatricality and relationship between the manufactured and the organic are central themes in the photographs of Lynn Cazabon. Cazabon was also drawn to Houston by the Core Residency Program, which she entered in 1991. A native of Detroit, she had attended the University of Michigan, Ann Arbor, and Cranbrook Academy of Art before coming to Texas. Cazabon's work of the early 1990s paid homage to the writings of Jacques Lacan, the French psychoanalyst, whose essays on the subjectivity of the "gaze" of the spectator had a widespread influence on critical theory in film and the visual arts. For her first series of works exhibited in Houston, Cazabon rephotographed sequences of images that suggested various ways of interpreting works of art, emphasizing the viewer's relationship to the object.[69]

Trace, 1993 (plate 137), is among a subsequent series of photographs where Cazabon turned her camera on a more immediate environment. The upper half of the diptych displays a taut segment of a woman's neck, the bottom half the scraped crescent left on the floor by an ill-fitting door. The pairing of the two images suggests a temporal sequence, like two film stills. Working in the wake of Cindy Sherman, whose *Untitled Film Stills* of 1977–80 revolutionized conceptual photography, Cazabon strips away the anecdotal frame favored by Sherman to examine the physical presence—and absence—of the body in space. She has stated:

The work I have done over the past three years has been largely concerned with the invention of a form that is a hybrid of organic and mechanical matter. . . . My most recent work incorporates my own fabricated forms with particular found elements, like the prosthetic eye in the untitled "egg" piece. In an effort to further investigate the relationship between nature and science this work explores a peculiar biotechnical breed of object/entity that brings into question our own physiology. Where and what is the bridge between the organic and the manufactured?[67]

Engelstein featured a series of related sculptures in the *3-D Rupture* exhibition at the Contemporary Arts Museum in 1993; grouped together on the floor, these pieces achieved an intimate theatricality, analogous to Tony Oursler's video projections on sculpted forms. Susie Kalil observed of this installation that it is impossible to regard Engelstein's work without a degree of self-

The piece *Trace* comes from a series of diptychs from 1993 in which a body fragment is paired alongside a detail of a lived-in domestic, architectural space. I think of the images in this series as revolving around absence and presence, and objectivity and subjectivity. In one image, a fragment of a body is objectified almost to a point of misrecognition. In the other, an object becomes anthropomorphized in the process of locating its meaning—a fragment of an object shows a trace of human presence through the absence of a body. The frailty of the human body, its fleeting and ever-changing state, is (falsely) made static in a singular still photograph and these diptychs point to this inadequacy of the medium while at the same time seeing to "correct" it.[70]

The internal workings of the body, its vulnerability to disease, and its locus as a generative force, have also been of interest to a number of artists. The cultural historian Thomas Laqueur has noted that "The body since the eighteenth century has become a site to be explored, opened up, revealing what is hidden below the surface and therefore profoundly true. The first stages of this exploration go back to the extravagant public dissections of the Renaissance in which the opened body, as opposed to a venerated text, was proclaimed to be the font of truth.... In fact, dead bodies spoke, as if alive, inviting viewers to explore beneath the skin, beneath even the muscle, to the very depths of being."[71] Texas artists Bert Long, Kyle Young, and Jesse Amado have explored this aspect of corporeal aesthetics in their art. Less concerned with how the body is perceived than the artists discussed above, they have concentrated on how it functions.

Bert Long came to art indirectly, following a career as a master chef and ice sculptor. Raised in Houston's historic Fifth Ward, he attended the Los Angeles Trade-Technical College and the University of California, Los Angeles. He began to exhibit his ice sculptures in the late 1970s, and encouraged by James Surls (see plates 24 and 63), Long began to explore folk art and assemblage to create a unique body of work. However, as Sue Graze has noted, "Bert Long is not a naïf or folk artist. His paintings and sculptures incorporate both a high level of skill and a sophisticated knowledge of art history and complex philosophical issues. Ultimately, Long is both a visionary and a realist, a seeming paradox in our time of narrow specialization."[72]

Kidney Stone, 1983–85 (plate 138), is a remarkable self-portrait. Created shortly after the artist recovered from a kidney stone operation, the composition is focused on the massive image of a stone that menacingly fills the foreground. This image is complemented by the actual stones and bones embedded in the surrounding frame, while Long's silhouette is a shadowy presence in the background of the canvas. To be afflicted by kidney stones is one of the most painful experiences that the human frame can withstand, indicated by the bloodlike streaks that drip across the composition. Long presents his subject free of editorial comment—instead, he confronts the viewer with the raw fact of his experience. The

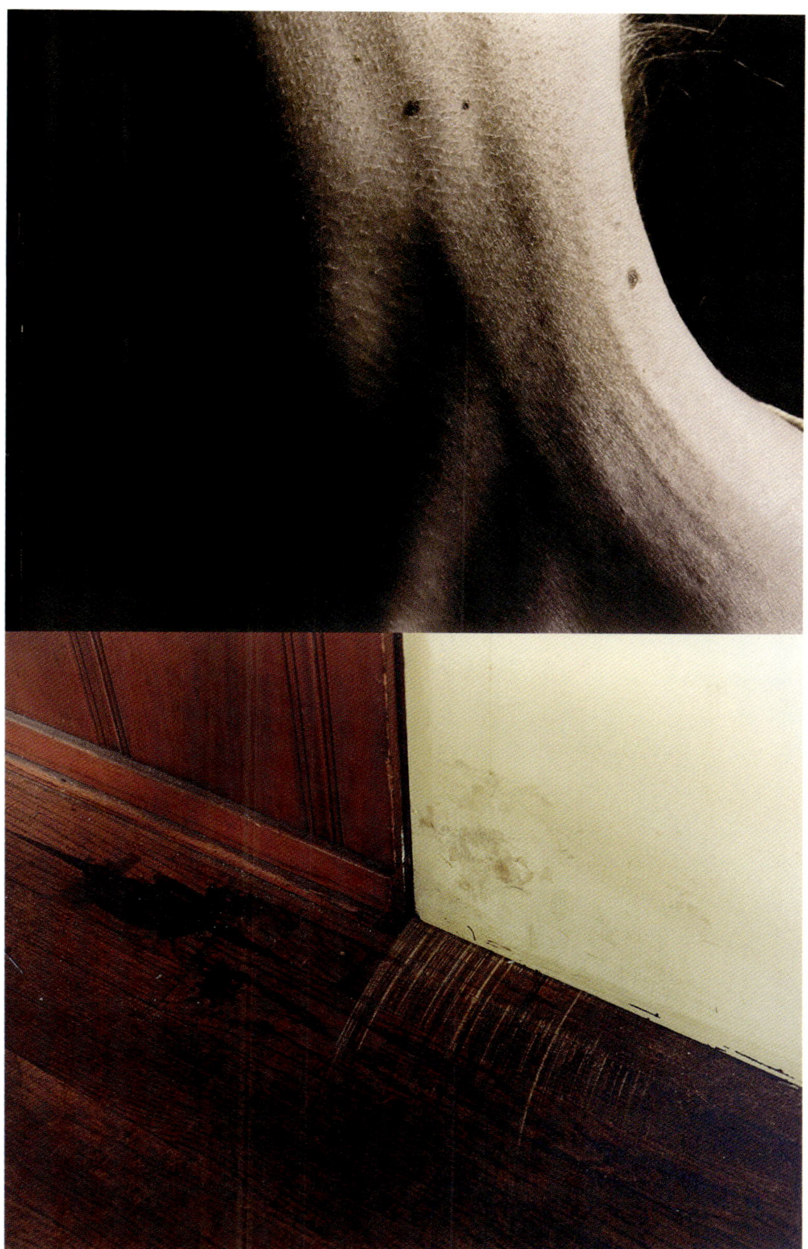

137
Lynn Cazabon
Trace, 1993
Color coupler photograph diptych, 30½ x 18¾ in. (77.47 x 47.6 cm). Gift of Fredericka Hunter and Ian Glennie, 93.129.

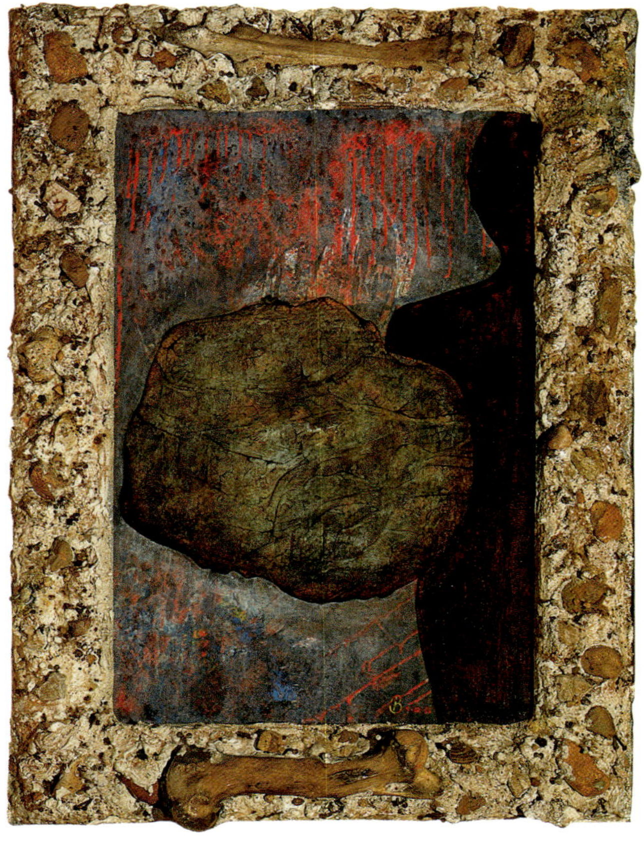

138
Bert Long
Kidney Stone, 1983–85
Acrylic on canvas, bones, nails, stones, fiberglass resin on plaster, and cement, 47 1/2 x 35 x 5 3/4 in. (120.6 x 88.9 x 14.6 cm). Gift of James Surls and Charmaine Locke, 87.360.

139
Kyle Young
Plastos Endon, 1995
Ink, gesso, and graphite on paper, 31 x 53 in. (78.1 x 134 cm). Museum purchase with funds provided by Jerry Williams in memory of Robert Todd Bucks and Charles V. Hooks, 96.616.

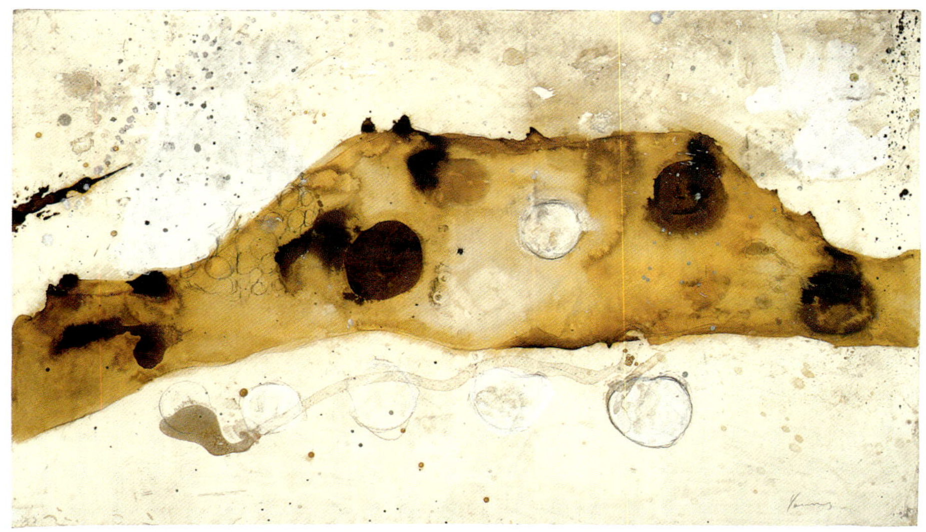

artist stated in 1985: "Communication is the sole reason for the existence of artists. I paint in order to help people understand their ills so that they might cure them. . . . My paintings are no longer rose-colored illusions. They are now reality, thus they are alive."[73]

Kyle Young's moodily evocative paintings and works on paper of the mid-1990s draw upon his experience as a medical technician. Born in Port Arthur, Texas, he attended Lamar University, and Paul Manes (see plate 31) was among his early mentors. He was introduced to Houston audiences with a remarkable solo exhibition titled *Genos Vita* (Source of Life) at Hooks-Epstein Galleries in 1995. The paintings and drawings of this presentation took as their sources the X rays and lab samples Young tracked during the twelve years he worked as a technical assistant at various medical laboratories.

Plastos Endon, 1995 (plate 139), takes medical imagery into the realm of art. The horizontal stretch of the composition is reinforced by the arterial wash of ink that crosses the sheet. Tissue-like cellular clusters appear to be on the verge of formation or dissolution within this flow, offering a metaphor for the process of creation. Young has discussed this work:

> The piece is about two years old from conception to conclusion. Different mediums are used just as different organs and fluids are used in the body. The basic composition was conceived as an artery or vein, perhaps even a river moving across the paper. . . . This particular piece is combining and flowing, outside and inside. The title means "formed within," giving reference to the creative process, reproduction, feelings or whatever. Not only formed within myself but formed within the history of painting.[74]

The rituals of tending to the body have inspired San Antonio artist Jesse Amado. A graduate of the English department at the University of Texas at Austin, Amado became interested in the visual arts in the early 1980s, and later returned to his studies at the University of Texas in San Antonio, where he received an M.F.A. in 1990. As Patricia C. Johnson has recorded, Amado remained aloof from the Chicano art movements that dominated the San Antonio scene of the 1980s; instead, he looked to such Conceptual artists as Joseph Beuys for inspiration, and his first mature works embraced Beuys's use of felt as a sculptural medium.[75]

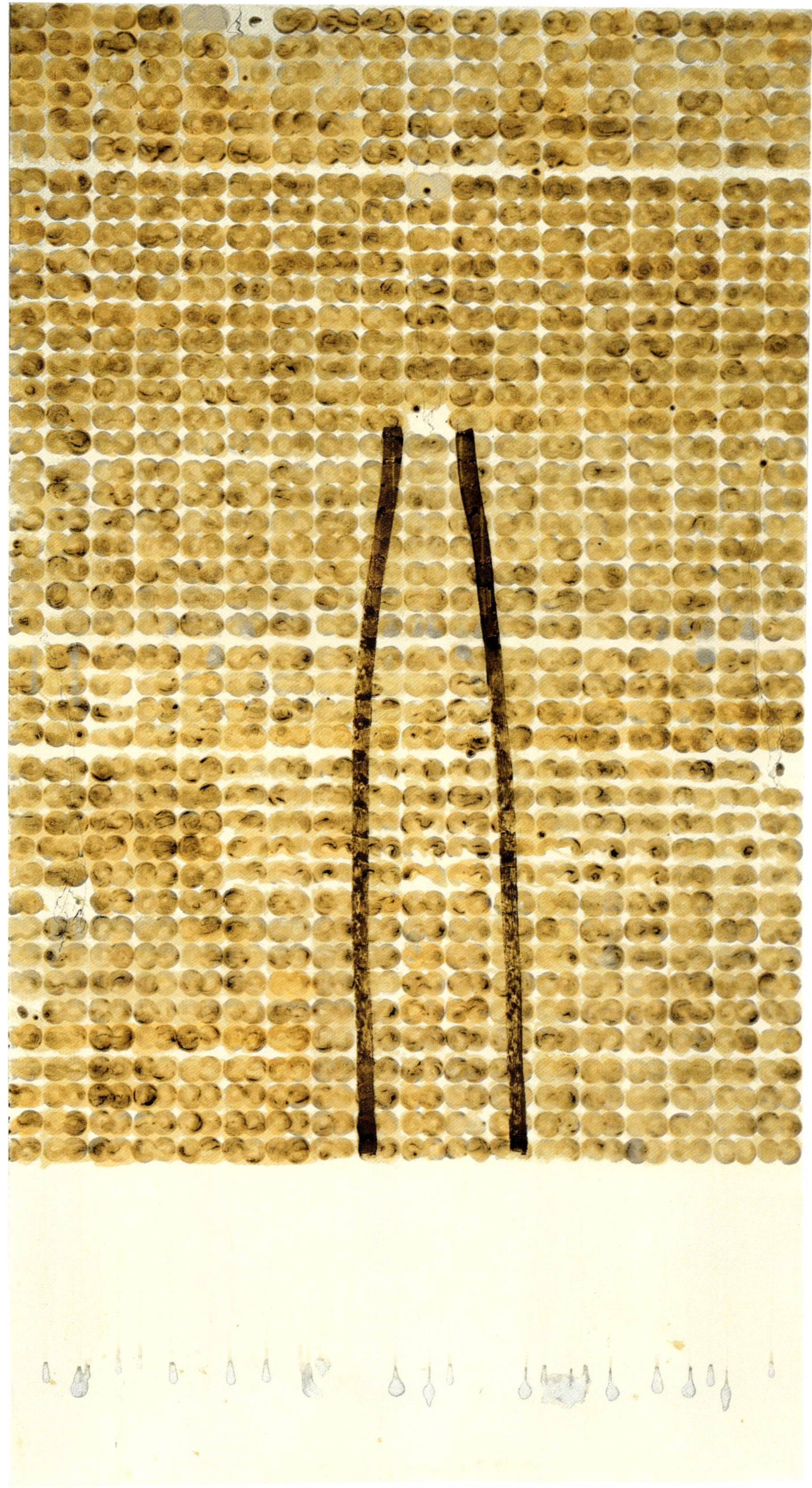

140
Jesse Amado
Stains and Symptoms #2,
1996
Tire black, milk paint,
graphite, and oil bar on paper,
91 x 47½ in. (230.8 x 120.3
cm). Museum purchase with
funds provided by an anonymous donor and Beverly and
John Berry, 97.123.

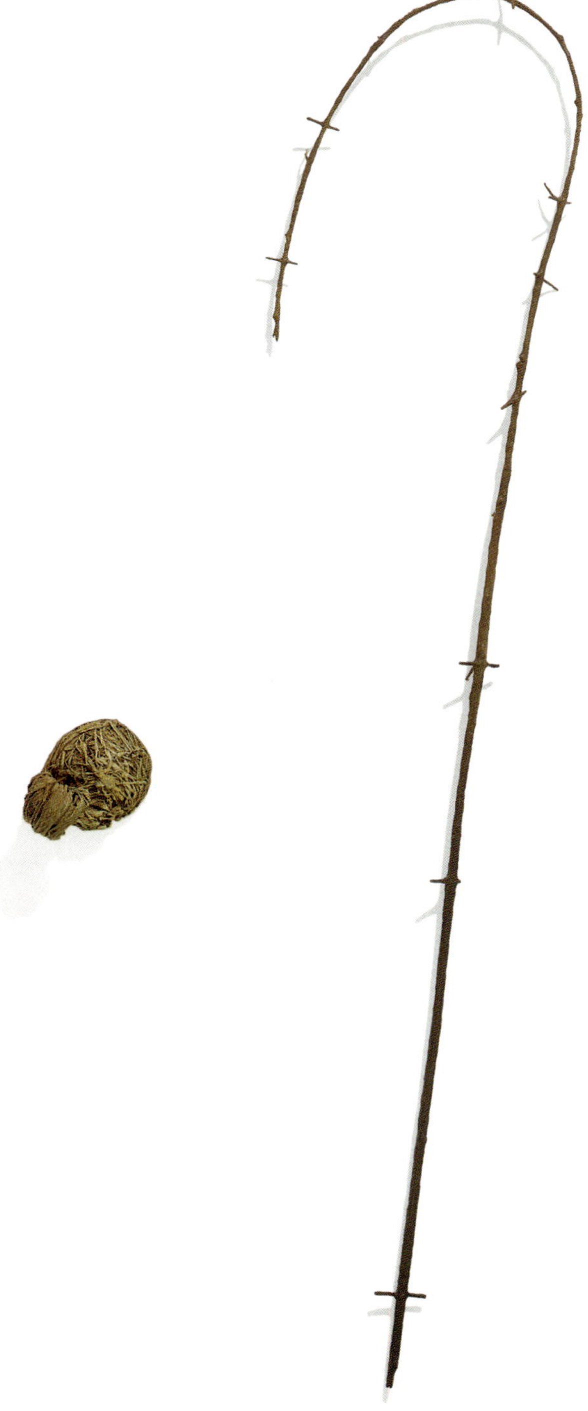

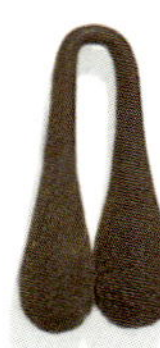

Amado's *White Floating* installation at ArtPace Foundation for Contemporary Art in San Antonio in 1994 signaled a new direction in his art. This ambitious presentation used plumbing fixtures, mirrors, garments, water, and soap to create an environment of ceremonial purification. In an era marked by the AIDS pandemic, the analogue between cleansing and healing had particular resonance, and the artist has stated of the work, "It has to do with a societal syntax and with a personal syntax, and most of all with a visual syntax. The theme is the washing and the cleansing of all those things."[76]

Stains and Symptoms #2, 1996 (plate 140), evolved out of a second installation project, the Contemporary Arts Museum's *Jesse Amado: Renascence* exhibition of 1996. At the invitation of the curator Dana Friis-Hansen, Amado was allowed to deconstruct the downstairs "Perspectives" gallery shortly before the museum closed for major renovations, and the artist literally breached the walls and floor of the space. Central to this installation was an assemblage of severed calla lilies lying on a standard paper cutter; on the walls hung a series of drawings that echoed the forms of the wilting flowers.[77] Although *Stains and Symptoms #2* was not included in the Contemporary Arts Museum's presentation, it is closely related to the *Renascence* series. The large format of *Stains and Symptoms #2*, engulfs the viewer; the sinister title—with its suggestion of bodily decay—is redeemed by the sheer beauty of the composition. Dana Friis-Hansen wrote of the *Renascence* series: "The artist has put forth a life-affirming body of work under the title 'Renascence,' signifying a rebirth, a rising to vigor, which finds signs of renewal in hidden structures, physical frailty, and even echoes of death. It is through a sensitive selection of materials, their deft manipulation, and charge imagery related to the body that he is able to address these themes so powerfully, so poetically."[78]

Linda Ridgway, David McGee, and Rachel Ranta share a common interest in charting existential issues through imagery drawn from the anatomy and nature. Using a broad range of compositional methods, they seek to identify the self in the context of social and cultural interchange.

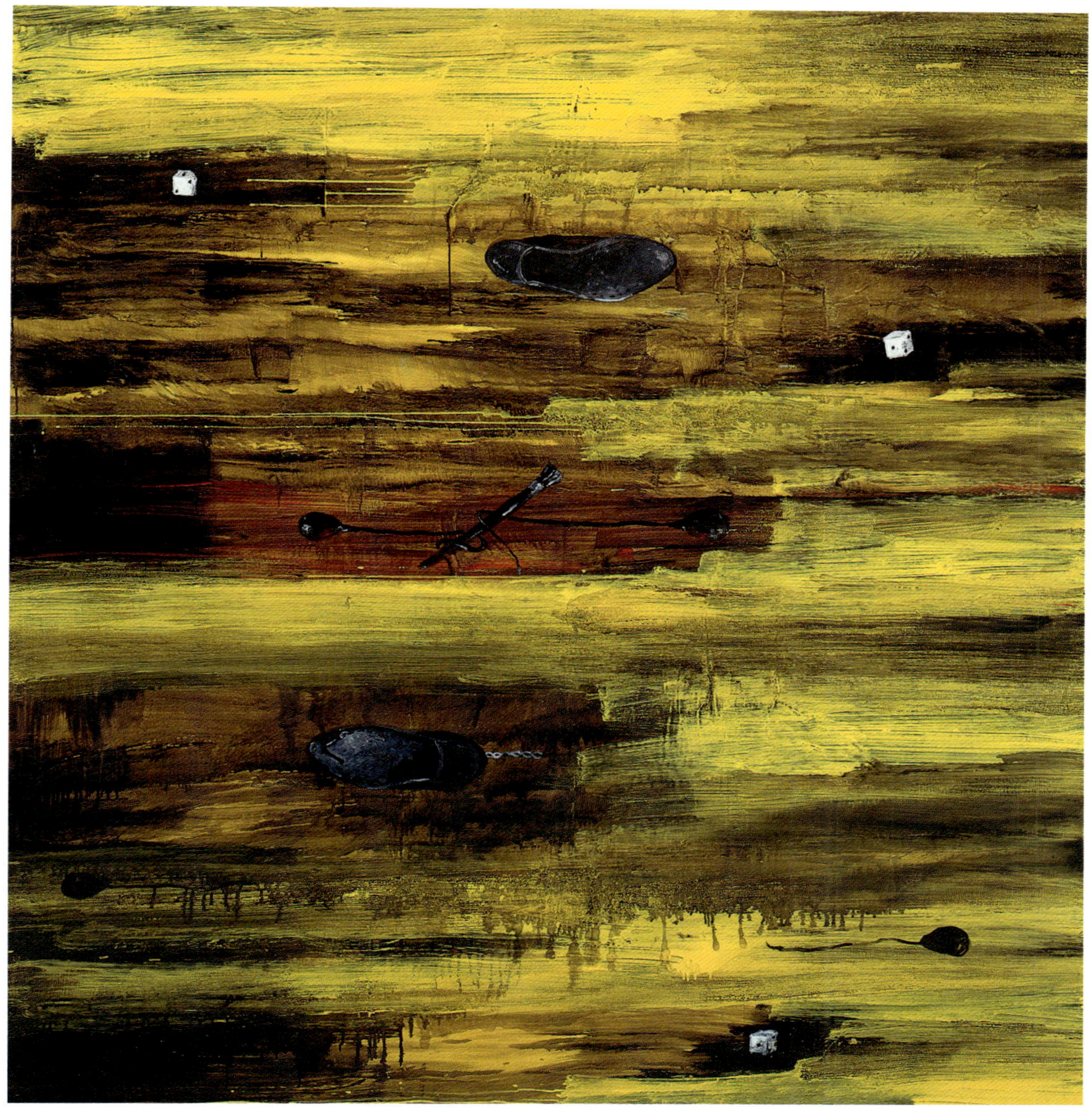

Born in Jeffersonville, Indiana, Ridgway attended the Louisville School of Art, and received an M.F.A. in 1973 from Tulane University in New Orleans. She subsequently made her home in Dallas, and throughout the 1980s her work evolved from Minimalist constructions made out of ephemeral materials to sculptures cast in bronze. However, as Sue Graze has noted, in Ridgway's hands "...bronze is the most delicate and fragile of materials, thus, she has transformed the medium into something uniquely personal and eccentric. Her forms have grown intentionally awkward and clumsy, yet at the same time moody and evocative."[79]

Border Line, 1993 (plate 141), typifies Ridgway's mastery of both form and content. Working with Harry Geffert (see plate 38) at Green Mountain Foundry, Ridgway created three exquisitely cast bronze elements, each one patinated uniquely. The composition can be read as an investigation of sexual polarities; two abstract forms—one feminine, the other masculine—are separated by a barbed-wire border. The possibility of reconciliation is suggested, however, by the graceful arc of the dividing element. Rather than being a didactic paradigm of the war of the sexes, *Border Line* is a meditative statement that encompasses both an abstract sensibility and a slyly feminist wit. Ridgway has commented on her work:

Recently, I read a statement by Christopher Wilmarth about art which was, "If it is not magic, it is merchandise." Both he and I have enjoyed the making of an object. But to give the object a humanness, a sense of being, a feeling of existence, that's the magic. To transplant that internal knowing through an external object can take a lifetime. I consider my work a dialogue of forms that interact with one another as people who meet are naturally curious to learn more about each other. My measure of success is the fine line between the beautiful and the ugly that I like to walk.[80]

142
David McGee
Sperm Rush, from the *Wastelands* series, 1994
Oil and enamel on newsprint on canvas, 69 ¾ x 66 ¼ in. (177.1 x 168.3 cm). Museum purchase with funds provided by Mr. and Mrs. I. H. Kempner III and Jeanne and Michael Klein, 94.107.

141 *opposite*
Linda Ridgway
Border Line, 1993
Bronze, 66 x 39 x 5 in. (167.6 x 99 x 12.7 cm) overall. Museum purchase with funds provided by Bryant M. and Nancy C. Hanley and Nona and Richard Barrett, 94.137.

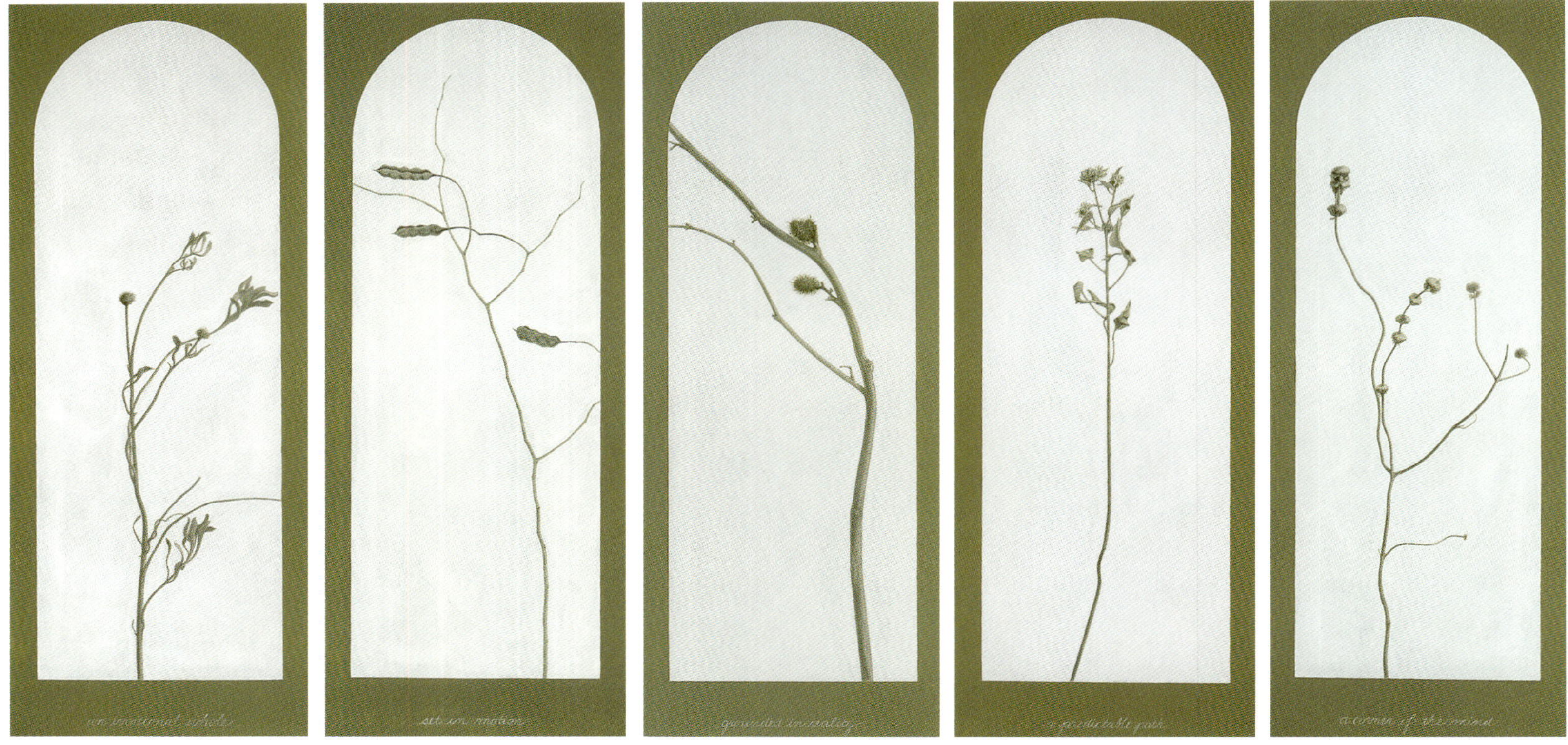
an irrational whole
set in motion
grounded in reality
a predictable path
a corner of the mind

Drawing on memory and desire, David McGee maps the emotional and physical territories that surround him. A native of Louisiana, McGee grew up in Detroit, Michigan. He attended Prairie View A&M University, and shortly after his graduation in 1986 he made Houston his home. In 1992, his work was featured in the *Fresh Visions/New Voices: Emerging African-American Artists in Texas* exhibition at the Glassell School of Art, where McGee introduced the themes of anatomical interiority and terror that were to characterize his work of the following two years. In the catalogue, McGee cited Dante's lines from *The Divine Comedy*: "And I, who looked, saw an ensign, which whirling ran quickly that it seemed to scorn all pause; / and every man fixed his eyes to his feet. / And behind it came so long a train of people, that I should have never believed that death had undone so many."[81]

McGee's subsequent series of *Inferno* and *Wasteland* paintings probed more specifically the inevitable alienation of love in the time of AIDS.[82] *Sperm Rush*, from the *Wastelands* series, 1994 (plate 142), confronts the viewer with the tar black and acrid yellow field common to the series as a whole, aptly capturing the twilit realms of Dante's and T. S. Eliot's epic poems.[83] Floating in the foreground are symbols of the artist's life and trade—shoes, sperm, and a paintbrush—while three floating die suggest the chance reversals and gains of fortune. These images are rendered with remarkable painterly naturalism; not only are they emblematic of the artist's ambitions and fears, but by their vivid immediacy they invite a strong emotional response from the viewer. McGee has commented:

> I am primarily a painter and, as such, I have always tried to convey a private moment in the Landscape of the Soul—its passions, torments, and fears. I have tried to do this not by painterly decisions or with the process of mind, but through the process of feeling. I seek to somehow transcend any physical boundaries that stifle true feelings.[84]

While profoundly different in mood and technique, Rachel Ranta's paintings similarly shimmer with a literary and somewhat surreal intelligence. A graduate of Maryville College, St. Louis, and the University of Houston, Ranta has used fragments of text and elegantly rendered images to question the nature of objects and how we describe the intangible through language. Lynn M. Herbert has written, "The objects in Ranta's paintings are seemingly insignificant, small things the artist has around the house, things she lives with.... Toy figurines, weeds, a pair of dice, clouds.... The words Ranta employs are also part of our every day world. Her sources include newspapers, novels, even frozen food wrappers."[85]

In 1994, Ranta created a five-panel painting titled *Weed Series* (plate 143). In each panel a local Texas weed is framed by a simple niche inscribed with oblique phrases that suggest states of being: *an irrational whole, set in motion, grounded in reality, a predictable path,* and *a corner of the mind.* The contrast between the vividly individualized weeds—with the play of light across the surface of the plants magnificently captured—and the minimal frame throws the images into high relief; viewed as an ensemble, the weeds trace a delicate dance across the composition. The inscriptions are rendered with the meticulous calligraphy of the Palmer method taught to schoolchildren across America, emphasizing the fact that each phrase sounds like a careful lesson well learned.

The device of pairing image and text has appeared in the work of such Surrealists as René Magritte and his Conceptualist heir Marcel Broodthaers, and as Patricia C. Johnson has suggested, Magritte's famous maxim "This is not a pipe" inscribed under an image of a pipe offers an instructive parallel to Ranta's approach.[86] However, Ranta is less interested in the visual and verbal conundrums of Surrealism; rather, text and image enter into a subtle relationship that is openly associative. As Jim Edwards has observed, "Rachel Ranta's small oil paintings of simple objects...glow as if the subconscious mind is offering an X-ray of the conscious mind's flip side."[87]

A key aspect of Postmodernism, as defined by Fredric Jameson, was "the erosion of the older distinction between high culture and so-called mass or popular culture."[88] He noted further:

> This is perhaps the most distressing development of all from an academic standpoint, which has traditionally had a vested interest in preserving a realm of high or elite culture against the surrounding environment of philistinism, of schlock and kitsch, of TV series and

143
Rachel Ranta
Weed Series, 1994
Oil on wood, five panels,
24 x 9½ in. (60.9 x 24.1 cm)
each. Museum purchase
with funds provided by Mr.
and Mrs. Jack Blanton, Jr.,
Laura and Jim Martin, Mr.
and Mrs. James M. Vaughn,
Jr., The Wilder Foundation,
and friends of the artist,
94.246.1–5.

Reader's Digest culture.... But many of the newer post-modernisms have been fascinated precisely by that whole landscape of advertising and motels, of the Las Vegas strip, of the late show and Grade-B Hollywood film, of so-called paraliterature with its airport paperback categories of the gothic and the romance, the popular biography, the murder mystery and the science fiction or fantasy novel.[89]

A fascination with kitsch has characterized various movements across the twentieth century, from Dada to Pop Art; however, as the artists discussed in this concluding section demonstrate, their work takes for granted the manipulated and even fictive aspects of our contemporary information culture. Randy Twaddle, Mark Flood, Osamu James Nakagawa, and The Art Guys travel the "landscape of advertising and motels," while Nic Nicosia, Bill Thomas, and Helen Altman seem to be hooked on late-night television and infomercials. These artists cross the line between reality and simulation, in many cases not only in the subject matter of their works, but also in their strategies of presentation.

Randy Twaddle moved to Dallas in 1980, shortly after completing a degree in fine arts at Northwest Missouri State University. In the mid-1980s he embarked on a series of large-scale charcoal drawings that effectively employed silhouette, using charcoal to create a softly modulated ground within the varying fields of black—the medium also left traces of the artist's hand on the unworked areas of white. Charles Dee Mitchell wrote admiringly of these works: "One of the best things about Randy Twaddle's art is that you don't have to spend a lot of time looking at it.... If by no other means than their size, the drawings command attention, but their simplicity defies extended or enthralled gazing. The viewer is quickly pushed into a speculation on the artist's intentions."[90]

Survey, 1987 (plate 144), details the high and low technologies of contemporary urban culture. Twaddle juxtaposed silhouettes of a billboard, a radar antenna, and a satellite—all tools of mass communication—in order to highlight our appetite for simulated experience. At the same time, Twaddle withholds any information about what these instruments communicate; rather, he emphasizes the somewhat menacing presence they exert over our lives. The artist stated in 1988:

> With the increasing rate of speed our culture is changing, I find it necessary for my own understanding of the changes to find (or at least manufacture) some sort of structure or order in these changes. I believe that patterns exist and are representative of a natural evolution. I hope that by recognizing these patterns I will more clearly comprehend the significance of these changes and will be better able to participate in the transition.[91]

Mark Flood employs a subversive approach to the instruments of commerce.[92] A native Houstonian, Flood attended the Museum School and Rice University, and he had his first public exposure in such alternative

144
Randy Twaddle
Survey, 1987
Charcoal on wove paper, triptych, 53 x 53 in. each (134.6 x 134.6 cm). Museum purchase with funds provided by Duke Energy, 87.197.

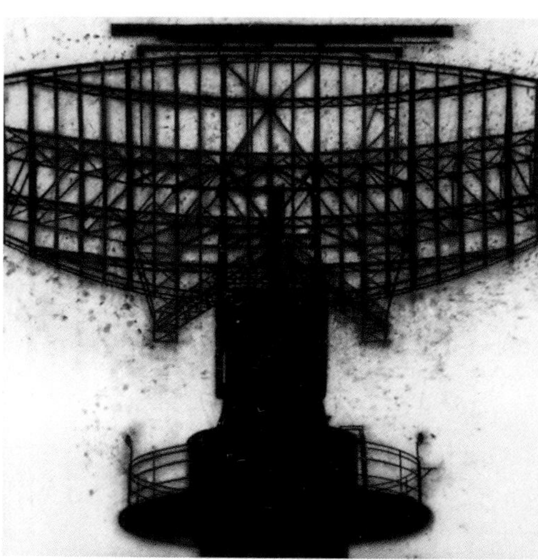
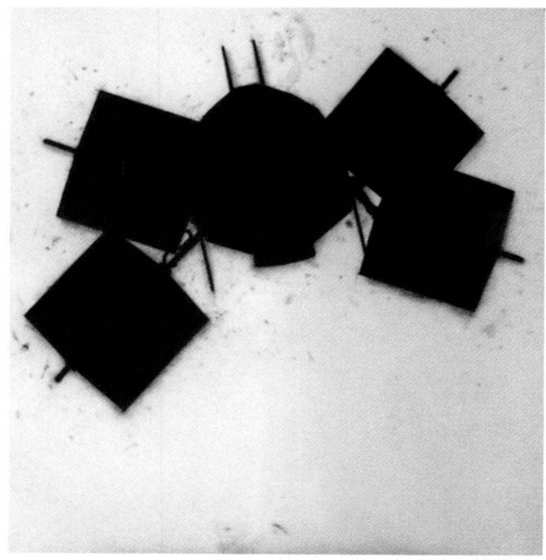

spaces as William Steen's Studio One in the early 1980s. Largely driven by conceptual rather than formal interests, Flood pursued a variety of media, from collage and appropriated imagery to an extended series of bluntly rendered diaristic drawings and paintings. In 1992 Flood reflected, "As an artist, I make work that asks as many questions as it answers. I am constantly striving to understand the nature of things, to make work that explores that in life for which no maps exist."[93]

In early 1989 Flood exhibited a series of silkscreens that examined the cult of celebrity, deliberately following in the footsteps of Andy Warhol. At the same time he began to promote a more commercially viable image of himself by inviting a younger and handsomer man to stand in for him in publicity photographs and public appearances. Later that year, Flood launched a project to sell advertising space within his artworks, and *Museum Piece*, 1989/91 (plate 145), documents the initial stage of this un-

dertaking.[94] Flood silkscreened onto canvas the phrase found on billboards across the country "Your Ad Here," followed by his actual telephone number of the time. The white expanse of the canvas effectively mimics the format of an unused billboard, while the slightly off-kilter text is applied with the seeming informality of Warhol's *Death and Disaster* silkscreens of the early 1960s.[95]

Flood took this project to the next level in a subsequent series of paintings that actually incorporated logos of various sponsors who took him up on the offer to place an ad in his work. In so doing, Flood made clear the self-interest of most art patronage, whether corporate, private, or government funded. These paintings were exhibited at Houston's Treebeard's restaurant in November 1989, along with similarly silkscreened works by other Houston artists, many of whom chose to remain anonymous. The exhibition was titled *Primal Screen* and proclaimed the establishment of a Fake Art Movement in

145
Mark Flood
Museum Piece, 1989/91
Silkscreen on canvas, 60 x 96 3/8 in. (152.4 x 244.8 cm). Museum purchase with funds provided by David Morris, Lynn Goode, the Vaughn Foundation Fund, and friends of the artist, 91.315.

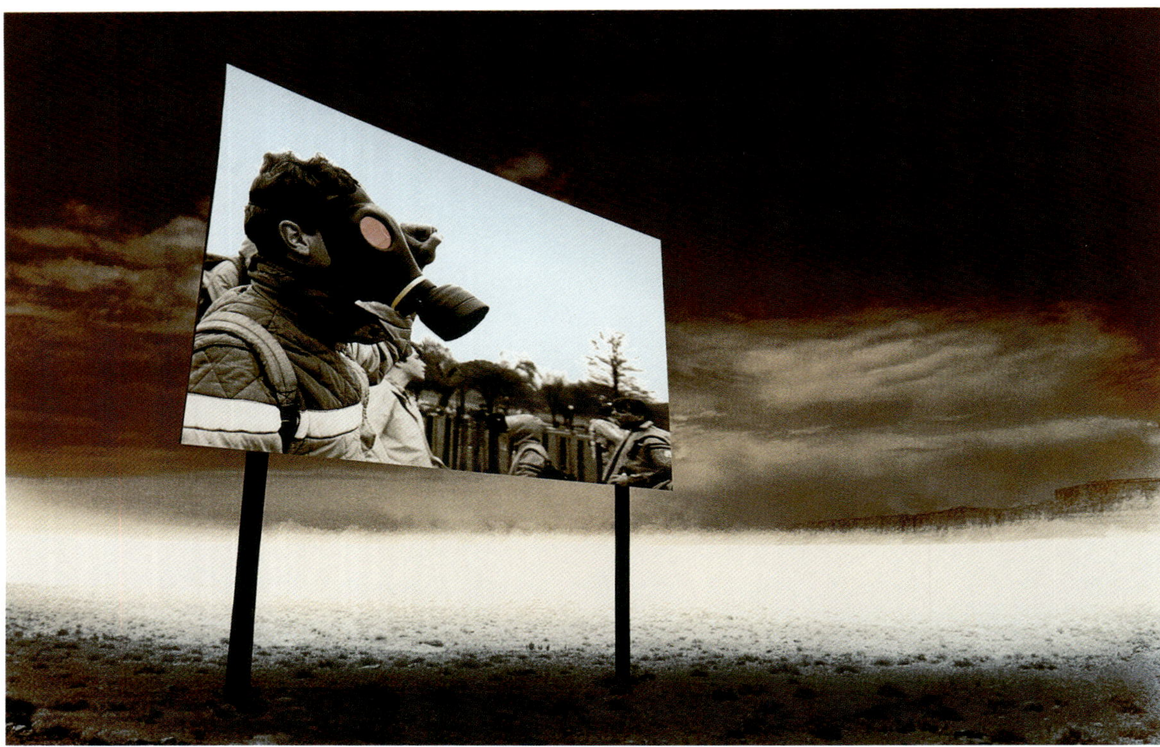

146
Osamu James Nakagawa
Gasmask, from the *Billboard*
series, 1993
Color coupler photograph,
26½ x 39½ in. (67 x 100.6
cm). Gift of Eleanor D.
McMurtrey in honor of
Clinton T. Willour, 94.124.

Houston. Flood issued a manifesto in the form of a mission statement that lampooned Barbara Rose's and Susie Kalil's preface from the 1985 *Fresh Paint* catalogue, opening with the phrase: "In contriving the first movement by Houston artists, our intent was to present a pessimistic and distorted selection that would fully conceal Houston from other major art centers."[96]

In an interview conducted shortly after the opening, Flood commented: "I think the media that surrounds art exhibits in Houston is as much a form as the art itself."[97] The press kit for *Primal Screen* included photocopies of articles purporting to be from the *Houston Post, Artforum, Art in America, Artscribe,* and even an Italian edition of *Flash Art,* written by Flood in a style that wittily simulated the tone of each publication. However, the mainstream press did take notice, and the *Wall Street Journal* reported: "Mark Flood's work gives new meaning to the phrase 'commercial art.'"[98] In the wake of these activities, *Museum Piece* stands on its own, chipping away at the boundaries between what is staged and what is real, exposing the fictions that are central to art and commerce.

The billboard is also a primary motif in the work of Osamu James Nakagawa. Born in New York, Nakagawa was raised in the United States and Japan, a divided cultural heritage that led him to explore visual dichotomies in his art. He attended the University of St. Thomas; later, as a student in the graduate program at the University of Houston he worked with the collaborative artists MANUAL (see plate 124), and followed their example in

utilizing the computer's capacity for creating nearly seamless photomontages through digital imaging. The cultural historian Geoffrey Batchen has written on this process:

> Photographers intervene in every photograph they make, whether by orchestrating or directly interfering in the scene being imaged; by selecting, cropping, excluding, and in other ways making pictorial choices as they take the photograph; by enhancing, suppressing, and cropping the finished print in the darkroom; and finally, by adding captions and other contextual elements to their image to anchor some potential meanings. . . . The thing about computers is that they let an operator do all these same things, but much more easily and in a less detectable way. The difference seems to be that, whereas photography claims a spurious objectivity, digital imaging remains an overtly fictional process. As a practice that is known to be nothing but fabrication, digitization abandons even the rhetoric of truth that has been such an important part of photography's cultural success.[99]

In his 1992 *Drive-In Theater* series Nakagawa found a naturalistic framework for his computer-generated fictions. *Gasmask,* from the subsequent *Billboard* series, 1993 (plate 146), offers a similarly convincing image: like a movie screen, a billboard is a *tabula rasa* for applied images. At a glance, *Gasmask* appears to be straight photography; only on closer examination do the toxic colors of the landscape and the incongruously heightened image of protesters at an environmental rally reveal the artificiality of the photograph and the polemical intent of the artist. Nakagawa remarked of these series:

Using the computer, I paste images I have photographed onto the drive-in screen, a major American icon and symbol of the "good life," or onto the billboard, upholder of the American lifestyle. From my view, as outsider (screen image) and insider (surrounding landscape), these images are representative of American society.[100]

In a related statement, the artist further observed: "The *Drive-in Theater/Billboard* series uses the idea of a frame within a frame…. The nostalgic mythology of the drive-in theater is juxtaposed with explicitly public and political messages. Similarly, the commercial nature of the billboard is subverted. The series as a whole proposes a critical inspection of Western society from my particular viewpoint, which is Eastern in origin and Western by immersion."[101]

Michael Galbreth and Jack Massing are The Art Guys, Houston artists who have worked collaboratively for close to two decades. They met in 1982 at an opening at the University of Houston's Lawndale Annex; at that time Galbreth was enrolled in the university's graduate program, and with the encouragement of James Surls (see plates 24 and 63), Massing subsequently enrolled in the university's undergraduate program. Galbreth and Massing enacted their first public performance in 1983; following the example of the performance artists of the 1960s Fluxus movement, including most notably George Maciunas, they made simple, everyday actions the subject of their many productions, from mowing the lawn at the Contemporary Arts Museum to spending twenty-four hours at a Denny's restaurant banquette, an event which Massing categorized as "This isn't performance, this is behavior."[102] Like Mark Flood (see plate 145), they have made the dynamics of commerce central to their work, from their 1984 flaunting of Texas's blue laws by pointedly selling goods in front of Houston's City Hall on a Sunday to their most recent marketing of advertising space on the suits they sport to public events.[103]

Aspects of performance have also characterized The Art Guys' prodigiously large production of objects. Typically, their work can be linked in some fashion to action, whether through the act of accumulation, appropriation, or destruction (for example, they have mounted ninety-nine bottles of beer on a wall; stolen and enshrined mementos from friends' and colleagues' homes; and hammered, burned,

and drowned a book). There is a perverse twist of humor to these activities, and Dave Hickey has commented: "As Michel Foucault has astutely pointed out, the great task of twentieth-century culture has been to make us feel good about feeling bad. The Art Guys turn the tables on this Puritan masochism and in so doing, make us uneasy about feeling good. They taunt our pretensions with innocent fun and indict us with amusement."[104]

Chastity, 1993 (plate 147), is one of an extended series of suitcase sculptures. An icon of travel, the function of a suitcase as a container offers a flexible metaphor for the function of art, both being capable of conveying more than is apparent to the eye. Inside an old-fashioned beat-up suitcase—more suggestive of a Greyhound bus journey than an exotic trek—The Art Guys have installed an audio chip, which at regular intervals emits the sounds of a trapped cat scratching and mewing in distress. Placed in an art setting, *Chastity* becomes particularly disruptive:

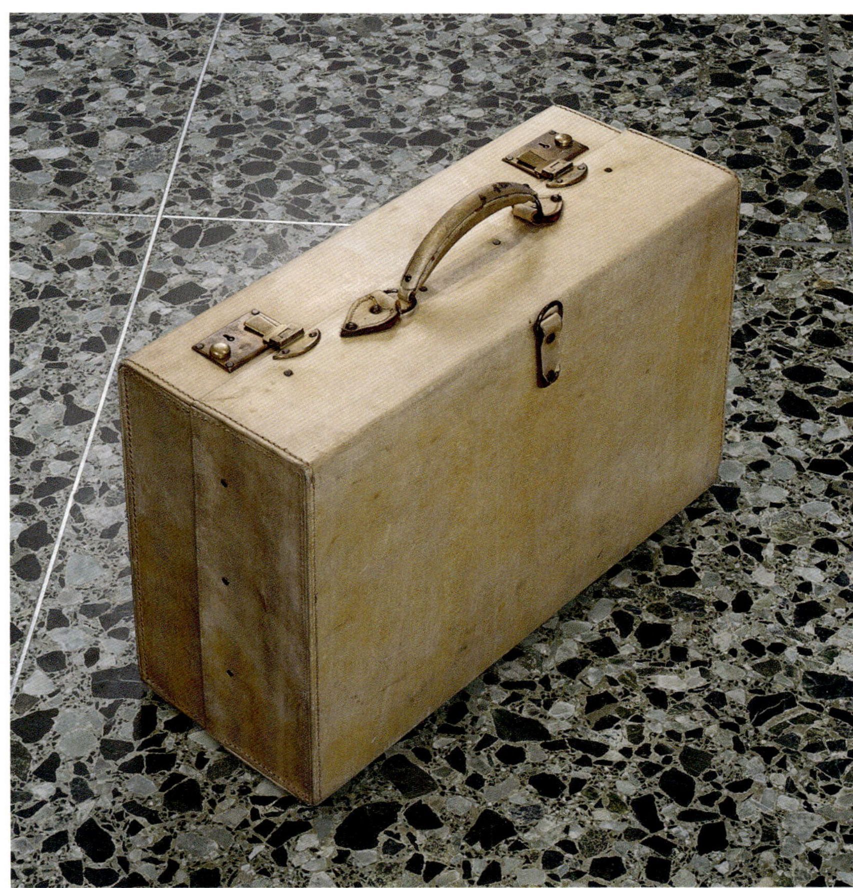

147
The Art Guys (Michael Galbreth and Jack Massing)
Chastity, 1993
Suitcase with electro-mechanical parts, 12 x 18 x 8 in. (30.5 x 45.7 x 20.3 cm). Gift of Michael A. Caddell and Cynthia Chapman, 98.227.

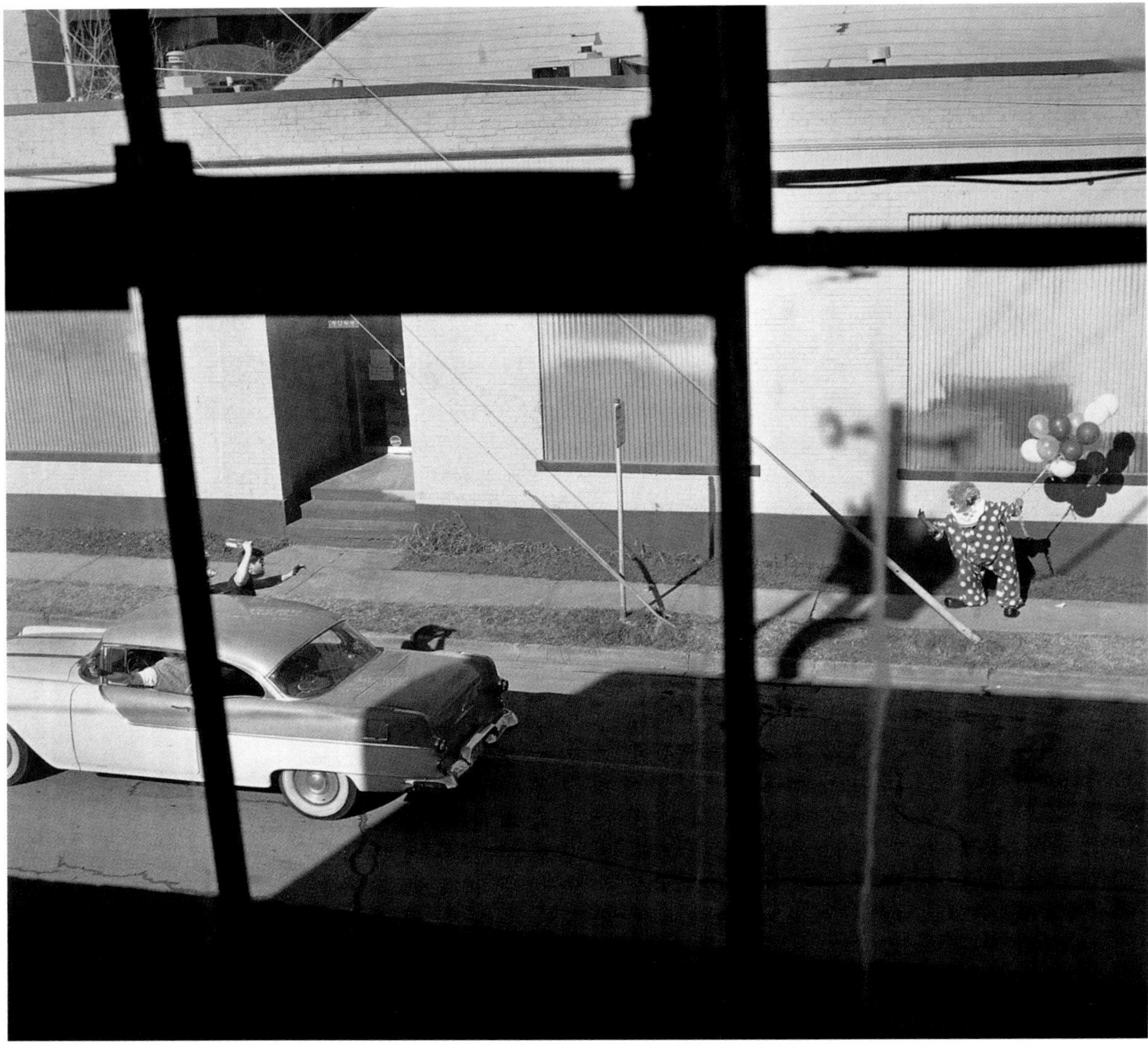

148
Nic Nicosia
Real Pictures #8, 1985
Gelatin silver photograph,
48¼ x 51¾ in. (122.5 x
131.4 cm). Museum pur-
chase with funds provided by
the National Endowment for
the Arts, Photo Forum, Anthony and Andrew Cochran,
and Joan Alexander in honor
of Margaret Skidmore's
birthday, 88.379.

since the initial impulse upon hearing these sounds is to literally "let the cat out of the bag," the viewer is placed in a
quandary, whether to obey the instinct to aid a frightened
animal or to behave with the propriety of a museum visitor
and maintain a proper distance.[105]

The tension between the documentary and the fabricated has always animated the work of Dallas photographer, filmmaker, and video artist Nic Nicosia. Nicosia
attended the University of North Texas in Denton, taking
a degree in filmmaking in 1974. In 1980, however, he
made photography his chief medium and returned to
school, where Al Souza (see plate 128) was among his
mentors. Nicosia commented on the importance of
Souza's example:

> My friend and teacher was Al Souza, well-known for his
> conceptual and humorous use of photographs that ex-
> pose the false information perceived through them. I
> was presented with a new view, *fabricated to be pho-
> tographed.* Ah ha! There is more than the snapshot and
> the 'decisive moment.' This was great by me; now I

could combine my film-making background, my new-
found interest in art, and still photography to create anything I want, any way I want.[106]

Nicosia's first important series, the *Domestic Dramas*
and the *Near (modern) Disaster* photographs of the early
1980s, were patently staged, combining Pop-Art aesthetics with the melodramatic theatricality of daytime soaps.
The subsequent series was also staged; however, as *Real
Pictures #8*, 1985 (plate 148), demonstrates, the artificiality of the scene is less readily apparent. The camera
seems to have captured from a second-story window the
chance altercation between a clown and a man in a car;
the dirty window, the interruptions created by the frame,
and the shadows falling across the street look like the
"mistakes" of a poorly planned shot. Only the improbable theatricality of the event suggests that the scene may
be staged—much like the crime reenactment videos that
have become a popular feature of network television—a
quality heightened by the large format of the print

(which is four feet high). Liz Ward has observed: "In the *Real Pictures* series, Nicosia actively challenges the notion of photographic truth. His use of black-and-white documentary modes underlies his strategy of forcing us to question the supposed veracity of all photographs and to examine our predisposition and our desire to accept the photograph as an objective document of the real."[107]

Bill Thomas places himself at the center of his staged fictions. A native of Houston, he attended the University of Texas at Austin, receiving a degree in psychology in 1973. After pursuing a career in social work, he became increasingly interested in photography, and he entered the graduate program at the University of Houston in 1990. Unlike Osamu James Nakagawa (see plate 146), who was among his contemporaries at the University of Houston, Thomas eschewed the manipulative techniques of digital imaging. Instead, in his first major series of works he adopted a bluntly straightforward approach, using black-and-white photography to document carefully arranged scenes of suicide. Peter Doroshenko has observed of these works: "While humor gives the viewer the option to turn away from the serious side of these tableaux and treat them as wacky street theater, the suicide set-ups are unnervingly believable.... Through his images, which he sees as life affirming, Thomas comes to his own personal understanding of death."[108]

Dog and Shotgun, 1991 (plate 149), is one of the more complicated images of the series, all of which feature Thomas as protagonist. The setting is a well-appointed living room (itself an ironic stage for such an activity), and the artist's function as documentary photographer is made clear by the shutter bulb he holds in his right hand, emphasizing his role as author of both image and arrangement. The suggested element of time (a melting block of ice or a slowly filling pool being the causal instruments in other works) is typical of Thomas's perilous scenarios. In *Dog and Shotgun*, however, the narrative frame is altered subtly: the viewer is left to wonder *if* rather than *when* the dog will snap at the bone tied to the string that will release the trigger of the gun aimed at Thomas's head.

The black humor of *Dog and Shotgun* lies in the contrast between the perfect orchestration of the Rube Goldbergian suicide mechanism, which depends upon the faithful dog, the carefully crafted support, and the well-oiled gun, and the terrifying chaos that would inevitably follow should this mechanism be released. Nevertheless, Thomas's Goldbergian stratagem has a redemptive element of humanism; Peter C. Marzio has noted of Goldberg's elaborate inventions: "While many Goldberg cartoons focused on the disruptive influence of machines, his larger message was brimming with optimism.... Their very rigidity assures us that human values can survive in a society of steam power, electrical wires, and atomic reactors, so long as man is willing to remain flexible and to laugh at his own creations."[109]

Where other artists engaged in critiquing Postmodern culture emphasize their self-conscious sense of estrangement, Helen Altman is fascinated by the rapture of the satisfied consumer. A native of Alabama, Altman came to Texas in 1986 to attend the graduate program at the University of North Texas in Denton. Vernon Fisher (see plates 26 and 125) was among her mentors, and Altman's first works embodied the narrative strategies promoted by Fisher.[110] Using actual appliances, such as refrigerators, gas ranges, and irons, Altman constructed scenarios of

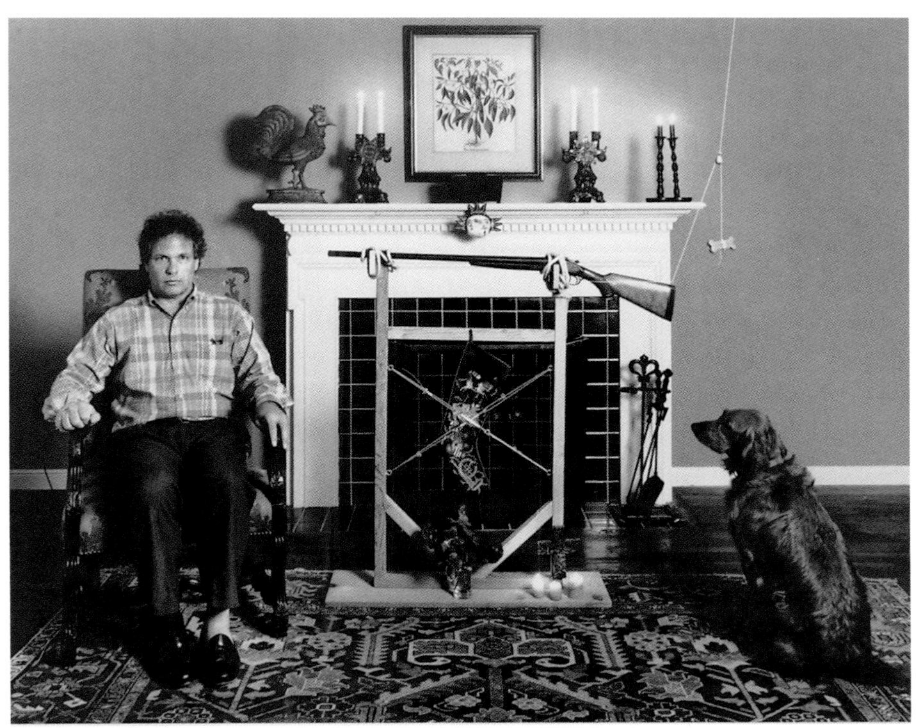

149
Bill Thomas
Dog and Shotgun, 1991
Gelatin silver photograph,
15½ x 19½ in. (39.4 x 49.3
cm). Museum purchase
with funds provided by
Mr. and Mrs. Joe S. Mundy,
94.21.

domesticity gone awry: food turned bad, water boiling away, shirts erupting into flames. Simulating common household furniture, these assemblages convince the viewer with their familiarity, and the artist has commented, "I start out with benign-looking objects like those I grew up with, things we've all held in our hands."[111]

These works in turn led to a series of sculptures made from electric fire logs, of which *Signal*, 1992 (plate 150), is the earliest.[112] Altman has stacked thirty-six sets of fire logs into a nine-foot wall of fire, an image at once daunting and deeply seductive. Altman has recalled:

> I first saw these types of logs as a child. The neighbors hauled them out at Christmas time. They had the same effect on me as the plastic display food in the refrigerators at Sears. I was fascinated.... The fire logs appealed to me for many reasons. I saw a sweet pathos in them, they were able to be both convincing and absurd.[113]

Signal prompts the viewer to question the levels of simulation exploited by Altman: fire logs are in themselves an artificial household fixture, and are mass produced to replicate the comforting but not always convenient amenity of a fire in the hearth. Constructed from actual wood kindling, electric bulbs, motors, and tinsel, they shed a dappled light and crackle like a real fire, but cast no heat. The artist's intervention has been minimal—and the artwork is a testament to accumulation, suggesting an out-of-hand Kmart shopping spree. Multiplied and wrested into the theatrical space of an art gallery, displayed with the electric wires and plugs clearly showing, the fire logs acquire a curious authenticity, and standing in front of *Signal* is a mesmerizing and ultimately ecstatic experience. Frances Colpitt has commented: "Beneath the playfulness of Altman's work is a thoughtful inquiry into domestic and social myths. The fire logs specifically reference the hearth and home—the center of the house—which provides warmth and cohesion for the family gathered round it. The bonfires for college homecomings also figure in our memories of youth, while the campfire and the storytelling it engenders typify our images of both Old West Cowboys and contemporary campers."[114]

It seems appropriate to conclude this survey with *Signal*, a work which taps into the mythic roots of Texas culture explored in the first chapter of this catalogue. Like Hermann Lungkwitz (see plate 2), Altman invites the viewer to experience the sublime aspect of our environment. The fact that the artist's frame of reference has shifted from the Texas Hill Country of the nineteenth century (an image colored in Lungkwitz's case by the conventions of German Romantic painting) to a highly artificial but actual substitute aptly reflects the changing perspective of our times.

Ultimately, Texas itself is a fictive construct, and any attempt to define an art that is uniquely Texan is an illusory pursuit. Nevertheless, as the paintings, sculptures, photographs, and works on paper gathered together in this book demonstrate, across Texas history, artists have helped shape our understanding of this state we're in.

150
Helen Altman
Signal, 1992
Mixed-media assemblage, 108 x 156 x 12 in. (274.3 x 396.5 x 30.5 cm). Gift of The Barrett Collection, Dallas, Texas, 98.720.

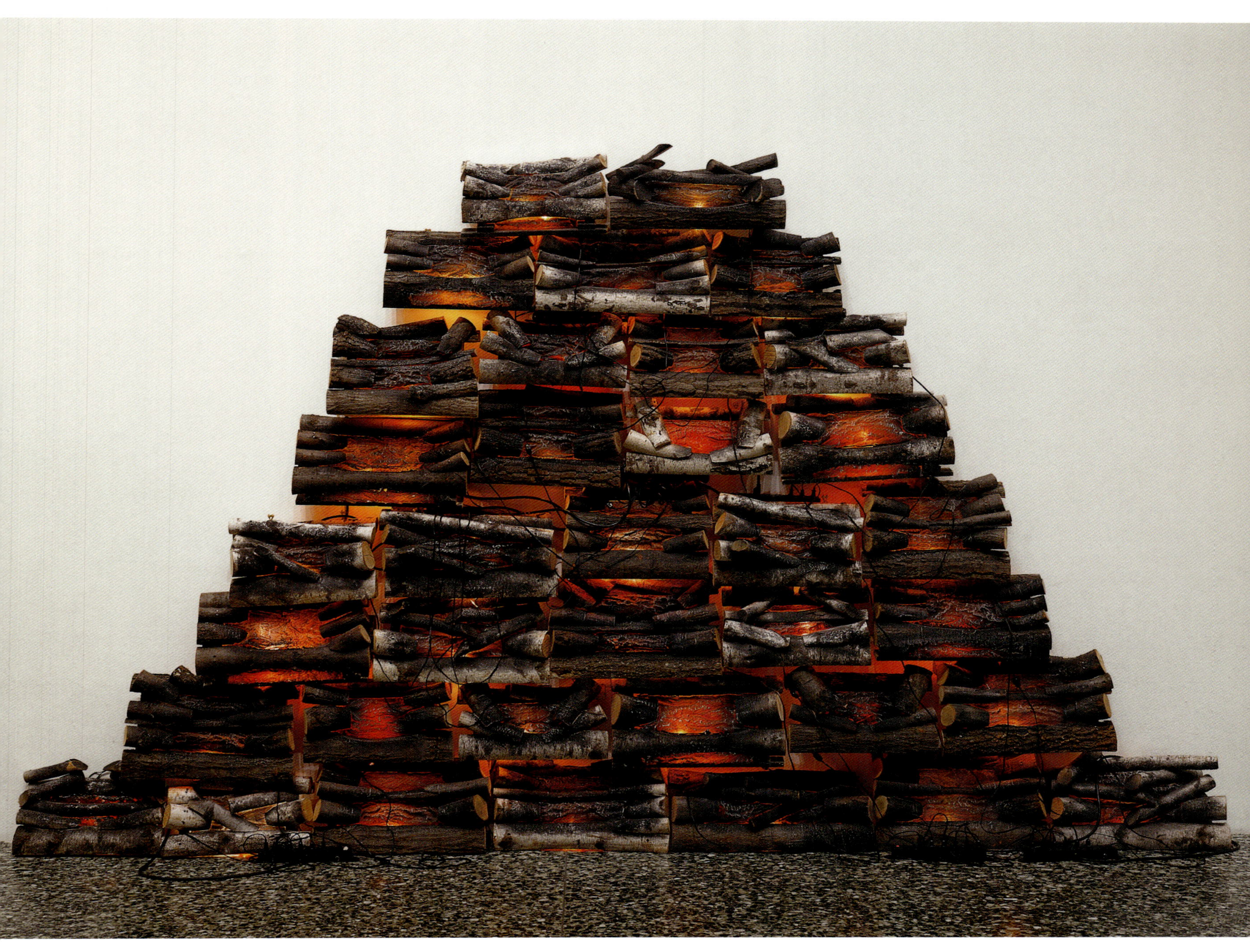

Notes

Introduction
pages 15–20

1. James Chillman, Jr., introduction to *14th Annual Exhibition of Works by Houston Artists* (Houston: The Museum of Fine Arts, Houston, 1938), 1. Chillman began employing this motto as early as the 1920s, attributing it at that time to an unnamed source. See Houston Art League Scrapbook, 130 (RG19, Series 1), MFAH archives. See also "Lecture Notes, 1932," Director's Records (RG2), Chillman Papers—Miscellaneous Subjects (SG1, Series 2, Folder 22), MFAH archives.

2. Although the museum's name has changed several times, for clarity it will be referred to by its present name in this book; abbreviated as appropriate to MFAH. From 1916 to 1923 the museum was called the Houston Art Museum; from 1924 to mid-1925, the Museum of Fine Arts; from 1925 to the early 1960s, the Museum of Fine Arts of Houston (this change was ratified by state charter in 1929). The Museum of Fine Arts, Houston, became the institution's formal title in the early 1960s.

3. Jean-Léon Gérôme, *Tiger on the Watch*, gift of the Art League of Houston, bequest of George M. Dickson, AL.21; James Abbott McNeill Whistler, *Black Lion Wharf*, lent by Joseph S. Cullinan; and Anton Mauve, *Landscape with Cattle*, gift of the Art League of Houston, bequest of George M. Dickson, AL.23.

4. For a detailed overview of William C. Hogg's Remington paintings, see Emily Ballew Neff, *Frederic Remington: The Hogg Brothers Collection of the Museum of Fine Arts, Houston* (Houston: The Museum of Fine Arts, Houston; Princeton: Princeton University Press, 2000).

5. James Chillman, Jr., director of the museum, invited the general public to select the most popular picture on loan from a private collection in the museum's inaugural installation. Ballots were handed out to each visitor to the museum on the weekend of 19–20 April 1924; the results were announced in the *Houston Chronicle* on 23 April 1924. Onderdonk's *Bluebonnets*, lent by Mrs. I. F. Carter, received 139 votes; George Inness's *Contentment*, lent by Ima Hogg, received 119 votes; and Frederic Remington's *The Emigrants*, lent by William C. Hogg, received 92 votes.

6. From 1917 to 1919 the Houston Art League's exhibition schedule included touring exhibitions of American art, loans from local collectors, and exhibitions focusing on regional talent. For a detailed study of the Houston Art League, see Theo M. Billings, "The Museum of Fine Arts, Houston: A Social History" (M.A. thesis, Department of History, The University of Houston, May 1994).

7. The Houston Art League also sponsored exhibitions at Houston area schools, the Mayor's and City Council offices, and in the homes of Art League members. For a detailed overview of the museum's architectural and education histories, see "The Museum of Fine Arts, Houston: An Architectural History 1924–1986," *The Museum of Fine Arts, Houston, Bulletin* 15, nos. 1–2 (April 1992); and Beth B. Schneider et al., "The Museum of Fine Arts, Houston: Education in the Arts," *The Museum of Fine Arts, Houston, Bulletin* 16, nos. 1–2 (February 1995).

8. James Chillman, Jr., "To the Membership," *Bulletin of the Museum of Fine Arts of Houston* 1, no. 2 (March 1930): n. p.

9. James Chillman, Jr., "Art in Houston," in *Houston: Text by Houstonians*, by Michel Cadoret and Sibylle De L'Epine (Marrero, La.: Hope Haven Press, 1949), 71.

10. "Annual Report of the Director for 1924–1925," Houston Art League Records (RG19), Miscellaneous Subjects (Series 5, Box 2, Folder 2), MFAH archives.

11. This exhibition featured, among others, Evelyn Byers Bessell, Grace Spaulding John, Margaret Brisbine, Emma Richardson Cherry, and Ruth Pershing Uhler. See "28 Houston Exhibitors Pass Jury of Museum of Fine Arts; Works Hung on Second Floor," *Houston Chronicle*, 29 March 1925.

12. In 1957 Ima Hogg donated her house, Bayou Bend, and her magnificent collection of Americana to the museum. Among Miss Hogg's many distinguished areas of collecting were her pioneering holdings of Texas decorative arts.

13. See Chronology of Exhibitions of Texas Art at the Museum of Fine Arts, Houston (pages 260–67), for a complete listing.

14. The first purchase prize went to Evelyn Byers Bessell for a still-life composition featured in the *4th Annual Exhibition of Works by Houston Artists*.

15. Chillman, introduction to *14th Annual Exhibition*, 1.

16. The Texas Centennial in 1936 was commemorated at the MFAH by a series of installations celebrating Texas and Southwestern themes, including a survey of the museum's purchase prize acquisitions, the Hogg brothers' collection of Remingtons, and loans from Houston collections. The most ambitious celebration of Texas art that year, however, was mounted in Dallas, as a part of its inauguration of Fair Park.

17. After 1961 the MFAH withdrew from *Texas Annual* exhibition schedule; however, the museum continued to be listed as a sponsor of the exhibition through its last tour in 1965.

18. James Chillman, Jr., *9th Texas General Exhibition* (Houston: The Museum of Fine Arts, Houston, 1947–48), 1.

19. "Museum of Fine Arts Fundraising Brochure," 1941, 3, the Museum of Fine Arts, Houston, Development Office Records (RG7), Annual Fund Drives (Series 5, Box 1, Folder 3), MFAH archives.

20. "The Eighteenth Annual Exhibition of Work by Houston Artists," *Bulletin of the Museum of Fine Arts of Houston* 5, no. 4 (winter 1943): 2. A review of all MFAH exhibitions from 1924 to 1959—its first thirty-five years—shows that the institution devoted twenty to twenty-five percent of its annual schedule to exhibiting the art of Texans.

21. "Green Hillside," *Bulletin of the Museum of Fine Arts of Houston* 7, no. 2 (summer 1944): 1.

22. James Johnson Sweeney, foreword to *The Galveston That Was*, by Howard Barnstone (New York: Macmillan; Houston: The Museum of Fine Arts, Houston, 1966; new, annotated ed., Houston: Rice University Press and the Museum of Fine Arts, Houston, 1993).

23. James Chillman, Jr., "The 22nd Annual Exhibition of Works by Houston Artists," *Bulletin of the Museum of Fine Arts of Houston* 9, no. 4 (winter 1947): 2.

24. "Museum of Fine Arts, Houston Collectors' Committee: Statement of Purpose," January 1957, 1, the Museum of Fine Arts, Houston, Board of Trustees Records (RG1), Trustee Committee Records, 1956–57 (Subgroup 2, Series 1, Box 1, Folder 22), MFAH archives.

25. See Susie Kalil's succinct introduction to the Houston gallery scene in "Dynamic Pioneers: A Brief History of Painting in Houston, 1900 to the Present," in *Fresh Paint: The Houston School*, by Barbara Rose and Susie Kalil (Austin: Texas Monthly Press; Houston: The Museum of Fine Arts, Houston, 1985), 11–46.

26. The Art League of Houston also became an independent entity in 1948.

27. For a detailed chronology of the Contemporary Arts Museum's history, see Cheryl A. Brutvan, Marti Mayo, and Linda L. Cathcart, *In Our Time: Houston's Contemporary Arts Museum 1948–1982* (Houston: Contemporary Arts Museum, 1982), 19–69. Also, see Marti Mayo, Bruce C. Webb, and Richard Howard, *Finders/Keepers* (Houston: Contemporary Arts Museum, 1997), 180–213.

28. "Contemporary Arts Association Annual Report for 1954–1955," 1, Contemporary Arts Museum Records (MS4), MFAH archives.

29. When the collection was dispersed in 1984, the MFAH received a gift of twenty-one works, including a number of prints by various American artists, a 1963 painting by Houstonian Dick Wray, and the 1971 *Cardbird* series of silkscreens on cardboard by Texas-born Robert Rauschenberg.

Introduction
pages 20–28

30. Miss Cullinan also stipulated that the new Mies van der Rohe gallery would "be made available to the CAA . . . for exhibitions of contemporary and modern art." Brutvan, Mayo, and Cathcart, *In Our Time*, 14.

31. One of the first installations to fully realize the potential of the new gallery was Jermayne MacAgy's historic *Totems Not Taboo: An Exhibition of Primitive Art*, her last project sponsored by the CAA and held at the MFAH in the spring of 1959.

32. Lee Malone, "Annual Report of the Director for 1956 and 1957," *Bulletin of the Museum of Fine Arts of Houston* 18–19, no. 1 (1957): 9.

33. It is interesting to note that the merits of this policy proved a matter of much debate among members of the board of trustees and that the museum's commitment to continue to collect regional work was not universally accepted. See "Accessions Policy Statement," c. 1958, the MFAH Board of Trustees Records (RG1), Full Board Records (SG1) Miscellaneous Subjects (Series 3, Box 1, Folder 1), MFAH archives.

34. For a detailed overview of the Sweeney years at the MFAH, see Toni Ramona Beauchamp, "James Johnson Sweeney and the Museum of Fine Arts, Houston: 1961–1967" (M.A. thesis, University of Texas at Austin, 1983).

35. Once the MFAH ceased to sponsor annual exhibitions, the Jewish Community Center, the Art League of Houston, and the Contemporary Arts Association offered alternative venues for juried exhibitions in the 1960s. However, only the CAA was able to offer a museum-quality exhibition space.

36. Matters began to improve for Houston artists toward the end of the 1960s. As the community grew larger and stronger, it received greater recognition from commercial galleries and art collectors, and donations of Texas art came to the museum from such leading patrons as Mrs. Robert Lee Blaffer and the McAshan Education and Charitable Trust.

37. Sweeney, foreword to Barnstone, *The Galveston That Was*, 11.

38. For an overview of MacAgy's career, see Dominique de Menil, *Jermayne MacAgy: A Life Illustrated by an Exhibition* (Houston: The University of St. Thomas, 1968).

39. Brutvan, Mayo, and Cathcart, *In Our Time*, 39.

40. Although the de Menil support of art department of the University of St. Thomas was largely transferred to the new Institute for the Arts at Rice University, the Jones Hall Gallery at St. Thomas continued to function as an active gallery space. For example, from 1969 to 1971, St. Thomas was the primary venue of the CAA while the Gunnar Birkerts building was under construction.

41. The MFAH received NEA funds annually for the purchase of the work of living American artists from 1973 to 1991 (excepting the years 1983 and 1987). These grants required that the MFAH raise matching funds on a dollar-for-dollar basis.

42. In 1982, for example, all NEA moneys were committed exclusively to Texas acquisitions.

43. Between 1974 and 1991, NEA funds were applied to more than three hundred contemporary art purchases and works by Texas painters Basilios Poulos, Philip Renteria, Charles Schorre, Gael Stack, Earl Staley, Richard Stout, and Robin Utterback were added to the collection with support from the NEA.

44. In 1972 the MFAH purchased a group of photographs at the auction that marked the closing of Houston's first photography gallery, Latent Image. Photographs by Geoff Winningham and Eve Sonneman (who were teaching at that time at Rice University) were among the works purchased from the Latent Image auction.

45. Private patrons, including Joe and Marion Mundy and Clinton T. Willour, led the museum's sponsorship of Texas photographers; NEA funds gave further impetus to this area of the collection. Over the next decade works by Texas photographers Gay Block, Keith Carter, George Krause, Al Souza, Wendy Watriss, Geoff Winningham, and Robert Ziebell, among others, were acquired with NEA support.

46. Rose and Kalil, *Fresh Paint*, 65.

47. Rose and Kalil, *Fresh Paint*, 76.

48. Charlotte Moser, "Regional Revisions: Houston and Chicago," *Art in America* 73, no. 7 (July 1985): 93.

49. Thomas McEvilley, "Double Vision in Space City," *Artforum* 23, no. 8 (April 1985): 53.

50. See Susie Kalil, "Houston Artists Would Rather Fight than Switch," *Artnews* 5, no. 10 (December 1981): 103–7; and Jamey Gambrell, "In the Third Coast Art Capital," *Art in America* 75, no. 4 (April 1987): 180–203.

51. Camfield's exhibition originated as a project in collaboration with Peter Weiermair, *New Art from a New City: Houston*, seen at the Frankfurter Kunstverein, Frankfurt, Germany, 8 June–3 July 1983, and accompanied by a catalogue published in German.

52. *Julian Schnabel: Paintings 1975–1987* was organized by Nicholas Serota for the Whitechapel Art Gallery, London, in 1986. Subsequently the exhibition had an extensive European and American tour.

53. The Menil Collection became the official name of the de Menil family collection only on the opening of the new building in 1987; while housed at Rice it was exhibited as part of the Rice Institute for the Arts in the Rice Museum.

54. In the 1980s The Menil Collection featured three significant regional exhibitions. *Ben Culwell: The Adrenaline Hour*, curated by director Walter Hopps, was one of the Menil's inaugural installations of 1987. The following year curator Neil Printz organized *Texas Art*, a survey made up of works drawn from the collections of the Menil, the MFAH, and the trustees of the Contemporary Arts Museum. In 1989 the Menil hosted *Michael Tracy: Terminal Privileges*, a retrospective organized by P.S. 1, The Institute for Art and Urban Resources, New York.

55. Among the alternative spaces that had brief histories were Studio One, founded by William Steen in 1980, and Midtown Art Center, founded in 1982. For detailed chronologies of Houston's alternative spaces see Rachel Ranta and Elizabeth Ward, *Lawndale Live! A Retrospective 1979–1990* (Houston: Lawndale Art and Performance Center, 1993) and Elizabeth McBride and Lorenzo Thomas, *DiverseWorks Artspace* (Houston: DiverseWorks Artspace, 1993).

56. A comprehensive history of Houston's gallery scene has yet to be written, but articles by Peter Schjeldahl, Charlotte Moser, and Susan Chadwick offer overviews of the gallery scene in the late 1970s and mid-1980s. See Peter Schjeldahl, "Art and Money in the City of Future-Think," *Houston City Magazine* 4, no. 2 (February 1980): 46–54, 97–101; Charlotte Moser, "But on the Other Hand," *Houston City Magazine* 4, no. 2 (February 1980): 54–57; Susan Chadwick, "Galleries Reveal Varied Personalities," *Houston Post*, 3 August 1986; and Susan Chadwick, "Local Art Galleries Keep Cultural Community Thriving," *Houston Post*, 10 August 1986.

57. The MFAH sponsored film screenings as early as the 1930s; the 1974 expansion of Mies van der Rohe's master plan for the Brown Pavilion included Brown Auditorium and gave Houston a state-of-the-art projection facility, funded in part by Dominique de Menil. The de Menils had earlier demonstrated their support of vanguard film in 1967 through the establishment of the Media Center at the University of St. Thomas; in 1969 the Media Center was transferred to Rice University. Gerald O'Grady and James Blue were the successive founding directors of the program, which drew to its faculty such luminaries as Roberto Rossellini, Frank Daniel, and Colin Young; among the visiting lecturers was Jean-Luc Godard. The Southwest Alternate Media Project (SWAMP) grew out of the Rice Media Center in 1977 and additionally promoted independent film and video in Houston.

58. Alison de Lima Greene, "Twentieth-Century Art in the Museum Collection: Direction and Diversity," *The Museum of Fine Arts, Houston, Bulletin* 11, no. 3 (summer 1988). This was the first collection publication to feature more than a token representation of Texas artists.

Introduction
pages 28–31

59. Illustrated in Gambrell, "In the Third Coast Art Capital": 202–3.

60. The most recent inventory of the Texas collection indicates that by the year 2000, the collection will number over 2000 objects.

61. While many Glassell exhibitions led to museum acquisitions, *Fresh Visions/New Voices* was unique in that the corporate sponsor, AT&T Foundation, also encouraged purchases from the exhibition, directly supporting the acquisition of two installation works by Annette Lawrence and Vicki Meek, and promoting the additional purchase of works by Michael Ray Charles, David McGee, and Bert Samples.

62. See Patricia C. Johnson, "Making Room for Art," *Houston Chronicle*, 27 June 1993.

63. McKissack began working on *The Orange Show* in 1956; it opened to the public in 1979, one year before McKissack's death. It has since been preserved by The Orange Show Foundation. For an overview of site-specific installations in Houston, see Stephanie Smith, "A Chronology of Public Art in Houston in the 20th Century," *ArtLies* 5 (February–March 1995): 6–9. Also worthy of note is "O" House, an ephemeral manifestation that was the result of a tight collaboration. In the spring of 1995 three artists—Dan Havel, Kate Petley, and Dean Ruck—transformed a West End house slated for demolition into a monumental and mysterious camera obscura that was open for public viewing for only two weeks. See Patricia C. Johnson, "The Art Shack," *Houston Chronicle*, 28 April 1995.

64. See Vicki Goldberg, "In Houston, Rebuilding by Creating," *New York Times*, 16 July 1995.

65. Chillman, "To the Membership," n.p.

66. Michael Ennis, "Texas Vision: Through the Looking Glass of History," 1992. This unpublished essay was written to place The Barrett Collection in the context of Texas history. The authors are grateful to Nona and Richard Barrett making this important text available, and to the author, who has kindly allowed us to quote from it.

Chapter 1: A Sense of Place
pages 34–39

1. Jerry Bywaters, "Texas Panorama," *Magazine of Art* 37, no. 8 (November 1944): 306.

2. For a detailed discussion of the image of Texas in films, see Don Graham, *Cowboys and Cadillacs: How Hollywood Looks at Texas* (Austin: Texas Monthly Press, 1983).

3. Dave Hickey, "The Texas to New York via Nashville Semi-Transcontinental Epiphany Tactic," *Art in America* 60, no. 5 (September–October 1972): 57.

4. Thomas McEvilley, "Yet Another Reality," in *Another Reality*, by Thomas McEvilley, Surpik Angelini, and Bert Long (Houston: Hooks-Epstein Galleries, Inc., 1989), 85.

5. For example, Frances Colpitt in her introduction to the *Texas Abstract* catalogue writes, "The twelve artists in this exhibition do not subscribe to regional attitudes, nor do they accommodate any stereotypes of provincial abstraction." Frances Colpitt, *Texas Abstract: New Painting in the Nineties* (San Antonio: ArtPace, 1995), 4.

6. Susie Kalil, *The Texas Landscape, 1900–1986* (Houston: The Museum of Fine Arts, Houston, 1986), 15.

7. Randolph B. Campbell, *An Empire for Slavery: The Peculiar Institution in Texas, 1821–1865* (Baton Rouge: Louisiana State University Press), 1989.

8. This shift from a Southern identity to a more independent one is reflected in the MFAH's institutional history. From 1924, the opening year of the museum building, the MFAH participated in the *Annual Circuit Exhibition of the Southern States Art League*, which featured Texas artists in the company of artists from the South. In 1940, however, the newly created *Texas General Exhibition* (later known as *The Annual Texas Exhibition of Painting and Sculpture*), organized by a consortium of Texas museums, began to draw more support, and after 1943 Houston ceased to host the *Southern States Art League* exhibition.

9. Debbie Nathan, "Forget the Alamo," *Texas Monthly* 25, no. 4 (April 1998): 126.

10. The daguerreotype process was one of the two photographic methods introduced in 1839. Unlike its competitor, the calotype, the daguerreotype had no negative, and each photograph was a one-of-a-kind image.

11. The city of Houston served as a temporary capital of the Republic of Texas from 1837 to 1839.

12. Although by its nature the daguerreotype is a unique image, a lithograph was produced after this photograph by E. C. Kellogg of Hartford, Connecticut, in 1852, most likely as a means of promoting Houston's bid for presidency; see "Full Length Portrait of Gen. Sam Houston to Be Given to

Cruiser Tonight," *Houston Chronicle*, 24 September 1934 (courtesy of the Sam Houston Regional Library and Research Center, Liberty, Texas). Anne Wilkes Tucker has noted that Houston's presidential ambitions are further underlined by his conservative attire in this portrait. Houston was known for his eccentricity of dress; he would sport flamboyant waistcoats and extravagantly spurred white beaver boots (MFAH curatorial files).

13. An 1860 daguerreotype portrait of Sam Houston's wife, Margaret, has been preserved in the MFAH's Bayou Bend Collection.

14. See David B. Warren, Michael K. Brown, Elizabeth Ann Coleman, and Emily Ballew Neff, *American Decorative Arts and Paintings in the Bayou Bend Collection* (Houston: The Museum of Fine Arts, Houston; Princeton: Princeton University Press, 1998), 211–12; and James Patrick McGuire, *Hermann Lungkwitz: Romantic Landscapist on the Texas Frontier* (San Antonio: The University of Texas Institute of Texan Cultures at San Antonio, 1983), 75, 109, 180, 185.

15. Michael K. Brown, curator of the Bayou Bend Collection, and Cecily Horton, Bayou Bend docent, have kindly shared their research on Colyer. The Bayou Bend Collection features twenty-six examples of Colyer's Indian Commission sketches, including four Texas landscapes and one detailed botanical study of Texas flora. See Warren et al., *Bayou Bend Collection*, 212–13.

16. The title *Sunlight and Shadow* is a common one among the American Impressionists. In the MFAH collection, for example, both Willard L. Metcalf (*Sunlight and Shadow*, 1888) and William Merritt Chase (*Sunlight and Shadow, Shinnecock Hills*, c. 1895) used this title to signal their allegiance to the principles of French Impressionism.

17. It is worth noting, however, that while most professional artists were drawn to Dallas or Houston in the 1920s and 1930s, the establishment of the Witte Memorial Museum in San Antonio in 1926, and the tenure of Eleanor Rogers Onderdonk as curator there from 1927 to 1958, saw the formation of the first great historical collection of Texas art.

18. "Dallas Exhibit Reveals World's Art and Significance of the Southwest," *Art Digest* 10, no. 7 (June 1936): 13–14. Other artists who participated in this exhibition included John Douglass, Otis Dozier, Lloyd L. Goff, William Lester, and Perry Nichols; however, the remaining two artists of the original "nine" were not recorded in this article.

19. Rick Stewart, *Lone Star Regionalism: The Dallas Nine and Their Circle, 1928–1945* (Austin: Texas Monthly Press; Dallas: Dallas Museum of Art, 1985), 22–23.

Chapter 1: A Sense of Place
pages 39–54

20. Henry Nash Smith, "A Note on the Southwest," *Southwest Review* 8 (January 1928), 257–78, quoted in Stewart, *Lone Star Regionalism*, 23.

21. Thomas Hart Benton, *An Artist in America*, 3rd ed. (Columbia, Missouri: University of Missouri Press, 1968), 44, 45.

22. Alexandre Hogue, "Rockwell Kent Exhibition, The Highland Park Municipal Art Gallery," *Southwest Review* 15 (autumn 1929): 129.

23. Alexandre Hogue, "Queen of the Valley," *Southwest Review* 15 (autumn 1929): 119–26. Ironically, Squaw Creek was dammed in the 1970s to provide cooling water for a nuclear power plant. See John Graves, "Our Own Piece of Country," *Cite* 39 (fall 1997): 12.

24. Alexandre Hogue to Carl Zigrosser, 19 August 1940, Archives of American Art, Smithsonian Institution, Washington, D.C.

25. Alexandre Hogue to Thomas Hart Benton, 16 March 1970, quoted in Sandra Lea Rosson [Lea Rosson DeLong], *The Career of Alexandre Hogue* (Ph.D. dissertation, University of Kansas; Ann Arbor, Mich.: University Microfilms International, 1983), 10–11.

26. Jerry Bywaters to Carl Zigrosser, 20 July 1940, quoted in Stewart, *Lone Star Regionalism*, 93.

27. Jerry Bywaters, "A Note on the Lone Star Printmakers," *Southwest Review* 26 (autumn 1940): 63, quoted in Francine Carraro, *Jerry Bywaters: A Life in Art* (Austin: University of Texas Press, 1994), 118. Among the museums that the exhibition circulated to was the MFAH.

28. Gibson Danes, "Everett Spruce: Painter of the Southwest," *Magazine of Art* 37, no. 1 (January 1944): 14–15.

29. As the third chapter of this publication documents, Houston in the 1930s was home to a hybrid form of synthetic Modernism that was distinct from Regionalist concerns.

30. Boynton and Love collaborated with Jermayne MacAgy in several of her exhibitions and, along with Bess, were featured in her personal collection; see de Menil, *Jermayne MacAgy*, 1968.

31. Jack Boynton, quoted in Jerry M. Daviee, *Jack Boynton: Retro/Spectrum* (Amarillo, Texas: Amarillo Art Center, 1980), 12.

32. Stella Hope Shurtleff, "Art Critic Praises Forrest Bess, Whose Exhibition Closes Today," *Houston Post*, 16 February 1941; I am grateful to Chuck Smith, coauthor and codirector of the 1998 documentary *Forrest Bess: Key to the Riddle*, for sharing this clipping and other research on Bess with me.

33. Although Bess only had two commercial gallery exhibitions in Texas during his lifetime, he had a second solo exhibition at the MFAH in 1951, followed in 1962 by a solo presentation at the Contemporary Arts Association.

34. Forrest Bess to Betty Parsons, 2 March 1962, Archives of American Art, Smithsonian Institution, Washington, D.C.

35. According to a letter from Bess to Schapiro dated 11 January 1954, preserved in the Archives of American Art, the original version of this painting was sent by Bess in the early 1950s to Schapiro to forward to Jung, but it was apparently lost in transit. The 1958 version in the museum's collection was featured in Bess's 1962 retrospective exhibition at Parsons.

36. Douglas MacAgy, *James Boynton* (New York: Barone Gallery, 1959), quoted in Daviee, *Jack Boynton*, 7.

37. Jermayne MacAgy, *The Age of the Thousand Flowers: An Exhibition of Works by Artists Past and Present* (Houston: University of St. Thomas, 1962), n.p.

38. Kalil, *The Texas Landscape*, 41.

39. Dave Hickey, quoted in Ron Gleason, "Interview: Dave Hickey," *Arts and Architecture* 1, no. 2 (winter 1981): 33.

40. The Oak Cliff artists took their name from the Oak Cliff suburb of Dallas, where many had found studios. By 1970, the Texas Funk movement had grown to the extent that Dave Hickey could organize an exhibition titled "South Texas Sweet Funk," which included artists from Austin and Houston, as well as the Oak Cliff group.

41. Bob Wade, letter to the author, 21 March 1992. The other, complementary view is now in The Menil Collection, Houston.

42. Wade also noted that *Whitney Texas Picturesque* owed a debt to the example of Robert Smithson and Richard Serra, and that this "found" installation particularly appealed to him in relation to their investigations of the picturesque. Indeed, Texas saw the creation of a number of earthworks and monumental installations over the following decade, from Robert Smithson's *Amarillo Ramp*, 1973, to Donald Judd's long-term development of Marfa. Projects such as Ant Farm's 1974 *Cadillac Ranch*, which has become one of the most beloved icons along Route 66, further brought a newly popular consciousness to the Texas landscape. Stanley Marsh, who sponsored *Amarillo Ramp* and *Cadillac Ranch*, among other earthworks, and the Dia Foundation, which underwrote a part of Judd's installations in Marfa, not only made these extraordinary undertakings possible, but also redefined art patronage. Susie Kalil chronicles this current in Texas art in greater detail; see *Texas Landscape*, 48–53.

43. Joan Seeman Robinson, *The Art of Robert Levers: A Retrospective* (Austin: Laguna Gloria Art Museum, 1991), 11.

44. Garry Winogrand, *Stock Photographs: The Fort Worth Fat Stock Show and Rodeo* (Austin: University of Texas Press, 1980), n.p.

45. Beaumont Newhall, *The History of Photography*, rev. ed. (New York: The Museum of Modern Art; Boston: New York Graphic Society Books, Little, Brown and Company, 1982), 292.

46. Anne Wilkes Tucker has recalled that shortly after taking this photograph, Winogrand was caught in the melee of the game and his leg was broken.

47. Geoff Winningham, *Going Texan: The Days of the Houston Livestock Show and Rodeo* (Houston: Mavis P. Kelsey, Jr., 1976), 116.

48. Wendy Watriss and Fred Baldwin, *Coming to Terms: The German Hill Country of Texas* (College Station, Texas: Texas A&M University Press, 1991), 137.

49. Robert D. Bullard, *Invisible Houston: The Black Experience in Boom and Bust* (College Station, Texas: Texas A&M University Press, 1987), 6.

50. I am grateful to Anne Wilkes Tucker for sharing this statement from her files on Gay Block.

51. Earlie Hudnall, quoted in Paul Rogers Harris, *Breaking into the Mainstream: Texas African-American Artists* (Irving, Texas: Irving Arts Center, 1996), 6.

52. Earlie Hudnall, unpublished statement, courtesy of Benteler-Morgan Galleries, MFAH curatorial files.

53. Wiley spent two weeks in Houston at the University of St. Thomas in 1969 at the invitation of Earl Staley, and returned to Houston several times over the following decade, embarking on several collaborative projects. See Janet Landay, *Collaborators: Artists Working Together in Houston, 1969–1986* (Houston: The Museum of Fine Arts, Houston, The Glassell School of Art, 1986), 3.

54. James Harithas and Michael Samuels, *James Surls: Sculptor* (Houston: Contemporary Arts Museum, 1975), n.p.

55. Mimi Crossley, "The World of John Alexander," *Houston Post*, 17 August 1975.

56. John Beardsley, "John Alexander," *Art International* 36, no. 3 (July–August 1983): 39.

57. John Alexander, quoted in Beardsley, "John Alexander," 39.

58. James Surls, quoted in Sue Graze, *Visions: James Surls, 1974–1984* (Austin: Texas Monthly Press; Dallas: Dallas Museum of Art, 1984), 30.

Chapter 1: A Sense of Place
pages 54–72

59. James Surls, quoted in Susan Freudenheim, "James Surls: The Power of Singular Belief," *Artspace* 9, no. 2 (spring 1985): 13.

60. O'Connor's collaborations with Thompson were surveyed in 1985 by the Contemporary Arts Museum in Houston. See Linda L. Cathcart, *Nancy O'Connor: Milam's Journey* (Houston: Contemporary Arts Museum, 1985).

61. Nancy O'Connor, unpublished statement, 10 May 1982, MFAH curatorial files.

62. William A. Fagaly and Monroe K. Spears, in *Southern Fictions*, by Linda L. Cathcart, Marti Mayo, William A. Fagaly, and Monroe K. Spears (Houston: Contemporary Arts Museum, 1983), 7–19; William H. Goetzmann, "Images of Texas," in *Texas Images and Visions*, by William H. Goetzmann and Becky Duval Reese (Austin: Archer M. Huntington Art Gallery, The University of Texas at Austin, 1983), 15–44; and Barbara Rose, "Painting is Dead, Long Live Painting in Houston," in Rose and Kalil, *Fresh Paint*, 65–93.

63. Rose, "Painting is Dead," 70.

64. Goetzmann, "Images of Texas," 44.

65. Dave Hickey, "The Code of the West," in *Vernon Fisher*, by Hugh M. Davis and Madeleine Grynsztejn (La Jolla, California: La Jolla Museum of Contemporary Art, 1989), 22.

66. The artist has disclosed that the original source of the image was a vintage safety manual for driving; interview by the author, 8 April 1999.

67. An expanded version of this text is published under the title "Amazing Grace," in Vernon Fisher, *Navigating by the Stars: Writings by Vernon Fisher* (Chicago: Landfall Press, Inc., 1988), 114–15.

68. This unpublished interview is from a panel discussion between Vernon Fisher and Madeleine Grynsztejn, sponsored by the Department of Education at the La Jolla Museum of Contemporary Art (now the Museum of Contemporary Art, San Diego) on the occasion of the exhibition *Vernon Fisher*, curated by Hugh M. Davis and Madeleine Grynsztejn and hosted by the La Jolla Museum of Contemporary Art, 3 February–2 April 1989. A tape of this discussion was provided by the artist and transcribed by G. Clifford Edwards for the MFAH.

69. Lee N. Smith III, quoted in Paul Rogers Harris, *Lee N. Smith III: Paintings* (Waco, Texas: The Art Center, 1984), n.p.

70. Emily Todd, *Lee N. Smith III: Recent Paintings* (Houston: Contemporary Arts Museum, 1986), n.p.

71. Derek Boshier, quoted in Patricia C. Johnson, "Boshier: Too Theatrical? Wray: Trying Too Hard?" *Houston Chronicle*, 18 September 1983.

72. Derek Boshier, statement, in Rose and Kalil, *Fresh Paint*, 106.

73. Mel Chin, letter to the author, 27 February 1990.

74. Mel Chin, quoted in Patricia C. Johnson, "Mel Chin: Poetic, Pragmatic, with a Rare Sensitivity," *Houston Chronicle*, 22 September 1985. The themes in the MFAH's landscape diptych were further explored in a subsequent sculpture, *Myrrha P.I.A.* [*Post-Industrial Age*], realized in 1985 as a commission for Bryant Park, New York.

75. Frank Martin, *Meeting Places*, an unpublished series of statements by the artist, 1990, MFAH curatorial files.

76. Keith Carter, *Keith Carter Photographs: Twenty-five Years* (Austin: University of Texas Press, 1997), n.p.

77. Carter Ratcliff, *Paul Manes* (New York: Kouros Gallery, 1989), 5.

78. Rosellen Brown, *Mojo: Photographs by Keith Carter* (Houston: Rice University Press, 1992), n.p.

79. These images were first exhibited under the series title *A Sense of Place. A Sense of Time*; the series was exhibited at Rice University's Farish Gallery in 1990. The photographs were recently published under a new title, *On the Plains*, with an introduction by Kathleen Norris (New York: DoubleTake Books/W. W. Norton & Co., 1999).

80. *Seasons of Light* appeared later in book form: Peter Brown, *Seasons of Light: Photographs and Stories by Peter Brown* (Houston: Rice University Press, 1988).

81. Norris, introduction to Brown, *On the Plains*, 15.

82. Opening narration of *This State I'm In*, 1990, quoted in Susan Chadwick, "Houstonian Debuts Fun, Wacko 'Oz' Film," *Houston Post*, 30 November 1990.

83. Elizabeth Ward, *Reinventing Reality: Five Texas Photographers* (Houston: Sarah Campbell Blaffer Gallery, University of Houston, 1990), 6–7.

84. Julie Bozzi, statement, in *Third Coast Review: A Look at Art in Texas* by Annette DiMeo Carlozzi (Aspen, Colorado: Aspen Art Museum, 1987), 10.

85. Dennis Blagg, letter to the author, 2 February 1994.

86. Dennis Blagg, in an interview published in *The Tyler Museum of Art Review* (Tyler, Texas) (September–November 1992), 4.

87. Hayden Herrera, *Rackstraw Downes: Recent Work* (New York: Marlborough Gallery, 1997), 5.

88. Rackstraw Downes, quoted ibid., 4.

89. Rackstraw Downes, letter to the author, 26 October 1992.

90. Green Mountain has since become Texas's premier fine arts foundry, and artists as diverse as Danny Williams, Joseph Havel, and Linda Ridgway have collaborated with Geffert (see plates 66, 116, and 139).

91. Harry Geffert, quoted in Alison de Lima Greene, *Genesis in Fire: Works from the Green Mountain Foundry* (Houston: The Museum of Fine Arts, Houston, The Glassell School of Art, 1995), n.p.

92. See Clint Willour, *Harry Geffert: New Work* (Dallas: Dallas Visual Art Center, 1998), n.p.

93. For an extended consideration of border politics and art, see Patricio Chávez and Madeleine Grynsztejn, *La Frontera/The Border: Art about the Mexico/United States Border Experience* (San Diego: Centro Cultural de la Raza and Museum of Contemporary Art, 1993).

94. A copy and translation of this text was provided by the artist.

95. In the CAM exhibition, Drake contrasted the brutality of contemporary events with one drawn from history by featuring a tableau incorporating a copy of Théodore Géricault's *Raft of the Medusa*, 1818–19 (Musée du Louvre, Paris).

96. Hans Staartjes, "Fiction, Sex, and Violence," *Spot* 12, no. 1 (spring 1993): 22.

97. For an overview of Texas women artists active during the first half of this century, see Susan Landauer and Becky Duval Reese, "Lone Star Spirits," in *Independent Spirits: Women Painters of the American West, 1890–1945*, by Patricia Trenton et al. (Los Angeles: Autry Museum of Western Heritage; Berkeley and Los Angeles: University of California Press, 1995), 183–207.

98. Admittedly, issues of ecological consciousness are not limited to Texas, or to women artists, as has been demonstrated by such exhibitions as *Fragile Ecologies: Contemporary Artists' Interpretations and Solutions*, hosted by the Queens Museum of Art in 1993, and featuring such diverse artists as Helen and Newton Harrison, Mel Chin, and Betty Beaumont.

99. Liz Ward, letter to the author, 11 August 1998.

100. One of only two surviving iron lighthouses on the Texas coast, the Bolivar Lighthouse was erected in 1873; during the Galveston hurricanes of 1900 and 1915, as many as 125 people found refuge inside the tower. It ceased operations in 1933.

101. Liz Ward, unpublished statement written in conjunction with the first installation of *To the Lighthouse* in the exhibition *Not for the Living Room* (Houston: DiverseWorks Artspace, February–April 1988), MFAH curatorial files. The last sentence was added by the artist in letter to the author, 11 August 1998.

Chapter 1: A Sense of Place
pages 72–77

102. Liz Ward, letter to the author, 25 May 1993.

103. Valerie Loupe Olsen, *In Situ: Responses from Charles Mary Kubricht and Ann Stautberg* (Houston: The Museum of Fine Arts, Houston, The Glassell School of Art, 1998), 8.

104. Eleanor Jones Harvey, *Jean Carruthers Wetta, A Survey: 1984–1998* (Galveston: Galveston Arts Center, 1998), n.p.

105. Jean Carruthers Wetta, letter to the author, 14 January 1998.

106. Page Kempner, letter to the author, 30 January 1994.

107. Kristin Musgnug, "Land Futures in America: Re-envisioning the Middle Landscape in England and America," unpublished statement, 1994, MFAH curatorial files.

108. Robert Ruello, letter to the author, 19 October 1994.

109. Ibid.

110. Susie Kalil, "Canyons and Cowboys," *Houston Press* (27 May–2 June 1999).

111. Charles Mary Kubricht, statement, in *Charles Mary Kubricht/Terrell James: New Art Series*, by Alison de Lima Greene and Daniel Stern (Corpus Christi: Museum of South Texas, 1997), n.p.

112. George F. Thompson, "The Value of Place," *Cite* 39 (fall 1997): 28.

Chapter 2: Another Reality
pages 80–89

1. Nancy Reddin Kienholz, "Chronology," in *Kienholz: A Retrospective*, by Walter Hopps et al. (New York: Whitney Museum of American Art and D.A.P./Distributed Art Publishers, 1996), 273.

2. Mircea Eliade, "Paradise and Utopia: Mythical Geography and Eschatology," *Utopias and Utopian Thought* (Boston: Houghton Mifflin Co., 1966), 265, quoted in Marcia Tucker, *Paradise Lost/Paradise Regained: American Visions of the New Decade* (Venice: 41a Biennale di Venezia, United States Pavilion, 1984), 12–13.

3. Alexis de Tocqueville, *Democracy in America*, vol. I, ed. Phillips Bradley (New York: Alfred A. Knopf, 1945), 308, quoted in Richard Francis, *Negotiating Rapture* (Chicago: The Museum of Contemporary Art, 1996), 2.

4. Maurice Tuchman's defining exhibition *The Spiritual in Art: Abstract Painting, 1890–1985* offers a succinct overview of this current in scholarship. See Maurice Tuchman et al., *The Spiritual in Art: Abstract Painting, 1890–1985* (Los Angeles: The Los Angeles County Museum of Art, 1986).

5. *Magiciens de la terre* was organized by the Centre Georges Pompidou, Paris, in 1989.

6. Rose, "Painting is Dead," 89.

7. Bert Long, "Another Reality," in McEvilley, Angelini, and Long, *Another Reality*, 9.

8. McEvilley, "Yet Another Reality," 83. Danny Williams, whose work is discussed below, has cited Iamblichus (died c. 330) as a specific influence: "In antiquity, ritual acts and potent visual metaphors were employed as means to approach deities and invoke sources of power. The philosopher Iamblichus wrote, 'It was not thinking which linked men with the divinity but the efficacy of the unspeakable acts performed in the appropriate manner, acts beyond comprehension and powerful because of … unutterable symbols which are clear only to the divinity.'" Letter to the author, 11 November 1998.

9. McEvilley, "Yet Another Reality," 86.

10. A selection of Charles Dellschau's notebooks were first brought to the public eye by Mary Jane Victor at the University of St. Thomas, Houston, in 1969; Dominique de Menil acquired several of the early notebooks, and four additional notebooks were later acquired by the San Antonio Museum Association. See Cecelia Steinfeldt, *Art for History's Sake: The Texas Collection of the Witte Museum* (San Antonio: Witte Memorial Museum of the San Antonio Museum Association, 1993), 49–55; and Cynthia Greenwood, "Secrets of the Sonora Aero Club," *Houston Press* 10, no. 50 (10–16 December 1998), 22–29.

11. André Breton, *Manifeste du Surréalisme* (Paris, 1924), quoted in William S. Rubin, *Dada, Surrealism, and Their Heritage* (New York: The Museum of Modern Art, 1968), 64.

12. Dorothy Hood, *Dorothy Hood: Recent Works* (Houston: University of Houston at Clear Lake, 1979), n.p. These comments were later expanded by Hood into an essay, "Sighting the Invisible Encounters," *Art Journal* 39, no. 4 (summer 1980): 268–69.

13. Frances Frigbourg Stillman and Ary Stillman, *Reminiscenes: The Personal Life of Artist Ary Stillman* (Houston: The Stillman-Lack Foundation, 1988), 142.

14. Johnson had his first solo exhibition in Houston in 1966 at David Gallery; by the early 1970s, he had a well-established reputation in the city.

15. Lucas Johnson, quoted in Susan Chadwick, "Houston Artist Returns to the Realm of Painting in Exceptional Show," *Houston Post*, 2 November 1991.

16. Carla Stellweg, *Lucas Johnson: Drawings from the Underworld/Dibujos del bahomundo* (Houston: Contemporary Arts Museum, 1994), 5.

17. In an interview of 1989, Tracy stated: "I wanted to do for art what Antonin Artaud did for the theater: make it a sacred ritual of transformation." Quoted in Susan Chadwick, "Art as a Sacred Ritual of Transformation," *Houston Post*, 25 February 1989.

18. Michael Tracy, notes on "Mexican Paperworks," 1979, quoted in Ed Leffingwell and Thomas McEvilley, *Terminal Privileges: Michael Tracy* (New York: P.S. 1, The Institute for Art and Urban Resources, Inc., 1987), 7.

19. Thomas McEvilley, "Your Flowers as My Hair: The Art of Michael Tracy," in Leffingwell and McEvilley, *Terminal Privileges*, 39.

20. Kermit Oliver, letter to the author, 11 February 1992.

21. The original frame for this painting was lost. In 1991, shortly after the painting was purchased, the MFAH commissioned Oliver to create a new frame.

22. Alvia J. Wardlaw, *Kermit Oliver* (Houston: Hooks-Epstein Galleries, 1997), n.p.

23. Marcia Tucker, "Earl Staley: Myth, Symbol, Dream," in *Earl Staley 1973–1983*, by Linda L. Cathcart and Marcia Tucker (Houston: Contemporary Arts Museum; New York: The New Museum of Contemporary Art, 1984), 25.

24. Melissa Miller, quoted in M. Tucker, *Paradise Lost/Paradise Regained*, 115.

25. Linda L. Cathcart, *Melissa Miller: A Survey 1978–1986* (Houston: Contemporary Arts Museum, 1986), 17.

26. Miller, quoted ibid.

27. M. Tucker, *Paradise Lost/Paradise Regained*, 22.

Chapter 2: Another Reality
pages 89–109

28. Ibid., 25.

29. Carlozzi, *Third Coast Review*, 5.

30. Jeff DeLude, statement, in Rose and Kalil, *Fresh Paint*, 120.

31. Jeff DeLude, "Statement," *Houston Art Scene* 1, no. 4 (January/February 1981): n.p.

32. William A. Fagaly, in Cathcart et al., *Southern Fictions*, 11.

33. Richard Stout has recalled that in the first state the painting was more generally abstract; he added the more figurative elements during the revisions he made in 1984. Conversation with the author, 25 January 1999.

34. Richard Stout, statement, in Rose and Kalil, *Fresh Paint*, 176.

35. Anne Wilkes Tucker, *George Krause: A Retrospective* (Houston: The Museum of Fine Arts, Houston, and Rice University Press, 1991), 15.

36. Ibid., 17.

37. In the early 1960s, Douglas MacAgy's program of exhibitions at the Dallas Museum for Contemporary Arts included *The Art of Assemblage* and Claes Oldenburg's *The Store*—as well as a "Happening" staged by Oldenburg titled *Injun*, which Fridge documented on film—all of which fed Fridge's increasing interest in exploring the evocative power of found objects and performance. For further documentation of this era, see Douglas MacAgy, *one i at a time* (Dallas: Southern Methodist University, Pollock Galleries, 1971).

38. These shrines were not meant as permanent structures. Although Fridge made a temporary home in the woods, once this series of work was completed, he deliberately abandoned the structures and allowed them to return to nature.

39. Michael Ennis, "The Shrine of the Bleached Skull: The Eerie Sculptures of South Texas Hermit Roy Fridge," *Texas Monthly* 10, no. 11 (November 1982): 256–57.

40. Ellipses are original to artist's text. The accompanying series of altered photographs are arranged in a cruciform around the text, showing a boat both afloat and propped in the woods like a shrine, with images of the artist gradually superimposed over the central shamanistic figure. *Shamanic Ritual Voyage*, 1983, mixed media collage on paperboard, 22⅛ x 18⅛ inches, the Museum of Fine Arts, Houston, gift of Moody Gallery, 85.139.

41. Madeline O'Connor, quoted in Annette DiMeo Carlozzi and Gay Block, *50 Texas Artists: A Critical Selection of Painters and Sculptors Working in Texas* (San Francisco: Chronicle Books, 1986), 75.

42. Frances Colpitt, *Madeline O'Connor* (Houston: Moody Gallery, 1994), n.p.

43. Fragments of this poem were first published in Janet Landay and Donald Barthelme, *One + One: Collaborations by Artists and Writers* (Houston: The Museum of Fine Arts, Houston, The Glassell School of Art, 1988), 15; an edited text was later published under the title "At the Round Earth's Imagin'd Corners: A Stack of Marriage Boxes," in Cynthia Macdonald, *Living Wills: New and Selected Poems* (New York: Alfred A. Knopf, 1991), 28–32. The original text is printed here with the courteous permission of the author.

44. For an overview of the exhibition, see Landay and Barthelme, *One + One*.

45. James Surls, quoted in Sue Graze, *Visions: James Surls, 1974–1984* (Austin: Texas Monthly Press; Dallas: Dallas Museum of Art, 1984), 27.

46. William Steen, "Affinity with a Madman," *Eleven x Fourteen* (August 1987): 23.

47. James Reaben, "Dream," quoted in John Harvey and William Steen, *In Fear and Rebellion: The Epistolary Art of James Reaben* (Houston: Brazos Bookstore, 1995), 30.

48. William Steen, interview by the author, 19 January 1990.

49. Louis Dobay, "The Passion of James Reaben," *Gulf Coast* 5, no. 1 (summer 1992): 51.

50. Danny Williams, letter to the author, 11 November 1998.

51. Danny Williams, "Travel in India," in *Danny Williams: Travels: 1977–1979*, by Gordon McConnell (Waco, Texas: The Art Center, 1980), n.p.

52. Williams, letter to the author.

53. Susan Chadwick, "No Fool's Gold: Houston Artist Waits Patiently for Recognition," *Houston Post*, 3 March 1990.

54. Ibid.

55. Susan Chadwick, "Home Is Where the Art Is," *Houston Post*, 14 November 1991.

56. Sharon Kopriva, letter to the author, 25 November 1991.

57. Sharon Kopriva, quoted in Susan Chadwick, "The Dark, Religious Imagery of Sharon Kopriva's Art," *Houston Post*, 4 May 1986.

58. Dee Wolff, letter to the author, 2 November 1991.

59. Ibid.

60. Octavio Paz, "Art and Identity: Hispanics in the United States," in *Hispanic Art in the United States: Thirty Contemporary Painters and Sculptors*, by John Beardsley and Jane Livingston (New York: Abbeville Press; Houston: The Museum of Fine Arts, Houston, 1987), 37.

61. Amalia Mesa-Bains, *Ceremony of Memory: New Expressions of Spirituality among Contemporary Hispanic Artists* (Santa Fe: Center for Contemporary Arts of Santa Fe, 1988), 7.

62. Huerta has acknowledged that as a child he felt privileged to be raised in a city designated "The Body of Christ." See Marilyn A. Zeitlin, *Benito Huerta: Attempted, Not Known* (New York: Artists Space, 1989), n.p. This exhibition was reorganized and expanded by the Contemporary Arts Museum in Houston in 1990; it then toured nationally through ExhibitsUSA.

63. Michael Ennis, "Sacred Meets Profane," *Texas Monthly* 18, no. 6 (June 1990): 136–38.

64. Benito Huerta, letter to the author, 7 March 1990.

65. As a child, Vargas assisted her uncle in his commercial photography business by hand-coloring the finished prints.

66. Diana Emery Hulick, "Kathy Vargas: Immortalizing Death," *Latin American Art* 6, no. 1 (fall 1994): 65.

67. Kathy Vargas, interview by the author, 8 February 1999.

68. The clothing and objects are actually those of Muñoz's children.

69. Moira Roth, *Personal Odysseys: The Photography of Celia Alvarez Muñoz, Clarissa T. Sligh, and María Martínez-Cañas* (New York: INTAR Gallery, 1990), 7; see also Anita Cramer, "An Artist of Two Worlds: Contradiction is Inspiration for Celia Muñoz," *Dallas Life Magazine* 7, no. 41 (22 January 1989): 18. The full text of the inscriptions in *"Ella" y 'El'* reads: "Two souls sought each other by fate. One was in love with life. The other with respect for death. He was tough, yet, clearly transparent. She was smoothed strength. She looked in the mirror. He didn't look back. He I call Jaime. She Caterina. Jaime collects *calaveras*. She fancies old funeraries. To start a new life together, they roamed the countrysides, looking for old cemeteries."

70. Ennis, "Texas Vision: Through the Looking Glass of History," n.p.

71. Diane Kett, *Karin Broker: Searching for a Saint* (Houston: Rice University, Sewall Art Gallery, 1992), n.p.

72. These biographical details were supplied by Karin Broker, interview by the author, 10 February 1999.

Chapter 2: Another Reality
pages 109–114

73. Steve Brudniak, unpublished statement, c. 1988, courtesy of the artist.

74. Steve Brudniak, letter to the author, 8 June 1992.

75. *Faces of the Gods: Art and Altars of Africa and the African Americas* traveled to the Contemporary Arts Museum in Houston in 1998.

76. Robert Farris Thompson, *Face of the Gods: Art and Altars of Africa and the African Americas*, (New York: The Museum of African Art; Munich: Prestel, 1993), 20–21.

77. Edmund Barry Gaither, "Heritage Reclaimed: An Historical Perspective and Chronology," in *Black Art—Ancestral Legacy: The African Impulse in African-American Art*, by Robert V. Rozelle, Alvia J. Wardlaw, and Maureen A. McKenna (Dallas: Dallas Museum of Art; New York: Harry N. Abrams, Inc., 1989), 18.

78. John Biggers, *Ananse: The Web of Life in Africa* (Austin: University of Texas Press, 1962), 31.

79. Illustrated in Alvia J. Wardlaw, *The Art of John Biggers: View from the Upper Room* (Houston: The Museum of Fine Arts, Houston; New York: Harry N. Abrams, Inc., 1995), 105 and 128 respectively.

80. John Biggers, interview by Alvia J. Wardlaw and Shannon Halwes, 22 April 1994.

81. Wardlaw, *The Art of John Biggers*, 73.

82. Bruce D. Kurtz, *Contemporary Identities: 1993 Phoenix Triennial* (Phoenix: Phoenix Art Museum, 1993), 70.

83. Vicki Meek, statement, in *Fresh Visions/New Voices: Emerging African-American Artists in Texas*, by Joseph Havel and Rick Lowe (Houston: The Museum of Fine Arts, Houston, The Glassell School of Art, 1992).

84. Howdy Doody was a puppet figure popularized by a children's television show in the late 1940s and 1950s; here Howdy Doody takes on the somewhat menacing aspect of a ventriloquist's dummy, a further reference to the artist (much as a ventriloquist speaks through a dummy, so too does the artist project his or her "voice" through art).

85. Walter Hopps has recalled that the Kienholzes used to say that "the fish is always Jesus" in reference to the fish symbol many drivers have chosen to place on their cars to indicate their Christian faith; conversation with the author, 22 February 1999.

86. Edward Kienholz, quoted in Hopps et al., *Kienholz: A Retrospective*, 242.

87. Marcus Raskin, "Ed Kienholz and the Burden of Being American," in Hopps et al., *Kienholz: A Retrospective*, 43.

88. Miguel Cervantes, *Mito y magia en América: Los Ochenta* (Monterrey: Museo de Arte Contemporáneo, 1991), 111.

89. Charles Merewether, "Like a Coarse Thread Through the Body: Transformation and Renewal," in Cervantes, *Mito y magia en América*, 122.

Chapter 3: Texas Modern
pages 118–122

1. Myron Stout, Journal, 9 June 1957, courtesy of the late Richard Bellamy and Miles Bellamy, Oil & Steel Gallery, New York. This extract from Stout's journal was published in slightly altered form in Sanford Schwartz, *Myron Stout* (New York: The Whitney Museum of American Art, 1980), 81.

2. Eva Hesse, quoted in Mark Rosenthal, *Abstraction in the Twentieth Century: Total Risk, Freedom, Discipline* (New York: The Solomon R. Guggenheim Museum, 1996), 1.

3. Clement Greenberg, "Avant-Garde and Kitsch," reprinted in *Art and Culture: Critical Essays by Clement Greenberg* (Boston: Beacon Press, 1961), 6.

4. Peggy Louise Jones, "Modern Art Evaluated by George Biddle," *Dallas Morning News*, 7 December 1947, quoted in Francine Carraro, *Jerry Bywaters: A Life in Art* (Austin: University of Texas Press, 1994), 162.

5. Martin Dreyer, "The Day Art Came to Houston," *Houston Chronicle: Texas Magazine*, 11 February 1968.

6. Stewart, *Lone Star Regionalism*, 31.

7. Julliette Grebin, "Artist Comes to Houston to Put City's Beauty Spots on Canvas," *Houston Post*, 12 April 1920; quoted in Patricia John Keightley, *Grace Spaulding John: Artist (1890–1972)* (Houston: The Pantile Press, 1993), n.p.

8. Patricia John Keightley, letter to the author, 21 August 1998.

9. See also Susan Landauer's and Becky Duval Reese's comments on Uhler's *Earth Rhythms*: "The paintings in this series impart the essence and pulse of the land in a manner reminiscent of O'Keeffe." Landauer and Reese, "Lone Star Spirits," in Trenton et al., *Independent Spirits*, 204.

10. Keightley, letter to the author.

11. Patricia D. Hendricks and Becky Duval Reese, *A Century of Sculpture in Texas: 1889–1989* (Austin: University of Texas Press and the Archer M. Huntington Art Gallery, 1989), 48. The primary role that Dallas held in the arts in the 1920s and 1930s was confirmed by the Texas Centennial celebrations of 1936. Dallas was selected over Houston and San Antonio as the site for the celebrations, and the city issued $500,000 in bonds for the completion of a new art museum as part of the development of Fair Park. Unlike Houston's earlier and essentially Beaux-Arts building, the new Dallas Museum of Fine Arts was a more modern, undecorated structure. See Jerry Bywaters, *Seventy-Five Years of Art in Dallas* (Dallas: The Dallas Museum of Fine Arts, 1978), n.p.

Chapter 3: Texas Modern
pages 123–134

12. Robert Preusser, quoted in "Exhibit of Abstractions at Museum is Drawing Praise of Young Artists," *Houston Post*, February 1938 [?], MFAH archives.

13. The importance of "The New Bauhaus" in Chicago cannot be underestimated for Texas artists in the 1940s. Not only did a number of Texans go to Chicago for instruction, but it also provided a link to the European avant-garde for many Texas institutions. For a summary description of "The New Bauhaus," see Peter Selz, "Modernism Comes to Chicago: The Institute of Design," in *Art in Chicago: 1945–1995,* by Lynne Warren et al. (Chicago: The Museum of Contemporary Art, 1996), 35–52.

14. For installation views of these exhibitions, which were held at the MFAH, see Mayo, Webb, and Howard, *Finders/Keepers*, 180.

15. While Jerry Bywaters brought few contemporary European artists to Dallas in the 1940s, he did profile both LaSelle and Corpron in solo exhibitions at the Dallas Museum of Fine Arts in 1947 and 1948 respectively.

16. Gyorgy Kepes, quoted in Martha A. Sandweiss, *Charlotta Corpron: Designer with Light* (Austin: University of Texas Press; Fort Worth: Amon Carter Museum, 1980), 5.

17. Charlotta M. Corpron, quoted ibid., 16.

18. Moholy-Nagy first visited Denton in the winter of 1941 as a guest lecturer; he returned to conduct summer workshops in sculpture in 1942 and 1943.

19. Toni LaSelle, telephone interview by Jason A. Goldstein, 30 June 1998.

20. Toni LaSelle, "Coincident to Hour and Place," February 1983, Provincetown, Mass., courtesy of Murray Smither.

21. Although Stout and LaSelle parted ways after the early 1950s, Stout paid the following tribute to LaSelle in his journal in 1953: "I think that Tony [*sic*] was my inspiration in this way: she helped me to see personal and particular possibilities, and Hofmann inspired me through the breadth of vision and understanding, and the vast range of possibilities he opened up. The penetration that Tony has into the impulsiveness and particulars of style in painting is a very powerful and impressive thing." Myron Stout, unpublished journal entry, 29 May 1953, courtesy of Oil & Steel Gallery, New York.

22. Sanford Schwartz, "Myron Stout," *Artforum* 13, no. 7 (March 1975): 40.

23. Stout, unpublished journal entry, 13 October 1965, courtesy Oil & Steel Gallery.

24. Ben Culwell, quoted in Dorothy Miller, *Fourteen Americans* (New York: The Museum of Modern Art, 1946), 16.

25. Ibid., 77.

26. *Salome*, 1955, oil on canvas, 79 3/4 x 66 3/4 inches, private collection. See Marti Mayo, Michael Berryhill, and Julian Schnabel, *Joseph Glasco: 1948–1986* (Houston: Contemporary Arts Museum, 1986), 41.

27. Although Glasco did not take up residence in Texas again until 1972, he was the focus of a solo exhibition at Kiko Gallery in Houston in 1968.

28. Joseph Glasco, quoted in Selden Rodman, *Conversations with Artists* (New York: The Devin-Adair Co., 1957), 113.

29. In contrast, the Dallas Museum of Fine Arts went through a deeply troubled period in the mid-1950s as charges of Communism were leveled against the staff for their support of such "Red" artists as Pablo Picasso, Diego Rivera, George Grosz, and Ben Shahn among others. See Carraro, *Jerry Bywaters*, 172–204.

30. For a detailed discussion of the American Federation of Arts convention, see Lauri G. Nelson, " 'This Kind of Circus, All in Cordiality': Marcel Duchamp's Speech 'The Creative Act' " (M.A. thesis, Rice University, 1994), 58–86.

31. American Federation of Arts, 1957 Convention Brochure, MFAH archives.

32. Nelson, *"This Kind of Circus,"* 82.

33. Richard Stout, interview by Sandra Curtis for the Archives of American Art, Texas Project, November 1979. *Irons in the Fire: An Exhibition of Metal Sculpture* was curated by Jermayne MacAgy and featured the work of Harry Bertoia, Julio González, David Hare, Seymour Lipton, Theodore Roszak, David Smith, and Richard Stankiewicz, among others. MFAH archives.

34. Artists from Arkansas, Oklahoma, Texas, New Mexico, Arizona, and Southern California were invited to participate in this exhibition. Among the featured artists was the young John Baldessari.

35. James Johnson Sweeney, *The Southwest: Painting and Sculpture* (Houston: The Museum of Fine Arts, Houston, 1962), n.p.

36. David E. Brauer, *Artists' Progress: Seven Houston Artists, 1943–1993* (Houston: The Museum of Fine Arts, Houston, The Glassell School of Art, 1993), 20.

37. Dick Wray, quoted in Charlotte Moser, "On Location: Four Interviews, Six Artists," *Art in America* 64, no. 4 (July/August 1976): 83.

38. James Harithas wrote of Wray's early work: "The paintings of this period are rigorously structured and brilliantly painted. At the same time, they exhibit a conceptual freedom characteristic of the best second generation abstract-expressionist paintings—particularly in the radical juxtaposition of linear forms and painted fields." James Harithas, *Dick Wray* (Houston: Contemporary Arts Museum, 1975), n.p.

39. *Dorothy Hood: Recent Paintings*, opened in 1970, during the period that the Contemporary Arts Museum was under construction. The exhibition was organized by the Contemporary Arts Association and hosted by the University of St. Thomas.

40. Dorothy Hood, quoted in Eleanor Stern, "Invasion of the Firmament," *Houston Post*, 3 May 1970.

41. Charles Schorre, statement, in Rose and Kalil, *Fresh Paint*, 168.

42. As Susie Kalil has observed, Schorre was a deeply reflective artist, one who imbued his work with internal correspondences: "It can be said that the artist set up equivalents, where a single line serves commensurately as a torso, a shell, cloud or rock formation. Yet the artist's penchant for employing cross-references within his own body of work is not a calculated measure inasmuch as an afterthought and outgrowth of loosely connected accidents." Susie Kalil, *Charles Schorre: Drawings and Notes* (Houston: Seashore Press, 1975), n.p.; reprinted in Jim Edwards et al., *Charles Schorre* (Houston: Herring Press and the Houston Artists Fund, 1997), 30–31.

43. Donald Judd, *Arts Yearbook* 8; reprinted in Donald Judd, *Complete Writings 1959–1975* (Halifax: The Press of the Nova Scotia College of Art and Design; New York: New York University Press, 1975), 187.

44. Barbara Haskell, *Donald Judd* (New York: Whitney Museum of American Art, 1988), 57.

45. Judd's collaboration with the Dia Foundation and the establishment of the Chinati Foundation has been exhaustively documented elsewhere. See Melissa Susan Gaido Allen, "From the Dia Foundation to the Chinati Foundation: Donald Judd in Marfa" (M.A. thesis, Rice University, 1995); Michael Ennis, "The Marfa Art War," *Texas Monthly* 12 (August 1984): 138–42, 186–92; and Haskell, *Donald Judd*, 118–45.

46. In an interview of 1971, Judd stated: "I like the color and I like the quality of cadmium red light. And then, also, I thought for a color it had the right value for a three-dimensional object." See John Coplans, *Don Judd* (Pasadena: Pasadena Art Museum, 1971), 25; reprinted in *Artforum* 9, no. 10 (June 1971): 50.

47. Judd, quoted in Coplans, *Don Judd*, 43.

48. Michael Fried, "Art and Objecthood," *Artforum* 5, no. 10 (summer 1967): 16.

Chapter 3: Texas Modern
pages 137–158

49. Trevor Fairbrother, *Robert Wilson's Vision* (Boston: Museum of Fine Arts, Boston; New York: Harry N. Abrams, Inc., 1991), 116. The cloth-covered chair was also a common motif in social realist paintings of the Soviet era. See Alanna Heiss et al., *The Aesthetic Arsenal: Socialist Realism under Stalin* (New York: P.S. 1, Institute for Art and Urban Resources, 1993).

50. Robert Stearns, *Robert Wilson: From a Theatre of Images* (Cincinnati: The Contemporary Arts Center, 1980), 52.

51. See Brauer, *Artists' Progress*, 6.

52. For a wittily succinct overview of the evolution of abstract painting, see Raphael Rubinstein, "The Life and Afterlife of Painting: A Descriptive Chronology of Six Decades (1920–1980)," in *Abstract Painting, Once Removed*, by Dana Friis-Hansen et al. (Houston: Contemporary Arts Museum, 1998), 28–33.

53. Glasco noted his affinity to Hofmann in an interview in 1983. See Vered Lieb, "An Interview with Joseph Glasco," *Arts Magazine* 57, no. 7 (March 1983): 120.

54. Ibid., 119.

55. William R. Thompson, in "The Lillie and Hugh Roy Cullen Sculpture Garden of the Museum of Fine Arts, Houston," by Alison de Lima Greene, Diane Planer Lovejoy, and William R. Thompson, *The Museum of Fine Arts, Houston, Bulletin* 17 (April 1996): 59.

56. Suzanne Delehanty, *Robin Utterback: Paintings 1989–1992* (Houston: Contemporary Arts Museum, 1992): n.p.

57. Ibsen Espada, quoted in Patrick McCracken, *Ibsen Espada: Veiled Messages* (Amarillo, Texas: Amarillo Art Center, 1990), n.p.

58. Lisa Phillips, *Vital Signs: Organic Abstraction from the Permanent Collection* (New York: The Whitney Museum of American Art, 1988), 11.

59. William Kelly Simpson, *Salle Werner Vaughn* (New York: La Boetie, 1983), n.p.

60. DeWitt Godfrey, unpublished statement, 1988, courtesy of the artist.

61. A related large-scale ink drawing in the museum's collection, created the following year, revisits the compositional theme of this sculpture.

62. Michael Kimmelman, "Biomorphic Profiles," *New York Times*, 21 October 1988.

63. The artist has commented that the title of the work advocates intellectual freedom, and was given in response to the climate of opinion that dominated the art world during the attacks on the National Endowment for the Arts. Terrell James, conversation with the author, 28 October 1998.

64. Terrell James, statement, in Greene and Stern, *Charles Mary Kubricht/Terrell James*, n.p.

65. Greene and Stern, *Charles Mary Kubricht/Terrell James*, n.p.

66. Marilyn A. Zeitlin, *Sally Gall: Tropical Landscapes* (Houston: Contemporary Arts Museum, 1988), n.p.

67. James Salter, *The Water's Edge: Photographs by Sally Gall* (San Francisco: Chronicle Books, 1995), n.p.

68. Michael Kennaugh, letter to the author, 29 August 1996.

69. Melvin Edwards, interview by the author, 24 June 1994.

70. Ibid. Damas was one of the leading authors to proclaim pride in his African heritage in the 1930s; he and Edwards met in New York in 1969.

71. Ibid.

72. Michael Brenson, "Lynch Fragments," in *Melvin Edwards Sculpture: A Thirty-Year Retrospective 1963–1993*, by Lucinda H. Gedeon et al. (Purchase, New York: Neuberger Museum of Art, 1993), 9.

73. The first work of this series is in the collection of the Modern Art Museum of Fort Worth.

74. Jane Livingston, "Recent Hispanic Art: Style and Influence," in Beardsley and Livingston, *Hispanic Art in the United States*, 127.

75. Thomas McEvilley, *George Smith: Sculpture and Drawings* (Burlington, Vermont: University of Vermont, Robert Hull Fleming Museum, 1999), 5.

76. George Smith, unpublished statement, c. 1994, courtesy of Sally K. Reynolds, Houston.

77. See McEvilley, *George Smith*, 7–9.

78. Rosalind Krauss, *Grids: Format and Image in Twentieth-Century Art* (New York: Pace Gallery, 1978), n.p.

79. In the early 1990s, Tracy was commissioned to create a chapel dedicated to San Martin de Porres in a Franciscan mission and medical clinic in San Miguel Pochuta, Guatemala.

80. Amy Blakemore, "Statement," *Photo Metro* 9 (September 1991): 12.

81. Susie Kalil, *Amy Blakemore, Ten Years* (Houston: Inman Gallery, 1999), 19.

82. Colpitt, *Texas Abstract*, 5–6.

83. Michael Ennis, "The Mod Squad," *Texas Monthly* 24, no. 3 (March 1996): 74.

84. Aaron Parazette, *Process, Strategy, Irony* (Houston: DiverseWorks Artspace, Inc., 1994), n.p.

85. Valerie Loupe Olsen, *Posttension: A Compelling Refinement by Joe Mancuso* (Houston: The Museum of Fine Arts, Houston, The Glassell School of Art, 1998), 14.

86. Michael Ennis, "Beneath the Surface," *Texas Monthly* [*Domain* Suppl.] 8, no. 3 (March 1990): 13.

87. Tracy Harris, quoted ibid., 13.

88. Oswald Mathia Ungers, "*Ordo, fondo et mensura*: The Criteria of Architecture," in *The Renaissance from Brunelleschi to Michelangelo: The Representation of Architecture*, by Henry A. Millon et al. (New York: Rizzoli International Publications, Inc.; Washington, D.C.: National Gallery of Art, 1994), 315.

89. Jackie Tileston, letter to the author, 23 July 1992.

90. The title is appropriated from an e.e. cummings poem, "love's function is to fabricate unknowingness." Ibid.

91. Colpitt, *Texas Abstract*, 6.

92. *Buttered Side Up*, Lawndale Art and Performance Center, Houston, 14 November–23 December 1994; *Analogs of Modernism*, McKinney Avenue Contemporary, Dallas, 7 April–21 May 1995; *Texas Abstract: New Paintings of the Nineties*, ArtPace Foundation for Contemporary Art, San Antonio, 18 November–22 December 1995; and *Abstract Painting, Once Removed*, Contemporary Arts Museum, Houston, 3 October–6 December 1998.

93. Tom Moody, *Analogs of Modernism* (Dallas: McKinney Avenue Contemporary, 1995), 3.

94. Dave Hickey, "Prom Night in Flatland," in *The Invisible Dragon: Four Essays on Beauty* (Los Angeles: Art Issues Press, 1993), 39–50.

95. David Pagel, "Once Removed from What?," in Friis-Hansen et al., *Abstract Painting, Once Removed*, 26.

96. Among the artists currently making important contributions to Postmodernist abstraction in Texas who as yet are not represented in the collection of the MFAH are Susie Rosemarin and Constance Lowe.

97. Bernard Brunon, *Buttered Side Up* (Houston: Lawndale Art and Performance Center, 1994), 6. *Buttered Side Up* subsequently traveled to the Arlington Museum of Art, Arlington, Texas; in 1996, the exhibition was reconfigured and expanded, and traveled to Hallwalls Contemporary Art Center, Buffalo, and The Koffler Gallery, Toronto.

Chapter 3: Texas Modern
pages 158–168

98. According to the artist, the title is taken from "How I Saved Roosevelt," a song in Stephen Sondheim's musical *Assassins*. Aylsworth has frequently taken titles from show tunes, and in this case he was attracted to the "singsong nature of that line … while the whole song had the mix of stirring grandeur and gross stupidity that I think I'm trying to go after in my painting." David Aylsworth, letter to the author, 9 February 1995.

99. Ibid.

100. Marek Bartelik, "Giles Lyon," *Artforum* 36, no. 8 (May 1998): 151.

101. John Goodman, "Giles Lyon at Alexandre de Folin," *Art in America* 86, no. 9 (September 1998): 134.

102. Peter Doroshenko, *Texas/Between Two Worlds* (Houston: Contemporary Arts Museum, 1993), 68.

103. Casey Williams, interviewed by the author, 10 November 1998.

104. Terrie Sultan, "The Realm of Forms as Objects of Knowledge," in *42nd Biennial Exhibition of American Painting* (Washington, D.C.: The Corcoran Gallery of Art, 1991), 15–17.

105. Michael Odom, "Michael Miller," *The New Art Examiner* 23, no. 7 (March 1996): 49.

106. Michael Miller, "To Make and Make Fun Of," unpublished statement, 1992, MFAH curatorial files.

107. Joseph Havel, letter to the author, 3 August 1994.

108. Tad Griffin, quoted in Friis-Hansen et al., *Abstract Painting, Once Removed*, 60. See also Tad Griffin, statement, in *Tad Griffin, Tom Moody, John Pomara, David Szafranski* (Dallas: Eugene Binder Gallery, 1994), 4.

109. Tad Griffin, quoted in Friis-Hansen et al., *Abstract Painting, Once Removed*, 60.

110. Rosenthal, *Abstraction in the Twentieth Century*, 1.

111. Pagel, "Once Removed from What?," 24.

112. Aaron Parazette, quoted in Friis-Hansen et al., *Abstract Painting, Once Removed*, 74.

113. Aaron Parazette, letter to the author, 1 August 1996.

114. Bill Davenport, statement, in *Irreverent Homage*, by Lynn Cazabon (Lewisburg, Pa.: Bucknell University Center Gallery, 1995), n.p.

115. Bill Davenport, unpublished statement, 1997, courtesy of Inman Gallery, Houston.

116. Randy Watson, "Simply Beautiful," *ArtLies* 16 (fall 1997): 41.

117. Robert Montgomery, letter to the author, 29 October 1998.

118. Paul Kittelson, quoted in Catherine Anspon, "Paul Kittelson Revisits Pop," *Public News* 826 (22 April 1998), 10. *Too Good to Be True* was hosted by Barbara Davis Gallery, 28 March–25 April 1998.

119. Anspon, "Paul Kittelson Revisits Pop," 10.

120. "Turning Japanese" was a 1980s hit song by The Vapors. However, the artist has disclosed that the primary inspiration for using the word "Japanese" was to refer to the paranoia many Americans feel over the Japanese dominance of computer technology.

121. Jeff Elrod, quoted in Friis-Hansen et al., *Abstract Painting, Once Removed*, 58.

122. An early version of the essay appeared in 1984 in *The Death of Art*, edited by Berel Lang (New York: Haven Publishers, 1984).

123. Arthur C. Danto, "Narratives of the End of Art," reprinted in *Encounters and Reflections: Art in the Historical Present* (Berkeley and Los Angeles: University of California Press, 1990), 344.

Chapter 4: This State I'm In
pages 172–173

1. Vernon Fisher, text accompanying *Easter Egg Hunt*, 1981 (plate 125). This text was reprinted as "When I Was a Kid," in *Navigating by the Stars: Writings by Vernon Fisher* (Chicago: Landfall Press, Inc.; Kansas City, Missouri: Karl Oskar Group, 1988), 12.

2. I am indebted to Douglas Crimp for pointing this out; see Douglas Crimp, "On the Museum's Ruins," *October* 13 (summer 1980); reprinted in Hal Foster, ed., *Postmodern Culture* (London: Pluto Press, 1983), 44.

3. Leo Steinberg, "Reflections on the State of Criticism," *Artforum* 10, no. 7 (March 1972): 49. This essay was based on a lecture originally given at the Museum of Modern Art in March 1968; it was reprinted as "Other Criteria," in Leo Steinberg, *Other Criteria: Confrontations with Twentieth-Century Art* (New York: Oxford University Press, 1972), 55–91.

4. Rosalind Krauss has written: "Almost everyone is agreed about '70s art. It is diversified, split, factionalized. Unlike the art of the last several decades, its energy does not seem to flow through a single channel for which a synthetic term, like Abstract-Expressionism, or Minimalism, might be found. In defiance of the notion of collective effort that operates behind the very idea of artistic 'movement,' '70s art is proud of its own dispersal." Rosalind Krauss, *The Originality of the Avant-Garde and Other Modernist Myths* (Cambridge, Massachusetts: The MIT Press, 1985), 196.

5. Hal Foster, "Postmodernism: A Preface," in Foster, *Postmodern Culture*, vii.

6. Ibid., xiii.

7. It is worth noting, however, that a number of earlier exhibitions explored currents that later came to be recognized as Postmodern; for example, *American Narrative/Story Art: 1967–1977*, curated by Paul Schimmel for the Contemporary Arts Museum in 1978, was among the first exhibitions to place Texas artists Terry Allen and Vernon Fisher in the larger context of the narrative and video art movements that were transforming the American scene during the 1970s.

8. Jim Edwards, *The Perfect World in Contemporary Texas Art* (San Antonio: San Antonio Museum of Art, 1991), 7.

9. Louise Dompierre, Peter Doroshenko, and James Fisher, foreword to *Texas/Between Two Worlds*, 5.

10. The title of this film was also used with the artist's permission for an exhibition of Texas art, curated by Annegreth Nill, at the Dallas Museum of Art in the fall of 1991. For a discussion of Ziebell's photographs, see the first chapter of this book.

Chapter 4: This State I'm In
pages 173–183

11. Charles Stuckey, "Rauschenberg's Everything, Everywhere Era," in *Robert Rauschenberg: A Retrospective*, by Walter Hopps and Susan Davidson (New York: Solomon R. Guggenheim Museum, 1997), 30–41.

12. Robert Rauschenberg, quoted in Richard Kostalanetz, *The Theatre of Mixed Means: An Introduction to Happenings, Kinetic Environments and Other Mixed Media Performances* (New York: The Dial Press, 1968), 93–94. See also Stuckey, "Rauschenberg's Everything, Everywhere Era," 31.

13. Acknowledging that he was treading the ground between painting and sculpture, Rauschenberg adopted the term "Combine" to describe these works.

14. Julia Blaut, "Transfer Drawings, Prints, and Silkscreened Paintings: 1958–70," in Hopps and Davidson, *Rauschenberg: A Retrospective*, 156. Rauschenberg's first large-scale essay into this technique resulted in thirty-five illustrations for *Dante's Inferno*, 1958–60 (The Museum of Modern Art, New York).

15. Esther Sparks, *Universal Limited Art Editions, A History and Catalogue: The First Twenty-Five Years* (Chicago: The Art Institute of Chicago; New York: Harry N. Abrams, 1989), 222.

16. In an interview of 1979, Suzanne Bloom noted that MANUAL had dual references: "Some of the projects we do *are* more didactic in nature, and they are more in the category of a manual toward reinvestigating or reconsidering art history, or various aspects of cultural history. The other type of activity that we seem to do as MANUAL is more phenomenological, more about experience, and so the touching aspect of the name still applies." Suzanne Bloom, quoted in Anne Wilkes Tucker, "Anne Tucker interview with Ed Hill and Suzanne Bloom (MANUAL)," *Suzanne Bloom and Ed Hill (MANUAL): Research and Collaboration* (Houston: The Museum of Fine Arts, Houston, 1980), 10.

17. Walter Benjamin, "The Work of Art in the Age of Mechanical Reproduction," in *Illuminations*, ed. Hannah Arendt, trans. Harry Zorn (New York: Random House, 1988), 217–51.

18. Ibid., 220.

19. Ed Hill, quoted in A. W. Tucker, "Anne Tucker interview with Ed Hill and Suzanne Bloom (MANUAL)," 30.

20. Grynsztejn, *Vernon Fisher*, 12–13.

21. Later that year, Fisher incorporated all three texts in an installation titled *Breaking the Code* in the Fort Worth Art Museum's *The Southern Voice* exhibition. The installation and accompanying texts are reproduced ibid., 84–85.

22. Fisher returned to this text again in 1983, creating *When I Was a Kid*, now in the collection of Arthur and Carol Goldberg. Illustrated in Marge Goldwater, *Past/Imperfect: Eric Fischl, Vernon Fisher, Laurie Simmons* (Minneapolis: Walker Art Center, 1987), 25.

23. Ibid., 19.

24. This unpublished interview is from a panel discussion between Vernon Fisher and Madeleine Grynsztejn. See Chapter 1, note 68.

25. Allen's *Juarez* exhibition was a remarkable multimedia event. One half of the museum was devoted to the *Juarez* series of paintings and drawings; the other half was set up as an impromptu theater, with a slide-show of the *Juarez* series timed to coordinate with a recording of Allen's *Juarez* country-western song cycle. See Paul Schimmel, Michael Walls, and David Hickey, *Terry Allen: Juarez Series* (Houston: Contemporary Arts Museum, 1975).

26. The series has extended over eight years and has comprised over sixty works. The title is a pun on "euthanasia"; the subtitles of individual works within the *Youth in Asia* series usually have similar double entendres. *Truth Are Consequences*, for example, refers to the New Mexico town, Truth or Consequences, near where Allen currently lives, as well as to the popular television contest show.

27. Craig Adcock, "Image/Music/Text: Terry Allen's *Youth in Asia* Series," in *Terry Allen: Youth in Asia*, by Craig Adcock, Roxy Gordon, and Dave Hickey. (Winston-Salem, North Carolina: Southeastern Center for Contemporary Art, 1993), 14.

28. Terry Allen, quoted in Kristine McKenna, "Death and Taxes," *L. A. Weekly*, 24–30 June 1988.

29. Charles Jencks, quoted in Marti Mayo, *Gael Stack* (Houston: University of Houston, Sarah Campbell Blaffer Gallery, 1989), 17.

30. Gael Stack, statement, in Rose and Kalil, *Fresh Paint*, 170.

31. Mayo, *Gael Stack*, 18. Mayo traces the thematic origins of *The Christmas Picture* to a painting of 1987 titled *Beloved*, inspired by Toni Morrison's novel of the same title, where a lost child haunts the narrative. This work was created in collaboration with Houston poet Olive Hershey. See also Landay and Barthelme, *One + One*, 23.

32. Gael Stack, quoted in Patricia C. Johnson, "Painter Gael Stack's Webs of Meaning," *Houston Chronicle*, 19 February 1989.

33. Sue Graze, *Al Souza: Concentrations 6* (Dallas: Dallas Museum of Fine Arts, 1982), n.p.

34. Sergei Eisenstein, *Film Form*, 1949, quoted in Michael M. Floss, *Matrix 124: Al Souza* (Berkeley, California: University Art Museum, 1989), n. p.

35. Interview by the author, 12 July 1989.

36. Owen Jones, *The Grammar of Ornament*, 1856, quoted in Ernst Gombrich, *The Sense of Order: A Study in the Psychology of Decorative Art* (Ithaca, New York: Cornell University Press, 1979), 52.

37. Craig Owens, "The Discourse of Others: Feminists and Postmodernism," in Foster, *Postmodern Culture*, 57.

38. Dana Friis-Hansen, "Other Narratives," in *Other Narratives*, by Dana Friis-Hansen, Robert Atkins, and Greg Tate (Houston: Contemporary Arts Museum, 1999), 12.

39. John Beardsley, "And/Or: Hispanic Art, American Culture," in Beardsley and Livingston, *Hispanic Art in the United States*, 58.

40. César Augusto Martínez, quoted in Beardsley and Livingston, *Hispanic Art in the United States*, 206.

41. César Augusto Martínez, letter to the author, 1 August 1992.

42. Ibid.

43. Jacinto Quirarte, *César Martínez: Reflejos Mestizos* (El Paso: El Paso Museum of Art, 1994), n.p.

44. Benito Huerta, *Luis Jiménez: Working-Class Heroes, Images from the Popular Culture* (Kansas City, Missouri: ExhibitsUSA, 1997), 7.

45. Dave Hickey, "Luis Jiménez and the Incarnation of Democracy," in Huerta, *Luis Jiménez: Working-Class Heroes*, 27.

46. The plight of the Mexican laborer has a strong history in the work of such Mexican artists as David Alfaro Siqueiros, who in the early 1930s similarly paid tribute to those threatened by deportation. See Siqueiros's *Peasant Mother [Madre Campesina]*, c. 1931 (Museo de Arte Moderno, INBA, Mexico City).

47. The artist's paternal grandparents entered the United States in this fashion. Madeleine Grynsztejn has remarked of *Border Crossing [Cruzando el Rio Bravo]*: "Joined within a single uninterrupted Fiberglas column, a man, a woman, and a child are caught at the very moment of transition between two worlds, a sort of 'Chicano-ized' *Flight into Egypt.*" Grynsztejn, *La Frontera: Art About the Mexico/United States Border Experience*, 35.

48. Luis Jiménez, statement, in *Man on Fire/El Hombre en llamas: Luis Jiménez* by James Moore et al. (Albuquerque, New Mexico: The Albuquerque Museum, 1994), 146.

Chapter 4: This State I'm In
pages 183–198

49. Greg Tate, "In Praise of Shadow Boxers: The Crises of Originality and Authority in African-American Visual Arts vs. The Wu-Tang Clan," in Friis-Hansen, Atkins, and Tate, *Other Narratives*, 39.

50. The artist has noted "*Josephine* is my theme of the dance.... I've always been an admirer of the late Josephine Baker, and was compelled by the [recently aired] HBO version of her life to do the painting." Floyd Elbert Newsum, Jr., letter to the author, 3 February 1992.

51. Andrea D. Barnwell, "Like the Gypsy's Daughter," in *Rhapsodies in Black: Art of the Harlem Renaissance*, by David A. Bailey et al., (London: Hayward Gallery, 1997), 87–88.

52. The phrase originated with a comment from a friend as she and Lawrence were forced to wait unduly for a table in a restaurant. See Peter Doroshenko and Lynn M. Herbert, *3-D Rupture: Gallery Notes* (Houston: Contemporary Arts Museum, 1993), n.p.

53. Annette Lawrence, letter to the author, July 1993.

54. Marilyn Kern-Foxworth has pointed out that the title *Forever Free* is common among African-American artists, citing examples by Sargent Johnson and Edmonia Lewis. See Marilyn Kern-Foxworth, "Painting Positive Pictures of Images that Injure: Michael Ray Charles' Dueling Dualities," in *Michael Ray Charles: An American Artist's Work, 1989–1997*, by Don Bacigalupi et al. (Houston: The University of Houston, Sarah Campbell Blaffer Gallery, 1997), 10.

55. Michael Ray Charles, quoted in Calvin Reid, *Michael Ray Charles* (New York: Tony Shafrazi Gallery, 1998), 8.

56. See Susan Chadwick, "Artist Updates Black Images of Yesteryear," *Houston Post*, 13 July 1993.

57. Michael Ray Charles, letter to the author, 22 July 1994.

58. Reid, *Michael Ray Charles*, 6–7.

59. *Corporeal Politics* originated at the MIT List Visual Arts Center, in Cambridge, Massachusetts; *Post Human* originated at FAE Musée d'Art Contemporaine in Lausanne, Switzerland; and *Identity and Alterity: Figures of the Body 1895–1995* originated at Palazzo Grassi and the Museo Correr in Venice, Italy.

60. Linda Nochlin, *The Body in Pieces: The Fragment as a Metaphor of Modernity* (New York: Thames and Hudson, 1994), 54–55.

61. Rachel Hecker, unpublished statement, 1992, courtesy of Texas Gallery, MFAH curatorial files.

62. Hecker has revealed, for example, that the illustrator and caricaturist Jack Hamm provided the source for the leering face. See Annegreth Nill, *Encounters 6: Rachel Hecker* (Dallas: The Dallas Museum of Art, 1995), n.p.

63. Ann Cvetkovich, "Almost Heaven," *Grand Street* 14, no. 4 (spring 1996): 185.

64. Gary McKay, "Young at Art," *Houston Metropolitan* 17, no. 3 (December 1990): 50.

65. Originally titled *My Gang Will Get You*, this series was retitled by Cowie in 1993. The original title in part referred to the hate-crime attack on Paul Broussard, a gay man who was murdered in Houston's Montrose district; the artist chose the later title to get away from the fact that "My Gang" could be understood as the collages themselves. (Jeffrey Cowie, letter to the author, 5 May 1993.) The dedication is in tribute to Sheila Rosenstein, wife of the art critic Harris Rosenstein, who in her own right was one of the chief champions of young artists in Houston.

66. Jeffrey Cowie, letter to the author, 5 May 1993.

67. Sharon Engelstein, letter to the author, 30 January 1993.

68. Susie Kalil, "3-D Falls Flat," *Houston Press*, 4 March 1993.

69. Cazabon's photographic sequences of this period reflected Lacan's statement: "I must, to begin with, insist on the following: in the scopic field, the gaze is outside, I am looked at, that is to say, I am the picture." Jacques Lacan, *Four Fundamentals of Psychoanalysis*, quoted in Lynn Cazabon, statement, *1992 Core Fellows Exhibition* (Houston: The Museum of Fine Arts, Houston, The Glassell School of Art, 1992), n.p.

70. Lynn Cazabon, letter to the author, 1 June 1999.

71. Thomas Laqueur, "Clio Looks at Corporeal Politics," in *Corporeal Politics*, by Donald Hall, Thomas Laqueur, and Helaine Posner (Cambridge, Massachusetts: MIT List Visual Arts Center; Boston: Beacon Press, 1992), 18.

72. Sue Graze, *Concentrations: Bert Long* (Dallas: Dallas Museum of Art, 1988), n.p.

73. Bert Long, statement, in Rose and Kalil, *Fresh Paint*, 148.

74. Kyle Young, letter to the author, 23 August 1996.

75. Patricia Covo Johnson, *Contemporary Art in Texas* (Roseville East, New South Wales, Australia: Craftsman House, 1995), 36.

76. Jesse Amado, interview by Frances Colpitt in *ArtPace: New Works for a New Space*, by Robert Storr (San Antonio: The Pace Roberts Foundation for Contemporary Art, 1995), 16.

77. Amado has commented that "I've always thought of drawing as one of the most intimate art practices." Jesse Amado, quoted in Dana Friis-Hansen, *Jesse Amado: Renascence* (Houston: Contemporary Arts Museum), n.p.

78. Friis-Hansen, *Jesse Amado*, n.p.

79. Sue Graze, "Linda Ridgway: Lines of Contemplation," in *Linda Ridgway: A Survey, The Poetics of Form*, by Sue Graze and Charles Wylie (Houston: The Museum of Fine Arts, Houston, The Glassell School of Art; Dallas: Dallas Museum of Art, 1997), 20.

80. Linda Ridgway, unpublished statement, c. 1993, MFAH curatorial files.

81. Dante Alighieri, *The Divine Comedy*, canto III, quoted in David McGee, statement, in Havel and Lowe, *Fresh Visions/New Voices*, 18.

82. See Doroshenko, *Texas/Between Two Worlds*, 44.

83. Like other works of these series, *Sperm Rush* is painted on newsprint mounted on canvas, a technique which not only offers a variegated surface, but also, as McGee has pointed out, prompted him to further contextual readings: "The daily newspapers became an interesting source of irritation for me in regards to the making of my own work—it became impossible for me to ignore all the different social ills of society while painting about mine." David McGee, letter to the author, April 1994.

84. David McGee, *Landscape of the Soul* (Houston: Project Row Houses, 1994).

85. Lynn M. Herbert, *Rachel Ranta: The Discrete Inquiry* (Houston: The Contemporary Arts Museum, 1994), n.p.

86. Patricia C. Johnson, "Discrete Work Reveals Intriguing Images," *Houston Chronicle*, 26 May 1994.

87. Jim Edwards, *The Perfect World in Contemporary Texas Art* (San Antonio: The San Antonio Museum of Art, 1992), 9.

88. Fredric Jameson, "Postmodernism and Consumer Culture," in Foster, *Postmodern Culture*, 112.

89. Ibid.

90. Charles Dee Mitchell, "Thoughts on Randy Twaddle," *Dallas Observer*, 12 September 1985.

91. Randy Twaddle, unpublished statement, 25 January 1988, courtesy of DWG Gallery, Dallas, MFAH curatorial files.

92. In a post-Duchampian gesture, Mark Flood is the name that John Peters formally adopted early in his career as his *nom d'atelier*, signifying his production as a visual artist; he has also used the name Perry Webb to signify his work as a musician. The artist has also offered alternate versions of his life, citing, for example, varying birth dates and places of birth in interviews and biographical statements. In 1999, Peters legally changed his name to Flood.

Chapter 4: This State I'm In
pages 199–204

93. Mark Flood, statement, in *Avenues of Departure: Twelve Houston Artists*, by William Steen (New Orleans: Contemporary Arts Center, 1992), 17.

94. The first version of the painting was created in 1989 and was titled *Your Ad Here* (this work is presently in a private collection in Houston); at the invitation of the Museum of Fine Arts, Houston, Flood created a second version in 1991, making clear the commissioned status of the work by the title *Museum Piece*.

95. Andy Warhol's *Death and Disaster* silkscreens were exhibited in Houston at The Menil Collection in 1988. Flood, working as an exhibition technician at the Menil during this period, would have become intimately aware of Warhol's example.

96. Mark Flood, writing as Fake Barbara Rose and Fake Susie Kalil, "Preface: Primal Screen" (Houston: Treebeard's Restaurant, 1989), courtesy of the artist, MFAH curatorial files. Flood had lampooned museums earlier, in the lyrics of Culturecide's single, "Consider Museums as Concentration Camps," released in 1980.

97. Mark Flood, quoted in Susan Chadwick, "'Primal Screen' Lampoons Local Art Movement," *Houston Post*, 8 December 1989.

98. Dianna Solis, "He Avoids the Risk of Censorship Just by Not Needing Endowments," *The Wall Street Journal*, 9 August 1990. See also Kevin Cunningham, "This is Not an Art Show," *Houston Press*, 7 December 1989.

99. Geoffrey Batchen, "Phantasm: Digital Imaging and the Death of Photography," *Aperture* 136 (summer 1994): 48.

100. Osamu James Nakagawa, unpublished statement, 1994, courtesy of McMurtrey Gallery, Houston.

101. Osamu James Nakagawa, "Portfolios: Computer Photomontage," *Aperture* 136 (summer 1994): 27.

102. Jack Massing, quoted in Sam Howe Verhovek, "In Performance: Life Imitates Art Imitating Life," *New York Times*, 9 August 1995.

103. In 1998, The Art Guys collaborated with designer Todd Oldham to create *SUITS: The Clothes Make the Man*. Oldham tailored two gray business suits for The Art Guys, who in turn marketed the project to potential clients, who for a fee could have their logos embroidered on the suits. See Mimi Swartz, "The Creative Life," *The New Yorker* (3 November 1997): 47; and Shaila Dewan, "Absolutely for Sale," *Houston Press*, 19–25 March 1998.

104. Dave Hickey, "Laughter Takes the Bus," in *The Art Guys: Think Twice 1983–1995*, by Lynn M. Herbert et al. (Houston: Contemporary Arts Museum, 1995), 16.

105. The title *Chastity* confers a sexual aura on the artwork, and further suggests the hesitant balance between inaction and commitment.

106. Nic Nicosia, quoted in Carlozzi and Block, *50 Texas Artists*, 75.

107. Elizabeth Ward, *Reinventing Reality: Five Texas Photographers* (Houston: University of Houston, Sarah Campbell Blaffer Gallery, 1990), 6.

108. As the artist has revealed, his fascination with death stems in part from the traumatic experience of witnessing the aftermath of the notorious mass-murder/suicide bombing in 1959 at Houston's Poe Elementary School. See Doroshenko, *Texas/Between Two Worlds*, 56.

109. Peter C. Marzio, *Rube Goldberg: His Life and Work* (New York: Harper & Row Publishers, 1973), 197.

110. In 1988 Altman began to work as Fisher's studio assistant in Fort Worth; over the following decade she has continued to work with him.

111. Helen Altman, quoted in Janet Kutner, "The Reality Factor," the *Dallas Morning News*, 31 May 1990.

112. As Altman has documented, *Signal* was commissioned by Dallas collectors Nona and Richard Barrett, who encouraged Altman to expand a work in process. Letter to the author, 16 September 1999.

113. Ibid.

114. Frances Colpitt, "Helen Altman at Barry Whistler," *Art in America* 83, no. 6 (June 1995): 110.

pages 220–221
North facade of the Caroline Wiess Law Building, designed by Ludwig Mies van der Rohe in 1954–56, completed in 1973. Photograph c. 1973.

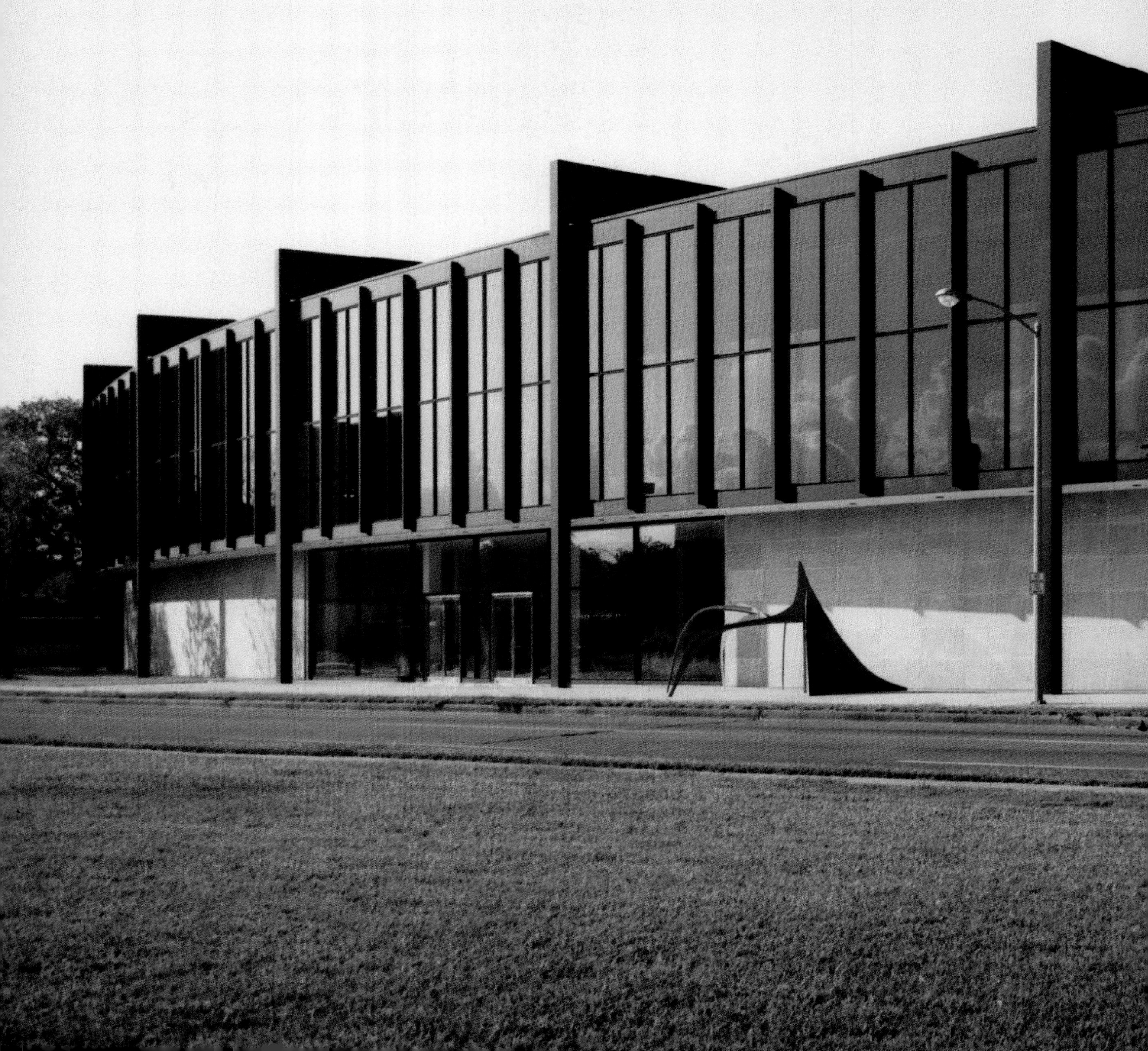

Biographies
Chronology of Exhibitions of Texas Art
Selected Bibliography

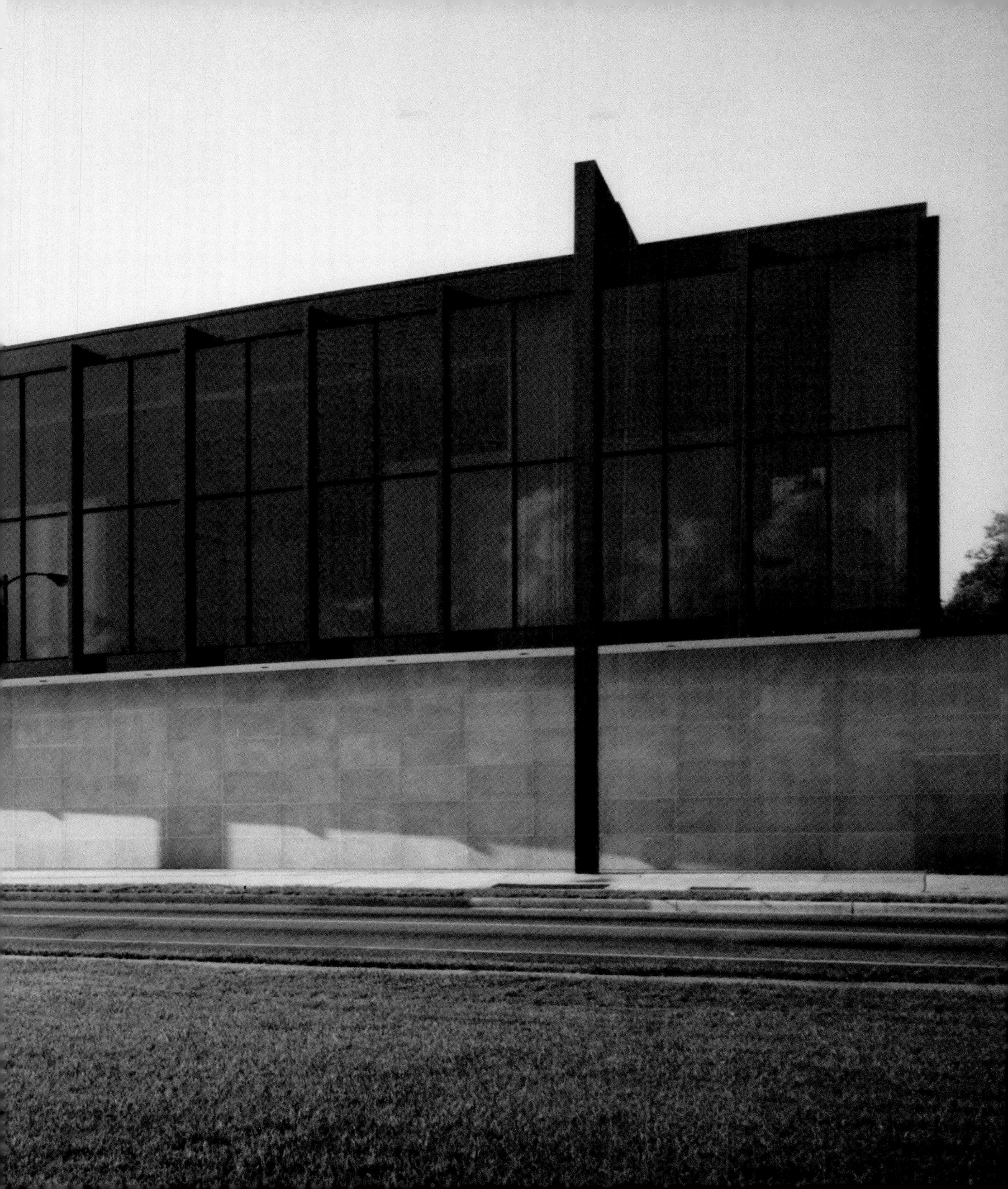

Biographies

Robert Montgomery, Monica Garza,
Jason A. Goldstein, and Alison de Lima Greene

❏ **JOHN ALEXANDER**
  Born 1945, Beaumont, Texas
  Lives in Amagansett, New York

John Alexander brings the gestural intensity of Abstract Expressionism to his dynamic figurative compositions. Alexander received a B.F.A. in 1968 from Lamar University in Beaumont, Texas, and an M.F.A. in 1970 from Southern Methodist University in Dallas. He moved to Houston in 1972 to join the faculty of the University of Houston. In 1975, Alexander was the focus of a solo exhibition at the Contemporary Arts Museum in Houston. Coinciding with this exhibition, his friend James Surls had a solo show in an adjoining gallery at the museum. When Surls joined Alexander on the faculty of the University of Houston the following year, the pair became a dynamic and influential force on the Houston art scene. In 1979, however, Alexander left Houston for New York, where he was included in a group exhibition at Betty Parsons Gallery later that year. The following year, the Corcoran Gallery of Art in Washington, D.C., recognized him with a solo exhibition. His profile in New York grew throughout the 1980s, but he also maintained links with Houston, participating in a 1981 exhibition at the Lawndale Annex of the University of Houston. Alexander was awarded a Solomon R. Guggenheim Memorial Foundation Fellowship in 1984. The Metropolitan Museum of Art in New York included his work in presentations of their new acquisitions in 1984 and 1985. His work also was featured in *Fresh Paint: The Houston School* at the MFAH in 1985. The museum featured him again in *Directions and Diversity: Twentieth-Century Art in the Museum Collection* in 1988. The following year, Alexander had a solo exhibition at the Art Museum of Southeast Texas in his hometown of Beaumont. He completed a commission for the National Dance Institute in New York in 1992, participated in Leo Castelli Gallery's thirtieth anniversary exhibition in New York in 1993, and had a solo show at Meredith Long & Company in Houston in 1995. In the mid-1990s, Alexander turned his attention from overt Expressionism. Exhibitions at Marlborough Gallery in New York in 1996 and Gerald Peters Gallery in Dallas in 1997 revealed a more reflective vision, alluding to the landscape of Alexander's Southeast Texas childhood.   —*RM*

Selected References:
Livingston, Jane. *John Alexander*. Washington,
  D.C.: Corcoran Gallery of Art, 1980.
Beardsley, John. "John Alexander." *Art International* 26, no. 3 (July–August 1983): 38–42.
Rose, Barbara, and Susie Kalil. *Fresh Paint: The
  Houston School*. Austin: Texas Monthly Press;
  Houston: The Museum of Fine Arts, Houston, 1985.
Plimpton, George. *John Alexander*. New York:
  Marlborough Gallery, 1994.

❏ **TERRY ALLEN**
  Born 1943, Wichita, Kansas
  Lives in Santa Fe, New Mexico

Terry Allen has established a strong identity both as a visual artist and as a singer/songwriter. Allen grew up in Lubbock, Texas, where he briefly attended Texas Tech University. In 1962, he married his high-school sweetheart, the writer and actress Jo Harvey Koontz, and they moved to Los Angeles. Allen studied at the Chouinard Art Institute, where he received a B.F.A. in 1966, and taught briefly before joining the faculty of California State University in Fresno in 1971. During 1975, he exhibited his *Juarez* series at the Contemporary Arts Museum in Houston and released a record of his songs with the same title. *Juarez* introduced tales of contemporary drifters wandering aimlessly through the Southwest, a theme that continually recurs in his work. Allen was included in the 1977 Whitney Biennial, signifying a growing national reputation. In the early 1980s, he began a series titled *Youth in Asia* (a pun on "euthanasia") dealing with the social consequences of America's involvement in the Vietnam War. He participated in the 1982 Sydney Biennial and was the focus of an exhibition at the La Jolla Museum of Contemporary Art in La Jolla, California, the following year. During these years, he also began an affiliation with Moody Gallery in Houston. In 1987, Allen was included in the *Documenta* exhibition in Kassel, Germany. He left California that year to settle in Santa Fe, New Mexico. Allen had a solo show at the San Francisco Art Institute in 1989, and he was the focus of a 1992 traveling exhibition organized by the Southeastern Center for Contemporary Art in Winston-Salem, North Carolina. In 1993, *Chippy (Diaries of a West Texas Hooker)*, Allen's theatrical collaboration with his wife, Jo Harvey Allen, premiered at the American Music Theatre Festival in Philadelphia. The following year, *Poison Amor*, his collaboration with James Drake, was presented at Blue Star Art Space in San Antonio and the Sarah Campbell Blaffer Gallery at the University of Houston. In 1999, he completed a commission for Terminal B of the George Bush Intercontinental Airport in Houston and Moody Gallery exhibited the working drawings for this project.   —*RM*

Selected References:
Schimmel, Paul, et al. *Terry Allen: Juarez Series*.
  Houston: Contemporary Arts Museum, 1975.
Forsha, Linda. *Rooms and Stories: Recent Works
  by Terry Allen*. La Jolla, California: La Jolla
  Museum of Contemporary Art, 1983.
Margolis, Nancy H. *Terry Allen: Youth in Asia*.
  Winston-Salem, North Carolina: Southeastern
  Center for Contemporary Art, 1992.
Brooks, Rosetta. *Poison Amor*. San Antonio: Blue
  Star Art Space, 1994.

❏ **HELEN ALTMAN**
  Born 1958, Tuscaloosa, Alabama
  Lives in Fort Worth, Texas

Helen Altman creates assemblages and installations using ready-made domestic objects. Altman received a B.F.A. from the University of Alabama in Tuscaloosa in 1981 and an M.A. from the same institution in 1986. Later that year, she moved to Denton, Texas, and entered the graduate program at the University of North Texas, Denton, where she studied with Vernon Fisher and received an M.F.A. in 1989. The following year, she won the Juror's Choice Award in the Texas Fine Arts Association's *New American Talent* exhibition at the Laguna Gloria Art Museum in Austin. In 1991, Altman was represented in the group show *The Perfect World in Contemporary Texas Art* at the San Antonio Museum of Art. That same year, she moved to Fort Worth, where she began working as Vernon Fisher's studio assistant. In the early 1990s, Altman became recognized widely around Texas for her distinctive assemblages of electric fire log components. During these years, she began affiliations with Barry Whistler Gallery in Dallas and Hiram Butler Gallery in Houston. In 1994, she was featured in *Texas/Between Two Worlds* at the Contemporary Arts Museum in Houston. During 1996, Altman was seen in *Schemata: Drawings by Sculptors* at the Glassell School of Art and in *Transformers: A Moving Experience* at the Auckland City Art Gallery in New Zealand. In 1997, she was a visiting professor at the University of Texas at Arlington, and her solo exhibition, *Just Ahead: Installations by Helen Altman*, was presented at the Art Museum of Southeast Texas in Beaumont and at the Galveston Arts Center. In 1999, Altman was featured in the inaugural exhibition of Dunn and Brown Contemporary in Dallas.   —*RM*

Selected References:
Doroshenko, Peter. *Texas/Between Two Worlds*.
  Houston: Contemporary Arts Museum, 1993.
Colpitt, Frances. "Helen Altman at Barry Whistler."
  Art in America 83, no. 6 (June 1995): 110–11.
______. *Just Ahead: Installations by Helen Altman*.
  Beaumont, Texas: Art Museum of Southeast
  Texas, 1997.

❏ **JESSE AMADO**
  Born 1951, San Antonio, Texas
  Lives in San Antonio, Texas

Jesse Amado's sculptures, drawings, and installations balance reductive and decorative elements to create a subtle and elegant language. In 1974, Amado began studying English at the University of Texas at

Austin. After graduating in 1977, he returned to San Antonio, where he began working as a firefighter. In 1981, he enrolled in art classes at San Antonio College, thus marking the beginning of his career as an artist. Amado studied art at the University of Texas at San Antonio in the mid-1980s and received a B.F.A. in 1987. In 1989, he had his first solo show at the Koehler Cultural Art Center in San Antonio and he also was included in the Texas Fine Arts Association's touring exhibition *New American Talent.* Amado continued part-time studies at the University of Texas at San Antonio, receiving an M.F.A. in 1990. During the 1990s, he emerged as one of San Antonio's most prominent artists. He had solo exhibitions at the Philadelphia Fabric Workshop in 1991 and the Galveston Arts Center in 1992. He began showing with Davis/McClain Gallery in Houston in 1993 and with Milagros Contemporary in San Antonio in 1994. That same year, Amado was selected, along with Annette Messager and Felix Gonzalez-Torres, to be among the first artists-in-residence at the ArtPace Foundation for Contemporary Art in San Antonio. He had a solo show at Carla Stellweg Gallery in New York in 1995. The following year, he created an installation, *Renascence,* for the Contemporary Arts Museum in Houston. In 1997, he presented a solo show at Sala Diaz, San Antonio, and was featured in the Kwangju Biennale in South Korea.   —RM

Selected References:
Doroshenko, Peter. *Texas/Between Two Worlds.* Houston: Contemporary Arts Museum, 1993.
Storr, Robert. *For Immediate Occupancy: ArtPace/ New Works for a New Space.* San Antonio: ArtPace Foundation for Contemporary Art, 1995.
Friis-Hansen, Dana. *Jesse Amado: Renascence.* Houston: Contemporary Arts Museum, 1996.

❏ THE ART GUYS

Michael Galbreth
Born 1956, Philadelphia, Pennsylvania
Lives in Houston, Texas

Jack Massing
Born 1959, Buffalo, New York
Lives in Houston, Texas

The Art Guys create pieces inspired by the Fluxus movement's principle of transforming ordinary actions into works of art, and their objects and performances often contain subtle wordplays and visual puns. Michael Galbreth studied art and creative writing at Middle Tennessee State University in Murfreesboro before receiving a B.F.A. from Memphis State University in 1980. He entered the graduate program of the University of Houston in 1981. Jack Massing studied at Niagara Community College in Niagara Falls in the late 1970s and moved to Houston in 1980. Galbreth and Massing met in 1982, at the opening of an exhibition at the Lawndale Annex of the University of Houston in which James Surls had included Massing's work. Surls encouraged Massing to complete his B.F.A. studies in Houston, and Galbreth and Massing began collaborating shortly thereafter. In 1983, they staged their first performance as the Art Guys, *The Art Guys*

Agree on Painting, at Lawndale and presented an installation of collaborative work at Studio One in Houston. They completed their respective degrees at the University of Houston in 1984. That same year, they presented a performance, *Blue Sunday,* selling objects outside Houston City Hall that were banned by local laws from sale on Sundays. They had exhibitions at Hiram Butler Gallery and the Midtown Art Center in 1985. The following year, they were included in *Collaborators: Artists Working Together in Houston, 1969–1986,* at the Glassell School of Art. Continuing a series of performances integrated into the urban environment of Houston, in 1988 the Art Guys spent an entire twenty-four hours in a booth in a Denny's restaurant for a piece marking the winter solstice. They were featured in *Project Diomede,* a 1989 exhibition at P.S. 1 in New York, and the following year they began an affiliation with Barry Whistler Gallery in Dallas. In 1992, they created the performance piece *Keep a Dime between Your Knees* at the Dallas Museum of Art, and in 1994 they presented *Art Guise Unplugged* at the Modern Art Museum of Fort Worth. During 1995, the Art Guys completed a residency at Capp Street Project in San Francisco and they were the focus of a major retrospective at the Contemporary Arts Museum in Houston, a show that traveled to the Tyler Museum of Art. The following year, they had exhibitions at Blue Star Art Space in San Antonio and the Kempner Museum of Contemporary Art and Design in Kansas City. They were the focus of 1997 exhibitions at Hallwalls Contemporary Art Center in Buffalo, New York, and the Austin Museum of Art. In 1998, the Art Guys launched their *SUITS* project in collaboration with fashion designer Todd Oldham, providing a commentary on the ubiquitous nature of commerce and the role of the artist as celebrity by selling advertising spaces on their own clothes.   —RM

Selected References:
Landay, Janet. *Collaborators: Artists Working Together in Houston, 1969–1986.* Houston: The Museum of Fine Arts, Houston, The Glassell School of Art, 1986.
Doroshenko, Peter. *Texas/Between Two Worlds.* Houston: Contemporary Arts Museum, 1993.
Mayo, Marti, Lynn M. Herbert, Dave Hickey, Walter Hopps, and David Levi-Strauss. *The Art Guys: Think Twice, 1983–1995.* Houston: Contemporary Arts Museum, 1995.
Thompson, William R. "Just between Guys: The Art Guys Think Twice at the Contemporary Arts Museum." *Spot* 15, no. 1 (spring 1996): 8–9.

❏ DAVID AYLSWORTH

Born 1966, Tiffin, Ohio
Lives in Houston, Texas

David Aylsworth brings a dynamic sense of play and an art-historical savvy to his painterly abstractions. After graduating from the B.F.A. program at Kent State University, Ohio, in 1989, Aylsworth moved to Houston to attend the Core Residency Program at the Glassell School of Art. He had his first solo exhibition at Inman Gallery in 1992, and also was featured that year in *The Big Show* at Lawndale Art and

Performance Center in Houston. In 1993, Aylsworth participated in the *Texas Biennial Exhibition,* sponsored by Dallas Artists Research and Exhibition (DARE). The following year, he collaborated with Bill Davenport and Giles Lyon in presenting *Buttered Side Up,* a three-person exhibition at Lawndale; during 1996 and 1997, this exhibition toured in expanded form to Hallwalls Contemporary Art Center in Buffalo, New York, and the Koffler Gallery in North York, Ontario. In 1996, Aylsworth was included in *Texas Modern and Postmodern* at the MFAH and *The Houston Area Exhibition* at the Sarah Campbell Blaffer Gallery at the University of Houston. He was featured in *Critic's Choice* at the Dallas Visual Art Center in 1997. The following year, he exhibited in New York in *The Texas Show* at ABC No Rio and in Galveston in *Organic Produce* at the Galveston Arts Center. In 1999, Aylsworth was featured in the *Five Artists: New Work* exhibition curated by Bill Lassiter for DiverseWorks Artspace in Houston.   —ALG

Selected References:
Brunon, Bernard. "Basic Attitude." In *Buttered Side Up: David Aylsworth, Bill Davenport, Giles Lyon,* by Bernard Brunon. Houston: Lawndale Art and Performance Center, 1994.
Emenhiser, Karen. "Puerile Utopias." In *Buttered Side Up: David Aylsworth, Bill Davenport, Giles Lyon,* by Bernard Brunon. Buffalo, New York: Hallwalls Contemporary Art Center; North York, Ontario: Koffler Gallery, 1996.

❏ FRED BALDWIN and WENDY WATRISS

Fred Baldwin
Born 1929, Lausanne, Switzerland
Lives in Houston, Texas

Wendy Watriss
Born 1943, San Francisco, California
Lives in Houston, Texas

Together and individually, the photographers Fred Baldwin and Wendy Watriss have completed important documentary projects that eloquently record aspects of Texas life and the evolution of diverse Texan cultures. Baldwin received a B.A. from Columbia University in New York in 1955, and Watriss earned a B.A. from New York University a decade later. Before they met, both photographers pursued independent careers. During the late 1950s, Baldwin did freelance work for *Sports Illustrated* and *National Geographic.* In 1963, working as a volunteer, he documented the coming of age of the Civil Rights movement in Savannah, Georgia. Reflecting his commitment to social issues, Baldwin served as the administrative director for a branch of the Peace Corps in Sarawak, Borneo, from 1964 to 1966. He returned to New York in 1967 and resumed work as a freelance photojournalist. Watriss began her career as a newspaper reporter in St. Petersburg, Florida, where she worked from 1965 to 1967. In the late 1960s, she worked for National Educational Television in New York and as a foreign correspondent for *Newsweek* in Eastern Europe. Watriss and Baldwin met in 1970, and in 1971 they began a collaborative project, planning to travel through the back roads of the southern United States to record life in small towns. After touring Tennessee, Arkansas, and Mississippi that year, they entered Texas. They realized the state concealed layers of cultural diversity that challenged its stereotype as the "western frontier," and decided to adapt their project to focus on the complexity of the Texas experience. Returning to Texas in 1975, they set up a makeshift darkroom in Grimes County, about seventy miles northwest of Houston. Over the next two years, they minutely documented life in the area, and their photographs of this community remain on permanent exhibition at the courthouse in Anderson, Texas. Baldwin and Watriss subsequently moved to Houston, and in 1978 they received a fellowship from the National Endowment for the Humanities to photograph the Hill Country around Austin (this part of their Texas project was published in 1991 in the book *Coming to Terms: The German Hill Country of Texas*). In the early 1980s, they each completed important individual projects. Baldwin published his photographs of the Civil Rights movement in the book "*. . . We Ain't What We Used To Be . . .*" and Watriss completed projects documenting such controversial subjects as the effects of Agent Orange on Vietnam veterans and the U.S. government's support of guerrilla warfare in Nicaragua. Her Vietnam veterans project was awarded the Oskar Barnack Prize in 1982 from the World Press Foundation. In 1984, Baldwin and Watriss joined forces with the Houston community to found FotoFest, a biennial festival of photography that attracts an international audience to Houston.—*RM*

Selected References:

Rosenstein, Harris. *Frederick Baldwin and Wendy Watriss: Photographs from Grimes County, Texas.* Houston: Rice University Institute for the Arts, 1977.

Horne, Jed. "Tracking Agent Orange." *Life* 4, no. 12 (December 1981): 65–70.

Baldwin, Frederick. "*. . .We Ain't What We Used To Be . . .*" Savannah, Georgia: Telfair Press, 1983.

Watriss, Wendy, and Fred Baldwin. *Coming to Terms: The German Hill Country of Texas.* College Station, Texas: Texas A&M Press, 1991.

❏ DAVID BATES
Born 1952, Dallas, Texas
Lives in Dallas, Texas

David Bates has made the landscape and people of the Gulf Coast the central subjects of his affectionate and vivid paintings and sculptures. Bates studied at Southern Methodist University in Dallas, where he received a B.F.A. in 1975 and an M.F.A. in 1976. During 1977, he participated in the Independent Study Program at the Whitney Museum of American Art in New York, where he experimented with abstract painting and performance art. He returned to Dallas in 1978 and began making figurative wooden sculptures depicting Texas themes. Bates shifted his focus to painting around 1980, and in the early 1980s he developed his distinctive impasto technique. He achieved national exposure in 1983, when his work was featured in the thirty-eighth Corcoran Biennial, which toured nationwide the following year. In Texas

during the mid-1980s, he showed with Eugene Binder Gallery in Dallas and with Texas Gallery in Houston. Bates was included in the 1987 Whitney Biennial and he had a major solo exhibition organized by the Modern Art Museum of Fort Worth in 1988. In the early 1990s, he focused increasingly on depictions of the Gulf Coast, which he exhibited regularly in New York at Charles Cowles Gallery. He began showing with Gerald Peters Gallery in Dallas in 1996. In 1997, the Galveston Arts Center organized a major survey of his work that toured statewide through 1999. Also in 1999, he began exhibiting with D. C. Moore Gallery in New York.   —*RM*

Selected References:

Price, Marla. *David Bates: Forty Paintings.* Fort Worth: Modern Art Museum of Fort Worth, 1988.

Cohen, Ronny. *David Bates.* New York: Charles Cowles Gallery, 1990.

Graze, Sue. *David Bates.* Dallas: Gerald Peters Gallery, 1996.

Willour, Clint, and Charles Dee Mitchell. *David Bates: The Gulf Coast.* Galveston: Galveston Arts Center, 1997.

❏ FORREST BESS
Born 1911, Bay City, Texas
Died 1977, Bay City, Texas

The son of an itinerant oil laborer, Forrest Bess developed a deeply personal style of painting that supported his fascination with the visionary and the unconscious. In 1929, he enrolled at Texas A&M University to study architecture, but in 1931 he transferred to the University of Texas at Austin, where he became interested in psychology and was deeply influenced by Havelock Ellis's *Psychology of Sex*. In 1933, Bess left school to work in the oil fields. After a number of temporary jobs and several trips to Mexico, he set up a studio in Bay City, Texas, in 1934. Drawing inspiration for his early paintings from the work of Vincent van Gogh and Albert Pinkham Ryder, Bess had solo exhibitions at the Witte Memorial Museum in San Antonio in 1938 and the MFAH in 1941. From 1941 to 1945, he served in the Army Corps of Engineers. Before returning to Bay City in 1947, Bess maintained a small studio in San Antonio and taught painting at the local Veterans Affairs Hospital. In 1948, he visited New York and joined the Betty Parsons Gallery, where he exhibited in 1954, 1957, and 1959; in 1962, Betty Parsons mounted a retrospective of his work with a catalogue essay by Meyer Schapiro. Bess also had solo shows at the MFAH in 1951 and at the Contemporary Arts Museum in Houston in 1962. In 1950, he began an extensive correspondence with Carl Jung regarding Jung's theories on the collective unconscious. Bess began what he referred to as "Phase II" of his career in 1965. His 1967 exhibitions at the Witte Memorial Museum and the Parsons Gallery displayed a more clearly defined personal symbolism. In 1973, Meyer Schapiro assisted Bess in receiving a grant for older artists from the Mark Rothko Foundation. Despite living and working outside the mainstream art community, Bess developed a powerful body of paintings that earned him national recognition, including a

posthumous retrospective at the Whitney Museum of American Art in New York in 1981.   —*JAG*

Selected References:

Schapiro, Meyer. *Forrest Bess.* New York: Betty Parsons Gallery, 1962.

Haskell, Barbara. *Forrest Bess.* New York: Whitney Museum of American Art, 1981.

Ennis, Michael. "His Name Was Forrest Bess." *Texas Monthly* 10, no. 6 (June 1982): 141–43, 240–47.

Luhring, Lawrence, and David Reed. *"I Knew It To Be So," Forrest Bess, Alfred Jensen, Myron Stout: Theory and the Visionary.* New York: New York Studio School, 1984.

Yau, John, et al. *Forrest Bess.* New York: Hirschl and Adler Modern, 1988.

❏ JOHN BIGGERS
Born 1924, Gastonia, North Carolina
Lives in Houston, Texas, and Gastonia, North Carolina

John Biggers has created a body of work that stirringly chronicles African-American culture and history. Biggers grew up in rural North Carolina and enrolled at Lincoln Academy, Kings Mountain, in 1937. In 1941, he entered the Hampton Institute (now Hampton University) in Hampton, Virginia, where he studied with Viktor Lowenfeld and the muralist Charles White, who became important early influences. Biggers completed his first mural project, *Dying Soldier*, at Hampton in 1942. During 1943, he was included in *Young Negro Art*, an exhibition Lowenfeld curated for the Museum of Modern Art in New York. Three years later, Biggers followed Lowenfeld to Pennsylvania State University, where in 1948 he received a B.S. and an M.S. in art education. That same year, he married Hazel Hales in Philadelphia, and in 1949 the couple moved to Houston, where Biggers accepted a position at the Texas State University for Negroes (now Texas Southern University). Biggers soon established the art department at that university. In 1950, he broke the color barrier at the MFAH when his work was awarded the Purchase Prize in the museum's *25th Annual Exhibition of Work by Houston Artists*. In 1954, he was awarded a Ph.D. in art education from Penn State. He received a 1957 UNESCO fellowship to study traditional cultural patterns in West Africa. Biggers visited Ghana, Togo, the Republic of Benin, and Nigeria, returning through Rome, where he saw the great mural cycles of the Renaissance. He published a record of his African travels, *Ananse: The Web of Life in Africa*, in 1962, and his groundbreaking reconsideration of African heritage encouraged a new holistic vision of African-American identity. During the late 1970s and early 1980s, Biggers developed a rich allegorical language exemplified in public murals throughout the Houston area, as well as in Paris, Texas. In 1991, he completed major mural projects for Winston-Salem State University in North Carolina and Hampton University in Virginia. Biggers was the subject of a major 1995 retrospective organized by the MFAH, an exhibition that traveled nationally. He completed a mural for the University of Houston,

Downtown, in 1998, and another for Texas Southern University in 1999.   —RM

Selected References:
Biggers, John. *Ananse: The Web of Life in Africa.* Austin: University of Texas Press, 1962.
Driskell, David A. *Two Centuries of Black American Art.* New York: Alfred A. Knopf in association with the Los Angeles County Museum of Art, 1976.
Wardlaw, Alvia J., et al. *John Biggers: View from the Upper Room.* New York: Harry N. Abrams in association with the Museum of Fine Arts, Houston, 1995.

❏ **DENNIS BLAGG**
   Born 1951, Oklahoma City, Oklahoma
   Lives in Fort Worth, Texas

Dennis Blagg's paintings evoke the rich landscape of Texas. Blagg spent his early childhood on a cotton farm outside of Seminole, Texas. He lived in Dallas and then Fort Worth during high school and regularly visited the Dallas Museum of Art and the Fort Worth Art Museum (now the Modern Art Museum of Fort Worth). Blagg left Fort Worth briefly for military service in 1971, but returned the following year. In the early 1970s, he concentrated on portrait painting. He had his first solo show in 1974 at Carr Gallery in Fort Worth. Toward the end of the 1970s, Blagg was introduced to the landscape of Big Bend by fellow Fort Worth artist Jim Malone. Within a few years, landscape became his favored subject, and in the 1980s he frequently visited Big Bend, accompanied by Malone or Vernon Fisher. Blagg participated in *At the Edge of Town* at the Nave Museum in Victoria, Texas, in 1985 and in *Texas Realism* at the Texas Fine Arts Association in Austin in 1987. He had a solo show that same year at Barry Whistler Gallery in Dallas and was the focus of exhibitions at the Amarillo Art Center in 1991 and the Tyler Museum of Art in 1992. In 1995, he presented a solo exhibition at Artspace III in Fort Worth. That same year, he began showing with Meredith Long & Company in Houston.   —RM

Selected References:
Blagg, Dennis. "Statement." *Review* (Tyler Museum of Art, Texas), September/November 1992.
Otton, William G. *Dennis Blagg: A Desert Journal.* Fort Worth: Open Studio Catalogues, 1999.

❏ **AMY BLAKEMORE**
   Born 1958, Tulsa, Oklahoma
   Lives in Houston, Texas

Amy Blakemore limits the range of focus in her photographs to create atmospheric images imbued with the sense of memories. Blakemore attended Drury College in Springfield, Missouri, where she received a B.S. in psychology before completing a B.A. in art in 1982. She moved to Austin in 1982, entered the graduate program at the University of Texas at Austin, and had her first solo show at the Accent Photographic Gallery, before receiving an M.F.A. in 1984. Blakemore moved to Houston in 1985 to accept a Core Residency Fellowship at the Glassell School of Art. That same year, she was featured in the annual *New American Talent* exhibition at the Laguna Gloria Art Museum in Austin. She joined the faculty of the Glassell School in 1986 and was included annually in *New American Talent* from 1987 to 1990. Blakemore also was featured in *Reinventing Reality* at the University of Houston's Sarah Campbell Blaffer Gallery in 1990, and she participated in the 1993 group show *Stairway to Heaven* at the Galveston Arts Center. In 1994, she began an affiliation with Inman Gallery in Houston, and the following year she had a solo show at the Kansas City Art Institute in Missouri. During 1997, Blakemore was awarded two grants from the Cultural Arts Council of Houston/Harris County. The following year, she traveled to Bosnia and France to photograph pilgrimage sites and was featured in *Field of Vision: Five Gulf Coast Photographers* at the Contemporary Arts Museum in Houston. In 1999, Blakemore had a solo show at Inman Gallery that traveled to the Galveston Arts Center.   —RM

Selected References:
Greene, Alison de Lima, and Clint Willour. *Stairway to Heaven.* Galveston: Galveston Arts Center, 1993.
Irvine, Alexandra L. *Field of Vision: Five Gulf Coast Photographers.* Houston: Contemporary Arts Museum, 1998.
Kalil, Susie, and Anne Wilkes Tucker. *Amy Blakemore: 10 Years.* Houston: Inman Gallery, 1999.

❏ **GAY BLOCK**
   Born 1942, Houston, Texas
   Lives in Santa Fe, New Mexico

Gay Block has developed a distinctive style of portrait photography and has realized a number of important documentary projects. Block attended Tulane University in New Orleans from 1959 to 1961 and studied architecture at the University of Houston from 1971 to 1972. She found her vocation as a photographer in 1973, and subsequently studied with Geoff Winningham, Garry Winogrand, Ed Hill, Anne Wilkes Tucker, and Lee Friedlander. From the beginning of her career, Block felt a deep interest in subjects related to Jewish culture, and in 1975 Houston's Congregation Beth Israel commissioned her, along with the writer Lind May, to assemble a visual and oral history of the congregation. Block was included in a group exhibition at the Contemporary Arts Museum in Houston in 1975. Her first solo show in Houston was at Cronin Gallery in 1979. At the beginning of the 1980s, she taught photography at the University of Houston. She was featured in a 1982 solo exhibition at the Contemporary Arts Museum. In the early 1980s, Block spent winters in Miami, photographing the senior citizens who make their home there, and she exhibited her *Miami* series at William A. Graham Gallery in Houston in 1985. The following year, she was commissioned by H.E.B. Pantry Foods to create portraits of workers in the company's Texas grocery stores. Her *H.E.B. Texas* series accompanied the *Miami* series in a solo exhibition at the Visual Studies Workshop in Rochester, New York, in 1986. Block had a solo exhibition at the College of the Mainland in Texas City that same year, before leaving Houston for Los Angeles, where she taught at the California Institute of the Arts. She moved to Santa Fe, New Mexico, in 1992, and that same year a significant book she created with the writer Malka Drucker was published. Titled *Rescuers: Portraits of Moral Courage in the Holocaust*, the book recorded heroes of the struggle against Nazism. Block's rescuer portraits were showcased at the Museum of Modern Art in New York and the MFAH in 1992, and they embarked on a major international tour. In 1994, the Jewish Museum in New York honored her with a solo exhibition.   —RM

Selected References:
Goldwater, Marge. *Four Texas Photographers.* Fort Worth: Fort Worth Art Museum, 1977.
Carlozzi, Annette DiMeo, and Gay Block. *50 Texas Artists: A Critical Selection of Painters and Sculptors Working in Texas.* San Francisco: Chronicle Books, 1986.
Sandweiss, Martha, ed. *Contemporary Texas: A Photographic Portrait.* Austin: Texas Monthly Press, 1986.
Block, Gay, and Malka Drucker. *Rescuers: Portraits of Moral Courage in the Holocaust.* New York and London: Holmes and Meier Publishers Inc., 1992.

❏ **DEREK BOSHIER**
   Born 1937, Portsmouth, England
   Lives in Los Angeles, California

Derek Boshier's figurative paintings present powerful allegories of contemporary urban life. Boshier attended Yeovil School of Art in Somerset, England, from 1953 to 1957 and the Royal College of Art in London from 1959 to 1962. He emerged onto London's vibrant Pop Art scene in the 1960s, among a group of artists including Richard Hamilton, Peter Blake, and Eduardo Paolozzi. Boshier's early work involves a sharp political commentary, and his first solo exhibition, *Image in Revolt* at Grabowski Gallery in London in 1962, underlined these concerns. That same year, Boshier was awarded a prestigious Arts Council Prize at the *Young Contemporaries* national student exhibition in Britain. In 1964, his work was featured in the Whitechapel Art Gallery's high-profile group show *The New Generation*, and a related travel award allowed him to make an early visit to America. In the late 1960s, he shifted his focus from painting. Over the next decade, Boshier experimented with installation, photographic documentation, and printmaking. In 1980, he accepted a one-year visiting artist position at the University of Houston and subsequently returned his focus to painting. The following year, he joined the faculty of the university and was featured in an exhibition at the Contemporary Arts Museum in Houston. The skyline of Houston looms as a dramatic background in many of Boshier's canvases from the 1980s, which are dark and ironic reflections of American culture in that decade. In 1982, his Houston paintings were featured in *Derek Boshier: Texas Works* at the Institute for Contemporary Arts in London. He was included in *Fresh Paint: The Houston School* at the MFAH in 1985. Throughout these years he maintained an affiliation with Houston's Texas Gallery. Boshier remained an influential teacher at the University of Houston until 1992, when he returned to England. In 1995, his Texas paintings were surveyed in *Derek Boshier: The Texas Years* at the Contemporary Arts Museum. He moved to Los Angeles and joined the faculty of the California Institute of the Arts in 1997. Boshier's installation *Journey/Israel Project* was seen at the Holocaust Museum in Houston in 1998.

—RM

Selected References:
Brutvan, Cheryl A. *Derek Boshier: Paintings from 1980–1981*. Houston: Contemporary Arts Museum, 1981.
Bloom, Suzanne, and Ed Hill. "Derek Boshier, Texas Gallery." *Artforum* 24, no. 1 (September 1985): 131.
Cotter, Holland. "Derek Boshier at TotahStelling." *Art in America* 74, no. 10 (October 1986): 157–59.
Livingstone, Marco, et al. *Pop Art*. London: Royal Academy of Arts, 1991.
Mayo, Marti, Lynn M. Herbert, and Guy Brett. *Derek Boshier: The Texas Years*. Houston: Contemporary Arts Museum, 1995.

❏ **JAMES (JACK) BOYNTON**
   Born 1928, Fort Worth, Texas
   Lives in Houston, Texas

Jack Boynton has displayed a unique connection to the Texas landscape and images of Texana paralleled by few artists in this region. In 1949, he earned his B.F.A. in commercial art from Texas Christian University. His first exhibition in New York was at Knoedler Gallery in 1952. While working as a technical illustrator for Convair Aircraft in Fort Worth, Boynton decided to return to Texas Christian for graduate work in painting. In 1955, he received an M.F.A. and moved to Houston, where he joined the faculty of the University of Houston. That same year, he won the Purchase Prize in the annual Texas exhibition at the MFAH, and he also received a solo exhibition at the Fort Worth Art Museum. He was featured in a number of group exhibitions, including *Made in Texas by Texans* at the Dallas Museum for Contemporary Arts in 1959 and *Recent Painting: The Figure* at the Museum of Modern Art in New York in 1962. During 1967, Boynton obtained a fellowship at the Tamarind Institute, where he began making prints. Around 1969, he started focusing on printmaking and drawing—a decision that shifted the subject of his art from introspective, visionary landscapes to a Dadaist embrace of the commercial imagery of Texas. At the same time, he began exhibiting under the name "Jack" rather than the more formal "James," which he had used in earlier years. Throughout his studio career, Boynton also has enjoyed success as an art educator. He held a variety of teaching positions at the Art Institute of San Francisco, the University of New Mexico, the Museum School of the MFAH, and the Northwood Institute in Dallas, and from 1969 to 1985 he served on the faculty of the University of St. Thomas in Houston. The University of St. Thomas held a solo exhibition of his work in 1971, and the following year Boynton had a solo exhibition at the Fort Worth Art Center. In 1980, the Amarillo Art Center organized *Jack Boynton: Retro/Spectrum*, an exhibition that traveled to museums across Texas. Boynton had a two-person show with Bob Fowler at Robinson Galleries in Houston in 1999.

—JAG

Selected References:
Bywaters, Jerry. *James W. Boynton*. Fort Worth: Fort Worth Art Museum, 1955.
MacAgy, Douglas. *James Boynton*. New York: Barone Gallery, 1959.
Daviee, Jerry M. *Jack Boynton: Retro/Spectrum*. Amarillo, Texas: Amarillo Art Center, 1980.
Goetzmann, William H., and Becky Duval Reese. *Texas Images and Visions*. Austin: University of Texas at Austin, Archer M. Huntington Art Gallery, 1983.

❏ **JULIE BOZZI**
   Born 1943, San Jose, California
   Lives in Fort Worth, Texas

Julie Bozzi is best known for her paintings that depict the American landscape in miniature, often surrounded by vast framing borders, enhancing a sensation of distance or even loneliness. Bozzi grew up in San Jose, California, and in 1961 she was awarded a scholarship to the University of California at Los Angeles to study painting. She attended San Jose State University in 1962, but in 1963 suspended her studies and began working as a laboratory technician at Stanford University. In 1971, she returned her focus to painting and resumed her studies, attending the University of California at Davis, where she received a B.A. in 1974. The following year, Bozzi won a scholarship to the Skowhegan School of Painting and Sculpture in Maine. She returned to the University of California to receive her M.F.A. in 1976. Her first solo exhibition was held at the Candystore Gallery in Folsom, California, in 1978. Bozzi moved to Fort Worth in 1980. She subsequently developed her landscape paintings with a concurrent series titled *American Food*, which featured miniature sculptures of popular food products. She had her first solo exhibitions in Texas in 1983, at Texas Christian University in Fort Worth and Delahunty Gallery in Dallas. Bozzi was included in a group exhibition at the New Museum in New York in 1984, and that same year began showing with Texas Gallery in Houston. During 1986, she was featured in the group show *Natural Settings* at the Corcoran Gallery of Art in Washington, D.C., and in the *Texas Landscape* exhibition at the MFAH. In 1989, she was included in *A Century of Sculpture in Texas* at the Archer M. Huntington Art Gallery at the University of Texas at Austin. In 1992, the San Diego Museum of Contemporary Art organized a major national touring exhibition of Bozzi's *American Food* series. She continued showing with Texas Gallery in the 1990s, and in 1994 began an affiliation with Gerald Peters Gallery in Dallas. That same year, Bozzi was awarded a fellowship from the Art Matters Inc. Foundation in New York.   —RM

Selected References:
Goetzmann, William H., and Becky Duval Reese. *Texas Images and Visions*. Austin: University of Texas at Austin, Archer M. Huntington Art Gallery, 1983.
Davies, Hugh. *Julie Bozzi: American Food*. San Diego: San Diego Museum of Contemporary Art, 1992.

❏ **GEARY BROADNAX**
   Born 1952, Norfolk, Virginia
   Lives in Houston, Texas

Geary Broadnax's documentary photographs vividly capture ordinary scenes of everyday life. Broadnax pursued studies in electrical engineering and architecture at the Virginia Polytechnic Institute and State University in Blacksburg, Virginia, from 1970 to 1976; he moved to Houston in 1977. His early work as a freelance photographer and as a photojournalist for United Press International prepared him for a position in the early 1980s with the photography staff at the *Houston Post*, where he soon was appointed an assistant photo chief and eventually the director of photography. After working with the *Houston Post* for eleven years, Broadnax delved into computer services. In 1992, he developed All-Source, a computer services organization. Three years later, he founded Insync Internet Services Inc., a Houston-based Internet provider. Broadnax was one of nine photographers included in *A Photographic Journey: Three Houston Neighborhoods*, a 1998 exhibition at the MFAH.   —MG

Selected References:
Patrick, Mignette Y. "15 Minutes: Geary Broadnax Has Developed Eye for Style." *Houston Chronicle*, 26 October 1995.
Kever, Jeannie. "More Alike Than Different/Nine Photographers Set Out to Portray Life in Three Houston Neighborhoods. Here's a Sample of What They Found for an Exhibition at the Museum of Fine Arts." *Houston Chronicle*, 31 May 1998.

❏ **KARIN BROKER**
   Born 1950, Philadelphia, Pennsylvania
   Lives in Houston, Texas

Karin Broker's work crosses traditional boundaries between printmaking and drawing. Broker studied printmaking with Mauricio Lasansky at the University of Iowa from 1968 until 1972. She spent the following year in Paris, where she studied with the influential master of modern intaglio printing, Stanley William Hayter. Broker received an M.F.A. from the University of Wisconsin in 1980. That same year, she came to Houston and joined the faculty of Rice University. She exhibited internationally in the early 1980s; her first solo show was in Germany at the Studio-Galerie, Rastede, in 1982. The following year, she was featured in the *Biennial Internacional de Gravura e Arte Grafica* in Cabo Frio, Brazil. Broker was awarded grants from the National Endowment for the Arts in 1985 and 1987. She had solo exhibitions at the University of Corpus Christi in 1988 and at Keuka College in New York State in 1991. During 1992, she was the subject of a retrospective at the Sewall Art Gallery at Rice University. Broker was associated briefly with a number of Houston galleries, including Molina, Hadler/Rodriguez, Susanna Sheffield, and McMurtrey. In 1994, she began showing with Gerhard Wurzer Gallery. That same year, the Art League of Houston nominated her as Texas Artist of the Year.   —*RM*

Selected References:
Rose, Carey. *Karin Broker.* Corpus Christi: Corpus Christi State University, Weil Gallery, 1988.
Brauer, David E. *Karin Broker: Searching for a Saint.* Houston: Sewall Art Gallery, Rice University, 1992.
Walker, Barry. *Karin Broker: Etchings.* Houston: Gerhard Wurzer Gallery, 1994.

❏ **PETER BROWN**
  Born 1948, Northampton, Massachusetts
  Lives in Houston, Texas

Peter Brown's photographic work has concentrated on two subjects: the light of interior spaces, and the vast open expanses of the North American plains. When Brown was thirteen, his family moved from New York to California. While traveling across the country each summer to his family's holiday home in Massachusetts, Brown established an affection for the western plains that would deeply influence his vision as a photographer. He studied at Stanford University in California, where he received a B.A. in English before completing his M.F.A. in 1977. The following year, he began teaching at Rice University and had a solo exhibition at the Rice Media Center. In 1983, Brown published a portfolio titled *Seasons of Light,* a collection of his photographs of interiors accompanied by his own prose. Around this time, he began photographing the high plains of Texas, New Mexico, Oklahoma, and Kansas. He had solo exhibitions in Texas at the Art Center, Waco, in 1983 and the Tyler Museum of Art in 1985. In 1988, Rice University Press published his *Seasons of Light* in book form, and in 1990 Brown had a solo exhibition at the university's Farish Gallery. His work was featured in the 1991 *The Pleasures and Terrors of Domestic Comfort* at the Museum of Modern Art in New York. Throughout the 1990s, Brown continued his photographic study of the Great Plains. A selection from this series was published in the photography journal *DoubleTake* in 1998 and the series became the focus of a full-length book published the following year. *On the Plains* was the focus of an exhibition at the Galveston Arts Center in 1999; also that year he received the national Alfred Eisenstaedt Award for Magazine Photography.   —*RM*

Selected References:
Brown, Peter, and Denise Levertov. *Seasons of Light.* Houston: Rice University Press, 1988.
Brown, Peter. "The Great Plains." *DoubleTake* 4, no. 1 (winter 1998): 66–75.
Brown, Peter, and Kathleen Norris. *On the Plains.* New York: DoubleTake Books/W. W. Norton, 1999.

❏ **STEVE BRUDNIAK**
  Born 1961, Topeka, Kansas
  Lives in Austin, Texas

Steve Brudniak, a former musician, composer, and poet, explores the tradition of assemblage to create eccentric constructions. Largely self-taught, Brudniak exhibited widely in Houston in the 1980s and early 1990s, including four annual *Texas Art Celebration* exhibitions sponsored by the Assistance League of Houston. In 1987, Brudniak was featured in *Found,* an exhibition at DiverseWorks Artspace in Houston that presented sixty-two artists working with found objects. That same year, he had his first solo show at the Blue Collar Gallery in San Antonio and also exhibited *Imogene Icon,* a large structure that incorporated high volts of electricity, at the Museum of Neon Art in Los Angeles. In 1989, Brudniak was included in group shows at the Archer M. Huntington Art Gallery at the University of Texas at Austin, the Dallas Museum of Art, and Hooks-Epstein Galleries in Houston, as well as *High Tech Art* at the Discovery Hall Science Museum in Austin. The Judy Youens Gallery in Houston presented Brudniak in two solo shows in 1989 and 1990. During 1991, he had solo exhibitions at Concordia Lutheran College in Austin and also was included in *The Perfect World in Contemporary Texas Art* at the San Antonio Museum of Art. That same year, Brudniak began exhibiting at Lynn Goode Gallery in Houston, which in 1992 represented him at the ArtFair in Seattle, Washington. Eeka-Beeka Gallery in Austin highlighted his work in a solo show in 1997. Brudniak was featured in a 1999 two-person exhibition at the Yukiko Lunday Gallery in Houston.   —*MG*

Selected References:
Edwards, Jim, et al. *The Perfect World in Contemporary Texas Art.* San Antonio: San Antonio Museum of Art, 1991.
McBride, Elizabeth. "Steve Brudniak: Lynn Goode." *Artnews* 91, no. 4 (April 1992): 129.

❏ **JERRY BYWATERS**
  Born 1906, Paris, Texas
  Died 1989, Dallas, Texas

Artist, art critic, art educator, and museum director, Jerry Bywaters played a pivotal role in defining the early Texas art scene and in championing the art and artists of the Lone Star Regionalist movement. After obtaining a B.A. in comparative literature at Southern Methodist University in 1926, Bywaters briefly attended the Dallas Art Institute and then toured Europe. In 1928, he traveled to Mexico, where he observed and wrote about Mexican muralists, including Diego Rivera, David Alfaro Siqueiros, and José Clemente Orozco. During that year, Bywaters also studied at artist colonies in Woodstock, New York, and Provincetown, Massachusetts, as well as under Bruce Crane at the Old Lyme Art Colony in Connecticut. In the fall of 1928, he attended the Art Students League in New York, where he took classes from Ivan Olinsky and John Sloan, returning to Dallas at the beginning of 1929. Bywaters's Regionalist paintings earned mural commissions for post-office buildings in Quanah, Houston, Farmersville, and Trinity, Texas, between 1937 and 1942. During that period, he also was active as a writer for the *Dallas Morning News* and the *Southwest Review,* and as an editor for *Southwestern News.* From 1942 until 1964, Bywaters served as director of the Dallas Museum of Art. During his twenty-one years at the museum, he also taught at Southern Methodist University, wrote on Texas artists, and exhibited at national institutions, including the Metropolitan Museum of Art in New York and the Art Institute of Chicago. Between 1965 and 1970, Bywaters served as director of the Pollock Galleries at Southern Methodist University, where he received a major retrospective in 1976. He instituted the Jerry Bywaters Research Collection on American Art at that university. Until his death in 1989, Bywaters served as regional director of the Archives of American Art for the Smithsonian Institution.   —*JAG*

Selected References:
Goetzmann, William H., and Becky Duval Reese. *Texas Images and Visions.* Austin: University of Texas at Austin, Archer M. Huntington Art Gallery, 1983.
Stewart, Rick. *Lone Star Regionalism: The Dallas Nine and Their Circle, 1928–1945.* Austin: University of Texas Press; Dallas: Dallas Museum of Art, 1985.
Carraro, Francine. *Jerry Bywaters: A Life in Art.* Austin: University of Texas Press, 1994.

❏ **KEITH CARTER**
  Born 1948, Madison, Wisconsin
  Lives in Beaumont, Texas

Keith Carter's black-and-white photographs offer evocative portraits and symbolic reflections of life in the South. Carter spent his childhood in Beaumont, where his mother worked as a commercial photographer. During the late 1960s, he studied business management at Lamar University in that city. In 1970, he embarked on a trip across Europe with a fellow student, the artist Paul Manes. The following year, Carter studied at the Winona School of Professional Photographers in Atlanta, Georgia. He had an early exhibition at Afterimage Gallery in Dallas in 1973 and a solo exhibition at the Galveston Arts Center in 1975. Carter's first museum show came three years later, at the Art Museum of South Texas in Corpus Christi. His work appeared regularly in *Texas Monthly* throughout the 1980s, and Texas Monthly Press published his first book of photographs, *From Uncertain to Blue,* in 1988. Carter began teaching at Lamar University in 1988. His wistful depictions of life in remote parts of the South found an international audience in the 1990s, and he presented an average of eight solo exhibitions annually between 1993 and 1997. Carter continued living and teaching in Beaumont throughout this time, however, showing a resolute commitment to the region. The University of Texas Press published a survey of his photographs in 1997 to coincide with his retrospective at Southwest Texas State University in San Marcos. In 1998, Carter received Lamar University's Distinguished Faculty Lecture Award.   —*RM*

Selected References:
Carter, Keith. *The Blue Man.* Houston: Rice University Press, 1990.
Clibborn, Edward. *American Photography 9.* New York: Rizzoli, 1993.
Carter, Keith. *Keith Carter Photographs: Twenty-five Years.* Austin: University of Texas Press; San Marcos, Texas: Southwest Texas State University, 1997.
Stout, D. J., Nancy MacMillan, and Anne Wilkes Tucker. *The Pictures of Texas Monthly: Twenty-five Years.* New York: Stewart, Tabori and Chang, 1998.

❏ **LYNN CAZABON**
  Born 1964, Detroit, Michigan
  Lives in Lewisburg, Pennsylvania

Lynn Cazabon's multimedia work raises important questions regarding self-representation. Cazabon received a B.F.A. in photography in 1986 and a B.A. in arts and ideas in 1987 from the University of Michigan at Ann Arbor. In 1990, she graduated with an M.F.A. from the Cranbrook Academy of Art in Bloomfield Hills, Michigan, and that same year she was awarded a Smithsonian Graduate Fellowship from the National Museum of American Art. She joined the Core Residency Program at the Glassell School of Art in Houston in 1991. The following year, Cazabon participated in numerous group exhibitions, including *20/20 Vision* at the Cranbrook Academy of Art Museum and *Slouching towards 2000: The Politics of Gender* at Women and Their Work in Austin. In 1993, she was awarded an Individual Artist Grant from the Mid-America Arts Alliance/National Endowment for the Arts. That same year, she presented work at Houston's DiverseWorks Artspace and the Pyramid Arts Center in Rochester, New York. After completing her residency at the Glassell School, Cazabon moved to Pennsylvania, where she began teaching photography at Bucknell University, Lewisburg. She had her first solo exhibition at the Filmmakers Gallery in Pittsburgh, Pennsylvania, in 1993. Subsequently, Cazabon had one-person exhibitions at the Lawndale Art and Performance Center, Houston; the Mattress Factory, Pittsburgh; the Kansas City Art Institute; and the CEPA Gallery, Buffalo, New York. She was appointed an artist-in-residence at the Anderson Ranch Arts Center, Colorado, in 1996 and at the Bucknell Art Gallery two years later. Cazabon was featured in *Rushes,* a solo exhibition at the Bucknell Art Gallery in 1999. —*MG*

Selected References:
Slouching towards 2000: The Politics of Gender. Austin: Women and Their Work, 1992.
Batchen, Geoffrey. "Lynn Cazabon." *Creative Camera,* no. 357 (April/May 1999): 28–33.

❏ **MICHAEL RAY CHARLES**
  Born 1967, Lafayette, Louisiana
  Lives in Austin, Texas

Michael Ray Charles's bold and confrontational images force the viewer to reconsider the social forces that shape the character of African-American culture. A native of Louisiana, Charles graduated from McNeese State University in Lake Charles in 1989 with a B.A. in advertising. Shortly thereafter, he began studying art at the University of Houston, receiving an M.F.A. in 1993. During 1992, Charles was featured in the *Fresh Visions/New Voices* exhibition at the Glassell School of Art and quickly became known as an outstanding young artist in the Houston community. In 1993, he presented the *Forever Free* series in an *Introductions* exhibition at Moody Gallery, and also began teaching art at the University of Texas at Austin. The following year, he participated in various national and international group exhibitions and was awarded a Regional Visual Arts Fellowship from the National Endowment for the Arts. In 1995, Charles's work was featured in shows in the United States, Germany, and Switzerland. During 1996, he showed at Barry Whistler Gallery in Dallas, Dishman Art Gallery at Lamar University in Beaumont, and the MFAH. In 1997, the Sarah Campbell Blaffer Gallery at the University of Houston hosted his first solo museum exhibition, which traveled to the Austin Museum of Art and the Contemporary Arts Center in Cincinnati, Ohio. That same year, Charles also had solo shows at Tony Shafrazi Gallery in New York, Moody Gallery in Houston, and the Albright-Knox Art Gallery in Buffalo, New York. —*MG*

Selected References:
Havel, Joseph, and Rick Lowe. *Fresh Visions/ New Voices: Emerging African-American Artists in Texas.* Houston: The Museum of Fine Arts, Houston, The Glassell School of Art, 1992.
Bacigalupi, Don, et al. *Michael Ray Charles, 1989–1997: An American Artist's Work.* Houston: Sarah Campbell Blaffer Gallery, 1997.
Reid, Calvin. *Michael Ray Charles.* New York: Tony Shafrazi Gallery, 1998.

❏ **MEL CHIN**
  Born 1951, Houston, Texas
  Lives in New York, New York

Mel Chin's sculptures and installations reflect his deep concerns for ecology and transcultural understanding. Chin grew up in Houston's Fifth Ward and attended the George Peabody College for Teachers in Nashville, Tennessee. After graduating in 1975, he returned to Houston, where in 1976 he had his first solo show at Robinson Galleries. He moved to New York in 1984, but maintained strong links with his hometown. DiverseWorks Artspace in Houston presented a survey of his early work in 1985. Toward the end of the 1980s, Chin emerged onto the national stage, with solo shows at the Hirshhorn Museum and Sculpture Garden in Washington, D.C., in 1989 and the Walker Art Center in Minneapolis in 1990. With the support of the Houston-based Citizens' Environment Coalition, he began developing a major project called *Revival Field,* thereby initiating a method of cleaning toxic-waste sites using plants capable of absorbing contamination from soil. In 1991, a grant awarded to Chin by the National Endowment for the Arts to support this project was withdrawn by NEA chairman John Frohnmayer, but subsequently reinstated. Soon after the national controversy surrounding *Revival Field,* The Menil Collection in Houston hosted an exhibition of Chin's work from the Walker Art Center, which also traveled to Cincinnati and New York. *Revival Field* finally was realized on the Pig's Eye Landfill in St. Paul, Minnesota, in 1991. Chin completed two additional major collaborative projects during the 1990s. In 1996, he assembled the GALA Committee, a group including Houston artist Mark Flood, to execute *In the Name of the Place.* This project surreptitiously placed artworks on the set of the television show *Melrose Place.* Documentation of the project was shown at the Museum of Contemporary Art in Los Angeles in 1997 and traveled to Lawing Gallery in Houston the following year. During 1998, Chin completed a collaboration with Houston schoolchildren, creating illuminated pillars based on the children's drawings as a commission for the city's Sesquicentennial Park. —*RM*

Selected References:
Rifkin, Ned. *Mel Chin.* Washington, D.C.: Hirshhorn Museum and Sculpture Garden, 1989.
Boswell, Peter. *Viewpoints: Mel Chin.* Minneapolis, Minnesota: Walker Art Center, 1990.
Kozik, K. K. "Mel Chin." *Journal of Contemporary Art* 6, no. 2 (winter 1993): 5–15.
Huerta, Benito, and Lucy Lippard. *Inescapable Histories: Mel Chin.* Kansas City, Missouri: ExhibitsUSA, 1997.
Koshalek, Richard. *Uncommon Sense.* Los Angeles: Museum of Contemporary Art, 1997.

❏ **VINCENT COLYER**
  Born 1825, Bloomington, New York
  Died 1888, Contentment Island, Darien, Connecticut

Vincent Colyer was among the first artists to record the topography and flora of North Texas. Colyer studied under John R. Smith in the Life and Antique School of the National Academy of Design from 1844 to 1848 and was elected an associate of the academy in 1849. He established a successful career as a portraitist in New York, although much of his time was dedicated to humanitarian campaigns. Colyer was strongly opposed to slavery, and during the Civil War he organized an African-American volunteer regiment to support the Unionist cause. After the war, he was elected secretary of the Board of Indian Commissioners, and in 1869 the commission asked him to assemble a report on the conditions of Native American tribes in Kansas, Texas, New Mexico, Arizona, Colorado, and areas of what is now Oklahoma. Colyer made watercolor sketches of the territories during this assignment and his watercolors of the Texas Panhandle date from this time. A number of these watercolors were included in the reports he submitted to Congress; others were published in *Harper's Weekly*. Following his service as commissioner, Colyer returned to the Northeast, settling near Darien, Connecticut. He subsequently enlarged his sketches of the Southwest into landscape paintings, which were featured in a general exhibition at the National Academy of Design in 1875. Colyer remained active both as an artist and in government service until his death in 1888.   —JAG

Selected References:
Dawdy, Doris Ostrander. *Artists of the American West*. Vol. 1. Chicago: Swall Press, Inc., 1974.
Warren, David B., Michael K. Brown, Elizabeth Ann Coleman, and Emily Ballew Neff. *American Decorative Arts and Paintings in the Bayou Bend Collection*. Houston: The Museum of Fine Arts, Houston; Princeton, New Jersey: Princeton University Press, 1998.

❏ **CARLOTTA M. CORPRON**
Born 1901, Blue Earth, Minnesota
Died 1988, Denton, Texas

Carlotta M. Corpron stretched the limits of photography and light with her dazzling abstractions. When she was a small child, Corpron and her family moved to India, where her father worked as a missionary surgeon. At the age of nineteen, she returned to the United States and enrolled at Michigan State Normal College (now Eastern Michigan State University), where she received a B.S. in art education in 1925. After earning an M.A. from the Teachers College of Columbia University in 1926, she accepted a teaching post at Woman's College of Alabama (now Huntington College). In 1928, Corpron moved to Ohio to teach at the School of Applied Arts at the University of Cincinnati. She purchased her first camera in 1933 as an aid to her teaching. In 1935, Corpron joined the faculty of Texas State College for Women (now Texas Woman's University in Denton), where she taught design, creative photography, and the history of art until her retirement in 1968. During László Moholy-Nagy's visits to Denton in 1941 and 1942, Corpron worked as his assistant, conducting a light workshop with her students in 1942. In 1944, she studied in Denton with Moholy-Nagy's associate, Gyorgy Kepes. That same year, her work was reproduced in Kepes's book *Languages of Vision*. Corpron received solo exhibitions at the Dallas Museum of Art in 1948 and the Art Institute of Chicago in 1953. She also participated in several group exhibitions, including *Contemporary Photography* at the Contemporary Arts Association in Houston in 1951 and *Abstraction in Photography* at the Museum of Modern Art in New York in 1952. Although declining health forced Corpron to abandon new photographic projects in the early 1950s, she continued exploring the nuances of light in prints she made from the negatives of her earlier work. Her photographs received acclaim in such group exhibitions as *Women of Photography: An Historical Survey* at the San Francisco Museum of Art in 1975. During 1980, Corpron was the focus of a retrospective at the Amon Carter Museum in Fort Worth. Upon her death in 1988, the Amon Carter Museum became heir to her negatives and related archives.   —JAG

Selected References:
Murdock, Robert M. *Works on Paper: Southwest 1978*. Dallas: Dallas Museum of Fine Arts, 1978.
Mitchell, Margaretta. *Recollections: Ten Women of Photography*. New York: Viking Press, 1979.
Sandweiss, Martha A. *Carlotta Corpron: Designer with Light*. Austin: University of Texas Press for the Amon Carter Museum, Fort Worth, 1980.
Traub, Charles H., et al. *Tradition and the Unpredictable: The Allan Chasanoff Photographic Collection*. Houston: The Museum of Fine Arts, Houston, 1994.

❏ **JEFFREY COWIE**
Born 1958, New Brunswick, New Jersey
Lives in New York, New York, and Hartford, Connecticut

Jeffrey Cowie's work has evolved from lyrical abstractions to vividly graphic collages of screenprints and found imagery. Cowie studied painting at the Rhode Island School of Design and spent a year in Rome on the school's European honors program before receiving a B.F.A. in 1982. He moved to Houston later that year to accept a Core Residency Fellowship at the Glassell School of Art. The following year, he participated in a group show at Square One Gallery in Houston, and in 1984 he was featured in *Texas Only* at the Laguna Gloria Art Museum in Austin. In 1986, Cowie began an affiliation with Hiram Butler Gallery in Houston, and the following year his work was introduced to Dallas audiences by Barry Whistler Gallery. During 1988, he was featured in *New American Talent* at the Laguna Gloria Art Museum and in the *First Texas Triennial Exhibition* at the Contemporary Arts Museum in Houston. He was included in the Assistance League of Houston's *Texas Art Celebration* 89 at the Cullen Center. In Houston in 1991, Cowie was featured in the group show *Out: Voices from a Queer Nation* at DiverseWorks Artspace and in *Creative Partners* at Rice University's Sewall Art Gallery. He accepted a fellowship at the Edward Albee Foundation in Montauk, New York, in 1993 and subsequently settled in New York City. Cowie created stage-set designs for the Samuel Beckett Theater and the Soho Rep Theater in New York in 1994, while continuing to exhibit regularly with Devin Borden Hiram Butler Gallery in Houston. In 1996, he designed the stage set for a production by the Alley Theatre in Houston of Tennessee Williams's *A Streetcar Named Desire*.   —RM

Selected References:
Zeitlin, Marilyn A., Marge Goldwater, and David Ross. *The First Texas Triennial Exhibition: 1988*. Houston: Contemporary Arts Museum, 1988.
McKay, Gary. "Young at Art." *Houston Metropolitan Magazine*, December 1990, 50–51.

❏ **BEN CULWELL**
Born 1918, San Antonio, Texas
Died 1992, Temple, Texas

As a unique proponent of Expressionism in Texas, Ben Culwell created highly personal paintings and drawings that transcend generational and art historical connections to both the Regionalist movement of the Southwest and the New York-based school of Abstract Expressionism. After growing up in Houston, Culwell moved to Dallas in 1934, where he attended the Dallas Art Institute and Southern Methodist University. He left for New York in 1935 and remained there for a year, studying painting at Columbia University under Walter Pach. Returning to Dallas in 1937, he continued painting while selling insurance for a living. Culwell enlisted in the Navy in 1941, serving in the South Pacific on the USS *Pensacola* from 1942 to 1944. During his active duty, he kept a diary of drawings that poignantly recorded all aspects of his experience at war; in 1945, these works were exhibited at the Dallas Museum of Art. He received national exposure in *Fourteen Americans*, a 1946 exhibition at the Museum of Modern Art in New York, which also featured Arshile Gorky, Robert Motherwell, and Mark Tobey, among others. Although the Museum of Modern Art purchased two of his works in 1947, Culwell was not able to build a career as an artist in Dallas. He turned again to the insurance business to support his family. However, over the following four decades, he continued developing a unique body of abstract paintings and drawings. Focusing exclusively on art after his retirement in 1974, Culwell ultimately earned critical attention in the Texas art scene with a retrospective at the McNay Institute in San Antonio in 1977 and an exhibition of drawings at The Menil Collection in Houston in 1987.   —JAG

Selected References:
Miller, Dorothy C., ed. *Fourteen Americans*. New York: Museum of Modern Art, 1946.
Goetzmann, William H., and Becky Duval Reese. *Texas Images and Visions*. Austin: University of Texas at Austin, Archer M. Huntington Art Gallery, 1983.
Hopps, Walter. *Adrenaline Hour: The South Pacific, World War II*. Houston: The Menil Collection, 1987.

❏ **BILL DAVENPORT**
Born 1962, Greenfield, Massachusetts
Lives in Houston, Texas

Bill Davenport questions both the form and the content of Modernism, looking to popular culture, craft, and folk art to create wittily hybrid sculptures. Davenport received a B.F.A. from the Rhode Island School of Design in 1986 and an M.F.A. from the University of Massachusetts in 1990, before coming to Houston to participate in the Core Residency Program later that year. In 1993, he had his first solo exhibition at Wierzbowski Gallery in Houston. The following year, he began an association with Inman Gallery and also collaborated with David Aylsworth and Giles Lyon in presenting *Buttered Side Up*, a three-person exhibition at Lawndale Art and Performance Center in Houston. In 1996 and 1997, this exhibition toured in expanded form to Hallwalls Contemporary Art Center in Buffalo, New York, and the Koffler Gallery in North York, Ontario. Davenport began editing and publishing *Artletter*, a biweekly journal of contemporary art, in 1995, when he also began contributing critical writing to *Artnews* and Houston's *ArtLies*. In 1997, he was awarded a grant from the Louis Comfort Tiffany Foundation, had his first solo exhibition in New York at Cristinerose Gallery, and was featured in *Simply Beautiful* at the Contemporary Arts Museum in Houston. That same year, he and Francesca Fuchs cocurated *Fish and Chips*, an exhibition of British artists for DiverseWorks Artspace in Houston. Davenport's work was seen in solo exhibitions at Sala Diaz in San Antonio in 1998, and at Angstrom Gallery in Dallas and Inman Gallery in Houston in 1999.   —ALG

Selected References:
Brunon, Bernard. "Basic Attitude." In *Buttered Side Up: David Aylsworth, Bill Davenport, Giles Lyon*, by Bernard Brunon. Houston: Lawndale Art and Performance Center, 1994.
Colpitt, Frances. "Bill Davenport at Inman." *Art in America* 84, no. 3 (March 1996), 105.
Emenhiser, Karen. "Puerile Utopias." In *Buttered Side Up: David Aylsworth, Bill Davenport, Giles Lyon*, by Bernard Brunon. Buffalo, New York: Hallwalls Contemporary Art Center; North York, Ontario: Koffler Gallery, 1996.
Moody, Tom. "Bill Davenport at Cristinerose." *Artforum* 35, no. 8 (April 1997): 95.

❏ **JEFF DeLUDE**
    Born 1955, New York, New York
    Lives in Houston, Texas

Jeff DeLude's figurative paintings chart unreal and psychologically charged realms. DeLude received a B.F.A. from the Middle Tennessee State University in Murfreesboro in 1978 and an M.F.A. from the University of Houston in 1981. During 1984, he was featured in concurrent exhibitions at DiverseWorks Artspace and William A. Graham Gallery in Houston. The following year, his work was included in a juried show at Lawndale Art and Performance Center in Houston, an invitational exhibition at Main Gallery at the University of Texas at El Paso, and *Fresh Paint: The Houston School* at the MFAH. In 1986, he participated in *Texas Time Machine*, a group show at the Cullen Center in Houston that illustrated the history of Texas for the state's sesquicentennial celebration. DeLude had a solo exhibition that same year at William A. Graham Gallery, where he showed a series of allegorical paintings influenced by Mexican folk traditions. During 1988, he was featured in the *Texas Art* exhibition cosponsored by The Menil Collection, the Contemporary Arts Museum, and the MFAH. In 1991, he was included in *Creative Partners*, an exhibition at Rice University's Sewall Art Gallery. DeLude also helped open Houston's Ocotillo Gallery in 1995. During 1999, No tsu oh Gallery in Houston exhibited a survey of his work.   —MG

Selected References:
DeLude, Jeff. "Statement." *Houston Art Scene* 1, no. 4 (January/February 1981), n.p.
Rose, Barbara, and Susie Kalil. *Fresh Paint: The Houston School.* Austin: Texas Monthly Press; Houston: The Museum of Fine Arts, Houston, 1985.

❏ **RACKSTRAW DOWNES**
    Born 1939, Kent, England
    Lives in New York, New York

The panoramic paintings of Rackstraw Downes present the contemporary landscape with the interventions of industry poignantly apparent, subverting the viewer's preconceptions of the picturesque. Downes studied English literature at Cambridge University in England, where he graduated in 1961. He came to the United States later that year to study painting at Yale, where he was taught by Alex Katz and Al Held, and received an M.F.A. in 1964. Downes was awarded a postgraduate fellowship to the University of Pennsylvania. He had his first solo show at Swarthmore College in Pennsylvania in 1969. Later that year, he began exhibiting in New York, and his studies of the urban landscapes of the Northeast garnered widespread critical acclaim in the 1970s. He knew and greatly admired the realist painter and writer Fairfield Porter and he edited an anthology of Porter's writings that was published in 1979. Downes first encountered the landscape around Texas City during a visit to the College of the Mainland in the early 1980s, and he was fascinated by its confluence of heavy industry and animal life. He returned to the area to paint in 1986, and his compelling records of the Gulf Coast were featured in exhibitions in New York in 1987, 1991, and 1997. During these years, Texas Gallery introduced his work to Houston audiences. Although he maintained a home in New York, until 1997 Downes spent his winter months in Galveston. In 1998 and 1999, he undertook residencies at the Chinati Foundation in Marfa, Texas, where he made a series of works documenting Donald Judd's architectural projects set in the plains of West Texas.   —RM

Selected References:
Downes, Rackstraw, ed. *Fairfield Porter: Art in Its Own Terms.* New York: Taplinger Publishing Company, 1979.
Glueck, Grace. "Art: Rackstraw Downes and the Unspectacular." *New York Times*, 10 February 1984.
Yau, John. *Rackstraw Downes.* New York: Hirschl and Adler Modern, 1984.
Anderson Spivy, Alexandra. "Local Knowledge: Rackstraw Downes Paints Things as They Are." *ArtsMagazine* 66, no. 7 (March 1992): 38–41.
Herrera, Hayden. *Rackstraw Downes.* New York: Marlborough Gallery, 1997.

❏ **JAMES DRAKE**
    Born 1946, Lubbock, Texas
    Lives in El Paso, Texas

The border culture of El Paso and its neighboring Ciudad Juárez has provided inspiration for James Drake's stark, elegant installations and powerful drawings. Drake moved with his family from the Texas Panhandle to El Paso in the 1960s. He studied at the Art Center College of Design in Pasadena, California, where he received a B.F.A. in 1969 and an M.F.A. in 1970, before returning to El Paso. Significantly, Drake had his first solo museum exhibition across the border in Ciudad Juárez, at the Museo de Arte y Historia, in 1976. Five years later, the Amarillo Art Center organized another solo exhibition of his work, which traveled throughout Texas. In 1983, he was included in the New Orleans Triennial at the New Orleans Museum of Art and in *Southern Fictions* at the Contemporary Arts Museum in Houston; he also began an affiliation with Texas Gallery in Houston. During the mid-1980s, Drake began a project titled *Juárez/El Paso*, which formed the basis for his solo exhibition at the Contemporary Arts Museum in 1988. He had further solo exhibitions that year at the Alternative Museum in New York and the University of Texas at San Antonio. In 1990, the Corcoran Gallery of Art in Washington, D.C., showcased his work. He received a major commission in 1991 from the Civil Rights Institute and the Historic Preservation Authority of Birmingham, Alabama. Drake had a solo show at the El Paso Museum of Art in 1994, and later that year he presented *Poison Amor*, a collaboration with Terry Allen, at Blue Star Art Space in San Antonio and the Sarah Campbell Blaffer Gallery at the University of Houston. In 1996, Drake presented his first installation employing video in his solo exhibition *Tongue-Cut Sparrows* at DiverseWorks Artspace in Houston. In 2000, he was among the artists to be featured in the Whitney Biennial.   —RM

Selected References:
Sultan, Terrie. *James Drake: Place and Passage.* Washington, D.C.: Corcoran Gallery of Art, 1990.
Brooks, Rosetta. *Poison Amor.* San Antonio: Blue Star Art Space, 1994.
Reese, Becky Duval, and Marilyn A. Zeitlin. *James Drake: The Sky Was Swirling Like a Snake.* El Paso, Texas: El Paso Museum of Art, 1994.
Kalil, Susie. *James Drake, Tongue-Cut Sparrows.* Houston: DiverseWorks Artspace, 1996.

❏ **MELVIN EDWARDS**
    Born 1937, Houston, Texas
    Lives in New York, New York

Melvin Edwards makes assembled metal sculptures that are outwardly abstract but contain subtle references to traditional African designs. When Edwards was seven, he and his family moved from MacNair, Texas, to Dayton, Ohio, but they returned to Texas and settled in Houston when he was twelve. Edwards attended Wheatley Senior High School, where he excelled as an athlete. In 1953, he became one of the first black students to attend art classes at the school of the MFAH. He moved to Los Angeles in 1955 and entered the University of Southern California in 1957. There he studied under Hal Gebhardt, and in 1960 he began working with welded metals. That same year, Edwards exhibited his first sculpture in a group exhibition at the Los Angeles County Museum of Art. In 1963, he created the first in his ongoing series of wall-mounted pieces called *Lynch Fragments*. He graduated with a B.F.A. in 1965 and immediately was offered a solo show at the Santa Barbara Museum of Art. The following year, Edwards moved to New York, where he temporarily laid aside his *Lynch Fragments* series to develop free-standing geometric sculptures. In 1969, he completed his first large public sculpture, for the campus of Cornell University in Ithaca, New York. Edwards quickly built a reputation in New York, and in 1970 he was featured in a solo exhibition at the Whitney Museum of American Art. In 1975, he was awarded a Guggenheim Fellowship. Over the subsequent two decades, Edwards shifted his focus periodically between the ongoing *Lynch Fragments* series and freestanding geometric works. In 1993, he was the focus of a major retrospective organized by the Neuberger Museum of Art at the State University of New York in Purchase.   —*RM*

Selected References:
Gedeon, Lucinda H., et al. *Melvin Edwards Sculpture: A Thirty Year Retrospective 1963–1993*. Purchase, New York: Neuberger Museum of Art, State University of New York, 1993.
Edwards, Melvin, and Jayne Cortez. *Fragments*. New York: Bola Press, 1994.

❏ JEFF ELROD
Born 1966, Irving, Texas
Lives in New York, New York

Jeff Elrod's use of the computer as a means of creative release has produced witty and seductive work that eloquently captures the current debates of painting. Elrod attended the University of North Texas, Denton, where he received a B.F.A. in 1991. Later that year, he came to Houston and entered the Core Residency Program at the Glassell School of Art. In 1993, he continued his residency at the Rijksakademie van Beeldende Kunsten and had a solo exhibition at the Rijksakademie Exhibits Gallery in Amsterdam. Back in Houston in 1994, Elrod participated in group shows at DiverseWorks Artspace and Commerce Street Warehouse and also had a solo exhibition at New Gallery. In 1996, he had a solo show at Art of This Century, a Houston gallery founded by the artist in collaboration with Mark Flood. During 1997, he exhibited his first series of *Analog* paintings at Texas Gallery in Houston and was awarded a grant from the Louis Comfort Tiffany Foundation. The following year, Elrod undertook a residency at the Chinati Foundation in Marfa, Texas, where he presented work in two solo exhibitions. During this period, Elrod also participated in *Painting, Now and Forever, Part I* at the Pat Hearn Gallery in New York, an exhibition that also featured such senior artists as Kenneth Noland and Larry Poons, and in *Abstract Painting, Once Removed*, an exhibition at the Contemporary Arts Museum in Houston. In 1999, Elrod was featured with artist Lisa Ruyter at Pat Hearn Gallery; in a solo exhibition at ArtPace Foundation for Contemporary Art in San Antonio; and in *Fabstraction*, a traveling group exhibition organized by Dave Hickey, seen in Houston at Texas Gallery.   —*MG*

Selected References:
Colpitt, Frances. "Going against the Grain." *Art in America* 83, no. 4 (April 1995): 43–47.
Friis-Hansen, Dana, David Pagel, and Raphael Rubinstein. *Abstract Painting, Once Removed*. Houston: Contemporary Arts Museum, 1998.
Dailey, Meghan. "Jeff Elrod/Lisa Ruyter: Pat Hearn Gallery." *Artforum* 37, no. 10 (summer 1999): 157.

❏ SHARON ENGELSTEIN
Born 1965, Montreal, Canada
Lives in Houston, Texas

Sharon Engelstein's biomorphic sculptures examine the human anatomy through metaphor, fragmentation, and dissection. After receiving a B.A. in journalism and fine arts at the University of South Florida, Tampa, Engelstein received an M.F.A. from the Claremont Graduate Program in Claremont, California, in 1990. That same year, she moved to Houston to join the Core Residency Program at the Glassell School of Art. She was featured in the 1991 *Introductions* exhibition at William A. Graham Gallery and quickly became one of the rising talents on the Houston art scene. In 1992, she participated in the *Texas Art Celebration* exhibition sponsored by the Assistance League of Houston and was awarded a third-place prize. During 1993, Engelstein exhibited in group shows in Houston at Texas Gallery, the MFAH, the Contemporary Arts Museum, and the Glassell School of Art; outside of Houston she was seen at Women and Their Work in Austin, Blue Star Art Space in San Antonio, and Lyons Wier Gallery in Chicago. In 1994, she was featured in exhibitions hosted by the Satellite Space of the University of Texas at San Antonio and by the Museum of Surgical Science in Chicago. That same year, she received a Creative Artist Program Award from the Cultural Arts Council of Houston/Harris County. In 1995, she was honored with a grant from the Louis Comfort Tiffany Foundation. Engelstein participated actively in many nationwide group shows, including exhibitions at Hunter Gallery in Austin, Barry Whistler Gallery in Dallas, and the Nexus Contemporary Art Center in Atlanta. In 1996, she was featured in solo exhibitions at Houston's Project Row Houses and Texas Gallery. She was among the artists profiled by the *Texas Draws* exhibition at the Contemporary Arts Museum in Houston in 1999.   —*MG*

Selected References:
Johnson, Patricia Covo. *Contemporary Art in Texas*. Roseville East, New South Wales, Australia: Craftsman House, 1995.
Herbert, Lynn M. *Texas Draws*. Houston: Contemporary Arts Museum, 1999.

❏ IBSEN ESPADA
Born 1952, New York, New York
Lives in Houston, Texas

Ibsen Espada has developed an expressive yet structured abstract vocabulary through his calligraphically vivid paintings and drawings. Espada spent his childhood in Puerto Rico. When he was thirteen, he met exiled Cuban muralist Rolando Lopez Dirube, with whom he subsequently studied in Puerto Rico and the Dominican Republic. Espada received a B.F.A. from the University of the Sacred Heart in Puerto Rico in 1975 and later that year he moved to Texas. He was awarded a Frank Freed Memorial Scholarship to study at the Glassell School of Art in 1977, and the following year he had his first solo show in Houston, at the Christ Church Cathedral. He was featured by the MFAH in the 1985 exhibition *Fresh Paint: The Houston School* and in the major 1987 exhibition *Hispanic Art in the United States*, which embarked on a national tour. That same year, Espada was included in *The Third Coast: A Look at Art in Texas* at the Aspen Art Museum in Colorado; he also began an affiliation with McMurtrey Gallery in Houston. In 1990, he had solo shows in Texas at the Art Museum of Southeast Texas in Beaumont and at the Amarillo Art Center. In the early 1990s, he completed a number of artist residencies, including periods at Texas A&M University in College Station and Bellaire High School in Houston. In 1995, he participated in *Texas Art for Russia*, an exchange exhibition organized by the Art League of Houston, which toured Russian venues. That same year, Espada was an artist-in-residence in the MFAH program "A Place for All People." He was featured in the museum's "Artists at Work" program the following year, completing a large-scale mural for the Flores Branch of the Houston Public Library.   —*RM*

Selected References:
Rose, Barbara, and Susie Kalil. *Fresh Paint: The Houston School*. Austin: Texas Monthly Press; Houston: The Museum of Fine Arts, Houston, 1985.
Beardsley, John, and Jane Livingston. *Hispanic Art in the United States: Thirty Contemporary Painters and Sculptors*. New York: Abbeville Press; Houston: The Museum of Fine Arts, Houston, 1987.

❏ VERNON FISHER
Born 1943, Fort Worth, Texas
Lives in Fort Worth, Texas

Vernon Fisher explores Postmodern narrative forms, using images and text with a remarkable sense of poetry and an endless appetite for formal experimentation. Fisher received a B.A. from Hardin-Simmons University in Abilene, Texas, in 1967 and undertook graduate studies at the University of Illinois in Champaign-Urbana. He received an M.F.A. in 1969 and returned to Texas to teach at Austin College in Sherman. In 1978, he joined the faculty of the University of North Texas, Denton. With their combination of intriguing narratives and absorbing images, Fisher's works of the early 1980s soon gathered critical acclaim and national recognition. In 1981, Fisher was included in the Whitney Biennial and in exhibitions at the Guggenheim Museum in New York and the Hirshhorn Museum and Sculpture Garden in Washington, D.C. In 1984, he began an affiliation with Hiram Butler Gallery in Houston; subsequently he exhibited with Barry Whistler Gallery and Gerald Peters Gallery in Dallas, as well. His work also traveled to international venues, including the Centro Cultural Arte Contemporáneo in Mexico City in 1986 and the Institute for Contemporary Arts in London in 1987. During 1989, he was the subject of a major touring exhibition, organized by the La Jolla Museum of Contemporary Art in California, which visited the Contemporary Arts Museum in Houston and the Modern Art Museum of Fort Worth. In 1990, Fisher became the first Texas artist to be honored with a solo show at the Museum of Modern Art in New York, where he presented his installation *Movements among the Dead*. He was also the subject of solo exhibitions at the Museum of Contemporary Art in Chicago in 1992 and Blue Star Art Space in San Antonio in 1994. Fisher was awarded a Guggenheim Fellowship in 1995. In 1998, the Miami Art Museum presented *Map*, an installation featuring the artist's text and cast-epoxy flies. Devin Borden Hiram Butler Gallery in Houston presented recent paintings in 1999. In 2000, Fisher was among the artists to be featured in the Whitney Biennial.   —*RM*

Selected References:
Mayo, Marti. *Vernon Fisher: Forty Paintings and Drawings*. Houston: Contemporary Arts Museum, 1980.
Graze, Sue. *Vernon Fisher: Lost for Words*. Dallas: Dallas Museum of Art, 1988.
Davis, Hugh M., and Madeleine Grynsztejn. *Vernon Fisher*. La Jolla, California: La Jolla Museum of Contemporary Art, 1989.
Fisher, Vernon. *Navigating by the Stars: Writings by Vernon Fisher*. Chicago: Landfall Press, 1989.
Dabrowski, Magdalena. *Vernon Fisher: Movements among the Dead*. New York: Museum of Modern Art, 1990.
Graze, Sue. *Vernon Fisher*. Dallas: Gerald Peters Gallery, 1997.

❑ **MARK FLOOD**
    Born 1957, Houston, Texas
    Lives in Houston, Texas

Mark Flood's paintings and drawings embody a wryly subversive attitude toward contemporary culture, echoing the irreverence of punk rock music. Flood studied at Rice University from 1976 until 1981, when he left college and began exhibiting his work in alternative spaces. He participated in group shows at Studio One in Houston in 1981 and at DiverseWorks Artspace and the Midtown Art Center in 1985. During the late 1980s, Flood provided a catalyst for alternative exhibitions in Houston, often acting in the dual role of curator and artist. He organized and participated in the group show *Vandalism: Defacements and Other Alterations* at Screen Memories in 1987. The following year, he had a solo show of his *Billboard Alterations* series at DiverseWorks Artspace, and in 1989 he organized *Primal Screen* at Treebeard's in Houston. Flood invented the ironic gesture of selling advertising space on his canvases, and in 1990 he attained notoriety in the national press when his *Your Ad Here* series was featured in the *Wall Street Journal*. That same year, Flood began showing with Lynn Goode Gallery in Houston. In 1991, he was featured in the group show *Animals* at Max Fish Gallery in New York and in *The Perfect World in Contemporary Texas Art* at the San Antonio Museum of Art. He was included in *Primarily Paint* at the Laguna Gloria Art Museum in Austin in 1992 and had a solo exhibition at Zero One Gallery in Los Angeles in 1993. During 1995, Flood was seen in the group exhibitions *Changing Perspectives* at the Contemporary Arts Museum in Houston and *City Folk* at Holly Solomon Gallery in New York. He curated the exhibition program for Houston artist Jeff Elrod's alternative space, Art of This Century, in 1996. The following year, he collaborated with Mel Chin on *In the Name of the Place*, presented at the Museum of Contemporary Art in Los Angeles, and also had a two-person exhibition with Mark Allen at the Lawndale Art and Performance Center in Houston. In 1998, Flood curated *Local Heroes*, an exhibition of Houston underground photographers, for The Menil Collection and began exhibiting with Texas Gallery in Houston. Originally, "Mark Flood" was the name that John Peters used to signify his production as a visual artist, while he used "Perry Webb" to signify his work as a musician. Throughout the 1980s and 1990s, he was known by all three names in Houston. In 1999, however, Peters legally changed his name to Mark Flood.   —*RM*

Selected References:
Kalil, Susie. "Art and Commerce: Mark Flood Looks at the Uneasy Alliance." *Houston Press*, 27 February 1992.
Flood, Mark. *By and about Mark Flood*. Houston: Artists' Publication, 1995.
Dewan, Shaila. "Playing Around: A Quartet of Current Exhibits Show Art Can Be Fun and Challenging." *Houston Press*, 2–8 October 1997.

❑ **ROY FRIDGE**
    Born 1927, Beeville, Texas
    Lives in Port Aransas, Texas

Roy Fridge has developed a symbolic language in sculpture and assemblage to express the mystical roots of his native landscape. Fridge attended the University of Texas at Austin from 1944 until 1946, when he was drafted into the U.S. Navy. In 1948, he entered Baylor University in Waco, where he studied theater with the director Paul Baker and befriended Jim Love, who was also a student of Baker's at that time. Fridge received a B.A. in 1950, and in the early 1950s he established his own film company, among the first in Texas to produce color commercials for television. During the mid-1950s, he designed stage sets for the Dallas Little Theater. He began making sculpture in 1957, and later that year had his first exhibition at the Baylor Theater in Waco. He continued experimenting with film and, during 1959, made three films of his sculptures in motion. That same year, he had a solo show at the Waco Museum of Art. In 1962, Fridge's film *Theater USA* won Best National Presentation at the São Paulo Arts Festival in Brazil. Despite the success of his films, during the 1960s Fridge focused increasingly on sculpture. In 1963, he moved to Port Aransas, where he built a simple studio on the beach and began working as a virtual recluse. He rented a studio in Houston from Jim Love in 1966 and split his time between Houston and Galveston until 1969, when he accepted a teaching position at the University of Oklahoma. Fridge gave up teaching in 1973 and returned to his home in Port Aransas. He had a solo show at the Art Museum of South Texas in Corpus Christi in 1979 and participated in *Southern Fictions* at the Contemporary Arts Museum in Houston in 1983. Throughout the 1980s he maintained an affiliation with Moody Gallery in Houston. Fridge was honored with a second solo show at the Art Museum of South Texas in 1985.   —*RM*

Selected References:
Platt, Susan. "Roy Fridge: Moody Gallery." *Artforum* 19, no. 1 (September 1980): 77.
Ennis, Michael. "The Shrine of the Bleached Skull: The Eerie Sculptures of South Texas Hermit Roy Fridge." *Texas Monthly* 10, no. 11 (November 1982): 254–57.
Freudenheim, Susan. *Heroes, Hermits, Shamans, and Boats: Roy Fridge Selected Works, 1959–1985.* Corpus Christi: Art Museum of South Texas, 1985.

❑ **SALLY GALL**
    Born 1956, Washington, D.C.
    Lives in New York, New York

Sally Gall makes meditative black-and-white photographs that take images of water and landscape as their central motifs. Gall moved to Houston at the age of ten and began taking photographs in the early 1970s. She studied briefly at Reed College in Portland, Oregon, and at the San Francisco Art Institute, before graduating with a B.F.A. from the Rhode Island School of Design in 1978. She returned to Houston, where she had her first solo exhibition at Rice Media Center in 1978. Gall served as the associate director of Cronin Gallery between 1978 and 1981. She was featured in a survey of contemporary Texas photography at the Corcoran Gallery of Art in Washington, D.C., in 1981. During the early 1980s, she taught at the Glassell School of Art and the University of Houston. She received a fellowship from the National Endowment for the Arts in 1983, and began exhibiting with Texas Gallery in Houston that same year. Gall was awarded a grant by the Cultural Arts Council of Houston/Harris County in 1986, and began showing with Lieberman & Saul Gallery in New York the following year. A survey of Gall's work was presented in 1988 at the Contemporary Arts Museum in Houston to celebrate FotoFest. She moved to New York that same year, and her exhibitions at Julie Saul Gallery in New York garnered broad critical attention during the early 1990s. A book of Gall's photographs was published by Umbra Editions in 1995 to coincide with a traveling exhibition organized by the Southeast Museum of Photography in Daytona Beach, Florida.   —*RM*

Selected References:
Zeitlin, Marilyn A., and Christina West. *Sally Gall: Tropical Landscapes.* Houston: Contemporary Arts Museum, 1988.
Salter, James. *The Water's Edge: Photographs by Sally Gall.* San Francisco: Chronicle Books; New York: Umbra Editions, 1995.

❑ HARRY GEFFERT
Born in Live Oak County, Texas, 1934
Lives in Crowley, Texas

Harry Geffert's bronze sculptures unite technical brilliance with narrative complexity; using a broad range of casting techniques, he has explored the mythologies and everyday experiences that shape our lives. Geffert received a B.S. from the Southwest Texas State University in San Marcos, Texas, in 1957 and an M.A. from the New Mexico Highlands University in Las Vegas, New Mexico, in 1961. Geffert had his first solo exhibition, *Project South by Southwest,* at the Fort Worth Art Museum in 1971. He established the Green Mountain Foundry in Crowley, Texas, in 1980, and over the following decade it emerged as the state's premier fine arts foundry. In 1989, Geffert was included in *A Century of Sculpture in Texas 1889–1989* at the Archer M. Huntington Art Gallery at the University of Texas at Austin. He received a fellowship from the National Endowment for the Arts in 1990, when he also was featured in *Harry Geffert: Bronze Allegories,* a solo exhibition at the Dallas Museum of Art. In 1992, Geffert had his first Houston solo exhibition at Moody Gallery. The Art Museum of Southeast Texas in Beaumont featured him in a solo exhibition in 1994. His work and his association with other Texas artists were the focus of *Genesis in Fire: Works from the Green Mountain Foundry,* a 1995 exhibition at the Glassell School of Art in Houston. In 1998, the Dallas Visual Art Center honored Geffert with a Legend Award and a solo exhibition.   —MG

Selected References:
Freudenheim, Susan. "Harry Geffert." *Artforum* 25, no. 6 (February 1987): 123–24.
Davidow, Joan. *Harry Geffert: Bronze Allegories.* Dallas: Dallas Museum of Art, 1990.
Castle, Lynn P. *Harry Geffert: Pursuit.* Beaumont, Texas: Art Museum of Southeast Texas, 1994.
Greene, Alison de Lima. *Genesis in Fire: Works from the Green Mountain Foundry.* Houston: The Museum of Fine Arts, Houston, The Glassell School of Art, 1995.
Willour, Clint. *Harry Geffert: New Work.* Dallas: Dallas Visual Art Center, 1998.

❑ JOSEPH GLASCO
Born 1925, Paul's Valley, Oklahoma
Died 1996, Galveston, Texas

Joseph Glasco developed a distinctive abstract style characterized by a brilliant palette and syncopated compositional structures. Glasco moved with his family from Oklahoma to Tyler, Texas, in 1931, and entered the University of Texas at Austin in 1942. He was drafted into the Army in 1943 and saw combat duty in Germany toward the end of World War II. When the war ended in 1945, he enrolled in Portsmouth Art School in Bristol, England, returning later that year to Texas and to his family's new home in Dallas, where he worked as a commercial artist for the Dreyfuss department store. In 1946, he left Dallas for Los Angeles, where he studied at the Art Center School and later with Rico Lebrun at the Jeppson Art Institute. He moved to New York in 1949 and enrolled at the Art Students League. Glasco took New York by storm. By 1950, he had presented a successful one-person show at Perls Gallery and become the youngest artist represented in the collection of the Museum of Modern Art. In 1952, he was featured in the landmark *Fifteen Americans* exhibition at the Museum of Modern Art, along with Jackson Pollock and Mark Rothko. Glasco had frequent solo shows in New York in the 1950s and 1960s, while he lived briefly in Taos, New Mexico; Bucks County, Pennsylvania; and Boston. He began visiting Texas in the early 1970s, and in 1972 he settled in Galveston. There he developed his mature abstract style, collaging cut pieces of canvas to create graphic compositions. Glasco exhibited in Houston in the mid-1970s and established an affiliation with Meredith Long & Company. After a nine-year hiatus from New York galleries, he presented a solo show at Gimpel + Weitzenhoffer to critical acclaim in 1979. He was included in the MFAH exhibition *Fresh Paint: The Houston School* in 1985 and had a retrospective at the Contemporary Arts Museum in Houston in 1986. Glasco was featured in the 1991 Whitney Biennial. In 1995, he had a ten-year survey exhibition at the Galveston Arts Center, which traveled to Moody Gallery in Houston.   —RM

Selected References:
Miller, Dorothy C. *Fifteen Americans.* New York: Museum of Modern Art, 1952.
Leib, Vered. "Joseph Glasco: Painting Under Construction." *Artforum* 18, no. 3 (November 1979): 35–37.
Mayo, Marti, Michael Berryhill, and Julian Schnabel. *Joseph Glasco 1948–1986: A Sesquicentennial Exhibition.* Houston: Contemporary Arts Museum, 1986.
Greene, Alison de Lima. *New Work: Joseph Glasco.* Norman, Oklahoma: University of Oklahoma Museum of Art, 1990.
Willour, Clint, and Marti Mayo. *Joseph Glasco: A Celebration.* Galveston: Galveston Arts Center, 1995.

❑ DeWITT GODFREY
Born 1960, Houston, Texas
Lives in New York, New York

DeWitt Godfrey's sculptures balance biomorphic abstraction with a measured and nuanced geometry. Born in Houston, Godfrey grew up in Kalamazoo, Michigan. He received a B.A. from Yale University in 1982 and an M.F.A. from the Edinburgh College of Art in Scotland in 1996. Godfrey moved to Houston in 1982 as a fellow in the newly established Core Residency Program at the Glassell School of Art. In 1984, he had his first solo show at Hadler/Rodriguez Gallery in Houston. A year later, he created *Bayou Drawings,* his first major outdoor installation, which was placed along Buffalo Bayou as part of the annual Houston Festival. Godfrey moved to New York in 1986, but continued working in Texas on numerous projects. In the early 1990s, he presented work at nationwide venues, including Hiram Butler Gallery in Houston and David Beitzel Gallery in New York. A 1989 Luce Fellowship and a 1993 Artist's Fellowship from the Japan Foundation permitted Godfrey to study traditional stonecutting techniques in Japan. In 1994, he was awarded a Fulbright Fellowship that enabled him to complete graduate work in Scotland. He received a grant from the Louis Comfort Tiffany Foundation in 1997 and was featured in a solo exhibition at Devin Borden Hiram Butler Gallery that same year. In 1998, Godfrey was the focus of solo presentations at the Contemporary Arts Museum in Houston and the Sculpture Center in New York. He joined the faculty of Amherst College in Massachusetts in 1999.   —RM

Selected References:
Kotik, Charlotta. *Third Western States Exhibition.* Brooklyn, New York: Brooklyn Museum of Art, 1986.
Kimmelman, Michael. "Biomorphic Profiles." *New York Times,* 21 October 1988, 24(C).
Greene, Alison de Lima, Diane Planer Lovejoy, and William R. Thompson. "The Lillie and Hugh Roy Cullen Sculpture Garden of the Museum of Fine Arts, Houston." *The Museum of Fine Arts, Houston, Bulletin* 17 (April 1996), 54–55.
Mayo, Marti. *DeWitt Godfrey: A Sculpture and Two Drawings.* Houston: Contemporary Arts Museum, 1998.

❑ TAD GRIFFIN
Born 1966, Houston, Texas
Lives in Houston, Texas

A compelling tension between structure and gesture characterizes Tad Griffin's compositions. After receiving his B.F.A. from Texas A&M University at Commerce in 1991, Griffin returned to live and work in his native Houston. He participated in the Cheekwood National Contemporary Painting Competition in Nashville, Tennessee, that same year. In 1993, he was included in the *Texas Biennial Exhibition* organized by the McKinney Avenue Contemporary in Dallas and in the *34th Annual Invitational* exhibition at the Longview Museum of Fine Art in Longview, Texas. The Center for Research in Contemporary Art at the University of Texas at Arlington organized *A Project for Public Space,* Griffin's first solo exhibition, in 1994. That same year, Griffin also was featured in *Process, Strategy, Irony,* an exhibition curated by artist Aaron Parazette at DiverseWorks Artspace in Houston. In 1995, he participated in the exhibition *Texas Abstract, New Painting in the Nineties,* curated by Frances Colpitt for ArtPace Foundation for Contemporary Art in San Antonio. Griffin was featured in group exhibitions at Texas Gallery in Houston and Barry Whistler Gallery in Dallas in 1996 and 1997. The following year, he was among the artists featured in *Abstract Painting, Once Removed* at the Contemporary Arts Museum in Houston. In 1999, he was included in the exhibition *Post-Hypnotic*, curated by Barry Blinderman for the Illinois State University Gallery.   —MG

Selected References:
Colpitt, Frances. "Going against the Grain." *Art in America* 83, no. 4 (April 1995): 43–47.
Mitchell, Charles Dee. "Tad Griffin at the Center for Research in Contemporary Art." *Art in America* 83, no. 2 (February 1995): 100.
Friis-Hansen, Dana, David Pagel, and Raphael Rubinstein. *Abstract Painting, Once Removed.* Houston: Contemporary Arts Museum, 1998.
Blinderman, Barry, and Tom Moody. *Post-Hypnotic.* Normal, Illinois: Illinois State University, 1999.

❏ **VIRGIL GROTFELDT**
    Born 1948, Decatur, Illinois
    Lives in Houston, Texas, and New York, New York

Virgil Grotfeldt's paintings, drawings, and sculptures tap into mystical and subconscious sources of creativity. Grotfeldt grew up in a small Illinois town and graduated from Eastern Illinois University, Charleston, in 1971. He received an M.F.A. from the Tyler School of Art in Philadelphia in 1973 and moved to Houston in 1977. His early paintings followed a realist style, but in the 1980s he began striving for spiritual resonance and adopted an improvisational manner. He participated in group shows at the Glassell School of Art and DiverseWorks Artspace in Houston in 1985. Two years later, he had a solo exhibition at Gallery D'Theeboom in Amsterdam, Holland. Grotfeldt's 1988 exhibition at Hiram Butler Gallery in Houston began a six-year affiliation with that gallery. In 1991, he presented a solo exhibition at Lamar University in Beaumont. Grotfeldt began showing with Barbara Davis Gallery in Houston in 1995, and that same year he was included in *Genesis in Fire: Works from the Green Mountain Foundry* at the Glassell School of Art. In an extraordinarily active period, he participated in nine group shows during 1996. The following year, he was included in the *Second Texas Annual* at the Contemporary Art Center of Fort Worth and his work was showcased in a solo exhibition at Jason McCoy Gallery in New York.   —RM

Selected References:
Johnson, Patricia Covo. *Contemporary Art in Texas.* Roseville East, New South Wales, Australia: Craftsman House, 1995.
Hopps, Walter, et al. *American Images: The SBC Collection of Twentieth-Century American Art.* New York: Harry N. Abrams, Inc., 1996.
Willour, Clint. *With a Quiet Strength: Virgil Grotfeldt/Terrell James.* Galveston: Galveston Arts Center, 1997.

❏ **TRACY HARRIS**
    Born 1958, Lawton, Oklahoma
    Lives in Dallas, Texas

Tracy Harris's paintings combine the delicacy of architectural drawing with sensuous paint surfaces. Harris moved to Dallas with her family in 1960, when her father, an architect, began working for the Dallas firm of George Dahl. She studied at Southern Methodist University in Dallas, where she received a B.F.A. in 1980 and an M.F.A. in 1983. Harris had her first solo show that same year, at the Action/Influence Gallery in Dallas, and in 1994 she had a solo exhibition at Eastfield College in Mesquite, Texas. Throughout the mid-1980s, she participated in group exhibitions at DW Gallery in Dallas, where she had a solo exhibition in 1987. She was featured in the *First Texas Triennial Exhibition* at the Contemporary Arts Museum in Houston in 1988, and the following year had a solo exhibition at the Longview Museum of Fine Art in Longview, Texas. She began showing with William A. Graham Gallery in Houston in 1990. Harris had a solo show at Benton Gallery in Southampton, New York, in 1993, when she also began an affiliation with McMurtrey Gallery in Houston. She had a two-person exhibition, *Surface Pleasures*, with Otis Jones at the Galveston Arts Center in 1994. Harris was featured in solo exhibitions at McMurtrey Gallery in 1997 and 1999.   —RM

Selected References:
Zeitlin, Marilyn A., Marge Goldwater, and David Ross. *The First Texas Triennial Exhibition: 1988.* Houston: Contemporary Arts Museum, 1988.
Ennis, Michael. "Beneath the Surface." *Texas Monthly* [*Domain* suppl.] 8, no. 3 (March 1990): 12–14.
McBride, Elizabeth. "Tracy Harris." *Artnews* 90, no. 10 (December 1991): 137.

❏ **JOSEPH HAVEL**
    Born 1954, Minneapolis, Minnesota
    Lives in Houston, Texas

Joseph Havel's sculptures have a conceptual depth developed from his examination of existential issues, and a formal integrity derived from his investigation of materials. Havel received a B.F.A. from the University of Minnesota in Minneapolis in 1975 and an M.F.A. from Pennsylvania State University in 1979. He moved to Texas later that year to join the faculty of Austin College in Sherman. His first solo exhibition was in 1979 at the University of North Texas, Denton. In 1983, he participated in a group show at the Sculpture Center Gallery in New York, and the following year he had a solo exhibition at 500x Gallery in Dallas. Havel became an established figure in the Dallas-area art scene in the mid-1980s, with solo exhibitions at Texas Woman's University in Denton in 1985 and DW Gallery in Dallas in 1987. He began an affiliation with Barry Whistler Gallery in Dallas in 1988, and the following year began showing with Davis/McClain Gallery in Houston. Havel was included in *100 Years of Texas Sculpture* at the Archer M. Huntington Art Gallery of the University of Texas at Austin in 1989. He moved to Houston in 1991 to become associate director of the Glassell School of Art, where he took

charge of the Core Residency Program. In the 1990s, Havel increasingly became recognized throughout Texas, and his work was featured in exhibitions at Rice University in Houston and the Dallas Museum of Art in 1991, the Laguna Gloria Art Museum in Austin and the Arlington Museum of Art in 1992, and the Contemporary Arts Museum in Houston in 1993. He began an affiliation with Devin Borden Hiram Butler Gallery in Houston in 1994. The following year, he had a solo exhibition at the Satellite Space of the University of Texas at Blue Star Art Space in San Antonio. Also that year, he was invited to participate in the third exhibition in the series *Twentieth-Century American Sculpture at the White House*, installed in the First Ladies' Garden at the White House in Washington, D.C., and was awarded a grant from the Louis Comfort Tiffany Foundation. Havel was the subject of a solo exhibition at the Huntington Beach Art Center in California in 1996, when he also participated in the project *Shopping*, organized by Deitch Projects in New York. He became director of the Glassell School in 1996 and had a solo exhibition in Paris at Galerie Gabrielle Maubrie in 1997. During 1999, he realized an installation for Project Row Houses in Houston and was featured in a solo exhibition at the Galveston Arts Center. For the opening of the Audrey Jones Beck Building at the MFAH in 2000, Havel was commissioned to create two monumental bronze reliefs to flank the museum's Main Street entrance. Also in 2000, he was among the artists to be featured in the Whitney Biennial.   —RM

Selected References:
Doroshenko, Peter, and David Pagel. *Joseph Havel.* Huntington Beach, California: Huntington Beach Art Center, 1996.
Youngs, Christopher. *Interactions: Susan Schelle, Mark Gomes, Lisa Ludwig, Joseph Havel.* Reading, Pennsylvania: Freedman Gallery, 1996.
Sans, Jerome. *Joseph Havel: Commun.* Paris: Galerie Gabrielle Maubrie, 1997.
Smith, Roberta. "Hudson Valley Conversation." *New York Times*, 18 July 1997.

❏ **RACHEL HECKER**
    Born 1958, Providence, Rhode Island
    Lives in Houston, Texas

Rachel Hecker uses a graphic airbrush technique to create montages of nudes, cartoon characters, and advertising slogans, exposing a subconscious sexual drive within pop culture and commerce. Hecker received a B.F.A., summa cum laude, from the Moore College of Art in Philadelphia in 1980 and an M.F.A. from the Rhode Island School of Design in 1982. She moved to Houston that same year to join the faculty of the Glassell School of Art, where she later became associate director. In 1984, Hecker began an affiliation with Texas Gallery in Houston, where she had her first solo show in 1988. She was featured in the *First Texas Triennial Exhibition* at the Contemporary Arts Museum in Houston that same year. In 1989, Hecker was awarded a fellowship from the National Endowment for the Arts. A mural commission she completed that year for DiverseWorks Artspace in Houston was a protest against censorship. During

1990, she participated in group shows at Women and Their Work in Austin and at the University of West Florida in Pensacola. Hecker was represented in *Out: Voices from a Queer Nation* at DiverseWorks Artspace in 1991. She participated in *Public Pictures*, a billboard project for the 1992 Houston International Festival, and that same year began teaching at the University of Houston. In 1993, she had a solo exhibition at the Galveston Arts Center. During 1995, Hecker was featured in a two-person exhibition with Peter Halley at the Dallas Museum of Art and was also the focus of a solo exhibition at the Contemporary Arts Museum in Houston. The following year, she had a solo show at the ArtPace Foundation for Contemporary Art in San Antonio. Her work was featured in the exhibition *Finders/Keepers* at the Contemporary Arts Museum in 1997. In 1999, Hecker completed a commission for Terminal B of the George Bush Intercontinental Airport in Houston.   —*RM*

Selected References:
Cvetkovich, Ann. *Rachel Hecker: Pleasure and Commerce*. Houston: Contemporary Arts Museum, 1995.
Nill, Annegreth. *Rachel Hecker: Encounters 6*. Dallas: Dallas Museum of Art, 1995.
Cvetkovich, Ann. "Almost Heaven." *Grand Street* 15, no. 4 (1996): 178–85.

❑ RICHARD HINSON
Born 1955, Beaumont, Texas
Lives in Houston, Texas

Richard Hinson presents his photographs of urban sites alongside texts that describe violent incidents that have occurred in each locale, uncovering a vision of the modern American city in which danger looms as a perpetual threat. Hinson studied music theory and composition at Lamar University in Beaumont, where he received a B.S. in 1983. While studying music he became seriously interested in photography, and he began post-baccalaureate studies at Lamar University in 1984. He had a solo show at the John Gray Library at Lamar in 1987, and briefly taught photography classes in the university's continuing education program before moving to Houston in 1988. Hinson participated in a 1990 group exhibition at the Houston Center for Photography. He completed an M.F.A. in 1991 at the University of Houston, where George Krause was among his mentors. The following year, he was included in the group exhibition *Critical Fictions* at the Dishman Art Gallery at Lamar University. He was featured in the 1993 exhibition *Visible Language* at the University of Illinois in Chicago and in the 1994 Arena Productions exhibition *Loop to Loop* at Foster/Freeman Gallery in San Antonio. In 1995, he had solo shows at Texas Tech University in Lubbock and at Amarillo College. During 1996, Hinson participated in the Design Industries Foundation Fighting Aids benefit exhibition, *Proof of Love*, at Lynn Goode Gallery in Houston. The following year, he had a solo show of his *Victims* series at the University of Texas Health Science Center at Houston. In 1998, Hinson was featured in a solo exhibition at the Houston Center for Photography.   —*RM*

Selected References:
Staartjes, Hans. "Fiction, Sex, and Violence." *Spot* 12, no. 1 (spring 1993): 22.
Calledare, Donald. "Decoding Violence: A Few Texas Photographers." *ArtLies* 2 (May/June 1994): 10.

❑ ALEXANDRE HOGUE
Born 1898, Memphis, Missouri
Died 1994, Tulsa, Oklahoma

Creating powerful images of the desolation of farmland in rural America, Alexandre Hogue became one of Texas's premier artists and a leader of the Lone Star Regionalist movement. When Hogue was six weeks old, his family moved from Missouri to Denton, Texas, and as a youth he began formal art training in the Saturday drawing classes of Denton artist Elizabeth Hillyar. After graduating from high school in 1918, he attended the Minneapolis College of Art and Design. From 1921 to 1925, he worked in New York as a commercial illustrator, studied at the Art Students League, and visited the Woodstock Artists Colony. During this period, he returned to Texas every summer to accompany Frank Reaugh on his sketching tours. Beginning in 1926, Hogue divided his time between teaching design at YMCA camps near Dallas and working in Taos, New Mexico, where he became acquainted with Ernest Blumenschein and other New Mexico Modernists. In 1929, he had his first solo exhibition at the MFAH. During the 1930s, he taught at Texas State College for Women (later Texas Woman's University) and Hockaday Junior College. Acting as a principal spokesman for the Regionalist movement, Hogue helped found the Dallas Artists League in 1932, served as charter member of the Lone Star Printmakers in 1938, and received commissions from the art program of the Works Progress Administration for post-office murals from 1939 to 1941. He earned national attention in 1937, when his depictions of Dust Bowl landscapes were featured in *Life* magazine. In 1942, he contributed to the war effort as a technical illustrator for North American Aviation. He moved to Oklahoma after World War II and headed the art department at the University of Tulsa from 1945 to 1963. Following his retirement in 1968, Hogue continued painting scenes of the Southwest from a farm outside of Big Bend. In 1984, the Philbrook Art Center at the University of Tulsa organized a major retrospective of his work, which toured nationally.   —*JAG*

Selected References:
Goetzmann, William H., and Becky Duval Reese. *Texas Images and Visions*. Austin: University of Texas at Austin, Archer M. Huntington Art Gallery, 1983.
Rosson DeLong, Lea. *Nature's Forms/Nature's Forces: The Art of Alexandre Hogue*. Tulsa, Oklahoma: Philbrook Art Center; University of Oklahoma Press, 1984.
Stewart, Rick. *Lone Star Regionalism: The Dallas Nine and Their Circle, 1928–1945*. Austin: University of Texas Press; Dallas: Dallas Museum of Art, 1985.

❑ DOROTHY HOOD
Born 1919, Bryan, Texas
Lives in Houston, Texas

Dorothy Hood's paintings evoke the color and texture of vast geological landscapes, while alluding to interior, psychological spaces. Hood attended the Rhode Island School of Design from 1937 to 1940 on a national scholastic scholarship and completed her studies at the Art Students League in New York in 1941. Between 1943 and 1961, she spent most of her time in Mexico City and Puebla, Mexico. The poet Pablo Neruda introduced her to the great muralist José Clemente Orozco, who became her close friend. She also befriended other avant-garde artists of the Mexican Renaissance, including Diego Rivera, Frida Kahlo, Leanora Carrington, and Rufino Tamayo. Reflecting these associations, her drawings from the 1950s distill Surrealist influences with her own graphic simplicity. Hood visited New York in 1956 and 1957, and her work was included in exhibitions at the Museum of Modern Art in New York in 1958 and 1959. She married Bolivian composer Velasco Maidana, and in 1961 the couple settled in Houston, where Hood joined the faculty of the Museum School. She began showing with Meredith Long & Company and was the focus of a solo show at the MFAH in 1963. Hood also was featured in solo exhibitions in Houston at the Contemporary Arts Museum in 1970 and at Rice University in 1971. In 1973, the American Academy of Arts and Letters awarded her the prestigious Childe Hassam Prize and showcased her work in New York. Hood was the focus of a second solo exhibition at the MFAH in 1975. She was included in the museum's 1985 exhibition *Fresh Paint: The Houston School*. In 1988, she received the Outstanding Achievement in Visual Arts award from the Women's National Caucus for Art. She was awarded an honorary doctorate from the Rhode Island School of Design in 1990. In the fall of 1998, Hood was honored by three simultaneous exhibitions in Houston when the Lawndale Art and Performance Center, Transco Tower, and MD Modern each celebrated her work and her important contribution to the cultural life of the city.   —*RM*

Selected References:
Harithas, James. *Dorothy Hood Recent Paintings*. Houston: Contemporary Arts Museum, 1970.
Montebello, Philippe de. "A Surrealist Abstraction: Dorothy Hood's Haiti." *The Museum of Fine Arts, Houston, Bulletin* 2, no. 4 (spring 1971): 48–49.
Harithas, James. *Dorothy Hood Paintings*. Syracuse, New York: Everson Museum of Art, 1972.
______. *Dorothy Hood Drawings*. Syracuse, New York: Everson Museum of Art, 1974.
Hobbs, Robert. *Dorothy Hood's Collages: Connecting Change*. Washington, D.C.: Wallace Wentworth Gallery, 1988.

❑ EARLIE HUDNALL, JR.
Born 1946, Hattiesburg, Mississippi
Lives in Houston, Texas

Earlie Hudnall, Jr.'s photographs chronicle the rhythms and continuities of African-American communities in Houston. Hudnall served with the Marines in Vietnam from 1966 until 1968. Soon afterward, he moved to Houston to attend Texas Southern University, where he received a B.A. in 1976. After graduation, he worked as staff photographer at Texas Southern University, while developing his studies of local neighborhoods. He was awarded an Art in Community Places Grant by the Cultural Arts Council of Houston/Harris County in 1981, when he also presented his first solo exhibition at the Kashmere Gardens Branch of the Houston Public Library. In 1984, he was included in the exhibition *African Photographers of the Southwest* at Texas Southern University and also presented a second solo exhibition at Houston Public Library branches. He collaborated with the writer Robert D. Bullard on the 1987 book *Invisible Houston*, which highlighted the gap between the rich and the poor citizens of the city. In 1990, Hudnall was featured in the exhibition *Home: Contemporary Urban Images by Black Photographers* at the Studio Museum in Harlem, New York. The following year, he published a photo essay, *Sisters*, in the *Houston Press*. During Houston's 1992 FotoFest, he had exhibitions at Benteler-Morgan Galleries and Texas Southern University. The following year, Hudnall was honored with a solo exhibition at the Museum for Contemporary Photography in Chicago. In 1996, he was included in the Irving Arts Center exhibition *Breaking into the Mainstream: Texas African-American Artists.*   —RM

Selected References:
Bullard, Robert D. *Invisible Houston.* College Station, Texas: Texas A&M University Press, 1987.
Hudnall, Earlie. "Sisters: A Photo Essay by Earlie Hudnall." *Houston Press,* 4 July 1991.
Harris, Paul Rogers. *Breaking into the Mainstream: Texas African-American Artists.* Irving, Texas: Irving Arts Center, 1996.

❑ BENITO HUERTA
Born 1952, Corpus Christi, Texas
Lives in Arlington, Texas

Benito Huerta probes the stereotypical images of contemporary visual culture in his delicately structured paintings. A native of south Texas, Huerta moved to Houston when he was thirteen and received a B.F.A. from the University of Houston in 1975. He continued his studies at New Mexico State University in Las Cruces, where he received an M.F.A. in 1978. He returned to Houston in 1981 and participated in *Latin Spirit of the 80s* at the Lawndale Art and Performance Center later that year. In 1983, he had a solo exhibition at Texas A&M University in College Station. Huerta took an active role in the Houston art community in the mid-1980s, curating the *Chulas Fronteras* exhibition for the Midtown Art Center in 1985 and serving on the artist advisory board of DiverseWorks Artspace

from 1985 to 1987. During 1987, he was included in *Four Houston Artists* at the Glassell School of Art, *Abstract Visions* at the Museum of Contemporary Hispanic Art in New York, and *The Third Coast: A Look at Art in Texas* at the Aspen Art Museum in Colorado. *Benito Huerta: Attempted, Not Known,* his 1989 solo show at Artists Space in New York, subsequently was reorganized and expanded by the Contemporary Arts Museum in Houston. Huerta was among the founding directors of the Houston art journal *ArtLies* in 1993, and the following year he was featured in *Benito Huerta: Preserve, Negate, Transcend,* an extensive survey exhibition at the Arizona State University in Tempe. In 1997, he joined the faculty of the University of Texas at Arlington, where he also oversees the exhibition program at the University's Center for Research in Contemporary Art. Huerta curated the 1997 retrospective *Luis Jiménez: Working-Class Heroes, Images from the Popular Culture.* The exhibition embarked on a national tour, visiting the Sarah Campbell Blaffer Gallery at the University of Houston in 1999. In 1999, Huerta's recent paintings were featured at MD Modern in Houston.   —RM

Selected References:
Zeitlin, Marilyn A. *Benito Huerta: Attempted, Not Known.* New York: Artists Space, 1989.
Lippard, Lucy. *Mixed Blessings: New Art in a Multicultural America.* New York: Pantheon Books, 1990.
Lineberry, Heather Sealy, Alberto Ríos, and Marilyn A. Zeitlin. *Benito Huerta: Preserve, Negate, Transcend.* Tempe, Arizona: Arizona State University Art Museum, 1994.

❑ TERRELL JAMES
Born 1955, Houston, Texas
Lives in Houston, Texas

Terrell James creates subtly gestural abstract paintings and drawings that approach spiritual reflection through an abstraction of the organic world. James attended the Museum School of the MFAH in 1972, and the following year she studied in Mexico at the Instituto Allende and the Universidad de México in San Miguel de Allende. She returned to the United States in 1974 and entered the University of the South in Sewanee, Tennessee, where she received a B.A. in fine arts in 1977, graduating magna cum laude with departmental honors. Returning to Houston, she had her first solo show at Christ Church Cathedral in 1978, and the following year took part in the inaugural exhibition of the Lawndale Annex of the University of Houston. In the first half of the 1980s, James was assistant director of the Smithsonian Institution Archives of American Art Texas Project, based at the MFAH, while also developing her career as an artist. She had solo exhibitions at William A. Graham Gallery in Houston and Delgado College Gallery in New Orleans in 1985. James quickly gained recognition beyond the Gulf Coast. She was featured in group exhibitions at the Southern California Gallery for Contemporary Arts in Los Angeles in 1985 and at the Jack Tilton Gallery in New York in 1988. During 1991, she began an affili-

ation with Hiram Butler Gallery in Houston and also presented a solo show, *The Lure of Things That Are Seen and Heard,* at the C. G. Jung Educational Center in Houston. In 1993, she joined the faculty of the Glassell School of Art and was featured in the group exhibition *Seeing the Forest through the Trees* at the Contemporary Arts Museum in Houston. James was included in a 1994 exhibition of works on paper at the Centro Cultural Arte Contemporáneo in Mexico City. In 1997, she had two-person exhibitions with Virgil Grotfeldt at the Galveston Arts Center and with Charles Mary Kubricht at the Art Museum of South Texas in Corpus Christi.   —RM

Selected References:
Snow, Edward. *Shroud of Field and Stone.* Houston: Hiram Butler Gallery, 1991.
Davenport, Bill. "Terrell James." *Artnews* 95, no. 5 (May 1996): 142.
Greene, Alison de Lima, and Daniel Stern. *New Art Series: Charles Mary Kubricht and Terrell James.* Corpus Christi: Art Museum of South Texas, 1997.
Willour, Clint. *With a Quiet Strength: Virgil Grotfeldt/Terrell James.* Galveston: Galveston Arts Center, 1997.

❑ LUIS JIMÉNEZ
Born 1940, El Paso, Texas
Lives and works in Hondo, New Mexico

Luis Jiménez creates vivid fiberglass sculptures that interpret myths of the American West from a Chicano perspective. His father was a sign-maker who crossed the Rio Grande into Texas in 1922 and earned a national reputation for the neon signs he created in El Paso. Jiménez assisted in the family business from the age of six, and he credits his father's craft as a major influence on his own desire to create popularly accessible sculptures. After attending Texas Western College in El Paso from 1958 until 1959, Jiménez entered the University of Texas at Austin, where he received a B.S. in art and architecture in 1964. Shortly afterward, he traveled to Mexico City to study with the sculptor Francisco Zúñiga and explore his Mexican heritage firsthand. In 1966, Jiménez moved to New York, where he was employed as a social worker in the city's barrios and as a studio assistant to sculptor Seymour Lipton. During the late 1960s, much of his work dealt explicitly with the social upheavals of the period and specifically with the police brutality surrounding the 1968 Democratic Party Convention. His return to El Paso in 1971 prompted an exploration of Southwestern myth and folklore. Using the facilities of his father's workshop, he created a watershed series of large illuminated fiberglass sculptures. This series, *End of the Trail,* depicts a tragic lone Native American warrior in ironic Day-Glo colors, anticipating the thematic concerns of the artist's public sculptures over the subsequent three decades. Jiménez completed commissions supported by the National Endowment for the Arts for the city of Fargo, North Dakota, in 1977, and for the city of Albuquerque, New Mexico, in 1981. Also in 1981, his sculpture *Vaquero* was installed in Moody Park, on the north side of Houston. Jiménez created public sculptures for San Jacinto Plaza in El Paso in 1986 and for the City of Corpus Christi in 1993. He began exhibiting regularly with Moody Gallery in Houston in 1987, and that same year he was featured in the landmark MFAH exhibition *Hispanic Art in the United States: Thirty Contemporary Painters and Sculptors*. In 1994, Jiménez was featured in a major retrospective organized by the Albuquerque Museum. He became a part-time faculty member of the University of Houston in 1995. Jiménez was nominated as Texas Artist of the Year by the Art League of Houston in 1998. His retrospective exhibition, *Luis Jiménez: Working-Class Heroes, Images from the Popular Culture*, traveled to Houston at the Sarah Campbell Blaffer Gallery of the University of Houston in 1999.   —*RM*

Selected References:
Harithas, James. *Luis Jiménez: (Progress 1)*. Houston: Contemporary Arts Museum, 1974.
Beardsley, John, and Jane Livingston. *Hispanic Art in the United States: Thirty Contemporary Painters and Sculptors*. New York: Abbeville Press; Houston: The Museum of Fine Arts, Houston, 1987.
Moore, James, et al. *Man on Fire/El Hombre en llamas: Luis Jiménez*. Albuquerque, New Mexico: Albuquerque Museum, 1994.
Huerta, Benito, et al. *Luis Jiménez: Working-Class Heroes, Images from the Popular Culture*. Kansas City, Missouri: ExhibitsUSA, 1997.

❏ **GRACE SPAULDING JOHN**
   Born 1890, Battle Creek, Michigan
   Died 1972, Houston, Texas

Grace Spaulding John was among a few pioneer women artists who were responsible for establishing the art community of Houston. At the age of thirteen, she moved to Beaumont, Texas, where she received her first art lessons from the local portraitist Penelope Lingan. In 1909, she entered the St. Louis School of Fine Arts at Washington University in St. Louis, Missouri, and in late 1912 she transferred to the School of the Art Institute of Chicago, where she studied with Antonin Sterba. She interrupted her studies in 1913 to marry Roy Keehnel, a jeweler in Pine Bluff, Arkansas. After the failure of the marriage, she moved to Houston in 1918 and worked as a window dresser in Munn's department store. In 1920, she established a studio in an attic on the 1700 block of San Jacinto in Houston. She married Alfred Morgan John in 1921 and adopted the name Grace Spaulding John, which she used for the rest of her professional career. In 1921, John attended both the Parsons School of Design and the National Academy of Design in New York, before entering the summer school of the Pennsylvania Academy of the Fine Arts. Nominated by Daniel Garber, her instructor at the Pennsylvania Academy, she won a prestigious grant from the Louis Comfort Tiffany Foundation to work at Tiffany's Long Island estate in 1923. She had solo exhibitions at the Schleuter's Studio Building in Houston and the Hotel Galvez in Galveston in 1924, and soon established herself as a prominent figure in the blossoming Houston art community. John traveled to Europe in 1927, visiting Paris, Rome, Venice, and Collieure. She was

included in the *4th Annual Exhibition of Work by Houston Artists* at the MFAH in 1928, and claimed the museum's Portrait Award in both 1930 and 1931. John completed three frescoes for the Sidney Lanier Middle School in the 1930s. Significant exhibitions of her work were presented by the MFAH in 1936, the National Arts Club in New York in 1943, and the Museum of Art of the American West in Houston in 1988.   —*RM*

Selected References:
John, Grace Spaulding. *Memo: A Book of Poetry and Drawings*. New York: Golden Eagle Press, 1949.
Keightley, Patricia John. *Grace Spaulding John: Artist 1890–1972*. Houston: Pantile Press, c. 1993.

❏ **LUCAS JOHNSON**
   Born 1940, Hartford, Connecticut
   Lives in Houston, Texas

Lucas Johnson has absorbed characteristics of Latin American Modernism into his metaphysical landscape paintings. Johnson spent most of his childhood in Southern California, where in the 1950s he briefly studied marine biology at the University of California in Los Angeles. In 1964, he moved to Mexico, where he met a generation of artists who shared a humanist outlook, including José Luis Cuevas, Francisco Corzas, and Artemio Sepúlveda. That same year, Johnson was the focus of solo exhibitions at the Instituto Mexicano-Norteamericano in both Monterrey and San Luis Potosi. He began exhibiting in Houston at David Gallery in 1966, and in 1973 left Mexico to settle in that city. Johnson was the focus of solo exhibitions at the College of the Mainland in Texas City in 1976 and the University of Houston in 1977. He began an affiliation with Moody Gallery, and during 1979 and 1980, he taught watercolor and drawing classes at the Glassell School of Art. He was featured in the 1985 MFAH exhibition *Fresh Paint: The Houston School*. Drawings from his *Estuary Series* were the focus of an exhibition at London's prominent Serpentine Gallery in 1987. Johnson's drawings also were showcased at the Museo Ex-Convento del Carmen in Guadalajara in 1990, but he did not receive a solo museum exhibition in Texas until 1994, when the Contemporary Arts Museum in Houston presented *Lucas Johnson: Drawings from the Underworld*. The Art League of Houston honored him as Texas Artist of the Year in 1996, and that same year the University of Texas at San Antonio organized a major exhibition surveying Johnson's career to date.   —*RM*

Selected References:
Rose, Barbara, and Susie Kalil. *Fresh Paint: The Houston School*. Austin: Texas Monthly Press; Houston: The Museum of Fine Arts, Houston, 1985.
Stellweg, Carla. *Lucas Johnson: Drawings from the Underworld (Dibujos del Bajomundo)*. Houston: Contemporary Arts Museum, 1994.
Johnson, Patricia Covo. *Contemporary Art in Texas*. Roseville East, New South Wales, Australia: Craftsman House, 1995.

❏ **DONALD JUDD**
   Born 1928, Excelsior Springs, Missouri
   Died 1994, New York, New York

Donald Judd was one of the preeminent artists of the second half of the twentieth century. He created objects of radical simplicity with an elegant sense of geometry, establishing the use of industrial processes as a basis for art making. Judd became world renowned as a protagonist of Minimalism, although he did not embrace that term, nor the term sculpture, preferring to refer to his works as specific objects. Between 1949 and 1953, Judd studied philosophy and art history at the Art Students League in New York. He began exhibiting as an artist in 1952, and for much of the 1950s experimented with abstract painting. He entered the masters program in art history at Columbia University in 1957, and in 1959 began writing as an art critic for *Artnews* and for *ArtsMagazine*, where he was a contributing editor for the next six years. Judd reached a breakthrough in 1961, when he created his first three-dimensional wall-mounted works. The following year, he made his first freestanding objects. In 1963, he participated with Frank Stella, Robert Morris, and Ellsworth Kelly in *New Work: Part 1*, an influential exhibition at Green Gallery in New York. Later that year, Judd had a solo show at the same venue. In 1966, he began an affiliation with Leo Castelli Gallery in New York. During the second half of the 1960s, he emerged as a major figure in the New York art world, recognized by a solo exhibition at the Whitney Museum of American Art in 1968. Judd's connection to Texas dates from the early 1970s, when he began looking for a second home outside of New York. He visited West Texas and, in 1972, bought a block of buildings in the small town of Marfa in Presidio County, about 180 miles southeast of El Paso. Judd developed a vision for an integrated environment of sculpture and architecture in Marfa. In 1978, he secured the collaboration of the Dia Foundation to develop his projects there. Together they purchased the property of an old army base, Fort D. A. Russell, and an adjoining 340 acres of land, in 1981. Judd realized his redesign of the artillery sheds at Fort Russell, where he created a major installation of one hundred aluminum boxes in 1984. That same year, he founded the Chinati Foundation, which took over from the Dia Foundation as the trustee of projects at Marfa. As well as Judd's works, the Chinati Foundation sponsored permanent installations in Marfa of works by John Chamberlain, Claes Oldenburg, Ilya Kabakov, Roni Horn, and Dan Flavin. Judd introduced an artist residency program and a schedule of temporary exhibitions in 1984. His own work maintained a prominent position in international museums throughout the 1970s and 1980s. He had a second solo exhibition at the Whitney Museum in 1988, and in the 1980s and 1990s maintained affiliations with Paula Cooper Gallery and Pace Gallery in New York, as well as with Texas Gallery in Houston. Judd died in 1994. Marianne Stockebrand organized a 1999 exhibition of his work, alongside that of his friend Dan Flavin, at The Menil Collection in Houston.   —*RM*

Selected References:
Agee, William C., and Dan Flavin, and Donald Judd. *Don Judd.* New York: Whitney Museum of American Art, 1968.
Boggs, Jean Sutherland, et al. *Donald Judd: Catalogue Raisonné.* Ottawa: National Gallery of Canada, 1975.
Judd, Donald. *Complete Writings 1959–1975.* Halifax, Canada: Press of the Nova Scotia College of Art and Design; New York: New York University Press, 1975.
Ennis, Michael. "The Marfa Art War." *Texas Monthly* 12, no. 8 (August 1984): 138–42, 186–92.
Haskell, Barbara. *Donald Judd.* New York: Whitney Museum of American Art and W. W. Norton & Company, 1988.

❏ **MABEL FAIRFAX KARL**
  Born 1901, Glenview, Oregon
  Died 1990, San Diego, California

Mabel Fairfax Karl created sculptures of stylized figures in wood and bronze and dealt with classical subjects, such as characters from Greek mythology, that were unusual in Texas art of the period. Karl began her artistic career as Mabel Fairfax Smith in San Diego, where she lived from 1919 until 1926, when she traveled with three other San Diego artists to study at the Santa Barbara School of the Arts. She studied bronze casting in Santa Barbara with the Glasgow artist Archibald Dawson, and also at the Art Students League in New York with Leo Lentelli, Joseph Pennell, George Bridgeman, and Frank V. DuMond. After her marriage in 1927, Karl divided her time between San Diego and Houston. She was included regularly in annual exhibitions of Southern California artists at the Fine Arts Gallery of San Diego (now the San Diego Museum of Art), where she received first prize for sculpture in 1931, honorable mentions in 1932 and 1933, and the Purchase Prize in 1934. She received an honorable mention in the *8th Annual Exhibition of Work by Houston Artists* at the MFAH in 1932. At the *10th Annual Exhibition of Work by Houston Artists* in 1934, the museum awarded her the Purchase Prize for her sculptures *Orpheus* and *Eurydice.* Karl was included in the California Pacific International Exposition at the Fine Arts Gallery of San Diego in 1935. She sent a self-portrait carved from Texas limestone back to California, for exhibition at the San Diego Art Guild in its annual exhibition of 1938–39. There was a revival of interest in Karl's work in the late 1980s. She was included in *A Century of Sculpture in Texas, 1889–1989,* a 1989 exhibition at the Archer M. Huntington Art Gallery in Austin. The Panhandle-Plains Historical Museum featured Karl in its 1993 exhibition *Women Artists of Texas, 1850–1950.*   —RM

Selected References:
Hendricks, Patricia D., and Becky Duval Reese. *A Century of Sculpture in Texas: 1889–1989.* Austin: University of Texas Press and Archer M. Huntington Art Gallery, 1989.
Grauer, Michael. *Women Artists of Texas, 1850–1950.* Canyon, Texas: Panhandle-Plains Historical Museum, 1993.

❏ **PAGE KEMPNER**
  Born 1961, Houston, Texas
  Lives in Houston, Texas

Page Kempner's bronze sculptures explore issues of femininity and nature. A 1984 Phi Beta Kappa graduate of Pomona College in Claremont, California, Kempner undertook postgraduate work at the University of Houston from 1984 through 1986. In the 1980s, she was featured in various group exhibitions at Houston's DiverseWorks Artspace, Lawndale Art and Performance Center, and the Glassell School of Art. Kempner was included in the 1988 *Houston Area Exhibition* at the Sarah Campbell Blaffer Gallery at the University of Houston. In 1992, she participated in a group exhibition at Hiram Butler Gallery and had her first solo exhibition, *Introductions,* at Moody Gallery in Houston. The following year, she presented work in *Seeing the Forest through the Trees* at the Contemporary Arts Museum in Houston and *Conventional Forms/Insidious Vision* at the Glassell School of Art. Her 1993 exhibition at Moody Gallery introduced her first monumental work. In 1994, Kempner participated in the *Second Annual Sculpture on the Green* show at the Omni Hotel in Houston, in *Stories* at Moody Gallery, and in a solo exhibition at the Galveston Arts Center. She was included in the 1995 exhibition *Texas Myths and Realities* at the MFAH. In 1996, Kempner was featured in *Convergence* at Barbara Davis Gallery in Houston and in *Art and Art Adventures* at the Galveston Arts Center. She had solo exhibitions at the Nave Museum, Victoria, in 1996, and Moody Gallery in 1998.   —MG

Selected References:
Kienholz, Edward, et al. *Houston Area Exhibition.* Houston: Sarah Campbell Blaffer Gallery, 1988.
Kalil, Susie. "Words and Pictures." *Houston Press,* 6 August 1992, 32–33.
Whitney, Kathleen. "Calculated Risks: Showing the Big Stuff." *Sculpture* 17, no. 10 (December 1998): 34–39.

❏ **MICHAEL KENNAUGH**
  Born 1964, Casper, Wyoming
  Lives in Houston, Texas

Michael Kennaugh creates nuanced paintings that explore the sensuality and fluidity of forms. Raised in East Texas, Kennaugh received a B.F.A. from Lamar University in Beaumont, Texas, in 1986 and an M.F.A. from the University of North Texas, Denton, in 1990. During the mid-1980s, he worked as a studio assistant to artist Paul Manes in New York. Kennaugh had his first solo exhibition in 1990 at the American College of Switzerland, Leysin, where he briefly studied. In the mid 1990s, he participated in numerous group exhibitions, at venues including the Dishman Art Gallery at Lamar University, and 500x Gallery in Dallas. In Houston, Kennaugh was featured in a 1994 *Introductions* exhibition organized by Sally Sprout at the Transco Tower Gallery, and in the 1996 *Vernacular* show at the Lawndale Art and Performance Center. Also in 1996, he was appointed an artist-in-residence at the William Flanagan

Memorial Creative Persons Center in Montauk, New York. Kennaugh held teaching positions at Lamar University, the Gold Coast Art League in Beaumont, and the University of North Texas, Denton. He was featured in a 1997 solo exhibition at the Galveston Arts Center. In 1998, his work was shown at Sally Sprout Gallery in Houston and in the exhibition *Edward Albee Curates: 5 Artists* at the Art League of Houston. In 1999, Kennaugh was featured in *Six* at the Kouros Gallery in New York and *Four Painters* at the Hong Kong Visual Arts Center in China. Also that year, he was among the artists selected by the Albright-Knox Art Gallery in Buffalo to be featured in its *New York Collection* series.   —MG

Selected References:
Lundee, Paige. "Albee's Seescape: An Interview with Edward Albee." *ArtLies,* no. 14 (spring 1997): 4–6.
Albee, Edward. *Edward Albee Curates: 5 Artists.* Houston: Art League of Houston, 1998.

❏ **EDWARD KIENHOLZ and
NANCY REDDIN KIENHOLZ**

  Edward Kienholz
  Born 1927, Fairfield, Washington
  Died 1994, Sandpoint, Idaho

  Nancy Reddin Kienholz
  Born 1943, Los Angeles, California
  Lives in Hope, Idaho

Edward Kienholz was among the generation of American artists who pioneered the art of assemblage, creating vivid tableaux out of the real stuff of everyday life. Kienholz was raised on his family's farm near Fairfield, Washington. He briefly studied art at Eastern Washington College of Education and Whitworth College in Spokane. After traveling throughout the country in the late 1940s, he moved to Los Angeles in 1952. His early works of this era were gestural abstractions, but by 1954 he had begun to incorporate found materials into his compositions. In 1955, Café Galleria in Los Angeles hosted his first solo show. Kienholz met Walter Hopps in 1956, and the following year they opened Ferus Gallery, which was to become one of Los Angeles's most dynamic galleries, introducing the work of such artists as Wallace Berman, Jay DeFeo, and Robert Irwin, as well as Kienholz himself. He was featured in his first solo museum exhibition at the Pasadena Art Museum in 1961, when he also participated in *The Art of Assemblage* at the Museum of Modern Art in New York. In 1964, Kienholz began working on *The Beanery,* an assemblage that took six months to complete. He was awarded the Watson F. Blair prize in the *68th American Exhibition* at the Art Institute of Chicago in 1966 for this submission. Also in 1966, Maurice Tuchman at the Los Angeles County Museum of Art organized the first retrospective exhibition devoted to the artist. Kienholz met Nancy Reddin, a native Californian, in Los Angeles in 1972. This meeting marked the beginning of a twenty-two-year partnership and collaboration, formally acknowledged by Kienholz in 1981 when he stated that all works from his studio since 1972 should be signed Edward Kienholz and Nancy Reddin Kienholz. The two artists moved to Berlin in 1973 and began dividing their time between Germany and Idaho. Among their first major collaborations was *The Art Show,* which premiered at the Berliner Künstlerprogramm/DADD in 1977 and later traveled to the Centre Georges Pompidou in Paris. Also in 1977, the Kienholzes presented *The Middle Islands No. 1* at the Venice Biennale. The San Francisco Museum of Modern Art organized *Edward and Nancy Reddin Kienholz: Human Scale* in 1984, which traveled to the Contemporary Arts Museum in Houston, and the Kunsthalle Düsseldorf presented *Edward and Nancy Kienholz: Works from the 1980s* in 1989. During 1991 and 1992, the Kienholzes purchased and renovated a studio in Houston. Throughout the early 1990s, they divided their time between Idaho, Texas, and Berlin. Their artworks increasingly reflected their global interests and travels: *The Merry-Go-World or Begat by Chance and the Wonder Horse Trigger,* begun in Berlin in 1986, was completed in Idaho in 1992 and featured at the MFAH the following year. On June 10, 1994, Edward died of a massive heart attack; he was buried in a 1940 Packard on Howe Mountain, Idaho. The following year, *Edward Kienholz: 1954–1962,* an exhibition organized by Walter Hopps, was presented at The Menil Collection in Houston. In 1996, Hopps curated *Kienholz: A Retrospective,* a major exhibition organized by the Whitney Museum of American Art in New York. The show traveled to the Museum of Contemporary Art, Los Angeles, and the Berlinische Galerie, Berlin.   —*MG*

Selected Readings

Pincus, Robert L. *On a Scale That Competes with the World: The Art of Edward and Nancy Reddin Kienholz.* Los Angeles: University of California Press, 1990.

Kienholz, Edward, and Nancy Reddin Kienholz. *Edward and Nancy Kienholz: The Merry-Go-World or Begat by Chance and the Wonder Horse Trigger.* Venice, California: L. A. Louver, 1992.

Hopps, Walter. *Edward Kienholz: 1954–1962.* Houston: The Menil Collection, 1995.

————, et al. *Kienholz: A Retrospective.* New York: Whitney Museum of American Art, 1996.

❏ **PAUL KITTELSON**
    Born 1959, Wheaton, Minnesota
    Lives in Houston, Texas

Paul Kittelson's sculptures always discover an aspect of the precious and absurd in what otherwise might seem mundane. Kittelson received a B.A. from the University of California at Santa Barbara in 1982 and an M.F.A. from the University of Houston in 1985. He first captured the attention of Houston with his improbable public sculptures: *Stegosaurus,* a life-size dinosaur made from discarded foam in 1986, and *Mindless Competition,* which stood in front of the Contemporary Arts Museum for the *First Texas Triennial Exhibition* in 1988. His first solo exhibition was held at Hiram Butler Gallery in Houston that same year. Kittelson was awarded a

grant from the Dallas Museum of Art's Anne Giles Kimbrough Fund in 1988 and a fellowship from the Mid-America Arts Alliance/National Endowment for the Arts in 1989. He joined the faculty at the University of Houston in 1990 and had solo exhibitions at the Art Museum of Southeast Texas in Beaumont, Texas, in 1993 and at Milagros Contemporary in San Antonio in 1995. During 1994, he was featured in *Lesser Gods of Earth,* a solo show at Hiram Butler Gallery. The University of Houston, Downtown, permanently installed *Passage* in 1997, which Kittelson created with his wife, the sculptor Carter Ernst. Kittelson has undertaken projects in Houston in collaboration with the Wortham Center, DiverseWorks Artspace, and Lawndale Art and Performance Center. He was featured in a 1998 solo exhibition at Barbara Davis Gallery in Houston.   —*MG*

Selected References:

Zeitlin, Marilyn A., Marge Goldwater, and David Ross. *The First Texas Triennial Exhibition: 1988.* Houston: Contemporary Arts Museum, 1988.

Kalil, Susie. "Plastic Jesus: With His Poetic Kitsch Gods, Paul Kittelson Is One of Houston's Most Important Artists." *Houston Press,* 14 July 1994, 30.

Johnson, Patricia Covo. *Contemporary Art in Texas.* Roseville East, New South Wales, Australia: Craftsman House, 1995.

❏ **SHARON KOPRIVA**
    Born 1948, Houston, Texas
    Lives in Houston, Texas

Sharon Kopriva has explored issues of mortality and transcendence in her sculptures and paintings. Kopriva received a B.S. in art education from the University of Houston in 1970. She taught in Houston high schools for nine years before entering the graduate program at the University of Houston, where John Alexander and James Surls became guiding influences. Kopriva received an M.F.A. in 1981 and had a solo show that year at the Brazosport Fine Arts Center in Lake Jackson. During the early 1980s, she created dark, expressionistic paintings. In 1985, she was included in *Fresh Paint: The Houston School* at the MFAH. She had her first solo show in Houston at William A. Graham Gallery in 1986. During 1988, she presented a solo exhibition at the C. G. Jung Educational Center in Houston and won first prize in the *Houston Area Exhibition* at the University of Houston's Sarah Campbell Blaffer Gallery. Kopriva began focusing increasingly on sculpture in the late 1980s and was included in *A Century of Texas Sculpture* at the Archer M. Huntington Art Gallery in Austin in 1989. She was the focus of a number of exhibitions at Texas institutions in the early 1990s, with solo shows at the Art Center in Waco and the Art Museum of Southeast Texas in Beaumont in 1991. She began showing with Barbara Davis Gallery in Houston in 1996. Kopriva had solo exhibitions in 1998 at the Art Museum of South Texas in Corpus Christi and the Utah Art Center in Salt Lake City.   —*RM*

Selected References:

Rose, Barbara, and Susie Kalil. *Fresh Paint: The Houston School.* Austin: Texas Monthly Press; Houston: The Museum of Fine Arts, Houston, 1985.

Hendricks, Patricia D., and Becky Duval Reese. *A Century of Sculpture in Texas: 1889–1989.* Austin: University of Texas Press and Archer M. Huntington Art Gallery, 1989.

McBride, Elizabeth. *Sharon Kopriva: Sculptures and Paintings.* Houston: Graham Gallery, 1989.

Rose, Carey. *Sharon Kopriva: Conflicting Rituals.* Corpus Christi: Corpus Christi State University, 1992.

❏ **GEORGE KRAUSE**
    Born 1937, Philadelphia, Pennsylvania
    Lives in Wimberly, Texas

George Krause's photographs deal with some of the classic themes of Western art: religion, sexuality, and death. Krause studied at the Philadelphia College of Art on a Board of Education Scholarship from 1954 to 1957. There he was introduced to photography by his instructor, John Codax. Krause nurtured his passion for the medium during a period in the army between 1957 and 1959. After returning to the Philadelphia College of Art in 1959, he began traveling regularly to New York to participate in the discussions of a group of young photographers, including Walter Rosenblum and Jack Lessinger, who were particularly interested in photography as a means of social documentary. Krause's early work shared the documentary concerns of his young colleagues, and he met with some success. Edward Steichen purchased his work for the Museum of Modern Art in 1960, and *Art in America* elected him a member of its *Young Talent USA* list in 1963. That same year, however, Krause turned his back on social documentary to explore instead the idea of fantasy. While traveling in San Francisco in 1960, he photographed an Italian-American cemetery. This laid the foundation for two extended series, *Qui Riposa* and *Saints and Martyrs,* depicting graves and religious statutory. While teaching at Brooklyn College in New York, Krause developed two further series: *The Street,* which he had begun in the late 1950s, and *I Nudi,* his work with nude models begun in 1972. He moved to Houston in 1975 to establish a photography program at the University of Houston. Krause received both a Guggenheim Fellowship and a Prix de Rome prize in 1976. He was the subject of a major retrospective at the MFAH in 1991 and remained an influential professor at the University of Houston until his retirement in 1998. In 1999, his recent work was jointly presented by John Cleary Gallery and Hooks-Epstein Galleries in Houston.   —*RM*

Selected References:

Krause, George, and Mark Power. *George Krause: 1.* Haverford, Pennsylvania: Toll and Armstrong, 1972.

Krause, George, and Carol Kismaric. *Saints and Martyrs.* Philadelphia: Photopia Gallery, 1976.

Krause, George, and Mark Power. *George Krause 1960–1970.* Philadelphia: Photopia Gallery, 1980.

Sandweiss, Martha, ed. *Contemporary Texas: A Photographic Portrait.* Austin: Texas Monthly Press, 1986.

Tucker, Anne Wilkes. *George Krause: A Retrospective*. Houston: Rice University Press; The Museum of Fine Arts, Houston, 1991.
Brierly, Dean. "George Krause: In the Darkroom." *Camera and Darkroom* 16, no. 12 (December 1994): 42–47.

❏ **CHARLES MARY KUBRICHT**
Born 1946, Houston, Texas
Lives in Houston, Texas

Charles Mary Kubricht's paintings segment and deconstruct views of nature, so that the landscape appears as both a formal motif and a distant memory. Kubricht enrolled at Queens College in Charlotte, North Carolina, in 1965. She attended the Institute for European Studies in Vienna in 1967, before returning to Queens College to receive a B.A. in 1969. She emerged onto the Houston art scene in 1975, when she was included in the *International Woman's Year Exhibition* at the Contemporary Arts Museum. Between 1981 and 1983, while studying for an M.F.A. at the University of Houston, Kubricht participated in group exhibitions at the university's Sarah Campbell Blaffer Gallery and Lawndale Annex. After completing her graduate studies, she entered the Core Residency Program at the Glassell School of Art. Her first solo exhibition was held in 1985 at Hadler/Rodriguez Gallery in Houston. She taught at the High School for the Performing and Visual Arts in Houston during 1985–86, and subsequently spent a year on the faculty of the Glassell School of Art. Kubricht had a number of solo exhibitions in the 1990s, including shows at Harris Gallery in Houston in 1990 and 1991, Adair Margo Gallery in El Paso in 1993, Eugene Binder Gallery in Dallas in 1994, and Lynn Goode Gallery in Houston in 1995. She had significant two-person exhibitions with Terrell James at the Art Museum of South Texas in Corpus Christi in 1997 and with Ann Stautberg at the Glassell School of Art in 1998. Kubricht began an affiliation with Moody Gallery in Houston in 1998.
                                                    —RM

Selected References:
Binder, Eugene, and Tom Moody. *Charles Mary Kubricht: Recent Paintings*. Dallas: Eugene Binder Gallery, 1994.
Brauer, David E. *Soundless Journey*. Houston: Lynn Goode Gallery, 1995.
Greene, Alison de Lima, and Daniel Stern. *New Art Series: Charles Mary Kubricht and Terrell James*. Corpus Christi: Art Museum of South Texas, 1997.
Olsen, Valerie Loupe. *In Situ: Responses from Charles Mary Kubricht and Ann Stautberg*. Houston: The Museum of Fine Arts, Houston, The Glassell School of Art, 1998.

❏ **DOROTHY ANTOINETTE (TONI) LaSELLE**
Born 1901, Beatrice, Nebraska
Lives in Denton, Texas, and Provincetown, Massachusetts

As the first woman working in this region to show nonobjective paintings on a national level, Toni LaSelle was instrumental in introducing the principles of planar abstraction to her students and fellow Texas artists. After receiving her B.A. from Nebraska Wesleyan University in 1923, she attended graduate school at the University of Chicago, where she earned her M.A. in 1926. Frequent visits to the Art Institute of Chicago exposed her to the work of Paul Cézanne, Vincent van Gogh, and Paul Gauguin. In 1928, she joined the Fine Arts Department at the Texas State College for Women in Denton (now Texas Woman's University), where she remained on the faculty until 1972. LaSelle was named director of the Little Chapel in the Woods at Texas State College for Women in 1938 and spent much of her tenure designing the chapel with her students. During her forty-four years of teaching, she continued to broaden her own range of study. LaSelle took courses under László Moholy-Nagy at Chicago's Institute of Design and was responsible for bringing the artist to lecture in Denton in 1942. While taking a leave of absence in 1932 to study sculpture at the California School of Fine Arts in San Francisco, she heard about the teaching methods of Hans Hofmann. In 1944, she enrolled in Hofmann's summer class in Provincetown, Massachusetts. Through working with Hofmann that year and during subsequent summers in Provincetown, LaSelle realized the connections between her art and her studies in the sciences and humanities, which brought a painterly sophistication to her compositions. Although exhibiting rather infrequently over the past six decades, LaSelle achieved a considerable reputation as a force in Texas Modernism.   —JAG

Selected References:
Kutner, Janet. "Discovery Theme Reflected at TWU." *Dallas Morning News*, 23 April 1972.
Stedman, Jarie. "Dorothy LaSelle, a Teaching Artist." *Advocate*, 17 August 1989.

❏ **ANNETTE LAWRENCE**
Born 1965, New York, New York
Lives in Denton, Texas

Annette Lawrence's poetic constructions collect and preserve the ephemeral. Lawrence received a B.F.A. from the University of Hartford in West Hartford, Connecticut, in 1986 and an M.F.A. from the Hoffberger School of Painting at the Maryland Institute in Baltimore, Maryland, in 1990. That same year, she moved to Austin and later to Houston, where she was named an artist-in-residence for the Community Artists' Collective. In 1992, Lawrence was featured in the *Fresh Visions/New Voices* exhibition at the Glassell School of Art in Houston and also was appointed an artist-in-residence for the Houston Housing Authority's BRIDGE She joined the Glassell's Core Residency Program in 1993, when she also was

featured in exhibitions at the Contemporary Arts Museum, Barnes-Blackman Galleries, and Inman Gallery in Houston, as well as the Houston International Festival. Two years later, ArtPace Foundation for Contemporary Art in San Antonio organized her first solo exhibition. Lawrence had solo shows during 1996 at Women and Their Work in Austin, Gerald Peters Gallery in Dallas, and the Art League of Houston. In 1997, she presented work in a number of group shows, including the Whitney Biennial in New York. Throughout her career, Lawrence has been honored with numerous prestigious awards and grants, including the W. E. B. Dubois Fellowship in 1987–88 and the Skowhegan Camille Hanks Cosby Fellowship for African-American Artists in 1996. She held teaching positions at the Houston Community College; the High School for Performing and Visual Arts, Houston; the University of Houston, Downtown; and the University of North Texas, Denton. In 1999, she was featured in *Faultlines* at Houston's ArtScan Gallery and *Other Narratives* at the Contemporary Arts Museum.   —MG

Selected References:
Havel, Joseph, and Rick Lowe. *Fresh Visions/New Voices: Emerging African-American Artists in Texas*. Houston: The Museum of Fine Arts, Houston, The Glassell School of Art, 1992.
Phillips, Lisa, and Louise Neri. *1997 Biennial Exhibition*. New York: Whitney Museum of American Art, 1997.
Friis-Hansen, Dana, Robert Atkins, and Greg Tate. *Other Narratives*. Houston: Contemporary Arts Museum, 1999.

❏ **RUSSELL LEE**
Born 1903, Ottawa, Illinois
Died 1986, Austin, Texas

From Depression-era farm life, to the American oil industry, to the Appalachian coalfields, Russell Lee photographed the nation with an expressiveness and sensitivity to the immediacy of the moment. In 1925, Lee graduated from Lehigh University in Bethlehem, Pennsylvania, with a degree in chemical engineering and returned to the Midwest to work in Kansas City, Missouri. In 1927, he married his first wife, a painter named Doris Emrick, whose artistic interests inspired him to leave chemical engineering in 1929 and become a painter himself. For the next six years, Lee and Emrick traveled frequently to Europe and Mexico. During this period, Lee also spent several winters at the Art Students League in New York and summers at the Woodstock Artists Colony. Hoping to improve his ability to paint facial features, he purchased a camera in 1935, and a year later his growing interest in photography led him to abandon painting entirely. In 1936, his friend the painter Ben Shahn introduced him to Roy Stryker. A few weeks later, Stryker hired Lee to work on the historic Farm Security Administration (FSA) project that documented conditions in Depression-era rural America. In 1938, Lee met his second wife, Jean Smith, who accompanied him on numerous assignments. Lee left the FSA in 1942 to work for the Air Transport Commission, taking aerial photographs for the war effort in South America, Europe, and the Far East. During 1946 and 1947, he worked for the Coal Mines Administration as a photographer for a medical survey of the bituminous coal industry. In 1947, Lee and his wife moved to Austin, where he became a freelance photographer. Following a major retrospective of his work at the University Art Museum at the University of Texas at Austin in 1965, he joined the faculty there. Lee ended his career as a photographer in 1973, but his work continued to receive national acclaim.   —JAG

Selected References:
Hurley, F. Jack. "Russell Lee." *Image* 16, no. 3 (September 1973): 1–8.
——. *Russell Lee Photographer.* Dobbs Ferry, New York: Morgan and Morgan, 1978.

❏ ROBERT LEVERS
   Born 1930, Brooklyn, New York
   Died 1992, Austin, Texas

Robert Levers's paintings and drawings explore apocalyptic themes in strangely pastoral settings. Levers studied at Yale University, where he received a B.F.A. in 1952 and an M.F.A. in 1961. Later that year, he joined the faculty of the University of Texas at Austin and was included in the prestigious Corcoran Biennial. Despite such early national recognition, Levers was deeply committed to the art community in Texas, and most of his subsequent exhibitions were concentrated inside the state. He contributed regularly to faculty exhibitions at the University of Texas and presented an important solo exhibition at the university's museum in 1979. Levers was awarded a fellowship from the National Endowment for the Arts in 1980. He was among a small group of artists selected to represent the United States at the forty-first Venice Biennale in 1984. The biennale exhibition, *Paradise Lost/Paradise Regained: American Visions of the New Decade*, subsequently embarked on a major international tour. In 1991, the Laguna Gloria Art Museum in Austin honored Levers with a major retrospective, which traveled to the Amarillo Art Center and the Galveston Arts Center.   —RM

Selected References:
Schmandt-Besserat, Denise, and Terence Grieder. *Robert Levers, Paintings, Drawings, and Constructions.* Austin: University Art Museum, University of Texas, 1979.
Tucker, Marcia, et al. *Paradise Lost/Paradise Regained: American Visions of the New Decade.* Venice: La 41a Biennale di Venezia, United States Pavilion, 1984.
Mears, Peter, Terence Grieder, and Joan Seeman Robinson. *The Art of Robert Levers: A Retrospective.* Austin: Laguna Gloria Art Museum, 1991.

❏ BERT LONG
   Born 1940, Houston, Texas
   Lives in Houston, Texas

Bert Long embraces folk art and art history to express a vivid and visionary identity. Long grew up in Houston's Fifth Ward. His father died in 1943, and as a teenager Long worked in catering to help support his family. He joined the Marine Corps in 1959, serving until he received an honorable discharge in 1964. Between 1966 and 1972, Long studied cuisine at the Los Angeles Trade-Technical College and at the University of California in Los Angeles. He enjoyed a successful career as a chef in the 1970s, receiving an Augie award from the Chefs de Cuisine Association of America in 1972. During this period, he pursued his passion for painting on a part-time basis. In 1977, he returned to Houston, working as executive sous-chef for the Hyatt Regency Hotel. The following year, Long decided to abandon his culinary career and focus on painting. In 1979, he founded the magazine *Artscene*, which for the next decade remained an important voice on art in Houston. He collaborated with his friend, the artist James Surls, to organize a 1980 gala fundraiser for the Lawndale Art and Performance Center, Surls's fledging alternative space at the University of Houston. Long soon found himself at the center of Houston's art community, and his work was included in the 1985 exhibition *Fresh Paint: The Houston School* at the MFAH. In 1988, the Art League of Houston nominated him as Texas Artist of the Year and he was featured in a solo exhibition at the Dallas Museum of Art. Long was awarded the coveted Prix de Rome in 1990 and spent a year in Italy as a fellow of the American Academy of Arts and Letters in Rome. His European work was showcased in Houston in *Bert Long Jr.: Looking and Seeing in Rome*, a 1992 exhibition at the Contemporary Arts Museum. Subsequently, Long and his wife, Connie, divided their time between Texas and the town of Berzocana in Spain. The death of Connie Long in 1998 sadly cut short her own burgeoning career as an artist.—RM

Selected References:
Rose, Barbara, and Susie Kalil. *Fresh Paint: The Houston School.* Austin: Texas Monthly Press; Houston: The Museum of Fine Arts, Houston, 1985.
Graze, Sue. *Bert Long.* Dallas: Dallas Museum of Art, 1988.
Ennis, Michael. "Long Shot." *Texas Monthly* 20, no. 2 (February 1992): 42–45.

❏ JIM LOVE
   Born 1927, Amarillo, Texas
   Lives in Houston, Texas

With a playful attitude and an inventive eye, Jim Love absorbed a variety of Surrealist and Pop Art influences to develop his own language in assemblage. Love spent most of his childhood in Amarillo, though during the Depression his family spent a brief period living outside of Lubbock, Texas. He joined the Army in 1946, planning to take advantage of the G.I. Bill, and was posted to Kumamoto in Japan. When his military service ended in 1948, he returned to Amarillo. Love attended junior college and later that year enrolled at Baylor University in Waco, where he majored in accounting. Elective classes in theater at Baylor, under the director Paul Baker, inspired Love to turn his back on a business career. In 1953, he was offered a job stage-lighting for the Houston-based company Theatre Inc., and he consequently moved to Houston. He began working as a set designer for the Alley Theatre in 1955. While working on a production of *The Glass Menagerie*, Love began to explore working with metal. In 1956, he became an installation technician for the Contemporary Arts Association, where director Jermayne MacAgy encouraged him to pursue sculpture seriously. Shortly after, he created a screen welded from found materials, which he submitted to a juried exhibition at the association, thereby launching his career as an artist. The Dallas Museum for Contemporary Arts included him in group exhibitions in 1957, 1959, and 1961. He also was included in *The Art of Assemblage*, a 1961 exhibition at the Museum of Modern Art in New York. John and Dominique de Menil donated his *Paul Bunyan Bouquet No. 1* to the MFAH in 1962, and the following year the museum included it in an exhibition of recent acquisitions. Love exhibited regularly in Texas throughout the 1960s, and the Whitney Museum of American Art in New York included him in its annual exhibition of 1968. He was featured in a solo exhibition, *Jim Love: In Pursuit of the Bear*, organized by the Contemporary Arts Museum in 1973. The Institute for the Arts at Rice University presented a major 1980 retrospective of his work, which traveled to the Amarillo Art Center in Texas, the San Francisco Museum of Modern Art, and the Hudson River Museum in Yonkers, New York. A large commissioned sculpture he created for Hobby Airport in Houston was unveiled in 1985. During the 1980s, he was affiliated with Janie C. Lee Gallery in Houston; in 1994, he began exhibiting with Moody Gallery in Houston. Love undertook another major commission, this time for the Cullen Sculpture Garden at the MFAH, in 1990.   —RM

Selected References:
MacAgy, Douglas. *one i at a time.* Dallas: Southern Methodist University, Pollock Galleries, 1971.
Belloli, Jay, and Douglas MacAgy. *Jim Love: In Pursuit of the Bear.* Houston: Contemporary Arts Museum, 1973.
Barthelme, Donald, and Dominique de Menil. *Jim Love up to Now.* Houston: Rice Institute for the Arts, 1980.
Goetzmann, William H., and Becky Duval Reese. *Texas Images and Visions.* Austin: University of Texas at Austin, Archer M. Huntington Art Gallery, 1983.
Greene, Alison de Lima, Diane Planer Lovejoy, and William R. Thompson. "The Lillie and Hugh Roy Cullen Sculpture Garden at the Museum of Fine Arts, Houston." *The Museum of Fine Arts, Houston, Bulletin* 17 (April 1996).

❑ **HERMANN LUNGKWITZ**
   Born 1813, Halle-an-der-Saale, Germany
   Died 1891, Austin, Texas

Hermann Lungkwitz was among the first professional artists working in Texas. Lungkwitz trained at the Dresden Akademie der Bildenden Kunste under Ludwig Richter. He left Germany in 1850, in the wake of the political unrest that drove many men and women of his generation to immigrate to the United States. After a brief visit to New York and Virginia, he joined the great German migration to the Texas Hill Country, making Fredericksburg his home in 1852. Lungkwitz became an American citizen in 1857. Along with William De Ryee and William C. A. Thielepape, he presented magic lantern shows nationwide in 1861. During 1864, when Civil War aggressions were making the rural areas of Texas unsafe, he moved his family to San Antonio. He and photographer Carl von Iwonski opened a photography studio in 1866. Between 1870 and 1874, Lungkwitz worked as an official photographer for the General Land Office in Austin. In the late 1870s, he taught at Jacob Bickler's German-American Select School for Boys, Bickler's German and English Academy, and the Texas Female Institute in Austin. Lungkwitz died of influenza in 1891. Samuel E. Gideon from the University of Texas at Austin began the first scholarly research on the artist in 1913. James Patrick McGuire organized *Hermann Lungkwitz: German Romantic Landscapist on the Texas Frontier*, a 1986 traveling exhibition at the University of Texas Institute of Texan Cultures at San Antonio.   —*MG*

Selected References:
McGuire, James Patrick. *Hermann Lungkwitz: German Romantic Landscapist on the Texas Frontier.* Austin: University of Texas Press for the Institute of Texan Cultures at San Antonio, 1983.
Warren, David B., Michael K. Brown, Elizabeth Ann Coleman, and Emily Ballew Neff. *American Decorative Arts and Paintings in the Bayou Bend Collection.* Houston: The Museum of Fine Arts, Houston; Princeton, New Jersey: Princeton University Press, 1998.

❑ **GILES LYON**
   Born 1967, New York, New York
   Lives in New York, New York

Giles Lyon balances chaos and order, as well as representation and abstraction, in his sprawling and monumental canvases. After receiving a degree in 1989 from the Rhode Island School of Design, Lyon moved to Houston to enter the Core Residency Program at the Glassell School of Art. In 1991, he was also an artist-in-residence at the Edward F. Albee Foundation in Montauk, New York. The following year, he had his first solo exhibition in Houston at Lynn Goode Gallery. His work was seen further at Michael Walls Gallery in New York, at the Contemporary Arts Center in New Orleans, and in *The Houston Area Exhibition* at the Sarah Campbell Blaffer Gallery at the University of Houston. In 1994, Lyon collaborated with David Aylsworth and Bill Davenport in presenting *Buttered Side Up*, a three-person exhibition at Lawndale Art and Performance Center in Houston. During 1996 and 1997, this exhibition toured in expanded form to Hallwalls Contemporary Art Center in Buffalo, New York, and the Koffler Gallery in North York, Ontario. Throughout this period, Lyon exhibited widely in New York and in Texas, including most notably *Texas Abstract: New Paintings of the Nineties* at ArtPace Foundation for Contemporary Art in San Antonio in 1995. He had his first solo exhibition in New York at Alexandre de Folin Gallery in 1997 and was featured in another solo exhibition at Angstrom Gallery in Dallas in 1998. Lyon began an affiliation with Richard Feigen Gallery in New York in 1999.   —*ALG*

Selected References:
Brunon, Bernard. "Basic Attitude." In *Buttered Side Up: David Aylsworth, Bill Davenport, Giles Lyon,* by Bernard Brunon. Houston: Lawndale Art and Performance Center, 1994.
Emenhiser, Karen. "Puerile Utopias." In *Buttered Side Up: David Aylsworth, Bill Davenport, Giles Lyon,* by Bernard Brunon. Buffalo, New York: Hallwalls Contemporary Art Center; North York, Ontario: Koffler Gallery, 1996.
Bartelik, Marek. "Giles Lyon." *Artforum* 36, no. 8 (May 1998): 151–52.
Goodman, John. "Giles Lyon at Alexandre de Folin." *Art in America* 86, no. 9 (September 1998): 133–34.

❑ **CYNTHIA MACDONALD**
   Born 1928, New York, New York
   Lives in Houston, Texas

Cynthia Macdonald's poetry vividly charts the nuances of our present-day environment. Macdonald received a B.A. from Bennington College, Vermont, in 1950 and an M.A. from Sarah Lawrence College, New York, in 1970. Subsequently, she taught at Sarah Lawrence and at Johns Hopkins University in Baltimore. In 1972, she published *Amputations*, her first collection of poems. Macdonald subsequently published five books of poetry, including *Living Wills: New and Selected Poems*, a 1991 publication recognized by the *New York Times Book Review*. She also published extensively in periodicals and anthologies, including the *New Yorker*, the *New Republic*, *American Poetry Review*, and the *Paris Review*. Over the years, she received numerous prestigious fellowships and awards, such as a Guggenheim Fellowship, Rockefeller Fellowship, P.E.N. Syndicated Fiction Award, and O. B. Hardison, Jr., Poetry Prize from the Folger Shakespeare Library. In 1979, Macdonald helped establish the highly esteemed Creative Writing Program at the University of Houston and was appointed its first director. She pursued her personal interest in psychoanalysis during the mid-1980s, receiving a graduate degree from the Houston-Galveston Psychoanalytic Institute in 1986. Macdonald collaborated in 1988 with artist James Surls to produce *At the Round Earth's Imagin'd Corners* for an exhibition at the Glassell School of Art in Houston. A sequence of twelve poems written by Macdonald accompanied three drawings by Surls. In 1997, Macdonald published *I Can't Remember*, her sixth book of poetry.   —*MG*

Selected References:
Macdonald, Cynthia. *Amputations.* New York: George Braziller, Inc., 1972.
______. *Pruning the Annuals.* West Hartford, Connecticut: Bartholomew's Cobble, 1976.
______. *Transplants.* New York: George Braziller, Inc., 1976.
______. *(W)holes.* New York: Alfred A. Knopf, 1980.
______. *Alternate Means of Transport.* New York: Alfred A. Knopf, 1985.
Landay, Janet, and Donald Barthelme. *One + One: Collaborations by Artists and Writers.* Houston: The Museum of Fine Arts, Houston, The Glassell School of Art, 1988.
Macdonald, Cynthia. *Living Wills: New and Selected Poems.* New York: Alfred A. Knopf, 1991.
______. *I Can't Remember.* New York: Alfred A. Knopf, 1997.

❑ **JOE MANCUSO**
   Born 1954, Hibbing, Minnesota
   Lives in Houston, Texas

Joe Mancuso investigates materials and processes normally associated with the construction trade to create minimal sculptures that uncover the beauty of concrete, wood, and industrial paint. Mancuso received a B.F.A. from Colorado State University in Fort Collins in 1977 and an M.F.A. from Indiana University in Bloomington in 1980. He had early exhibitions in Pennsylvania and Indiana, before moving to Houston in 1982. His work was introduced to Houston audiences in 1985, when he began showing with Davis/McClain Gallery. In 1987, he was seen in the Assistance League of Houston's annual juried exhibition and in a group show at the Laguna Gloria Art Museum in Austin. Mancuso was featured in *Synergy '89* at the Glassell School of Art in 1989 and in a group exhibition at New York University in 1990. He had a 1991 solo exhibition at the University of Texas Health Science Center at Houston. During the 1990s, his work increasingly became prominent in group exhibitions around the state. Mancuso was featured in *Darkness + Light* at the Sarah Campbell Blaffer Gallery at the University of Houston in 1993. The following year, his work was exhibited in *Essentials* at the Glassell School of Art, in *Low Tech* at the Center for Research in Contemporary Art at the University of Texas at Arlington, in *Process, Strategy, Irony* at DiverseWorks Artspace in Houston, and in a solo exhibition at the C. G. Jung Educational Center in Houston. Mancuso was featured in the 1995 exhibition *Texas Abstract: New Painting in the Nineties* at ArtPace Foundation for Contemporary Art in San Antonio and in the 1997 group exhibition *Simply Beautiful* at the Contemporary Arts Museum in Houston. That same year, he completed a commission from the Texas Department of Transportation for the bridge crossing U.S. Highway 59 at Hazard Street in Houston. Mancuso was the subject of a 1998 solo exhibition at the Glassell School of Art, which was accompanied by a catalogue surveying his work over the previous decade. In 1999, the University of Houston commissioned Mancuso to collaborate on the renovation of the main building of its downtown campus.   —*RM*

Selected References:
Colpitt, Frances. *Texas Abstract: New Painting in the Nineties.* San Antonio: ArtPace Foundation for Contemporary Art, 1995.
Friis-Hansen, Dana. *Simply Beautiful.* Houston: Contemporary Arts Museum, 1997.
Olsen, Valerie Loupe. *Posttension: A Compelling Refinement by Joe Mancuso.* Houston: The Museum of Fine Arts, Houston, The Glassell School of Art, 1998.

❑ **PAUL MANES**
Born 1948, Austin, Texas
Lives in Brooklyn, New York

Paul Manes has developed his own pictorial language within a tradition of Expressionism, and his paintings display sensuous surface textures and a dramatic sense of light. Manes spent most of his childhood in Beaumont, Texas, where he entered Lamar University in 1966 to study business. In 1970, he embarked on a trip across Europe with a fellow student, the photographer Keith Carter. Manes practiced photography during the 1970s, but in 1978 he realized his true vocation was painting. He returned to Lamar University to study painting in 1980 and received a B.F.A. in 1983. Manes had his first solo exhibition at the Beaumont Art Museum shortly after his graduation and moved to New York later that year. He attended graduate school at Hunter College and also worked as a studio assistant to the painter John Alexander. Manes had his first New York solo exhibition at Getler Saper Gallery in 1985. Two years later, he had an exhibition at the FIAC Grand Palais in Paris. His first solo show in Houston was held at Moody Gallery in 1988. In the 1990s, he developed a simpler abstract language, but ultimately returned to still-life compositions. These developments characterized solo exhibitions in New York at Kouros Gallery in 1990 and Marisa del Re Gallery in 1992. Later that year, the Art Museum of Southeast Texas in Beaumont honored Manes with a survey exhibition that documented his work from 1986 to 1992. In the mid-to-late 1990s, Manes maintained a schedule of regular solo exhibitions in New York and in Palm Beach, Florida.—*RM*

Selected References:
Ratcliff, Carter. *The Paintings of Paul Manes.* New York: Kouros Gallery, 1987.
Tuchman, Phyllis. *Paul Manes.* New York: Kouros Gallery, 1989.
del Re, Marisa, and Alison de Lima Greene. *Paul Manes.* New York: Marisa del Re Gallery, 1992.
Stewart, Sheila L., et al. *Paul Manes.* Beaumont, Texas: Art Museum of Southeast Texas, 1992.

❑ **MANUAL**

Suzanne Bloom
Born 1943, Philadelphia, Pennsylvania
Lives in Houston, Texas

Ed Hill
Born 1935, Springfield, Massachusetts
Lives in Houston, Texas

MANUAL is the duo of Suzanne Bloom and Ed Hill, whose close collaboration has yielded photographs and digital images that often reflect their concern for the environment. Hill studied painting at the Rhode Island School of Design, graduating with a B.F.A. in 1957. He then studied under Josef Albers and Rico Lebrun at Yale University, where he received an M.F.A. in 1960. Bloom graduated with a B.F.A. from the Pennsylvania Academy of the Fine Arts and the University of Pennsylvania in 1965. She completed an M.F.A. at the University of Pennsylvania in 1968. Hill turned to photography in 1967, inspired initially by Michelangelo Antonioni's movie *Blow Up,* while Bloom began experimenting with the medium during a trip to Europe in 1970. The two met in 1970, while both were teaching at Smith College in Northampton, Massachusetts, and in 1973 they began developing the idea of working collaboratively. They coined the name MANUAL in 1974, and that same year began the project *Art in Context: Homage to Walter Benjamin,* siting works of art within specific cultural situations outside museums and galleries. At this time, they also began exploring video. MANUAL had early solo exhibitions at Amherst College in Massachusetts in 1975 and at the University of Massachusetts in 1978. Bloom and Hill became professors of art together at the University of Houston in 1976. They have continued to work consistently, but not exclusively, as a team. In 1980, the MFAH featured the *Art in Context: Homage to Walter Benjamin* series alongside separate individual projects by each artist: Bloom's *White Oak Bayou* and Hill's *A Phenomenological Study of Life Drawing.* During the 1980s, MANUAL increasingly focused on the new experimental area of digital imaging. The duo participated in a number of group exhibitions that explored digital media, including *Photo-Technology: An Exploration of the Electronic Imaging Environment* at the Houston Center for Photography in 1987; *Digital Photography* at Camerawork in San Francisco in 1988; and *Digitale Fotografie* at the Museum Volkwang in Essen, Germany, in 1989. Throughout the 1980s, the artists also helped to establish a critical voice for the Houston art scene as contributors to *Artforum* and other periodicals and exhibited their work locally at Moody Gallery. In 1991, MANUAL was the focus of an exhibition at the Contemporary Arts Museum in Houston, and in 1992 the duo was awarded a fellowship in photography from the National Endowment for the Arts. During the 1990s, Bloom and Hill continued their experiments with digital media and video. They remained influential professors at the University of Houston, where they also initiated an internet web site, "digital imaging forum," supported by the university's Sarah Campbell Blaffer Gallery.   —*RM*

Selected References:
Tucker, Anne Wilkes. *Suzanne Bloom and Ed Hill (MANUAL): Research and Collaboration.* Houston: Seashore Press, 1980.
McBride, Elizabeth. "MANUAL at the Contemporary Arts Museum." *Artnews* 90, no. 5 (May 1991): 162.
Morgan, Anne Barclay. "Art & Technology: Tomorrow's Palette." *Art in America* 82, no. 4 (April 1994): 36–41.

❑ **FRANK MARTIN**
Born 1942, New Orleans, Louisiana
Died 1994, Houston, Texas

Frank Martin created an expressive style of photographic monoprinting by adapting conventional darkroom techniques. Martin studied philosophy and aesthetics at Louisiana State University in the mid-1960s. He lived in Oaxaca, Mexico, in the mid-1970s and first visited Houston while returning from Oaxaca to New Orleans in 1977. Two years later, he made Houston his home. In the early 1980s, Martin worked as a commercial photographer, often commissioned to document other artists' work. He began pursuing his own artistic vision in the mid-1980s. Martin participated in group exhibitions in 1987 at On Waugh Gallery in Houston and Mexi-Arte in Austin. In 1988, he was included in the *First Texas Triennia! Exhibition* at the Contemporary Arts Museum in Houston and in the exhibition *Black and White* at the Glassell School of Art. The MFAH included his work in a presentation of new acquisitions in 1989, and Martin was featured in the Phoenix Triennial at the Phoenix Art Museum in 1990. Lynn Goode Gallery represented his work in Houston in the 1990s. Martin was featured in the 1993 exhibition *Paradoxical Scale* at the Glassell School of Art. In 1994, he participated in *Romancing the Land,* which was seen at Blue Star Art Space in San Antonio and the Galveston Arts Center. Martin died unexpectedly of a heart attack in his studio in December of that year. The Art League of Houston honored him with a retrospective in 1998.   —*RM*

Selected References:
Zeitlin, Marilyn A., Marge Goldwater, and David Ross. *The First Texas Triennial Exhibition: 1988.* Houston: Contemporary Arts Museum, 1988.

❑ **CÉSAR AUGUSTO MARTÍNEZ**
Born 1944, Laredo, Texas
Lives in San Antonio, Texas

César Augusto Martínez depicts characters from various Chicano communities in strong, iconographic figural compositions. Martínez grew up in Laredo, and many of his paintings are based on people recalled from his childhood there. He studied at Laredo Junior College and in 1968 received a B.S. from the Texas Arts and Industries University in Kingsville. After completing military service in 1971, he settled in San Antonio, where he worked as a commercial photographer. Martínez became interested in Chicano political movements in the 1970s and participated in various community organizations, including the Chicano periodical *Caracol*. In the mid-1970s, he joined the visual arts organization Con Safos, founded by Mel Casas and Felipe Reyes, and began focusing on painting. Martínez was included in the 1977 group exhibition *Dále Gas: Chicano Art of Texas* at the Contemporary Arts Museum in Houston. During 1978, he began his *Pachuco/Bato* series, documenting Hispanic youth subcultures across two generations. He was featured in *Showdown* at the Alternative Museum in New York in 1983 and in *Hispanic Art in the United States* at the MFAH in 1987. Martínez was included in the 1993 exhibition *Art of the Other Mexico: Sources and Meanings* at the Mexican Fine Arts Center Museum in Chicago and the Museum of Modern Art in Mexico City, a show that toured the United States the following year. In the mid-1990s, visionary landscapes emerged as a secondary theme in his work. Martínez had solo exhibitions at Lynn Goode Gallery in Houston in 1996 and at ArtPace Foundation for Contemporary Art in San Antonio in 1997.   —RM

Selected References:
Beardsley, John, and Jane Livingston. *Hispanic Art in the United States: Thirty Contemporary Painters and Sculptors.* New York: Abbeville Press; Houston: The Museum of Fine Arts, Houston, 1987.
Gaspar de Alba, Alicia. *Chicano Art Inside/Outside the Master's House.* Austin: University of Texas Press, 1998.

❏ **DAVID McGEE**
   Born 1962, Lockhart, Louisiana
   Lives in Houston, Texas

David McGee's paintings reflect his personal fears, conflicts, and anxieties regarding the construction of history. McGee studied at Prairie View A&M University, where he received a B.A. in 1985. He had his first solo exhibition at Barnes-Blackman Galleries in Houston in 1986 and was featured in solo exhibitions at Houston's Irene Pagan Gallery and GVG Gallery in 1991. The following year, his work was included in the *Fresh Visions/New Voices* exhibition at the Glassell School of Art in Houston. In 1993, McGee was featured in *Texas/Between Two Worlds*, a traveling exhibition organized by the Contemporary Arts Museum in Houston. He presented the *Wastelands* series of paintings in a solo show at Texas Gallery in Houston in 1994. That same year, he was included in *I Remember: Images of the Civil Rights Movement, 1963–1993* at the Sarah Campbell Blaffer Gallery at the University of Houston. McGee also was featured at Houston's Project Row Houses in 1994. He had solo exhibitions at Texas Gallery in 1995 and at the Galveston Arts Center in 1996. During 1998, the Contemporary Arts Museum in Houston hosted his first solo museum show, *David McGee: Black Comedies and Night Music*, which later traveled to the Southeastern Center for Contemporary Art in Winston-Salem, North Carolina. McGee participated in the 1999 exhibition *Re-Righting History: Work by Contemporary African-American Artists* at the Katonah Museum of Art in New York. —MG

Selected References:
Havel, Joseph, and Rick Lowe. *Fresh Visions/New Voices: Emerging African-American Artists in Texas.* Houston: The Museum of Fine Arts, Houston,
   The Glassell School of Art, 1992.
Doroshenko, Peter. *Texas/Between Two Worlds.* Houston: Contemporary Arts Museum, 1993.
Herbert, Lynn M. *David McGee: Black Comedies and Night Music.* Houston: Contemporary Arts Museum, 1998.

❏ **MEADE BROTHERS**
   Henry William Matthew Meade
   Born 1823, London, England
   Died 1865, Albany, New York

   Charles Richard Meade
   Born 1826, London, England
   Died 1858, Albany, New York

Henry William Matthew Meade and Charles Richard Meade immigrated to the United States from their native England in 1833. Together with their father, Henry R. Meade, they opened their first daguerreotype studio in Albany, New York, in 1842. The following year, they moved into a larger building and opened studios in Buffalo and Saratoga Springs. In 1850, they opened an additional studio in New York City. Their distinguished sitters included Daniel Webster, Kit Carson, Sam Houston, and Louis Daguerre, founder of the daguerreotype process. The Meade brothers received national recognition from the American Institute for their advancements of the daguerrean process in the early 1850s. They presented a series of daguerreotypes featuring the *Four Quarters of the World* in the Great Exhibition at the Crystal Palace in London in 1851, and another featuring Shakespeare's *Seven Ages of Man* at the Crystal Palace in New York in 1853. That same year, they opened a branch studio in Williamsburg, Brooklyn. In 1855, the brothers were awarded a medal for their submissions at the Paris Exposition. After Charles's death in 1858, Mary Ann Meade helped her brother Henry manage the studios and open another in uptown Manhattan. She continued to run the business after Henry's death in 1865. —MG

Selected References:
Lyons, Volina Valentine. "The Brothers Meade." *History of Photography* 14, no. 2 (April/June 1990), 113–34.

❏ **VICKI MEEK**
   Born 1950, Philadelphia, Pennsylvania
   Lives in Dallas, Texas

Vicki Meek creates poignant installations that explore the cultural memories of African-American people. Meek completed a B.F.A. at the Tyler School of Art in Philadelphia, Pennsylvania, in 1971 and received an M.F.A. from the University of Wisconsin in 1973. She did postgraduate work in art history at Queens College, New York, and moved to Dallas in 1980. That year, Meek was included in the traveling exhibition *Forever Free: Art by African American Women 1862–1980*, organized by Illinois State University in Normal. Her work first was seen in Houston in 1984, when she participated in *Diverse Idioms* at the Lawndale Art and Performance Center. From 1986 to 1988, she served as curator of the Dallas Visual Art Center. In 1989, Meek created the installation *Mask Controlled* at the Bath House Cultural Center in Dallas, and the following year she presented her installation *In Homage to Lady Day* at venues around Texas. She was featured in *Narrative Constructs: Contemporary Women of Color*, a 1990 exhibition curated by Kathy Vargas for Women and Their Work in Austin. In 1992, Meek was represented in *Fresh Visions/New Voices* at the Glassell School of Art by her installation *The Crying Room: A Memorial to the Ancestors*. The following year, she was featured in the Phoenix Triennial at the Phoenix Art Museum in Arizona. Meek began working as adjunct curator at the African American Museum in Dallas in 1994. She completed an installation for Project Row Houses in Houston in 1996, and that same year was featured in *The Heart That Sings, the Spirit That Soars* at the Dallas Museum of Art. Meek became director of the South Dallas Cultural Center in 1997. In 1999, she created the installation *quoteADVICEunquote* for Women and Their Work in Austin.   —RM

Selected References:
Havel, Joe, and Rick Lowe. *Fresh Visions/New Voices: Emerging African-American Artists in Texas.* Houston: The Museum of Fine Arts, Houston, The Glassell School of Art, 1992.
Kurtz, Bruce D., and Karen C. Hodges. *Contemporary Identities: 1993 Phoenix Triennial.* Phoenix, Arizona: Phoenix Art Museum, 1993.
Greene, Alison de Lima. *Vicki Meek: quoteadviceunquote.* Austin: Women and Their Work, 1999.

❏ **MELISSA MILLER**
   Born 1951, Houston, Texas
   Lives in Austin, Texas

Melissa Miller's paintings offer allegories of the human condition through the symbolism of animals. Miller attended the University of Texas at Austin and the Museum School of the MFAH, before completing a B.F.A. at the University of New Mexico in 1974. That year she attended Yale University's Summer School, where she encountered Philip Guston and Charles Burchfield. She returned to Texas in 1975, settling in Austin. Her first solo exhibition was at the Amarillo Art Center in 1978. She was the focus of 1981 exhibitions at the Art Museum of South Texas in Corpus Christi and the Contemporary Arts Museum in Houston. Miller began showing with Texas Gallery in Houston in 1983 and quickly came to the fore amidst the new figurative painters of the 1980s. She was included in the Whitney Biennial in 1983 and in the Venice Biennale the following year. Miller had solo exhibitions at Holly Solomon Gallery in New York in 1984 and 1985. A survey exhibition of her work organized in 1986 by the Albright-Knox Art Gallery in Buffalo, New York, traveled to the Contemporary Arts Museum in Houston and the

Modern Art Museum of Fort Worth. Miller was featured in the forty-third Corcoran Biennial in 1993. Her 1995 solo exhibition was presented at Holly Solomon Gallery in New York and Texas Gallery in Houston. She began exhibiting with Gerald Peters Gallery in Dallas in 1997; in 1999, a survey of her paintings was the opening exhibition of the renovated Dallas Visual Art Center.   *—RM*

Selected References:
Tucker, Marcia, et al. *Paradise Lost/Paradise Regained: American Visions of the New Decade.* Venice: La 41a Biennale di Venezia, United States Pavilion, 1984.
Cathcart, Linda L., and Doug Schultz. *Melissa Miller: A Survey, 1978–1986.* Houston: Contemporary Arts Museum, 1986.
Holly Solomon Gallery. *Melissa Miller: Paintings, 1986–1995.* New York: Holly Solomon Gallery, 1995.

❏ **MICHAEL MILLER**
Born 1962, Denison, Texas
Lives in Commerce, Texas

Michael Miller's paintings wittily play with decorative motifs, balancing the familiar and the abstract with ease. After attending Austin College in Sherman, Texas, Miller received a B.F.A. from Southwest Texas State University, San Marcos, in 1984 and an M.F.A. from the University of California, Davis, in 1986. Among his mentors in graduate school was visiting artist Jürgen Partenheimer. Following graduation, he joined the Core Residency Program at the Glassell School of Art in Houston. In 1988, he was awarded a fellowship from the Skowhegan School of Painting and Sculpture in Maine. He was featured in the forty-second Corcoran Biennial in Washington, D.C., in 1991. The following year, he was honored with a fellowship from the Mid-America Arts Alliance/National Endowment for the Arts. In 1992, Miller joined the faculty at Texas A&M University in Commerce. He was featured in solo shows at Barry Whistler Gallery in Dallas in 1992 and 1994 and at Inman Gallery in Houston in 1995. That same year, he also was included in *Texas Abstract, New Painting in the Nineties,* curated by Frances Colpitt at ArtPace Foundation for Contemporary Art in San Antonio, and in the *East Texas Drawing Exhibition,* organized by the Richland College in Dallas. In 1999, Miller again was featured in solo exhibitions at Barry Whistler Gallery and Inman Gallery. *—MG*

Selected References:
Sultan, Terrie, et al. *42nd Biennial Exhibition of Contemporary American Painting.* Washington, D.C.: Corcoran Gallery of Art, 1991.
Greene, Alison de Lima, and Clint Willour. *Stairway to Heaven.* Galveston: Galveston Arts Center, 1993.
Colpitt, Frances. *Texas Abstract: New Painting in the Nineties.* San Antonio: ArtPace Foundation for Contemporary Art, 1995.
Odom, Michael. "Michael Miller." *New Art Examiner* 23, no. 7 (March 1996): 49.
______. *Michael Miller: New Paintings.* Houston: Inman Gallery; Dallas: Barry Whistler Gallery, 1999.

❏ **ROBERT MONTGOMERY**
Born 1972, Bellshill, Scotland
Lives in London, England

Light is central to the aesthetic of Robert Montgomery, who has explored performance, installation art, and video, as well as more traditional media. Montgomery attended the Edinburgh College of Art at Heriot-Watt University, where he received a B.A. in 1993 and an M.F.A. in 1995. He had his first solo exhibition at 369 Gallery in Edinburgh in 1992 and was featured in exhibitions at Transmission Gallery in Glasgow and the Collective Gallery in Edinburgh in 1994 and 1995. At the advice of DeWitt Godfrey, a former Houstonian who also attended the Edinburgh College of Art, Montgomery entered the Core Residency Program at the Glassell School of Art in the fall of 1995. In Houston, his work was introduced by Art of This Century in 1996. The following year, Montgomery was featured in numerous exhibitions around Texas: he created a light installation in the Hudson Room at ArtPace Foundation for Contemporary Art in San Antonio, contributed two sculptural installations to the *Simply Beautiful* exhibition at the Contemporary Arts Museum in Houston, and also was seen in the *Space* exhibition at the Arlington Museum of Art. Also in 1997, Montgomery had his first solo exhibition at Inman Gallery in Houston and joined both the faculty of the Glassell School of Art and the curatorial staff of the MFAH. In 1998, he was invited to exhibit at the Talbot Rice Gallery at the University of Edinburgh and at DiverseWorks Artspace in Houston. That same year, Montgomery was visiting lecturer at Rice University. A video and light installation that he created at Lawndale Art and Performance Center in 1999 addressed his sense of distance from his homeland. Later that year, Montgomery moved to London, England.   *—ALG*

Selected References:
Colpitt, Frances. "Robert Montgomery at Inman." *Art in America* 85, no. 9 (September 1997): 116–17.
Friis-Hansen, Dana. *Simply Beautiful.* Houston: Contemporary Arts Museum, 1997.
Ogilvie, Liz, and Sean Watson. *In Situ.* Edinburgh: Talbot Rice University, 1998.

❏ **JESÚS BAUTISTA MOROLES**
Born 1950, Corpus Christi
Lives in Rockport, Texas

Jesús Bautista Moroles's carved abstract sculptures transform Texas granite with an unmatched technical virtuosity. Moroles grew up in Dallas and spent summers in Rockport, Texas, assisting his uncle, who was a master stonemason from Mexico. After completing military service in 1973, he spent two years at El Centro Junior College in Dallas. He subsequently enrolled at the University of North Texas, Denton, where he studied sculpture and industrial arts and received a B.F.A. in 1978. Later that year, he moved to El Paso, where he worked as apprentice to the sculptor Luis Jiménez. In 1979, Moroles traveled to Carrara in Italy to study the traditional methods of stone carving cultivated there. He had two solo exhibitions in Texas during 1982, one at the

Amarillo Art Center and the other at the Nave Museum in Victoria. In 1983, Moroles established a large studio complex in Rockport; he also began exhibiting with Davis/McClain Gallery in Houston. He completed a commission for the Albuquerque Museum in 1984 and was showcased in *Hispanic Art in the United States: Thirty Contemporary Painters and Sculptors* at the MFAH in 1987. His major public sculptures in the late 1980s and early 1990s included commissions for the E. F. Hutton–CBS Plaza in New York in 1987 and the City Hall of Corpus Christi in 1992. His *Houston Police Officers Memorial,* completed in 1992, quickly became a landmark in that city. In 1995, Moroles was featured in the exhibition series *Twentieth-Century American Sculpture at the White House,* presented in the First Ladies' Garden at the White House in Washington, D.C. *—RM*

Selected References:
Beardsley, John, and Jane Livingston. *Hispanic Art in the United States: Thirty Contemporary Painters and Sculptors.* New York: Abbeville Press; Houston: The Museum of Fine Arts, Houston, 1987.
McEvilley, Thomas. *Art at the Gateway: Jesús Bautista Moroles.* Houston: Davis/McClain Gallery, 1990.
Johnson, Patricia Covo. *Contemporary Art in Texas.* Roseville East, New South Wales, Australia: Craftsman House, 1995.
Little, Carol Morris. *A Comprehensive Guide to Outdoor Sculpture in Texas.* Austin: University of Texas Press, 1996.

❏ **CELIA ALVAREZ MUÑOZ**
Born 1937, El Paso, Texas
Lives in Arlington, Texas

Celia Alvarez Muñoz's photographs and installations explore her identity as a Mexican-American woman. Muñoz earned a B.A. from the University of Texas at El Paso in 1964. At the end of the 1960s, she lived briefly in Albany, New York, and Washington, D.C. In 1971, she returned to El Paso, where she taught art in high school until 1974. Later that year, she joined her husband in Portland, Oregon, where he was a federal employee working to counter discrimination against Spanish-speaking workers. During this period, Muñoz became involved in the Chicano movement and designed posters for documentary films highlighting the plight of immigrants. She returned to Texas in 1975 to live in Arlington. Two years later, Muñoz entered the University of North Texas, Denton, where she studied with Vernon Fisher. She received an M.F.A. in 1982 and had her first solo exhibition the following year at the University of Texas at El Paso. In 1984, she participated in *New Talent in Texas: Eight Texas Artists* at Texas Christian University in Fort Worth. During the first half of the 1980s, she created artist's books that were included in 1985 exhibitions at the Brand Library in Glendale, California, and at the Center for Book Arts in New York City. In 1987, she was included in *Third Coast Review: A Look at Art in Texas* at the Aspen Art Museum in Colorado. The following year, she participated in the *First Texas Triennial Exihibition* at the Contemporary Arts Museum in Houston. Toward the end of the 1980s, Muñoz discovered large-format photography. She created ambitious installations for two Texas museums, the Tyler Museum of Art and the San Angelo Museum of Art. Her prominence grew in 1991, when she had a solo show at the Dallas Museum of Art and was showcased in the Whitney Biennial. Her projects during the second half of the 1990s, including a 1996 installation for the Roswell Museum and Art Center, increasingly included the direct collaboration of local Hispanic communities.   —RM

Selected References:
Zeitlin, Marilyn A., Marge Goldwater, and David Ross. *The First Texas Triennial Exhibition: 1988.* Houston: Contemporary Arts Museum, 1988.
Armstrong, Richard, John G. Hanhardt, Richard Marshall, and Lisa Phillips. *1991 Biennial Exhibition.* New York: Whitney Museum of American Art; W. W. Norton & Company, 1991.
Johnson, Patricia Covo. *Contemporary Art in Texas.* Roseville East, New South Wales, Australia: Craftsman House, 1995.
Lippard, Lucy R. *Celia Alvarez Muñoz, Herencia: Now What?* Roswell, New Mexico: Roswell Museum and Art Center, 1996.

❏ **KRISTIN MUSGNUG**
   Born 1959, Buffalo, New York
   Lives in Fayetteville, Arkansas

Kristin Musgnug's scenes of suburban and industrial environments redefine the Romantic tradition of landscape painting. Musgnug received a B.A. in art history from Williams College in Williamstown, Massachusetts, in 1981 and an M.F.A. in painting from Indiana University, Bloomington, in 1988. She moved to Houston in 1988, when she joined the Core Residency Program at the Glassell School of Art. In 1990, Musgnug had her first solo show at Inman Gallery in Houston, where she had three subsequent exhibitions. During 1991, she participated in several group exhibitions, including *Profiles I: The Land* at the Arlington Museum of Art and *The Big Show* at the Lawndale Art and Performance Center in Houston. That same year, she joined the faculty at the University of Arkansas in Fayetteville. Musgnug was featured in *Freedom of Expression* at Lawndale in 1992 and *Light and Water* at the Artist's Loft in Galveston in 1994. A 1994 Fulbright Fellowship enabled her to work for a year at Lucy Cavendish College in Cambridge, England. Musgnug was featured in the 1994 exhibition *Nature/Culture* at Inman Gallery in Houston. In 1996, she presented drawings and collages in a traveling solo show at the Marko Cepenkov Center of Culture in Prilep, Macedonia, and also presented her *Land Futures in Arcadia* series at Inman Gallery. During 1998, her *Uses of Nature* series was featured in solo exhibitions at the University of Arkansas in Fayetteville, the Galveston Arts Center, and Inman Gallery. —MG

Selected References:
Ward, Elizabeth. *Nature/Culture.* Houston: Inman Gallery, 1994.
Harvey, Eleanor Jones. *Kristin Musgnug: Land Futures in Arcadia.* Houston: Inman Gallery, 1996.

❏ **OSAMU JAMES NAKAGAWA**
   Born 1962, New York, New York
   Lives in Bloomington, Indiana

Osamu James Nakagawa's digitally altered images expose the conflicts and tensions of his bicultural identity. Although born in the United States, Nakagawa was raised in Japan. His family returned to the United States in 1977, a move that enabled him to attend Houston-area schools. Nakagawa received a B.A. from the University of St. Thomas in Houston in 1986 and an M.F.A. from the University of Houston in 1993. His first solo exhibition was a 1993 *Introductions* show at McMurtrey Gallery in Houston, where he had two additional shows in 1997 and 1998. He was awarded a fellowship from the Houston Center for Photography in 1993 and two grants from the Cultural Arts Council of Houston/Harris County in 1994 and 1995. During 1995, he was featured in *Metamorphosis: Photography in the Electronic Age* at the Sarah Campbell Blaffer Gallery at the University of Houston and in the first Tokyo International Photo-Biennale at the Tokyo Metropolitan Museum of Photography. Nakagawa presented work at the Amarillo Museum of Art in Texas, the American Photography Institute in New York City, and the Silver Eye Center for Photography in Pittsburgh, Pennsylvania. He held teaching positions at the University of Houston, Lamar University in Beaumont, and Indiana University in Bloomington. In 1997, Nakagawa had a solo show at the Art Museum of Southeast Texas in Beaumont and was honored with two awards in *Current Works '97*, an exhibition organized by the Society for Contemporary Photography in Kansas City, Missouri. During 1998, he was featured in *New Realities: From Collage to Digital* at the MFAH and *Field of Vision: Five Gulf Coast Photographers* at the Contemporary Arts Museum in Houston.   —MG

Selected References:
Sand, Michael, ed. *Metamorphosis: Photography in the Electronic Age.* New York: Aperture Foundation, 1994.
Irvine, Alexandra L. *Field of Vision: Five Gulf Coast Photographers.* Houston: Contemporary Arts Museum, 1998.

❏ **FLOYD ELBERT NEWSUM, JR.**
   Born 1950, Memphis, Tennessee
   Lives in Houston, Texas

Floyd Elbert Newsum, Jr.'s colorful, semiabstract compositions draw both on his African-American heritage and on European Modernism. Newsum received a B.F.A. from the Memphis Academy of Arts in 1973 and an M.F.A. from the Tyler School of Art in Philadelphia, Pennsylvania, two years later. In

1976, he moved to Houston to accept a teaching position at the University of Houston. Newsum began participating in group exhibitions in Houston in 1977. He had a two-person show with Bert Long at the O'Kane Gallery in 1981 and a solo exhibition at the same venue in 1984. Further afield, he was featured in *Emerging Artists of the Southwest* at the Studio Museum in Harlem, New York, in 1986. During the mid-1980s, he also participated in group shows at the African American Museum in Dallas and at DiverseWorks Artspace in Houston. Newsum had solo exhibitions at Barnes-Blackman Galleries in Houston in 1988 and at the Art Museum of Southeast Texas in Beaumont in 1992. He was the focus of a 1993 exhibition at the Amarillo Art Center in Texas. During the mid-1990s, Lynn Goode Gallery represented his work in Houston. In 1994, as part of Project Row Houses in Houston, Newsum covered the outside of a row house in animated marks, thereby underlining his work's relationship to West African cultures that traditionally decorate exterior walls. He was included in *Breaking into the Mainstream: Texas African-American Artists*, a 1996 exhibition at the Irving Arts Center.   —RM

Selected References:
Castle, Lynn P. *Floyd Newsum: Women That Soar.* Beaumont, Texas: Art Museum of Southeast Texas, 1990.
Harris, Paul Rogers. *Breaking into the Mainstream: Texas African-American Artists.* Irving, Texas: Irving Arts Center, 1996.

❏ **NIC NICOSIA**
   Born 1951, Dallas, Texas
   Lives in Dallas, Texas

Nic Nicosia creates disconcerting photographs and videos from carefully staged scenarios. Nicosia studied radio, television, and film at the University of North Texas, Denton, where he received a B.A. in 1974. He briefly undertook graduate studies at the University of North Texas and subsequently at the University of Houston. Nicosia began exhibiting in 1981, when his photographs were included in *The New Photography* at the Contemporary Arts Museum in Houston. In 1984, he received a grant from the Louis Comfort Tiffany Foundation. He was featured in the *Concentrations* series at the Dallas Museum of Art in 1986. Nicosia was included in *Emerging Artists: 1978–1986*, a 1987 exhibition at the Guggenheim Museum in New York. The following year, he was featured in *Contemporary Art from Texas* at the Groninger Museum in Groningen, the Netherlands. He exhibited the *Real Pictures* series at Texas Gallery in Houston and Bruno Facchetti Gallery in New York in 1988, and at Barry Whistler Gallery in Dallas and Dart Gallery in Chicago in 1989. With his reputation growing, Nicosia was included in *Pleasures and Terrors of Domestic Comfort*, a 1991 traveling exhibition from the Museum of Modern Art in New York. The following year, he participated in the *Documenta* exhibition in Kassel, Germany. He exhibited his *Love + Lust* series widely in the 1990s, followed by two other thematic series, *Acts* and *Sex Acts*, first shown in 1997. His video work *Middletown* was seen at the Contemporary

Arts Museum in Houston and at Stephen Wirtz Gallery in San Francisco during 1998; in 1999 the Contemporary Arts Museum mounted a mid-career survey of his work. In 2000, Nicosia was among the artists to be featured in the Whitney Biennial.—*RM*

Selected References:
Freudenheim, Susan. *Nic Nicosia: Real Pictures.* New York: Facchetti Gallery, 1988.
Haks, Frans, and Alison de Lima Greene. *Hedendaagse Kunst uit Texas/Contemporary Art from Texas.* Groningen, the Netherlands: Groninger Museum, 1988.
Friis-Hansen, Dana, Lynn M. Herbert, and Dave Hickey. *Nic Nicosia: Real Pictures 1979–1999.* Houston: Contemporary Arts Museum, 1999.

❏ MADELINE O'CONNOR
Born 1931, San Antonio, Texas
Lives in Victoria, Texas

Madeline O'Connor has developed a remarkably understated poetic language to evoke the nature and wildlife surrounding her South Texas home. O'Connor is largely self-taught as an artist, although friendships with Donald Judd and Roy Fridge have influenced her development. She began participating in group exhibitions in Austin and Corpus Christi during the late 1960s, and had her first solo shows in 1970 at the McNamara Museum in Victoria and Bee College in Beeville. O'Connor was featured in solo exhibitions at Texas Tech University in Lubbock in 1973 and at the Art Museum of South Texas in Corpus Christi in 1977. During the 1980s, she extended her activities to New York, showing her *Purple Gallinule Series* at Donald Judd's Spring Street building in 1986 and creating an installation of her *Ibis* series for P.S. 1 in Long Island City in 1987; locally she maintained an affiliation with Moody Gallery in Houston. O'Connor presented a solo exhibition at the Stamford Museum and Nature Center in Connecticut in 1988. Two years later, she was included in *Revered Earth*, an exhibition from the Contemporary Arts Museum in Houston that traveled throughout the nation. O'Connor was featured in solo shows at the University of Texas at San Antonio in 1992 and at the Nave Museum in Victoria in 1995. A two-person exhibition highlighting her work alongside that of her daughter, artist Nancy O'Connor, was presented at Blue Star Art Space in San Antonio in 1997. In 1999, the Art Museum of South Texas in Corpus Christi mounted a twenty-year survey of her work.   —*RM*

Selected References:
Edwards, Jim. *Jay deFeo/Madeline O'Connor: Paintings and Drawings.* Victoria, Texas: Nave Museum, 1986.
Colpitt, Frances. *Madeline O'Connor.* Houston: Moody Gallery, 1994.
———. *Color + Spirit: Madeline O'Connor and Nancy O'Connor.* San Antonio: Blue Star Art Space, 1997.
Otton, William G., and Frances Colpitt. *Madeline O'Connor: A Survey, 1980–1999.* Corpus Christi: Art Museum of South Texas, 1999.

❏ NANCY O'CONNOR
Born 1957, Victoria, Texas
Lives in Houston, Texas

Nancy O'Connor uses poetry, photographs, and found objects to animate the narratives of her mixed-media works. While her mother, artist Madeline O'Connor, finds the subject for her work in the native wildlife of Texas, Nancy O'Connor focuses on human stories. She studied filmmaking at Trinity University before receiving a B.A. in journalism in 1979 from the University of Texas at Austin, where she studied photojournalism with Garry Winogrand. O'Connor had her first solo exhibition at Robert Molina Gallery in Houston in 1980. The following year, she had solo shows at the Tyler Museum of Art and the Nave Museum in Victoria. In 1983, she was featured in the New Orleans Triennial at the New Orleans Museum of Art and in the group exhibition *Showdown* at the Alternative Museum in New York. Her project *Milam's Journey*, which traced the life story of a black Texas cowboy, was the focus of a 1985 exhibition at the Contemporary Arts Museum in Houston. This exhibition traveled to the Art Museum of South Texas in Corpus Christi and the Tyler Museum of Art. In 1987, O'Connor was included in the Phoenix Biennial at the Phoenix Art Museum in Arizona. She began an affiliation with Moody Gallery in Houston in 1990. During 1993, she had a solo exhibition at the Alternative Museum in New York. In 1996, O'Connor created a video installation, *To the Silenced*, for the Sculpture Center in New York. She had a two-person exhibition with Madeline O'Connor at Blue Star Art Space in San Antonio in 1997 and a solo exhibition at Moody Gallery in Houston in 1998.   —*RM*

Selected References:
Harithas, Ann. *Showdown.* New York: Alternative Museum, 1983.
Cathcart, Linda L. *Nancy O'Connor: Milam's Journey.* Houston: Contemporary Arts Museum Perspectives Series, 1985.
Colpitt, Frances. *Color + Spirit: Madeline O'Connor and Nancy O'Connor.* San Antonio: Blue Star Art Space, 1997.

❏ KERMIT OLIVER
Born 1943, Refugio, Texas
Lives in Waco, Texas

Kermit Oliver creates refined realist paintings, incorporating symbols that relate to his childhood in Southeast Texas. In 1962, Oliver was awarded a Jesse Jones Scholarship and entered Texas Southern University, where he studied with John Biggers; he received a B.F.A. in 1967. An additional scholarship allowed him to attend summer classes taught by Elaine de Kooning at Rice University. In 1968, the Texas Pavilion of the Hemisfair in San Antonio commissioned him to create a series of paintings depicting black Texas history. He completed a related commission for the Teacher Retirement System of Texas in Austin in 1975. During the late 1970s and early 1980s, he had three solo exhibitions with DuBose Gallery in Houston. Oliver designed the official poster of the 1980 Houston Festival. He participated in 1981 group exhibitions at the University of Houston's Sarah Campbell Blaffer Gallery and the San Antonio Museum of Art. In 1982, Lawrence Marcus of the Neiman Marcus department store introduced Oliver's work to the firm of Hermès of Paris, which subsequently commissioned the artist to create patterns for a series of scarves. Oliver settled in Waco in 1984. His work was featured in *Fresh Paint: The Houston School* at the MFAH in 1985. He had a 1989 solo exhibition at the Laguna Gloria Art Museum in Austin and was featured in 1990 solo shows at the Art Museum of Southeast Texas in Beaumont and the Art Center in Waco. During 1993, Oliver had a solo show at the Longview Museum of Fine Art in Longview, Texas, and was included in *Texas Contemporary: Acquisitions of the '90s* at the MFAH. In 1995, the MFAH again featured his work in *Texas Myths and Realities*. Oliver had a solo show at the Museum of the Southwest in Midland, Texas, in 1997. He maintained an affiliation with Hooks-Epstein Galleries in Houston during the 1990s.   —*RM*

Selected References:
Biggers, John, and Carroll Simms, with John Edward Weems. *Black Art in Houston: The Texas Southern University Experience.* College Station, Texas: Texas A&M University Press, 1978.
Rose, Barbara, and Susie Kalil. *Fresh Paint: The Houston School.* Austin: Texas Monthly Press; Houston: The Museum of Fine Arts, Houston, 1985.
Wardlaw, Alvia J. *Kermit Oliver.* Houston: Hooks-Epstein Galleries, 1998.

❏ (ROBERT) JULIAN ONDERDONK
Born 1882, San Antonio, Texas
Died 1922, San Antonio, Texas

Julian Onderdonk's paintings of the Southwest Texas landscape blanketed in bluebonnets occupy a special place in the popular imagination, comparable to that of Frank Reaugh's pastels of the plains. The artist's father, Robert Jenkins Onderdonk, celebrated as the "Dean of Texas Artists," inaugurated a school of San Antonio landscape painters whose most notable followers included his two children, (Robert) Julian and Eleanor. Julian Onderdonk first studied under his father in a drawing class in 1898. With the support of the influential San Antonio banker G. Bedell Moore, he went to New York in 1901 to study at the Art Students League. He received further training in a summer course taught by his father's instructor, William Merritt Chase, at Shinnecock in Southampton, Long Island. After marrying Gertrude Shipman in 1902, Onderdonk struggled to earn a living by doing commercial work and selling his impressionistic portraits and landscapes. In spite of financial difficulties, he continued his art education through a night course in life drawing taught by Robert Henri. In 1906, Onderdonk was invited by the State Fair of Texas to organize exhibitions of local and national artists. He returned permanently to San Antonio in 1909. Although arranging exhibitions took time away from his studio, it enabled Onderdonk to tour the country in search of innovative art and to elevate and promote his own painting in the process. Unfortunately, Onderdonk's life ended early when he failed to recuperate from an operation. Despite a career compressed into less than two decades, Onderdonk earned the rare distinction in 1922 of having his work posthumously included in the annual winter exhibition of contemporary artists at the National Academy of Design in New York.

—JAG

Selected References
Steinfeldt, Cecilia. *The Onderdonks: A Family of Texas Painters*. San Antonio: Trinity University Press for the San Antonio Museum Association, 1976.
————. *Art for History's Sake: The Texas Collection of the Witte Museum*. San Antonio: Texas State Historical Association for the Witte Museum of the San Antonio Museum Association, 1993.

❏ **AARON PARAZETTE**
   Born 1960, Ventura, California
   Lives in Houston, Texas

Aaron Parazette's carefully constructed abstractions critique the charges made by Modernism regarding authenticity and heroism. Parazette received a B.A. from the University of South Florida in Tampa in 1987 and an M.F.A. from the Claremont Graduate Program in Claremont, California, in 1990. Shortly thereafter, he moved to Houston and joined the Core Residency Program at the Glassell School of Art. In 1991, Parazette was featured in solo exhibitions at the Lloyd Shin Gallery in Chicago and the Davis/McClain Gallery in Houston. He curated *Process, Strategy, Irony*, a 1994 exhibition at DiverseWorks Artspace in Houston, and was awarded a fellowship from the Mid-America Arts Alliance/National Endowment for the Arts that same year. In 1994 and 1997, Texas Gallery in Houston presented his work in solo exhibitions. Parazette also was featured in group exhibitions at the University of Texas at San Antonio, Bucknell University in Lewisburg, Pennsylvania, and the San Francisco Art Institute. He was included in *Texas Abstract: New Painting in the Nineties* at ArtPace Foundation for Contemporary Art, San Antonio, in 1997, and *Abstract Painting, Once Removed* at the Contemporary Arts Museum, Houston, in 1998. In 1999, Parazette was presented in *Fabstraction*, a traveling group exhibition organized by Dave Hickey, seen in Houston at Texas Gallery, and in the *Post-Hypnotic* exhibition curated by Barry Blinderman for the Illinois State University Gallery.

—MG

Selected References:
Colpitt, Frances. "Going against the Grain." *Art in America* 83, no. 4 (April 1995): 43–47.
————. *Texas Abstract: New Painting in the Nineties*. San Antonio: ArtPace Foundation for Contemporary Art, 1997.
Friis-Hansen, Dana, David Pagel, and Raphael Rubinstein. *Abstract Painting, Once Removed*. Houston: Contemporary Arts Museum, 1998.
Blinderman, Barry, and Tom Moody. *Post-Hypnotic*. Normal, Illinois: Illinois State University, 1999.

❏ **BRIAN PORTMAN**
   Born 1960, Woonsocket, Rhode Island
   Lives in Houston, Texas

Brian Portman's deeply sonorous abstractions combine an architectural sense of space with a sensual command of paint. Portman received a B.F.A. from the Rhode Island School of Design, Providence, in 1983. Later that year, he moved to Houston to join the Core Residency Program at the Glassell School of Art. In 1984, he was featured in *The Next Show* at the Gallery Yves Arman in New York, and in 1985 he was included in *Emerging Artists* at the Art League of Houston. He had his first Houston solo exhibition at Hiram Butler Gallery in 1988; he was also featured that year in the Contemporary Arts Museum's *First Texas Triennial Exhibition*. Portman was awarded a grant from the Anne Giles Kimbrough Fund of the Dallas Museum of Art in 1988 and a fellowship from the National Endowment for the Arts in 1989. Hiram Butler Gallery again featured him in solo shows in 1990 and 1992. He was included in *Presence*, a 1992 exhibition at the Center for Research in Contemporary Art at the University of Texas at Arlington, and in *Darkness + Light: Twentieth-Century Works from Texas Collections*, a 1993 exhibition curated by artist Liz Ward at the Sarah Campbell Blaffer Gallery at the University of Houston. Portman was featured in solo shows at Barry Whistler Gallery in Dallas in 1993, at Robert McClain & Co. in Houston in 1994 and 1996, and at the Amarillo Museum of Art in 1997. In 1999 he began an affiliation with Barbara Davis Gallery in Houston.

—MG

Selected References:
Zeitlin, Marilyn A., Marge Goldwater, and David Ross. *The First Texas Triennial Exhibition: 1988*. Houston: Contemporary Arts Museum, 1988.
Robinson, Joan Seeman. "Brian Portman." *Artforum* 28, no. 9 (May 1990): 196.
Ennis, Michael. "The Mod Squad." *Texas Monthly* 24, no. 3 (March 1996): 74–79.
McCracken, Patrick. *Brian Portman: Atrium Installation*. Amarillo: Amarillo Museum of Art, 1997.

❏ **ROBERT PREUSSER**
   Born 1919, Houston, Texas
   Died 1992, Cambridge, Massachusetts

Robert Preusser was a pioneer abstract artist in Houston, as well as an influential teacher and advocate of Modernist aesthetics. He began studying art as a child in 1930, under the tutelage of McNeill Davidson, then the most prominent art teacher in Houston. In 1939, Preusser left Houston to attend the Institute of Design in Chicago, recently founded by László Moholy-Nagy and Gyorgy Kepes, which was dubbed "The New Bauhaus." In 1940, three of his works submitted to the *16th Annual Exhibition of Works by Houston Artists* at the MFAH were awarded the museum's Purchase Prize. World War II interrupted Preusser's studies in Chicago in 1942, and he served as a camouflage technician in the U.S. Army until 1945. After the war, he studied briefly at Tulane University in New Orleans and then at the Art

Center School in Los Angeles from 1946 until 1947. Preusser returned to Houston in 1947, and in 1948 he was given a solo exhibition at the MFAH. That same year, he became a founding member of the Contemporary Arts Association (now the Contemporary Arts Museum). In the succeeding years, he became a central figure in the growing Houston art community. From 1947 to 1954, he was an influential teacher at the MFAH school, where Frank Freed was among his students. Preusser codirected the Contemporary Arts Association from 1949 until 1951. He taught at the University of Houston from 1951 until 1954 and served as associate curator of education at the MFAH from 1952 until 1954. Preusser left Houston in 1954 to accept a position at the Massachusetts Institute of Technology (MIT) in Cambridge. In 1956, *Art in America Review* included him in its list of "promising new talents in the USA." He had one-person exhibitions in Boston and Houston in 1960. Preusser continued teaching at MIT until his retirement in 1985. In 1990, two exhibitions in Houston, at Parkerson Gallery and at Transco Tower, surveyed his work from the 1930s through the 1950s. He was honored with a retrospective of his paintings at the MIT Museum in Cambridge in 1991.

—RM

Selected References:
Recent Paintings by Robert Preusser. Boston: Boris Mirski Gallery, 1960.
Johnson, Patricia C. "Early Houston Abstract Artist Subject of Two Exhibitions." *Houston Chronicle*, 28 October 1990.
Chadwick, Susan. "Dual Show Features City Abstract Pioneer." *Houston Post*, 14 November 1990.

❏ **RACHEL RANTA**
   Born 1953, Ely, Minnesota
   Lives in Houston, Texas

Rachel Ranta examines the dialects of image and language in her paintings, depicting isolated objects with inscriptions that confound the images or suggest metaphorical interpretations. She received a B.F.A. from Maryville College in St. Louis, Missouri, in 1977 and moved to Houston in 1981. Ranta participated in a group show at the Lawndale Art and Performance Center in 1986. Her first solo exhibition was at the Firehouse Gallery in Houston in 1988. That same year, she was awarded an M.F.A. from the University of Houston and was featured in *Introductions '88* at Transco Tower. During the early 1990s, Ranta exhibited with William A. Graham Gallery in Houston. In 1991, she was featured in *The Perfect World in Contemporary Texas Art* at the San Antonio Museum of Art. Ranta began working as assistant director of the Lawndale Art and Performance Center in 1991. She was featured in group exhibitions in Houston at West End Gallery and University of Houston's Sarah Campbell Blaffer Gallery in 1993. Also in 1993, she curated with Liz Ward *Lawndale Live! A Retrospective* at the Lawndale Art and Performance Center. Ranta left Lawndale in 1994, and that same year was featured in solo exhibitions in Houston at the Contemporary Arts Museum and at the Sewall Art Gallery at Rice

University. In the mid-1990s, she participated in group exhibitions at Texas Gallery, where she had a solo exhibition in 1997.   —RM

Selected References:
Edwards, Jim. *The Perfect World in Contemporary Texas Art.* San Antonio: San Antonio Museum of Art, 1991.
Herbert, Lynn M. *Rachel Ranta: The Discrete Inquiry.* Houston: Contemporary Arts Museum, 1994.

❏ **ROBERT RAUSCHENBERG**
Born 1925, Port Arthur, Texas
Lives in Captiva, Florida

Robert Rauschenberg is among the few artists who can be credited with altering the course of American art in this century. Raised on the Gulf Coast of Texas, Rauschenberg briefly studied pharmacology at the University of Texas at Austin in 1943. He was drafted into the U.S. Navy in 1944 and dismissed the following year. Rauschenberg took advantage of the GI Bill, studying art at the Kansas City Art Institute in 1947–48; at the Académie Julian, Paris, in 1948; at the Black Mountain College, North Carolina, in 1948–49; and at the Art Students League, New York, in 1949–51. He returned to Black Mountain in 1952, and through such teachers as Merce Cunningham and John Cage, as well as such contemporaries as Cy Twombly, he forged his radical approach to art, embracing the real stuff of everyday life. In 1951, he had his first solo show at the Betty Parsons Gallery in New York. The following year, Cunningham and Cage featured him in *Theater Piece #1*, a 1952 performance piece at Black Mountain College, which is now considered to be the first Happening. In 1954, Rauschenberg adopted the term "Combine" to describe his painting/sculpture works. During these years, he established an important friendship with the painter Jasper Johns and began exhibiting with Leo Castelli Gallery in New York in 1958. He was included in *L'Exposition Internationale de Surréalisme: 1959–1960*, a 1959 exhibition organized by Marcel Duchamp and André Breton for the Galerie Daniel Cordier in Paris. In 1963, the Jewish Museum in New York offered the artist what was to be the first of many museum survey exhibitions. Over the following decade, Rauschenberg pursued performance and technological works as his major interests. In 1981, he embarked on one of his most ambitious projects, the *1/4 Mile or 2 Furlong Piece*, which the artist has continued to extend. From 1984 to 1991, Rauschenberg's attention was focused primarily on the creation of artworks for his ROCI (Rauschenberg Overseas Culture Interchange) exhibition project, which engaged artists around the world. Although he never again made his home in Texas, his work received significant exposure in his native state. Solo exhibitions were seen at the Contemporary Arts Museum in Houston in 1964, 1984, 1985, and 1986; Walter Hopps organized a landmark show of his early work for The Menil Collection in Houston in 1991; and Julia Brown Turrell undertook a groundbreaking examination of his sculpture for the Modern Art Museum of Fort Worth in 1995. The artist also has maintained a long-term affiliation with

Texas Gallery in Houston. In 1998, the three major museums of Houston—The Menil Collection, the Contemporary Arts Museum, and the MFAH—united to present Walter Hopps's and Susan Davidson's *Robert Rauschenberg: A Retrospective*, a presentation organized by the Solomon R. Guggenheim Museum that subsequently traveled internationally.   —MG

Selected References:
Solomon, Alan R. *Robert Rauschenberg.* New York: Jewish Museum, 1963.
Hopps, Walter. *Robert Rauschenberg.* Washington D.C.: National Collection of Fine Arts, Smithsonian Institution, 1977.
Turrell, Julia Brown. *Rauschenberg Sculpture.* Fort Worth: Modern Art Museum of Fort Worth, 1995.
Hopps, Walter, and Susan Davidson. *Robert Rauschenberg: A Retrospective.* New York: Guggenheim Museum Publications, 1997.

❏ **JAMES REABEN**
Born 1956, Houston, Texas
Died 1989, Houston, Texas

James Reaben's assemblages and journal-like drawings reveal a deep interest in symbology, expressing a need for a personal iconography to offer spiritual transcendence over the harsh realities of life and death. Reaben studied art and philosophy at the University of St. Thomas in Houston in 1976. Early in his career, he created abrasive and confrontational works, including a work titled *Minefield*, in which a grid of black circles actually was wired to an explosive charge and detonator. This early work was seen in a solo exhibition at Studio One in Houston in 1983. Reaben's mature work emerged in the mid-1980s. He participated in the 1986 group show *Prisoners of Conscience* at DiverseWorks Artspace in Houston. In 1987, a solo exhibition was organized by William Steen at Brazos Bookstore. The following year, Reaben had a solo exhibition at Moody Gallery in Houston and also began participating widely in local group exhibitions. In 1989, he was included in the Assistance League of Houston's *Texas Art Celebration '89* at the Cullen Center, *Messages From the South* at Rice University Art Gallery, and a solo exhibition at the C. G. Jung Educational Center in Houston. That same year, Reaben died of complications due to AIDS. In 1990, his work was featured in *Direct References: Drawings by Houston Artists* at the Glassell School of Art and in solo exhibitions at The Menil Collection and the MFAH in conjunction with *A Day without Art 1990*. Reaben's work appeared in *Avenues of Departure* at the Contemporary Arts Center in New Orleans in 1992 and in *Darkness + Light* at the Sarah Campbell Blaffer Gallery at the University of Houston in 1993. William Steen curated for Brazos Bookstore *In Fear and Rebellion: The Epistolary Art of James Reaben*, a 1995 exhibition that focused on Reaben's correspondence.
                —RM

Selected References:
Johnson, Patricia C. "Aura and Magic Surrounds Artist James Reaben's Work." *Houston Chronicle,* 16 July 1988.

Dobay, Louis. "The Passion of James Reaben." *Gulf Coast* 5, no. 1 (summer 1992): 32–53.
Steen, William, and John Harvey. *In Fear and Rebellion: The Epistolary Art of James Reaben.* Houston: Brazos Bookstore, 1995.

❏ **CHARLES FRANKLIN [FRANK] REAUGH**
Born 1860, Morgan County, Illinois
Died 1945, Dallas, Texas

Popularly referred to as the "Rembrandt of the Longhorns," Frank Reaugh celebrated the Texas landscape of rolling prairie and roaming cattle. In 1876, Reaugh came to Texas with his family and settled at a farm in Terrell, southeast of Dallas. From 1884 to 1885, he received formal training at the School of Fine Arts in St. Louis, Missouri. With the financial support of the Frank Reaugh Art Study Club, a Terrell group of art enthusiasts, he completed his education at the Académie Julian in Paris from 1888 to 1889. Reaugh moved to Dallas in 1890 and established a studio in Oak Cliff. His pastels began to receive acclaim in exhibitions held regularly at the National Academy of Design in New York, the Art Institute of Chicago, the State Fair of Texas, and the World's Fairs of 1893 and 1904 in Chicago and St. Louis, respectively. At the same time, his influence grew in the Southwest as he traveled each summer with students through West Texas and the Panhandle. Among those who accompanied him on these sketching trips were Alexandre Hogue, Otis Dozier, and other noteworthy artists who would later lead the Lone Star Regionalist movement of the 1930s. Though he enjoyed market successes, Reaugh held on to many of his pastels, hoping these works would remain together as testimony to a bygone era. Upon his death, a board of trustees appointed by Reaugh honored the artist's wishes by donating this collection of more than six hundred of his works to the Panhandle-Plains Historical Museum in Canyon, Texas.   —JAG

Selected References:
Haley, J. Evetts. *F. Reaugh: Man and Artist.* El Paso, Texas: Carl Hertzog Press, 1960.
Goetzmann, William H., and Becky Duval Reese. *Texas Images and Visions.* Austin: University of Texas at Austin, Archer M. Huntington Art Gallery, 1983.
Steinfeldt, Cecilia. *Art for History's Sake: The Texas Collection of the Witte Museum.* San Antonio: Texas State Historical Association for the Witte Museum of the San Antonio Museum Association, 1993.

❏ **LINDA RIDGWAY**
Born 1947, Jefferson, Indiana
Lives in Dallas, Texas

Linda Ridgway's subtle and poetic sculptures and drawings have been a significant presence in the Dallas art community since the mid-1970s. Ridgway received a B.A. in 1970 from the Louisville School of Art in Anchorage, Kentucky, and an M.A. in 1973 from Tulane University in New Orleans. The following year, she moved to Dallas. In 1977, she joined the Dallas Women's Cooperative Gallery, where she exhibited regularly until the cooperative disbanded in 1988. During 1979, she was included in the exhibition *FIRE!*, curated by James Surls, at the Contemporary Arts Museum in Houston, as well as *Twelve Artists Working in North Texas* at the Dallas Museum of Art. Ridgway was inspired to begin working in bronze in 1985, after a trip to Washington, D.C., where she encountered Alberto Giacometti's bronzes at the Hirshhorn Museum and Sculpture Garden. Soon after, she began collaborating with Harry Geffert at his foundry in Crowley, Texas, and her experiments there led to some of the strongest work of her career. In 1987, she became a professor of art at Cedar Valley College in Lancaster, Texas. She began showing with Gerald Peters Gallery in Dallas in 1991; subsequently, she exhibited with Inman Gallery in Houston and in 1999 began an affiliation with Dunn and Brown Contemporary in Dallas. Ridgway's prominence grew in the 1990s, and her bronzes were included in the 1995 exhibition *Genesis in Fire: Works from the Green Mountain Foundry* at the Glassell School of Art. In 1997, the Glassell School and the Dallas Museum of Art organized a major survey exhibition of her work.   —RM

Selected References:
Moody, Tom. "Linda Ridgway." *Artforum* 30, no. 2 (October 1991): 133–34.
Mitchell, Charles Dee. "Linda Ridgway at Gerald Peters." *Art in America* 82, no. 9 (September 1994): 121.
Greene, Alison de Lima. *Genesis in Fire: Works from the Green Mountain Foundry.* Houston: The Museum of Fine Arts, Houston, The Glassell School of Art, 1995.
Graze, Sue, and Charles Wylie. *Linda Ridgway: A Survey, The Poetics of Form.* Houston: The Museum of Fine Arts, Houston, The Glassell School of Art, 1997.

❏ **ROBERT RUELLO**
  Born 1958, New Orleans, Louisiana
  Lives in New Orleans, Louisiana

Robert Ruello has been fascinated by the mechanics of reproduction, incorporating collage techniques and photographic imagery into his densely layered paintings. Ruello received a B.A. in psychology from Loyola University in New Orleans in 1982 and a B.F.A. from the School of the Art Institute of Chicago in 1987. He moved to Houston later that year to join the Core Residency Program at the Glassell School of Art. In 1990, Ruello received a fellowship to the Skowhegan School of Painting and Sculpture in Maine, and the following year he was featured in *6 Houston Artists* at the Lafayette Art Center in Louisiana. During 1992, he was included in the Assistance League of Houston's *Texas Art Celebration* at the Cullen Center in Houston and had his first solo show at Inman Gallery. The following year, Ruello was featured in *Stairway to Heaven* at the Galveston Arts Center. In 1994, he was seen in *Nature/Culture* at Inman Gallery in Houston,

where he had a second solo exhibition in 1995. Later that year he enrolled in the graduate program at Columbia University and in 1996 he participated in the group exhibition *24 Degrees* at Columbia University. Ruello received an M.F.A. in 1997, and that same year he was included in the exhibition *Carousel* at New York's Leo Castelli Gallery. —RM

Selected References:
Greene, Alison de Lima, and Clint Willour. *Stairway to Heaven.* Galveston: Galveston Arts Center, 1993.
Ward, Elizabeth. *Nature/Culture.* Houston: Inman Gallery, 1994.
Schachter, Kenny. *24 Degrees.* New York: School of the Fine Arts, Columbia University, 1996.

❏ **CHARLES SCHORRE**
  Born 1925, Cuero, Texas
  Died 1996, Houston, Texas

Charles Schorre spent his career improvising on the classic themes of the figure, the still life, and the landscape. Schorre received a B.F.A. from the University of Texas at Austin in 1948. That same year, he married Margaret Storm and the couple moved to Houston, where Schorre started working as a commercial illustrator. In 1949, he began teaching at the school of the MFAH. During the 1950s, Schorre developed a series of paintings depicting stylized, crucifix-like forms with a clear relationship to Christian iconography. This series was presented in *Charles Schorre: Cruciforms*, a 1964 exhibition at Rice University in Houston. Schorre was an influential teacher at Rice from 1960 until 1972. In 1974, Schorre was featured in a solo exhibition at the Laguna Gloria Art Museum in Austin. He accepted an artist-in-residence award from Mobil Oil Corporation in 1979, and consequently traveled to Saudi Arabia. Schorre was included in *Fresh Paint: The Houston School*, the 1985 exhibition at the MFAH. In 1986, he was named Texas Artist of the Year by the Art League of Houston, and also honored with the City of Houston Mayor's Award for Outstanding Contribution to the Arts. After 1985, he continued exhibiting regularly with Meredith Long & Company in Houston until his death. In 1997, the Houston Artists Fund honored him with a major publication, celebrating Schorre's career as an important artist and influential educator.   —RM

Selected References:
Schorre, Charles. *Life Class.* New York: Wittenborn; Houston: Rice University, 1968.
Herring, Jerry, ed. *Charles Schorre.* Houston: Herring Press and Houston Artists Fund, 1997.

❏ **GEORGE SMITH**
  Born 1941, Buffalo, New York
  Lives in Houston, Texas

With strong roots in the American Minimalist tradition of the 1960s, George Smith looks toward African visual culture as a fresh source of inspiration. Smith studied with two of the greatest American sculptors of

his era: Bruce Nauman at the San Francisco Art Institute, where Smith received a B.F.A. in 1969, and Tony Smith at Hunter College in New York, where he received an M.F.A. in 1972. Smith's own career took off rapidly, and he was included in the 1970 Whitney Biennial while still in graduate school. In 1972, he had a solo exhibition at the Everson Museum of Art in Syracuse, New York, and began teaching at the State University of New York at Buffalo. Smith completed his first major outdoor sculpture at the Art Park in Lewiston, New York, in 1976. He had a major exhibition at Cornell University's Herbert F. Johnson Museum of Art in 1979, and a survey of his work from the 1970s was presented at the Studio Museum in Harlem in 1980. Smith moved to Houston in 1981 to become a professor at Rice University. He continued creating outdoor sculptures, winning commissions from the Metropolitan Atlanta Rapid Transit Authority in 1981 and the Niagara Frontier Transit Authority in Buffalo, New York, in 1983. He completed major commissions for the University of Houston in 1989 and the Belo Corporation in Dallas in 1991. In 1999, the Robert Hull Fleming Museum in Burlington, Vermont, organized an exhibition of his recent sculptures and drawings.   —RM

Selected References:
Rouse, Terrie S. *Architectural Sculpture by George Smith.* New York: Studio Museum in Harlem, 1980.
Grayson, Marion L. *George Smith: New Works.* Houston: Sewall Art Gallery, Rice University, 1983.
McEvilley, Thomas. *George Smith: Sculpture and Drawings.* Burlington, Vermont: Robert Hull Fleming Museum, 1999.

❏ **LEE N. SMITH III**
  Born 1950, New Orleans, Louisiana
  Lives in Dallas, Texas

Lee N. Smith III creates mysterious paintings, describing dreamlike worlds inhabited by enigmatic children. In 1956, Smith moved with his family to a newly built home in the suburbs of Dallas, and many of his paintings are based on memories of that environment. He briefly studied architectural drawing at El Centro Junior College, Dallas, in 1969 and 1970. Smith began painting in 1976 and had his first solo exhibition two years later at Eastfield College in Mesquite, Texas. He was included in the 1980 New Orleans Triennial at the New Orleans Museum of Art and in the 1983 exhibition *Southern Fictions* at the Contemporary Arts Museum in Houston. In 1984, Smith was among a small group of artists selected to represent the United States at the forty-first Venice Biennale. The biennale exhibition, *Paradise Lost/Paradise Regained: American Visions of the New Decade*, curated by Marcia Tucker of the New Museum in New York, subsequently embarked on a major international tour. Also in 1984, Smith had a solo exhibition at the Art Center in Waco. He was affiliated with Texas Gallery in Houston in the mid-1980s. During 1986, he was featured in a solo exhibition at the Contemporary Arts Museum in Houston, and also included in *The Texas Landscape 1900–1986* at the MFAH.

Smith garnered further international recognition in the late 1980s. He was invited to participate in the fifth *Bienale Americana de Artes Graficos* at the Museo de Arte Moderno la Tertulia in Cali, Colombia, in 1986, and to visit the American Center in Paris as artist-in-residence in 1988. During the 1990s, he divided his time between Dallas and France, primarily focusing on private commissions. Smith had exhibitions at Stiebel Modern in New York in 1994 and at Lyons Matrix Gallery in Austin in 1994 and 1997. —*RM*

Selected References:
Tucker, Marcia, et al. *Paradise Lost/Paradise Regained: American Visions of the New Decade.* Venice: La 41a Biennale di Venezia, United States Pavilion, 1984.
Todd, Emily. *Lee N. Smith III: Recent Paintings.* Houston: Contemporary Arts Museum, 1986.

❑ **AL SOUZA**
  Born 1944, Plymouth, Massachusetts
  Lives in Houston, Texas

With an attitude grounded in conceptual art, Al Souza has deconstructed the language of pictures in innovative works that span photography, painting, and assemblage. Souza originally studied engineering at the University of Massachusetts in Amherst, where he earned a B.S. before attending the Art Students League in New York. He subsequently attended the School of the Visual Arts in New York and in 1972 completed an M.F.A. at the University of Massachusetts. His first solo show was in New York, at OK Harris Gallery, in 1975. He exhibited in Houston with Cronin Gallery in the mid-1970s. Souza emerged onto the international stage in 1976, when he was included in the Venice Biennale. Two years later, he was awarded a fellowship from the National Endowment for the Arts. In 1980, he participated in group shows at both the Museum of Modern Art and the Alternative Museum in New York. Souza taught at the University of North Texas, Denton, in 1980 and at the University of Houston in 1981. The following year, he had solo shows at the New Museum in New York and the Dallas Museum of Art. He continued exhibiting in the United States and in Europe throughout the 1980s, and began showing with Moody Gallery in Houston in 1985. Souza lived in Texas in 1987, teaching at Texas A&M University at Commerce. He had a solo show at the Contemporary Arts Museum in Houston in 1988, before moving to California to teach at San Diego State University. Four years later, he returned to Texas, joining the faculty of the University of Houston. In the 1990s, Souza had solo exhibitions at the Art Museum of Southeast Texas in Beaumont, the Galveston Arts Center, Blue Star Art Space in San Antonio, and the Roswell Museum and Art Center in Roswell, New Mexico. In 2000, he was among the artists to be featured in the Whitney Biennial. —*RM*

Selected References:
Graze, Sue. *Concentrations VI: Al Souza.* Dallas: Dallas Museum of Fine Arts, 1982.
Zeitlin, Marilyn A. *Al Souza: Paintings.* Houston: Contemporary Arts Museum, 1988.

Castle, Lynn P. *Al Souza: Old News.* Beaumont, Texas: Art Museum of Southeast Texas, 1996.
Colpitt, Frances. *Morph: Meta(morph)osis and Bio(morph)ism in Contemporary Sculpture.* San Antonio: Blue Star Art Space, 1996.

❑ **EVERETT FRANKLIN SPRUCE**
  Born 1908, near Conway, Arkansas
  Lives in Austin, Texas

Everett Spruce painted with a rugged individualism that expressed his deep connection to the land of the Southwest and made him arguably the most independent of the Lone Star Regionalists. In 1925, Spruce graduated from high school in Mulberry, Arkansas. That same year, he met Dallas artist Olin H. Travis, whose Ozark Summer Art School was in nearby Cass. In 1926, Spruce moved to Dallas to study with Travis and Thomas Stell at the Dallas Art Institute. Through his acquaintance with the museum's director, Dr. John S. Ankeny, he became a gallery assistant at the Dallas Art Association Museum (later the Dallas Museum of Art, DMA) in 1931, eventually working his way up to assistant director in 1936. As a member of the Dallas Artists League, Spruce had his first solo exhibition at the DMA in 1932. He soon was established as a member of the Dallas Nine circle of Lone Star Regionalists, receiving shows at the Dallas Art Institute in 1933 and Joseph Sartor Galleries in 1934. Having earned a national reputation in group exhibitions at the Whitney Museum of American Art in New York and the Corcoran Gallery of Art in Washington, D.C., he left the DMA in 1940 to join the faculty of the University of Texas at Austin. Two years later, Spruce earned the honor of being one of two Texans selected for the exhibition *18 Artists from 9 States* at the Museum of Modern Art, New York. Along with Charles Umlauf, Spruce was featured in a joint exhibition at the Witte Memorial Museum in 1943, and that same year both artists were included in the *Artists for Victory Show* at the Metropolitan Museum of Art. In 1946, Spruce garnered the Painting of the Year award in the Pepsi-Cola Competition. He became chair of the art department at the University of Texas in 1949, retaining the position until 1951. Since his retirement from the university in 1974, Spruce has continued living in Austin, where he remained active as a painter until the late 1980s. —*JAG*

Selected References:
Danes, Gibson. "Everett Spruce: Painter of the Southwest." *Magazine of Art* 37, no. 1 (January 1944): 14–15.
Leeper, John Palmer. *Everett Spruce.* New York: American Federation of Arts for the Marion Kugler McNay Institute, San Antonio, 1959.
Stewart, Rick. *Lone Star Regionalism: The Dallas Nine and Their Circle, 1928–1945.* Austin: University of Texas Press; Dallas: Dallas Museum of Art, 1985.

❑ **GAEL STACK**
  Born 1942, Chicago, Illinois
  Lives in Houston, Texas

Gael Stack creates dense, atmospheric paintings in which she blends abstract and figurative elements, displaying a distinctive sense of calligraphic line. Stack entered the University of Illinois in 1959, initially to study journalism; however, she quickly switched her focus to fine art. After her marriage in 1963, she interrupted her studies for five years to begin raising her two sons. Divorced in 1968, Stack continued caring for her children and returned to the University of Illinois in Champaign, where she received a B.F.A. in 1970. She attended graduate school at Southern Illinois University in Carbondale, where she received an M.F.A. in 1972. After briefly teaching at the University of La Crosse in Wisconsin, she moved to Houston in 1973. Upon arriving in the city, she taught art classes in the after-school program at the Contemporary Arts Museum and also at the High School for the Performing and Visual Arts. In 1974, she accepted a teaching position at the University of Houston. The following year, Stack had her first solo exhibition in Houston, at Meredith Long & Company. In the early 1970s, she primarily worked in mixed media on paper, but in 1978 she began working in oil on canvas while retaining a strong element of drawing. Stack achieved a national reputation in the 1980s. Her work was included in the exhibition *19 Artists—Emergent Americans* at the Guggenheim Museum in New York in 1981, garnering critical attention in *Art in America*, *Artnews*, and *Artforum*. She had her first solo show in New York in 1985, and that same year was included in two exhibitions at the MFAH, *Fresh Paint: The Houston School* and *Eleven Houston Artists: Works on Paper.* Stack received fellowships from the Louis Comfort Tiffany Foundation in 1986 and the National Endowment for the Arts in 1989. That same year, the University of Houston's Sarah Campbell Blaffer Gallery highlighted her work in a major survey exhibition that traveled to the Dallas Museum of Art. In Houston in the 1980s she exhibited with Janie C. Lee Gallery and Hiram Butler Gallery; in 1989 she began an affiliation with Moody Gallery. She was nominated as Texas Artist of the Year in 1997 by the Art League of Houston. Throughout the late 1990s, Stack remained one of Houston's most distinguished artists and an influential professor at the University of Houston. —*RM*

Selected References:
Cathcart, Linda L., and Marti Mayo. *Four Painters: Jones, Smith, Stack, Utterback.* Houston: Contemporary Arts Museum, 1981.
Rose, Barbara, and Susie Kalil. *Fresh Paint: The Houston School.* Austin: Texas Monthly Press; Houston: The Museum of Fine Arts, Houston, 1985.
Mayo, Marti, Rosellen Brown, and Elizabeth Ward. *Gael Stack: A Survey 1974–1989.* Houston: University of Houston, 1989.

❏ EARL STALEY
Born 1938, Oak Park, Illinois
Lives in Houston, Texas

Earl Staley has embraced a range of subjects, from Mexican folklore to classical mythology, in his vividly expressive paintings. Staley received a B.F.A. from Illinois Wesleyan University in 1960. He attended graduate school at the University of Arkansas in Fayetteville, where he was awarded an M.F.A. in 1963. For the following three years, he worked as an instructor of drawing and printmaking at Washington University in St. Louis, Missouri. In 1966, Staley moved to Houston to teach at Rice University. Soon after arriving in Texas, he began making frequent sketching trips to Big Bend, and many of his paintings of the mid-1970s depict shaman figures set in the desert landscapes of West Texas. Staley left Rice in 1969 to accept a position as associate professor at the University of St. Thomas in Houston. Subsequently, he began a series of collaborative works with David Folkman, Bob Camblin, and Joe Tate. Long interested in indigenous American symbols and culture, Staley began visiting Mexico in 1975. His paintings from the following year clearly borrow from imagery associated with the celebration of the Day of the Dead in Mexico. Although seemingly out of step with Modernism, Staley's paintings captured the spirit of the late 1970s. He was included in the 1978 group show *'Bad' Painting* at the New Museum of Contemporary Art in New York. In 1981, Staley was awarded the coveted Prix de Rome, and in 1984 he was among a small group of artists selected to represent the United States at the forty-first Venice Biennale. Also in 1984 he was the focus of a survey exhibition seen at the New Museum of Contemporary Art and at the Contemporary Arts Museum in Houston. During 1985, he embarked on a major commission from the Houston Grand Opera to create set designs for a production of Gounod's *Faust*. That same year, he was featured in the MFAH exhibition *Fresh Paint: The Houston School*. A 1990 exhibition at the University of Texas at San Antonio reflected the influence of Mexico on his work. Staley presented his *Memories of Italy* at the Italian Cultural and Community Center in Houston in 1996.   —RM

Selected References:
Cathcart, Linda, and Marcia Tucker. *Earl Staley 1973–83.* New York: New Museum for Contemporary Art; Houston: Contemporary Arts Museum, 1984.
Tucker, Marcia, et al. *Paradise Lost/Paradise Regained: American Visions of the New Decade.* Venice: La 41a Biennale di Venezia, United States Pavilion, 1984.
Rose, Barbara, and Susie Kalil. *Fresh Paint: The Houston School.* Austin: Texas Monthly Press; Houston: The Museum of Fine Arts, Houston, 1985.

❏ ANN STAUTBERG
Born 1944, Houston, Texas
Lives in Galveston, Texas

Ann Stautberg creates large photographs that lyrically evoke the landscape of the Gulf Coast. Stautberg received a B.F.A. from Texas Christian University, Fort Worth, in 1971 and an M.A. from the University of Dallas in 1972. While studying painting in college, she experimented with photoemulsion. In 1973, she began to make black-and-white photography her chief medium. Stautberg had an early two-person show with Peter Yenne at the Laguna Gloria Art Museum in Austin in 1976, and soon after began exhibiting regularly in Dallas. During the late 1970s, she began adding her signature translucent, colored glazes to her photographs. Stautberg had a 1981 solo show at the Dallas Museum of Art and continued participating energetically in group exhibitions in Dallas, where she lived throughout the 1980s. She was the focus of an exhibition at the Tyler Museum of Art in 1987 and was included in *Texas Women* at the National Museum of Women in the Arts in Washington, D.C., in 1988. During 1990, she began showing with Barry Whistler Gallery in Dallas. She had a solo exhibition at the Galveston Arts Center in 1991. Charmed by the coastal landscape, Stautberg and her husband, artist Frank Tolbert, moved to Galveston that year. She subsequently began exhibiting regularly in Houston, and was featured in group exhibitions at the Houston Center for Photography in 1994 and the MFAH in 1996. Stautberg had a two-person show with Charles Mary Kubricht at the Glassell School of Art in 1998. That same year, she was included in the Contemporary Arts Museum's FotoFest exhibition, *Field of Vision: Five Gulf Coast Photographers*, and she also began an affiliation with James Gallery in Houston. —RM

Selected References:
Graze, Sue. *Concentrations II: Ann Lee Stautberg.* Dallas: Dallas Museum of Art, 1981.
Irvine, Alexandra L. *Field of Vision: Five Gulf Coast Photographers.* Houston: Contemporary Arts Museum, 1998.
Olsen, Valerie Loupe. *In Situ: Responses from Charles Mary Kubricht and Ann Stautberg.* Houston: The Museum of Fine Arts, Houston, The Glassell School of Art, 1998.

❏ ARY STILLMAN
Born 1891, near Minsk, Belarus
Died 1967, Houston, Texas

Ary Stillman progressed from early figurative work, influenced by Post-Impressionism, to an abstract calligraphic style of painting. In 1906, Stillman attended the Imperial Art School in Vilnius, in present-day Lithuania. He left for the United States the following year, living in Sioux City, Iowa, from 1907 until 1919. During his years in Sioux City, Stillman worked in a jewelry store and painted during his free time, except for an interlude in 1912 when he studied full-time at the Art Institute of Chicago. In 1919, he moved to New York, where he studied at the National Academy of Design, the Art Students League,

and the Jewish Educational Alliance. Stillman went to Europe in 1921 and spent the next twelve years traveling the continent, visiting England, Germany, Holland, and Spain, and briefly establishing a studio in Paris. He had his first solo exhibition in 1928, at Galerie Bernheim-Jeune in Paris. In 1933, Stillman returned to New York, where he exhibited extensively during the 1930s. By the mid-1940s, he had begun to exhibit his experiments with abstraction. Between 1957 and 1962, he lived in Mexico, where he adopted a symbolically rich abstract style that showed affinities with Surrealism and Mexico's ancient cultures. Stillman moved to Houston in 1962, contributing to the continuous exchange of ideas between Mexico and Texas. He died in 1967. In 1972, the MFAH organized a major retrospective survey of his career.   —RM

Selected References:
Montebello, Philippe de, and Richard Teller Hirsch. *Ary Stillman, 1891–1967.* Houston: The Museum of Fine Arts, Houston, 1973.
Stillman, Frances Frigbourg and Ary Stillman. *Reminiscenes: The Personal Life of Artist Ary Stillman.* Houston: The Stillman-Lack Foundation, 1988.
Stillman, Frances Frigbourg. *Ary Stillman in Mexico.* San Antonio: Jansen-Perez Gallery, 1990.

❏ MYRON STOUT
Born 1908, Denton, Texas
Died 1987, Chatham, Massachusetts

Myron Stout has come to be recognized as one of the outstanding artists among the American nonobjective painters who emerged in the 1950s. During his senior year at the University of North Texas, Denton, Stout decided to become an artist. He spent the summer of 1933 studying with Carlos Merida at the Academía San Carlos in Mexico City. In 1937, he enrolled at Teacher's College, Columbia University. After receiving his master's degree in 1939, he taught at a private art school in Honolulu before being drafted in 1943. Stout served in the war and in 1946 returned to Denton, where he was prompted by Toni LaSelle to attend Hans Hofmann's summer classes in Provincetown, Massachusetts, that same summer. In 1947, Stout moved to New York and divided his time between teaching and studying with Hofmann in Provincetown. He moved to Provincetown in 1952 and devoted his career to his studio. Stout was included in numerous group exhibitions, including the *Annual Exhibition of Contemporary American Painting* at the Whitney Museum of American Art in New York in 1958, *100 Works on Paper* at the Institute of Contemporary Art, Boston, in 1959, and *Geometric Abstraction in America* at the Whitney in 1962. Over the course of his working career, he received only two gallery exhibitions, the first at the Stable Gallery in New York in 1954 and the second at the Hansa Gallery in New York in 1957. Nevertheless, in more recent years Stout's work was the focus of numerous solo exhibitions. The Contemporary Arts Museum in Houston held the first overview of his career in 1977, and the Whitney organized a full-scale retrospective in 1980.
                                   —JAG

Selected References:
Schwartz, Sanford. *Myron Stout.* New York: Whitney Museum of American Art, 1980.
Luhring, Lawrence, and David Reed. *"I Knew It To Be So," Forrest Bess, Alfred Jensen, Myron Stout: Theory and the Visionary.* New York: New York Studio School, 1984.
Geldzahler, Henry. *Myron Stout.* New York: Flynn, Kent Fine Art, and Oil and Steel Gallery, 1990.
Nesbitt, Paul, and Mel Gooding. *Myron Stout.* Edinburgh: Royal Botanic Garden, 1998.

❏ **RICHARD STOUT**
   Born 1934, Beaumont, Texas
   Lives in Houston, Texas

Richard Stout's reflective and atmospheric paintings evolve from a delicate balance of abstract and figurative concerns. Stout spent his childhood in Beaumont, where as a high-school student he was impressed greatly by the work of Morris Graves. He entered the Art Academy of Cincinnati in 1952. The following year, he transferred to the renowned School of the Art Institute of Chicago, where he received a B.F.A. in 1957. After graduation he moved to Houston, where he rented a small apartment close to the MFAH. Stout quickly was embraced by the art community and soon joined the faculty of the Museum School. In 1958, he was invited to have his first solo show at New Arts Gallery, run by Katherine Swenson, a protégé of Jermayne MacAgy. He met artist Dick Wray in 1959, beginning a long friendship. In 1964, while studying at the University of Texas at Austin, he met another close friend, artist Michael Tracy. Stout married Anne Winkler in 1965, and that same year became acting dean of the school of the MFAH. He received an M.F.A. from the University of Texas in 1969, and began a long and influential teaching career at the University of Houston. Stout was a deep admirer of the nineteenth-century German Romantics, especially the painter Caspar David Friedrich and the architect Karl Friedrich Schinkel. In 1976, he visited Berlin, where he was deeply impressed by Friedrich's paintings at the Charlottenburg Palace. Stout's subsequent paintings fuse the influence of the Romantics with a deep affinity for his native Gulf Coast landscape. His drawings were featured in William A. Camfield's 1983 exhibition *New Art from a New City: Houston,* which was seen at the Frankfurter Kunstverein in Frankfurt, Germany, before traveling to the MFAH in 1985. Also in 1985, his work was included in the *Fresh Paint: The Houston School* exhibition at the MFAH. Stout retired from the University of Houston in 1996. He had a solo exhibition that year at the Museum of East Texas in Lufkin, followed by a second solo show in 1997 at Texas A&M University in College Station. In 1999, the Art Museum of Southeast Texas in Beaumont paid tribute to Stout with a major exhibition of his recent paintings.   —*RM*

Selected References:
Camfield, William A. *New Art from a New City: Houston.* Frankfurt: Frankfurter Kunstverein, 1983.
Rose, Barbara, and Susie Kalil. *Fresh Paint: The Houston School.* Austin: Texas Monthly Press; Houston: The Museum of Fine Arts, Houston, 1985.

Mansbach, Steven. *Structures of Intimacy.* Houston: Technigrafiks, Inc., 1997.
Kalil, Susie. *Richard Stout: Soul's Journey.* Beaumont: Art Museum of Southeast Texas, 1999.

❏ **JAMES SURLS**
   Born 1943, Terrell, Texas
   Lives in Splendora, Texas, and Basalt, Colorado

James Surls is renowned for his energetic line drawings and his twisting wooden figures, which exploit the tension between representation and rhythmic abstraction. Surls received a B.S. in 1966 from Sam Houston State College in Hunstville and an M.F.A. in 1969 from the Cranbrook Academy of Art in Bloomfield Hills, Michigan, where he studied with Julius Schmidt. He returned to Texas in 1970 to join the faculty at Southern Methodist University in Dallas. Surls had his first solo museum exhibition at the Tyler Museum of Art in Tyler, Texas, in 1974. The following year, he was the focus of a solo show at the Contemporary Arts Museum in Houston. He established a home and studio in Splendora, north of Houston, in 1976, and two years later married artist Charmaine Locke. Surls taught at the University of Houston from 1976 until 1982, and during this period was a vital catalyst in the local art scene. In 1979, he founded the Lawndale Art and Performance Center as an extension of the University of Houston art department. That same year, he curated *FIRE!*, an exhibition for the Contemporary Arts Museum, which included work by some one hundred Texas artists. Surls also was included in the 1979 Whitney Biennial, and the Whitney honored him in 1985 with a second invitation. In 1984, the Dallas Museum of Art organized a ten-year survey of his work, which traveled to the La Jolla Museum of Contemporary Art, the Seattle Art Museum, and the University of Oklahoma Museum of Art. Also in 1984, Surls began an affiliation with Hiram Butler Gallery in Houston; subsequently he exhibited with Barry Whistler Gallery and Gerald Peters Gallery in Dallas. Surls completed a public commission for Market Square in downtown Houston in 1991. He was awarded a Living Legend Award by the Dallas Visual Art Center in 1993. Surls established a second home in Basalt, Colorado, in 1997. During fall 1999 in Houston, the Glassell School of Art presented a retrospective of his drawings while the Barbara Davis Gallery organized a solo exhibition of his work; concurrently the El Paso Museum of Art presented an exhibition of his more recent sculptures.   —*RM*

Selected References:
Harithas, James. *James Surls: Sculptor.* Houston: Contemporary Arts Museum, 1975.
Surls, James. *FIRE!* Houston: Contemporary Arts Museum, 1979.
Graze, Sue. *Visions: James Surls, 1974–1984.* Dallas: Dallas Museum of Art, 1984.
Kalil, Susie. *James Surls: Walking with Diamonds.* El Paso, Texas: El Paso Museum of Art in collaboration with Houston Artists Fund, 1999.
Olsen, Valerie Loupe. *Innate Contours: The Drawings of James Surls.* Houston: The Museum of Fine Arts, Houston, The Glassell School of Art, 1999.

❏ **BILL THOMAS**
   Born 1948, Houston, Texas
   Lives in Houston, Texas

Bill Thomas's photographs illustrate the absurdly complex methods of committing suicide that Thomas devises, often posing himself in a tragicomic manner as someone about to take his own life. Thomas grew up in Houston in the 1950s, attending Poe Elementary School. Two key childhood experiences underlie his interest in suicide: the regular duck-and-cover drills enacted at his school in anticipation of nuclear war, and the actual horror of a murder-suicide bombing that took place on the grounds of Poe Elementary in 1959. With these events etched on his memory, Thomas studied psychology at the University of Texas at Austin, receiving a B.A. in 1973. Between 1975 and 1989, he worked with the Department of State to help resettle refugees in Houston, while occasionally working as a freelance photographer. Thomas began studying photography at the University of Houston in 1990 and received an M.F.A. in 1993. He was included in *Texas/Between Two Worlds* at the Contemporary Arts Museum in Houston in 1993. From 1993 to 1996, Thomas was a lecturer at Rice University in Houston. In 1994, he received a fellowship from the Houston Center for Photography. Thomas became director of photography and digital imaging at the Anderson Ranch Arts Center in Aspen, Colorado, in 1996. He returned to Houston in 1998 to join the faculty of the University of Houston.   —*RM*

Selected References:
Doroshenko, Peter. *Texas/Between Two Worlds.* Houston: Contemporary Arts Museum, 1993.

❏ **JACKIE TILESTON**
   Born 1960, Manila, Philippines
   Lives in Albuquerque, New Mexico

Jackie Tileston creates rich and sensual paintings that combine a bright palette with imagery drawn from nature. Born in the Philippines, Tileston grew up in England and France. She received a B.A. from Yale University, New Haven, in 1983 and an M.F.A. from Indiana University, Bloomington, in 1988. Tileston moved to Houston in 1988 to join the Core Residency Program at the Glassell School of Art. She immediately found a forum in a number of Houston-area exhibitions, including the *Texas Art Celebration* in 1989 and again in 1990. Her first solo show was a 1990 *Introductions* exhibition at Houston's William A. Graham Gallery, where she also had a solo exhibition in 1992. During 1993, Tileston and Sharon Engelstein were featured in a two-person exhibition at Women and Their Work in Austin. Tileston also was included in *New American Talent* at the Laguna Gloria Art Museum in Austin that same year. In 1994, the Longview Museum of Fine Art in Longview, Texas, organized a solo exhibition of her work. Tileston was seen in *Texas Abstract: New Painting in the Nineties,* a 1995 exhibition curated by Frances Colpitt at ArtPace Foundation for Contemporary Art in San Antonio. The Contemporary Arts Museum in Houston hosted *Hybrid Vigor,* a 1996 exhibition that presented

Tileston's paintings with the sculptures of Kirk McCarthy. During 1995 and 1997, Lawing Gallery in Houston featured Tileston in solo exhibitions. In 1998, Tileston accepted a teaching position at the University of New Mexico in Albuquerque.   —MG

Selected References:
Colpitt, Frances. *Texas Abstract: New Painting in the Nineties.* San Antonio: ArtPace Foundation for Contemporary Art, 1995.
Herbert, Lynn M. *Kirk McCarthy and Jackie Tileston: Hybrid Vigor.* Houston: Contemporary Arts Museum, 1996.

❑ **MICHAEL TRACY**
  Born 1943, Bellevue, Ohio
  Lives in San Ygnacio, Texas, and Mexico City, Mexico

Michael Tracy's vividly expressive works employ a vocabulary drawn from religious sources that range from Catholic altars to Congo fetishes. While still in high school, Tracy took classes at the Cleveland Institute of Art. A trip to Europe in 1961 solidified his interest in Italian art, which has remained an important touchstone throughout his career. Later in 1961, Tracy entered St. Edward's University in Austin, where he received a B.A. in English literature in 1964. He briefly attended the Cleveland Institute of Art before completing graduate studies at the University of Texas at Austin in 1969. In Austin, he met the painter Richard Stout, who became a close friend. Tracy made the first of many trips to Mexico in 1972, visiting a Penitente procession during Holy Week in Valenciana, Guanajuato. For much of the 1970s, he chose as his base Galveston, where Joseph Glasco was already working. In 1974, Tracy opened the Stella Maris bar there, and also staged a fabled performance/ritual titled *Sacrifice I: 9.13.74 (The Sugar)* in a Galveston sugar warehouse. In 1978, he established a studio in the small historic town of San Ygnacio, near the Mexican border on the Rio Grande. Tracy achieved international recognition in the 1980s, participating in the 1982 Venice Biennale and in the 1983 *New Art* exhibition at the Tate Gallery in London, as well as the *New Art from a New City: Houston* exhibition organized by William A. Camfield for the Frankfurter Kunstverein in Frankfurt, Germany. In 1983, he was the focus of a solo show at the Contemporary Arts Museum in Houston. In 1984, he began an affiliation with Hiram Butler Gallery and Hadler/Rodriguez Gallery in Houston. A major retrospective of his work, organized by P.S. 1 in Long Island City in 1987, traveled to The Menil Collection in Houston in 1989. Tracy also had a solo exhibition at the Centro Cultural Arte Contemporáneo in Mexico City in 1989. During the 1990s, he divided his time between Mexico City and San Ygnacio. In the mid-1990s, Tracy turned his attention to film projects. His first film, *Flower Warrior*, was released in 1994, and an exhibition of related works was presented at Moody Gallery in Houston. In 1998, his *Culture Water and Money: The Passion of the Frontier* won the award for Best Economic Documentary at the New York International Film and Video Festival.   —RM

Selected References:
Gallander, Cathleen, and Michael Tracy. *Michael Tracy: Six Paintings.* Corpus Christi: Art Museum of South Texas, 1973.
Stout, Richard. *Michael Tracy: Paintings and Drawings.* Houston: University of Houston, Sarah Campbell Blaffer Gallery, 1973.
Camfield, William A. *New Art from a New City: Houston.* Frankfurt: Frankfurter Kunstverein, 1983.
Mayo, Marti. *Requiem Para los Olvidados.* Houston: Contemporary Arts Museum, 1983.
Leffingwell, Edward, and Thomas McEvilley. *Terminal Privileges: Michael Tracy.* New York: P.S. 1, 1987.
Christophel, Joan, and Edward Leffingwell. *The River Pierce: Sacrifice II, 13.4.90.* Houston: River Pierce Foundation and Rice University Press, 1992.

❑ **RANDY TWADDLE**
  Born 1957, Elmo, Missouri
  Lives in Houston, Texas

Randy Twaddle's stark charcoal drawings treat industrial subjects such as pylons and satellite dishes as flat calligraphic silhouettes; his interest in the iconic images of contemporary culture later evolved into a fascination with anagrams and wordplay. Twaddle studied at the University of Missouri in Colombia before receiving a B.F.A. from Northwest Missouri State University in Maryville in 1980. He moved to Dallas later that year. In 1984, Twaddle was included in group exhibitions at the Laguna Gloria Art Museum in Austin and the Art Museum of South Texas in Corpus Christi, as well as in the inaugural exhibition of Hiram Butler Gallery in Houston. He had his first solo exhibition in 1985, at Moody Gallery in Houston. The following year, he had a solo show at the Tyler Museum of Art in Tyler, Texas. Twaddle garnered national recognition in 1986, when he was featured in group exhibitions at the Corcoran Gallery of Art in Washington, D.C., and the Brooklyn Museum of Art in New York. In 1987, he received a grant from the National Endowment for the Arts, and the following year he was featured in the *First Texas Triennial Exhibition* at the Contemporary Arts Museum in Houston. He began an affiliation with Barry Whistler Gallery in Dallas in 1989, while continuing to show with Moody Gallery in Houston, and moved to Houston that same year. In 1990, Twaddle was visiting assistant professor at the University of North Carolina in Chapel Hill. He lived in France for a short time before returning to Houston in 1991. Twaddle had solo shows that year at the University of North Carolina and Damon Brandt Gallery in New York. In 1993, he was featured in *Seeing the Forest through the Trees* at the Contemporary Arts Museum and in *Darkness + Light* at the Sarah Campbell Blaffer Gallery at the University of Houston. He had a solo show in 1995 at Moody Gallery. In 1996, Twaddle switched his focus from two-dimensional work to film production. He and David Thompson formed the multimedia production company Ttweak in 1998. Twaddle and Thompson were awarded a commission for the Fine Arts Building of the University of Houston in 1999.   —RM

Selected References:
Kotik, Charlotta. *Monumental Drawing: Works by 22 Contemporary Americans.* Brooklyn, New York: Brooklyn Museum of Art, 1986.
Rifkin, Ned. *Spectrum: Drawn Out.* Washington, D.C.: Corcoran Gallery of Art, 1986.
Zeitlin, Marilyn A., Marge Goldwater, and David Ross. *The First Texas Triennial Exhibition: 1988.* Houston: Contemporary Arts Museum, 1988.

❑ **RUTH PERSHING UHLER**
  Born 1895, Gordon, Pennsylvania
  Died 1967, Houston, Texas

Ruth Pershing Uhler not only was an accomplished painter of abstractions of the Southwestern landscape, but also played a critical role in the early years of the MFAH. In 1909, Uhler's family moved from Pennsylvania to Houston. After completing her high-school education, Uhler returned to the Northeast, where she attended the Philadelphia School of Design for Women. As a student of Leopold Seyffert and Jean Charlot in fresco painting, she was awarded the Daniel Bough Prize for Still Life Painting and the John Sartain Scholarship for Achievement and Ability. Upon receiving her degree, she did graduate work at the Henry Snell Art School in Boothbay Harbor, Maine, before returning to Houston in 1925. Uhler received first prize for still-life painting at the 1927 exhibition of *Works of Texas Artists* held in Nashville, Tennessee. In 1931, she earned an honorable mention in an exhibition of Texas artists at the MFAH. From 1935 to 1936, Uhler lived in Santa Fe, New Mexico, where she studied Native American arts and crafts. She came to the MFAH as a teacher of design classes in 1937, serving as curator of education from 1941 until her death in 1967. During her early years at the museum, Uhler continued her career as an artist. She assisted Daniel MacMorris in painting the Rozelle Court in the Nelson Gallery in Kansas City, Missouri, and also painted frescoes in Houston's City Hall and a mural in the Central Public Library. In the early 1940s, however, Uhler quit painting entirely. She devoted her complete attention to her many duties at the MFAH, where she was instrumental in establishing educational programs and serving as principal assistant to the museum's directors.   —JAG

Selected References:
Fisk, Frances Battaile. *A History of Texas Artists and Sculptors.* Abilene, Texas: Fisk Publishing Company, 1928.
Forrester-O'Brien, Esse. *Art and Artists of Texas.* Dallas: Tardy Publishing Company, 1935.
Trenton, Patricia, et al. *Independent Spirits: Women Painters of the American West, 1890–1945.* Berkeley and Los Angeles: Autry Museum of Western Heritage in association with University of California Press, 1995.

❏ **ROBIN UTTERBACK**
  Born 1949, Holton, Kansas
  Lives in Houston, Texas

Robin Utterback has questioned the structure of painting itself and developed his own delicately gestural language. Utterback was among the first artists to emerge from the B.F.A. program at Rice University, where he graduated in 1974. During the second half of the 1970s, he had regular solo exhibitions at Tibor de Nagy Gallery (later Watson/de Nagy & Company) in Houston. In 1981, he had a solo exhibition at Delahunty Gallery in Dallas. Utterback was featured in *New Art from a New City: Houston*, curated by William A. Camfield for the Frankfurter Kunstverein in Frankfurt, Germany, in 1983. Two years later, he was featured in *Fresh Paint: The Houston School* at the MFAH. In the late 1980s, Utterback garnered national exposure and critical acclaim. Over the following decade, he had more solo shows in New York than in his home city, showing regularly with Tibor de Nagy Gallery in New York. However, Utterback remained committed to living and working in Houston, where he served on the board of the Friends of Rice University Gallery and on the board of trustees of the Contemporary Arts Museum. Texas audiences were given the opportunity to appreciate fully Utterback's achievements in 1992, when he was featured in solo shows at the Contemporary Arts Museum and Moody Gallery in Houston, as well as in a significant survey exhibition at the Galveston Arts Center. He ended his affiliation with Tibor de Nagy, New York, in 1993. In 1995, Utterback had a solo exhibition with Hiram Butler Gallery in Houston, and in 1996 he began showing with E. M. Donahue Gallery (later Donahue/Sosinski Gallery) in New York. In 1999, his recent paintings were featured in the *Five Artists: New Work* exhibition curated by Bill Lassiter for DiverseWorks Artspace in Houston.   —*RM*

Selected References:
Cathcart, Linda L., and Marti Mayo. *Four Painters: Jones, Smith, Stack, Utterback.* Houston: Contemporary Arts Museum, 1981.
Camfield, William A. *New Art from a New City: Houston.* Frankfurt: Frankfurter Kunstverein, 1983.
Rose, Barbara, and Susie Kalil. *Fresh Paint: The Houston School.* Austin: Texas Monthly Press; Houston: The Museum of Fine Arts, Houston, 1985.
Zeitlin, Marilyn A., Marge Goldwater, and David Ross. *The First Texas Triennial Exhibition: 1988.* Houston: Contemporary Arts Museum, 1988.

❏ **KATHY VARGAS**
  Born 1950, San Antonio, Texas
  Lives in San Antonio, Texas

Kathy Vargas creates photographic works that build on the traditional layering of images and mementos found in Mexican shrines. Vargas began photographing yard shrines in her east San Antonio neighborhood while an undergraduate at the University of Texas at San Antonio, where she received a B.F.A. in 1981. Subsequently, she began creating her own shrine-like assemblages in the studio as a basis for her photographs. In 1984, Vargas received an M.F.A. from the University of Texas at San Antonio. The following year, she became director of the Guadalupe Cultural Arts Center, one of the largest community-based centers for Chicano studies in the United States. Vargas had an early solo exhibition at the University of California at Santa Barbara in 1985, and she participated in group shows at San Antonio's newly established Blue Star Art Space in 1986. During the late 1980s, she exhibited internationally, with a solo exhibition at the Universidad Nacional Autónoma de México in 1987 and another at the Universität Erlangen-Nürnberg in Germany in 1988. Vargas was featured in the 1990 touring exhibition *Chicano Art: Resistance and Affirmation*, organized by the University of California, Los Angeles, which received broad national press and visited the National Museum of American Art in Washington, D.C. In 1991, she had a solo show at the University of Texas at El Paso, and in 1993 she was the subject of a solo exhibition, *Images of Loss and Hope*, at the Houston Center for Photography and the Galveston Arts Center. During 1997, Vargas was an artist-in-residence at the ArtPace Foundation for Contemporary Art in San Antonio, where she created a major installation, *State of Grace: Angels for the Living/Prayers for the Dead*. The San Antonio Art League nominated her as Artist of the Year for 1998.   —*RM*

Selected References:
Lippard, Lucy R. *Mixed Blessings: New Art in a Multicultural America.* New York: Pantheon Books, 1990.
Kathy Vargas 97.1. San Antonio: ArtPace Foundation for Contemporary Art, 1997.
Kathy Vargas "I Was Little They Were Big." San Antonio: San Antonio Art League Museum, 1998.

❏ **SALLE WERNER VAUGHN**
  Born 1939, Ennis, Texas
  Lives in Houston, Texas

Salle Werner Vaughn's mystical paintings and whimsical installations lure the viewer into a carefully constructed dreamworld. Vaughn, who studied at the Texas Woman's University in Denton with distinguished artists Toni LaSelle and Carlotta M. Corpron, received a B.A. in 1961. After living briefly in San Francisco, she returned to Dallas and continued studying graphic and theater design. Vaughn was featured in *Texas Painting and Sculpture*, her first group exhibition, at the Dallas Museum of Art in 1968. She received national exposure when she was included in the 1973 Whitney Biennial. During the 1970s, Vaughn relocated to Houston. In the 1980s, she acquired several Victorian cottages in Houston's Magnolia Grove neighborhood. These houses since have been the sites of various installations exploring themes and characters from ancient literature. In 1983, Vaughn was featured at La Boetie, Inc., in New York. She had a 1984 solo exhibition at LYC Museum in Banks, Cumbria, England. Parkerson Gallery in Houston organized a solo show of her work in 1986 and the McAlpine Gallery in London featured her in 1987. Hiram Butler Gallery in Houston showcased her work in a 1988 solo exhibition.

In 1995, Robert McClain & Co. in Houston presented another solo exhibition, *Salle Werner Vaughn: Ut Pictura Poesis.*   —*MG*

Selected References:
Simpson, William Kelly. *Salle Werner Vaughn.* New York: La Boetie, 1983.
Chadwick, Susan. "Artist transforms two old homes into graceful works of art," *Houston Post*, 15 March 1993.
Johnson, Patricia C. "Symbol Little Bungalow: Inside, Artist Tells Persephone Myth One Room at a Time." *Houston Chronicle*, 6 March 1994.

❏ **BOB WADE**
  Born 1943, Austin, Texas
  Lives in Austin, Texas

Nicknamed "Daddy-O," Bob Wade has created heroic incarnations of popular images of Texas and cultivated a self-styled identity as the "good ole boy" of Texas art. On his mother's side of the family, Wade is a second cousin of Leonard Slye, who became Roy Rogers. Wade spent his childhood living in towns throughout Texas, and as a teenager in El Paso in the late 1950s he developed a passion for automobile customizing. He began studying art at the University of Texas at Austin in 1961, receiving a B.F.A. there in 1965 and then an M.A. from the University of California at Berkeley in 1966. After graduate school, he became a founding faculty member of the art department at McClennan Community College in Waco, Texas. Wade lived in Oak Cliff, across the river from downtown Dallas, in the early 1970s, when he and the artists Jack Mims, Jim Roche, and George Green together became known as "The Oak Cliff Four." In 1975, Wade began a humorous land art project, *A Bicentennial Map of the United States*, in Farmers Branch, off Interstate 635. During 1977, he took his *Texas Mobile Home Museum* to the Musée d'Art Moderne de la Ville de Paris for the *Biennale de Jeunes Artistes*. Among his most notorious and controversial outdoor sculptures were a giant iguana, installed on the roof of the Lone Star Café in Manhattan in 1978, and a sculpture of six dancing frogs, placed on the roof of a Dallas nightclub, which caused debate among city officials in 1983. Wade established a studio in Tesuque, New Mexico, in 1988. His sculpture of a giant saxophone for the roof of Billy Blues, a Houston nightclub, created a further civic controversy in 1993. Wade returned to Texas and settled in Austin in 1996. His traveling exhibition *Daddy-O's Stuff*, organized by the Art Center of Waco in 1997, was presented at the Lawndale Art and Performance Center in Houston in 1999.   —*RM*

Selected References:
Harithas, James. *12/Texas.* Houston: Contemporary Arts Museum, 1974.
Smith, Roberta. "Twelve Days of Texas." *Art in America* 64, no. 4 (July–August 1976), 44–48.
Wade, Bob, with Keith Zimmerman and Kent Zimmerman. *Daddy-O: Iguana Head and Texas Tails.* New York: St. Martins Press, 1995.
Province, Shannon. *Daddy-O's Stuff.* Waco, Texas: Art Center of Waco, 1997.

❏ LIZ WARD

Born 1959, Lafayette, Louisiana
Lives in Galveston and San Antonio, Texas

Liz Ward's conceptually rigorous and intimately scaled works serve as diaristic studies of nature. Ward completed undergraduate studies at the University of New Mexico, Albuquerque, in 1982. After graduation, a curatorial fellowship enabled her to work at the distinguished Tamarind Institute in Albuquerque, where she studied printmaking. In 1984, a Harriet Hale Woolley Scholarship allowed Ward to study printmaking further at Atelier 17 in Paris, France. During her stay in Paris, she had her first solo show at the Galerie Woolley, Fondation des Etats-Unis. Ward then moved to Houston, completing an M.F.A. at the University of Houston in 1990. Over the following decade, she built a body of work that ranged over a variety of media, from cyanotypes to silverpoint to sculpture to painting. Ward was awarded numerous grants and fellowships, including a National Endowment for the Arts Interarts Grant from Houston's Lawndale Art and Performance Center in 1986 and two fellowships from the Mid-America Arts Alliance/National Endowment for the Arts in 1991 and 1992. She was included in *The Perfect World in Contemporary Texas Art* at the San Antonio Museum of Art in 1991 and in *Seeing the Forest through the Trees* at the Contemporary Arts Museum in Houston in 1993. Ward was featured in solo exhibitions at the Ida Green Gallery at Austin College in Sherman, Texas, in 1994 and at Moody Gallery in Houston in 1995. Aside from producing art, she curated two exhibitions in 1990 and 1991 at the Glassell School of Art, and in 1993 *Darkness + Light: Twentieth-Century Works from Texas Collections* at the Sarah Campbell Blaffer Gallery at the University of Houston. Also in 1993, she curated with Rachel Ranta *Lawndale Live! A Retrospective* at the Lawndale Art and Performance Center. She held teaching positions at the High School for the Performing and Visual Arts in Houston, the University of Houston, and the Glassell School of Art. In 1998, the Contemporary Arts Museum in Houston presented *Liz Ward: The Present of Past Things,* her first solo show in a museum. In 1999, Ward accepted a teaching position at Trinity University in San Antonio; also that year, she was featured in the inaugural exhibition of Dunn and Brown Contemporary in Dallas.
— *MG*

Selected References:
Gambrell, Jamey. "In the Third Coast Art Capital." *Art in America* 75, no. 4 (April 1987): 186–203.
Edwards, Jim, et al. *The Perfect World in Contemporary Texas Art.* San Antonio: San Antonio Museum of Art, 1991.
Herbert, Lynn M. *Liz Ward: The Present of Past Things.* Houston: Contemporary Arts Museum, 1998.

❏ JEAN CARRUTHERS WETTA

Born 1944, St. Louis, Missouri
Lives in Ormond Beach, Florida

Jean Carruthers Wetta has tackled the classic genre subjects of landscape, still life, and portraiture with eloquent restraint. She graduated from Webster College in St. Louis, Missouri, in 1966 and studied at Louisiana State University in Baton Rouge, where she received an M.A. in painting in 1970. Wetta moved to Galveston in 1971 and led painting classes at the Galveston Arts Center from 1972 until 1977. She had her first solo exhibition in 1978, at the North Florida Community College in Madison. In 1979, she won the Purchase Prize at the *Fifth Biennial Five State Art Exhibition,* held in Port Arthur, Texas. That same year, Wetta began teaching at the College of the Mainland in Texas City, and in 1980 she became director of the college's gallery. During her tenure there, she brought Rackstraw Downes to Texas City, encouraging his engagement with the local landscape. Wetta did not exhibit in Houston until 1985, the year she gave up her post at the College of the Mainland, when she took part in *Houston Area Introductions '85* at Transco Tower. She began exhibiting regularly in Houston thereafter, establishing an affiliation with McMurtrey Gallery in 1987. Wetta left Galveston in 1993 to live in Ormond Beach, Florida. She received a State of Florida Individual Artists Fellowship in 1995 and had a solo exhibition at the Ormond Beach Memorial Art Museum two years later. A traveling exhibition surveying fifteen years of Wetta's career was organized by the Galveston Arts Center in 1998.
— *RM*

Selected References:
Hopps, Walter, et al. *American Images: The SBC Collection of Twentieth-Century American Art.* New York: Harry N. Abrams, Inc., 1996.
Willour, Clint, and Eleanor Jones Harvey. *Jean Wetta: A Survey 1984–1996.* Galveston: Galveston Arts Center, 1998.

❏ JOHN WILCOX

Born 1954, Denison, Texas
Lives in Dallas, Texas

John Wilcox takes a conceptual approach to his monochromatic paintings, with an interest in reinvesting a personal spirituality into the process of painting itself. Wilcox spent most of his childhood in Denison, Texas, moving to Austin at the age of 15. In 1973, he entered Colorado College in Colorado Springs, where he received a B.A. in fine arts in 1977. He subsequently undertook graduate studies at the University of Texas at Austin. Between 1978 and 1985, Wilcox lived alternately in Lake Texoma, Texas; Fort Worth; and Carpinteria, California. In 1983, he moved to Dallas, where he worked as an installation assistant at the Dallas Museum of Art. From 1985 until 1990, Wilcox lived in New York. In 1986, he had a two-person exhibition with DeWitt Godfrey at Barry Whistler Gallery in Dallas, and also was included in a group exhibition at Michael Klein Inc. in New York. During the late 1980s, he exhibited regularly with Barry Whistler Gallery in Dallas and with Fawbush Gallery in New York. He returned to Dallas in 1990. Wilcox had a solo exhibition at Fawbush Gallery in 1992. The following year, he participated in the group exhibition *Darkness + Light* at the University of Houston's Sarah Campbell Blaffer Gallery. Wilcox was featured in *Essentials* at the Glassell School of Art in 1994 and in *Literally Abstract* at the Center for Research in Contemporary Art at the University of Texas at Arlington in 1995. In 1996, he had a solo exhibition at Barry Whistler Gallery and also was featured in *Texas Abstract: New Painting in the Nineties* at the ArtPace Foundation for Contemporary Art in San Antonio. Wilcox was included in *A Cool Show* at the Arlington Museum of Art in 1998.
— *RM*

Selected References:
Ward, Elizabeth. *Darkness + Light: Twentieth-Century Works from Texas Collections.* Houston: University of Houston, Sarah Campbell Blaffer Gallery, 1993.
Colpitt, Frances. *Texas Abstract: New Painting in the Nineties.* San Antonio: ArtPace Foundation for Contemporary Art, 1995.
Mitchell, Charles Dee. "John Wilcox at Barry Whistler." *Art in America* 84, no. 12 (December 1996): 109.

❏ CASEY WILLIAMS

Born 1947, Houston, Texas
Lives in Houston, Texas

Casey Williams has explored the photograph's potential for abstraction. Williams studied at the University of Texas at Austin, where he took photography classes with Russell Lee, and graduated in 1970. He taught photography at the High School for the Performing and Visual Arts in Houston during the early 1970s, before entering the San Francisco Art Institute, where he received an M.F.A. in 1976. Williams returned to Houston and in 1979 began teaching at the Glassell School of Art, where he established darkroom facilities in the school's new building. During the early 1980s, he was affiliated with Texas Gallery in Houston. Williams was featured in *Big Pictures by Contemporary Photographers* at the Museum of Modern Art, New York, in 1983; in *The Texas Landscape 1900–1986* at the MFAH in 1986; and in the *First Texas Triennial Exhibition* at the Contemporary Arts Museum in Houston in 1988. He had a 1990 solo show at the Laguna Gloria Art Museum in Austin. In 1991, Williams taught at the University of North Texas, Denton, and he spent 1994 as visiting artist at the University of Texas at San Antonio. He was among the artists featured in the *Texas/Between Two Worlds* exhibition at the Contemporary Arts Museum in 1993. During the second half of the 1990s, he devoted his time to Houston, where he began showing with Barbara Davis Gallery in 1995. Williams had a solo exhibition at the Galveston Arts Center in 1998, and that same year his images of Houston's ship channel were featured in the 1998 New Orleans Triennial.
— *RM*

Selected References:
Kalil, Susie. *The Texas Landscape: 1900–1986.*
    Houston: The Museum of Fine Arts, Houston,
    1986.
Zeitlin, Marilyn A., Marge Goldwater, and David
    Ross. *The First Texas Triennial Exhibition: 1988.*
    Houston: Contemporary Arts Museum, 1988.
Doroshenko, Peter. *Texas/Between Two Worlds.*
    Houston: Contemporary Arts Museum, 1993.
Kotik, Charlotta. *1998 New Orleans Triennial.*
    New Orleans: New Orleans Museum of Art,
    1998.

❏ **DANNY WILLIAMS**
    Born 1950, Waco, Texas
    Lives in Dallas, Texas

Danny Williams's paintings and sculptures record
his fascination with the signs and symbols of ancient
and foreign cultures. Before finding his vocation as
an artist, Williams studied anthropology at Southern
Methodist University in Dallas, where he graduated
with a B.A. in 1972. He shifted his focus to art while
in graduate school, receiving an M.A. in painting
from the University of Iowa in 1976. Williams subsequently returned to Dallas, where he had a two-
person show with Ron Moody at the DW Gallery
later that year. In 1977, he received a Fulbright grant
that allowed him to travel extensively around India.
Williams was featured in *Twelve Artists Working in
North Texas* at the Dallas Museum of Art in 1979.
He had his first solo shows in 1980, when he was the
focus of exhibitions at Delahunty Gallery in Dallas
and the Art Center in Waco. Williams found national recognition in 1983 with his inclusion in the
thirty-eighth Corcoran Biennial in Washington, D.C.
In 1985, he began showing with Barry Whistler
Gallery in Dallas and Hiram Butler Gallery in
Houston. He also began a collaboration with Harry
Geffert at the Green Mountain Foundry in Crowley,
Texas. Some of his most alluring works of the 1990s
were the results of bronze-casting experiments at
Green Mountain. Williams's bronze works were
showcased in *Genesis in Fire: Works from the Green
Mountain Foundry* at the Glassell School of Art in
1995. His most recent paintings were seen at Barry
Whistler Gallery in 1998.   *—RM*

Selected References:
McConnell, Gordon. *Danny Williams: Travels
    1977–1979.* Waco, Texas: Art Center, 1980.
Carlozzi, Annette DiMeo, and Gay Block. *50 Texas
    Artists: A Critical Selection of Painters and Sculp-
    tors Working in Texas.* San Francisco: Chronicle
    Books, 1986.
Mitchell, Charles Dee. *Danny Williams Paintings:
    Travels Real and Imagined.* Dallas: Barry
    Whistler Gallery, 1998.

❏ **ROBERT WILSON**
    Born 1941, Waco, Texas
    Lives in New York, New York

As an artist, theater director, and stage designer,
Robert Wilson has expressed a grand vision, tran-
scending the boundary between visual art and theater. Wilson attended the University of Texas at
Austin from 1959 until 1962. He then was drawn to
New York, where he studied at the Pratt Institute.
In the mid-1960s, Wilson began designing sets and
lighting for off-Broadway productions and also staging his own performances in his Soho loft. He first
received serious recognition, however, in Europe.
In 1971, the Paris presentation of his *Deafman Glance*
won the French Critics Award for Best Foreign Play
and grand praise from the great Surrealist poet Louis
Aragon. Wilson had a solo exhibition at Paula
Cooper Gallery in New York in 1975. *Einstein on
the Beach*, his 1976 collaboration with the composer
Philip Glass, quickly became a landmark in experimental theater. In 1977, he collaborated with
Lucinda Childs to present *I was sitting on my patio
this guy appeared I thought I was hallucinating* at
the University of Houston at Clear Lake. Recognition of his artwork grew increasingly in the early 1980s,
with exhibitions at the Boymans-van Beuningen
Museum in Rotterdam in 1983 and the Walker Art
Center in Minneapolis in 1984. His epic *the Civil
warS: a tree is best measured when it is down*, originally created for the 1984 Olympic Arts Festival in
Los Angeles, was partially realized in separate
sections in Europe, Minneapolis, and Los Angeles
during the mid-1980s; drawing related to this production were exhibited at Texas Gallery in Houston.
In 1991, the Contemporary Arts Museum in Houston presented *Robert Wilson's Vision*, organized by
the Museum of Fine Arts, Boston. The exhibition
was complemented by Wilson's version of Henrik
Ibsen's *When We Dead Awaken* at the Alley Theatre.
Wilson visited Houston again in 1992, directing
Richard Wagner's *Parsifal* at the Houston Grand
Opera and exhibiting at Hiram Butler Gallery. His
installation at the 1993 Venice Biennale won the
prestigious Golden Lion Award for Sculpture. In
1995, the Art League of Houston voted him Texas
Artist of the Year, and that same year he directed
and performed in *HAMLET: a monologue* for the
Alley Theatre. Wilson directed Virgil Thompson
and Gertrude Stein's *Four Saints in Three Acts* for
the Houston Grand Opera in 1996. In 1999, he premiered *the days before: death destruction & detroit III*
at Lincoln Center; Wilson subsequently exhibited
works related to this production at Devin Borden
Hiram Butler Gallery in Houston.   *—RM*

Selected References:
Stearns, Robert. *Robert Wilson: From a Theatre of
    Images.* Cincinnati, Ohio: Contemporary Arts
    Center, 1980.
Johnston, Jill. "Family Spectacles." *Art in America*
    74, no. 12 (December 1986): 94–107.
Fairbrother, Trevor, et al. *Robert Wilson's Vision.*
    Boston, Massachusetts: Museum of Fine Arts,
    Boston; New York: Harry N. Abrams, Inc., 1991.
James, Jamie. "From Lohengrin to Catherine
    Deneuve." *Artnews* 95, no. 11 (December 1996):
    98–102.

❏ **GEOFF WINNINGHAM**
    Born 1943, Jackson, Tennessee
    Lives in Houston, Texas

Geoff Winningham's photographs have captured the
spirit of contemporary life in Texas and Mexico.
Winningham moved to Houston in 1961 to attend
Rice University, where he received a B.A. in English
in 1965. He chose photography over graduate opportunities in English and law, and in 1966 began
studying with Aaron Siskind at the Illinois Institute
of Technology. Winningham received an M.F.A. in
1968 and returned to Houston, first teaching at the
University of St. Thomas. He joined the faculty of
Rice University in 1969. Winningham founded
Latent Image, Houston's first professional photography gallery, in 1970. During the 1970s, he became
known widely for his black-and-white documentary
photographs. In 1971, he published *Friday Night
at the Coliseum*, a study of wrestlers and their audiences, and produced a 30-minute documentary of
the same title. The following year, he received a
Guggenheim Fellowship and in 1974 he was the
subject of a solo exhibition at the MFAH. In 1976,
he published *Going Texan: The Days of the Houston
Livestock Show and Rodeo*. Winningham was included in *Four American Photographers*, a 1977
exhibition at the Whitney Museum of American Art
in New York. *Rites of Fall*, his study of Texas high-
school football, was published in 1979. During a trip
to Mexico in 1981, Winningham began concentrat-
ing on color photography. He had a solo exhibition
in 1983 at the San Antonio Museum of Art. In 1986,
he published *A Place of Dreams*, which recorded contrasting aspects of life in Houston. A vivid use of color
characterized Winningham's later series, such as the
photographs of Mexican fiestas collected in his 1997
publication, *In the Eye of the Sun: Mexican Fiestas*.
                                      —RM

Selected References:
Tucker, Anne Wilkes. *Geoff Winningham: Pho-
    tographs.* Houston: The Museum of Fine Arts,
    Houston, 1974.
Winningham, Geoff. *Going Texan: The Days of the
    Houston Livestock Show and Rodeo.* Houston:
    Mavis P. Kelsey, Jr., 1976.
______. *A Place of Dreams.* Houston: Rice University
    Press, 1986.
______. *In the Eye of the Sun: Mexican Fiestas.*
    New York: Norton and Company, 1997.

❏ **GARRY WINOGRAND**
    Born 1928, New York, New York
    Died 1984, Tijuana, Mexico

Garry Winogrand developed an informal style of
photography that eloquently captured fleeting im-
pressions of the modern city. Winogrand studied
painting at City College of New York in 1947 and
1948 and at Columbia University in 1948. While
enrolled in painting classes at Columbia, he began
experimenting with photography. In 1951, he studied photography with Alexey Brodovitch at the New
School for Social Research in New York. Soon afterward, he began working as a photojournalist, receiv-

ing his first editorial assignment for *Harper's Bazaar* in 1952. While working as a magazine photographer, Winogrand also became recognized in the world of fine art. He was included in three group exhibitions at the Museum of Modern Art in New York between 1955 and 1963. Although he cannot be identified exclusively as a Texas artist, Winogrand created and published some of his most important work while he lived in the state. He made a visit to Texas in 1964 while traveling on a Guggenheim Fellowship, and returned in 1973 to join the faculty at the University of Texas at Austin. His most recognizably Texan images were the result of a 1974 commission from the Fort Worth Art Museum to document the Fort Worth Fat Stock Show and Rodeo for the exhibition *The Great American Rodeo Show*. Winogrand recognized that his images formed the nucleus of a book and, with the assistance of the Fort Worth Art Museum, he photographed the rodeo again in 1976 and 1977. He published two important series of urban street photographs, *Women Are Beautiful* and *Public Relations*, both in book form, before leaving Austin for Los Angeles in 1978. The University of Texas Press published *Stock Photographs* in 1980. The Houston Center for Photography presented a collection of Winogrand's most recent work in February 1984, shortly before his untimely death in March of that year.   —*RM*

Selected References:
Winogrand, Garry. *Women Are Beautiful*. New York: Light Gallery Books, 1975.
————. *Public Relations*. New York: Museum of Modern Art, 1977.
————. *Stock Photographs: The Fort Worth Fat Stock Show and Rodeo*. Austin and London: University of Texas Press, 1980.
Szarkowski, John, and Garry Winogrand. *Figments from the Real World*. New York: Museum of Modern Art, 1988.

❏ **DEE WOLFF**
   Born 1948, Springfield, Minnesota
   Lives in Houston, Texas

Dee Wolff has created a personal iconography with sources in both Western and Eastern religions. Wolff earned a B.A. from the University of Houston in 1970 and studied at the Museum School from 1974 to 1977. She began participating in local group exhibitions in 1976. Wolff had a solo exhibition at the Galveston Arts Center in 1977 and exhibited with Covo de Iongh Gallery in Houston that same year. In 1978, she began an affiliation with Watson/de Nagy in Houston. Wolff was featured in *New Art from a New City: Houston,* curated by William A. Camfield for the Frankfurter Kunstverein in Frankfurt, Germany, in 1983. She had solo exhibitions at Texas A&M University, College Station, in 1986 and Stephen F. Austin State University, Nacogdoches, the following year. In 1988, Wolff was awarded a National Endowment for the Arts Interdisciplinary Arts Grant for her collaboration with composer Stewart Wallace on the stage piece *Kabbalah*, which premiered at the Dance Theatre Workshop, New York, in 1989. She had solo exhibitions at DiverseWorks Artspace in Houston in both 1989 and 1990. During 1990, she presented solo shows at the C. G. Jung Educational Center in Houston, the Art Museum of Southeast Texas in Beaumont, and the Galveston Arts Center. Wolff participated in various group exhibitions in the mid-1990s, including the Art League of Houston's *Texas Art for Russia,* which toured Russia in 1995, and *Proof of Love* at Lynn Goode Gallery in Houston in 1996.   —*RM*

Selected References:
Camfield, William A. *New Art from a New City: Houston*. Frankfurt: Frankfurter Kunstverein, 1983.
Robinson, Joan Seeman. *Dee Wolff—Explorations: Then and Now*. Beaumont, Texas: Art Museum of Southeast Texas, 1990.

❏ **DICK WRAY**
   Born 1933, Houston, Texas
   Lives in Houston, Texas

Dick Wray creates distinctive and energetic paintings and works on paper, poised between graphic simplicity and gestural abstraction. As a teenager, Wray attended Lamar High School in Houston and worked part-time in the drafting department of a gas company. With his interest in drafting established, he entered the School of Architecture at the University of Houston in 1955. Still uncertain about a career in architecture after three years of study, Wray traveled to Europe in 1958 and enrolled at the renowned Kunstakademie in Düsseldorf. He returned to Houston the following year resolving to become a painter, and met fellow painter Richard Stout, who became a close friend. The Contemporary Arts Association included Wray in a group show in 1961, and the following year his submission to the MFAH exhibition *The Southwest: Painting and Sculpture* received the Ford Foundation Purchase Award. Between 1964 and 1966, he lived in Los Angeles, where he was guest artist at the Tamarind Institute in 1964. Returning to Houston, Wray served on the faculty of the Museum School from 1969 to 1982. He had solo exhibitions in Texas at the Contemporary Arts Museum in Houston in 1975, the Tyler Museum of Art in 1978, and the Galveston Arts Center in 1979. Wray was a guest artist at the Anderson Ranch Arts Center in Aspen, Colorado, in 1983. That same year, he was featured in *New Art from a New City: Houston*, a traveling exhibition curated by William A. Camfield for the Frankfurter Kunstverein in Frankfurt, Germany. In 1985, an exhibition surveying Wray's paintings since the mid-1970s was shown at Midtown Art Center in Houston. Wray was featured in *Fresh Paint: The Houston School* at the MFAH that same year, and in *Texas Art* at The Menil Collection in 1988. Following a long affiliation with Moody Gallery in Houston, he began to show his work independently in the late 1990s; in 1999 he exhibited his recent paintings at ArtScan Gallery in Houston.   —*RM*

Selected References:
Moser, Charlotte. "Philip Renteria and Dick Wray." *Art in America* 64, no. 4 (July–August 1976): 82–83.
Camfield, William A. *New Art from a New City: Houston*. Frankfurt: Frankfurter Kunstverein, 1983.
Johnson, Patricia. "Dick Wray." *Artspace* 7, no. 2 (spring 1983): 53–54.
Printz, Neil, Alison de Lima Greene, and Marilyn A. Zeitlin. *Texas Art*. Houston: The Menil Collection, 1988.

❏ **KYLE YOUNG**
   Born 1966, Port Arthur, Texas
   Lives in Houston, Texas

Kyle Young's moodily evocative paintings unite abstraction and the study of nature. Young received a B.F.A. from Lamar University in Beaumont, Texas, in 1990 and continued with postgraduate studies the following year. He moved to Houston in 1991 and began an affiliation with Hooks-Epstein Galleries in 1993. Young was featured in a solo exhibition at the Texas Artists Museum in Port Arthur in 1994. That same year, he was invited to participate in *Miniatures* and in *Boxes*, two exhibitions at Hooks-Epstein Galleries. In 1995, Hooks-Epstein sponsored *Genos Vita*, Young's first solo exhibition in Houston. *Poros*, a second presentation at Hooks-Epstein, followed in 1996, and the Galveston Arts Center organized *Genos to Poros* in 1997. Also in 1997, Young was included in *Figuring the Body* at the MFAH and in the *Dishman Competition*, juried by Sally Sprout for the Dishman Art Gallery at Lamar University. He was awarded a Visual Arts Fellowship from the Edward F. Albee Foundation in 1998. Young was included in *Six*, a 1999 exhibition curated by Paul Manes at Kouros Gallery in New York. He introduced a series of monochromatic paintings and drawings in another 1999 exhibition, *White*, at Hooks-Epstein Galleries. In 1999, Young was also among the artists selected by the Albright-Knox Art Gallery in Buffalo to be featured in its *New York Collection* series.   —*MG*

Selected Readings:
Lokensgard, Lynne. "Kyle Young at TAMS." *Beaumont Art League Magazine*, October 1994, 3.
Davenport, Bill. "Kyle Young at Hooks-Epstein." *Artletter*, no. 43 (15 December 1996): n.p.

❏ **ROBERT ZIEBELL**
   Born 1956, Chicago, Illinois
   Lives in Galveston and San Antonio, Texas

Robert Ziebell is perhaps best known for his photographs that record segments of the Gulf Coast landscape. He also has experimented with still-life photography and throughout his career has been active as a filmmaker. Ziebell studied at the University of Michigan in Ann Arbor, where he received a B.F.A. in 1979. He subsequently became director of the Cinema Guild Film Theater in Ann Arbor. His own film work was featured in the Ann Arbor Film Festival and the Athens International Film Festival in Athens, Georgia, in 1980. Ziebell taught photography at Prairie State College in Chicago, before moving to Houston in 1983 as a Core Artist in Residence at the Glassell School of Art. He had a solo show in 1984 at Rutger Gallery in Utica, New York. In 1987, he created a photo and video installation for the Dallas Film and Video Festival. Ziebell's film work was featured on KUHT TV's independent filmmaking program, *The Territory*, in 1988. His film portrait of life in Texas, *This State I'm In*, premiered at the MFAH in 1990. That same year, Ziebell was featured in the group exhibition *Reinventing Reality: Five Texas Photographers* at the Sarah Campbell Blaffer Gallery of the University of Houston. He had a solo show of his photographs at the Galveston Arts Center in 1992, and was included in the 1993 Phoenix Triennial at the Phoenix Art Museum in Arizona. The following year, he exhibited with Davis/McClain Gallery in Houston. He received artist fellowships from the Texas Commission of the Arts in Austin during 1994, 1995, and 1996; during this period he completed another film, *Stop Evil.* Ziebell was featured in the 1998 FotoFest exhibition *Field of Vision: Five Gulf Coast Photographers* at the Contemporary Arts Museum in Houston.   —*RM*

Selected References:

Gambrell, Jamey. "Texas: State of the Art." *Art in America* 75, no. 3 (March 1987): 114–131, 151.

Ward, Elizabeth. *Reinventing Reality: Five Texas Photographers*. Houston: University of Houston, Sarah Campbell Blaffer Gallery, 1990.

Kurtz, Bruce D., and Karen C. Hodges. *Contemporary Identities: 1993 Phoenix Triennial*. Phoenix, Arizona: Phoenix Art Museum, 1993.

Petr, Mark. "Robert Ziebell: Little Secrets." *ArtLies* 2 (May–June 1994): 14.

Irvine, Alexandra L. *Field of Vision: Five Gulf Coast Photographers*. Houston: Contemporary Arts Museum, 1998.

Chronology of Exhibitions of Texas Art
at the Museum of Fine Arts, Houston

Edited by Alejandra Jiménez

Note: The information assembled in this chronology was originally compiled by Kathleen Coleman, Jill Jackson, Kathleen Robinson, and Lorraine A. Stuart, with the assistance of Terry Brown, for the archives of the Museum of Fine Arts, Houston. Minor inconsistencies in annual exhibition titles have been regularized; permanent title changes of long-running annual exhibitions have been recorded when appropriate. Unless otherwise noted, all exhibitions after 1924 were held at the Museum of Fine Arts, Houston. In 1979, the atrium gallery of the new Glassell School of Art became the museum's chief venue for contemporary Texas exhibitions; however, this chronology does not reflect the annual faculty and student shows sponsored by the museum's school programs. Exhibitions marked with a star (★) are accompanied by a catalogue or related publication.

TEXAS EXHIBITIONS MOUNTED BY HOUSTON PUBLIC SCHOOL ART LEAGUE PRIOR TO THE OPENING OF MUSEUM OF FINE ARTS, HOUSTON

1917

Exhibition of Paintings by Texas Artists Arranged by the Houston Art League for the Texas Women's Fair
(location unknown)
November 5–10

1918

Paintings and Drawings by John Clark Tidden, James Henry Chillman, Jr., Agnes Lilienberg Tidden
Held at the University Club, Houston
April 25–27

John Clark Tidden
Held at Rice Institute, Houston
(precise dates unknown)

1922

Catalogue of Texas Paintings
Held at the Houston Public Library
March 6–20

1923

An Exhibition of Paintings by Mrs. E. Richardson Cherry and Percy W. Holt
Held at the YWCA, Houston
Spring

MUSEUM OPENS ON PRESENT SITE ON APRIL 12, 1924

1924

Percy Holt: Oils and Watercolors
May

Jose Arpa
May 24–June 7

Royston Nave
October 4–November 2

Paintings by Mrs. Charles Franklin (Hattie Virginia) Palmer
October 18–November 1

2nd Annual Circuit Exhibition of the Southern States Art League
(Selected from the 4th Annual Exhibition of the Southern States Art League)
October 23–November 10

John Clark Tidden
November 19–December 8

Paintings by Douglas R. Hansen
December

Agnes Lilienberg Tidden
Opened December 17

1925

Erwin Escher
January–February 16

Oil Paintings by Mrs. E. Richardson Cherry ★
January 31–February 28

Samuel E. Gideon: Watercolors
February 9–28

Julian Muench
March

Bertha Louise Hellman
Opened March 2

Paintings by Olin H. Travis
Opened March 7

1st Annual Exhibition of Work by Houston Artists ★
May 29–3

Collection of Articles Pertaining to the Early History of the Republic of Texas
May

Paintings of Texas Life
May

Paintings by Charles Bien
November 3–December 4

1926

Margaret Brisbine: Oil Paintings
January 31–February 28

6th Annual Exhibition of the Southern States Art League ★
March 4–April 4

Exhibition of Paintings by Margaret Fish
April 8–30

[1st] Exhibition of Work by Houston Photographers
May 9–June 9

2nd Annual Exhibition of Work by Houston Artists ★
May 9–June 9

1927

Watercolors by Boyer Gonzales ★
March 5–31

3rd Annual Exhibition of Work by Houston Artists ★
April 3–May 1

Mary Bonner: Etchings
April 5–15

Etchings by L. O. Griffith
May 1–22

2nd Annual Exhibition of Work by Houston Photographers
(Combined with an exhibition of Houston Craftsmen)
May 8–June 10

Selected Paintings from Texas Wildflower Competition
June 12–July 3

Thesis Studies of 6 Rice Architecture Graduates
Opened July 10

Julian Onderdonk
August–October

Work by Students of the Sul Ross State Teachers College
September

Sculpture by Abraham Rosenberg
October

5th Annual Circuit Exhibition of the Southern States Art League
(Selected from the *7th Annual Exhibition of the Southern States Art League*)
December 4, 1927–January 1, 1928

1928

Everett Gee Jackson: Oils
March 4–25

4th Annual Exhibition of Work by Houston Artists ★
April 1–29

3rd Annual Exhibition of Work by Houston Photographers
May 6–June 3

Paintings of Texas Life
June–July 15

Julian Onderdonk: Bluebonnets
June–July

Historic Texas
Opened June 28

Drawings by Rice Students
August

Paintings by Frederic Browne
November 4–December 2

6th Annual Circuit Exhibition of the Southern States Art League
(Selected from the *8th Annual Exhibition of the Southern States Art League*)
December

1929

Watercolors by Samuel E. Gideon
March 3–31

A Collection of Texas and New Mexico Paintings by Alexandre Hogue ★
March 3–31

5th Annual Exhibition of Work by Houston Artists ★
April 7–28

4th Annual Exhibition of Photography by Texas Photographers ★
May 5–June 2

Prize Winning Canvasses from the 1929 Wildflower Competition
June 1–30

[1st] Annual Circuit Exhibition of Work by Texas Artists
June 3–August

Etchings by Mary Bonner
July 7–August 31

Paintings by Ralph S. Rowntree
November 3–December 1

7th Annual Circuit Exhibition of the Southern States Art League
(Selected from the *9th Annual Exhibition of the Southern States Art League*)
December 8–29

1930

6th Annual Exhibition of Work by Houston Artists ★
April 6–27

5th Annual Exhibition of Photography by Texas Photographers ★
May 3–25

[2nd Annual Circuit] Exhibition of Work by Texas Artists ★
June 8–September 1

8th Annual Circuit Exhibition of the Southern States Art League
(Selected from the *10th Annual Exhibition of the Southern States Art League*)
December 7–28

1931

William McVey: Bronzes
February

Exhibition of Watercolors by Mary Aubrey Keating
February 1–22

Illustrations of Ben Carlton Mead: J. Frank Dobie's "Coronado's Children"
March 1–29

7th Annual Exhibition of Work by Houston Artists ★
April 5–26

6th Annual Exhibition of Photography by Texas Photographers
May 3–31

3rd Annual Circuit Exhibition of the Work of Texas Artists
July 5–26

Paintings by Samuel P. Ziegler ★
October 4–25

Wood Carvings by Peter Mansbendel
November 1–29

Oils and Drawings by Watson Neyland
December 6–27

Watercolors by Edward B. Arrants
December 6–27

9th Annual Circuit Exhibition of the Southern States Art League
(Selected from the *11th Annual Exhibition of the Southern States Art League*)
December 6–27

1932

8th Annual Exhibition of Work by Houston Artists ★
January 10–31

Junior League Arts and Crafts Exhibition
February 16–20

Oils, Watercolors, Drawings, Prints by Mato Gjuranovic/Sculpture by Caroline Burton
March 1–15

7th Annual Exhibition of Photography by Texas Photographers
May 1–29

4th Annual Circuit Exhibition of Work by Texas Artists
June

Oil Paintings by Julian Onderdonk
July 3–August 28

Exhibition of Oils and Watercolors by Dawson Dawson-Watson
November 6–27

Exhibition of Oils by Robert Joy
November 6–27

Watercolors and Drawings by Edward M. Schiwetz
November 6–27

10th Annual Circuit Exhibition of the Southern States Art League ★
(Selected from the *12th Annual Exhibition of the Southern States Art League*)
December 4–25

1933

9th Annual Exhibition of Work by Houston Artists ★
January 8–29

Exhibition of Work by Texas Alumni of the Fountainbleau School of Fine Arts
April 16–30

8th Annual Exhibition of Photography by Texas Photographers
May 7–28

Oils and Watercolors by Mato Gjuranovic
October 15–29

Paintings and Drawings by Clara Beard Northington
November 5–26

Watercolors and Drawings by Angela MacDonnell
November 5–26

Drawings by Coreen Mary Spellman
November 5–26

Oils by Vallie Fletcher and Arthur Thompson
December 1–10

11th Annual Circuit Exhibition of the Southern States Art League
(Selected from the *13th Annual Exhibition of the Southern States Art League*)
December 3–27

1934

10th Annual Exhibition of Work by Houston Artists ★
January 14–February 4

Etchings, Lithographs and Block Prints by Members of the Southern States Art League
Opened February 17

Photographs by Frederic Browne
Closed October 28

9th Annual Exhibition of Photography by Texas Photographers
October 10–28

Paintings by Beulah Schiller Ayars
November 4–25

12th Annual Circuit Exhibition of the Southern States Art League
(Selected from the *14th Annual Exhibition of the Southern States Art League*)
December 9–30

1935

11th Annual Exhibition of Work by Houston Artists ★
January 13–February 3

Watercolors by J. Ward Lockwood
March 31–April 28

10th Annual Exhibition of Photography by Texas Photographers
October 6–27

1936

12th Annual Exhibition of Work by Houston Artists ★
January 12–February 2

Memorial Exhibition of Watercolors by Boyer Gonzales
March 1–22

Oil Paintings by Grace Spaulding John
March 1–22

16th Annual Exhibition of the Southern States Art League ★
April 3–30

Texas Centennial Exhibition
June 14–August 31 (closing date unconfirmed)

11th Annual Exhibition of Photography by Texas Photographers
October 11–November 1

1937

13th Annual Exhibition of Work by Houston Artists ★
January 10–31

Oils by Three San Antonians: Paul Cook, Boyer Gonzales, Jr., and Caroline Durieux
March 7–28

12th Annual Exhibition of Photography by Texas Photographers ★
October 10–24

Work by Southeast Texas Artists
October 31–November 28

1938

14th Annual Exhibition of Work by Houston Artists ★
March 5–27

1st Annual Exhibition of the Houston Camera Club
April 3–24

2nd Annual Exhibition of Work by Artists of Southeast Texas ★
November 6–27

Lone Star Printmakers Exhibition
December 3–30

1939

Painting and Metal Plastics by Edmund Kinzinger ★
January 8–29

15th Annual Exhibition of Work by Houston Artists ★
April 12–30

2nd Annual Exhibition of the Houston Camera Club
June 4–25

17th Annual Circuit Exhibition of the Southern States Art League
(Selected from the *19th Annual Exhibition of the Southern States Art League*)
July 1–August 28

3rd Annual Exhibition of Work by Artists of Southeast Texas
November 5–26

1940

[1st] Texas General Exhibition ★
February 4–18

3rd Annual Exhibition of the Houston Camera Club
June 2–30

16th Annual Exhibition of Work by Houston Artists ★
November 3–24

Wood Carvings by Andrew Larsen
November 24–December 15

Lone Star Printmakers Exhibit
December 1–15

1941

One Man Show by Forrest Bess
February 1–16

Historic and Modern Examples of "Cattle in Art"
February 2–16

2nd Texas-Oklahoma General Exhibition ★
February 23–March 9

Oils of the Southwest and Mexico
April 13–May 4

4th Annual Exhibition of the Houston Camera Club
June 7–July 6

3rd Texas General Exhibition
November 1–16

19th Annual Circuit Exhibition of Southern States Art League
(Selected from the *21st Annual Exhibition of the Southern States Art League*)
November 22–December 7

Exhibition of Watercolors by Ward Lockwood
December 10, 1941–January 4, 1942

1942

17th Annual Exhibition of Work by Houston Artists ★
February 8–March 1

5th Annual Exhibition of the Work of Members of the Houston Camera Club
March 25–April 8

Woodcarvings by Carter Howard
October 4–25

4th Texas General Exhibition ★
November 8–22

1943

18th Annual Exhibition of Work by Houston Artists ★
February 14–28

6th Annual Exhibition of the Houston Camera Club
March 24–April 7

Purchase Prize Winners by Houston Artists
July 4–September 12

5th Texas General Exhibition ★
October 24–November 7

21st Annual Circuit Exhibition of the Southern States Art League
(Selected from the *23rd Annual Exhibition of the Southern States Art League*)
December 5–22

1944

19th Annual Exhibition of Work by Houston Artists ★
February 27–March 12

Mexican Canvases: Paintings by Hari Kidd
March 15–26

7th Annual Houston Camera Club Exhibition
March 19–April 2

Frederic Browne: Paintings of France
October 8–29

6th Texas General Exhibition ★
November 5–26

Lithographs by Caroline Durieux
November 22–December 13

1945

20th Annual Exhibition of Work by Houston Artists ★
February 25–March 11

8th Annual Houston Camera Club Exhibition
March 18–April 1

7th Texas General Exhibition ★
December 16, 1945–January 6, 1946

1946

21st Annual Exhibition of Work by Houston Artists ★
January 27–February 10

9th Annual Houston Camera Club Exhibition
February 17–March 3

8th Texas General Exhibition ★
November 10–December 1

1947

Exhibition of Sculpture by Charles Umlauf ★
January 12–February 2

22nd Annual Exhibition of Work by Houston Artists ★
February 9–March 2

Non-objective Painting by Nione Carlson
April 2–May 4

9th Texas General Exhibition ★
October 26–November 16

Paintings by Xavier Gonzales
December 7–28

1948

23rd Annual Exhibition of Work by Houston Artists ★
February 15–March 7

Watercolors by 16 Texas Artists
March 14–28

Robert O. Preusser ★
March 14–April 4

First Southwestern Print Exhibition ★
June 6–27

Photography by Paul Gittings
July 4–25

Paintings by Gene Charlton ★
October 10–24

10th Texas General Exhibition ★
November 21–December 12

1949

12th Annual Houston Camera Club Exhibition
February 27–March 13

Paintings by Frances Skinner
February 27–March 13

24th Annual Exhibition of Work by Houston Artists ★
March 20–April 3

An Exhibition of Seventeen Texas and Mexico Watercolor Landscapes by Amy Freeman Lee ★
October 16–30

11th Annual Texas Exhibition of Painting and Sculpture ★
(Formerly the *Texas General Exhibition*)
December 18, 1949–January 8, 1950

1950

Historic Houston: An Exhibit of Watercolors by Mary Ellen Shipnes
February 5–19

13th Annual Houston Camera Club Exhibition
February 12–26

25th Annual Exhibition of Work by Houston Artists ★
March 12–26

Exhibition of Drawings and Prints by Janet Turner
March 26–April 9

Work by Boleslaw Jan Czedekowski
October 20–November 19

12th Annual Texas Painting and Sculpture Exhibition ★
December 17, 1950–January 7, 1951

1951

Paintings by Forrest Bess
April 15–29

26th Annual Exhibition of Work by Houston Artists ★
April 22–May 6

14th Annual Houston Camera Club Exhibition
May 27–June 17

*13th Annual Exhibition of Texas Painting
and Sculpture* ★
October 28–November 11

*Designs for Murals, Petroleum Club by
Seymour Fogel* ★
November 18–December 2

Paintings by Frank Dolejska
November 25–December 9

Paintings and Drawings by David Adickes ★
December 16–30

1952

3rd Annual Texas Watercolor Society Exhibition ★
April 6–27

27th Annual Exhibition of Work by Houston Artists ★
April 13–27

Latin American Paintings by Mildred Dixon
October 19–November 2

Paintings and Drawings by Lowell Collins
November 9–23

*14th Annual Exhibition of Texas Painting
and Sculpture*★
December 14, 1952–January 4, 1953

1953

28th Annual Exhibition of Work by Houston Artists ★
February 1–22

4th Annual Texas Watercolor Society Exhibition ★
April 12–26

Houston Camera Club Exhibition
May 17–31

*15th Annual Exhibition of Texas Painting
and Sculpture* ★
November 8–29

*Two Approaches in Painting: Buck Schiwetz
and Robert Preusser*
November 9–December 1

1954

*Paintings and Drawings by John Biggers and
James Boynton* ★
January 13–February 14

Pastels by Howard Cook
February 17–March 14

29th Annual Exhibition of Work by Houston Artists ★
February 28–March 14

Jewelry by Electra Waggoner Biggs
March 1–31

Houston Camera Club Exhibition
May 23–June 6

*16th Annual Exhibition of Texas Painting
and Sculpture* ★
December 5–26

1955

*Two Texas Artists: Kelly Fearing and
Mildred Wood Dixon*★
February 6–27

30th Annual Exhibition of Work by Houston Artists ★
March 5–27

*17th Annual Exhibition of Texas Painting
and Sculpture* ★
September

31st Annual Exhibition of Work by Houston Artists ★
December 4–24

1956

*The D. D. Feldman Collection of Contemporary
Texas Art* ★
Held at the Texas National Bank Gallery, Houston
February 3–29

6th Southwestern Exhibition of Prints and Drawings
September 30–October 28

1957

*18th Annual Texas Painting and Sculpture
Exhibition* ★
January 9–30

32nd Annual Houston Artists Exhibition ★
Held at the Art League of Houston
November 20–December 11

1958

*19th Annual Texas Painting and Sculpture
Exhibition* ★
January 20–February 6

Texas Heroes ★
September 27–November 23

*Texas Oil '58: A Salute to the Oil Industry by Texas
Painters* ★
Held at the Bank of The Southwest, Houston
November 3–14

33rd Annual Houston Artists Exhibition ★
December 3–31

1959

*20th Annual Texas Painting and Sculpture
Exhibition* ★
April 5–19

Everett Spruce
April 5–19

*10th Anniversary Exhibition of the Texas
Watercolor Society* ★
May 1–15

34th Annual Houston Artists Exhibition ★
December 9, 1959–January 3, 1960

1960

*21st Annual Texas Painting and Sculpture
Exhibition* ★
May 18–June 19

35th Annual Houston Artists Exhibition ★
December 28, 1960–January 22, 1961

1961

*22nd Annual Texas Painting and Sculpture
Exhibition* ★
April 6–May 28

Houston Camera Club Exhibition
June 4–July 2

*23rd Annual Texas Painting and Sculpture
Exhibition* ★
Cosponsored by the MFAH, but did not travel
to Houston
October 7, 1961–May 15, 1962

1962

Drawings from West Africa: Dr. John Biggers ★
April 11–29

*24th Annual Texas Painting and Sculpture
Exhibition* ★
Cosponsored by the MFAH, but did not travel
to Houston
October 7, 1962–May 12, 1963

The Southwest: Painting and Sculpture ★
December 7, 1962–January 20, 1963

1963

University of Texas Art Faculty: Past and Present ★
April 16–May 15

25th Annual Texas Painting and Sculpture Exhibition ★
Cosponsored by the MFAH, but did not travel to Houston
October 5, 1963–June 28, 1964

Dorothy Hood: Paintings and Drawings ★
November 3–December 8

1964

Paintings and Drawings by William Anzalone
February 2–March 1

26th Annual Texas Painting and Sculpture Exhibition ★
Cosponsored by the MFAH, but did not travel to Houston
October 28, 1964–July 4, 1965

1965

Photography by Henri Cartier-Bresson and Ezra Stoller for "The Galveston That Was" ★
November 30, 1965–January 9, 1966

1966

Photographs by Ted A. Rozumalski ★
April 27–May 29

1968

John Biggers
September 21–November 24

1970

Drawings from Nine States ★
April 28–May 31

Jewelry by William Steffy and His Students
December 4, 1970–January 22, 1971

Dick Wray: Recent Paintings and Graphics
December 12–17

1971

Arthur Turner: Recent Works
March 4–28

Southern Exposure: The Architecture of Galveston
August 1–September 15

1972

Ary Stillman Retrospective ★
February 23–March 26

1974

Geoff Winningham: Photographs ★
March 23–June 30

Abstract Painting and Sculpture in Houston
May 25–July 7

1975

Dorothy Hood Drawings ★
February 27–March 30

Texas Public Buildings of the 19th Century
March 8–April 10

1978

George Krause Photographs
February 11–April 2

1979

Some Houston Photographers: A Guest Curator's Choice
The Glassell School of Art
February 23–April 12

A Survey of Texas Naive Artists
April 13–May 27

Houston Artists' Kites
The Glassell School of Art
June 4–July 19

1980

Suzanne Bloom and Ed Hill (MANUAL): Research and Collaboration ★
February 20–April 13

Fiber/Creative Forces: Fiber Designers All-Texas Show
The Glassell School of Art
March 11–28

Glassell Graduate Exhibition: Lu Ellis
The Glassell School of Art
June 9–28

Texas Artists: Clay
The Glassell School of Art
September 5–October 10

Houston CETA Artist-in-Residence Exhibition
The Glassell School of Art
September 5–October 10

Bernard Brunon: Notebooks
September 9–November 2

1982

Synergy '82
The Glassell School of Art
October 17–31

Core Fellows/Work in Progress
The Glassell School of Art
November 18–December 3

1983

Ezekiel Gibbs
March 4–May 15

1st Annual Core Fellows Exhibition
The Glassell School of Art
April 8–29

Synergy '83
The Glassell School of Art
October 9–20

Core Fellows/Work in Progress
The Glassell School of Art
November 30–December 30

1984

1984 Core Fellows Exhibition: I
The Glassell School of Art
March 22–April 7

1984 Core Fellows Exhibition: II
The Glassell School of Art
May 10–27

Synergy '84
The Glassell School of Art
October 22–November 4

Core Fellows/Work in Progress
The Glassell School of Art
November 8–30

1985

Fresh Paint: The Houston School ★
January 26–April 7

Works on Paper: Eleven Houston Artists ★
January 26–March 8

1985 Core Fellows Exhibition
The Glassell School of Art
March 28–April 26

Houston Drawing
The Glassell School of Art
September 30–October 23

Synergy '85
The Glassell School of Art
November 3–24

Core Fellows/Work in Progress
The Glassell School of Art
November 29–December 21

1986

George Bunker in Houston: 1974–1986 ★
The Glassell School of Art
February 6–27

1986 Core Fellows Exhibition
The Glassell School of Art
April 3–27

The Texas Landscape, 1900–1986 ★
May 17–September 7

*Collaborators: Artists Working Together in Houston,
1969–1986* ★
The Glassell School of Art
September 18–October 19

Synergy '86
The Glassell School of Art
October 26–November 20

1987

From the Object: Still-Life Themes and Variations ★
The Glassell School of Art
January 9–February 6

1987 Core Fellows Exhibition
The Glassell School of Art
March 18–April 5

*Hispanic Art in the United States: Thirty
Contemporary Painters and Sculptors* ★
May 3–August 2

Houston Hispanic Artists: New Views ★
The Glassell School of Art
May 28–June 28

Four Houston Artists
The Glassell School of Art
May 28–June 28

Synergy '87
The Glassell School of Art
October 19–November 15

1988

One + One: Collaborations by Artists and Writers ★
The Glassell School of Art
January 19–February 21

1988 Core Fellows Exhibition
The Glassell School of Art
March 1–May 5

*Twentieth-Century Art in the Museum Collection:
Direction and Diversity* ★
May 21–September 4

Julian Schnabel: Paintings, 1975–1987 ★
May 27–August 14

Synergy '88
The Glassell School of Art
November 1–23

1989

1989 Core Fellows Exhibition ★
The Glassell School of Art
March 16–April 30

*The New American Landscape:
Selections from the Museum's Collection* ★
The Glassell School of Art
August 19–October 15

Synergy '89
The Glassell School of Art
November 7–December 30

1990

Recent Acquisitions: Houston Photographers
February 3–April 29

*Tradition and Innovation: A Museum Celebration of
Texas Art*
February 17–April 29

1990 Core Fellows Exhibition ★
The Glassell School of Art
March 13–April 29

Direct References: Drawings by Texas Artists
The Glassell School of Art
October 16–November 26

1991

1991 Core Fellows Exhibition ★
The Glassell School of Art
March 14–April 25

The Big Show: A Lawndale Juried Exhibition
The Glassell School of Art
October 5–November 21

1992

Iconoclasm in Contemporary Texas Art
The Glassell School of Art
January 21–March 2

George Krause: Universal Issues ★
March 8–May 17

1992 Core Fellows Exhibition ★
The Glassell School of Art
March 17–April 23

Rescuers of the Holocaust: Portraits by Gay Block ★
August 9–November 1

*Fresh Visions/New Voices: Emerging African-American
Artists in Texas* ★
The Glassell School of Art
September 13–November 29

1993

Traditional Forms/Insidious Visions
The Glassell School of Art
January 19–March 1

1993 Core Fellows Exhibition ★
The Glassell School of Art
March 16–April 22

*Texas Focus: Recent Acquisitions from the Mundy
and Willour Collections*
September 5–November 21

Texas Contemporary: Acquisitions of the '90s
September 19–November 21

*Edward and Nancy Kienholz: The Merry-Go-World
or Begat by Chance and The Wonder Horse Trigger* ★
September 19–November 28

Artists' Progress: Seven Houston Artists, 1953–1993 ★
The Glassell School of Art
October 21–November 28

1994

Speaking of Artists: Words and Works from Houston
January 1–July 10

Essentials ★
The Glassell School of Art
January 28–April 25

1994 Core Fellows Exhibition ★
The Glassell School of Art
March 15–April 24

Call and Response: The Artist and the Museum
September 25, 1994–January 1, 1995

Paradoxical Scale
The Glassell School of Art
November 3–December 4

1995

Images from Space ★
The Glassell School of Art
January 21–March 5

Worlds Apart: Core 1995 Exhibition ★
The Glassell School of Art
March 17–April 23

The Art of John Biggers: View from the Upper Room ★
April 2–September 3

*Genesis in Fire: Works from the Green
Mountain Foundry* ★
The Glassell School of Art
December 15, 1995–February 18, 1996

Texas Myths and Realities
October 29–December 31

1996

Artists at Work
January 6–June 30

Texas Modern and Post-Modern
January 21–March 3

Photographs by Core Residents, Past and Present
The Glassell School of Art
February 29–March 17

Core 1996 Exhibition ★
The Glassell School of Art
March 29–April 28

*More Than a Constructive Hobby:
The Paintings of Frank Freed* ★
June 30–September 8

Reconfigured: Six Approaches to Figurative Painting
The Glassell School of Art
September 6–November 24

Schemata: Drawing by Sculptors ★
The Glassell School of Art
December 13, 1996–February 16, 1997

1997

Core 1997 Exhibition ★
The Glassell School of Art
March 7–April 13

Linda Ridgway: A Survey, The Poetics of Form ★
The Glassell School of Art
October 10–December 7

1998

*Classical Sensibilities: Images by Alain Gerard
Clement and George Dureau* ★
The Glassell School of Art
January 9–March 8

Robert Rauschenberg: A Retrospective ★
A joint presentation of The Menil Collection,
the Contemporary Arts Museum, and
the Museum of Fine Arts, Houston
February 13–May 17

Core 1998 Exhibition ★
The Glassell School of Art
March 20–April 26

Photographic Journeys: Three Houston Neighborhoods
May 17–August 2

*In Situ: Responses from Charles Mary Kubricht
and Ann Stautberg* ★
The Glassell School of Art
July 9–August 23

*Posttension: A Compelling Refinement by
Joe Mancuso* ★
The Glassell School of Art
September 11–October 25

1999

Core 1999 Exhibition ★
The Glassell School of Art
March 5–April 23

Intrinsic Radiance: The Paintings of Philip Renteria
August 7–September 12

Innate Contours: The Drawings of James Surls ★
The Glassell School of Art
September 9–November 28

2000

Vernon Fisher's File 00 ★
The Glassell School of Art
January 13–March 5

Core 2000 Exhibition ★
The Glassell School of Art
March 10–April 23

Selected Bibliography

Note: References for individual artists are listed with the artists' biographies.

Anderson, Adrian, and Ralph A. Wooster. *Texas and Texas Artists*. Austin: Steck-Vaughn, 1972.

Baldridge, Melissa, et al. *Visions of the West: Art and Artifacts from the Private Collections of J. P. Bryan, Torch Energy Advisors Incorporated, and Others*. Salt Lake City, Utah: Gibbs-Smith Publishers, 1999.

Beardsley, John, and Jane Livingston. *Hispanic Art in the United States: Thirty Contemporary Painters and Sculptors*. New York: Abbeville Press; Houston: The Museum of Fine Arts, Houston, 1987.

Beauchamp, Toni Ramona. "James Johnson Sweeney and the Museum of Fine Arts, Houston: 1961–1967." M.A. thesis, University of Texas at Austin, 1983.

Biggers, John, and Carroll Simms, with John Edward Weems. *Black Art in Houston: The Texas Southern University Experience*. College Station, Texas: Texas A&M University Press, 1978.

Billings, Theo M. "The Museum of Fine Arts, Houston: A Social History." M.A. thesis, The University of Houston, 1994.

Block, Diana. *Revelation*. Dallas: Dallas Visual Art Center, 1997.

Brauer, David E. *Art from Houston in Norway*. Stavanger, Norway: Stavanger Kunstforening, 1982.

______. *Artists' Progress: Seven Houston Artists, 1953–1993*. Houston: The Museum of Fine Arts, Houston, The Glassell School of Art, 1993.

Brettell, Richard R. *Now/Then/Again: Contemporary Art in Dallas, 1949–1989*. Dallas: Dallas Museum of Art, 1989.

Brettell, Richard R., Charles Dee Mitchell, and Gail Thomas. *The Vessel*. Dallas: D-Art Visual Art Center, 1990.

Brimmer, Henry. "Photography in Houston." *Photo Metro* 8, no. 76 (February 1990): 7–43.

Brunon, Bernard. *Buttered Side Up: David Aylsworth, Bill Davenport, Giles Lyon*. Houston: Lawndale Art and Performance Center, 1994.

Brutvan, Cheryl A., Marti Mayo, and Linda L. Cathcart. *In Our Time: Houston's Contemporary Arts Museum, 1948–1982*. Houston: Contemporary Arts Museum, 1982.

Butterfield, Jan. "Texas." *Arts Magazine* 45, no. 8 (summer 1971): 45.

Bywaters, Jerry. "The New Texas Painters." *Southwest Review* 21, no. 3 (April 1936): 330–42.

______. *Texas Panorama*. Dallas: Dallas Museum of Fine Arts, 1945. An earlier version of this text appeared as "Texas Panorama" in *Magazine of Art* 37, no. 8 (November 1944): 306–9.

______. *Seventy-Five Years of Art in Dallas*. Dallas: The Dallas Museum of Fine Arts, 1978.

Bywaters, Jerry, et al. *Texas Painting and Sculpture: The 20th Century*. Dallas: Southern Methodist University, Pollock Galleries, 1971.

Camfield, William A. *New Art from a New City: Houston*. Frankfurt: Frankfurter Kunstverein, 1983. Revised as *Works on Paper: Eleven Houston Artists*. Houston: The Museum of Fine Arts, Houston, 1985.

Carlozzi, Annette DiMeo. *Third Coast Review: A Look at Art in Texas*. Aspen, Colorado: Aspen Art Museum, 1987.

Carlozzi, Annette DiMeo, and Gay Block. *50 Texas Artists: A Critical Selection of Painters and Sculptors Working in Texas*. San Francisco: Chronicle Books, 1986.

Cathcart, Linda L., and Marti Mayo. *Four Painters: Jones, Smith, Stack, Utterback*. Houston: Contemporary Arts Museum, 1981.

Cathcart, Linda L., Marti Mayo, William A. Fagaly, and Monroe K. Spears. *Southern Fictions*. Houston: Contemporary Arts Museum, 1983.

Chávez, Patricio, and Madeleine Grynsztejn. *La Frontera/The Border: Art about the Mexico/United States Border Experience*. San Diego: Centro Cultural de la Raza and Museum of Contemporary Art, 1993.

Colpitt, Frances. "Report from Texas: Going Against the Grain." *Art in America* 83, no. 4 (April 1995): 43–47.

______. *The Home Show*. San Antonio: The University of Texas at San Antonio, 1995.

______. *Texas Abstract: New Painting in the Nineties*. San Antonio: ArtPace Foundation for Contemporary Art, 1995.

Davidow, Joan. *Odd Realities: Realistic Paintings and Sculpture by Ten Texas Artists*. Arlington, Texas: Arlington Museum of Art, 1997.

Davidow, Joan, and Michael Odom. *Boys Toys*. Arlington, Texas: Arlington Museum of Art, 1998.

Donovan, Kevin, et al. *Capirotada: Eight El Paso Artists*. El Paso, Texas: El Paso Museum of Art, 1991.

Doroshenko, Peter. *Texas/Between Two Worlds*. Houston: Contemporary Arts Museum, 1993.

Edwards, Jim, et al. *The Perfect World in Contemporary Texas Art*. San Antonio: San Antonio Museum of Art, 1991.

Ennis, Michael. "We Are the World." *Texas Monthly* 23, no. 12 (December 1995): 54–61.

______. "The Mod Squad." *Texas Monthly* 24, no. 3 (March 1996): 74–79.

______. *Texas: Art of the State*. New York: Harry N. Abrams, 1999.

Fisher, James L. *Forty Texas Printmakers*. Fort Worth: Modern Art Museum of Fort Worth, 1990.

Fisk, Frances Battaile. *A History of Texas Artists and Sculptors*. Abilene, Texas: Fisk Publishing Company, 1928.

Forrester-O'Brien, Esse. *Art and Artists of Texas*. Dallas: Tardy Publishing Company, 1935.

Friis-Hansen, Dana. *Simply Beautiful*. Houston: Contemporary Arts Museum, 1997.

Friis-Hansen, Dana, Robert Atkins, and Greg Tate. *Other Narratives*. Houston: Contemporary Arts Museum, 1999.

Friis-Hansen, Dana, David Pagel, and Raphael Rubinstein. *Abstract Painting, Once Removed*. Houston: Contemporary Arts Museum, 1998.

Gambrell, Jamey. "Texas: State of the Art." *Art in America* 75, no. 3 (March 1987): 114–31, 151.

______. "In the Third Coast Art Capital." *Art in America* 75, no. 4 (April 1987): 180–203.

Goetzmann, William H., and Becky Duval Reese. *Texas Images and Visions.* Austin: University of Texas at Austin, Archer M. Huntington Art Gallery, 1983.

González, Patricia. *Houston Hispanic Artists: New Views.* Houston: The Museum of Fine Arts, Houston, The Glassell School of Art, 1987.

Graham, Don. *Cowboys and Cadillacs: How Hollywood Looks at Texas.* Austin: Texas Monthly Press, 1983.

Grauer, Michael. *Women Artists of Texas: 1850–1950.* Canyon, Texas: Panhandle-Plains Historical Museum, 1993.

Grauer, Paula L., and Michael R. Grauer. *Dictionary of Texas Artists, 1800–1945.* College Station, Texas: Texas A&M University Press, 1999.

Greene, Alison de Lima. "Twentieth-Century Art in the Museum Collection: Direction and Diversity." *The Museum of Fine Arts, Houston, Bulletin* 11, no. 3 (summer 1988).

———. *Genesis in Fire: Works from the Green Mountain Foundry.* Houston: The Museum of Fine Arts, Houston, The Glassell School of Art, 1995.

Greene, Alison de Lima, Diane Planer Lovejoy, and William R. Thompson. "The Lillie and Hugh Roy Cullen Sculpture Garden of the Museum of Fine Arts, Houston." *The Museum of Fine Arts, Houston, Bulletin* 17 (April 1996).

Greene, Alison de Lima, and Clint Willour. *Stairway to Heaven.* Galveston: Galveston Arts Center, 1993.

Grynsztejn, Madeleine. *La Frontera/The Border: Art about the Mexico/United States Border Experience.* San Diego: Centro Cultural de la Raza and Museum of Contemporary Art, 1993.

Haks, Frans, and Alison de Lima Greene. *Hedendaagse Kunst uit Texas/Contemporary Art from Texas.* Groningen, the Netherlands: Groninger Museum, 1988.

Harrigan, Stephen. *Contemporary Texas: A Photographic Portrait.* Austin: Texas Monthly Press, 1986.

Harris, Paul Rogers. *Breaking into the Mainstream: Texas African-American Artists.* Irving, Texas: Irving Arts Center, 1996.

Havel, Joseph, and Rick Lowe. *Fresh Visions/New Voices: Emerging African-American Artists in Texas.* Houston: The Museum of Fine Arts, Houston, The Glassell School of Art, 1992.

Hendricks, Patricia D., and Becky Duval Reese. *A Century of Sculpture in Texas: 1889–1989.* Austin: University of Texas Press and Archer M. Huntington Art Gallery, 1989.

Hickey, Dave. "The Texas to New York via Nashville Semi-Transcontinental Epiphany Tactic." *Art in America* 60, no. 5 (September–October 1972): 54–58.

———. *Air Guitar: Essays on Art and Democracy.* Los Angeles: Art Issues Press, 1997.

Huerta, Benito. *Chulas Fronteras: An Exhibition of Contemporary Texas Hispanic Art.* Houston: Midtown Art Center, 1986.

———. *Establishment and Revelation.* Dallas: Dallas Visual Art Center, 1997.

Irvine, Alexandra L. *Field of Vision: Five Gulf Coast Photographers.* Houston: Contemporary Arts Museum, 1998.

Janosco, Jerry, Judy Pollock, and Barbara Simcoe. *1993 Texas Biennial Exhibition: Eight Texas Artists.* Dallas: DARE (Dallas Artists Research and Exhibition), 1993.

Johnson, Patricia Covo. *Contemporary Art in Texas.* Roseville East, New South Wales, Australia: Craftsman House, 1995.

Kalil, Susie. "Houston Artists Would Rather Fight Than Switch." *Artnews* 80, no. 10 (December 1981): 103–7.

———. "Texas Ranges: Houston." *Artnews* 81, no. 10 (December 1982): 82–85.

———. *The Texas Landscape: 1900–1986.* Houston: The Museum of Fine Arts, Houston, 1986.

Kurtz, Bruce D. *Contemporary Identities: 1993 Phoenix Triennial.* Phoenix: Phoenix Art Museum, 1993.

Kutner, Janet. "The Houston-Dallas Axis." *Art in America* 60, no. 5 (September–October 1972): 59–61.

———. "Texas Ranges: Dallas." *Artnews* 81, no. 10 (December 1982): 86–89.

Landay, Janet. *Collaborators: Artists Working Together in Houston, 1969–1986.* Houston: The Museum of Fine Arts, Houston, The Glassell School of Art, 1986.

Landay, Janet, and Donald Barthelme. *One + One: Collaborations by Artists and Writers.* Houston: The Museum of Fine Arts, Houston, The Glassell School of Art, 1988.

Lemaire, Gérard-Georges. *Cinq x cinq: Houston, Texas.* Paris: Galerie Dario Boccara, 1986.

MacAgy, Douglas. *one i at a time.* Dallas: Southern Methodist University, Pollock Galleries, 1971.

Mayo, Marti, Bruce C. Webb, and Richard Howard. *Finders/Keepers.* Houston: Contemporary Arts Museum, 1997.

McBride, Elizabeth, and Lorenzo Thomas. *DiverseWorks Artspace.* Houston: DiverseWorks Artspace, Inc., 1993.

McClintic, Miranda. *Directions, 1981.* Washington, D.C.: Hirshhorn Museum and Sculpture Garden, Smithsonian Institution, 1981.

McEvilley, Thomas. "Double Vision in Space City." *Artforum* 23, no. 8 (April 1985): 52–56.

McEvilley, Thomas, Surpik Angelini, and Bert Long. *Another Reality.* Houston: Hooks-Epstein Galleries, Inc., 1989.

de Menil, Dominique. *Jermayne MacAgy: A Life Illustrated by an Exhibition.* Houston: University of St. Thomas, 1968.

Mesa-Bains, Amalia. *Ceremony of Memory: New Expressions in Spirituality among Contemporary Hispanic Artists.* Santa Fe, New Mexico: Center for Contemporary Arts of Santa Fe, 1988.

Moody, Tom. *Analogs of Modernism,* Dallas: McKinney Avenue Contemporary, 1995.

Moser, Charlotte. "But on the Other Hand." *Houston City Magazine* 4, no. 2 (February 1980): 54–57.

———. "Playing Cowboys and Artists in Houston." *Artnews* 79, no. 10 (December 1980): 124–28.

———. "Regional Revisions: Houston and Chicago." *Art in America* 73, no. 7 (July 1985): 90–99.

The Museum of Fine Arts, Houston. "The Museum of Fine Arts, Houston: An Architectural History 1924–1986." *The Museum of Fine Arts, Houston, Bulletin* 15, nos. 1–2 (April 1992).

Nathan, Debbie. "Forget the Alamo." *Texas Monthly* 25, no. 4 (April 1998): 105, 126–28.

Nelson, Lauri G. "'This Kind of Circus, All in Cordiality': Marcel Duchamp's Speech 'The Creative Act.'" M.A. thesis, Rice University, 1994.

Olsen, Valerie Loupe. *Schemata: Drawings by Sculptors*. Houston: The Museum of Fine Arts, Houston, The Glassell School of Art, 1997.

Parazette, Aaron. *Process, Strategy, Irony*. Houston: DiverseWorks Artspace, Inc., 1994.

Printz, Neil, Alison de Lima Greene, and Marilyn A. Zeitlin. *Texas Art*. Houston: The Menil Collection, 1988.

Ranta, Rachel, and Elizabeth Ward. *Lawndale Live! A Retrospective, 1979–1990*. Houston: Lawndale Art and Performance Center, 1993.

Reese, Becky Duval. *Made in Texas*. Austin: University of Texas at Austin, Archer M. Huntington Art Gallery, 1979.

Robinson, William A., and Toni Beauchamp. *1980 Houston Area Exhibition and Recapitulation 1928–1960, with The Visual Arts in Houston: A Selected Overview*. Houston: University of Houston, Sarah Campbell Blaffer Gallery, 1980.

Rogers, John William. "Southwestern Culture Must Not Be a Cult." *Southwest Review* 14 (July 1929): 485–88.

Rose, Barbara, and Susie Kalil. *Fresh Paint: The Houston School*. Austin: Texas Monthly Press; Houston: The Museum of Fine Arts, Houston, 1985.

Rozelle, Robert V., Alvia J. Wardlaw, and Maureen A. McKenna. *Black Art—Ancestral Legacy: The African Impulse in African American Art*. Dallas: Dallas Museum of Art; New York: Harry N. Abrams, Inc., 1989.

Schjeldahl, Peter. "Art and Money in the City of Future-Think." *Houston City Magazine* 4, no. 2 (February 1980): 46–54, 97–101.

Schneider, Beth B., with Daniel J. Gorski, Joseph P. Havel, and Norma R. Ory. "The Museum of Fine Arts, Houston: Education in the Arts." *The Museum of Fine Arts, Houston, Bulletin* 16, nos. 1–2 (February 1995).

Smagula, Howard. *Texas Currents*. San Antonio: San Antonio Art Institute, 1985.

Smith, Henry Nash. "A Note on the Southwest." *Southwest Review* 8 (January 1928): 257–78.

Smith, Roberta. "Twelve Days of Texas." *Art in America* 64, no. 4 (July–August 1976): 42–48.

Smith, Stephanie. "A Chronology of Public Art in Houston in the 20th Century." *ArtLies* 5 (February–March 1995): 6–9.

Steen, William. *Avenues of Departure: Twelve Houston Artists*. New Orleans: Contemporary Arts Center, 1993.

Steinfeldt, Cecilia. *Art for History's Sake: The Texas Collection of the Witte Museum*. San Antonio: Texas State Historical Association for the Witte Museum of the San Antonio Museum Association, 1993.

Stewart, Rick. *Lone Star Regionalism: The Dallas Nine and Their Circle, 1928–1945*. Austin: University of Texas Press; Dallas: Dallas Museum of Art, 1985.

Sweeney, James Johnson. *The Southwest: Painting and Sculpture*, Houston: The Museum of Fine Arts, Houston, 1962.

Trenton, Patricia, et al. *Independent Spirits: Women Painters of the American West 1890–1945*. Berkeley and Los Angeles: Autry Museum of Western Heritage in association with University of California Press, 1995.

Trotty, Sarah A. *Forerunners and Newcomers Revisited: Houston's African-American Artists in the Lead*. Beaumont, Texas: Lamar University, Dishman Gallery, 1991.

Tucker, Anne Wilkes. "Lone Star Statement: A Vision Bound by Diversity." *American Photographer* (May 1987): 66–75.

Tucker, Marcia, et al. *Paradise Lost/Paradise Regained: American Visions of the New Decade*. Venice: La 41a Biennale di Venezia, United States Pavilion, 1984.

Turnbull, Betty. *A Glimpse of Houston: Works on Paper by Nine Texas Artists*. Newport Beach, California: Newport Harbor Art Museum, 1978.

Utterback, Martha. "Texas." *Artforum* 9, no. 1 (September 1970): 88–89.

Van der Marck, Jan. "Houston's 'Clean Machine': Contemporary Arts Museum." *Art in America* 60, no. 5 (September–October 1972): 50–51.

Vander Lee, Jana, and John Perreault. *A Sense of Spirit*. Houston: University of Houston, Lawndale Annex, 1982.

Ward, Elizabeth. *Reinventing Reality: Five Texas Photographers*. Houston: University of Houston, Sarah Campbell Blaffer Gallery, 1990.

______. *Darkness + Light: Twentieth-Century Works from Texas Collections*. Houston: University of Houston, Sarah Campbell Blaffer Gallery, 1993.

______. *Nature/Culture*. Houston: Inman Gallery, 1994.

Warren, David B., Michael K. Brown, Elizabeth Ann Coleman, and Emily Ballew Neff. *American Decorative Arts and Paintings in the Bayou Bend Collection*. Houston: The Museum of Fine Arts, Houston; Princeton: Princeton University Press, 1998.

Willour, Clint. *Ship Shapes*. Galveston: Galveston Arts Center, 1991.

______. *Observations/Notations*. Galveston: Galveston Arts Center, 1993.

______. *In Body and Spirit*. Galveston: Galveston Arts Center, 1994.

Zeitlin, Marilyn A. *Establishment Exposed*. Dallas: Dallas Visual Art Center, 1996.

Zeitlin, Marilyn A., Marge Goldwater, and David Ross. *The First Texas Triennial Exhibition: 1988*. Houston: Contemporary Arts Museum, 1988.

Zigrosser, Carl. "Prints in Texas." *Southwest Review* 26 (autumn 1940–summer 1941): 50–64.

Index

*Page numbers in boldface italic
type refer to illustrations*

■ A

ABC No Rio, 223
Academía San Carlos, 252
Académie Julian, 37, 173, 249
Accent Photographic Gallery,
225
Action/Influence Gallery, 234
Adcock, Craig, 177
Adickes, David, 264
Adler, Sebastian J., 22–23, 131
Aesop, 88
African American Art Advisory
Association (the Museum of
Fine Arts, Houston), 29, 110
African American Museum, 111,
244, 246
Afterimage Gallery, 48, 227
Agee, William C., 24, 137
Albee, Edward, 229, 242, 258
Albers, Josef, 173, 243
Albright-Knox Art Gallery, 228,
238, 244, 258
Albritton, Claude, 72
Albuquerque Museum, 237, 245
Alechinsky, Pierre, 131, 141
Alexander, Joan, 202
Alexander, John, 23, 51–52, **52,**
54–55, 62, 89, 103, 133, 222,
239, 243
Alighieri, Dante, 197, 217n. 14,
218n. 81
Allen, Jo Harvey, 222
Allen, Mark, 232
Allen, Terry, 23, 30, 174, 176–79,
177, 216n. 7, 222, 230
Allen Center, 27
Alley Theatre, 44, 137, 229, 241,
257
Alternative Museum, 230, 244,
247, 251
Altman, Helen, *170–71,* 198,
203–4, *205,* 222
Alvarado, Pablo, 84, 181
Amado, Jesse, 173, 191–94, *193,*
222–23
Amarillo Art Center, 225–26,
230–31, 241, 244–46
Amarillo College, 235
Amarillo Museum of Art, 246,
248
American Academy (Rome), 92
American Academy of Arts and
Letters, 235, 241
American Center, Paris, 251
American College of
Switzerland, 238
American Federation of Arts
(AFA), 129, 251
American Institute, 244
American Music Theatre
Festival, 222

American Photography Institute,
246
Amherst College, 233, 243
Amon Carter Museum, 229
Anderson Ranch Arts Center,
228, 253, 258
Angelini, Surpik, 81
Angstrom Gallery, 230, 242
Ankeny, John S., 251
Ann Arbor Film Festival, 258
Anspon, Catherine, 167
Ant Farm, 209n. 42
Antonioni, Michelangelo, 243
Anzalone, William, 265
Aragon, Louis, 257
Archives of American Art (Smith-
sonian Institution), 227
Archives of American Art Texas
Project (Smithsonian Insti-
tution), 144, 236
Arcidiacono, Patsy, 93
Arena Productions, 235
Arizona State University, 236
Arlington Museum of Art, 234,
245–46, 256
Arpa, Jose, 260
Arrants, Edward B., 261
Art Academy of Cincinnati, 90,
253
Art Center (Waco), 227, 239,
247, 250, 255, 257
Art Center College of Design
(Calif.), 68, 230
Art Center School (Dallas), 233,
248
Art Guys, The (Michael
Galbreth and Jack Massing),
30, 198, 201–2, *201,* 223
Art Institute of Chicago, 75, 82,
90, 227, 229, 237–38, 240,
249–50, 252–53
Art Institute of San Francisco,
226
Art League of Houston, 15, 30,
37, 130, 206n. 6, 206n. 7,
206n. 26, 207n. 35, 227, 231,
237–38, 240–41, 243, 248,
250, 251, 257–58, 260, 264
Art Matters Inc. Foundation,
226
Art Museum of South Texas,
227, 232, 236, 239–40, 244,
247, 254
Art Museum of Southeast Texas,
222, 231, 233, 239, 243,
246–47, 251, 258
Art of This Century, 231–32, 245
Art Park, 250
Art Students League, 36, 82,
173, 179, 227, 233, 235,
237–38, 240, 247, 249,
251–52
Artaud, Antonin, 81, 84, 96, 100,
211n. 17

Artist's Loft, 246
Artists Space, 236
ArtPace Foundation for
Contemporary Art, 194, 223,
231, 233, 235, 240, 242,
244–45, 248, 253, 255–56
ArtScan Gallery, 240, 258
Artspace III, 225
Aspen Art Museum, 231, 236,
245
Assistance League of Houston,
59, 227, 229, 231, 242,
249–50
Associated American Artists, 40
Associated Artists of Houston, 19
AT&T Foundation, 208n. 61
AT&T New Art/New Visions,
113, 184
Atelier 17 (Paris), 71, 108, 256
Athens International Film
Festival, 258
Auckland City Art Gallery, 222
Austin College, 160, 231, 234,
245, 256
Austin Museum of Art, 223, 228
Ayars, Beulah Schiller, 262
Aylsworth, David, 157–59, *158,*
223, 229, 242

■ B

Bacigalupi, Don, 30
Baker, Diane S., 155
Baker, Josephine, 184, 218n. 50
Baker, Paul, 44, 93, 232, 241
Baldessari, John, 214n. 34
Baldwin, Fred, 27, 48–49, *49,*
223–24
Ballard, Carol C., 100, 164
Bank of the Southwest, 83, 264
Barnes-Blackman Galleries, 184,
240, 244, 246
Barnstone, Howard, 22
Barnwell, Andrea D., 184
Barrett, Nona and Richard, 101,
163, 195, 208n. 66, 219n. 112
Barrett Collection, Dallas, 107,
204, 208n. 66
Bartelik, Marek, 158
Barthelme, Donald, 95, 131
Batchen, Geoffrey, 200
Bates, David, 89–90, *91,* 224
Bateson, Gregory, 130
Bath House Cultural Center,
244
Baudrillard, Jean, 172
Bauhaus, 124, 214n. 13, 248.
See also New Bauhaus
Baylor Theater, 232
Baylor University, 44, 93, 232,
241
Bayou Bend Collection
(the Museum of Fine Arts,
Houston), 16, 35–36
Bearden, Romare, 184

Beardsley, John, 26, 52, 181
Beaumont, Betty, 210n. 98
Beaumont Art Museum, 243
Beck, Audrey Jones, 30
Beck Collection, John A. and
Audrey Jones (the Museum of
Fine Arts, Houston), 24
Bee College, 247
Beitzel Gallery, David, 233
Bell, Randal E., 163
Bellaire High School, 231
Bellini, Giovanni, 92
Bellows, George, 119
Benjamin, Walter, 175, 243
Bennington College, 242
Benteler-Morgan Galleries, 236
Benton, Thomas Hart, 39–40,
119, 209n. 25
Benton Gallery, 234
Berliner Künstlerprogramm
/DADD, 239
Berlinische Galerie, 239
Berman, Wallace, 238
Berry, Beverly and John, 193
Bertoia, Harry, 214n. 33
Bess, Forrest, 18, 28, 42–44, *42,*
62, 81, 93, 118, 130, 144, 224,
263
Bessell, Evelyn Byers, 18, 206n.
11, 206n. 14
Beuys, Joseph, 150, 192
Bickler, Jacob, 242
Biddle, George, 118
Bien, Charles, 260
Bierstadt, Albert, 35
Biggers, John, *19,* 22, 29, *40–41,*
41–42, 51, 86, *110,* 111,
224–25, 247, 264–65, 267
Biggs, Electra Waggoner, 264
Billy the Kid, 183
Binder Gallery, Eugene, 224,
240
Birkerts & Associates, Gunnar,
23, 207n. 40
Black Mountain College, 173,
249
Blackshear, Kathleen, 122
Blaffer, Robert Lee, 15, 20
Blaffer, Mrs. Robert Lee, 207n.
36
Blaffer Gallery, Sarah Campbell
(University of Houston), 23,
26, 30, 113, 222–23, 225, 228,
230, 236–40, 242–44,
246–49, 251, 254, 256, 259
Blagg, Dennis, 66–67, *66,* 225
Blake, Peter, 225
Blakemore, Amy, 71, 150–52,
152, 225
Blanton, Mr. and Mrs. Jack S.,
Jr., 68, 197
Blaut, Julia, 173
Blinderman, Barry, 234, 248

Block, Gay, 29, 49–51, **50,** 207n.
45, 225, 266
Bloom, Suzanne. *See* MANUAL
Blue, James, 207n. 57
Blue Collar Gallery, 227
Blue Star Art Space, 222–23,
230–32, 234, 243, 247, 251,
255
Blumenschein, Ernest, 39, 119,
235
Böcklin, Arnold, 88
Bonner, Mary, 261
Boshier, Derek, 28, 58–61, *59,*
89, 225–26
Bourgeois, Louise, 29, 140
Boymans-van Beuningen
Museum, 257
Boynton, Jack (James), 22, 43–44,
44, 62, 130–31, 226, 264
Bozzi, Julie, 65–66, *65,* 226
BP America, 76, 158
Brancusi, Constantin, 118, 167
Brand Library, 245
Brandt Gallery, Damon, 254
Braque, Georges, 45
Brauer, David E., 29, 131
Brazos Bookstore, 249
Brazosport Fine Arts Center,
239
Brenson, Michael, 148
Breton, André, 81, 249
Bridgeman, George, 238
Brisbine, Margaret, 206n. 11, 261
Broadnax, Geary, 49–50, **50,** 226
Brodovitch, Alexey, 257
Broker, Karin, 108–9, *108,*
226–27
Broodthaers, Marcel, 197
Brooklyn College, 239
Brooklyn Museum of Art, 254
Brooks, James, 22, 130
Broussard, Paul, 218n. 65
Brown, Michael K., 208n. 15
Brown, Peter, 63–65, *63,* 227
Brown, Roger, 57
Brown, Rosellen, 63
Brown Foundation, 134
Browne, Frederic, 261–63
Bruce, Patrick Henry, 137
Brudniak, Steve, 109–10, *109,* 227
Brunon, Bernard, 158, 265
Bucknell University, 228, 248
Bühler, Wolf-Eckart, 177
Bullard, Robert D., 50, 236
Bunker, George, 23, 92, 266
Bunker Living Trust, George,
141, 151, 176, 189
Burchfield, Charles, 244
Burton, Caroline, 262
Butler Gallery, Hiram, 222–23,
229, 232–34, 236, 238–39,
248, 251, 253–55, 257. *See
also* Devin Borden Hiram
Butler Gallery

Bywaters, Jerry, 19, 34, 39–40, **39**, 42, 124, 214n. 15, 227
Bywaters Research Collection on American Art, Jerry (Southern Methodist University), 227

■ **C**

Caddell, Michael A., 189, 201
Cadillac Ranch, 209n. 42
Café Galleria, 238
Cage, John, 173, 249
Calame, Ingrid, 157
Calder, Alexander, 21–22, 118, 123, 130
California Institute of the Arts (Los Angeles), 225–26
California School of Fine Arts (San Francisco), 240
California State University at Fresno, 222
Calk, Olin, 29
Camblin, Bob, 252
Cambridge University, 230
Camerawork, 243
Camfield, Virginia, 71, 128
Camfield, William A., 26, 71, 128, 207n. 51, 253–55, 258
Camp, William R., 66
Campbell, Randolph B., 35
Candystore Gallery, 226
Capp Street Project, 223
Carlos, Edward, 144
Carlozzi, Annette DiMeo, 89
Carlson, Nione, 263
Carmean, E. A., Jr., 24
Carr Gallery, 225
Carrington, Leanora, 235
Carson, Kit, 35, 244
Carter, Mrs. I. F., 206n. 5
Carter, Keith, 62–63, **63**, 207n. 45, 227–28, 243
Cartier-Bresson, Henri, 22, **23**, 130, 265
Casas, Mel, 244
Castelli Gallery, Leo, 222, 237, 249–50
Cathcart, Linda L., 26, 29, 88
Cavendish College, Lucy, 246
Cazabon, Lynn, 187, 190, **191**, 228
Cedar Valley College, 250
Celmins, Vija, 57
Center for Book Arts, 245
Center for Research in Contemporary Art, 233, 236, 242, 248, 256
Centre Georges Pompidou, 239
Centro Cultural Arte Contemporáneo (Mexico City), 232, 236, 254
CEPA Gallery, 228
Cepenkov Center of Culture, Marko, 246
Cervantes, Miguel, 114
Cézanne, Paul, 240
Chamberlain, John, 237
Chapman, Cynthia, 189, 201
Charles, Michael Ray, 30, 183–86, **186**, 208n. 61, 228
Charlot, Jean, 254
Charlton, Gene, 263
Chasanoff Photographic Collection, Allan, 125, 146

Chase, William Merritt, 15, 36, 208n. 16, 247
Chefchis, Kay and James, 108
Cherry, Emma Richardson, 15, 17, 122, 206n. 11, 260
Childs, Lucinda, 137, 257
Chillida, Eduardo, 21, 118
Chillman, James, Jr., 15–19, 21, 123, 129, 206n. 4, 260
Chilton, Barbara, 93
Chin, Mel, 27, **60**, 61–62, 81, 210n. 98, 228, 232
Chinati Foundation, 134, 137, 214n. 45, 230–31, 237
Chouinard Art Institute, 177, 222
Christ Church Cathedral (Houston), 231, 236
Cinema Guild Film Theater, 258
City College of New York, 257
Civil Rights Institute, 230
Claremont Graduate Program, 164, 189, 231, 248
Clean Well-Lighted Place, A, 46
Clearman, Jennifer and Scott, 68
Cleary Gallery, John, 239
Clement, Alain Gerard, 267
Cleveland Institute of Art, 254
Cochran, Anthony and Andrew, 202
Cocteau, Jean, 142
Codax, John, 239
Collective Gallery, 245
College of the Mainland, 225, 230, 237, 256
Collins, Lowell, 264
Colorado College, 152, 256
Colorado State University, 242
Colpitt, Frances, 94–95, 152, 157, 204, 208n. 5, 233, 245, 253
Columbia University, 223, 229, 237, 250, 252, 257
Colyer, Vincent, 35–36, **36**, 63, 228–29
Commerce Street Warehouse, 231
Community Artists' Collective, 184, 240
Concordia Lutheran College, 227
Congregation Beth Israel (Houston), 51, 225
Contemporary Art Center of Fort Worth, 234
Contemporary Arts Association (CAA) (Houston), 19–23, 42, 44, 81, 83, 118, 124, 129–31, 207n. 35, 209n. 33, 214n. 39, 229, 241, 248, 258. *See also* Contemporary Arts Museum
Contemporary Arts Center (Cincinnati), 228
Contemporary Arts Center (New Orleans), 242, 249
Contemporary Arts Museum (CAM) (Houston), 19, 23, 26, 29–30, 42, 51–52, 54–55, 61, 70, 87, 130, 137, 141, 151, 167, 173, 177, 180, 190, 194, 201, 210n. 95, 214n. 39, 216n. 7, 222–26, 229–59, 267. *See also* Contemporary Arts Association
Cook, Howard, 264

Cook, Paul, 262
Cooper Gallery, Paula, 237, 257
Corcoran Gallery of Art, 160, 222, 224, 226, 230, 232, 241, 245, 251, 254, 257
Core Residency Program (the Glassell School of Art), 27, 65, 74, 76, 143, 151, 153, 156–57, 164, 166–67, 187, 189–90, 223, 225, 228–29, 231, 233–34, 240, 242, 245–46, 248, 250, 253, 258, 265–67
Cornell University, 231, 250
Corpron, Carlotta M., 28, 119, 123–25, **125**, 142, 229, 255
Corzas, Francisco, 237
Cosimo, Piero di, 92
Covo de Iongh Gallery, 258
Cowie, Jeffrey, 187–89, **189**, 229
Cowles Gallery, Charles, 224
Cragg, Tony, 29
Cranbrook Academy of Art, 54, 190, 228, 253
Crane, Bruce, 227
Cravens, Patsy, 47
Crawford, Ralston, 160
Crimp, Douglas, 172, 216n. 2
Crispin, Andre and Sylvia, 72
Cristinerose Gallery, 230
Cronin Gallery, 48, 49, 225, 232, 251
Cronin Memorial Collection, Anthony G., 49
Crossley, Mimi, 52
Crowley, Marks & Douglas, 84, 104, 109, 161, 181, 183, 190
Crowley, Tim, 157
Cuevas, José Luis, 83, 237
Cullen Center, 27, 229–30, 249–50
Cullen Sculpture Garden, Lillie and Hugh Roy (the Museum of Fine Arts, Houston), 28, 140, 144, 161, 241
Cullinan, Joseph S., 15
Cullinan, Nina, 20, 129, 207n. 30
Cultural Arts Council of Houston/Harris County, 225, 231–32, 236, 246
Culwell, Ben, 28, 119, 123, 127–28, **128**, 207n. 54, 229
cummings, e. e., 215n. 90
Cunningham, Merce, 173, 249
Current Literature Club of Houston, 15
Curry, John Steuart, 40
Cushman, Mr. and Mrs. Louis B., 155
Cvetkovich, Ann, 187
GVG Gallery, 244
Czedekowski, Boleslaw Jan, 263

■ **D**

Daguerre, Louis J. M., 35, 244
Dahl, George, 234
Dallas Art Association Museum, 251
Dallas Art Institute, 39–40, 119, 127, 227, 229, 251
Dallas Artists League, 39, 235, 251
Dallas Artists Research and Exhibition (DARE), 223

Dallas Film and Video Festival, 259
Dallas Little Theater, 232
Dallas Museum for Contemporary Arts, 42, 118, 212n. 37, 226, 241. *See also* Dallas Museum of Art
Dallas Museum of Art, 17, 40, 110, 137, 216n. 10, 223, 225, 227, 229, 233–35, 239, 241, 244, 246, 248, 250–53, 255–57
Dallas Museum of Fine Arts, 19, 39–40, 42, 83, 124, 213n. 11, 214n. 29. *See also* Dallas Museum of Art
Dallas Public Art Gallery, 39
Dallas Visual Art Center, 111, 223, 233, 244–45, 253
Dallas Women's Cooperative Gallery, 250
Damas, Léon Gontran, 147
Dance Theatre Workshop, 258
Danes, Gibson, 41
Daniel, Frank, 207n. 57
Dante, 197, 217n. 14, 218n. 81
Danto, Arthur C., 168
Dart Gallery, 246
Dasburg, Andrew, 119
Davenport, Bill, 157, 164–66, **166**, 223, 229–30, 242
Davenport, Kimberly, 30
David Gallery, 131, 211n. 14, 237
Davidson, McNeill, 123, 248
Davidson, Susan, 249
Davis, Stuart, 129–30
Davis Gallery, Barbara, 234, 238–39, 248, 253, 256
Davis/McClain Gallery, 223, 234, 242, 245, 248, 259
Dawson, Archibald, 238
Dawson-Watson, Dawson, 262
de Kooning, Elaine, 86, 247
De Ryee, William, 242
Dee, Charles, 198
Defenbacher, Daniel, 19
DeFeo, Jay, 238
Deitch Projects, 234
Delahunty Gallery, 226, 255, 257
Delehanty, Suzanne, 29, 141
Delgado College Gallery, 236
Dellschau, Charles, 81
DeLude, Jeff, 89–90, **89**, 230
Demuth, Charles, 121
Design Industries Foundation Fighting Aids (DIFFA), 235
Devin Borden Hiram Butler Gallery, 229, 232–34, 257. *See also* Butler Gallery, Hiram
Dewey, John, 39
Dia Foundation, 134, 209n. 42, 214n. 45, 237
Dickson, George M., 15, 37
Dirube, Rolando Lopez, 141, 231
Discovery Hall Science Museum, 230
Dishman Art Gallery (Lamar University), 228, 235, 238, 258
Disney, Walt, 187
DiverseWorks Artspace, 27, 30, 223, 227–36, 238–39, 242, 245–46, 248–49, 255, 258

Dixon, Mildred, 264
Dobay, Louis, 100
Dobie, J. Frank, 261
Dolejska, Frank, 264
Dompierre, Louise, 173
Donahue Gallery, E. M., 255
Doroshenko, Peter, 159, 173, 203
Douglas, Aaron, 110
Douglass, John, 208n. 18
Dove, Arthur, 19, 122, 142
Downes, Rackstraw, **4–5**, 66–68, **67**, 73, 230, 256
Dozier, Otis, 18, 208n. 18, 249
Drake, James, 26, 30, 68–70, **69**, 222, 230
Dresden Akademie der Bildenden Kunste, 35, 242
Drucker, Malka, 225
Drury College, 225
Du Bois, W. E. B., 110
DuBose Gallery, 247
Dubuffet, Jean, 90, 131
Duchamp, Marcel, 21, 129–30, 164, 168, 176, 218n. 92, 249
Duchamp-Villon, Raymond, 130
Duke Energy, 25, 39, 42, 52, 57, 61, 65, 88, 90, 92, 97, 133, 140, 144, 156, 180, 198. *See also* Texas Eastern Corporation
DuMond, Frank V., 238
Dunn and Brown Contemporary, 222, 250, 256
Dureau, George, 267
Durieux, Caroline, 262–63
Dutton, Bernie, 93
DW Gallery, 234, 257

■ **E**

East Texas State University, 163
Eastern Illinois University, 101, 234
Eastern Michigan State University, 229
Eastern Washington College of Education, 238
Eastfield College, 234, 250
Edinburgh College of Art, 233, 245
Edwards, Jim, 172–73, 197
Edwards, Melvin, 119, 147–48, **148**, 230
Eeka-Beeka Gallery, 227
Eisenman, Nicole, 30
Eisenstein, Sergei, 179
El Centro Junior College, 58, 245, 250
El Paso Museum of Art, 230, 253
Eliade, Mircea, 80
Elias, Mark, 37
Eliot, T. S., 101, 197
Elkins, Leslie, 30
Ellis, Havelock, 224
Ellis, Lu, 265
Elrod, Jeff, 164, 167–68, **169**, 231–32
Emrick, Doris, 240
Engelhard Foundation, Charles, 143
Engelstein, Sharon, 187, 189–90, **190**, 231, 253
Ennis, Michael, 30, 93, 105, 108, 153, 155, 224, 255
Ernst, Carter, 239
Ernst, Jimmy, 129
Ernst, Max, 19, 44

■ F

Escher, Erwin, 260
Espada, Ibsen, 26, 141, *142,* 231
Evans, Walker, 41
Everson Museum of Art, 250

Fabrigas, Ramona, 27
Facchetti Gallery, Bruno, 246
Factor Family Collection, Betty and Monte, 113
Fagaly, William A., 55, 90
Fairbrother, Trevor, 137
Fall, Henry B., 15
Farish Gallery (Rice University), 210n. 79, 227
Farm Security Administration (FSA), 41, 63, 240
Farris, Kirk, 27
Fawbush Gallery, 256
Fearing, Kelly, 264
Feigen Gallery, Richard, 242
Feininger, Lyonel, 123
Feldman Collection of Contemporary Texas Art, D. D., 264
Ferus Gallery, 238
FIAC Grand Palais, Paris, 243
Fields, Dr. and Mrs. Clive, 155
Filmmakers Gallery, 228
Fine Arts Gallery of San Diego, 238
Finger family, 36
Firehouse Gallery, 248
Fish, Margaret, 261
Fish Gallery, Max, 232
Fisher, James, 173
Fisher, Vernon, 28, *56,* 57, 63, 66, 73, 106, 118, 172–76, *176,* 203, 216n. 7, 219n. 110, 222, 225, 231–32, 245, 267
500x Gallery, 234, 238
Flanagan Memorial Creative Persons Center, William, 238
Flavin, Dan, 237
Fleming Museum, Robert Hull, 250
Fletcher, Vallie, 262
Flood, Mark (John Peters; Perry Webb), 198–201, *199,* 218n. 92, 228, 231–32
Floss, Michael M., 179
Fogel, Seymour, 264
Folin Gallery, Alexandre de, 242
Folkman, David, 252
Fontana, Lucio, 140
Ford, John, 34, 183
Fore, Demian, 76
Fort Worth Art Association, 19
Fort Worth Art Center, 226
Fort Worth Art Museum, 217n. 21, 225, 226, 233, 258
Fort Worth Fat Stock Show and Rodeo, 258
Foster, Hal, 172
Foster/Freeman Gallery, 235
FotoFest, 27, 224, 232, 236, 252, 259
Foucault, Michel, 201
Fountainbleau School of Fine Arts, 262
Fowler, Bob, 226
Francis, Richard, 80
Frankenthaler, Helen, 131, 137
Frankfurter Kunstverein, 207n. 51, 253–55, 258
Franklin Furnace, 176

Franzheim, Kenneth, 20
Frazer, Sir James George, 101
Freed, Eleanor, 89
Freed, Frank, 19, *19, 21,* 22, 29, 248, 267
Freed Foundation, Eleanor and Frank, 19, 21
Freed Memorial Painting Fund, Frank, 126
Fridge, Roy, 44, 90, 93–94, *94,* 232, 247
Fried, Michael, 134
Friedlander, Lee, 225
Friedrich, Caspar David, 36, 253
Friis-Hansen, Dana, 30, 163, 180, 194
Frohnmayer, John, 228
Fuchs, Francesca, 230

■ G

Gabo, Naum, 123
Gaither, Edmund Barry, 111
Galbreth, Michael. *See* Art Guys
Galerie Bernheim-Jeune, 252
Galerie Daniel Cordier, 249
Galerie Gabrielle Maubrie, 234
Galerie Woolley, Fondation des Etats-Unis, 256
Gall, Sally, 144–46, *146,* 232
Gallery D'Theeboom, 234
Gallery Yves Arman, 248
Galveston Arts Center, 222–25, 227, 233–36, 238, 241, 243–44, 246, 250–52, 255–56, 258–59
Garber, Daniel, 237
Garden Club of Houston, 17
Gauguin, Paul, 114, 240
Gebhardt, Hal, 231
Geffert, Harry, 68, *68,* 74, 101, 161, 195, 210n. 90, 233, 250, 257
Géricault, Théodore, 210n. 95
Gérôme, Jean-Léon, 15, 206n. 3
Getler Saper Gallery, 243
Giacometti, Alberto, 250
Gibbs, Ezekiel, 265
Gideon, Samuel E., 242, 260–61
Gimpel + Weitzenhoffer, 233
Gittings, Paul, 263
Gjuranovic, Mato, 262
Glasco, Joseph, 22, 25–26, 119, 123, 127–29, *129,* 137–41, *138–39,* 233, 254
Glass, Philip, 257
Glassell School of Art (the Museum of Fine Arts, Houston), 24, 26, 27, 29, 65, 74, 76, 95, 111, 157, 184, 187, 197, 208n. 61, 222–23, 225, 228–29, 231–34, 236–38, 240, 242–46, 248–50, 252–53, 256–58, 260, 265–67. *See also* Core Residency Program; Museum School
Glennie, Ian, 58, 191
Godard, Jean-Luc, 207n. 57
Godfrey, DeWitt, 29, *116–17,* 143–44, *144,* 233, 245, 256
Goetzmann, William H., 55
Goff, Lloyd L., 208n. 18
Gogh, Vincent van, 19, 43, 224, 240
Gold Coast Art League, 238

Goldberg, Arthur and Carol, 217n. 22
Goldwater, Marge, 176
Gombrich, Ernst, 179
Gongolas, Christopher J., 155
Gonzales, Boyer, 261–62
Gonzales, Xavier, 263
González, Julio, 147, 214n. 33
Gonzalez, Patricia, 26
Gonzalez-Torres, Felix, 223
Goode, Lynn, 157, 199
Goode Gallery, Lynn, 227, 232, 235, 240, 242–44, 246, 258
Goodman, John, 159
Gorky, Arshile, 127, 164, 229
Gorski, Dan, 29
Gounod, Charles, 252
Goya, Francisco de, 103
Grabowski Gallery, 225
Graham Gallery, William A., 225, 230–31, 234, 236, 239, 248, 253
Graves, Audrey, 160
Graves, Morris, 253
Graves, P. F., 160
Gray Library, John, 235
Graze, Sue, 179, 191, 195, 224
Green, George, 46, 255
Green Gallery, Ida, 237, 256
Green Mountain Foundry, 29, 68, 101, 161, 195, 210n. 90, 233, 250, 257, 267
Greenberg, Clement, 118
Greene, Alison de Lima, 28
Griffin, Tad, 157, 163, *163,* 233–34
Griffith, L. O., 261
Groninger Museum, 246
Grooms, Red, 90
Grosman, Tatyana, 173–74
Grosz, George, 128, 214n. 29
Grotfeldt, Virgil, 100–103, *102,* 234, 236
Grünewald, Mathias, 152
Grynsztejn, Madeleine, 175
Guadalupe Cultural Arts Center, 105, 255
Guggenheim Museum, Solomon R., 44, 130, 232, 246, 249, 251
Guston, Philip, 244

■ H

H. E. B. Pantry Foods, 51, 225
Habermas, Jürgen, 172
Hacklin, Allan, 27, 187
Hadler/Rodriguez Gallery, 227, 233, 254
Hadra, Ida Weisselberg, 71
Hales, Hazel, 224
Halley, Peter, 235
Hallwalls Contemporary Art Center, 223, 230, 242
Hamilton, Richard, 225
Hampton University, 41, 224
Hanley, Bryant M. and Nancy C., 68, 195
Hansa Gallery, 252
Hansen, Douglas R., 260
Hardin-Simmons University, 231
Hare, David, 214n. 33
Harithas, James, 23, 51
Harris, Tracy, 153, 155–56, *156,* 234
Harris Gallery, 240

Harrison, Helen and Newton, 210n. 98
Hartley, Marsden, 119, 122, 157
Harvey, Eleanor Jones, 73
Haskell, Barbara, 134, 224
Havel, Dan, 208n. 63
Havel, Joseph, 29–30, 157, 160–63, *162,* 210n. 90, 234
Hayter, Stanley William, 226
Hearn Gallery, Pat, 231
Hecker, Rachel, 187, *188,* 234–35
Heiss, Alanna, 25
Held, Al, 230
Helion, Jean, 123
Hellman, Bertha Louise, 260
Hendricks, Patricia D., 122
Henfrey, Dr. and Mrs. Anthony, 143
Hennings, E. Martin, 119
Henri, Robert, 247
Hepworth, Barbara, 167
Herbert, Lynn M., 30, 197
Heriot-Watt University, 245
Herrera, Hayden, 67, 230
Hershey, Olive, 217n. 31
Herzstein, Max H. and Isabell Smith, 68, 137, 163–64
Hesse, Eva, 118
Hickey, Dave, 34, 46, 57, 157, 183, 201, 209n. 40, 231, 248
High School for the Performing and Visual Arts, 240, 251, 256
Hill, Ed, 225. *See also* MANUAL
Hill, Gary, 30
Hill, William James, 100, 176–77
Hillyar, Elizabeth, 235
Hinson, Richard, 70, *70,* 235
Hirshhorn Museum and Sculpture Garden, Washington, D.C., 164, 228, 232, 250
Historic Preservation Authority of Birmingham, 230
Hockaday Junior College, 235
Hoffberger School of Painting, 240
Hofmann, Hans, 123, 125, 127, 137, 240, 252
Hogg, Ima, 15, 36, 123, 206n. 12
Hogg, William C., 15, 206n. 5
Hogg brothers, 206n. 16
Hogue, Alexandre, 17–18, 28, *38,* 39, *39,* 40, 235, 249, 261
Holding, Eileen, 123
Holloway, Patti Jones, 73
Holocaust Museum, 226
Holt, Percy W., 260
Hong Kong Visual Arts Center, 238
Hood, Dorothy, 19, 22, 24, 81–83, *82,* 96, 119, 131, *132,* 141, 235, 265
Hooks-Epstein Galleries, 192, 227, 239, 247, 258
Hopps, Walter, 27, 81, 113, 207n. 54, 213n. 85, 238–39, 249
Horn, Roni, 237
Horrigan, Sally, 93
Horton, Cecily, 208n. 15
Houston, Margaret, 16, 208n. 13
Houston, Sam, 16, 35, 119, 244
Houston Art League, 15, 30, 37, 130, 206n. 6, 206n. 7, 206n. 26, 207n. 35, 227, 231, 237–38, 240–41, 243, 248, 250, 251, 257–58, 260, 264

Houston Artists Fund, 250, 253
Houston Artists' Gallery, 19
Houston Camera Club, 16, 262–64
Houston Center for Photography, 27, 235, 243, 246, 252–53, 255, 258
Houston Community College, 240
Houston Endowment, 21
Houston Festival, 233, 247
Houston Friends of Art, 17, 40
Houston-Galveston Psychoanalytic Institute, 242
Houston Grand Opera, 137, 252, 257
Houston International Festival, 143, 235, 240
Houston Lighting & Power Company, 67
Houston Livestock Show and Rodeo, 48–49
Houston Public Library, 231, 236, 260
Houston Public School Art League, 260
Howard, Carter, 263
Hudnall, Earlie, Jr., 49, 51, *51,* 236
Hudson River Museum, 241
Huerta, Benito, 105, *105,* 182, 236
Hulick, Diana Emery, 106
Hunter, Fredericka, 58, 191
Hunter College, 148, 243, 250
Hunter Gallery, 231
Huntington Art Gallery, Archer M., 55, 226–27, 233–34, 238–39
Huntington Beach Art Center, 234
Huntington College, 229
Huntington Library (Pasadena, Calif.), 173

■ I

Iamblichus, 81, 211n. 8
Ibsen, Henrik, 257
Illinois Institute of Technology, 257
Illinois State University, 244
Illinois State University Gallery, 234, 248
Illinois Wesleyan University, 87, 252
Imperial Art School (Vilnius), 252
Indiana University, 75, 242, 246, 253
Ingres, Jean-Auguste-Dominique, 175
Inman, Kerry F., 75, 158
Inman Gallery, 223, 225, 229–30, 240, 245–46, 250
Inness, George, 73, 206n. 5
Institute for Contemporary Arts (London), 225, 232
Institute for European Studies (Vienna), 240
Institute for the Arts, Rice University, 23, 241
Institute of Contemporary Art (Boston), 252
Institute of Design (Chicago), 124–25, 240, 248

Institute of Texan Cultures (San Antonio), 242
Instituto Allende, 236
Instituto Mexicano-Norte-americano, 237
Irving Arts Center, 236, 246
Irwin, Robert, 238
Italian Cultural and Community Center, 252
Iwonski, Carl von, 242

J

Jackson, Everett Gee, 261
James, Terrell, 44, 71, 144, *145*, 153, 236, 240
James Gallery, 252
Jameson, Fredric, 172, 197–98
Janson, H. W., 175
Japan Foundation, 233
Jarrell, Randall, 130
Jeffers, Susan, 87
Jencks, Charles, 179
Jensen, Bill, 142
Jensen, Sandra, 61
Jeppson Art Institute, 233
Jewish Community Center, 207n. 35
Jewish Educational Alliance, 252
Jewish Museum, 225, 249
Jiménez, Luis, 23, 26, *26*, 148, 181–83, *182*, 236–37, 245
John, Alfred Morgan, 119, 237
John, Grace Spaulding, 16, 119–22, *121*, 206n. 11, 237, 262
Johns, Jasper, 105, 173, 249
Johns Hopkins University, 242
Johnson, Mr. and Mrs. John W., 159
Johnson, Lucas, 83–84, *84*, 113, 133, 237
Johnson, Patricia Covo, 192, 197
Johnson Museum of Art, Herbert F., 250
Jones, Lois Mailou, 110
Jones, Otis, 234
Jones, Owen, 179–80
Jones Hall Gallery, University of St. Thomas, 207n. 40
Joy, Robert, 262
Judd, DeForrest, *19*
Judd, Donald, 94, 119, 133–37, *135*, 164, 230, 237–38, 247
Jung, Carl, 43, 209n. 35, 224
Jung Educational Center, C. G., 103, 236, 239, 242, 249, 258
Junior League of Houston, 262

K

Kabakov, Ilya, 237
Kahlo, Frida, 82, 235
Kalil, Susie, 25–26, 35, 45, 76, 152, 190, 200
Kamrath, Karl, 19
Kandinsky, Wassily, 123
Kansas City Art Institute, 173, 225, 228, 249
Kant, Immanuel, 82
Karl, Mabel Fairfax, 18, 119, 122, *123*, 238
Karp, Ivan, 106
Katonah Museum of Art, 244
Katz, Alex, 230
Keating, Mary Aubrey, 261
Keehnel, Roy, 237

Keightley, Patricia John, 121–22
Kellogg, E. C., 208n. 12
Kelly, Ellsworth, 140, 237
Kelsey, Mavis P., 257
Kempner, Mr. and Mrs. I. H., III, 195
Kempner, Page, 74, *74*, 238
Kempner Museum of Contemporary Art and Design, 223
Kennaugh, Michael, 144, 146–47, *147*, 153, 238
Kennedy, John F., 174
Kent, Rockwell, 39, 119
Kent State University, 157, 223
Kepes, Gyorgy, 123–25, 229, 248
Kett, Diane, 108
Keuka College, 227
Kidd, Hari, 263
Kiefer, Anselm, 57
Kienholz, Edward, 103, 113–14, *115*, 238–39, 266
Kienholz, Nancy Reddin, 81, 103, 113–14, *115*, 238–39, 266
Kiko Gallery, 131, 214n. 27
Kimmelman, Michael, 144
King, Ken, 101
King, Rodney, 184
Kinzinger, Edmund, 262
Kitchen, Katie Kaim, 99
Kittelson, Paul, 29, 164, 167, *168*, 239
Klee, Paul, 123, 128, 131, 146
Klein, Michael (Mickey) and Jeanne, 164, 195
Klein Inc., Michael, 256
Kline, Franz, 118
Knoedler Gallery, 19, 44, 226
Koehler Cultural Art Center, 223
Koffler Gallery, 223, 230, 242b
Koontz, Jo Harvey, 222
Kopriva, Sharon, 100, 103, *103*, 113, 239
Kosuth, Joseph, 179
Kouros Gallery, 238, 243, 258
Krause, George, 23, 29, 90–93, *93*, 207n. 45, 235, 239–40, 265–66
Krauss, Rosalind, 150, 216n. 4
Kress Collection, the Museum of Fine Arts, Houston, 17
Kubricht, Charles Mary, 29, 76, *77*, 236, 240, 252, 267
Kulman, Walter, 130
Kunstakademie Düsseldorf, 131, 258
Kunsthalle Düsseldorf, 239
Kurtz, Bruce D., 111

L

La Boetie, Inc., 255
La Jolla Museum of Contemporary Art, 222, 232, 253. *See also* San Diego Museum of Contemporary Art
La Tour, Maurice Quentin de, 37
Lacan, Jacques, 190
Lack, Mr. and Mrs. A. I., 83
Lafayette Art Center, 250
Laguna Gloria Art Museum, 137, 222, 225, 229, 232, 234, 241–42, 247, 250, 252–54, 256
Lamar High School, 258

Lamar University, 52, 62, 70, 146, 192, 222, 227–28, 234–35, 238, 243, 246, 258
Landay, Janet, 26, 95
Lange, Dorothea, 41
Lanier Middle School, 237
Laqueur, Thomas, 191
Laredo Junior College, 181, 243
Larsen, Andrew, 262
Lasansky, Mauricio, 226
LaSelle, Dorothy Antoinette (Toni), 28, 119, 123–25, *126*, 142, 240, 252, 255
Lassiter, Bill, 223, 255
Lawing Gallery, 228, 254
Lawndale Annex (University of Houston), 27, 30, 89, 103, 201, 222–23, 236, 240. *See also* Lawndale Art and Performance Center
Lawndale Art and Performance Center, 30, 157, 223, 228, 230, 232, 235–36, 238–39, 241–42, 244–46, 248, 253, 255–56, 266. *See also* Lawndale Annex
Lawrence, Annette, 183–84, *185*, 208n. 61, 240
Le Corbusier, 156
Lebrun, Rico, 233, 243
Lee, Amy Freeman, 263
Lee, Russell, 41, *41*, 63, 159, 240–41, 256
Lee Gallery, Janie C., 241, 251
Léger, Fernand, 140
Lehigh University, 240
Lentelli, Leo, 238
Leonardo da Vinci, 156
Lessinger, Jack, 239
Lester, William, 208n. 18
Levers, Robert, 47, *47*, 241
Levine, Robert, 48
Levy, Bubba, 61
LeWitt, Sol, 30
Lichtenstein, Roy, 164
Lieberman & Saul Gallery, 232
Lincoln, Abraham, 186
Lincoln Academy, 224
Lingan, Penelope, 237
Lipton, Seymour, 214n. 33, 236
Livingston, Jane, 26, 148
Locke, Alain, 110
Locke, Charmaine, 103, 192, 253
Lockwood, J. Ward, 262, 263
Lone Star Printmakers, 40, 235, 262
Long, Bert, 81, 191, *192*, 241, 246
Long, Connie, 241
Long, Meredith J., 100, 133
Long, Mrs. Meredith J., 133
Long & Company, Meredith, 130, 222, 225, 233, 235, 250–51
Long, Richard, 184
Longview Museum of Fine Art, 233–34, 247, 253
Lopez Dirube, Rolando, 141, 231

Los Angeles County Museum of Art, 231, 238
Los Angeles Trade-Technical College, 191, 241
Louis, Morris, 131
Louisiana Gallery, 131
Louisiana State University, 243, 256
Louisville School of Art, 195, 249
Love, Jim, 22, 29, 43–45, *45*, 93, 140, *140*, 232, 241
Lowe, Constance, 215n. 96
Lowe, Rick, 29–30
Lowenfeld, Viktor, 224
Lowry, Malcolm, 83
Loyola University, 75, 250
Lungkwitz, Hermann, *32–33*, *36*, 35–36, 204, 242
Luntz, Marian, 28
LYC Museum, 255
Lyon, Giles, 157–59, *159*, 223, 229, 242
Lyons Matrix Gallery, 251
Lyons Wier Gallery, 231

M

MacAgy, Douglas, 42, 44, 212n. 37, 226, 241
MacAgy, Jermayne, 20–22, 42, 44–45, 81, 129–31, 207n. 31, 207n. 38, 209n. 30, 214n. 33, 241, 253
Macdonald, Cynthia, 95–98, *96–98*, 242
MacDonnell, Angela, 262
Maciunas, George, 201
MacMorris, Daniel, 254
Magritte, René, 197
Maidana, Velasco, 235
Main Gallery, University of Texas at El Paso, 230
Main Street Festival, 61
Malevich, Kasimir, 118, 157
Malone, Jim, 225
Malone, Lee, 21, 129
Mancuso, Joe, 153, 155, *155*, 242–43, 267
Mandell, Mr. and Mrs. Arthur J., 41
Manes, Paul, 62, *62*, 146, 192, 227, 238, 243, 258
Mansbendel, Peter, 261
MANUAL (Suzanne Bloom and Ed Hill), 23, 173–75, *175*, 200, 243, 265
Mapplethorpe, Robert, 187
Marcus, Lawrence, 247
Marcus, Stanley, 129
Margo Gallery, Adair, 240
Margulies, Anne and Martin Z., 57
Marlborough Gallery, 222, 230
Márquez, Gabriel García, 106
Marsh, Stanley, 209n. 42
Marshall, Alexandra, 61
Martin, Agnes, 118, 166
Martin, Frank, 61–62, *61*, 243
Martin, Laura and Jim, 197
Martínez, César Augusto, 26, 181–82, *181*, 243–44
Martinez, Roman and Paula, 105
Marvins Portrait Collection, Sonia and Kaye, 51
Maryland Institute, 184, 240

Maryville College, 197, 248
Marzio, Peter C., 25, 28, 203
Massachusetts Institute of Technology Museum, 248
Massing, Jack. *See* Art Guys
Masson, André, 82, 128
Matisse, Henri, 45, 184
Mattress Factory, 228
Mauve, Anton, 15, 37, 206n. 3
May, L. O. Griffith, 261
May, Lind, 225
May Department Stores Company Foundation, 155, 158
Mayo, Marti, 26, 29, 179
McAlpine Gallery, 255
McAshan, Mr. and Mrs. Maurice, 61–62
McAshan, Mrs. Susan, 151
McAshan Education and Charitable Trust, 207n. 36
McCarthy, Kirk, 254
McClain & Co., Robert, 248, 255
McClennan Community College, 255
McClung, Florence, 71
McCoy Gallery, Jason, 234
McCracken, Patrick, 248
McCullough, Jewel, 93
McEvilley, Thomas, 25, 34, 81, 84, 148
McGee, David, 194, *195*, 197, 208n. 61, 244
McGuire, James Patrick, 242
McKay, Ralph, 28
McKinney Avenue Contemporary, 233
McKissack, Jeff, 30, 208n. 63
McLanahan, Muffy, 93
McMurtrey, Eleanor D., 73, 200
McMurtrey Gallery, 227, 231, 234, 246, 256
McNamara Museum, 247
McNay Institute, Marion Kugler, 229
McNeese State University, 184, 228
McPherson, Dr. Alice, 87
McVey, William, 17, 261
MD Modern, 235–36
Mead, Ben Carlton, 261
Meade, Charles Richard, *10*, 35, 244
Meade, Henry R., 244
Meade, Henry William Matthew, *10*, 35, 244
Meade, Mary Ann, 244
Media Center. *See* Rice Media Center
Meek, Vicki, 111, *112*, 113, *113*, 208n. 61, 244
Memphis Academy of Arts, 184, 246
Memphis State University, 223
Menil Collection, The, 27, 30, 81, 113, 150, 207n. 53, 207n. 54, 228–30, 232, 237, 239, 249, 254, 258, 267
Menil, Dominique de, 21–23, 27, 44, 61, 81, 129, 131, 207n. 57, 211n. 10, 241
Menil, John de, 22–23, 27, 44, 129, 131, 241
Merewether, Charles, 114
Merida, Carlos, 125, 252

Mesa-Bains, Amalia, 104
Messager, Annette, 223
Metcalf, Willard L., 208n. 16
Metropolitan Museum of Art, 176, 222, 227, 251
MexiArte, 184, 243
Mexican Fine Arts Center Museum, 244
Miami Art Museum, 232
Michelangelo, 156, 243
Michigan State Normal College, 229
Mid-America Arts Alliance, 228, 239, 245, 248, 256
Middle Tennessee State University, 223, 230
Midtown Art Center, 105, 207n. 55, 223, 232, 236, 258
Mies van der Rohe, Ludwig, 20, 23, 129–30, 207n. 57
Milagros Contemporary, 223, 239
Miller, Dorothy, 127–28
Miller, Melissa, 26, 28, 71, *78–79*, 86, 88–89, *88*, 244–45
Miller, Michael, 157, 160–61, *161*, 245
Mims, Jack, 46, 255
Minneapolis College of Art and Design, 235
Minneapolis College of Design, 39
Miró, Joan, 19, 21, 118
Mitchell, Charles Dee, 198, 224
Mobil Oil Corporation, 250
Modern Art Museum of Fort Worth, 89, 223–25, 232, 245, 249
Moderna Museet, Stockholm, 113, 173
Moholy-Nagy, László, 19, 123–25, 214n. 18, 229, 240, 248
Molina Gallery, Robert, 227, 247
Mondrian, Piet, 118, 123, 164
Moneo, Rafael, 30
Monte Factor Family Collection, 113
Montebello, Philippe de, 24
Montgomery, Robert, 164, 166–67, *167*, 222, 245
Moody, Betty, 178
Moody, Ron, 257
Moody, Tom, 157
Moody Gallery, 95, 222, 228, 232–33, 237–38, 240–41, 243, 247, 249, 251, 254–56, 258
Moore, G. Bedell, 247
Moore College of Art, 187, 234
Moore Gallery, D. C., 224
Moran, Thomas, 35
Morgenstern, Joan, 63, 72, 108
Moroles, Jesús Bautista, 26, 147–48, *149*, 245
Morris, David, 199
Morris, Robert, 237
Morrison, Toni, 217n. 31
Moser, Charlotte, 25
Motherwell, Robert, 118, 127, 173, 229
Muench, Julian, 260
Mundy, Mr. and Mrs. Joe S., 63, 160, 203, 207n. 45
Mundy Collection, 266
Muñoz, Celia Alvarez, 105–8, *107*, 245–46

Murphy, Gerald, 44
Murray, Elizabeth, 142
Musée d'Art Moderne de la Ville de Paris, 255
Musée d'Orsay, Paris, 187
Musée du Louvre, Paris, 175
Museo de Arte Contemporáneo (Monterrey), 114
Museo de Arte Moderno la Tertulia, 251
Museo de Arte y Historia, 230
Museo Dolores Olmedo Patiño, 82
Museo Ex-Convento del Carmen, 237
Museum Collectors, the Museum of Fine Arts, Houston, 28, 121
Museum for Contemporary Photography, 236
Museum Ludwig, 113
Museum of African Art (New York), 110
Museum of Art of the American West, 237
Museum of Contemporary Art (Los Angeles), 228, 232, 239
Museum of Contemporary Hispanic Art, 236
Museum of East Texas, 253
Museum of Fine Arts, Boston, 257
Museum of Fine Arts, Houston (MFAH), 15–31, 41–43, 48, 55, 61, 74, 83, 104, 111, 113, 118–19, 122–24, 129–30, 134, 137, 140, 219n. 94, 222–26, 228–31, 233–39, 241, 243–59, 260–67. *See also* African American Art Advisory Association; Bayou Bend Collection; Beck Collection, John A. and Audrey Jones; Cullen Sculpture Garden, Lillie and Hugh Roy; Glassell School of Art; Museum Collectors; Museum School; Photo Forum
Museum of Modern Art, Mexico City, 244
Museum of Modern Art, New York, 42, 127–28, 131, 164, 224–27, 229, 232–33, 235, 238–39, 241, 246, 249, 251, 256, 258
Museum of Neon Art, 227
Museum of Surgical Science, 231
Museum of the Southwest, 247
Museum School (the Museum of Fine Arts, Houston), 17, 19, 24, 82, 88, 103, 122, 141, 147, 198, 226, 235, 236, 244, 253, 258. *See also* Glassell School of Art
Museum Volkwang, 243
Musgnug, Kristin, 74–75, *75*, 246

■ N
Nakagawa, Osamu James, 198, 200–201, *200*, 203, 246
Nathan, Debbie, 35
National Academy of Design, 36, 82, 228–29, 237, 248–49, 252

National Arts Club, 237
National Dance Institute, 222
National Educational Television, 223
National Endowment for the Arts (NEA), 24, 28, 65, 87, 134, 202, 207n. 41, 207n. 42, 207n. 43, 207n. 45, 224, 226, 228, 232–34, 236, 239, 241, 243, 245, 248, 251, 254, 256, 258
National Endowment for the Humanities (NEH), 224
National Museum of American Art, 228, 255
National Museum of Women in the Arts, 252
Nauman, Bruce, 250
Nave, Royston, 260
Nave Museum, 225, 238, 245, 247
Nebraska Wesleyan University, 240
Nelson Gallery, 254
Neruda, Pablo, 235
Neuberger Museum of Art, 231
New Arts Gallery, 130, 253
New Bauhaus, 124, 214n. 13, 248
New Mexico Highlands University, 68, 233
New Mexico State University, 105, 236
New Museum, 25, 226, 250–52
New Orleans Museum of Art, 230, 247, 50
New School for Social Research, 257
New York International Film and Video Festival, 254
New York University, 223, 242
Newhall, Beaumont, 48
Newman, Barnett, 23, 43, 133, 150
Newsum, Floyd Elbert, Jr., 183–84, *183*, 246
Nexus Contemporary Art Center, 231
Neyland, Watson, 261
Niagara Community College, 223
Nichols, Perry, 208n. 18
Nicholson, Ben, 123
Nicosia, Nic, 198, 202–3, *202*, 246–47
Nill, Annegreth, 216n. 10
No tsu oh Gallery, 230
Nochlin, Linda, 187
Noguchi, Isamu, 28, 127
Noland, Kenneth, 167, 231
Nordbrock, Jeri, 189
Norris, Kathleen, 65
North Florida Community College, 256
North Texas State University, 124, 148
Northington, Clara Beard, 262
Northwest Missouri State University, 198, 254
Northwood Institute, 226

■ O
"O" House, 208n. 63
O'Connor, Madeline, 55, 71, 94–95, *95*, 247
O'Connor, Nancy, *54*, 55, 247

Ocotillo Gallery, 230
Odom, Michael, 160
O'Grady, Gerald, 207n. 57
OK Harris Gallery, 251
O'Kane Gallery (University of Houston), 246
O'Keeffe, Georgia, 44, 71, 80, 119, 122
Old Lyme Art Colony, 227
Oldenburg, Claes, 22, 167, 212n. 37, 237
Oldham, Todd, 219n. 103, 223
Olinsky, Ivan, 227
Oliver, Kermit, 80, 86, *86*, 247
Olsen, Valerie Loupe, 29, 72, 155
On Waugh Gallery, 243
Onderdonk, Eleanor Rogers, 36, 208n. 17, 247
Onderdonk, Julian, 15, 17, 36–37, *37*, 206n. 5, 247, 261–62
Onderdonk, Robert Jenkins, 36, 247
Onnasch, Reinhard, 113
Oomoto School of Traditional Art, 103
Orange Show, 30, 208n. 63
Ormond Beach Memorial Art Museum, 256
Orozco, José Clemente, 227, 235
Oshman, Marilyn, 100, 113
Oursler, Tony, 190
Ovid, 61, 92
Owens, Craig, 172, 180
Ozark Summer Art School, 251

■ P
P.S. 1, Institute for Art and Urban Resources, 25, 207n. 54, 223, 247, 254
Pace Gallery, 237
Pach, Walter, 229
Pagan Gallery, Irene, 244
Pagel, David, 157, 163–64
Palmer, Mrs. Charles Franklin, 260
Pan Texas Assembly, 176
Panhandle-Plains Historical Museum, 238, 249
Paolozzi, Eduardo, 225
Parazette, Aaron, 155, 164, *165*, 233, 248
Parkerson Gallery, 248, 255
Parsons, Betty, 43
Parsons Gallery, Betty, 43, 222, 224, 249
Parsons School of Design, 237
Pasadena Art Museum, 238
Partenheimer, Jürgen, 245
Pasolini, Pier Paolo, 84
Paz, Octavio, 244
Peabody College for Teachers, George, 228
Pennell, Joseph, 238
Pennsylvania Academy of the Fine Arts, 75, 237, 243
Pennsylvania State University, 42, 224, 234
Perls Gallery, 233
Perrault, Charles, 88
Perry, Commodore, 35
Peters, John. *See* Flood, Mark
Peters Gallery, Gerald, 222, 224, 226, 232, 240, 245, 250, 253
Peterson, Mark, 189

Petley, Kate, 208n. 63
Philadelphia College of Art, 92, 239
Philadelphia Fabric Workshop, 223
Philadelphia Museum of Art, 168
Philadelphia School of Design for Women, 122, 254
Philbrook Art Center, University of Tulsa, 235
Phillips, Lisa, 142
Phoenix Art Museum, 243–44, 247, 259
Photo Forum (the Museum of Fine Arts, Houston), 29, 202
Piano, Renzo, 27
Picasso, Pablo, 21, 45, 118, 214n. 29
Piranesi, Giovanni Battista, 153
Poe Elementary School, 253
Pollock, Jackson, 22, 43, 82, 118, 128, 141, 158, 233
Pollock Galleries (Southern Methodist University), 227
Pomona College, 74, 238
Pompidou, Centre Georges, 239
Poons, Larry, 231
Poor, Henry Varnum, 42
Porter, Fairfield, 230
Portman, Brian, 153, *154*, 248
Portsmouth Art School, 128, 233
Poulos, Basilios, 207n. 43
Pousette-Dart, Richard, 43
Prairie State College, 258
Prairie View A&M University, 197, 244
Pratt Institute, 257
Preusser, Robert, 18–19, 123–24, *124*, 248, 263, 264
Price, Vincent, 130
Prieto, Monique, 157
Printz, Neil, 207n. 54
Procter and Gamble, 17
Project Row Houses, 30–31, 231, 234, 244, 246
Prudential Insurance Company of America, 19
Pyramid Arts Center, 228

■ Q
Queens College (New York), 111, 244
Queens College (North Carolina), 76, 240
Quirarte, Jacinto, 182

■ R
Ranta, Rachel, 194, *196*, 197, 248–49, 256
Raskin, Marcus, 114
Ratcliff, Carter, 62
Rau, Marty, 93
Rauschenberg, Robert, 26, 30, 47, 172–75, *174*, 206n. 29, 249, 267
Re Gallery, Marisa del, 243
Reaben, James, 30, 44, 81, 96, 99–100, *99*, *100*, 249
Reaugh, Frank, 36–37, *37*, 39, 66, 74, 235, 247, 249
Redon, Odilon, 101
Reed College, 232
Reid, Calvin, 186
Reinhardt, Ad, 80

Remington, Frederic, 15, 34, 54, 206n. 16
Renteria, Philip, 207n. 43, 267
Resettlement Administration, 41
Reyes, Felipe, 244
Reynolds, Patrick H., 163
Rhode Island School of Design, 82, 144, 158, 187, 229, 232, 234–35, 242–43, 248
Ribelin, Frank, 148, 183
Rice Institute for the Arts, 16, 207n. 53, 241, 260
Rice Media Center, 23, 207n. 57, 227, 232
Rice Museum, 23
Rice University, 16, 20, 23, 27, 48, 63, 86, 108, 140, 148, 198, 207n. 40, 224, 226–27, 229–30, 232, 234–35, 241, 245, 247, 248–50, 252–53, 255, 257. *See also* Farish Gallery; Rice Institute for the Arts; Rice Media Center; Rice Museum; Rice University Art Gallery
Rice University Art Gallery (Sewall Art Gallery), 30, 227, 229–30, 248–50
Richland College, 245
Richter, Gerhard, 118
Richter, Ludwig, 242
Ridgway, Linda, 29, 194–95, *194,* 210n. 90, 249–50, 267
Rijksakademie, 167, 231
Rimbaud, Arthur, 100
Rivera, Diego, 42, 214n. 29, 227, 235
Rivers, Larry, 173
Robinson, Jerome, 159
Robinson, Joan Seeman, 47
Robinson, Minnette, 159, 168
Robinson, William, 23
Robinson Galleries, 226, 228
Roche, Jim, 46, 255
Rodin, Auguste, 187
Rogers, Roy, 255
Romansky, Mr. and Mrs. Alvin S., 39, 41
Roosevelt, Franklin D., 41
Rose, Barbara, 25–26, 55, 80, 174, 200
Rosemarin, Susie, 215n. 96
Rosenberg, Abraham, 261
Rosenblum, Walter, 239
Rosenquist, James, 187
Rosenstein, Harris, 218n. 65
Rosenstein, Sheila, 218n. 65
Rosenthal, Mark, 118, 163
Rossellini, Roberto, 207n. 57
Roswell Museum and Art Center, 246, 251
Roszak, Theodore, 214n. 33
Roth, Moira, 108
Rothko, Mark, 23, 42–43, 84, 94, 128, 131, 233
Rothko Chapel, 23, 84, 137
Rothko Foundation, Mark, 224
Roupe, Tom, 68
Rowntree, Ralph S., 261
Royal College of Art, 225
Rozumalski, Ted A., 265
Ruck, Dean, 27, 208n. 63
Ruello, Robert, 74–75, *76,* 250
Rutger Gallery, 259
Ruyter, Lisa, 231

Ryder, Albert Pinkham, 224
Ryman, Robert, 164

■ S
Sala Diaz, 223, 230
Salle, David, 187
Salter, James, 146
Sam Houston State College, 253
Sam Houston State University, 54
Samples, Bert, 25, 31, 208n. 61
Samuels, Michael, 52
San Angelo Museum of Art, 246
San Antonio Art League, 255
San Antonio College, 223
San Antonio Museum of Art, 172–73, 222, 227, 232, 247–48, 256–57
San Diego Art Guild, 238
San Diego Museum of Art, 238
San Diego Museum of Contemporary Art, 226. *See also* La Jolla Museum of Contemporary Art
San Diego State University, 251
San Francisco Art Institute, 222, 232, 248, 250, 256
San Francisco Museum of Art, 229
San Francisco Museum of Modern Art, 239, 241
San Jose State University, 226
San Martin de Porres, 215n. 79
Santa Barbara Museum of Art, 231
Santa Barbara School of the Arts, 238
São Paulo Arts Festival, 232
Sarah Lawrence College, 242
Sartor Galleries, Joseph, 251
Satellite Space, 231, 234
Saul Gallery, Julie, 232
Schapiro, Meyer, 43, 130, 209n. 35, 224
Scheffey, Dr. Eric, 103
Schimmel, Paul, 216n. 7
Schinkel, Karl Friedrich, 253
Schiwetz, Edward M. "Buck," 18, 262, 264
Schlanger, Beth, 93
Schleuter's Studio Building, 237
Schmidt, Julius, 253
Schnabel, Julian, 23, 26, 266
Schneck, Mr. and Mrs. Andrew, 159, 168
Schofield, Kevin, 75, 158
School of Fine Arts (St. Louis), 37, 237, 249
School of the Art Institute of Chicago, 75, 90, 237, 250, 253
School of the Visual Arts, 179, 251
Schorre, Charles, 131, 133, *133,* 207n. 43, 250
Schwartz, Sanford, 127
Schwarzkogler, Rudolph, 84
Screen Memories, 232
Sculpture Center, 233, 234, 247
Seattle Art Museum, 253
Seitz, William, 130
Sélavy, Rose, 21
Sepúlveda, Artemio, 83, 237
Serota, Nicholas, 207n. 52
Serpentine Gallery, 237
Serra, Richard, 150, 209n. 42
Seuss, Dr., 158

Sewall Art Gallery. *See* Rice University Art Gallery
Seyffert, Leopold, 254
Shafrazi Gallery, Tony, 228
Shahn, Ben, 214n. 29, 240
Shapiro, Joel, 29
Sheeler, Charles, 160
Sheffield Gallery, Susanna, 227
Sherman, Cindy, 187, 190
Shin Gallery, Lloyd, 248
Shipman, Gertrude, 247
Shipnes, Mary Ellen, 263
Shurtleff, Stella Hope, 43
Siegel, Bugsy, 183
Silver Eye Center for Photography, 246
Simmons and Company International, 143
Simpson, William Kelly, 143
Siqueiros, David Alfaro, 217n. 46, 227
Siskind, Aaron, 257
Skinner, Frances, 263
Skowhegan School of Painting and Sculpture, 65, 226, 245, 250
Sloan, John, 227
Slye, Leonard, 255
Smith, Chuck, 209n. 32
Smith, David, 214n. 33
Smith, George, 147–50, *150,* 250
Smith, Hassel, 130
Smith, Henry Nash, 39
Smith, Jean, 240
Smith, John R., 228
Smith, Lee N., III, 57–58, *58, 62,* 250–51
Smith, Tony, 148, 250
Smith College, 175, 243
Smither, Murray, 214n. 20
Smithson, Robert, 209n. 42
Smithsonian Institution, 144, 227, 236
Snell Art School, Henry, 254
Snook, Steven J., 147, 166–67
Society for Contemporary Photography, 246
Solomon Gallery, Holly, 232, 244–45
Sondheim, Stephen, 216n. 98
Sonneman, Eve, 207n. 44
South Dallas Cultural Center, 111, 244
Southeast Museum of Photography, 232
Southeastern Center for Contemporary Art, 222, 244
Southern California Gallery for Contemporary Arts, 236
Southern Illinois University, 179, 251
Southern Methodist University, 39–40, 52, 54, 90, 100, 222, 224, 227, 229, 234, 253, 257
Southern States Art League, 260–63
Southwest Alternate Media Project (SWAMP), 207n. 57
Southwest Texas State University, 68, 227, 233, 245
Souza, Al, 174, 179–80, *180,* 202, 207n. 45, 251
Sparks, Esther, 174
Spears, Monroe K., 55
Spellman, Coreen Mary, 71, 262

Spoleto Festival, Charleston, 30
Sprout, Sally, 238, 258
Sprout Gallery, Sally, 238
Spruce, Everett, 18, 39–41, *40,* 119, *120,* 251, 264
Square One Gallery, 229
St. Edward's University, 84, 254
St. Louis School of Fine Arts, 37, 237, 249
Staartjes, Hans, 70
Stable Gallery, 252
Stack, Gael, 23, 26, 28, 174–75, *178,* 179, 207n. 43, 251
Staley, Earl, 86–89, *87,* 207n. 43, 209n. 53, 252
Stalin, Joseph, 134, 137
Stamford Museum and Nature Center, 247
Stanford University, 226–27
Stankiewicz, Richard, 45, 147, 214n. 33
State Fair of Texas, 36, 247, 249
State University of New York, 231, 250
Stautberg, Ann, 29, 72–73, *72,* 240, 252, 267
Stearns, Robert, 137
Steen, William, 96, 99–100, 199, 207n. 55, 249
Steffy, Bill (William), 178, 265
Steichen, Edward, 92, 239
Stein, Gertrude, 45, 158, 257
Steinberg, Leo, 172
Steiner, Dr. Alton and Emily, 155, 158
Stell, Thomas, 119, 251
Stella, Frank, 167, 237
Stella, Joseph, 142
Stellweg, Carla, 84
Stellweg Gallery, Carla, 223
Stephen F. Austin State University, 258
Sterba, Antonin, 237
Stern, Daniel, 144
Stettheimer, Florine, 45
Stevens, George, 34
Stewart, Rick, 39, 119
Stiebel Modern, 251
Still, Clyfford, 42, 128
Stillman, Ary, 19, 24, 81–83, *83,* 252, 265
Stockebrand, Marianne, 237
Stoller, Ezra, 22, 265
Storm, Margaret, 250
Stout, Myron, 23, 118, 123–27, *127,* 130, 252–53
Stout, Richard, 90, *92,* 130, 207n. 43, 253, 254, 258
Stryker, Roy, 240
Stuckey, Charles, 173
Studio-Galerie, 226
Studio Museum of Harlem, 148, 236, 246, 250
Studio One, 96, 199, 207n. 55, 223, 232, 249
Sul Ross State Teachers College, 261
Sultan, Terrie, 160
Surls, James, 23, 26, 28, 51–52, 53, 54–55, 89, 95–98, *96–98,* 103, 133, 191–92, 201, 222–23, 239, 241–42, 250, 253, 267
Susman, Karen and Stephen, 164

Swarthmore College, 230
Sweeney, James Johnson, 21–22, 44, 130–31, 207n. 34
Swenson, Katherine, 253

■ T
Taafe, Phillip, 158
Tack, Augustus Vincent, 119
Talbot Rice Gallery (University of Edinburgh), 245
Tamarind Institute, 71, 226, 256, 258
Tamayo, Rufino, 83, 235
Tanguy, Yves, 142
Tàpies, Antoni, 131
Target Collection (the Museum of Fine Arts, Houston), 24
Target Stores, 24
Tartt, Blake, III, 37
Tate, Greg, 183
Tate, Joe, 252
Tate Gallery, 254
Texas A&M University at College Station, 43, 224, 231, 236, 258
Texas A&M University at Commerce, 233, 245, 251
Texas Artists Museum, Port Arthur, 258
Texas Arts and Industries University, 181, 243
Texas Centennial Exhibition, Dallas, 206n. 16, 262
Texas Center for Photographic Studies, 48
Texas Christian University, 44, 72, 226, 245, 252
Texas Commission for the Arts and Humanities, 24
Texas Commission on the Arts, 184, 259
Texas Eastern Corporation, 25, 28. *See also* Duke Energy
Texas Female Institute, 242
Texas Fine Arts Association, 17, 222–23, 225
Texas Gallery, 224, 226, 230–34, 237, 244–46, 248–50, 256–57
Texas National Bank Gallery, 264
Texas Southern University, 20, 41, 51, 86, 111, 224–25, 236, 247. *See also* Texas State University for Negroes
Texas State College for Women, 124–25, 229, 235, 240
Texas State University for Negroes, 41, 224, 227. *See also* Texas Southern University
Texas Tech University, 177, 222, 235, 247
Texas Watercolor Society, 264
Texas Western College, 236
Texas Woman's University, 124, 143, 229, 234, 235, 240, 255
Thielepape, William C. A., 242
Thomas, Bill, 198, 203, *203,* 253
Thompson, Arthur, 262
Thompson, David, 254
Thompson, George F., 76
Thompson, Milam, 55
Thompson, Robert Farris, 110
Thompson, Virgil, 257
Thompson, William R., 140
Thoreau, David Henry, 75

369 Gallery, 245
Tibor de Nagy Gallery, 255
Tidden, Agnes Lilienberg, 260
Tidden, John Clark, 260
Tiffany Foundation, Louis Comfort, 230–31, 233–34, 237, 246, 251
Tileston, Jackie, 153, 156–57, *157*, 253–54
Tilton Gallery, Jack, 236
Tinguely, Jean, 21–22, 118
Tobey, Mark, 82, 127, 146, 229
Tocqueville, Alexis de, 80
Todd, Mr. and Mrs. Anderson, 128
Todd, Emily, 58
Tokyo Metropolitan Museum of Photography, 246
Tolbert, Frank, 252
Tolstoy, Leo, 146
Tracy, Michael, 26, 28, 80–81, 83–86, *85*, 90, 109, 118, 150–51, *151*, 207n. 54, 253–54
Transco Tower Gallery, 27, 235, 238, 248, 256
Transmission Gallery, 245
Travis, Olin H., 17, 39–40, 251, 260
Treebeard's, 199, 232
Trinity University, 55, 247, 256
Tuchman, Maurice, 238
Tucker, Anne Wilkes, 24, 28, 92–93, 208n. 12, 209n. 46, 225
Tucker, Marcia, 25, 80, 87, 89, 250
Tulane University, 195, 225, 248, 250
Turner, Arthur, 265
Turner, Janet, 263
Turrell, James, 30, 80
Turrell, Julia Brown, 249
Twaddle, Randy, 198, *198*, 254
Twombly, Cy, 173, 249
Tyler Museum of Art, 223, 225, 227, 246–47, 252–54, 258
Tyler School of Art (Philadelphia), 101, 111, 184, 234, 244, 246

■ **U**

Uhler, Ruth Pershing, 16–17, 71, 119, 121–22, *122*, 206n. 11, 254
Umlauf, Charles, 251, 263
UNESCO, 111, 224
Ungers, Oswald Mathia, 156
Universal Limited Art Editions, 173–74
Universidad de México, 236
Universidad Nacional Autónoma de México, 255
Universität Erlangen-Nürnberg, 255
University Art Museum (University of Texas at Austin), 241
University Club (Houston), 260
University of Alabama, 222
University of Arkansas, 87, 246, 252
University of California, 46, 65, 71, 160, 191, 226, 237, 239, 241, 245, 255
University of Chicago, 125, 240
University of Cincinnati, 229

University of Corpus Christi, 227
University of Dallas, 72, 252
University of Edinburgh, 245
University of Hartford, 184, 240
University of Hawaii, 83
University of Houston, 23, 26–27, 30, 44, 50, 52, 54, 58, 70–71, 74, 76, 89–90, 92, 95, 103, 105, 131, 137, 167, 175, 179, 184, 187, 197, 200–201, 203, 222–26, 228, 230, 232, 235–44, 246–51, 253–54, 256–59. *See also* Blaffer Gallery, Sarah Campbell; Lawndale Annex; O'Kane Gallery
University of Illinois, 57, 179, 231, 235, 251
University of Iowa, 100, 108, 226, 257
University of La Crosse, 251
University of Massachusetts, 164, 179, 229, 243, 251
University of Michigan, 65, 190, 228, 258
University of Minnesota, 234
University of Missouri, 254
University of New Mexico, 71, 88, 226, 244, 254, 256
University of North Carolina, 254
University of North Texas, 106, 174–75, 202–3, 222, 231, 234, 238, 240, 245–46, 251–52, 256
University of Oklahoma, 232
University of Oklahoma Museum of Art, 253
University of Pennsylvania, 230, 243
University of South Florida, 189, 231, 248
University of Southern California, 231
University of St. Thomas, 22, 42, 45, 48, 200, 207n. 40, 207n. 57, 211n. 10, 214n. 39, 226, 246, 249, 252, 257
University of Texas at Austin, 40, 43, 46–48, 55, 84, 88, 90, 131, 134, 151–52, 159, 173, 182, 192, 203, 241–42, 244, 247, 249, 250–51, 253–58, 265. *See also* Huntington Art Gallery, Archer M.; University Art Museum
University of Texas at Arlington, 222, 233, 236, 242, 248, 256
University of Texas at El Paso, 106, 183, 230, 245, 255
University of Texas at San Antonio, 105, 192, 223, 230, 231, 237, 247, 248, 252, 255, 256
University of Texas Health Science Center, 235, 242
University of Texas Institute of Texan Cultures, 242
University of the Sacred Heart, 231
University of the South, 144, 236
University of Tulsa, 235
University of West Florida, 235

University of Wisconsin, 108, 111, 226, 244
Utah Art Center, 239
Utterback, Robin, 26, 140–42, *141*, 207n. 43, 255

■ **V**

Vapors, The, 216n. 120
Vargas, Kathy, 105–6, *106*, 244, 255
Vaughn, Mr. and Mrs. James M., 197
Vaughn, Salle Werner, 142–43, *143*, 255
Vaughn Foundation Fund, 199
Victor, Mary Jane, 211n. 10
Villon, Jacques, 130
Vinson & Elkins, L. L. P., 11
Virginia, Hattie, 260
Virginia Polytechnic Institute, 226
Visual Studies Workshop, 225
Vlaminck, Maurice de, 43

■ **W**

Waco Museum of Art, 232
Wade, Bob, 46–47, *46*, 255
Wagner, Mrs. Eugene, 82
Wagner, Richard, 88, 101, 257
Walker, Barry, 29
Walker, Kara, 186
Walker Art Center, Minneapolis, 228, 257
Wallace, Stewart, 258
Walls Gallery, Michael, 242
Ward, Liz, 29, 65, 71–72, *71*, 203, 248, 256
Wardlaw, Alvia J., 29, 86, 111
Warhol, Andy, 158, 164, 172, 176, 199, 219n. 95
Washington University, 237, 252
Watkin, William Ward, *14*, 15
Watriss, Wendy, 27, 48–49, *49*, 207n. 45, 223–24
Watson, Randy, 166
Watson/de Nagy & Company, 255, 259
Webb, Perry. *See* Flood, Mark
Webster, Daniel, 244
Webster College, 256
Weiermair, Peter, 207n. 51
Wenders, Wim, 28
West End Gallery, 248
Wetta, Jean Carruthers, 67, 72–74, *73*, 256
Wheatley High School, 147, 230
Whistler, James Abbott McNeill, 206n. 3
Whistler Gallery, Barry, 222–23, 225, 228–29, 231–34, 245–46, 248, 252–54, 256–57
White, Charles, 41
White, Pae, 157
Whitechapel Art Gallery, 225
Whitney Museum of American Art, 42, 44, 90, 137, 142, 222, 224, 230–34, 237, 239–41, 244, 246–47, 250–53, 255, 257
Whitworth College, 238
Wierzbowski Gallery, 229
Wilcox, John, 150, 152, *153*, 155, 256

Wilder Foundation, 113, 184, 187, 197
Wiley, William, 51, 209n. 53
Williams, Casey, 157, 159–60, *160*, 256
Williams, Danny, 100–101, *101*, 210n. 90, 211n. 8, 257
Williams, Jerry, 192
Williams, Tennessee, 229
Williams College, 75, 246
Willour, Clinton T., 49–50, 65, 70, 72, 76, 106, 152, 175, 200, 207n. 45, 266
Wilmarth, Christopher, 195
Wilson, Bob, 44
Wilson, Isabel B., 39, 52, 68, 100, 163
Wilson, Robert, 119, 134–37, *136*, 257
Wilson, Wallace S., 52
Winkler, Anne, 253
Winkler, Paul, 30
Winningham, Geoff, 24, 48–49, *49*, 207n. 44, 207n. 45, 225, 257, 265
Winogrand, Garry, 34, 48, *48*, 50, 55, 225, 247, 257–58
Winona School of Professional Photographers, 227
Winston-Salem State University, 224
Winters, Terry, 142
Wirtz Gallery, Stephen, 247
Witte Memorial Museum, 17, 36, 208n. 17, 224, 251
Wolff, Dee, 100, 103–4, *104*, 258
Woman's College of Alabama, 229
Women and Their Work, 228, 231, 235, 240, 244, 253
Women's National Caucus for Art, 235
Wood, Grant, 40
Woodstock Artists Colony, 235, 240
Woolf, Virginia, 71–72
Works Progress Administration, 235
World Press Foundation, 224
Wortham, Mr. and Mrs. R. W., III, 54
Wortham Center, 239
Wray, Dick, 22, 90, *130*, 131, 206n. 29, 253, 258, 265
Wurzer Gallery, Gerhard, 227
Wyeth, Andrew, 86

■ **Y**

Yale Summer School of Music and Art, 88
Yale University, 47, 67, 143, 230, 233, 241, 243–44, 253
Yenne, Peter, 252
Yeovil School of Art, 225
YMCA, 39, 235
Youens Gallery, Judy, 227
Young, Brigham, 183
Young, Colin, 207n. 57
Young, Kyle, 191–92, *192*, 258
Yukiko Lunday Gallery, 227
YWCA, 260

■ **Z**

Zeitlin, Marilyn A., 26, 144
Zero One Gallery, 232
Ziebell, Robert, 28, 65, **65**, 173, 207n. 45, 258–59
Ziegler, Samuel P., 261
Zigrosser, Carl, 209n. 24, 209n. 26
Zúñiga, Francisco, 236